BOLLINGEN SERIES XXX

PAPERS FROM THE ERANOS YEARBOOKS

Edited by Joseph Campbell

Selected and translated from the *Eranos-Jahrbücher*
edited by Olga Froebe-Kapteyn

Volume 1

Spirit and Nature

PAPERS FROM THE ERANOS YEARBOOKS

Ernesto Buonaiuti • Friedrich Dessauer • C. G. Jung

Werner Kaegi • C. Kerényi • Paul Masson-Oursel

Fritz Meier • Adolf Portmann • Max Pulver

Hugo Rahner • Erwin Schrödinger • Walter Wili

BOLLINGEN SERIES XXX · 1

PANTHEON BOOKS

THIS IS THE FIRST VOLUME
OF PAPERS SELECTED FROM THE ERANOS YEARBOOKS.
THESE VOLUMES OF SELECTIONS CONSTITUTE NUMBER XXX
IN BOLLINGEN SERIES, SPONSORED BY AND PUBLISHED FOR
BOLLINGEN FOUNDATION

These papers were originally published in German in
Eranos-Jahrbücher V (1937), XIII (1945), and XIV (1946),
by Rhein-Verlag, Zurich, Switzerland

Library of Congress Catalog Card No. 54-5647

Manufactured in The United States of America

PRE

Translated by

RALPH MANHEIM

except for the papers by C. G. Jung

which were translated by

R. F. C. HULL

NOTE OF ACKNOWLEDGMENT

Grateful acknowledgment is herewith made to the following publishers for permission to quote as indicated: George Allen and Unwin, Ltd., London, for a passage from Andrew Lang's translation of *The Homeric Hymns;* the American-Scandinavian Foundation, New York, for a passage from Henry Adams Bellows's translation of *The Poetic Edda;* Harvard University Press, for material from Kathleen Freeman, *Ancilla to the Pre-Socratic Philosophers,* and for various passages from the Loeb Classical Library editions of Callimachus (tr. A. W. Mair), Petronius Arbiter (tr. M. Heseltine), Philo (tr. F. H. Colson and G. H. Whitaker), and Virgil (tr. H. R. Fairclough); Houghton Mifflin Company, Boston, for a passage from Charles Eliot Norton's translation of Dante's *Divine Comedy;* Luzac and Company, Ltd., London, for a passage from R. A. Nicholson's translation of the *Mathnawi* of Jalalu 'ddin Rumi; Oxford University Press, New York, for passages from Louis MacNeice's translation of Goethe's *Faust* and from the W. D. Ross translation of Aristotle; Princeton University Press, for passages from H. H. Hudson's translation of Erasmus's *Praise of Folly;* and Charles Scribner's Sons, New York, for extracts from L. E. Opdycke's translation of Castiglione's *Book of the Courtier.*

The advice and assistance of the following persons is gratefully acknowledged: Marie-Louise von Franz, Erwin R. Goodenough, Norbert Guterman, Max Knoll, Mrs. Erla Rodakiewicz, and Willard R. Trask.

CONTENTS

CONTENTS

LIST OF ILLUSTRATIONS

For C. Kerényi, "Apollo Epiphanies"

following page 72

1 *and* 2. Pergamum coin. 2nd–1st century B.C.

From British Museum Catalogue of Coins: *Mysia* (London, 1892), Pl. XXVII, 4.

3. Delphi coin. 4th century B.C.

From photograph of a plaster print by Friedrich Imhoof-Blumer in W. H. Roscher, *Neue Omphalosstudien* (Sächsische Gesellschaft der Wissenschaft, Philologische-historische Klasse, Abhandlungen; Leipzig, 1915), Pl. II, 14.

4. Marble omphalos. Delos.

From Marcel Bulard, *Peintures murales et mosaïques de Delos* (Institut de France: Académie des inscriptions et belles-lettres, Fondation E. Piot, Monuments et mémoires, XIV; Paris, 1908), fig. 19.

5. Relief. Theater of Miletus.

From Georg Kawerau and Albert Rehm, *Das Delphinion in Milet* (Königliche Museen zu Berlin, Milet: Ergebnisse der Ausgrabungen und Untersuchungen seit dem Jahre 1899, No. 3; Berlin, 1914), fig. 101.

6. Detail from a mural. Pompeii.

After a sketch from Bulard, op. cit., fig. 21.

7. Apollo Belvedere.

Vatican Museum, Rome. (Photo: Anderson.)

EDITOR'S FOREWORD

The Eranos meetings have been held annually late in August, since 1933, at the home of Frau Olga Froebe-Kapteyn, in a hall built for this purpose on the grounds of her residence, at the northern end of Lago Maggiore near Ascona, Switzerland. With the idea that her estate —which had formerly been a vineyard—should become the site of a perennial round table of ideas, a meeting place of East and West, Frau Froebe had built this auditorium in 1928, adjacent to her villa, Casa Gabriella. The two buildings are separated by a terraced garden, with a commanding view of the lake and its surrounding mountains. After the lectures each day the speakers gather at a large round table on the main terrace for meals and further discussion. The late Professor Rudolf Otto of the University of Marburg suggested the Greek word *Eranos* (meaning a meal to which each contributes his share) as a name evoking both the convivial spirit of an unsystematic interchange and the classical prototype of all such discussions, the Platonic symposium.

In August, 1933, a *pléiade* of speakers capable of initiating the shared feast assembled at Frau Froebe's invitation: Dr. Heinrich Zimmer, professor of Sanskrit at the University of Heidelberg; Mrs. Rhys Davids of London, president of the Pali Text Society; Dr. Erwin Rousselle, director of the China Institute at the University of Frankfort on the Main; Dr. C. G. Jung of Zurich; Dr. G. R. Heyer of Munich; Dr. Friedrich Heiler, professor of Christian theology at the University of Marburg; and Professor Ernesto Buonaiuti of the University of Rome. The common theme, proposed by Frau Froebe, was "Yoga and Meditation in East and West." The lectures were delivered in German, English, and Italian, from the contrasting standpoints of the several speakers. The members of the audience who had brought portions of their own opened these at the numerous café tables in nearby Ascona, and immediately the shared feast, which for two decades has annually renewed itself, began revealing its power to shape, as well as to be shaped by, the men and women who made it.

In the course of the first decade of Eranos, the interest of the participants shifted from the meeting of East and West to Europe's meeting with the multiple aspects of its own destiny. During the war years, in the sanctuary of the Alps, a nucleus of Swiss scholars, joined by a few distinguished refugees, carried the annual gatherings through the period of isolation from the rest of Europe, analyzing intensively and from many points of view the spiritual background of what appeared to be a disintegrating civilization. Following that interval, only a few of the earlier participants returned, the greater number having passed away. New themes were announced, new voices heard. Nevertheless, the tenor and character of the meetings remained unimpaired. This continuity was due, on the one hand, to the guidance of Frau Froebe, whose sense of the meaning and object of Eranos never wavered, and on the other, to the continuous presence and genial spirit of Dr. C. G. Jung, whose concept of the fundamental psychological laws of human life and thought supplied a criterion for both the recognition and the fostering of the perennial in a period of transformation.

The names and topics of the seventy-odd scholars who have contributed to Eranos are given at the conclusion of the present volume: a glance will reveal the range of their subjects as well as the variety of their points of view. Each—scientist, theologian, philosopher—has been free to represent as strongly as possible his own position; yet precisely this circumstance has made it evident that even apparently irreconcilable traditions are informed by common ideas. "Ever the same, yet changing ever," these ubiquitously visible invisibles have been the chief objects of interest at the Eranos round table. And because of an unwavering concentration upon them, these meetings stand—in a world sundered by strife—as living witness to the inevitability of a profound harmony among men where good will and intelligence prevail.

From the first year of Eranos, Dr. Daniel Brody, owner and director of the Rhein-Verlag of Zurich, has published the annual lectures in a series of yearbooks (*Eranos-Jahrbuch 1933, 1934, 1935,* etc.). An edition in English of this growing compendium of comparative scholarship is now inaugurated. As the editor of this edition, I have had the task, not of choosing a scholarly miscellany, but of composing books that will communicate to the contemporary English reader, remote from Lago Maggiore, a sense of significant participation in the Shared Feast. The articles in the present volume—the first in a series of perhaps eight or ten—have been drawn from the yearbooks of the meetings of 1945 and 1946, with the addition of two from 1937 that open the view to the wider horizon of the earlier years. Frau Froebe has been exceedingly generous, not only in permitting me to approach the series from this point of view, but also in offering the fundamental suggestions that have made it possible to attempt the re-formation without violating the spirit of her vineyard. Mr. Ralph Manheim has translated the majority of the selections; Mr. R. F. C. Hull, those by C. G. Jung. To them, and to the members of the Bollingen Series editorial staff who have assisted in the work of editorial detail—especially Miss Ximena de Angulo, for her meticulous review of the translations—my thanks.

JOSEPH CAMPBELL

PREFACE

Those who feel the truth of the old Chinese conception that all that happens in the visible world is the expression of ideas or images in the invisible might do well to consider Eranos from this point of view. An idea takes shape and becomes concrete by virtue of its inherent power and pattern. Eranos is such a concretization, as its development through more than twenty years has confirmed. Lacking any formal organization, it is held together and molded by its underlying idea and its integrating power. There are other orders of reality than the tangible and visible, and it is their vitality and regenerating quality which survive the great changes of culture and are responsible for the rebuilding of a broken world.

The lectures given at Eranos treat of such realities, indestructible and virtue-laden, the essence of traditions and their values, seen in their constructive aspect as the rich earth from which a new culture can spring. The years of experience since the beginning of Eranos have convinced me that the living quality and the continuity of any enterprise depend upon its essential *flowing* character, its capacity for change. This implies the absence of dogmatism and rigidity of form.

With a sense of these imperative conditions, the first Eranos meeting took place in 1933, on the subject "Yoga and Meditation in East and West." There was no definite plan of development. To most organizers, this method, or rather nonmethod, will seem unreasonable. It *is* unreasonable, but it works. I and those who collaborated with me felt that an idea was seeking expression, and we decided to let it take its course and to follow its direction. The factor of *pistis*, "faith," in the idea and in its power of integration, as well as in our experience of its workings, has been of fundamental importance. Scholars of reputation grew interested; their faith in and loyalty to Eranos, always exceptional, have remained. As colleagues in a scholarly undertaking which sought the highest levels, they have possessed courage and imagination. Now, after more than two decades, Eranos has established itself among the cultural activities of today.

The primary aim of the lectures has not been literary perfection nor necessarily a total treatment of the subject. Their value is *evocative*. In many cases, they carry us to the bounds of scholarly investigation and discovery, and point beyond. They touch upon unusual themes, facts, and analogies and in so doing evoke the great archetypal images. The atmosphere in which these things occur has established an unusual relationship between the speakers and the audience, because it draws from the highest values that are essential to man—values for whose sake, in truth, he lives.

Since the beginnings of Eranos, in 1933, Dr. Daniel Brody, of the Rhein-Verlag, Zurich, has published a faithful record of the lectures in the form of the *Eranos-Jahrbücher*. These volumes—twenty-two through 1953—constitute a document for history. They play a part in the *Geistesgeschichte* of our times. Selections from their contents are now to appear in English, and I wish to express my thanks to Mr. Joseph Campbell, as editor, for his part in the publication of the present volume and those to follow.

OLGA FROEBE-KAPTEYN

SPIRIT AND NATURE

C. G. Jung

The Phenomenology of the Spirit in Fairy Tales[1]

Foreword

One of the unbreakable rules of the game in science is to take the object as known only so far as the inquirer is in a position to make scientifically valid statements about it. "Valid" in this sense simply means what can be verified by facts. The object of inquiry is the natural phenomenon. In psychology, one of the most important phenomena is the *statement*, and in particular its manifest form and content, the latter aspect being perhaps the more significant in view of the nature of the psyche. The first task that ordinarily presents itself is the description and arrangement of events, then comes the closer examination into the laws of their living behavior. To inquire into the *substance* of what has been observed is possible in natural science only where there is an Archimedean point outside. But for the psyche no such outside standpoint exists, since only the psyche can observe the psyche. Consequently, knowledge of the psychic substance is impossible for us, at least with our present resources. This does not rule out the possibility that the atomic physics of the future may supply us with the said Archimedean point. For the time being, however, our subtlest lucubrations can establish no more than is contained in the statement: this is how the psyche behaves. The honest investigator will piously refrain from meddling with questions of substance. I do not think it superfluous to acquaint my reader with the necessary limitations that psychology voluntarily imposes on itself, for he will then be in a position to appreciate the phenomenological point of view of modern psychology,

---

1 Expanded version of the lecture "Zur Psychologie des Geistes," delivered at the 1945 Eranos meeting and first published in the *Eranos-Jahrbuch 1945*. The present version was originally published as "Zur Phänomenologie des Geistes im Märchen" in *Symbolik des Geistes* (Zurich, 1948).

which is not always understood. This point of view does not exclude
the existence of faith, conviction, and experienced certainties of whatever description, nor does it contest their possible validity. Great as is
their importance for the individual and for collective life, psychology
completely lacks the means to prove their validity in the scientific
sense. One may lament this incapacity on the part of science, but that
does not enable it to jump over its own shadow.

1. Concerning the Word 'Spirit'

The word "spirit" possesses such a wide range of application that it
requires considerable effort to make clear to oneself all the things it
can mean. Spirit, we say, is the principle that stands in opposition to
matter. By this we understand an immaterial substance or form of
existence which on the highest and most universal level is called
"God." We imagine this immaterial substance also as the vehicle of
psychic phenomena or even of life itself. As against the latter view
there stands the opposition: spirit and nature. Here the concept of
spirit is restricted to the supernatural or antinatural, and has lost its
substantial connection with psyche and life. A similar restriction is
implied in Spinoza's view that spirit is an attribute of the One Substance. Hylozoism goes even further, taking spirit to be a quality of
matter.

A very widespread view conceives spirit as a higher and psyche as a
lower principle of activity, and conversely the alchemists thought of
spirit as the *ligamentum animae et corporis,* obviously regarding it as
a *spiritus vegetativus* (the later life spirit or nerve spirit). Equally
common is the view that spirit and psyche are essentially the same and
can be separated only arbitrarily. Wundt takes spirit as "the inner
being, regardless of any connection with an outer being." Others
restrict spirit to certain psychic capacities or functions or qualities,
such as the capacity to think and reason in contradistinction to the
more "psychic" sentiments. Here spirit means the sum total of all the
phenomena of rational thought, or of the intellect, including the will,
memory, imagination, creative power, and aspirations motivated by
ideals. Spirit has the further connotation of *sprightliness,* as when we
say that a person is "spirited," meaning that he is versatile and full of

4

ideas, with a brilliant, witty, and surprising turn of mind. Again, spirit denotes a certain attitude or the principle underlying it; for instance one is "educated in the spirit of Pestalozzi," or one says that the "spirit of Weimar is the immortal German heritage." A special instance is the time spirit, or spirit of the age, which stands for the principle and motive force behind certain views, judgments, and actions of a collective nature. Then there is the "objective spirit,"[2] by which is meant the whole stock of man's cultural possessions with particular regard to his intellectual and religious achievements.

As linguistic usage shows, spirit in the sense of an attitude has unmistakable leanings towards personification: the spirit of Pestalozzi can also be taken concretistically as his ghost or imago, just as the spirits of Weimar are the personal specters of Goethe and Schiller; for spirit still has the spookish meaning of the soul of one departed. The "cold breath of the spirits" points on the one hand to the ancient affinity of ψυχή with ψυχρός and ψῦχος, which both mean "cold," and on the other hand to the original meaning of πνεῦμα, which simply denoted "air in motion"; and in the same way animus and anima were connected with ἄνεμος, "wind." The German word *Geist* probably has more to do with something frothing, effervescing, or fermenting; hence affinities with *Gischt* (foam), *Gäscht* (yeast), "ghost," "gas," and also with the emotional "ghastly" and "aghast," are not to be rejected. From time immemorial emotion has been regarded as possession, which is why we still say today, of a hot-tempered person, that he is possessed of a devil or that an evil spirit has entered into him.[3]

Just as, according to the old view, the spirits or souls of the dead are of a subtle disposition like a vapor or a smoke, so to the alchemist *spiritus* was a subtle, volatile, active, and vivifying essence, such as alcohol was understood to be, and all the arcane substances. On this level, spirit includes spirits of salts, spirits of ammonia, formic spirit, etc.

This score or so of meanings and shades of meaning attributable to the word "spirit" makes it difficult for the psychologist to delimit his subject conceptually, but on the other hand they lighten the task

2 [An Hegelian term, roughly equivalent to our "spirit of man."—TRANS.]
3 See my "Spirit and Life," in *Contributions to Analytical Psychology,* tr. H. G. and Cary F. Baynes (New York and London, 1928).

of describing it, since the many different aspects go to form a vivid and concrete picture of the phenomenon in question. We are concerned with a functional complex which originally, on the primitive level, was apprehended as an invisible, breathlike "presence." William James has given us a lively account of this primordial phenomenon in his *Varieties of Religious Experience*. Another well-known example is the wind of the Pentecostal miracle. The primitive mentality finds it quite natural to personify the invisible presence as a ghost or demon. The souls or spirits of the dead are identical with the psychic activity of the living; they merely continue it. The view that the psyche is a spirit is implicit in this. When therefore something psychic happens in the individual which he feels as belonging to himself, that something is his own spirit. But if anything psychic happens which seems to him strange, then it is somebody else's spirit, and it may be causing a possession. The spirit in the first case corresponds to the subjective attitude, in the latter case to public opinion, to the time spirit, or to the original, not yet human, anthropoid disposition which we also call the *unconscious*.

In keeping with its original wind-nature, spirit is always an active, winged, swift-moving being as well as that which vivifies, stimulates, incites, fires, and inspires. To put it in modern language, spirit is the dynamic principle, forming for that very reason the classical antithesis of matter—the antithesis, that is, of its stasis and inertia. Basically it is the contrast between life and death. The subsequent differentiation of this contrast leads to the actually very remarkable opposition of spirit and nature. Even though spirit is regarded as essentially alive and enlivening, one cannot really feel nature as unspiritual and dead. We must therefore be dealing here with the (Christian) postulate of a spirit whose life is so vastly superior to the life of nature that in comparison with it the latter is no better than death.

This special development in man's idea of spirit rests on the recognition that the invisible presence is a psychic phenomenon, i.e., one's own spirit, and that the latter consists not only in uprushes of life but in formal contents too. Among the first, the most prominent are the images and shadowy presentations that occupy our inner field of vision; among the second, thinking and reason, which organize the world of images. In this way a transcendent spirit superimposed itself upon the original, natural life-spirit and even swung over to the opposite position, as though the latter were merely naturalistic. The transcendent spirit became the supranatural and transmundane cosmic principle of order and as such was given the name of "God," or at least it became an attribute of the One Substance (as in Spinoza) or one Person in the Godhead (as in Christianity).

The corresponding development of spirit in the reverse, hylozoistic direction—*a maiori ad minus*—took place under anti-Christian auspices in materialism. The premise underlying this reaction is the exclusive certainty of the spirit's identity with psychic functions, whose dependence upon brain and metabolism became increasingly clear. One had only to give the One Substance another name and call it "matter," to produce the idea of a spirit which was entirely dependent on nutrition and environment, and whose highest form was the intellect or reason. This meant that the original pneumatic presence had taken up its abode in man's physiology, and a writer like Klages could arraign the spirit as the "adversary of the soul."[4] For it was into this latter concept that the age-old spontaneity of the spirit withdrew after it had sunk down to a servile attribute of matter. Somewhere or other the *deus ex machina* quality of spirit had to be preserved—if not in the spirit itself, then in its synonym the soul, that glancing, Aeolian[5] thing, elusive as a butterfly (anima, ψυχή).

Even though the materialistic view did not prevail everywhere, the conception of spirit nevertheless remained outside the religious sphere, caught in the realm of conscious phenomena. Spirit as "subjective spirit" came to mean a purely endopsychic phenomenon, while "objective spirit" did not mean the universal spirit, or God, but merely the sum-total of intellectual and cultural possessions which make up our human institutions and the content of our libraries. Spirit had forfeited its original nature, its autonomy and spontaneity over a very wide area, with the solitary exception of the religious field, where, at least in principle, its pristine character remained unimpaired.

In this résumé we have described an entity which presents itself to us as an immediate psychic phenomenon distinguished from other psy-

4 Ludwig Klages, *Der Geist als Widersacher der Seele* (Leipzig, 1929–32; 3 vols.).

5 "Soul," from the Old German *saiwalô,* may be cognate with αἰόλος, "quick-moving, changeful of hue, shifting." It also has the meaning of "wily" or "shifty"; hence an air of probability attaches to the alchemical definition of *anima* as Mercurius.

chisms whose existence is naïvely believed to be causally dependent upon physical influences. A connection between spirit and physical conditions is not immediately apparent, and for this reason it was credited with immateriality to a much higher degree than was the case with psychic phenomena in the narrower sense. Not only is a certain physical dependence attributed to the latter, but they are themselves thought of as possessing a certain materiality, as the idea of the subtle body and the Chinese *kuei*-soul clearly show. In view of the intimate connection that exists between certain psychic processes and their physical parallels we cannot very well accept the total immateriality of the psyche. As against this, the *consensus omnium* insists on the immateriality of spirit, although by no means everybody also allows it a real substantiality. It is, however, not easy to see why our hypothetical "matter," which looks quite different from what it did even thirty years ago, alone should be real, and spirit not. Although the idea of immateriality does not in itself exclude that of reality, popular opinion invariably associates reality with materiality. Spirit and matter may well be forms of one and the same transcendental being. For instance the Tantrists, with as much right, say that matter is nothing other than the clothing of God's thoughts. The sole immediate reality is the psychic reality of conscious contents, which are as it were labelled with a spiritual or material origin as the case may be.

The hallmarks of spirit are, firstly, the principle of spontaneous movement and activity; secondly, the spontaneous capacity to produce images independently of sense perception; and thirdly, the autonomous and sovereign manipulation of these images. This spiritual entity approaches primitive man from outside; but with increasing development it gets lodged in man's consciousness and becomes a subordinate function, thus apparently forfeiting its original character of autonomy. That character is now retained only in the most conservative views, namely in the religions. The descent of spirit into the sphere of human consciousness is expressed in the myth of the divine νοῦς that was caught in the embrace of φύσις. This process, continuing over the ages, is probably an unavoidable necessity, and the religions would find themselves in a very forlorn situation if they believed in the attempt to hold up evolution. Their task, if they are well advised, is not to impede the ineluctable march of events, but to shape it in

8

such a way that it can proceed without fatal damage to the soul. The religions should therefore constantly remind us of the origin and original character of the spirit, lest man should forget what he is drawing into himself and with what he is filling his consciousness. He himself did not create the spirit, rather the spirit makes *him* creative, always spurring him on, giving him happy ideas, staying power, "enthusiasm" and "inspiration." So much, indeed, does it pervade his whole being that he is in gravest danger of thinking that he actually created the spirit and that he "has" it. In reality it has him, and what is more, it possesses him in exactly the same way that the physical world appears to be the willing object of his designs and yet in reality turns into an obsessive idée-force, binding his freedom with a thousand chains. Spirit threatens the naïve-minded man with inflation, of which our own times have given us the most horribly instructive examples. The danger becomes all the greater the more our interest fastens upon external objects and the more we forget that the differentiation of our relations to nature should go hand in hand with a correspondingly differentiated relation to the spirit, so as to establish the necessary balance. If the outer object is not offset by an inner, unbridled materialism results, coupled with maniacal arrogance or else the extinction of the autonomous personality, which is in any case the ideal of the totalitarian mass state.

As can readily be seen, the common modern idea of spirit ill accords with the Christian view, which regards it as the *summum bonum,* as God himself. To be sure, there is also the idea of an evil spirit. But the modern idea cannot be equated with that either, since for us spirit is not necessarily evil; we would have to call it morally indifferent or neutral. When the Bible says "God is a spirit," it sounds more like the definition of a substance, or like a qualification. But the devil too, it seems, is endowed with the same peculiar spiritual substance, albeit an evil and corrupt one. The original identity of substance is still expressed in the idea of the fallen angel, as well as in the close connection between Jehovah and Satan in the Old Testament. There may be an echo of this primitive connection in the Lord's Prayer, where we say "Lead us not into temptation"—for is not this really the business of the *tempter,* Old Nick himself?

This brings us to a point we have not considered at all in the course

9

of our observations so far. We have availed ourselves of cultural and everyday conceptions which are the product of human consciousness and its reflections, in order to form a picture of the psychic modes of manifestation of the factor "spirit." But we have yet to consider that because of its original autonomy,[6] about which there can be no doubt in the psychological sense, the spirit is quite capable of staging its own manifestations spontaneously.

2. Self-Representation of the Spirit in Dreams

The psychic manifestations of the spirit at once indicate that they are of an archetypal nature—in other words, the phenomenon we call spirit depends on the existence of an autonomous primordial image which is universally present in the preconscious makeup of the human psyche. As usual, I first came up against this problem when investigating the dreams of my patients. It struck me that a certain kind of father complex has a "spiritual" character, so to speak, in the sense that the father image gives rise to statements, actions, tendencies, impulses, opinions, etc., to which one could hardly deny the attribute "spiritual." In men a positive father complex very often produces a certain credulity with regard to authority and a distinct willingness to bow down before all spiritual dogmas and values; while in women it induces the liveliest spiritual aspirations and interests. In dreams it is always the father figure from whom the decisive beliefs, prohibitions, and wise counsels emanate. The invisibility of this source is frequently emphasized by the fact that it consists only in an authoritative voice which passes final judgments.[7] Mostly, therefore, it is the figure of a "wise old man" who symbolizes the spiritual factor. Sometimes the part is played by a "real" spirit, namely the ghost of one dead, or, more rarely, by grotesque gnomelike figures or talking animals. The dwarf forms are found, at least in my experience, mainly in women; hence it seems to me logical that in Ernst Barlach's play *Der tote Tag* (1912), the gnomelike figure of Steissbart ("Rump-

---

6 Even if one accepts the view that a self-revelation of spirit—an apparition for instance—is nothing but an hallucination, the fact remains that this is a spontaneous psychic event not subject to our control. At any rate it is an autonomous complex, and that is quite sufficient for our purpose.

7 Cf. *Psychology and Alchemy* (*Coll. Works*, Vol. 12; New York and London, 1953), pp. 49ff.

beard") is associated with the mother, just as Bes is associated with the mother-goddess at Karnak. In both sexes the spirit can also take the form of a boy or a youth. In women he corresponds to the so-called "positive" animus who indicates the possibility of conscious spiritual effort. In men his meaning is not so simple. He can be positive, in which case he signifies the "higher" personality, the self or *filius regius* as conceived by the alchemists.[8] But he can also be negative, and then he signifies the infantile shadow.[9] In both cases the boy means spirit of a sort.[10] Graybeard and boy belong together. The pair of them play a considerable role in alchemy as symbols of Mercurius.

It can never be established with one-hundred-per-cent certainty whether the spirit figures in dreams are morally good. Very often they show all the signs of duplicity, if not of outright malice. I must emphasize, however, that the grand plan on which the unconscious life of the psyche is constructed is so inaccessible to our understanding that we can never know what evil may not be necessary in order to produce good by enantiodromia, and what good may very possibly lead to evil. Sometimes the *probate spiritus* recommended by John cannot, with the best will in the world, be anything other than a cautious and patient waiting to see how things will finally turn out.

The figure of the Wise Old Man can appear so plastically, not only in dreams but also in visionary meditation (or what we call "active imagination"), that, as is sometimes apparently the case in India, it takes over the role of a guru.[11] The Wise Old Man appears in dreams in the guise of a magician, doctor, priest, teacher, professor, grandfather, or any other person possessing authority. The archetype of spirit in the shape of a man, hobgoblin, or animal always appears in a situation where insight, understanding, good advice, determination, planning, etc., are needed but cannot be mustered on one's own re-

8 Cf. the vision of the "naked boy" in Meister Eckhart.

9 The reader is reminded of the "boys" in Bruno Goetz's novel *Das Reich ohne Raum* (Potsdam, 1919; 2nd enlarged edn., Constance, 1925).

10 Cf. the "divine child" in my and C. Kerényi's *Essays on a Science of Mythology* (Bollingen Series XXII; New York, 1949).

11 Hence the many miraculous stories about rishis and mahatmas. A cultured Indian with whom I once conversed on the subject of gurus told me, when I asked him who his guru had been, that it was Shankaracharya (who lived in the 8th and 9th centuries). "But that's the celebrated commentator," I remarked in amazement. Whereupon he replied, "Yes, so he was; but naturally it was his spirit," not in the least perturbed by my Western bewilderment.

sources. The archetype compensates this state of spiritual deficiency by contents designed to fill the gap. An excellent example of this is the dream about the white and black magicians, which tried to compensate the spiritual difficulties of a young theological student. I did not know the dreamer myself, so the question of my personal influence is ruled out. He dreamed he was standing in the presence of a sublime hieratic figure called the "white magician," who was nevertheless clothed in a long black robe. This magician had just ended a lengthy discourse with the words "And for that we require the help of the black magician." Then the door suddenly opened and another old man came in, the "black magician," who however was dressed in a white robe. He too looked noble and sublime. The black magician evidently wanted to speak with the white, but hesitated to do so in the presence of the dreamer. At that the white magician, pointing to the dreamer, said, "Speak, he is an innocent." So the black magician began to relate a strange story of how he had found the lost keys of Paradise and did not know how to use them. He had, he said, come to the white magician for an explanation of the secret of the keys. He told him that the king of the country in which he lived was seeking a suitable monument for himself. His subjects had chanced to dig up an old sarcophagus containing the mortal remains of a virgin. The king opened the sarcophagus, threw away the bones, and had the empty sarcophagus buried again for later use. But no sooner had the bones seen the light of day than the being to whom they once had belonged— the virgin—changed into a black horse that galloped off into the desert. The black magician pursued it across the sandy wastes and beyond, and there after many vicissitudes and difficulties he found the lost keys of Paradise. That was the end of his story, and also, unfortunately, of the dream.

Here the compensation certainly did not fall out as the dreamer would wish, by handing him a solution on a plate; rather it confronted him with a problem to which I have already alluded, and one which life is always bringing us up against: namely, the uncertainty of all moral valuation, the bewildering interplay of good and evil, and the remorseless concatenation of guilt, suffering, and redemption. This path to the primordial religious experience is the right one, but how many can recognize it? It is like a still small voice, and it sounds from

12

afar. It is ambiguous, questionable, dark, presaging danger and hazardous adventure; a razor-edged path, to be trodden for God's sake only, without assurance and without sanction.

3. The Spirit in Fairy Tales

I would gladly present the reader with more modern dream material, but I fear that the individualism of dreams would make too high a demand upon our exposition and would claim more space than is here at our disposal. We shall therefore turn to folklore, where we need not get involved in the grim confrontations and entanglements of individual case histories and can observe the variations of the spirit motif without having to consider conditions that are more or less unique. In myths and fairy tales, as in dreams, the psyche tells its own story, and the interplay of the archetypes is revealed in its natural setting as "formation, transformation / the eternal Mind's eternal recreation."

The frequency with which the spirit type appears as an old man is about the same in fairy tales as in dreams.[12] The old man always appears when the hero is in a hopeless and desperate situation from which only profound reflection or a happy idea—in other words, a spiritual function or an endopsychic automatism of some kind—can extricate him. But since, for internal and external reasons, the hero cannot accomplish this himself, the knowledge needed to compensate the deficiency comes in the form of a personified thought, i.e., in the shape of this sagacious and helpful old man. An Esthonian fairy tale,[13] for instance, tells how an ill-treated little orphan boy who had let a cow escape was afraid to return home again for fear of more punishment. So he ran away, chancing to luck. He naturally got himself into a hopeless situation, with no visible way out. Exhausted, he fell into a deep sleep. When he awoke, "it seemed to him that he had something liquid in his mouth, and he saw a little old man with a long

12 I am indebted to Mrs. H. von Roques and Dr. Marie-Louise von Franz for the fairy-tale material used here.

13 *Finnische und estnische Volksmärchen* (Die Märchen der Weltliteratur, ed. Friedrich von der Leyen and Paul Zaunert; Jena, 1922), No. 68, p. 208 ["How an Orphan Boy Unexpectedly Found His Luck"]. [All of the German collections of tales here cited are in this series. English titles of tales are given in brackets, though no attempt has been made to locate published translations.—ED.]

gray beard standing before him, who was in the act of replacing the stopper in his milk flask. 'Give me some more to drink,' begged the boy. 'You have had enough for today,' replied the old man. 'If my path had not chanced to lead me to you, that would assuredly have been your last sleep, for when I found you, you were half dead.' Then the old man asked the boy who he was and where he wanted to go. The boy recounted everything he could remember happening to him up to the beating he had received the previous evening. 'My dear child,' said the old man, 'you are no better and no worse off than many others whose dear nurses and comforters lie coffined under the earth. You can no longer turn back. Now that you have run away, you must seek a new fortune in the world. As I have neither house nor home, nor wife nor child, I cannot go on looking after you, but I will give you some good advice for nothing.' "

So far the old man has been expressing no more than what the boy, the hero of the tale, could have thought out for himself. Having given way to the stress of emotion and simply run off like that into the blue, he would at least have had to reflect that he needed food. It would also have been necessary, at such a moment, to consider his position. The whole story of his life up to the recent past would then have passed before his mind, as is usual in such cases. An anamnesis of this kind is a purposeful process whose aim it is to gather the assets of the whole personality together at the critical moment, when all one's spiritual and physical forces are challenged, and with this united strength to fling open the door of the future. No one can help the boy to do this; he has to rely entirely on himself. There is no going back. This realization will give the necessary resolution to his actions. By forcing him to face the issue, the old man spares him the trouble of making up his mind. Indeed the old man is himself this purposeful reflection and concentration of moral and physical forces that comes about spontaneously in the psychic space outside consciousness when conscious thought is not yet—or is no longer—possible. The concentration and tension of psychic forces have something about them that always looks like magic: they develop an unexpected power of endurance which is often superior to the conscious effort of will. One can observe this experimentally in the artificial concentration induced by hypnosis: in my demonstrations I used regularly to put

14

an hysteric, of weak bodily build, into a deep hypnotic sleep and then get her to lie with the back of her head on one chair and her heels resting on another, stiff as a board, and leave her there for about a minute. Her pulse would gradually go up to 90. A husky young athlete among the students tried in vain to imitate this feat with a conscious effort of will. He collapsed in the middle with his pulse racing at 120.

When the clever old man had brought the boy to this point he could begin his good advice, i.e., the situation no longer looked hopeless. He advised him to continue his wanderings, always to the eastward, where after seven years he would reach the great mountain that betokened his good fortune. The bigness and tallness of the mountain are allusions to his grown personality.[14] Concentration of his powers brings assurance and is therefore the best guarantee of success.[15] From now on he will lack for nothing. "Take my scrip and my flask," says the old man, "and each day you will find in them all the food and drink you need." At the same time he gave him a burdock leaf that could change into a boat whenever the boy had to cross water.

Often the old man in fairy tales asks questions like who? why? whence? and whither?[16] for the purpose of inducing self-reflection and concentrating the moral forces, and more often still he gives the necessary magical talisman,[17] the unexpected and improbable power

14 The mountain stands for the goal of the pilgrimage and ascent, hence it often has the psychological meaning of the self. The *I Ching* describes the goal thus: "The king introduces him / To the Western Mountain" (tr. Richard Wilhelm–Cary F. Baynes, Bollingen Series XIX; New York, 1950: Vol. I, p. 78—Hexagram 17, *Sui*, "Following"). Cf. Honorius of Autun (*Speculum de mysteriis ecclesiae*, in J. P. Migne, *Patrologiae cursus completus*, Latin Series, Vol. CLXXII, p. 345): "The mountains are patriarchs and prophets." Richard of St. Victor says: "*Vis videre Christum transfiguratum? Ascende in montem istum, disce cognoscere te ipsum*" (Do you wish to see the transfigured Christ? Ascend that mountain and learn to know yourself). (*Benjamin minor*, in Migne, *Patr.*, Lat., Vol. CXCVI, coll. 53–56.)

15 In this respect we would call attention to the phenomenology of yoga.

16 There are numerous examples of this: *Spanische und portugiesische Volksmärchen* (1940), pp. 158, 199 ["The White Parrot" and "Queen Rose, or Little Tom"]; *Russische Volksmärchen* (1914), p. 149 ["The Girl with No Hands"]; *Balkanmärchen* (1915), p. 64 ["The Shepherd and the Three Samovilas (Nymphs)"]; *Märchen aus Iran* (1939), pp. 150ff. ["The Secret of the Bath of Windburg"]; *Nordische Volksmärchen*, Vol. I (1915), p. 231 ["The Werewolf"].

17 To the girl looking for her brothers he gives a ball of thread that rolls towards them (*Finnische und estnische Volksmärchen*, p. 260 ["The Contending Brothers"]). The prince who is searching for the kingdom of heaven is given a boat that propels itself (*Deutsche Märchen seit Grimm*, 1912, pp. 381f. ["The

to succeed, which is one of the peculiarities of the unified personality in good or bad alike. But the intervention of the old man—the spontaneous objectivation of the archetype—would seem to be equally indispensable, since the conscious will by itself is hardly ever capable of uniting the personality to the point where it acquires this extraordinary power to succeed. For that, not only in fairy tales but in life generally, the objective intervention of the archetype is needed, which checks the purely affective reactions with a chain of inner confrontations and realizations. These cause the who? where? how? why? to emerge clearly and in this wise bring knowledge of the immediate situation as well as of the goal. The resultant enlightenment and untying of the fatal tangle often has something positively magical about it—an experience not unknown to the psychotherapist.

The old man's fondness for prompting reflection also takes the form of urging people to "sleep on it." Thus he says to the girl who is searching for her lost brothers: "Lie down: morning is cleverer than evening."[18] He also sees through the gloomy situation of the hero who has got himself into trouble, or at least can give him such information as will help him on his journey. To this end he makes ready use of animals, particularly birds. To the prince who has gone in search of the kingdom of heaven the old hermit says: "I have lived here for three hundred years, but never yet has anybody asked me about the kingdom of heaven. I cannot tell you myself; but up there, on another floor of the house, live all kinds of birds, and they at any rate can tell you."[19] The old man knows what roads lead to the goal and points them out to the hero.[20] He warns of dangers to come and supplies the means of meeting them effectively. For instance, he tells the boy who has gone to fetch the silver water that the well is guarded

---

Iron Boots"]). Another gift is a flute that sets everybody dancing (*Balkanmärchen*, p. 173 ["The Twelve Crumbs"]), or the ball that points the way, the staff of invisibility (*Nordische Volksmärchen*, Vol. I, p. 97 ["The Princess with Twelve Pairs of Golden Shoes"]), miraculous dogs (ibid., p. 287 ["The Three Dogs"]), or a book of secret wisdom (*Chinesische Volksmärchen*, 1913, p. 258 ["Jang Liang"]).
18 *Finnische und estnische Volksmärchen*, loc. cit.
19 *Deutsche Märchen seit Grimm*, p. 382 [op. cit.]. In one Balkan tale (*Balkanmärchen*, p. 65 ["The Shepherd and the Three Samovilas"]) the old man is called the "Czar of all the birds." Here the magpie knows all the answers. Cf. the mysterious "master of the dovecot" in Gustav Meyrink's novel *Der weisse Dominikaner* (Vienna, 1921).
20 *Märchen aus Iran*, p. 152 [op. cit.].

by a lion who has the deceptive trick of sleeping with his eyes open and being awake with his eyes shut;[21] or he counsels the youth who is riding to a magic fountain in order to fetch the healing draught for the king, only to draw the water at a trot because of the lurking witches who lasso everybody that comes to the fountain.[22] He charges the princess whose lover has been changed into a werewolf to make a fire and put a caldron of tar over it. Then she must plunge her beloved white lily into the boiling tar, and when the werewolf comes, she must empty the caldron over its head, which will release her lover from the spell.[23] Occasionally the old man is a very critical old man, as in that Caucasian tale of the youngest prince who wanted to build a flawless church for his father, so as to inherit the kingdom. This he does, and nobody can discover a single flaw, but then an old man comes along and says, "That's a fine church you've built, to be sure! What a pity the main wall is a bit crooked!" The prince has the church pulled down again and builds a new one, but here too the old man discovers a flaw, and so for the third time.[24]

The old man thus represents knowledge, reflection, wisdom, cleverness, and intuition on the one hand, and on the other, moral qualities such as goodwill and readiness to help, which make his "spiritual" character sufficiently plain. Since the archetype is an autonomous content of the unconscious, the fairy tale, which usually concretizes the archetypes, can cause the old man to appear in a dream in much the same way as happens in modern dreams. In a Balkan tale the old man appears to the hard-pressed hero in a dream and gives him good advice about accomplishing the impossible tasks that have been imposed upon him.[25] His relation to the unconscious is clearly expressed in one Russian fairy tale, where he is called the "King of the Forest." As the peasant sat down wearily on a tree stump, a little old man crept out: "all wrinkled he was and a green beard hung down to his knees." "Who are you?" asked the peasant. "I am Och, King of the Forest," said the manikin. The peasant hired out his profligate son to him, "and the King of the Forest departed with the young man,

21 *Spanische und portugiesische Märchen*, p. 158 ["The White Parrot"].
22 Ibid., p. 199 ["Queen Rose, or Little Tom"].
23 *Nordische Volksmärchen*, Vol. I, pp. 231f ["The Werewolf"].
24 *Kaukasische Märchen* (1919), pp. 35f ["The False and the True Nightingale"].
25 *Balkanmärchen*, p. 217 ["The Lubi (She-Devil) and the Fair of the Earth"].

17

and conducted him to that other world under the earth and brought him to a green hut. . . . In the hut everything was green: the walls were green and the benches, Och's wife was green and the children were green . . . and the little water-women who waited on him were as green as rue." Even the food was green. The King of the Forest is here a vegetation or tree numen who reigns in the woods and, through the nixies, also has connections with water, which clearly shows his relation to the unconscious since the latter is frequently expressed through wood and water symbols.

There is equally a connection with the unconscious when the old man appears as a dwarf. The fairy tale about the princess who was searching for her lover says: "Night came and the darkness, and still the princess sat in the same place and wept. As she sat there lost in thought she heard a voice greeting her: 'Good evening, pretty maid! why are you sitting here so lonely and sad?' She sprang up hastily and felt very confused, and that was no wonder. But when she looked round there was only a tiny little old man standing before her, who nodded his head at her and looked so kind and simple." In a Swiss fairy tale the peasant's son who wants to bring the king's daughter a basket of apples encounters *"es chlis isigs Männdli, das frogt-ne, was er do i dem Chratte häig?"* (a little iron man who asked what he had there in the basket). In another passage the *"Männdli"* has *"es isigs Chlaidli a"* (iron clothes on). By *"isig"* presumably *"eisern"* (iron) is meant, which is more probable than *"eisig"* (icy). In the latter case it would have to be *"es Chlaidli vo Is"* (clothes of ice).[26] There are indeed ice men, and metal men too; in fact in a modern dream I have even come across a little black iron man who appeared at a critical juncture, like the one in this fairy tale of the country bumpkin who wanted to marry the princess.

In a modern series of visions in which the figure of the wise old man occurred several times, he was on one occasion of normal size and appeared at the very bottom of a crater surrounded by high rocky walls; on another occasion he was a tiny figure on the top of a

26 This occurs in the tale of the griffin, No. 84 in the volume of children's fairy tales collected by the brothers Grimm (Diederichs, 1912), Vol. II, pp. 84ff. The text swarms with phonetic mistakes. [The English text (tr. by Margaret Hunt, revised by James Stern, ed. by Joseph Campbell, New York, 1944, tale no. 165) has "hoary."—TRANS.]

mountain set inside a low, stony enclosure. We find the same motif in Goethe's tale of the dwarf princess who lived in a casket.[27] In this connection we might also mention the Anthroparion, the little leaden man of the Zosimos vision,[28] as well as the metallic men who dwell in the mines, the crafty dactyls of antiquity, the homunculi of the alchemists, and the gnomic throng of hobgoblins, brownies, gremlins, etc. How "real" such conceptions are became clear to me on the occasion of a serious mountaineering accident: after the catastrophe two of the climbers had the collective vision, in broad daylight, of a little hooded man who scrambled out of an inaccessible crevasse in the ice face and passed across the glacier, creating a regular panic in the two beholders. I have often encountered motifs which made me think that the unconscious must be the world of the infinitesimally small. Such an idea could be derived rationalistically from the dim feeling that in all these visions we are dealing with something endopsychic, the inference being that a thing must be exceedingly small in order to fit into the head. I am no friend of any such "rational" conjectures, though I would not say that they are all beside the mark. It seems to me more probable that this liking for diminutives on the one hand and for superlatives—giants, etc.—on the other is connected with the queer uncertainty of spatial and temporal relations in the unconscious.[29] Man's sense of proportion, his rational conception of big and small, is distinctly anthropomorphic, and it loses its validity not only in the realm of physical phenomena but also in those parts of the collective unconscious beyond the range of the specifically human. The atman is "smaller than small and bigger than big," he is "the size of a thumb" yet he "encompasses the earth on every side and rules over the ten-finger space."[29a] And of the Cabiri Goethe says: "little in length / mighty in strength." In the same way the archetype of the wise old man is quite tiny, almost imperceptible, and yet it possesses a fateful potency, as anyone can see when he gets down to fundamentals. The archetypes have this peculiarity in common with the atomic world, which is demonstrating before our eyes that the more deeply the

27 Goethe, "Die neue Melusine."
28 Cf. "Einige Bemerkungen zu den Visionen des Zosimos," *Eranos-Jahrbuch 1937.*
29 In one Siberian fairy tale (*Märchen aus Sibirien*, 2nd edn., 1940, no. 13 ["The Man Turned to Stone"]) the old man is a white shape towering up to heaven.
29a [Cf. "The Spirit of Psychology," infra, p. 409, note 103.—TRANS.]

investigator penetrates into the universe of microphysics the more devastating are the explosive forces he finds enchained there. That the greatest effect comes from the littlest things has become patently clear not only in physics but in the field of psychological research as well. How often in the critical moments of life everything hangs on what appears to be a mere nothing!

In certain primitive fairy tales the illuminating quality of our archetype is expressed by the fact that the old man is identified with the sun. He brings a firebrand with him which he uses for roasting a pumpkin. After he has eaten, he takes the fire away again, which causes mankind to steal it from him.[30] In a North American tale the old man is a witch doctor who owns the fire.[31] Spirit too has a fiery aspect, as we know from the language of the Old Testament and from the story of the Pentecostal miracle.

Apart from his cleverness, wisdom, and knowledge, the old man, as we have already mentioned, is also notable for his moral qualities; what is more, he even tests the moral qualities of others and makes his gifts dependent on this test. There is a particularly instructive example of this in the Esthonian fairy tale of the stepdaughter and the real daughter. The former is an orphan distinguished for her obedience and goodness. The story begins with her distaff falling into a well. She jumps in after it, but does not drown, and comes to a magic country where, continuing her quest, she meets a cow, a ram, and an apple tree whose wishes she fulfills. She now comes to a wash house where a dirty old man is sitting who wants her to wash him. The following dialogue develops: "Pretty maid, pretty maid, wash me, do, it is hard for me to be so dirty!" "What shall I heat the stove with?" "Collect wooden pegs and crows' dung and make a fire with that." But she fetches sticks, and asks, "Where shall I get the bath water?" "Under the barn there stands a white mare. Get her to piss into the tub!" But she takes clean water, and asks, "Where shall I get a bath switch?" "Cut off the white mare's tail and make a bath switch of that!" But she makes one out of birch twigs, and asks, "Where shall I get soap?" "Take a pumice stone and scrub me with that!" But she fetches soap from the village and with that she washes the old man.

30 *Indianermärchen aus Südamerika* (1920), p. 285 ["The End of the World and the Theft of Fire"—Bolivian].
31 *Indianermärchen aus Nordamerika* (1924), p. 74 [Tales of Manabos: "The Theft of Fire"].

As a reward he gives her a bag full of gold and precious stones. The daughter of the house naturally becomes jealous, throws her distaff into the well, where she finds it again instantly. Nevertheless she goes on and does everything wrong that the stepdaughter had done right, and is rewarded accordingly. The frequency of this motif makes further examples superfluous.

The figure of the superior and helpful old man tempts one to connect him somehow or other with God. In the German tale of the soldier and the black princess[32] it is related how the princess, on whom a curse has been laid, creeps out of her iron coffin every night and devours the soldier standing guard over the tomb. One soldier, when his turn came, tried to escape. "That evening he stole away, fled over the fields and mountains, and came to a beautiful meadow. Suddenly a little man stood before him with a long gray beard, but it was none other than the Lord God himself, who could no longer go on looking at all the mischief the devil wrought every night. 'Whither away?' said the little gray man, 'may I come with you?' And because the little old man looked so friendly the soldier told him that he had run away and why he had done so." Good advice follows, as always. In this story the old man is taken for God in the same naïve way that the English alchemist, Sir George Ripley,[33] describes the "old king" as *"antiquus dierum"*—"the Ancient of Days."

Just as all archetypes have a positive, favorable, bright side that points upwards, so also they have one that points downwards, partly negative and unfavorable, partly chthonic, but for the rest merely neutral. To this the spirit archetype is no exception. Even his dwarf-like shape points to a limiting diminutive, and so does his suggested character as a naturalistic vegetation numen sprung from the underworld. In one Balkan tale the old man is handicapped by the loss of an eye. It has been gouged out by the Vili, a species of winged demon, and the hero is charged with the task of getting them to restore it to him. The old man has therefore lost part of his eyesight—that is, his insight and enlightenment—to the daemonic world of darkness; this handicap is reminiscent of the fate of Osiris, who lost an eye at the sight of a black pig (his wicked brother Set), or again of Wotan, who sacrificed his eye at the spring of Mimir. Characteristically enough the

32 *Deutsche Märchen seit Grimm*, pp. 189ff.
33 In his "Cantilena" (17th cent.).

animal ridden by the old man of our fairy tale is a goat, a sign that he himself has a dark side. In a Siberian tale he appears as a one-legged, one-handed, and one-eyed graybeard who wakens a dead man with an iron staff. In the course of the story the latter, after being brought back to life several times, kills the old man by a mistake, and thus throws away his good fortune. The story is entitled "The One-sided Old Man," and in truth his handicap shows that he consists of one half only. The other half is invisible, but appears in the shape of a murderer who seeks the hero's life. Eventually the hero succeeds in killing his persistent murderer, but in the struggle he also kills the one-sided old man, so that the identity of the two victims is clearly revealed. It is thus possible that the old man is his own opposite, a life-bringer as well as a death-dealer—*"ad utrumque peritus"* (skilled in both), as is said of Hermes.[34]

In these circumstances, whenever the "simple" and "kindly" old man appears, it is advisable for heuristic and other reasons to scrutinize the context with some care. For instance in the Esthonian tale we first mentioned, about the hired boy who lost the cow, there is a suspicion that the helpful old man who happened to be on the spot so opportunely had surreptitiously made away with the cow beforehand in order to give his protégé an excellent reason for taking to flight. This may very well be, for everyday experience shows that a subliminal knowledge of the future may quite possibly contrive some annoying incident for the sole purpose of bullying our Simple Simon of an ego consciousness into the way he should go, which he would never have found by himself for sheer stupidity. Had our orphan guessed that it was the old man who had whisked off his cow as if by magic, he would have seemed like a spiteful troll or a devil. And indeed the old man has a wicked aspect too, just as the primitive medicine man is a healer and helper and also the dreaded concocter of poisons. The very word φάρμακον means "poison" as well as "antidote," and poison can in fact be both.

The old man, then, has a two-faced, elfin character—witness the

---

34 Prudentius, *Contra Symmachum*, I, 94 (tr. H. J. Thompson, Loeb Classical Library, Cambridge, Mass., 1949, Vol. I, p. 356). See Hugo Rahner, "Die seelen-heilende Blume," *Eranos-Jahrbuch 1944*.

extremely instructive figure of Merlin—seeming, in certain of his forms, to be good incarnate and in others to be an aspect of evil. Then again, he is the wicked magician who, from sheer egoism, does evil for evil's sake. In a Siberian fairy tale he is an evil spirit "on whose head were two lakes with two ducks swimming in them." He feeds on human flesh. The story relates how the hero and his companions go to a feast in the next village, leaving their dogs at home. These, acting on the principle "when the cat's away the mice do play," also arrange a feast at the climax of which they all hurl themselves on the stores of meat. The men return home and chase out the dogs, who dash off into the wilderness. "Then the Creator spoke to Ememqut [the hero of the tale]: 'Go and look for the dogs with your wife.' " But he gets caught in a terrible snowstorm and has to seek shelter in the hut of the evil spirit. There now follows the well-known motif of the biter bit. The "Creator" is Ememqut's father, but the father of the Creator is called the "Self-created" because he created himself. Although we are nowhere told that the old man with the two lakes on his head lured the hero and his wife into the hut in order to satisfy his hunger, it may be conjectured that a very peculiar spirit must have got into the dogs to cause them to celebrate a feast like the men and afterwards—contrary to their nature—to run away, so that Ememqut had to go out and look for them; and that the hero was then caught in a snowstorm in order to drive him into the arms of the wicked old man. The fact that the Creator, son of the Self-created, was a party to the advice raises a knotty problem whose solution we had best leave to the Siberian theologians.

In a Balkan fairy tale the old man gives the childless Czarina a magic apple to eat, from which she becomes pregnant and bears a son, it being stipulated that the old man shall be his godfather. The boy, however, grows up into a horrid little tough who bullies all the children and slaughters the cattle. For ten years he is given no name. Then the old man appears, sticks a knife in his leg, and calls him the "Knife Prince." The boy now wants to set forth on his adventures, which his father, after long hesitation, finally allows him to do. The knife in his leg is of vital importance: if he draws it out himself, he will live; if anybody else does so, he will die. In the end the knife becomes his doom, for an old witch pulls it out when he is asleep. He dies, but is restored to life by the friends he has won.[35] Here the old man is a helper, but also the giver of a dangerous fate which might just as easily have turned out for the bad. The evil showed itself early and plainly in the boy's villainous character.

In another Balkan tale there is a variant of our motif that is worth mentioning: a king is looking for his sister who has been abducted by a stranger. His wanderings bring him to the hut of an old woman who warns him against continuing the search. But a tree laden with fruit, ever receding before him, lures him away from the hut. When at last the tree comes to a halt, an old man climbs down from the branches. He regales the king and takes him to the castle where the sister is living with the old man as his wife. She tells her brother that the old man is a wicked spirit who will kill him. And sure enough, three days afterwards the king vanishes without trace. His younger brother now takes up the search and kills the wicked spirit in the form of a dragon. A handsome young man is thereby released from the spell and forthwith marries the sister. The old man, appearing at first as a tree numen, is obviously connected with the sister. He is a murderer. In an interpolated episode he is accused of enchanting a whole city by turning it to iron, i.e., making it immovable, rigid, and locked up.[36] He also holds the king's sister a captive and will not let her return to her relatives. This amounts to saying that the sister is animus-possessed. The old man is therefore to be regarded as her animus. But the manner in which the king is drawn into this possession, and the way he seeks for his sister, make us think that she has an anima significance for her brother. The fateful archetype (of the old man) has accordingly first taken possession of the king's anima—in other words, robbed him of the archetype of life which the anima personifies—and forced him to go in search of the lost charm, the "treasure hard to attain," thus making him the mythical hero, the higher personality who is an expression of the self. Meanwhile the old man acts the part of the villain and has to be forcibly removed, only to appear at the end as the husband of the sister anima, or more properly as the bridegroom

35 *Balkanmärchen*, pp. 34ff. ["The Deeds of the Czar's Son and His Two Companions"].
36 Ibid., pp. 177ff. ["The Son-in-Law from Abroad"].

of the soul, who celebrates the sacred incest that symbolizes the union of the opposite and equal. This bold enantiodromia, a very common occurrence, not only signifies the rejuvenation and transformation of the old man, but hints at a secret inner relation of evil to good and vice versa.

So in this story we see the archetype of the old man in the guise of an evildoer, caught up in all the twists and turns of an individuation process that ends suggestively with the *hieros gamos*. Conversely, in the Russian tale of the Forest King, he starts by being helpful and benevolent, but then refuses to let his hired boy go, so that the main episodes in the story deal with the boy's repeated attempts to escape from the clutches of the magician. Instead of the quest we have flight, which nonetheless appears to win the same reward as adventures valiantly sought, for in the end the hero marries the king's daughter. The magician, however, must rest content with the role of the biter bit.

4. Theriomorphic Spirit Symbolism in Fairy Tales

The description of our archetype would not be complete if we omitted to consider one special form of its manifestation, namely its animal form. This belongs essentially to the theriomorphism of gods and demons and has the same psychological significance. The animal form shows that the contents and functions in question are still in the extra-human sphere, i.e., on a plane beyond human consciousness, and consequently have a share on the one hand in the daemonically super-human and on the other in the bestially subhuman. It must be remembered, however, that this division is only true within the sphere of consciousness, where it is a necessary condition of thought. Logic says *tertium non datur,* meaning that we cannot envisage the opposites in their oneness. In other words, while the abolition of an obstinate antinomy can be no more than a postulate for us, this is by no means so for the unconscious, whose contents are without exception para-doxical or antinomial by nature, not excluding the category of being. If anyone unacquainted with the psychology of the unconscious wants to get a working knowledge of these matters, I would recommend a study of Christian mysticism and Indian philosophy. There he will find the most graphic elaboration of the antinomies of the unconscious.

Although the old man has, up to now, looked and behaved more or less like a human being, his magical powers and his spiritual superiority suggest that, in good and bad alike, he is outside, or above, or below the human level. Neither for the primitive nor for the unconscious does his animal aspect imply a diminution of value, for in certain respects the animal is superior to man. It has not yet blundered into consciousness nor pitted a self-willed ego against the power from which it lives; on the contrary, it fulfills the will that actuates it in a well-nigh perfect manner. Were it conscious, it would be morally better than man. There is deep doctrine in the legend of the Fall: it is the expression of a dim presentiment that the emancipation of ego consciousness was a Luciferian deed. Man's whole history consists from the very beginning in a conflict between his feeling of inferiority and his arrogance. Wisdom seeks the middle path and pays for this audacity by a questionable relationship to demon and beast, and consequently is open to moral misinterpretation.

Again and again in fairy tales we encounter the motif of helpful animals. These act like humans, speak a human language, and display a sagacity and a knowledge superior to man's. In these circumstances we can say with some justification that the archetype of the spirit is being expressed through an animal form. A German fairy tale[37] relates how a young man, while searching for his lost princess, meets a wolf, who says, "Do not be afraid! But tell me, where is your way leading you?" The young man recounts his story, whereupon the wolf gives him as a magic gift a few of his hairs, with which the young man can summon his help at any time. This intermezzo proceeds exactly like the meeting with the helpful old man. In the same story the archetype also displays its other, wicked side. In order to make this clear I shall give a summary of the story:

While the young man was watching his pigs in the wood he discovers a large tree whose branches lose themselves in the clouds. "How would it be," says he to himself, "if you were to look at the world from the top of that great tree?" So he climbs up, all day long he climbs, without reaching the branches. Evening comes and he has to pass the night in a fork of the tree. Next day he goes on climbing and by noon has

37 *Deutsche Märchen seit Grimm*, pp. 1ff. ["The Princess in the Tree"].

reached the foliage. Towards evening he comes to a village nestling in the branches. The peasants who live there give him food and shelter for the night. In the morning he climbs further. That afternoon he reaches a castle in which a young girl lives. Here he finds that the tree goes no higher. She is a king's daughter, held prisoner by a wicked magician. So the young man stays with the princess, and she allows him to go into all the rooms of the castle: one room alone she forbids him to enter. But curiosity is too strong. He unlocks the door, and there in the room he finds a raven fixed to the wall with three nails. One nail goes through his throat, the two others through the wings. The raven complains of thirst and the young man, moved by pity, gives him water to drink. At each sip a nail falls out, and at the third sip the raven is free and flies out at the window. When the princess hears of it she is very frightened and says, "That was the devil who enchanted me! It won't be long now before he fetches me again." And one fine morning she has indeed vanished.

The young man now sets out in search of her and, as we have described above, meets the wolf. In the same way he meets a bear and a lion, who also give him some hairs. In addition the lion informs him that the princess is imprisoned nearby in a hunting lodge. The young man finds the house and the princess, but is told that flight is impossible, because the hunter possesses a three-legged white horse that knows everything and would infallibly warn its master. Despite that the young man tries to flee away with her, but in vain. The hunter overtakes him but, because he had saved his life as a raven, lets him go, and rides off again with the princess. When the hunter has disappeared into the wood, the young man creeps back to the house and persuades the princess to wheedle from the hunter the secret of how he obtained his clever white horse. This she successfully does in the night, and the young man, who has hidden himself under the bed, learns that about an hour's journey from the hunting lodge there dwells a witch who breeds magic horses. Whoever can tend the foals for three days may choose a horse as a reward. In former times, said the hunter, she used to make a gift of twelve lambs into the bargain, in order to satisfy the hunger of the twelve wolves who lived in the woods near the farmstead, and prevent them from attacking; but to

27

him she gave no lambs. So the wolves followed him as he rode away, and while crossing the borders of her domain they succeeded in tearing off one of his horse's hoofs. That was why it had only three legs.

Then the young man made haste to seek out the witch and hired himself to her on condition that she gave him not only the horse but twelve lambs as well. To this she agreed. Instantly she commanded the foals to run away, and, to make him sleepy, she gave him brandy. He drinks, falls asleep, and the foals run away as commanded. On the first day he catches them with the help of the wolf, on the second day the bear helps him, and on the third the lion. He can now go and choose his reward. The witch's little daughter tells him which horse her mother rides. This is naturally the best horse, and it too is white. Hardly has he got it out of the stall when the witch pierces the four hoofs and sucks the marrow out of the bones. From this she bakes a cake and gives it to the young man for his journey. The horse grows deathly weak, but the young man feeds it on the cake, whereupon the horse recovers its former strength. He gets out of the woods unscathed after quieting the twelve wolves with the twelve lambs. He then fetches the princess and rides away with her. But the three-legged horse calls out to the hunter, who sets off in pursuit and quickly catches up with them, because the four-legged horse refuses to gallop. As the hunter approaches, the four-legged horse cries out to the three-legged, "Sister, throw him off!" The magician is thrown and trampled to pieces by the two horses. The young man sets the princess on the three-legged horse, and the pair of them ride away to her father's kingdom, where they get married. The four-legged horse begs him to cut off both their heads, for otherwise they would bring disaster upon him. This he does, and the horses are transformed into a handsome prince and a wonderfully beautiful princess, who after a while repair "to their own kingdom." They had been changed into horses by the hunter, long ago.

Apart from the theriomorphic spirit symbolism in this tale, it is especially interesting to note that the function of knowing and intuition is represented by a riding-animal. This is as much as to say that the spirit can be somebody's property. The three-legged white horse is thus the property of the daemonic hunter, and the four-legged one the property of the witch. Spirit is here partly a function, which can change its owner like any other thing (horse), and partly an autono-

28

mous subject (magician as owner of the horse). By obtaining the four-legged horse from the witch, the young man frees a spirit or a thought of some special kind from the grip of the unconscious. Here as elsewhere, the witch stands for a *mater natura* or the original "matriarchal" state of the unconscious, and this indicates a psychic constitution in which the unconscious is offset only by a feeble and not yet self-reliant consciousness. The four-legged horse shows itself superior to the three-legged, since it can command the latter. And since the quaternity is a symbol of wholeness and wholeness plays a considerable role in the picture world of the unconscious,[38] the victory of four-leggedness over three-leggedness is not altogether unexpected. But what is the meaning of the opposition between threeness and fourness, or rather, what does threeness mean as compared with wholeness? In alchemy this problem is known as the axiom of Maria and runs all through alchemical philosophy for more than a thousand years, finally to be taken up again in the Cabiri scene in *Faust*. The earliest literary version of it is to be found in the opening words of Plato's *Timaeus*,[39] of which Goethe gives us a reminder. Among the alchemists we can clearly see how the divine Trinity has its counterpart in a lower, chthonic triad (similar to Dante's three-headed devil). This consists in a principle which, by reason of its symbolism, betrays affinities with evil, though it is not at all sure that it expresses nothing but evil. Everything points rather to the fact that evil, or its familiar symbolism, belongs to the family of figures which describe the dark, nocturnal, lower, chthonic element. In this symbolism the lower stands to the higher as a correspondence[40] in reverse; that is to say it is conceived, like the upper, as a triad.

Three, being a masculine number, is logically correlated with the wicked hunter, who can be thought of alchemically as the lower triad.

38 With reference to the quaternity I would call attention to my earlier writings, and in particular to *Psychology and Alchemy, Coll. Works,* Vol. 12, and *Psychology and Religion* (London and New Haven, 1938; in German, expanded, Zurich, 1940).

39 The oldest representation I know of this problem is that of the four sons of Horus, three of whom are occasionally depicted with the heads of animals, and the other with the head of a man. Chronologically this links up with Ezekiel's vision of the four figures, which then reappear in the attributes of the four evangelists. Three have animal heads and one a human head (the angel).

40 According to the dictum in the "Tabula smaragdina," "Quod est inferius, est sicut quod est superius" (That which is below is like that which is above).

Four, a feminine number, is assigned to the old woman. The two horses are miraculous animals that talk and know and thus represent the unconscious spirit, which in one case is subordinated to the wicked magician and in the other to the old witch.

Between the three and the four there exists the primary opposition of male and female, but whereas fourness is a symbol of wholeness, threeness is not. The latter, according to alchemy, denotes polarity, since one triad always presupposes another, just as high presupposes low, lightness darkness, good evil. In terms of energy polarity means a potential, and wherever a potential exists there is the possibility of a current, a flow of events, for the tension of opposites strives for balance. If one imagines the quaternity as a square divided into two halves by a diagonal, one gets two triangles whose apices point in opposite directions. One could therefore say metaphorically that if the wholeness symbolized by the quaternity is divided into equal halves, it produces two opposing triads. This simple reflection shows how three can be derived from four, and in the same way the hunter of the captured princess explains how his horse, from being four-legged, became three-legged, through having one hoof torn off by the twelve wolves. The three-leggedness is due to an accident, therefore, which occurred at the very moment when the horse was leaving the territory of the dark mother. In psychological language we should say that when the unconscious wholeness becomes manifest, i.e., leaves the unconscious and crosses over into the sphere of consciousness, one of the four remains behind, held fast by the *horror vacui* of the unconscious. There thus arises a triad, which as we know—not from the fairy tale but from the history of symbolism—constellates a corresponding triad in opposition to it[41] —in other words, a conflict ensues. Here too we could ask with Socrates, "One, two, three—but, my dear Timaeus, of those who yesterday were the banqueters and today are the banquet-givers, where is the fourth?"[42] He has remained in the realm of the dark mother, caught by the wolfish greed of the unconscious, which is unwilling to let anything escape from its magic circle save at the cost of a corresponding sacrifice.

The hunter or old magician and the witch correspond to the nega-

---

41 Cf. *Psychology and Alchemy*, fig. 54 and par. 539; and, for a more detailed account, "Der Geist Mercurius," *Eranos-Jahrbuch 1942*, p. 215.

42 This unexplained passage has been put down to Plato's "drollery."

tive parental imagos in the magic world of the unconscious. The hunter first appears in the story as a black raven. He has stolen away the princess and holds her a prisoner. She describes him as "the devil." But it is exceedingly odd that he himself is locked up in the one forbidden room of the castle and fixed to the wall with three nails, as though *crucified*. He is imprisoned, like all jailers, in his own prison, and bound like all who curse. The prison of both is a magic castle at the top of a gigantic tree, presumably the world tree. The princess belongs to the upper region of light near the sun. Sitting there in captivity on the world tree, she is a kind of *anima mundi* who has got herself into the power of darkness. But this catch does not seem to have done the latter much good either, seeing that the captor is crucified and moreover with three nails. The crucifixion evidently betokens an agonizing thralldom and suspension, fit punishment for one foolhardy enough to venture like a Prometheus into the ambit of the counter principle. This was what the raven, who is identical with the hunter, did when he ravished a precious soul from the upper world of light; and so, as a punishment, he is nailed to the wall in that upper world. That this is an inverted reflection of the primordial Christian image should be obvious enough. The Saviour who freed the soul of humanity from the dominion of the prince of this world was nailed to a cross down below on earth, just as the thieving raven is nailed to the wall in the celestial branches of the world tree for his presumptuous meddling. In our fairy tale the peculiar instrument of the magic spell is the triad of nails. Who it was that made the raven captive is not told in the tale, but it sounds as if a spell had been laid upon him in the triune name.[43]

Having climbed up the world tree and penetrated into the magic castle, where he is to rescue the princess, our young hero is permitted to enter all the rooms but one, the very room in which the raven is imprisoned. Just as in paradise there was one tree of which it was forbidden to eat, so here there is one room that is not to be opened, with the natural result that it is entered at once. Nothing excites our interest more than a prohibition. It is the surest way of provoking disobedience.

43 In *Deutsche Märchen seit Grimm* (Vol. I, p. 256 ["The Mary-Child"]) it is said that the "Three-in-One" is the forbidden room, which seems to me a fact worth noting.

Obviously there is some secret scheme afoot to free not so much the princess as the raven. As soon as the hero catches sight of him, the raven begins to cry piteously and to complain about his thirst,[44] and the young man, moved by the virtue of compassion, slakes it, not with hyssop and gall, but with quickening water, whereupon the three nails fall out and the raven escapes through the open window. Thus the evil spirit regains his freedom, changes into the hunter, steals the princess for the second time, but this time locks her up in his hunting lodge on earth. The secret scheme is partially unveiled: the princess must be brought down from the upper world to the world of men, which was evidently not possible without the help of the evil spirit and man's disobedience.

But since in the human world too the hunter of souls is the princess's master, the hero has to intervene anew, to which end, as we have seen, he filches the four-legged horse from the witch and breaks the three-legged spell of the magician. It was the triad that first transfixed the raven, and the triad also represents the power of the evil spirit. These are the two triads that point in opposite directions.

Turning now to quite another field, namely that of psychological experience, we know that three of the four functions of consciousness can become differentiated, i.e., conscious, while the other remains connected with the matrix, the unconscious, and is known as the "inferior" function. It is the Achilles heel of even the most heroic consciousness: somewhere the strong man is weak, the clever man foolish, the good man bad, and the reverse is also true. In our fairy tale the triad appears as a mutilated quaternity. If only one leg could be added to the other

44 Aelian (*De natura animalium*, I, 47) relates that Apollo condemned the ravens to thirst because a raven sent to fetch water took too long over it. In German folklore the raven has to suffer thirst in June or August, the reason given being that he alone was not troubled at the death of Christ, or that he failed to return when Noah sent him forth from the ark. (Friedrich Panzer in *Zeitschrift für deutsche Mythologie*, II (1855), 171; and Reinhold Köhler, *Kleinere Schriften zur Märchenforschung* (Weimar, 1898, p. 3). For the raven as an allegory of evil, see the exhaustive account by Hugo Rahner, "Earth Spirit and Divine Spirit in Patristic Theology," in the present volume. On the other hand the raven is closely connected with Apollo as his sacred animal, and in the Bible too he has a positive significance. See Psalm 147:9: "He giveth to the beast his food, and to the young ravens which cry"; Job 38:41: "Who provideth for the raven his food? when his young ones cry unto God, they wander for lack of meat." Cf. also Luke 12:24. Ravens appear as true "ministering spirits" in I Kings 17:6, where they bring Elijah the Tishbite his daily fare.

three, it would make a whole. The enigmatic axiom of Maria runs: ". . . from the third comes the one as the fourth" (ἐκ τοῦ τρίτου τὸ ἕν τέταρτον)—which presumably means, when the third produces the fourth it at once produces unity. The lost component which is in the possession of the wolves belonging to the Great Mother is indeed only a quarter, but, together with the three, it makes a whole which does away with division and conflict.

But how is it that a quarter, on the evidence of symbolism, is at the same time a triad? Here the symbolism of our fairy tale leaves us in the lurch, and we are obliged to have recourse to the facts of psychology. I have said previously that three functions can become differentiated, and only one remains under the spell of the unconscious. This statement must be defined more closely. It is an empirical fact that only *one* function becomes more or less successfully differentiated, which on that account is known as the superior or main function, and together with extraversion or introversion determines the type of conscious attitude. This function is flanked by one or two partially differentiated auxiliary functions which hardly ever attain the same degree of differentiation as the main function, that is, the same degree of applicability by the will. Accordingly they possess a higher degree of spontaneity than the main function, which displays a large measure of reliability and is amenable to our intentions. The fourth, inferior function proves on the other hand to be inaccessible to our will. It appears now as a teasing and distracting imp, now as a *deus ex machina*. But always it comes and goes of its own volition. From this it is clear that even the differentiated functions have only partially freed themselves from the unconscious; for the rest they are still rooted in it and to that extent they operate under its rule. Hence the three "differentiated" functions at the disposal of the ego have three corresponding unconscious components that have not yet broken loose from the unconscious.[45] And just as the three conscious and differentiated parts of these functions are confronted by a fourth, undifferentiated function which acts as a painfully disturbing factor, so also the superior function seems to have its worst enemy in the unconscious. Nor should we omit to mention one final turn of the screw: like the devil who delights in disguising

---

45 Pictured as three princesses, buried neck deep, in *Nordische Volksmärchen*, Vol. II (1922), pp. 126ff. ["The Three Princesses in the White Land"].

himself as an angel of light, the inferior function secretly and mischievously influences the superior function most of all, just as the latter represses the former most strongly.[46]

These unfortunately somewhat abstract formulations are necessary in order to throw some light on the tricky and allusive associations in our—save the mark!—"childishly simple" fairy tale. The two antithetical triads, the one banning and the other representing the power of evil, tally to a hair's breadth with the functional structure of the conscious and unconscious psyche. Being a spontaneous, naïve, and uncontrived product of the psyche, the fairy tale cannot very well express anything except what the psyche actually is. It is not only *our* fairy tale that depicts these structural psychic relations, but countless other fairy tales do the same.[47]

Our fairy tale reveals with unusual clarity the essentially antithetical nature of the spirit archetype, while on the other hand it shows the bewildering play of antinomies all aiming at the great goal of higher consciousness. The young swineherd who climbs from the animal level up to the top of the giant world tree and there, in the upper world of light, discovers his captive anima, the high-born princess, symbolizes the ascent of consciousness, rising from almost bestial regions to a lofty perch with a broad outlook, which aptly describes the enlargement of the conscious horizon.[48] Once the masculine consciousness has attained this height, it comes face to face with its feminine counterpart, the anima.[49] She is a personification of the unconscious. The meeting shows how inept it is to designate the latter as the "subconscious": it is not merely "below" consciousness but also above it, so far above it indeed that the hero has to climb up to it with considerable effort. This "upper" unconscious, however, is far from being a "superconscious" in the sense that anyone who reaches it,

46 For the function theory see *Psychological Types* (London and New York, 1923).
47 I would like to add, for the layman's benefit, that the theory of the psyche's structure was not derived from fairy tales and myths, but is grounded on empirical observations made in the field of medicopsychological research and was corroborated only secondarily through the study of comparative symbology, in spheres very far removed from ordinary medical practice.
48 A typical enantiodromia is played out here: as one cannot go any higher along this road, one must now realize the other side of one's being, and climb down again.
49 The young man asks himself, on catching sight of the tree, "How would it be if you were to look at the world from the top of that great tree?"

like our hero, would stand as high above the "subconscious" as above the earth's surface. On the contrary, he makes the disagreeable discovery that his high and mighty anima, the Princess Soul, is bewitched up there and no freer than a bird in a golden cage. He may pat himself on the back for having soared up from the flatlands and from almost bestial stupidity, but his soul is in the power of an evil spirit, a grim father imago of the subterrene sort in the guise of a raven, the celebrated theriomorphic figure of the devil. What use now is his lofty perch and his wide horizon, when his own dear soul is languishing in prison? Worse, she plays the game of the underworld and ostensibly tries to stop the young man from discovering the secret of her imprisonment, by forbidding him to enter that one room. But secretly she leads him to it by the very fact of her veto. It is as though the unconscious had two hands of which one always does the opposite of the other. The princess wants and does not want to be rescued. But the evil spirit too has got himself into a fix, by all accounts: he wanted to filch a fine soul from the shining upper world—which he could easily do as a winged being—but had not bargained on being shut up there himself. Black spirit though he is, he longs for the light. That is his secret justification, just as his being spellbound is a punishment for his transgression. But so long as the evil spirit is caught in the upper world, the princess cannot get down to earth either, and the hero remains lost in paradise. So now he commits the sin of disobedience and thereby enables the robber to escape, thus causing the abduction of the princess for the second time—a whole chain of calamities. In the result, however, the princess comes down to earth and the devilish raven assumes the human shape of the hunter. The otherworldly anima and the evil principle both descend to the human sphere, that is, they dwindle to human proportions and thus become approachable. The three-legged, all-knowing horse represents the hunter's own power: it corresponds to the unconscious components of the differentiated functions.[50] The hunter himself personifies the inferior function, which also manifests itself in the hero as his inquisitiveness and

50 The "omniscience" of the unconscious function components is naturally an exaggeration. Nevertheless they do have at their disposal—or are influenced by— the subliminal perceptions and memories of the unconscious, as well as by its instinctive archetypal contents. It is these that give the unconscious activities their unexpectedly correct information.

sense of adventure. As the story unfolds he becomes more and more like the hunter: he too obtains his horse from the witch. But, unlike him, the hunter omitted to obtain the twelve lambs in order to feed the wolves, who then injured his horse. He forgot to pay tribute to the chthonic powers because he was nothing but a robber. Through this omission the hero learns that the unconscious lets its creatures go only at the cost of sacrifice.[51] The number 12 is presumably a time symbol, with the subsidiary meaning of the twelve labors (ἆθλα)[52] which have to be performed for the unconscious before one can get free.[53] The hunter looks like a previous unsuccessful trying out of the hero to gain possession of his soul through robbery and violence. But the conquest of the soul is in reality a work of patience, self-sacrifice, and devotion. By gaining possession of the four-legged horse the hero steps right into the shoes of the hunter and carries off the princess as well. The quaternity in our tale proves to be the greater power, for it integrates into its totality the component which this lacked in order to be whole.

The archetype of the spirit in this, be it said, by no means primitive fairy tale is expressed theriomorphically as a system of three functions which is subordinated to a unity, the evil spirit, in the same way that some unnamed authority has crucified the raven with a triad of three nails. The two superordinate unities correspond in the first case to the inferior function which is the archenemy of the main function, namely to the hunter; and in the second case to the main function, namely to the hero. Hunter and hero are ultimately equated with one another, so that the hunter's function is resolved in the hero. As a matter of fact, the hero lies dormant in the hunter from the very beginning, egging him on, with all the unmoral means at his disposal, to carry out the rape of the soul, and then causing him to play her into the hero's hands against the hunter's will. On the surface a furious conflict rages between them, but down below the one goes about the other's business. The knot is unraveled directly the hero succeeds in

51 The hunter has reckoned without his host, as generally happens. Seldom or never do we think of the price exacted by the spirit's activity.
52 Cf. the Herakles cycle.
53 The alchemists stress the long duration of the work and speak of the *"longissima via," "diuturnitas immensae meditationis,"* etc. The number 12 may be connected with the ecclesiastical year, when the redemptive work of Christ is fulfilled. The lamb sacrifice probably comes from this source too.

getting hold of the quaternity—or in psychological language, when he assimilates the inferior function into the ternary system. That puts an end to the conflict at one blow, and the figure of the hunter melts into thin air. After this victory the hero sets his princess upon the three-legged steed and together they ride away to her father's kingdom. From now on she rules and personifies the realm of spirit that formerly served the wicked hunter. Thus the anima is and remains the representative of that part of the unconscious which can never be assimilated into a humanly attainable whole.

Postscript. Only after the completion of my manuscript was my attention drawn by a friend to a Russian variant of our story. It bears the title "Maria Morevna."[54] The hero of the story is no swineherd, but Czarevitch Ivan. There is an interesting explanation of the three helpful animals: they form a correspondence to Ivan's three sisters and their husbands, who are really birds. The three sisters represent an unconscious triad of functions related to the animal or spiritual realm. The bird men are a species of angel and emphasize the auxiliary nature of the unconscious functions. In the story they intervene at the critical moment when the hero—unlike his German counterpart—gets into the power of the evil spirit and is killed and dismembered (the typical fate of the God-man!).[55] The evil spirit is an old man who is often shown naked and is called Koschei[56] the Deathless. The corresponding witch is the well-known Baba Yaga. The three helpful animals of the German variant are doubled here, appearing first as the bird men and then as the lion, the strange bird, and the bees. The princess is Queen Maria Morevna, a redoubtable martial leader—Mary the queen of heaven is lauded in the Russian Orthodox hymnal as "leader of hosts"! —who has chained up the evil spirit with twelve chains in the forbidden room in her castle. When Ivan slakes the old devil's thirst he makes off with the queen. The magic riding animals do not in the end turn into human beings. This Russian story has a distinctly more primitive character.

54 "Daughter of the sea."—*Russian Fairy Tales* (New York, 1945), pp. 553ff.
55 The old man puts the dismembered body into a barrel which he throws into the sea. This is reminiscent of the fate of Osiris (head and phallus).
56 From *kost,* "bone," and *pakost, kapost,* "disgusting, dirty."

5. *Supplement*

The following remarks lay no claim to general interest, being in the main technical. I wanted at first to delete them from this revised version of my essay, but then I changed my mind and appended them in a Supplement. The reader who is not specifically interested in psychology can safely skip this section. For, in what follows, I have dealt with the abstruse-looking problem of the three- and four-leggedness of the magic horses, and presented my reflections in such a way as to demonstrate the method I have employed. This piece of psychological reasoning rests firstly on the irrational data of the material, that is, of the fairy tale, myth, or dream, and secondly on the conscious realization of the "latent" rational connections which these data have with one another. That such connections exist at all is something of an hypothesis, like that which asserts that dreams have a meaning. The truth of this assumption is not established a priori: its usefulness can only be proved by application. It therefore remains to be seen whether its methodical application to irrational material enables one to interpret the latter in a meaningful way. Its application consists in approaching the material as if it had a coherent inner meaning. For this purpose most of the data require a certain amplification, that is, they need to be clarified, generalized, and approximated to a more or less general concept in accordance with Cardan's rule of interpretation. For instance the three-leggedness, in order to be recognized for what it is, has first to be separated from the horse and then approximated to its specific principle—the principle of threeness. Likewise the four-leggedness in the fairy tale, when raised to the level of a general concept, enters into relationship with the threeness, as a result of which we have the enigma mentioned in the *Timaeus,* the problem of three and four. Triads and tetrads represent archetypal structures that play a significant part in all symbolism and are equally important for the investigation of myths and dreams. By raising the irrational datum (three-leggedness and four-leggedness) to the level of a general concept we elicit the universal meaning of this motif and encourage the inquiring mind to tackle the problem seriously. This task involves a series of reflections and deductions of a technical nature which I would not wish to withhold from the psychologically interested reader and especially from the professional, the less so as this labor of the intellect represents a typical unraveling of symbols and is indispensable for an adequate understanding of the products of the unconscious. Only in this way can the nexus of unconscious relationships be made to yield their own meaning, in contrast to those deductive interpretations derived from a preconceived theory, e.g., interpretations based on astronomy, meteorology, mythology, and—last but not least—the sexual theory.

The three-legged and four-legged horses are in truth a recondite matter worthy of closer examination. The three and the four remind us not only of the dilemma we have already met in the theory of psychological functions, but also of the axiom of Maria Prophetissa, which plays a considerable part in alchemy. It may therefore be rewarding to examine more closely the meaning of the miraculous horses.

The first thing that seems to me worthy of note is that the three-legged horse which is assigned to the princess as her mount is a mare, and is moreover herself a bewitched princess. Threeness is unmistakably connected here with femininity, whereas from the dominating religious standpoint of consciousness it is an exclusively masculine affair, quite apart from the fact that 3, as an uneven number, is masculine in the first place. One could therefore translate threeness as "masculinity" outright, this being all the more significant when one remembers the ancient Egyptian triunity of God, Ka-mutef,[57] and Pharaoh.

Three-leggedness, as the quality of some animal, denotes the unconscious masculinity immanent in a female creature. In a real woman it would correspond to the animus who, like the magic horse, represents "spirit." In the case of the anima, however, threeness does not coincide with any Christian idea of the Trinity but with the "lower triangle," the inferior function triad that constitutes the "shadow." The inferior half of the personality is for the greater part unconscious. It does not denote the whole of the unconscious, but only the personal segment of it. The anima, on the other hand, so far as she is distinguished from the shadow, personifies the collective unconscious. If

57 Ka-mutef means "bull of his mother." See Helmuth Jacobsohn, "Die dogmatische Stellung des Königs in der Theologie der alten Aegypter," *Aegyptologische Forschungen* (Glückstadt), No. 8 (1939), pp. 17, 35, 41ff.

threeness is assigned to her as a riding-animal, it means that she "rides" the shadow, is related to it as "Mara."[58] In that case she possesses the shadow. But if she herself is the horse, then she has lost her dominating position as a personification of the collective unconscious and is "ridden"—possessed—by Princess A, spouse of the hero. As the fairy tale rightly says, she has been changed by witchcraft into the three-legged horse (Princess B).

We can sort out this imbroglio more or less as follows:

1. Princess A is the anima[59] of the hero. She rides—that is, possesses —the three-legged horse, who is the shadow, the inferior function triad of her later spouse. To put it more simply: she has taken over the inferior half of the hero's personality. She has caught him on his weak side, as so often happens in ordinary life, for where one is weak one needs support and completion. In fact, a woman's place is on the weak side of a man. This is how we would have to formulate the situation if we regarded the hero and Princess A as two ordinary people. But since it is a fairy story played out mainly in the world of magic, we are probably more correct in interpreting Princess A as the hero's anima. In that case the hero has been wafted out of the profane world through his encounter with the anima, like Merlin by his fairy: as an ordinary man he is like one caught in a marvelous dream, viewing the world through a veil of mist.

2. The matter is now considerably complicated by the unexpected fact that the three-legged horse is a mare, an equivalent of Princess A. She (the mare) is Princess B, who in the shape of a horse corresponds to Princess A's shadow (i.e., her inferior function triad). Princess B, however, differs from Princess A in that, unlike her, she does not ride the horse but is contained in it: she is bewitched and has thus come under the spell of a masculine triad. Therefore, she is possessed by a shadow.

3. The question now is, *whose* shadow? It cannot be the shadow of the hero, for this is already taken up by the latter's anima. The fairy tale gives us the answer: it is the hunter or magician who has be-witched her. As we have seen, the hunter is somehow connected with

58 Cf. *Symbole der Wandlung* (Zurich, 1952), pp. 427–30 and 475.
59 The fact that she is no ordinary girl, but is of royal descent and moreover the *electa* of the evil spirit, proves her nonhuman, mythological nature. I must assume that the reader is acquainted with the idea of the anima.

the hero, since the latter gradually puts himself in his shoes. Hence one could easily arrive at the conjecture that the hunter is at bottom none other than the shadow of the hero. But this supposition is contradicted by the fact that the hunter stands for a formidable power which extends not only to the hero's anima but much further, namely to the royal brother-sister pair of whose existence the hero and his anima have no notion, and who appear very much out of the blue in the story itself. The power that extends beyond the orbit of the individual has a more than individual character and cannot therefore be identified with the shadow, if we conceive and define this as the dark half of the personality. As a supra-individual factor the numen of the hunter is a dominant of the collective unconscious whose characteristic features—hunter, magician, raven, miraculous horse, crucifixion or suspension high up in the boughs of the world tree[60]—touch the Germanic psyche very closely. Hence the Christian *Weltanschauung*, when reflected in the ocean of the (Germanic) unconscious, logically takes on the features of Wotan.[61] In the figure of the hunter we meet an *imago dei*, a God-image, for Wotan is also a god of winds and spirits, on which account the Romans fittingly interpreted him as Mercury.

4. The Prince and his sister, Princess B, have therefore been seized by a pagan god and changed into horses, i.e., thrust down to the animal level, into the realm of the unconscious. The inference is that in their proper human shape the pair of them once belonged to the sphere of collective consciousness. But who are they?

In order to answer this question we must proceed from the fact that these two are an undoubted counterpart of the hero and Princess A. They are connected with the latter also because they serve as their

60 "I ween that I hung / on the windy tree,
   Hung there for nights full nine;
With the spear I was wounded, / and offered I was
   To Othin, myself to myself,
On the tree that none / may ever know
   What root beneath it runs."
   —*Hovamol*, 139 (tr. Henry Adams Bellows, in
      The Poetic Edda, New York, 1923, p. 60).
61 Cf. the experience of God as described by Nietzsche in "Ariadne's Lament":
   "I am but thy quarry,
   Cruellest of hunters!
   Thy proudest captive,
   Thou brigand back of the clouds!"
   —*Gedichte und Sprüche von Friedrich Nietzsche* (Leipzig, 1898), pp. 155ff.

41

mounts, and in consequence they appear as their lower, animal halves. Because of its almost total unconsciousness the animal has always symbolized the psychic sphere in man which lies hidden in the darkness of the body's instinctual life. The hero rides the stallion, characterized by the even (feminine) number 4; Princess A rides the mare who has only three legs (3: a masculine number). These numbers make it clear that the transformation into animals has brought with it a modification of sex character: the stallion has a feminine attribute, the mare a masculine one. Psychology can confirm this development as follows: to the degree that a man is overwhelmed by the (collective) unconscious there is not only a more unbridled obtrusion of the instinctual sphere, but a certain feminine character also makes its appearance, which I have suggested should be called "anima." If, on the other hand, a woman falls victim to the unconscious, the darker side of her feminine nature emerges all the more strongly, coupled with markedly masculine traits. These latter are comprised under the term "animus."[62]

5. According to the fairy tale, however, the animal form of the brother-sister pair is "unreal" and due simply to the magic influence of the pagan hunter god. If they were nothing but animals, we could rest content with the interpretation given above. But that would be to pass over in unmerited silence the singular allusion to a modification of sex character. The white horses are no ordinary horses: they are miraculous beasts with supernatural powers. Therefore the human figures out of which the horses were magically conjured must likewise have had something supernatural about them. The fairy tale makes no comment here, but if our assumption is correct that the two animal forms correspond to the subhuman components of hero and princess, then it follows that the human forms—Prince and Princess B—must correspond to their superhuman components. The superhuman quality of the original swineherd is shown by the fact that he becomes a hero, practically a half-god, since he does not stay with his swine but climbs the world tree, where he is very nearly made its prisoner, like Wotan. Similarly, he could not have become like the hunter if he did not have a certain resemblance to him in the first place. In the same way the

---

62 Cf. Emma Jung, "Ein Beitrag zum Problem des Animus," in *Wirklichkeit der Seele*, ed. C. G. Jung (Zurich, 1934), pp. 296–354.

imprisonment of Princess A on the top of the world tree proves her electness, and in so far as she shares the hunter's bed, as stated by the tale, she is actually the bride of God.

It is these extraordinary forces of heroism and election, bordering on the superhuman, which involve two quite ordinary humans in a superhuman fate. Accordingly, in the profane world a swineherd becomes a king, and a princess gets an agreeable husband. But since, for fairy tales, there is not only a profane but also a magical world, human fate does not have the final word. The fairy tale therefore does not omit to point out what happens in the world of magic. There too a prince and princess have got into the power of the evil spirit, who is himself in a tight corner from which he cannot extricate himself without extraneous help. So the human fate that befalls the swineherd and Princess A is paralleled in the world of magic. But in so far as the hunter is a pagan god image and thus exalted above the world of heroes and paramours of the gods, the parallelism goes beyond the merely magical into a divine and spiritual sphere, where the evil spirit, the Devil himself—or at least *a* devil—is bound by the spell of an equally mighty or even mightier counter principle indicated by the three nails. This supreme tension of opposites, the mainspring of the whole drama, is obviously the conflict between the upper and lower triads, or, to put it in theological terms, between the Christian God and the devil who has assumed the features of Wotan.[63]

6. We must, it seems, start from this supreme authority if we want to understand the story correctly, for the drama takes its rise from the initial transgression of the evil spirit. The immediate consequence of this is his crucifixion. In that distressing situation he needs outside help, and as it is not forthcoming from above, it can only be summoned from below. A young swineherd, possessed with the boyish spirit of adventure, is reckless and inquisitive enough to climb the world tree. Had he fallen and broken his neck, no doubt everybody would have said, "What evil spirit could have given him the crazy idea of climbing up an enormous tree like that!" Nor would they have been altogether wrong, for that is precisely what the evil spirit

---

63 As regards the triadic nature of Wotan cf. Martin Ninck, *Wodan und germanischer Schicksalsglaube* (Jena, 1935), p. 142. His horse is also described as, among other things, three-legged.

was after. The capture of Princess A was a transgression in the profane world, and the bewitching of the—as we may suppose—semidivine brother-sister pair was just such an enormity in the magical world. We do not know, but it is possible, that this heinous crime was committed before the bewitching of Princess A. At any rate both episodes point to a transgression of the evil spirit in the magical world as well as in the profane.

It is assuredly not without a deeper meaning that the rescuer or redeemer should be a swineherd, like the Prodigal Son. He is of lowly origin and has this much in common with the curious conception of the redeemer in alchemy. His first liberating act is to deliver the evil spirit from the divine punishment meted out to him. It is from this act, representing the first stage of lysis, that the whole dramatic tangle develops.

7. The moral of this story is in truth exceedingly odd. The finale satisfies in so far as the swineherd and Princess A are married and become the royal pair. Prince and Princess B likewise celebrate their wedding, but this—in accordance with the archaic prerogative of kings —takes the form of incest, which, though somewhat repellent, must be regarded as more or less habitual in semidivine circles.[64] But what, we may ask, happens to the evil spirit, whose rescue from condign punishment sets the whole thing in motion? The wicked hunter is trampled to pieces by the horses, which presumably does no lasting damage to a spirit. Apparently he vanishes without trace, but only apparently, for he does after all leave a trace behind him, namely a hard-won happiness in both the profane and the magical world. Two halves of the quaternity, represented on one side by the swineherd and Princess A and on the other by Prince and Princess B, have each come together and united: two marriage-pairs now confront one another, parallel but otherwise divided, inasmuch as the one pair belongs to the profane and the other to the magical world. But in spite of this indubitable division, secret psychological connections, as we have seen, exist between them which allow us to derive the one pair from the other.

Speaking in the spirit of the fairy tale, which unfolds its drama from

---

64 The assumption that they are a brother-sister pair is supported by the fact that the stallion addresses the mare as "sister." This may be just a figure of speech; on the other hand sister means sister, whether we take it figuratively or non-figuratively. Apart from this incest plays a significant part in mythology as well as in alchemy.

44

the highest point, one would have to say that the world of half-gods is anterior to the profane world and produces it out of itself, just as the former must be thought of as proceeding from the world of gods. Conceived in this way, the swineherd and Princess A are nothing less than earthly simulacra of Prince and Princess B, who in their turn would be the descendants of heavenly prototypes. Nor should we forget that the horse-breeding witch belongs to the hunter as his female counterpart, rather like an ancient Epona (the Celtic goddess of horses). Unfortunately we are not told how the magical conjuration into horses happened. But it is evident that the witch had a hand in the game because both the horses were raised from her stock and are thus, in a sense, her productions. Hunter and witch form a pair—the reflection, in the nocturnal-chthonic part of the magical world, of a divine parental pair. The latter is easily recognized in the central Christian idea of *sponsus et sponsa,* Christ and his bride, the Church.

If we wanted to explain the fairy tale personalistically the attempt would founder on the fact that the archetypes are not whimsical inventions, but autonomous elements of the unconscious psyche which were there before any invention was thought of. They represent the unalterable structure of a psychic world whose "reality" is attested by the determining effects it has upon the conscious mind. Thus, it is a significant psychic reality that the human pair[65] is matched by another pair in the unconscious, the latter pair being only in appearance a reflection of the first. In reality the royal pair invariably comes first, as an a priori, so that the human pair has far more the significance of an individual concretization, in space and time, of an eternal and primordial image—at least in so far as its spiritual structure is imprinted upon the biological continuum.

We could say, then, that the swineherd stands for the "animal" man who has a soul mate somewhere in the upper world. By her royal birth she betrays her connection with the pre-existent, semidivine pair. Looked at from this angle, the latter stands for everything a man can become if only he climbs high enough up the world tree.[66] For to the degree that the young swineherd gains possession of the patrician,

---

65 Human in so far as the anima is replaced by a human person.
66 The great tree corresponds to the *arbor philosophica* of the alchemists. The meeting between an earthly human being and the anima, swimming down in the shape of a mermaid, is to be found in the so-called "Ripley Scrowle." Cf. *Psychology and Alchemy,* fig. 257.

feminine half of himself, he approximates to the pair of half-gods and lifts himself into the sphere of kingship, that is, of universal validity. We come across the same theme in Christian Rosencreutz's *Chymical Wedding*, where the king's son must first free his bride from the power of a Moor, to whom she has *voluntarily* given herself as a concubine. The Moor represents the alchemical *nigredo* in which the arcane substance lies hidden, an idea that forms yet another parallel to our mythologem, or, as we would say in psychological language, another variant of this archetype.

As in alchemy, our fairy tale depicts those unconscious processes that compensate the Christian, conscious situation. It describes the workings of a spirit who plies away at our Christian ideas, carrying them beyond the fixed confines of ecclesiasticism, to seek an answer to those questions which neither the Middle Ages nor the present day could answer. It is not difficult to see in the image of the second royal pair a correspondence to the ecclesiastical conception of bridegroom and bride, and in that of the hunter and witch a distortion of it, veering towards an atavistic, unconscious Wotanism. The fact that it is a *German* fairy tale makes the position particularly interesting, since the same Wotanism stood psychological godfather to National Socialism, which carried the distortion to the lowest pitch before the eyes of the world.[67] On the other hand the fairy tale makes it clear that it is possible for a man to reach wholeness, to become the total man, only with the co-operation of the spirit of darkness, indeed that the latter is actually a *causa instrumentalis* of redemption and individuation. In utter perversion of this goal of spiritual development, to which all nature aspires and which is also prefigured in Christian doctrine, National Socialism destroyed man's moral autonomy and set up the nonsensical totalitarianism of the State. The fairy tale tells us how to proceed if we want to overcome the power of darkness: we must turn his own weapons against him, which naturally cannot be done if the magical underworld of the hunter remains unconscious, and if the best men in the nation would rather preach dogmatisms and platitudes than take the human soul seriously.

6. Conclusion

When we consider the spirit in its archetypal form as it appears to us

67 Cf. *Essays on Contemporary Events* (London, 1947).

in fairy tales and dreams, it presents a picture that differs strangely from the conscious idea of spirit, which is split up into so many meanings. Spirit was originally a spirit in human or animal form, a *daimonion* that came upon man from without. But our material already shows traces of an expansion of consciousness which has gradually begun to occupy that originally unconscious territory and to transform those *daimonia,* at least partially, into voluntary acts. Man conquers not only nature, but spirit also, without realizing what he is doing. To the man of enlightened intellect it seems like the correction of a fallacy when he recognizes that what he took to be spirits is simply the human spirit and ultimately his own spirit. All the superhuman things, whether good or bad, that former ages predicated of the *daimonia,* are reduced to "reasonable" proportions as though they were pure exaggeration, and everything seems to be in the best possible order. But were the unanimous convictions of the past really and truly only exaggerations? If they were not, then the integration of the spirit means nothing less than its daemonization, since the superhuman spiritual agencies that were formerly tied up in nature are introjected into human nature, thus endowing it with a power which extends the bounds of the personality *ad infinitum,* in the most perilous way. I put it to the enlightened rationalist: has his rational reduction led to the beneficial control of matter and spirit? He will point proudly to the advances in physics and medicine, to the freeing of the mind from medieval stupidity and—as a well-meaning Christian —to our deliverance from the fear of demons. But we continue to ask: what have all our other cultural achievements led to? The fearful answer is there before our eyes: man has been delivered from no fear, a hideous nightmare lies upon the world. So far reason has failed lamentably, and the very thing that everybody wanted to avoid rolls on in ghastly progression. Man has achieved a wealth of useful gadgets, but, to offset that, he has opened out the abyss, and what will become of him now—where can he make a halt? After the last World War we hoped for reason: we go on hoping. But already we are fascinated by the possibilities of atomic fission and promise ourselves a Golden Age —the surest guarantee that the abomination of desolation will grow to limitless dimensions. And who or what is it that causes all this? It is none other than that harmless (!), ingenious, inventive, and sweetly reasonable human spirit who unfortunately is abysmally unconscious

47

of the daemonism that still clings to him. Worse, this spirit does everything to avoid looking himself in the face, and we all help him like mad. Only, heaven preserve us from psychology—*that* depravity might lead to self-knowledge! Rather let us have wars, for which somebody else is always to blame, nobody seeing that all the world is driven to do just what all the world flees from in terror.

It seems to me, frankly, that former ages did not exaggerate, that the spirit has not sloughed off its daemonisms, and that mankind, because of its scientific and technological development, has in increasing measure delivered itself over to the danger of possession. True, the archetype of the spirit is capable of working for good as well as for evil, but it depends upon man's free—i.e., conscious—decision whether the good also will be perverted into something satanic. Man's worst sin is unconsciousness, but it is indulged in with the greatest piety even by those who should serve mankind as teachers and examples. When will the time come when we shall not simply take man for granted in this barbarous manner, but shall in all seriousness seek for ways and means to exorcise him, to rescue him from possession and unconsciousness, and make this the most vital task of civilization? Can we not understand that all the outward tinkerings and improvements do not touch man's inner nature, and that everything ultimately depends upon whether the man who wields the science and the technics is *compos mentis* or not? Christianity has shown us the way, but, as the facts bear witness, it has not penetrated deeply enough below the surface. What depths of despair are still needed to open the eyes of the world's responsible leaders, so that at least they can refrain from leading themselves into temptation?

C. Kerényi

Apollo Epiphanies

1. Prefatory Remarks

I have been asked to speak of the "spirit," as it is manifested in Greek mythology. Seen from a mythological point of view, this theme presents a special aspect; it is not the aspect which is known to us from the history of philosophy but that which we encounter in the study of religions. And yet, do not both aspects, with all their shadings, with all the modifications that the word "spirit" has undergone in the course of its history, presuppose some common entity, which is independent of this term that I am compelled to use, a something that is universally human? The diverse meanings of the word are of varying origin, religious, philosophical, empirical, or purely theoretical, and can coexist only because those who use the word "spirit" have largely forgotten both the experience of the spirit and the theories concerning its nature. The meanings become intelligible only if we apprehend them in the moment of their genesis, as it were, in the work of philosophers, poets, or religious thinkers; otherwise, they are mere lexicographical material, and not the living substance of a scientific evocation. But from time to time those who merely utter the word "spirit" and even those who truly believe that they hold communion with the spirit in their daily lives, must be reminded that this word with its innumerable meanings can still refer to an immediate experience. Here I should like to quote a reminder of this sort, testifying that this word embodies a universal human reality, an experience of which all of us are capable.

"It is the mission of the university," said Professor H. Barth, at a congress of Swiss universities, in 1945,[1] "to engender knowledge and to

1 Printed in the *Basler Studentenschaft* (1945), pp. 131ff.

transmit knowledge. Where this mission is at all successful, the university does not, to be sure, engender and transmit spirit itself, but spiritual benefits and values, which may be looked upon as emanations of the spirit. In so far as the university is called upon to become the scene of spiritual experiences—especially the experience of intellectual insight—it may be regarded as the trustee of the spirit. But we must not venture beyond an honest admission that the best the university can do is to 'serve the spirit.' He who serves the spirit must not aspire to become its master. For the spirit bloweth where it listeth. Knowledge is not kindled where our desire and preference would have it, but where it is given to us. If the world insists on expecting the university to be the initiator of spiritual experiences, the university is entitled to take this expectation as an honor. But in all humility, the university must make it plain that the spiritual experience is never at its command, but must first be *given,* before it can be transmitted to the world."

It would be absurd for a serious scholar and philosopher to insist on the fact that the experience of the spirit cannot be had at will, that it is not at one's command, if he had in mind accidental, random notions, and not something expected and indeed, in the case of understanding scientifically sought and found, something even prepared for. This paradox—the fact that something awaited and prepared for is nonetheless not at one's command—endows spiritual experiences even of totally unreligious nature, oriented, as Rilke has said, towards the "here" *(das Hiesige),* with a character which they share with a certain kind of religious epiphany—a type of epiphany in which the higher principle, irrupting as it were into the Here, not only manifests itself but opens the Here and permeates it with light. Though the profane seeker after knowledge is oriented entirely towards the Here, it is a higher principle which impels him to search and enables him to see. At this point, even this modern scholar and philosopher, who has testified to the spirit in terms of the strictest formulation, could not help speaking the language of religion. He had recourse to a Christian phrase which leads us historically beyond the limits of the profane history of ideas, to a primal phenomenology of the spirit; for here the source of the spiritual event is a wind, a stormy presence that carries one away like the gale: "For the spirit [πνεῦμα = wind or spirit] bloweth where it listeth."

These words of the Gospel of St. John (3:8) and the story in Acts (2:1–4) of how this metaphor came into being, show us what a powerful, elemental language was originally demanded by the epiphanal character of such events, in memory of which even entirely profane experiences came, among peoples of Christian culture, to be known as "spiritual events." Regardless whether the dialogue with Nicodemus and the miracle of the Pentecost are taken to be historical, the psychological reality of this type of epiphany must be recognized on the basis of these two texts, which immediately capture the reader and arouse in him a human resonance which is not necessarily Christian. If in the ancient religions we look about us for epiphanies that are likewise phenomenologically characterized by the windlike manifestation of a principle that cannot be commanded, though awaited and prepared for, we must inevitably turn to Apollo, and particularly to Virgil's account of the Apollo epiphany in the sanctuary of Cumae, which, like the house in which the Apostles were gathered together, is shaken as the breath of the approaching God surrounds the priestess: "*adflata est numine quando / iam propiore dei*" (*Aen.*, VI, 50).

I have devoted earlier inquiries to the two New Testament passages and this pagan testimony to the spirit.[2] In my present prefatory remarks, I should like only to mention a phenomenologically similar account of the epiphany-experience by a modern poet: the words in which Rilke described the birth of his *Duino Elegies* in Duino and at the Château de Muzot: "All in a few days, it was a nameless storm, a hurricane in the spirit (like that time at Duino)."[3] The word "spirit" by itself did not strike the poet as stormy enough to capture the spiritual experience. — Instead of such hurricanes of the spirit, we shall here speak of Apollo epiphanies by Greek poets, which in a phenomenological sense have little or nothing to do with the blowing of the gale. The question is: How will they appear to us if we approach

2 *Die Geburt der Helena* (Albae Vigiliae, N. S., III; Zurich, 1945), pp. 29ff.
3 *Letters of Rainer Maria Rilke*, tr. Jane Bannard Greene and M. D. Herder Norton, Vol. II: 1910–26 (New York, 1948), p. 290. Similar passages occur on pp. 291 and 293; on the latter page we even read: "In a *radiant* after-storm" ("in einem *strahlenden* Nachsturm"—*Briefe aus Muzot*, p. 118).

them under the sign of the "spirit"? Let us begin with a text in which my earlier inquiries culminated, an evocation of the classical figure of Apollo:[4]

2. *Callimachus' Hymn to Apollo*

How the laurel branch of Apollo trembles! how trembles all the shrine! Away, away, he that is sinful! Now surely Phoebus knocketh at the door with his beautiful foot. Seest thou not? the Delian palm nods pleasantly of a sudden, and the swan in the air sings sweetly. Of yourselves now ye bolts be pushed back, pushed back of yourselves, ye bars! The god is no longer far away. And ye, young men, prepare ye for song and for the dance.

Not unto everyone doth Apollo appear, but unto him that is good. Whoso hath seen Apollo, he is great; whoso hath not seen him, he is of low estate. We shall see thee, O Archer, and we shall never be lowly. Let not the youths keep silent lyre or noiseless step, when Apollo visits his shrine, and if they think to accomplish marriage and to cut the locks of age, and if the wall is to stand upon its old foundations. Well done the
16 youths, for that the shell is no longer idle.

Be hushed, ye that hear, at the song to Apollo; yea, hushed is even the sea when the minstrels celebrate the lyre or the bow, the weapons of Lycoreian Phoebus. Neither doth Thetis his mother wail her dirge for Achilles, when she hears *Hië Paeëon, Hië Paeëon.*

Yea, the tearful rock defers its pain, the wet stone that is set in Phrygia, a marble rock like a woman open-mouthed in some sorrowful utterance. Say ye *Hië! Hië!* an ill thing it is to strive with the Blessed Ones. He who fights with the Blessed Ones would fight with my King; he who fights with my King would fight even with Apollo. Apollo will honor the choir, since it sings according to his heart; for Apollo hath power, for that he sitteth on the right hand of Zeus. Nor will the choir sing of
31 Phoebus for one day only. He is a copious theme of song; who would not readily sing of Phoebus?

Golden is the tunic of Apollo and golden his mantle, his lyre, and his Lyctian bow and his quiver: golden too are his sandals; for rich in gold is Apollo, rich also in possessions: by Pytho mightst thou guess. And ever beautiful is he and ever

---

4 Greek text in U. von Wilamowitz-Moellendorff, *Callimachi hymni et epigrammata* (Berlin, 1907).

young: never on the girl cheeks of Apollo hath come so much as the down of manhood. His locks distill fragrant oils upon the ground; not oil of fat do the locks of Apollo distill but
41 very Healing of All. And in whatsoever city those dews fall upon the ground, in that city all things are free from harm.

None is so abundant in skill as Apollo. To him belongs the archer, to him the minstrel; for unto Apollo is given in keeping alike archery and song. His are the lots of the diviner
46 and his the seers; and from Phoebus do leeches know the deferring of death.

Phoebus and Nomius we call him, ever since, fired with love of young Admetus, by Amphrysus he tended the yoke-mares. Lightly would the herd of cattle wax larger, nor would the she-goats of the flock lack young, whereon as they feed Apollo casts his eye; nor without milk would the ewes be nor barren, but all would have lambs at foot; and she that bare one would soon be the mother of twins.

54 And Phoebus it is that men follow when they map out cities. For Phoebus evermore delights in the founding of cities, and Phoebus himself doth weave their foundations. Four years of age was Phoebus when he framed his first foundations in fair Ortygia near the round lake.

Artemis hunted and brought continually the heads of Cynthian goats and Phoebus plaited an altar. With horns builded he the foundations, and of horns framed he the altar, and of horns were the walls he built around. Thus did Phoebus learn to raise his first foundations. Phoebus, too, it was who told Battus of my own city of fertile soil, and in guise of a raven—auspicious to our founder—led his people as they entered Libya and sware that he would vouchsafe a walled city to our kings. And the oath of Apollo is ever sure. O Apollo! many there be that call thee Boëdromius, and many there be that call thee Clarius: everywhere is thy name on the lips of many. But I call thee Carneius; for such is the manner of my fathers. Sparta, O Carneius! was thy first foundation; and next Thera; but third the city of Cyrene. From Sparta the sixth generation of the sons of Oedipus brought thee to their colony of Thera; and from Thera lusty Aristoteles set thee by the Asbystian land, and builded thee a shrine exceeding beautiful, and in the city established a yearly festival wherein many a bull, O Lord, falls on his haunches for the last time. *Hië, hië,* Carneius! Lord of many prayers—thine altars wear flowers in spring, even all the pied flowers which the Hours lead forth when Zephyrus breathes dew, and in winter the sweet crocus. Undying evermore is thy fire, and ever doth the ash feed about the coals of yester even. Greatly, indeed, did Phoebus rejoice as the belted warriors of Enyo danced with the yellow-haired Libyan women, when the appointed season of the Carneian feast came round. But not yet could the Dorians approach the fountains of Cyre, but dwelt in Azilis thick with wooded dells. These did the Lord himself behold and showed them to his bride, as he stood on horned Myrtussa where the daughter of Hypseus slew the lion that harried the kine of Eurypylus. No other dance more divine hath Apollo beheld, nor to any city hath he given so many blessings as he hath given to Cyrene, remembering his rape of old. Nor, again, is there any other god whom the sons of Battus have honored above Phoebus.

96   *Hië, hië, Paeëon,* we hear—since this refrain did the Delphian folk first invent, what time thou didst display the archery of thy golden bow. As thou wert going down to Pytho, there met thee a beast unearthly, a dread snake. And him thou didst slay, shooting swift arrows one upon the other; and the folk cried *"Hië, hië, Paeëon,* shoot an arrow!" A helper from the first thy mother bare thee, and ever since that is thy
104 praise.

     Spake Envy privily in the ear of Apollo: "I admire not the poet who singeth not things for number as the sea." Apollo spurned Envy with his foot and spake thus: "Great is the stream of the Assyrian river, but much filth of earth and much refuse it carries on its waters. And not of every water do the Melissae carry to Deo, but of the trickling stream that springs from a holy fountain, pure and undefiled, the very crown of waters."

113   Hail, O Lord, but Blame—let him go where Envy dwells![5]

In this poem a cult—event and action—is described (1–16), a cultic hymn is sung (17–104), and finally a scene among the gods is revealed (105–113); we have as it were a twofold stage—the earth below, the heavens above—but a stage which the poet himself builds by the magic power of his poetry, in order that he may appear on its lower, earthly level and sing his actual hymn, his cult song to Apollo. To this end, he even conjures up a boys' chorus and speaks *for* it in his song, as he would speak *through* it if he were Pindar or any other

---

5 Tr. A. W. Mair (Loeb Classical Library, New York and London, 1921).

choral poet.[6] The long middle part of the poem, the hymn proper, is an epic rendition of a chorus, that chorus which Callimachus as a poet of choruses would have made the boys sing. But actually he does not make them sing a chorus, as the poets in a land of organic Greek life would have done, whether in old Hellas or the newer Cyrene. For in the colony of Cyrene, a transplanted Greek life grew more genuinely and immediately than in the Hellenistic metropolis of Alexandria in Egypt, where Greek scholars garnered into their library and guarded the spiritual flower of the original life that had grown in the Greek homeland, and where poets (Callimachus of Cyrene was both scholar and poet) evoked what was preserved in the books in a new manner, more suited both to the books and their readers.[7]

He himself, in the final scene, characterizes the new spiritual place where he stands. From a purely formal point of view, this scene among the gods resembles similar scenes in Homer. And since Homer, such scenes have been viewed from the standpoint of the poet, in contrast to that of common mortals, who look upon the divine only in a general way as the working of a "god," of a "daimon."[8] Homer had dwelt in a "spiritual place," a place of clear knowledge. But the vantage point of Callimachus becomes spiritual in another, more special sense: it is a place of insight into the rules of art, into refined standards of taste, and a special, spiritual culture exalted above the general culture of the people. The learned poet knows that from his own spiritual standpoint he is one with Apollo; Apollo is for him the god who differentiates between sound artistic judgment—this most subtle of all spiritual values—and malicious blame (Momos), the companion of envy (Phthonos). With his knowledge of the great and small festive experiences of the Hellenic religion, and with his superior poetic art, he honors Apollo by recounting the supreme event enacted in one of his sanctuaries.

The introductory scene of the hymn (1–16) is devoted to the advent

---

6 Cf. Wilamowitz-Moellendorff, *Hellenistische Dichtung* (Berlin, 1924), Vol. II, pp. 77ff.

7 Cf. Kerényi, "Die Papyri und das Wesen der alexandrinischen Kultur," in *Apollon* (3rd edn., Düsseldorf and Cologne, 1953), pp. 152ff.

8 O. Jörgensen, *Hermes* 39 (1904), 357ff.; E. Heden, *Homerische Götterstudien* (Uppsala, 1912); M. P. Nilsson, *Geschichte der griechischen Religion*, Vol. I (Munich, 1941), p. 203; Kerényi, *Die antike Religion* (3rd edn., Düsseldorf and Cologne, 1952), p. 105.

of the god. On the human side the chorus of boys accompany this event by playing the lyre and in preparation for their dances and songs. With the very first verse, the poet directs our attention towards the god, whose arrival fills the scene. He came, as is generally known, to Delphi from the Hyperboreans, and to Delos from Lycia, whither he withdrew in the rhythm of his periodic disappearance and reappearance.[9] As he reappears, choruses are formed, the dances and songs begin:

> qualis ubi hibernam Lyciam Xanthique fluenta
> deserit ac Delum maternam invisit Apollo
> instauratque choros . . .[10]

Thus Virgil bears witness to the cult of Delos. In his account, the great Hellenic festival is attended by the most ancient of peoples:

> mixti altaria circum
> Cretesque Dryopesque fremunt pictique Agathyrsi[11]

It is the chorus which attests the presence of the god. In a hymn of salutation and invocation, a paean, Alcaeus announces the arrival of Apollo in Delphi: "the nightingales, swallows and cicadas sing," as though made even more musical than usual by the approach of the god.[12]

Callimachus' poem begins with the mark of the epiphany: οἶον . . ., ἐσείσατο δάφνινος—"How the laurel branch . . . trembles." And this is not merely "sensitive nature's" intimation of the sun's coming, it is something more. The trembling passed not only through the laurel tree, but also through "all the shrine," the whole temple: ὅλον τὸ μέλαθρον. And then the gently inclining palm tree! It is only with the hymn proper, with the word εὐφημεῖτε—"Be hushed, ye that hear, at the song to Apollo"—that the poet turns to the festive gathering which he himself has conjured up and gives himself entirely to

---

9 L. Preller and C. Robert, *Griechische Mythologie*, Vol. I (Berlin, 1894), pp. 244ff.; L. R. Farnell, *The Cults of the Greek States*, Vol. IV (Oxford, 1904), pp. 288ff.

10 "As when Apollo quits Lycia, his winter home, and the streams of Xanthus, to visit his mother's Delos, and renews the dance. . . ." *Aen.*, IV, 143, tr. H. R. Fairclough, *Virgil* (Loeb Classical Library, rev. edn., Cambridge, Mass., 1935).

11 ". . . mingling about his altars Cretans and Dryopes and painted Agathyrsians raise their voices." *Aen.*, IV, 145, tr. idem.

12 Cf. Himerius, *Orationes*, XIV, 10.

the illusion of the stage he has created. Here in the introduction we expect him to identify the place at which the chorus is evoked. And he does so, speaking directly to us, his listeners and readers. He names the Delian palm, the sacred tree to which the great goddess clung in the throes of her labor, when Apollo was born.[13] For Odysseus this palm was still young (φοίνικος νέον ἔρνος: *Od.*, VI, 163), but exceptionally beautiful; even then, in the archaic age, the famous Delian palm was beautiful. It should not surprise us that even on Delos this tree should be pointed out and addressed as the Delian palm, to distinguish it from other palms under which Apollo was not born. It was a part of Delos, the isle on which the god was born was unthinkable without it. At the beginning of the fourth century B.C., when it seemed unlikely that the old palm tree, sung by Homer, could survive very much longer, Nicias, the pious Athenian general, ordered a new Delian palm to be fashioned of bronze in honor of the god. This new palm lacked the roots of the old; on one occasion it was overthrown by the powerful sea winds (whose force is attested today by the slanting trees and windmills on the neighboring isle of Mykonos) and upset the colossal statue of Apollo donated by the people of Naxos.[14] Both were set back on their feet.[15] And thus it is a bronze palm tree which, in the poetic vision of Callimachus, inclines sweetly before the power of Apollo, as though animated by his approach.

All the mountains and islands which had not dared to shelter Leto as she wandered from place to place, big with child, feared this overwhelming power. They trembled at the mere thought that the great god would drop upon them and that they would sink beneath his greatness:

αἱ δὲ μάλ' ἐτρόμεον καὶ ἐδείδισαν

So runs the Homeric hymn to Apollo (47) which goes on to relate how Delos, the little rocky island, in one variant of the myth a floating island, makes the goddess promise that the newborn child will not cause it to vanish beneath the sea (66–74):

13 *Homeric Hymn to Apollo*, 117; Callimachus, *Hymn to Delos*, 210.
14 Plutarch, *Nic.*, 3; W. A. Laidlaw, *A History of Delos* (Oxford, 1933), pp. 69ff. According to the Delian Semos (in *Ath.*, XI 502), who wrote later than 250 B.C., the bronze palm had also been donated by the Naxians; cf. Ludwig Ross, *Inselreisen*, Vol. I (Stuttgart, 1840), p. 34.
15 Archaeological findings in Laidlaw, p. 72.

But at this Word, Leto, I tremble, nor will I hide it from thee, for the saying is that Apollo will be mighty of mood, and mightily will lord it over mortals and immortals far and wide over the earth, the grain-giver. Therefore, I deeply dread in heart and soul lest, when first he looks upon the sunlight, he disdain my island, for rocky of soil am I, and spurn me with his feet and drive me down in the gulfs of the salt sea. Then should a great sea-wave wash mightily above my head for ever . . .[16]

And Leto swears a solemn oath that Delos will remain for all time the sacred isle of Apollo; in the floating island variant, it then strikes roots in the bottom of the sea,[17] and is described as less subject to earthquakes than the other islands of the Greek archipelago.[18] Nevertheless, it is not Delos but Apollo whom Callimachus calls the "imperturbable," ἀστυφέλικτος.[19] Whenever the foot, which might trample the whole island beneath the waves, treads its shore, there occurs—not an earthquake: Apollo is no earthquake god—but a trembling from above, from the tops of the laurels and of the palm tree which, just as it witnessed the birth, the first epiphany of Apollo, will witness all future epiphanies.

With one foot, Apollo is already present:

Now surely Phoebus knocketh at the door with his beautiful foot.

Seen plastically, a colossal apparition. The god strikes the temple gate with his foot, for to strike it with his hand, he would have to bow low. And it is strange to reflect that this gigantic foot of an archaic deity will administer a kick to literary envy. No longer is he seen *only* plastically, *only* after the manner of the poet of the Homeric hymn, for whom it was still possible to capture the full power and content of the gods in colossal, statuary figures. Without any diminution in the power of the divine, the old gigantic stature is caught up in a beauty ("with his *beautiful* foot Phoebus strikes at the gate") which even makes the bronze palm tree incline in sweetness. This beauty is mani-

16 Tr. Andrew Lang, *The Homeric Hymns* (London, 1899).
17 Pindar, fr. 78–79 (C. M. Bowra, *Pindari carmina*, 2nd ed., Oxford, 1947).
18 Cf. Herodotus, VI, 98; Thucydides, II, 8; Pliny, *Naturalis historia*, IV, 12; Seneca, *Quaestiones naturales*, VI, 26.
19 *Hymn to Delos*, 26.

fested also in sound. In the Homeric hymn to Apollo, this first epiphany, the birth, is preceded by nine symbolic days of frightful pain. In the hymn of Callimachus, the swans, birds sacred to Apollo, circle round the island of Delos seven times—another symbolic number—and sing. The eighth time they do not sing and then the god is born. All the primal terror and darkness has vanished. Only the raven, as the one witness to the darkness that can surround Apollo,[20] still appears in the "hymn proper" (66). But with regard to the epiphany: "The swan in the air sings sweetly." The god is at hand with his power that makes the world tremble for man, and with his beauty that permeates it with music. But when he is fully present, that which is still closed will open. It is not for nothing that the poet cries out:

> Of *yourselves* now ye bolts be pushed back, pushed back of *yourselves*, ye bars! . . .

Here the onlooker and listener must change his point of view. Up till now he has turned his eyes towards the temple. Now he must turn to the human side: to the poet and the chorus. No turning inward, in the sense of a departure from the outer, surrounding world is here demanded, and the human element, which together with the ambient world becomes the area of the god's full presence, is by no means represented as a frantic inwardness. Particularly if we have in mind the frenzy of the priestess of Apollo at Cumae, her blowing hair, her heaving breast, her heart surging wildly with madness,[21] we feel, in turning to Callimachus, that his whole poem and its world are bathed in a tranquil clarity. And the poet refers explicitly to the supreme peace of the ordinarily so agitated elements:

> . . . hushed is even the sea when the minstrels celebrate the lyre or the bow, the weapons of Lycoreian Phoebus. Neither doth Thetis his mother wail her dirge for Achilles, when she hears *Hië Paeëon, Hië Paeëon.*

And whence comes this effect of the poet's song and the paean if not from the presence of the god to whom they are addressed? In the moment when song and paean ring out, Apollo ceases to be present

20 Kerényi, *Apollon*, pp. 43f.
21 Cf. *Aen.*, VI, 48: "*non comptae mansere comae, sed pectus anhelum et rabie fera corda tument . . .*"

only with the *one* foot. He comes indeed from outside, but something kindred rises from man to meet him, and only then is the epiphany complete.

Thus the verses which follow "Be pushed back of yourselves, ye bars" become intelligible. The god no longer dwells in the distance (ὁ γὰϱ θεὸς οὐϰέτι μαϰϱήν), and the poem continues:

> And ye, young men, prepare ye for song and for the dance.
>   Not unto everyone doth Apollo appear, but unto him that is good. Whoso hath seen Apollo, he is great; whoso hath not seen him, he is of low estate. We shall see thee, O Archer, and we shall never be lowly.

In these words the poet has begun to address his chorus. He conceives it no doubt as made up of Cyrenian boys, whom in this magically evoked world of an Apollo epiphany he has brought to Delos to sing in honor of the god arriving from the east. The words that he addresses to *his* chorus—and as a singing, dancing, musical chorus, the boys are his—carry a Homeric note: "ὡπόλλων οὐ παντὶ φαείνεται," sings Callimachus. And in the *Odyssey*, when Pallas Athene is seen only by Odysseus and the dogs (XVI, 161): οὐ γάϱ πως πάντεσσι θεοὶ φαίνονται ἐναϱγεῖς—"For the blessed gods are not visible to all." It is indeed a terror almost beyond the endurance of men when they do appear (*Iliad*, XX, 131): . . . Χαλεποὶ δὲ θεοὶ φαίνεσθαι ἐναϱγεῖς—"For gods are terrible when they show their presence openly." According to both passages in Homer, the gods must be clearly visible (ἐναϱγεῖς) for a full epiphany. And to such fortunate, favored mortals as the Phaeacians, it is granted to see the gods with impunity. King Alcinous boasts:

> αἰεὶ γὰϱ τὸ πάϱος γε θεοὶ φαίνονται ἐναϱγεῖς
> ἡμῖν, εὖτ᾽ ἔϱδωσιν ἀγαϰλειτὰς ἑϰατόμβας

> (For in the past they have always shown themselves to us without disguise when we have offered them their sumptuous sacrifices; . . .)[22]

Callimachus imputes the same privilege to *his* elect, a little band led by himself, the poet. If he did not so explicitly mention himself as one of

---

22 *Od.*, VII, 201, tr. E. V. Rieu (London, 1945). Cf. Kerényi, *Die antike Religion*, pp. 104 and 145.

those who behold the god, one might suppose him to be playing a pious pedagogic trick in telling the boys that only the noble (ἀλλ' ὅ τις ἐσθλός) can see Apollo, that he who sees him is great and he who does not see him is insignificant (λιτός). After such a harangue, who would dare not to see?

But the emphasis with which the poet, as ideal leader of the chorus, proclaims that he will obtain a full vision of the god—

ὀψόμεθ', ὦ Ἑκάεργε καὶ ἐσσόμεθ' οὔποτε λιτοί

(We shall see thee, O Archer, and we shall never be lowly)

—this emphasis lends special force to everything that follows, including the final literary scene in heaven. In so speaking he professes a vision which draws its justification from the conscious higher spirituality of the poet and from this same source derives the experience of the awaited epiphany. Callimachus, it must be remembered, is not speaking to modern man, but to Greeks, who attended the Delian festivals. And yet he believes that in this *spiritual* way he can evoke the Delian epiphany, the god's "advent"[23] in Delos, which he as a Cyrenian celebrates. He celebrates it in the old way and yet also in a new way, that is, from his consciously spiritual standpoint. But his new approach adds no new dimension of inwardness to the religious experience. For from time immemorial music and poetry have been inherent in the cult of Apollo, and have been its characteristic expression. The swan, the song bird of Apollo,[24] not only appears in the hymns of Callimachus, but is represented above the palm tree on Delian coins.[25] The music contests of Delphi have become even more celebrated than the choruses of Delos. But it is concerning the latter that we have a strange tradition which might justify us in citing them as the only Hellenic parallel to the Christian pneumatic miracle, the "speaking in tongues" of the Apostles. Speaking of the chorus of virgins in Delos, the Homeric hymn (158) tells us:

> They, when first they have hymned Apollo, and next Leto and Artemis the Archer, then sing in memory of the men and

23 In line 13 this is rendered by the elsewhere familiar locution φοίβου . . . ἐπιδημήσαντος. Cf. Menander, *De encomiis*, 4.
24 Plato, *Phaedo*, 85b.
25 British Museum Catalogue of Coins: *Delos*, p. 99, Nos. 2, 3; Pl. 23, 2.

women of old time, enchanting the tribes of mortals. And they are skilled to mimic the notes and dance music of all men, so that each would say himself were singing, so well woven is their fair chant.

Callimachus himself carries on the tradition of these spiritual, illusion-fostering artistic miracles. The spiritual dimension of this world, consisting of man and his environment, was self-evident to a Greek audience; the poet could evoke it in a few strokes. What was more difficult was to create a harmony between this refined spiritual element and its natural background. Thanks to the efforts of K. O. Müller to arrive at an historically correct view of Apollo, it has come to be considered unseemly among classical scholars to speak of the possible existence of such natural backgrounds, for example, of the role of the sun in the cult of Apollo. The tragedy of this great scholar is that his mistakes have gained far wider currency than the finest fruits of his scholarship, his sound interpretations of a good many mythological traditions.[26] He was surely aware that in denying any relation between Apollo and the natural power which the Greeks called Helios, he came into conflict with the opinions and utterances of various classical poets, among them Callimachus, who—as Müller himself tells us—"violently censures those 'Who distinguish Apollo from all-powerful Helios and fair-footed Deïone from Artemis.' "[27] We have no need to discuss the whole question of the connections which after Homer were intentionally concealed; we need not inquire into the "secret names of the gods" (τὰ σιγῶντα ὀνόματα δαιμόνων),[28] to observe how Callimachus diffuses his Apollo epiphanies with the gold of a real sunrise. This is particularly true of the episode of Apollo's birth. In Theognis (5–11) the island is filled with ambrosian fragrance

26 Contemporary scholars found a strange irony in a personal mishap that befell this scientific foe of the sun. "The poor man," wrote F. G. Welcker to J. D. Guigniot (quoted in Ernest Renan, *Études d'histoire religieuse*, 1857), "he had always refused to recognize the solar divinity of Apollo, and the god was bound to avenge himself. In the very ruins of his own temple, Apollo proved to him how formidable his rays have remained to this day for those who dare to brave them." He had stayed too long in the open on a visit to Delphi, and had suffered a sunstroke, which resulted in his death.

27 *Geschichten Hellenischer Stämme und Städte*, Vol. II: *Die Dorier*, I (Breslau, 1844), p. 291. The quotation is from the *Hekale* of Callimachus, fr. 48 (Schneider). (Tr. A. W. Mair, Loeb Classical Library, London, 1931.)

28 Apollo is believed to be such a name for Helios: Euripides, *Phaethon*.

at the birth of the god, and the earth laughs up at him. In Callimachus, the moment is characterized by a golden radiance which fills the whole scene:[29] the rocks of Delos, the round artificial pool characteristic of the sun cult, the sacred olive tree, which otherwise has only a silvery sheen[30]—unlike the palm tree, whose Greek name (φοῖνιξ) suggests a sun-red color—and the river Inopos. This poet surely does not distinguish his Apollo from the "all-powerful" sun. And a similar suggestion of the sun is easily discernible in his hymn to Apollo.

It is characteristic of this epiphany that it not only has a peculiar space, extending equally over the whole surrounding world and over the human world, the outward and the inward, but that it takes place in a time of its own. The time is the time of the cult, which we might identify as the first hour of morning, even if the growing presence of the god, who at first is present only with one foot, did not in itself point to this hour. He knocks before he appears fully: in the dawn, before sunrise, the power of Apollo, who has not yet shown himself to the eyes of the body, is perceived by the whole man, for the whole man is awake to the spiritual. At the proper moment in the epiphany *this* man will paradoxically obtain also a timeless perception of the god as "he sits to the right of Zeus" (29). It was to this timeless spiritual vision that the poet referred when he cried out: "We shall see thee, O Archer, and we shall never be lowly." And it is for this moment in the epiphany that he tells his chorus to be ready with music and dances:

> Let not the youths keep silent lyre or noiseless step, when Apollo visits his shrine . . .
> Well done the youths, for that the shell is no longer idle.

The poet Scythinos tells us that a prelude on the lyre is eminently suited to an Apollo epiphany, which becomes complete only when the sun rises, for the plectrum with which Phoebus strikes his lyre is the light of the sun.[31]

---

29 *Hymn to Delos*, 260–63. In this connection, see Kerényi, *Töchter der Sonne* (Zurich, 1944), p. 29; "Vater Helios," *Eranos-Jahrbuch 1943*, p. 97; and *The Gods of the Greeks* (London and New York, 1951), p. 134.

30 Cf. Euripides, *Iphigenia in Tauris*, 1098ff. with J. E. Harrison, *Themis* (Cambridge, 1927), pp. 191f., which not without justification ascribes the same olive tree to Artemis the moon goddess.

31 Scythinos, fr. 14.

The "hymn proper," the epically narrated paean of his ideal chorus
—"Now be silent and hear the song in Apollo's honor" (for it is the
festive gathering and not the chorus that is expected to be silent)—is
intended to convey, along with the illusion of the god's spiritual
presence, an illusion of sunrise. The cry *"Hië, Hië paeëon,"* which
halts even the plaint of Thetis and the tears of Niobe when they "hear"
(21) it, is addressed to the rising sun, which at the first words of the
song is barely beginning to be visible. "Cry: *Hië! Hië!*" (25), the poet
demands. With this he exacts both worship and intercession for the
god, who must still battle with the enemy.

> Say ye *Hië! Hië!* An ill thing it is to strive with the Blessed
> Ones.

Callimachus will tell us later of this battle, how and against whom it
was first fought. Here he is entirely taken up with the kingly quality
in his god, and with all the glory that it sheds upon the singers: the
honor and fullness of song. And a fullness not only for this day of his
epiphany:

> Nor will the choir sing of Phoebus for one day only. He is a
> copious theme of song. Who would not readily sing of Phoebus?

And here he stands before our spiritual eye, clothed as it were with
the sensory, visible sun:[32]

> Golden is the tunic of Apollo and golden his mantle,[33] his
> lyre, and his Lyctian bow and his quiver: golden too are his
> sandals; for rich in gold is Apollo, . . .

From this quality of the πολύχρυσος, richness in actual gold, the poet
passes to "wealth of possessions" (πολυκτέανος). Only in the last, the
mythological part of his song, does he go back to the epiphany (the
sole subject of our present discussion). Here (97) we read:

> ἰὴ ἰὴ παιῆον ἀκούομεν, οὕνεκα τοῦτο . . .
> (*Hië, hië, Paeëon,* we hear—since this . . .)

---

32 Parallels to the vision in Revelation (12:1)—"a woman clothed with the sun"—
have been sought in the Apollo myth cycle. Cf. Albrecht Dieterich, *Abraxas*
(Leipzig, 1891), pp. 118ff.; and for a contrary view, F. Boll, *Aus der Offenbarung
Johannis* (Leipzig, 1914), pp. 108ff.

33 The term used by Callimachus, τὸ ἔνδυτον, means garment of any sort.

The meaning is not that the festive gathering raises the cry only at this point, towards the end of the "hymn proper." Perhaps it is the poet's conception that the cry resounds most loudly now that the sun is high in the heavens. The form ἀκούομεν can also mean "we keep hearing." In any event, Callimachus is leading up to the mythological basis for the rite. Why is this cry raised?

> . . . since this refrain did the Delphian folk first invent, what time thou didst display the archery of thy golden bow. As thou wert going down to Pytho, there met thee a beast unearthly, a dread snake. And him thou didst slay, shooting swift arrows one upon the other; and the folk cried "*Hië, hië Paeëon*, shoot an arrow!" A helper from the first thy mother bare thee, and ever since that is thy praise.

Thus the archenemy is the monster (δαιμόνιος θήρ), the "terrible dragon" (αἰνὸς ὄφις), with whom the god battled in Delphi. It can hardly be doubted that Callimachus no more distinguished this mythical creature from the conquered darkness of night than he distinguished the approaching Apollo from the rising sun. For him the rays of the sun, the plectrum with which the god strikes his golden lyre, are also arrows, unremittingly shot from the golden bow. "How could the force that warms and animates be designated by so one-sided an image?" asked K. O. Müller,[34] forgetting that Callimachus explicitly uses the lyre and the bow—ἢ κίθαριν ἢ τόξα (19)—these two instruments[34a] so closely related in their structure, as an expression of Apollo's two contradictory aspects; and that the light itself, both the sensible and the spiritual light, can when it strikes upon darkness be as sharp and destructive as an arrow. . . .

3. Aeschylus: The Eumenides 179–82

In this brief lecture we cannot analyze all the passages in classical literature where the apparition of Apollo is described. Beside the epiphany in Delos, I shall here cite just one in Delphi. It is Aeschylus in his *Eumenides,* the third tragedy of the Orestes trilogy, who gives us this extraordinary vision.

On the stage we see the gate of Apollo's temple. The Pythoness,

34 *Die Dorier,* p. 286.
34a Cf. W. F. Otto, *Die Götter Griechenlands* (2nd edn., Frankfort, 1934), p. 95.

priestess and prophetess of the god, enters and moves towards the temple, where she means to proclaim the responses of the oracle. She opens the gate, disappears within, and comes running back. First she describes the terrible scene that has frightened her out of the temple, then she flings open the gate, and looking into the innermost sanctuary the audience discerns, seated on the omphalos, the navel stone, held to be the middle point of the earth—Orestes, who at Apollo's command has murdered his mother. The Furies, with terrifying Gorgons' faces, who have pursued him here, lie sunk in sleep. Apollo appears, as it is quite natural for him to do in his own temple. With him is Hermes his brother, to whom he has entrusted the suppliant Orestes for protection. At first Apollo is calm. Only when the ghost of the murdered Clytemnestra awakens the Furies and they rise to attack Hermes does Apollo reveal himself as in an epiphany, in all the fullness of his divine power, menacing with his bow:

> Out! I command you, from these halls with speed
> Depart—begone from my prophetic shrines,
> Lest, feeling the winged flashing serpent's sting,
> As from the golden-plaited string it leaps . . .[35]

Thus he begins his speech, and it is most particularly the last two verses that warrant our attention:

> μὴ καὶ λαβοῦσα πτηνὸν ἀργηστὴν ὄφιν,
> χρυσηλάτου θώμιγγος ἐξορμώμενον . . .[36]

Here Apollo appears as the god of light, driving the powers of darkness, the terrors of night, from his temple. His bow glistens gold. Compare this with his dark manifestation at the beginning of the *Iliad*. Here he comes (I, 44)

> Down from Olympos . . ., angry at heart, carrying bow and quiver: the arrows rattled upon his shoulders as the angry god moved on, looking black as night. He sank upon his heel not far from the ships, and let fly a shaft; terrible was the twang of the silver bow. First he attacked the mules and dogs, then he shot his keen arrows at the men, and each hit the mark:

35 Tr. Arthur S. Way, *Aeschylus in English Verse* (New York and London, 1908), Vol. III.
36 The following line reads: ἀνῇς ὑπ᾽ ἄλγους μέλαν᾽ ἀπ᾽ ἀνθρώπων ἀφρόν . . . (lit., "pain should vomit forth black gore from slaughtered men").

pyres of the dead began to burn up everywhere and never ceased.[37]

This version of an Apollo epiphany—the first in Greek literature—makes it clear that the great god, who in Homer is consistently invoked along with Zeus, had also a very sinister aspect. Golden as he may have appeared to Callimachus, he is here literally "like the night": ὁ δ' ἤϊε νυκτὶ ἐοικώς. It scarcely dispels the dark aspect of Apollo to point out that Hector's glance when he breaks into the Greek camp,[38] or the menacing attitude of Herakles in Hades,[39] is also likened to the night. The bright aspect also occurs in Homer; the god who in his dark manifestation has a silver bow, and accordingly bears the epithet ἀργυρότοξος, also appears as the god "with the golden sword" (χρυσάορος).[40] This second epithet in substantive form is elsewhere applied to the hero who sprang from the body of the beheaded Medusa: a mythical being whose relation to erupting light is perfectly clear.[41]

Apollo appeared to the Greeks—this would be evident from Homer even if Apollo the wolf-god were unknown to us[42]—by night as well as by day; by night he shoots his fatal arrows from a moon-silvery bow. In the *Eumenides* his bow glitters with the gold of the sun. But the poet uses a strange circumlocution for the arrow: he calls it a winged serpent (πτηνὸς ὄφις).[43] This might almost seem to be a kenning, a cryptic metaphor of the high tragic style.[44] We might incline to this view if this epithet for the god's arrow did not seem so paradoxical precisely here in Delphi, where the god's battle with the primal serpent was solemnized. Snakelike is the weapon that was once

37 Tr. W. H. D. Rouse, *The Story of Achilles* (London and New York, 1938).
38 *Iliad*, XII, 463: νυκτὶ θοῇ ἀτάλαντος ὑπώπια.
39 *Od.*, XI, 606; both references in Otto, p. 96.   40 *Iliad*, V, 509; XV, 256.
41 The same epithet to be sure is given to goddesses closely related to Medusa, such as Demeter (*Homeric Hymn to Demeter*, 4) and a manifestation of Artemis (Herodotus, VIII, 77), more or less comparable to the representation of the Gorgon in Corfu, where the goddess, beheaded but unharmed, takes pride in Chrysaor who is standing beside her.
42 Cf. Kerényi, *Apollon*, pp. 43f.; *The Gods of the Greeks*, pp. 131f.
43 The word ἀργηστής, often translated as "hissing" (here as "flashing"), is also a frequent epithet for lightning.
44 This was the ancient interpretation: τραγικώτερον ὄφιν εἶπεν τὸ βέλος διὰ τὸν ἰόν. Thus the similarity consisted in its venomous property. We shall have more to say of this.

67

wielded against the snake: this paradox inevitably follows from the designation of the arrow as a snake, if this is to be regarded as anything more than an individual whim on the part of the poet. And on the basis of the mythological material involved, it would seem to be more. The equivalence of arrow and snake occurs among the variants of a myth connected with the cult of Apollo.

Troy, protected by Apollo, the god with the silver bow, could not be taken without the bow of Herakles.[45] This bow was in the possession of Philoctetes, who was detained on a barren island by his terrible wound. The similarity between this wound and the incurable wound of Chiron, the wise centaur and first physician, the teacher of many heroes, goes so far that in one version of the myth Philoctetes, like Chiron, was wounded by one of the poisoned arrows of Herakles, which fell upon his foot.[46] In another version, he was bitten by the poison snake which guarded the secret sanctuary of the goddess Chryse.[47] Mysterious, too, is the goddess herself. She is explicitly identified only with Pallas Athene.[48] Her close relation to Apollo follows from the fact, among others, that one of the places named after her—the isle of Chryse where Philoctetes was bitten by the snake, is supposed to have later vanished beneath the sea[49]—was the city of Chryse, which was under the special protection of Apollo and whose priest Chryses, father of Chryseis, moved the god by his prayers (in the first book of the *Iliad*) to punish the Greeks with his arrows. And there is also a version according to which Philoctetes was bitten by the snake while offering a sacrifice to Apollo.[50]

Thus Troy was protected by Apollo's bow and arrows—it was he who directed the bow of Paris against Achilles—and in a more mysterious sphere, by snake bite. Perhaps it would not be impossible to gather some knowledge of the nocturnal Apollo through a study of the golden goddess "Chryse." But here, on the basis of what has been said, I should like merely to formulate the relation between poisoned arrow and poison snake a little more sharply than was done by ancient commentators. For this relation was not merely metaphorical; it was

45 Documentation of the following: Robert, in Preller and Robert, *Griechische Mythologie*, Vol. II, pp. 24, 1093ff. and 1207ff.
46 Servius in *Aen.*, III, 402.   47 Sophocles, *Philoct.*, 1326ff.
48 Schol. in *Iliad*, II, 722.   49 Pausanias, VIII, 33, 4.
50 Apollodorus, *Epitome*, 3, 27.

also very real, in that the poisoning of arrows was originally undertaken in imitation of poison snakes. In a sense the arrow was an image, a copy, of the snake. The arrow was then a winged snake, particularly when shot from the bow of a god who was himself related to the snakes. Concerning Apollo this is not too well known, but there is express evidence of it.[51] In one of his sacred groves in Epirus, snakes were kept for him, as for Asclepius in Epidaurus: the snakes of Asclepius were kept in a round *peribolos,* those of Apollo in the *tholos.* A virgin priestess fed the snakes and the manner in which they accepted the sacrificial food passed as a kind of oracle. They were said to be descended from the Delphic snake Python and to be the "playthings" (ἄθυρμα) of the god.

These snakes to be sure were harmless beasts such as occurred in the cult of Asclepius. The two deities are identified in cultic inscriptions, surely not without reason,[52] and the story[53] of how the snake of Asclepius which was brought to Rome had previously climbed a palm tree in Apollo's sanctuary at Antium shows the possibilities of a harmony between the Delian tree and the beast which played so considerable a role in the myth and cult of Delphi. Though even in the cult, in so far as it is known to us, the snake appears not as a tame, sacred animal, but as a primal monster, whose mythological destiny— his slaying by Apollo—is ritually solemnized and repeated.[54] The relation of hostility between this dragon and Apollo seems clear. According to the Homeric hymn to Apollo, where it is first mentioned, this primordial monster was a female snake: not δράκων, but δράκαινα (300). The hymn represents it as a

> dragoness, mighty and huge, a wild Etin,[54a] that was wont to wreak many woes on earthly men, on themselves, and their straight-stepping flocks, so dread a bane was she (304).

51 Aelian, *De natura animalium,* XI, 3.
52 Two inscriptions, 'Απόλλωνι 'Ασκληπίωι, in Farnell, *Cults,* IV, pp. 408, 209. And the "god" of the Epidaurus medical inscriptions is only intelligible as Apollo and Asclepius considered as one deity. More on this in Kerényi, *Der göttliche Arzt: Studien über Asklepios und seine Kultstätten* (Basel, 1948).
53 In Valerius Maximus, I, 8, 2.
54 At the festival of the "septerion," which belongs in a separate study devoted to the slaying of the dragon by Apollo.
54a [The translator has used an archaic term which, as Old English *eoten,* was applied to the monster Grendel in *Beowulf.*—ED.]

This female snake is chosen by Hera as the nurse of Typhaon, another mythical monster, as the hymn goes on to tell us. The poet names the dragon neither here nor elsewhere, but merely explains the place name Pytho and Apollo's surname Pythios (371–73).⁵⁵ The name "python" for the snake, first used by postclassical authors, comes from the same root, but its precise meaning is unclear. The name Delphyne⁵⁶ from the root δελφ, "belly," "uterus," accords with the "fat" (ζατρεφής) monster of the hymn, and is known to us from other traditions. A giant constrictor snake was vanquished⁵⁷ by Apollo soon after his birth at "Delphoi,"⁵⁸ a place similarly named after the womb.

There is no such clear tradition concerning the relation of the monster to the oracle itself. According to the Homeric hymn, Apollo conquers the dragon after establishing the oracle. Our second classical source, Aeschylus in the *Eumenides,* relates with the precision and completeness befitting a sacred tradition, how the oracle was passed down from its foundress, the earth-goddess Gaia, by way of Themis and Phoebe, to Phoebus Apollo (1–9). Aeschylus says nothing of any struggle for its possession. This does not exclude the possibility of another struggle, such as that described by the author of the Homeric hymn and by Callimachus. A primordial battle might well have been grounded in the essence of the two mythical contestants, without reference to a possession of any sort. And it is understandable that later, after the feeling for this kind of primal mythology had been lost, explanations should have arisen such as that of the Homeric hymn, which makes the primal devourer a devourer of sheep, or that of Euripides, who makes her a guardian of the oracle of the earth-goddess.⁵⁹ And yet it is noteworthy that in the tradition the character of aggressor clings to the guardian and protectress, who finally turns into a robber and highwayman named "Python."⁶⁰

55 From πύθεσθαι, "to rot" and "to smell of rot."
56 Apollonius Rhodius, II, 706, with Schol. The male form "Delphynes" is a derivative. The Homeric hymn makes clear that the female is the original form.
57 Cf. the passages in T. Schreiber, *Apollon Pythoktonos* (Leipzig, 1897), pp. 4ff.
58 The relation of the newborn god to a place of this name has also a positive aspect, cf. Kerényi, "The Primordial Child in Primordial Times," in C. G. Jung and Kerényi, *Essays on a Science of Mythology* (Bollingen Series XXII; New York, 1949), p. 70.
59 *Iph. in T.,* 1247.
60 At least since Ephoros, cf. Plutarch, *Quaestiones Graecae,* 12, with Commentary of W. R. Halliday (Oxford, 1928).

These are the two variants of the written tradition concerning the relation between dragon and oracle. Both in the earlier, which describes the battle in itself, and in the later, which associates it with the possession of the oracle, Apollo's female adversary meets an appropriate end, one indeed that is in keeping with the name of Python: she rots. The opinion was put forward[61] that the omphalos at Delphi is the tombstone of the snake, and we have strange traditions regarding the snake's skin, teeth, and bones, and their connection with the tripod[62] which is so mysterious in many ways. But none of these traditions[63] accords with a considerable number of monuments which show the omphalos in connection with the snake. Most of the representations of the omphalos[64] form a tradition of their own, a third variant of the relation between snake and oracle, manifested only since the postclassical period[65] in the material which has accidentally been preserved. The texts concerning the slaying of the dragon cannot be used to interpret the monuments without violence to the latter. The close connection revealed in the monuments between the serpent and the cult stone of Apollo, the snake-entwined omphalos, points to the possibility of a positive relation between god and snake, of a snake in the service of Apollo.

That an ancient, in beholding a serpent coiled round the omphalos, may well have conceived of a friendly, beneficent beast, is proved by a Pergamum coin, showing on one side the head of Asclepius, and on the other the serpent-entwined omphalos.[66] A Delphi coin with the same representation of snake and omphalos[67] shows that this snake friendly to the god—for only such a snake is possible on a coin com-

---

61 Varro, De lingua Latina, VII, 17, and Hesychius, s.v. Τοξίου βουνός.

62 Servius in Aen., III, 360 and VI, 347; Hyginus, Fabulae, 140.

63 Lucian, De astrologia, 23 is based on the observation of a constellation; Hesychius and the Suidas, s.v. πύθων, on no observation at all.

64 A compilation already in need of supplementation may be found in the three treatises of W. H. Roscher: I, Omphalos (Leipzig, 1913); II, Neue Omphalosstudien (Leipzig, 1915); III, Der Omphalosgedanke bei verschiedenen Völkern, besonders den semitischen (Leipzig, 1918). They are all publications of the Sächsische Akademie (or Gesellschaft) der Wissenschaft, Philologisch-historische Klasse.

65 An inquiry extending farther back would have to consider the votive offering of the Plataeans: a field in which much archaeological spadework remains to be done. Cf. A. B. Cook, Zeus, Vol. II (Cambridge, 1915), pp. 193ff.

66 See our figs. 1, 2.

67 See our fig. 3. Reverse: head of Demeter with veil.

memorating Asclepius—was intended as a Delphic snake. To the Delphic coin corresponds a small marble omphalos[68] found on Delos, and this in turn shows points of comparison with a relief from Delos[69] and a group of omphalos representations on Etruscan urns.[70] In a Pompeiian mural, the snake lowers its head before Apollo playing the lyre;[71] the snake, as the texts tell us, is vanquished, but the significance is similar to that of a relief on a Roman candelabrum,[72] in which Apollo rests his lyre on an omphalos entwined in a snake. Here the lyre is the victorious power and the snake seems to be subdued by it. In a relief from Miletus,[73] the snake rests coiled round the omphalos, as though sheltered beneath the god's bow. In a less known Pompeiian mural, the snake twined round the omphalos actually raises its head menacingly against an approaching giant serpent.[74] This shows that the snake can itself assume the role of snake fighter.[75] And here let us recall the snake in a famous work of art, which to be sure reveals no other special relation to Delphi, but which discloses the god in one of his most familiar epiphanies: the little, unassuming snake, with head

68 See our fig. 4.
69 Roscher, II, Pl. III, 3, after Marcel Bulard, in *Monuments et Mémoires* (Académie des inscriptions et belles-lettres, Fond. E. Piot, Paris), XIV (1908), fig. 20.
70 Roscher, II, Pl. IV, 1, 3, 5, after Heinrich von Brunn and Gustav Körte, *Rilievi delle urne etrusche* (Rome, 1870–96), Vol. II, Pl. XCIV, 2; I, Pl. XLVII; and II, Pl. LXXV, 1.
71 Roscher, I, p. 93, after Paul Herrmann, *Denkmäler der Malerei des Altertums* (Munich, 1904–34), Vol. III, pl. 20, Color Pl. II. It is the opinion of Roscher that the snake "is dying or has just died." J. E. Harrison, *Themis* (Cambridge, 1927), p. 424, speaks of a "wounded and bleeding" beast. The color plate in Herrmann shows blood streaming from the mouth of the snake.
72 Roscher, II, Pl. IV, 2, after the *Annali dell' Istituto archeologico* (Rome, 1850); in his description of the candelabrum found in the baths of Titus, Brunn says, "il serpente sagro ad Apollone."
73 See our fig. 5. A "large, conical marble omphalos, entwined by a snake, from the necropolis of Miletus, after a photograph of Br. Schröder," in Roscher, I, Pl. VI, 5.
74 Roscher, II, Pl. IV, 4, after Bulard, fig. 21, who has here published only a sketch "destinée a donner une idée suffisament précise de la representation"; see our fig. 6. Actually, the almost hemispherical omphalos on a rectangular base in the sketch conforms almost perfectly to the omphalos with "dying" snake in the mural. This refutes Bulard's combinations (p. 72).
75 Roscher, who likewise finds Bulard's combinations, deriving this motif from the Roman religion, so unjustified that he does not so much as mention them, declares on p. 55: "Perhaps the representation is based merely on a play of the imagination." This he believes because the picture represents a "completely singular motif." This hypothesis is based on the entirely unjustified assumption that all the variants of the Delphic myth have come down to us. But precisely this is not the case.

[1]   [2]   [3]

[4]

1 and 2.   Pergamum coin.   2nd — 1st century B.C.

3.   Delphi coin.   4th century B.C.

4.   Marble omphalos.   Delos

[5]

[6]

5. *Relief. Theater of Miletus*
6. *Detail from a mural. Pompeii*

7. *Apollo Belvedere*

upraised, which adorns the tree trunk in the background of the Apollo Belvedere, whether put here by the Greek master himself, or by the Roman copyist.[76]

The Apollo Belvedere has already shot his arrow from his bow.[77] But beside the arrows in his quiver, he also bears a snake. Aeschylus' easily solved riddle of the "winged flashing serpent" combines elements which are elsewhere found side by side, two instruments and manifestations of Apollo's nature. Both can be fatal: the biting snake, the pointed arrow. And both are also salutary: the arrow directed against forces of darkness and the snake of the physician and prophet, the ἰατρόμαντις, as the Pythia calls him in the *Eumenides* (62). The arrows could also have a spiritual sense, considered as light-bringing sunbeams. And the snake? We have not set out to interpret it, but to call attention to its polyvalence. It is—among other things—a metaphor for the sunlike. For one great tragedian[78] Helios was the "fire-born snake" (πυριγενὴς δράκων). In the light of the tradition as a whole, of which we have here been able to mention only a small part, there is, however, no need to reduce the light and dark aspects of Apollo to a being susceptible of being called by any other name—such as "Helios." To the Greeks, Apollo was a very special deity, transcending the sun as celestial body, transcending the male and paternal sun god. Like all the great Olympians,[79] he is a kind of universal center and vantage point, seen from which the whole of existence takes on a unique aspect. From the standpoint of Apollo, it appears brighter and darker, more transparent, richer in the dangers and sufferings whose source is the "spirit."

Such dangers are found in a record as early as the Homeric hymn

76 Our fig. 7. The snake is no modern addition; cf. the drawing made of the statue by an unknown artist of the late 15th century before it had been restored, in C. de Tolnay, *The Youth of Michelangelo* (Princeton, 1943), fig. 113. The vanquished giant python with dangling head in a Louvre statue of Apollo (Farnell, *Cults*, Vol. IV, pl. 45) is ancient. Cf. W. Fröhner, *Notice de la sculpture antique du Musée National du Louvre* (Paris, 1876), pp. 97ff., which to be sure also lists a number of statues of Apollo ("Roman copies" it is true) with the little "serpent familier." The existence of this attribute, well known to earlier archaeologists, has been as good as forgotten in the more recent literature.

77 In his right hand, which has been broken off, he presumably held the laurel branch; cf. Wolfgang Helbig, *Führer durch die öffentlichen Sammlungen klassischer Alterthümer in Rom* (Leipzig, 1912), pp. 105f.

78 Euripides, fr. 937; cf. Kerényi, "Vater Helios," p. 88; *Töchter der Sonne*, p. 18.

79 Kerényi, *Hermes der Seelenführer* (Albae Vigiliae, N. S., I, Zurich, 1944), pp. 64ff.

to Hermes, in which Apollo denies even to his brother Hermes the gift of the true prophecy which reveals the *nous* (νόος) of Zeus[80] (533):

> . . . But as touching the art prophetic, oh best of fosterlings of Zeus, concerning which thou inquirest, for thee it is not fit to learn that art, nay, nor for any other Immortal. That lies in the mind of Zeus alone. Myself did make pledge, and promise, and strong oath that, save me, none other of the eternal Gods should know the secret counsel of Zeus. And thou, my brother of the Golden Wand, bid me not tell thee what awful purposes is planning the far-seeing Zeus.
>
> One mortal shall I harm [δηλήσομαι] and another shall I bless, with many a turn of fortune among hapless men. . . .[81]

Concerning the suffering whose source is the spirit, let us in conclusion cite a source which is purely profane but profoundly Greek and at the same time universally human, a passage which speaks to us all. "I have felt the serpent's sting," says Alcibiades of his philosophical experience with Socrates, in Plato's *Symposium* (217e). "And he who has suffered, as they say, is willing to tell his fellow-sufferers only, as they alone will be likely to understand him, and will not be extreme in judging of the sayings or doings which have been wrung from his agony. For I have been bitten by a more than viper's tooth; I have known in my soul, or in my heart, or in some other part, that worst of pangs, more violent in ingenuous youth than any serpent's tooth, the pang of philosophy, which will make a man say or do anything. . . ."[82]

---

80 The interpretation of the passages containing νοεῖν, "to know," and "that which knows," νόος, in the Homeric writings and in Hesiod, is essential to any scientific inquiry into the "spirit" in the history of Greek philosophy, but does not form part of the present study. On both subjects, see Kerényi, *Die antike Religion*, pp. 112 and 150; *Prometheus* (Albae Vigiliae, N.S. 4, Zurich, 1946), p. 30. Here be it only mentioned that the νόος seems to be bound up with the god Zeus, while the realization of knowledge, the "blowing" of the spirit, the epiphany, seems associated with his son Apollo.

81 Tr. A. Lang (London, 1899).   82 Tr. Benj. Jowett.

Walter Wili

The History of the Spirit in Antiquity

1. Introduction

The psychologists of the old school took little interest in the "spirit." They banished it from the psyche and contented themselves with thought and the understanding. And even those psychologists of our generation who do acknowledge the spirit betray a certain reserve when confronted with it as a problem; they stress its many meanings and point out that the spirit is scarcely a part of the individual psyche, that it is "supraindividual," perhaps a kind of collective supraconsciousness, to use a word both magnificent and dangerous.

Students of the humanities have an easier time of it than the psychologists. They may and must start from the prodigious assumption that the spirit has shown itself to be the decisive force in the development of mankind, so that history should really be interpreted as the outcome of the duel between soul and spirit. Accordingly, various thinkers have attempted to write the history of philosophy as the story of the spirit,[1] and this is highly significant—but it is only a beginning. Even the life work of Wilhelm Dilthey, who devised a system of the *Geisteswissenschaften*,[2] appears in its very intention to represent no more than a fragment of the spirit, because Dilthey's purpose was to distinguish between the natural sciences, which can be explained, and the other manifestations of the spirit which according to him are not susceptible to explanation but can be understood only through experience.

Dilthey made himself our guide to the last great "spiritual" thinkers

1 E.g., Wilhelm Windelband.
2 [Humanities; lit., sciences of the mind, or spirit.—Trans.]

75

of the West, Schleiermacher, Fichte, and Hegel.[3] Throughout his work he never wearied of pointing out that cultural epochs, and even the course of history, have always taken their orientation from man's conception of the spirit. True, he rejected Hegel's analysis of the "sciences of the mind." Hegel had actually represented the entire historical process as an outgrowth of the spirit and its development. In this development, according to Hegel, there are three stages:[4] "As subjective spirit, it attains to the consciousness of its freedom. As objective spirit it realizes this freedom in the world of law, morality, the state, and history.[5] And as absolute spirit, it achieves the unity of its existence and its concept of being in art, religion, and philosophy."

Dilthey recognized this return of the spirit as a consequence of Hegel's mysticism[6] and traced it to the impact of Neoplatonism. (Hegel's enthusiasm for the Neoplatonists was all the more significant in that it followed his readings of Plato with Hölderlin at the Tübingen *Stift*.[7])

Thus in the "heroic age of understanding," the spirit, this "sublime concept" as Hegel called it, was a power of philosophy and religion, of the soul and of pure thought; it was the reason which embraces intuition and feeling and the secret of the past and of the primal past as immanent forces—and at the same time it was part of that world spirit *(Weltgeist)*[8] of which Herder spoke in his *Adrastea* (VI, 5):

> The world spirit, I call it ether or light,
> It makes thee see and hear, feel and think,
> It thinks in thee; thou art only its vessel.

---

3 Among these we should also include Gustav Theodor Fechner, author of *Das Büchlein vom Leben nach dem Tode* (1836; tr. Mary C. Wadsworth, *Life after Death*, New York, 1943), who can be called a moderate follower of Xenocrates and the Neoplatonists.

4 Wilhelm Dilthey, *Gesammelte Schriften* (Leipzig, 1921–36), Vol. IV, p. 248.

5 Following Windelband and Hegel, Hans Freyer, in his astonishing little introduction to the philosophy of culture, *Die Theorie des objektiven Geistes* (Berlin, 1923), refers to the period from Herder to Hegel as the "heroic age of understanding." As a proof of his direct succession from Dilthey, I quote: "All the universal truths in the *Geisteswissenschaften* are based on experience and understanding" (p. 7).

6 And for that very reason rejected it as "fundamentally wrong." Dilthey, op. cit., p. 249.

7 Ibid., p. 17.

8 Cf. *Die Religion in Geschichte und Gegenwart* (2nd edn., Tübingen, 1927–32), Vol. II, pp. 955ff.

These words of Herder are post-Platonic and Stoic, as is the thinking of Hegel. And here we have hit on a crucial point: in the German classical-romantic period, the concept of "spirit" drew vast riches of meaning from Plato, the Stoics, and the New Testament.

And now let us approach the spirit—not as mystics, who have certainty of it, and not as scholastics, for whom it crystallizes into concept and number, but as seekers, looking upon the spirit as a realm that is and should be forever experienced, and wishing merely to discover how the Greeks and Romans were impelled to the spirit and what they meant by spirit. But first we may be permitted a philological intermezzo.

2. Philological Intermezzo

The German word *Geist* goes back to the Indo-Iranian *gheizd*, whose root *ghei* means "to move powerfully." Thus its original meaning is: "motive force."[9] In early usage, *Geist* simply designates "vital force," and by derivation a vital principle, equivalent to soul and anima. At an early day, the meaning of the word *Geist* approached "breath," "breath of life," still presumably by extension from "motive force." Under the influence of the Roman Platonists and Stoics, of the Fathers of the Latin Church and the New Testament, it then acquired the explicit Stoic and Christian meanings of *animus* and *spiritus,* and also of *mens,* a term developed largely in academic parlance, with the sense of *mens divina,* "divine world intelligence." Cicero, the foremost coiner of Western words and concepts, used the terms *spiritus sacer, animus divinus,* and *mens divina* to designate the Academic and Stoic-Posidonian world spirit, and in this he was followed by Seneca as well as the Church Fathers, beginning with St. Augustine.

When Luther took up the word *Geist,* it was already deeply embedded in Greek and Roman thought; from then until Hegel, this symbol, with its dominant religious and Ciceronian implications, did not lose but rather gained in sharpness and force, particularly after revival of Greek thought had restored the purity of its source meanings: of πνεῦμα, which designates breath and spirit, of νοῦς (intelligence,

---

9 *Trübners Deutsches Wörterbuch* (1936–) correctly rejects the assertion, in Grimm's *Deutsches Wörterbuch,* Vol. IV, p. 678, that the original meaning of the German word *Geist* was "breath" or "wind."

mind), and of λόγος (the thought which has become word).[10] When
Fichte called God *Geist,* in the sense of eternal and primal action,
source of life, he was following Alcmaeon, the Greek physician,
Anaxagoras, and Aristotle, but at the same time he was unwittingly
returning to the original meaning of the word *Geist* (motive force).
Hegel did very much the same in designating God as absolute *Geist.*

For the last hundred and twenty years both the spirit and the world
spirit have been under constant attack; the lofty structure of their
tradition-laden concepts and even the meaning of the words have
been reduced and impaired. This work of destruction and confusion
is even greater than that which has assailed the concept of "nature."[11]
Even the representatives of the natural sciences have played their part
in it. Among them Baron von Reichenbach, the German chemist,
stands solitary and unique: exactly one hundred years ago, he believed
that he had discovered a material emanation of the spirit. In his
experiments, persons chosen for their hypersensitivity were placed in
an absolutely dark room; they saw a certain fluid radiating from
magnets, plants, and animals. As a chemist and Stoicizing materialist,
he called this subtle substance, this "spirit," by the newly coined term
"od," chemical abbreviation for *"Odem."*[12]

For the sake of linguistic clarity as it were, we have looked into
the origin and development, the greatness and decline of the German
word *Geist,* and thus gained a hint not only of the omnipresence of
the spirit but of the vast tradition surrounding the symbols by which
we refer to it. Let us now turn to the Greeks, confident that the very
word "spirit" cannot fail to infuse life even into the most rigorous
of philologists.[13]

10 [Hereafter *pneuma, nous, logos.*] Hans Leisegang, in *Der Heilige Geist* (Leipzig,
1919), pp. 38ff., cites detailed references for *pneuma.* As to *logos,* I should like to
cite the excellent remark of Max Pohlentz, in his *Hippokrates* (Berlin, 1938),
p. 104: "For the 'gathering,' connecting, and hence understanding activity of the
human mind, the Greeks primarily used the word *logos.* But there was no verb
which completely rendered its meaning. When Alcmaeon of Crotona wished to
distinguish between the nature of man and beast, he said that only man ξυνίησι,
τά δ'ἄλλα αἰσθάνεται μέν, οὐ ξυνίησι δέ [understands, the others perceive, but
do not understand (tr. Freeman, op. cit. in n. 16, infra)]."
11 This has been analyzed in detail by Thure von Üxküll in *Wirklichkeit als
Geheimnis und Auftrag* (Bern, 1945), pp. 15ff.
12 [German for "breath."—TRANS.]
13 I.e., paraphrasing St. Paul, Stoic and Apostle (II Cor. 3:6): "For the letter killeth,
but the spirit giveth life."

3. The Spirit in the Pre-Socratic Philosophers

The Greeks gained their vision of the spirit in three mighty impulses: in the period from 580 to 430 B.C., which we roughly call the age of the pre-Socratics; in the era of the aged Plato and his closest disciples; and finally in the age of the Stoa of Posidonius.

Let us first turn to the Ionian natural philosophers, those men of action and shrewd observation, living amidst the rich culture of Asia Minor. The Ionian coastal cities were foci of immense vitality; their leading men traveled through the entire *oikoumene* of that time, and from their voyages they carried home knowledge and intimation of the world. The boldness with which the Ionians conquered foreign worlds and assimilated them to their own native sphere; the daily requirements of a life eminently oriented towards the outside world; the destiny, finally, which placed this most open-minded of all Greek peoples in a position to compare the candid Homeric vision of the gods with the very different thinking of the Greek mother country, and with the utterly different ideas of the more distant Persians, Babylonians, and Egyptians: all these elements combined to produce a literature in Ionian Asia Minor which from the very first was preoccupied with the wonders of the universe, with *mirabilia*, θαυμάσια; Herodotus, writing in the middle of the fifth century, was its classical culmination. But it remains unquestionable that despite their joy in the discovery of rational thought, despite their inborn passion for this thought, the Ionians, situated as they were between their mother country and Persia (which gave their thinking its main impetus), were able to achieve no more than a nucleus of *logos* thinking. And accordingly, we do not here find any purely rational thinking, even of the most archaic kind, despite the assertions of well-nigh all the philologists and philosophers who have written of the Ionians in the past three generations; the first philosopher to attempt such thinking was Aristotle, the mightiest of the Greek rationalists, and even he made this attempt only for a time, and with ill success.

Even in ancient times it was observed, for example, that Anaximander plunged his thinking into the depths of Orphic irrationality,[14]

14 Wili, "Die Orphischen Mysterien und der griechische Geist," *Eranos-Jahrbuch 1944*, pp. 91ff.

thus lending it the power to carry on the tradition of Hesiod. Passionately the Ionians raised the truly philosophical question concerning the origin of things. Anaximenes, pupil and friend of Anaximander, found the unique origin of the cosmos in the air, and this was the beginning of Greek speculation in regard not only to the original substance but also to the spirit.[15]

Through condensation the air becomes darkness, water, earth, and stone; through rarefaction, it becomes fire, which is ultimately refined into the light of the sun.[16] Here a decisive relation is established between man and cosmos: both are formed and sustained by the one air, which is called πνεῦμα καὶ ἀήρ. This is clearly stated in the second fragment of Anaximenes:[17] "As our soul, being air, holds us together, so do breath and air surround the whole universe." To the breath of man corresponds the breath of the cosmos. The air is soul, and thus a world soul is postulated.

Air, which is the origin of the cosmos and of man: breath, which moves the cosmos as it moves man: *pneuma,* vapor, which is transformed to fire and from fire to pure sunlight: these are the principal new ideas of Anaximenes, and with them begins the archaic metaphysics of the Greeks. This is what makes Anaximenes—contrary to the general belief among scholars—so much greater than Thales and Anaximander. It was his ideas that were now taken over, developed, and sharpened, in four diverse quarters: by the Pythagoreans, by the Eleatics, by Heraclitus, and finally by the physicians, chief of whom was Hippocrates. In the two generations from 500 to 430, these lines of thought running from Ionian Asia Minor to lower Italy and Sicily, to southern and northern Greece, led to several inspired formulations of the spirit.

Closest to Anaximenes was Heraclitus, also of Miletus, who flour-

---

15 O. Gigon in *Der Ursprung der griechischen Philosophie* (Basel, 1945; pp. 100ff.), rightly points out that the chaos of Hesiod and the Limitless of Anaximander are spatial concepts, that the water of Thales is no true ἀρχή, but that Anaximenes must be regarded as having conceived the first ἀρχή. And Aristotle, in the first book of his *Metaphysics,* was guilty of dangerous inaccuracy in this connection.

16 Hermann Diels (tr.), *Die Fragmente der Vorsokratiker* (5th edn., Berlin, 1934–37 [henceforward referred to as D]), 13 A 14; 13 B 2. English translation of the B-sections (i.e., the fragments themselves) from Kathleen Freeman, *Ancilla to the Pre-Socratic Philosophers* (Oxford and Cambridge, Mass., 1948).

17 For a fine interpretation of the fragment: Walther Kranz, "Kosmos als philosophischer Begriff frühgriechischer Zeit," *Philologus* (Leipzig), XCIII (1939), N.S. 47, 430–48.

ished around 480. For him the original substance of the cosmos was fire, which Anaximenes had looked upon as the most important of the forms assumed by the *pneuma:* "There is an exchange: all things for Fire and Fire for all things, like goods for gold and gold for goods" (D 22 B 90). Hence the cosmos, which is increate and eternal, undergoes cyclic changes; it is "everliving Fire, kindled in measure and quenched in measure" (B 30). This is no purely rational insight; the Orphic element in Heraclitus is apparent from the style of such fragments as B 94: "The sun will not transgress his measures; otherwise the Furies, ministers of Justice, will find him out."[18] This Heraclitean fire, by the rarefaction and condensation of Anaximenes, becomes water, then earth, and then again water and fire, descending and ascending, forever changing, forever traveling the road that is "one and the same" (B 60); it is the cause which renews the cosmos and the cause which will end it. In eternal change, opposite resolves into opposite in reluctant harmony (". . . that which differs with itself is in agreement"—B 51). Heraclitus combines Orphism with an understanding of his master when he formulates: "all things are one."[19]

Heraclitus developed a theory of the spirit exactly parallel to this doctrine of fire with its eternal rise and fall and change. He calls the spirit *logos*. It is the principle governing all happenings (B 1).[20] It is the great mystery of the soul, its innermost essence (B 45): "You could not in your going find the ends of the soul, though you travelled the whole way: so deep is its Law *(logos).*" Thus the *logos* is spirit, which is thought and yet deeper than mere thought; it travels the same circle in the consciousness, even at the edge of consciousness, as fire in the cosmos. The *logos* runs in a circle from opposite to opposite, thus shattering the proposition that opposites exclude one another.

"We breathe this divine *logos* [spirit] with the air and through it we become intelligent."[21] This conception of the *logos* reveals the

18 This cannot be traced back merely to the Dike of Anaximander (as does Julius Stenzel in his *Metaphysik des Altertums,* Munich, 1931, p. 56), but is Hesiodic and Orphic (Wili, loc. cit., pp. 91ff.). If fragment 22 B 66—"Fire, having come upon them, will judge and seize upon (condemn) all things"—is really imputable to Heraclitus, the Orphic tone is unmistakable.

19 D 22 B 50; with regard to the "Orphic one and all," see Wili, loc. cit., pp. 78f.

20 Unfortunately the authenticity of fragment B 72, concerning the *logos* "which guides and orders all things" is in doubt.

21 D 22 A 16. The passage is emphatically ascribed to Heraclitus in Sextus Empiricus, *Adversus mathematicos,* VII, 129.

81

direct influence of Anaximenes' theory of the *pneuma:* for Heraclitus the soul is also air or vapor (ἀναθυμίασις).[22] This *logos* which we breathe with the air, and whereby we gain our faculty for a thinking that is adequate to it, is subtler than the air, it is pure fire.[23] Thus the parallels of the cosmological and psychological, of fire and spirit, meet in the metaphysical: fire is the original substance of the cosmos, and spirit is the helmsman of the universe. But through breathing, the inward lives in the outward, and participates in the outward; through the breath, vehicle of the *logos,* the microcosm is joined to the macrocosm;[24] the *logos* in us and the *logos* in the universe are one and the same.

The *logos* of Heraclitus is a unique synthesis of the most diverse elements: above all—and this has been insufficiently stressed in the history of philosophy—it could not have been conceived without the thinking of Anaximenes: but Heraclitus was also influenced, in his conception of the spirit, by the first Pythagoreans and Eleatics; he was indeed the first to apply the theory of the breath formulated by his contemporary, the physician Alcmaeon, to metaphysics. Particularly in his conception of the spirit, which is central to his entire thinking, Heraclitus would seem to be one of the great adapters of other people's ideas, an offense for which he bitterly reproached Pythagoras (B 129): "Pythagoras, son of Mnesarchus, practiced research most of all men, and making extracts from these treatises he compiled a wisdom of his own, an accumulation of learning, a harmful craft."

*

Heraclitus, and other Greek philosophers after him, drew heavily on the early medical writers for their conception of the spirit. The early Greek physicians combined the undogmatic thinking of the Ionians with the Pythagorean conception of harmony. Chief among them were Alcmaeon, of Crotona in lower Italy, physician and Pythagorean, flourishing about 480 B.C.; Hippocrates, who appears to have reached

22 D 22 A 15.   23 D 22 A 20.
24 A. F. von Pauly and Georg Wissowa, *Real-encyclopädie der classischen Altertums-wissenschaft* (Stuttgart), Vol. XIII (1927), p. 1052. [Henceforward, PW.]

the height of his activity in the middle of the fifth century; and his contemporary, the Cretan physician Diogenes of Apollonia.[25]

On the basis of his anatomical studies, Alcmaeon of Crotona recognized that neither the heart nor the Homeric diaphragm was the material seat of thought. As a Pythagorean, he sought to prove the immortality of the soul by showing it to be the vehicle of eternal motion,[26] and at the same time he likened the nature of the soul to the sun. He may have been the first great student of motion, for it is possible that he took up this problem before Heraclitus. In these studies he was followed by both Plato and Aristotle, who frequently mention him.[27] It is to him that we owe the magnificent phrase which might serve as a motto to the history of the spirit and which states the fundamental principle of cyclic thought: "Men perish because they cannot join the beginning to the end."[28]

The Cretan physician Diogenes of Apollonia was influenced by Alcmaeon, but he was also under the direct influence of the Ionian thought of Anaximenes. Profiting, it would seem, by the philosophical conversations of a century and by the observations of the physicians, he ventured to extend the air theory of Anaximenes. In this work his point of departure was the medical observation that without air and breath there can be no life.[29] As a physician, he made not the cosmos, but man, the starting point for his speculations. He began with the air as the principle of life; then, extending his thought on a cosmic plane—and also, it may be presumed, following Anaximenes—he made it the original substance, from which everything else issued.[30] And he went further, conceiving it as soul and spirit in one (ψυχή ἐστι καὶ νόησις: B 4). This original substance is a "body both everlasting and immortal; whereas of other things, some come into being and others pass away" (D 64 B 7).

But Diogenes of Apollonia not only saw the air (ἀήρ) as spirit, he also recognized that the forms of the spirit correspond to the forms of the air. Moreover, as is hinted by the predicates "everlasting and immortal," the air is really God himself (D 64 B 5): "And it seems

25 He is referred to as a contemporary of Anaxagoras by Aristophanes (*Clouds*, 225ff.) and Euripides (*Trojan Women*, 884ff.).
26 Pohlentz, *Hippokrates*, pp. 82ff.   27 See D 24 A 3, 7, 11 and 12.
28 D 24 B 2.   29 D 64 B 4.   30 D 64 B 2.

to me that that which has Intelligence is that which is called Air by mankind; and further, that by this all creatures are guided, and that it rules everything; for this in itself seems to me to be God and to reach everywhere and to arrange everything and be in everything. And there is nothing which has no share of it; but the share of each thing is not the same as that of any other, but on the contrary there are many forms both of the Air itself and of Intelligence. . . ."

Thus the air is not only individual soul and spirit; it permeates all living creatures and even all "inanimate" nature; all creatures and things partake of it: it is at once world breath, world soul, and world spirit. Heraclitus had said similar things of fire. For the Ionian, this was a cosmic vision which included man; for Diogenes the physician, the doctrine first grew out of medical experience and then, extended through the philosophical influence of Anaximenes and Heraclitus, embraced the whole cosmos.

This doctrine was taken over by the most celebrated of all physicians, Hippocrates, whose probable familiarity with the writings of Alcmaeon and Diogenes of Apollonia has recently been demonstrated.[31] He adopted this doctrine because his observations of the *pneuma* fitted in with it. Hippocrates revealed this most clearly in his book *Sacred Disease*. The *pneuma*, the mobile air that is present in all existing things, is also the motive force in man. Man takes in the *pneuma* through his nose and mouth, through his pores, and even in his food, which contains air. The air he breathes is most highly concentrated in the brain. In line with the doctrine of Alcmaeon, the *pneuma* here appears as vehicle of the intelligence and as intelligence itself. The soul is not differentiated from the spirit, but is "the inner *pneuma*, continuously renewed by inspiration and expiration, which lends the whole organism movement and life."[32] Hippocrates finds the ultimate cause of all diseases in the circulation of the *pneuma*. Disturbances of the *pneuma*, brought about by faulty breathing or faulty nutriment, provoke disturbances in the organism as a whole. Salubrious diet consists not only in the quantity and type of nourishment, but

31 Pohlentz, op. cit., pp. 83ff. It seems to me that Pohlentz has here given decisive arguments in support of his contention (to which the whole book is devoted) that *On the Surrounding World* and *Sacred Disease* are the work of Hippocrates. I shall frequently follow him below.
32 Ibid., p. 85.

above all in the grace of proper breathing.[33] This accounts for the much discussed Pythagorean prohibition of beans: the Pythagorean rule forbade the eating of beans because they were regarded as highly disturbing to the *pneuma*.

We have seen that Hippocrates found the ultimate basis of life and of man's spiritual existence in the *pneuma* and built his pneumatic diet on this conception. His theory of the pneuma soon gained influence in the West, and was taken up at the court of the younger Dionysius of Syracuse. It would seem to have been at the court of Syracuse that an "inborn *pneuma*," as vehicle of individual life, was differentiated from the atmospheric air.[34] This was the period in which proper breathing (εὐπνοεῖν) came to be regarded as prerequisite for spiritual and intellectual life, and, in Sicilian medicine, as the basis for all physical health as well.[35]

*

The physicians had drawn inspiration for their theory of the *pneuma* from the early Pythagoreans (though it must be added that, in their speculations based on actual observation, they were soon compelled to depart from these ideas). By the first half of the fifth century, the Pythagoreans had developed a highly remarkable conception of the spirit, with which the ancient world was to concern itself for centuries to come. Yet it should not be forgotten that neither Pythagoras nor the order which he founded in southern Italy would have been conceivable without the experience of Orphism.[36] It was Orphism which provided the man who passed among the ancients as a prodigious adapter of other men's ideas with the core of his doctrine: immortality of the soul, metempsychosis, his view that earthly life is a prison for the soul, and, in the ethical sphere, his insistence on guilt and purifica-

---

33 Pohlentz (ibid., p. 90), speaks of the great pleasure with which Goethe read Hippocrates' treatise *De aere, aquis et locis* ("airs, waters, places"), and refers to his letter to Heinrich Meyer of December 30, 1795. It might also be well to recall his poem "Im Atemholen sind zweierlei Gnaden" ("In breathing there are two kinds of grace").

34 Werner Jaeger, "Das Pneuma im Lykeion," *Hermes* (Berlin), XLVIII (1913), 29–74. This must have occurred through the influence of Diogenes of Apollonia; see supra, p. 83.

35 Jaeger, *Diokles von Karystos* (Berlin, 1938), 217.

36 Concerning the difficult relation of Orphism to Pythagoras, see my "Orphische Mysterien," pp. 92ff.

tion. For the Pythagoreans, to be sure, this purification followed the law and measure which also governed the cosmos, the rhythmic relations which on earth take the form of music, song, and dance. Rhythm can be measured and stated in mathematical proportions; hence the Pythagoreans devoted themselves with an almost inconceivable passion to the mystery of numerical relations. For archaic man thought and the object of thought were one; and thus, for the Pythagoreans whatever entered into numerical relations became number. Aristotle explains this attitude in a celebrated passage in his metaphysics: "Since, again, they saw that the modifications and the ratios of the musical scales were expressible in numbers;—since, then, all other things seemed in their whole nature to be modeled on numbers, and numbers seemed to be the first things in the whole of nature, they supposed the elements of numbers to be the elements of all things, and the whole heaven to be a musical scale and a number."[37]

From this archaic metaphysic of numbers and from their fundamental doctrine of the immortality of the soul, the early Pythagoreans took their conception of a spirit, which—unlike the *pneuma* of the contemporary physicians—stands in direct opposition to matter, which above all is not matter, not even of the most refined sort. To the God "who is pure spirit,"[38] the visible cosmos is juxtaposed. The numerical form which the Pythagoreans found for this spirit demonstrates not only the mathematical origin of their conception, but also the immaterial nature of their spirit. For the One, from which all things arise, is spirit and God, while four is justice, evidently because in the Pythagorean view the number four represented the perfect, the "harmonious" proportion.[39] When the Pythagorean Empedocles conceived of the four elements, water, fire, air, and earth, as the origin of the universe, this was perhaps an attempt, ingenious in its simplicity, to create a compromise between the doctrines of the Pythagoreans and those of Alcmaeon. But from the middle of the fifth century B.C. onward, it remained a favorite notion with the Greeks to see the spirit

37 Aristotle, *Metaphysics*, I, 5, 985b 30ff. (tr. W. D. Ross, Oxford, 1928).
38 ὅπερ ἐστι νοῦς ὁ θεός D 58 B 15 (Aëtius, I, 3, 8, in Diels, Vol. I, p. 454, 39).
39 The supreme oath of the Pythagoreans, "By him who gave the fourness to our soul," must be considered in the light of this harmonious proportion. See Thomas H. Heath, *The Thirteen Books of Euclid's Elements* (Cambridge, 1926), Vol. II, pp. 112f.

86

in numbers. Plato and the Academics concerned themselves with it, and the Gnostics never ceased to do so.

After Parmenides, the Eleatic philosopher, had fought his battle for being as against becoming, the conception of the pure spirit achieved its perfection in Anaxagoras. At the end of the Persian Wars, this philosopher came to Athens from Clazomenae in Asia Minor and was befriended by Pericles, by whose name we know the happiest age in the history of Greece, perhaps of the entire West. The work of Anaxagoras on nature reveals for the first time an Ionian entirely free from Orphism and the religion of metropolitan Greece. In this sense he should rightly be considered the first "pure Ionian." His view of the world is fundamentally Ionic. Over the infinite throng of atoms,[40] holding them down, rest two substances, superior to all others in quantity and in the size of their atoms; these are the air (ἀήρ) and the ether (αἰθήρ). The universe is enlarged to include things both larger and smaller than hitherto known, and for the first time it is recognized that there must be many similar worlds.[41] The cosmos has achieved its present form by a process of differentiation that occurs in a mighty whirling motion.[42] By this differentiation the primal small things, which are the germs of the universe,[43] are ordered. The whole whirling motion by which the universe comes into being is governed and maintained by the spirit (νοῦς); above all, the *nous* gives the impetus for this world-creating whirling motion. For "whatever they were going to be, and whatever things were then in existence that are not now, and all things that now exist and whatever shall exist—all were arranged by Mind."[44] In so far as the spirit initiates, orders, and foresees the whirling motion by which the world comes into being, it is outside of this motion and before it. It is a transcendent prime mover. Here Anaxagoras takes up the mightiest theme in Greek thought, that of becoming and of motion in the broader sense. In so far as his spirit is transcendent, he seems Parmenidean. And yet his conception is essentially different from that of Parmenides and the other thinkers

40 Anaxagoras and not Democritus is the creator of the infinitely small things: D 59 B 1. It is true that Democritus seems to have been first to use the word ἄτομα; Anaxagoras called his atoms ὁμοιομερῆ. Nevertheless it is in place to recall that the word itself has come down to us in no fragment of certain authenticity. See Walther Kranz, word index to Diels, op. cit., Vol. III, s.v.

41 D 59 B 3 and 4.   42 D 59 B 9.   43 D 59 B 3, 4.   44 D 59 B 12.

of the Eleatic school in that his spirit is identical neither with what is thought or with being, but is an autonomous entity distinct from everything that is: "Other things all contain a part of everything, but Mind is infinite and self-ruling, and is mixed with no Thing, but is alone by itself. If it were not by itself, but were mixed with anything else, it would have had a share of all Things, if it were mixed with anything."[45]

Regulator of all things, initiator of all movement, an entity standing outside the cosmos, the *nous* of Anaxagoras is a transcendent world spirit. It is the fourth fundamental form of the Greek spirit, after the *pneuma* of Anaximenes and the physicians, the spirit-number of the Pythagoreans, and the *logos* of Heraclitus. His must be regarded as the mightiest among Western conceptions of the world spirit, and it gives food for constant reflection that two of our greatest modern thinkers, Leibniz and Newton, should have given much thought to the *nous* of Anaxagoras.

It is as a transcendent reality that this spirit confronts all being. And it is a source of lasting astonishment that it was not perceived in Orphic, mystical vision, apprehended in religious exaltation, or arrived at through sense of guilt. This transcendent world spirit was derived, recognized, seen, and formulated by the purest of Greek thinkers, on the basis of a realization of the indestructibility of being, a mythless exposition of the universe, a critique of Parmenidean being, an understanding of becoming and of motion, the principles of logic.

In similar situations, Plato and Aristotle struggled with these fundamental problems of being, above all with the problem of becoming and motion. The *nous* of Anaxagoras exerted a decisive influence on Plato's theory of ideas and on Aristotle's conception of God as prime mover. Aristotle, to be sure, tries to gloss over his debt to Anaxagoras with a painfully gross simplification: "For Anaxagoras uses reason [*nous*] as a *deus ex machina* for the making of the world, and when he is at a loss to tell for what cause something necessarily is, then he drags reason in, but in all other cases ascribes events to anything rather than to reason."[45a] Since historians of philosophy were prone to follow

45 Ibid.   45a *Met.,* I, 4, 985a 18 (tr. Ross).

88

Aristotle without reflection, Anaxagoras' conception of the spirit was in urgent need of Leibniz' unique elucidation.

Thus before Plato the spirit was four times apprehended and expounded as authentic knowledge: (1) as *aer* and *pneuma* by Anaximenes and the Pythagoreanizing physicians of the West, and by Hippocrates; (2) as the *logos*—that is, pure fire—by Heraclitus, following Anaximenes; (3) as spirit-number by the Pythagorean order; (4) as transcendent *nous* by Anaxagoras. By the middle of the fifth century B.C. these forms of the spirit had begun to irradiate one another, and this interchange steadily increased in force. Much later, the first two, the *pneuma* of the physicians and the *logos* of Heraclitus, exerted a powerful influence upon the Stoics; while with no less force the two others, that of the Pythagorean order and that of Anaxagoras, influenced Plato and Aristotle.

The next doctrine of the spirit, that of Plato, was gained from the deepest depths of the irrational, but after a critical appraisal of these four basic forms of the spirit. The forms of the spirit voiced by later thinkers, from Speusippus to Plotinus and St. Augustine, from Xenocrates to Posidonius, Plutarch, and Boethius, are unique variations whose metaphysical structure could only have crystallized out of mystical experience. They are no more a product of "pure thought" than their pre-Platonic models.

4. Brief Note on Plato[46]

In the *Philebus* (28 c) the aged Plato calls the spirit (νοῦς) "the king of heaven and earth." He had come to this conclusion on the basis of cosmological considerations, but underlying it is also a grandiose psychological definition of pleasure (ἡδονή).[47] The great intellectual heritage of the Ionians combined with that of the physicians to form a conception of the spirit. When Plato discerned the objective world corresponding to the *nous*, it was as the "absolute good." At least in

---

46 A more detailed discussion of Plato's conception of the spirit will be found in my forthcoming *Formen des Geistes in der Antike und im Humanismus.* Here I shall restrict my remarks to what is essential for an understanding of the following.

47 With regard to the background of this definition of pleasure, see my "Probleme der Aristotelischen Seelenlehre," *Eranos-Jahrbuch 1944* (Festgabe C. G. Jung), pp. 78ff.

the *Republic,* this idea of the good is the reality-giving principle of all things, both thinkable and visible. But through the primal Orphic experience, the "absolute good" was raised to substantiality. Moreover, a road was found which led, as it were, from this highest godhead back to individual things, and this was the influence of the absolute good upon particular things. For the mature Plato, this perspective "from above" transformed all relations of the existent; in it, the spirit truly became godhead. In the *Republic* (508 e), Plato had compared the idea of the good with the sun, which he called a son of the good, but in the *Philebus* (22 c) he refers to this good as the "divine spirit."[48] By a certain simplification, the One, the Good, and the divine Spirit came to be called the metaphysical trinity of Plato. For all the Neoplatonic mystics, and particularly for Plotinus, this trinity became the center of all thought and endeavor; because of it Plato can be considered the father of the Western conception of the spirit.

And there are two other motifs through which Plato dominated the conceptions of the spirit of the following centuries:

One is the motif of generation. In thoroughly Orphic style he speaks in the *Symposium* (210 a–212 a) of the generation, or bringing forth, of beautiful words, of ideas, of the truth. In the supreme moment of exaltation toward the beautiful, the act of generation is transferred to the thinker, whose highest endeavor it now becomes to generate true thoughts. The act of generation and rebirth had found its most magnificent symbols in the Orphic and other mysteries, whence Plato took them. Thus we approach the emergence of the *logos spermatikos* of the Stoics.

The second motif through which Plato exerted a decisive influence on later conceptions of the spirit is of an artistic nature. As a thinker and artist, looking upon the world from his new idealist perspective, he for the first time, in the *Timaeus,* juxtaposed a cosmopoeia to the cosmogonies, and conceived of the world builder, the *demiourgos,* who creates the world as the copy of an eternal and immutable prototype. This myth of creation introduces an element alien to the Greeks. It

---

48 R. Heinze (*Xenocrates,* Leipzig, 1892, pp. 46ff.) describes the influence of this conception on Xenocrates.

has been recognized as Persian,[49] just as the creation of a good and bad world soul in the *Laws*[50] has been traced to Persian influence; and it is certain that Zoroaster was known in the Academy in the first third of the fourth century B.C.[51] One easily discerns that the Platonic demiurge of the *Timaeus* had taken certain essential features from the spirit of Anaxagoras. And the *Timaeus* is the basic work that determined the conception of the spirit of the ensuing centuries. This work, more than any other, was commented upon by the Academics and Stoics, and chief of all by Posidonius, the magus among the Stoics. These commentaries and elaborations played an essential part in preparing the way for the spirit religion of the New Testament.[52]

5. The First Academics and Xenocrates

We are now in a position to understand how it was possible for the great "systems" of speculation on the spirit to appear suddenly at the end of the fourth century B.C., for we know that fundamentally they were variations of Plato's doctrine of the spirit and of the pre-Socratic conceptions of the *pneuma* and the *logos*. True, they were systems of thought and speculation, and yet they seem to be rudiments of primal experience; we should do best perhaps to call them excrescences of the unconscious that have irrupted into thought.

Xenocrates, who directed the Academy after Speusippus, from 339 to 315, ventured a grandiose religious vision of the spirit. Perhaps the most meticulous and faithful of Plato's students, he was a man of thorough Socratic bearing.[53] In his basically religious mind, the thoughts of Plato tended to turn into a binding dogma of the spirit-God.[54]

49 R. Reitzenstein and H. H. Schaeder, *Studien zum antiken Synkretismus aus Iran und Griechenland* (Leipzig, 1926), pp. 213ff.

50 Plato, *Laws*, 886 a ff. In this connection, see Heinze, op. cit., pp. 26ff., and Plutarch, *De Iside et Osiride*, c 45–48.

51 Principally through Eudoxus, disciple of Plato, and the first among Greek thinkers to possess an accurate knowledge of Egypt (PW, VI 93 A1).

52 This has principally been demonstrated by Reitzenstein and Schaeder, op. cit., passim.

53 Diogenes Laertius, IV, 6ff.

54 The following is based on Heinze's aforementioned work, a collection of the fragments of Xenocrates. One of the most urgent projects of the Berlin Academy,

Speusippus, Plato's first successor as head of the Academy, had already begun to transform the school into an order such as that of the Pythagoreans, with a binding rule of life. In his work "Plato's Supper," he had exalted the founder into a hero, and made him the son of Apollo, the bestower of all spirit.[55] But then in his critique of the theory of ideas, a sharp conflict had arisen between religious and critical thought.

With Xenocrates there was no such conflict. This profoundly religious thinker strove to combine Plato's metaphysics and the vast astronomical knowledge of the early Academy. His inner need of order and certainty drove him towards a systematism hostile to inquiry and certainly alien to Plato. The essence of this systematization was the group of three, or triad. He was first to subdivide philosophy into physics, ethics, and dialectics.[56] He also subdivided the domain of epistemology, placing it at the summit of the spirit. He followed Plato in distinguishing sense perception, opinion, and knowledge; but in his view, perception was directed towards the things of the earth, opinion towards the heavens, while knowledge embraced the world of the spirit, which is above and outside of the heavens. To these three forms of cognition he seems to assign three forms of destiny, in a play on the names of the fates. He associated sense perception with Clotho, soul knowledge with Lachesis, and spiritual knowledge with Atropos, "the inexorable."

But as we have intimated, the core of Xenocrates' doctrine of the spirit is a religious dogmatization of what Plato had represented through the give and take of his dialogues as possible and probable. The spirit now becomes truly number; it is no longer the One, but in a Pythagoreanizing sense, oneness, the monad. This monad is pure spirit, the father of the universe, Zeus, the supreme God.[57] And with this personalization of the pure spirit and of the good, thinking has

---

announced thirty years ago, unfortunately has never advanced beyond the project stage: the publication of the fragments of the early Academy, with the exception of Aristotle—i.e., primarily, Speusippus, Xenocrates, Eudoxus of Cnidos, Heracleides Ponticus, Polemon, Crates, and Crantor.

55 Documentation in P. Lang, *De Speusippi Academici scriptis* (Bonn dissertation, 1911), pp. 14ff.

56 Heinze, op. cit., fr. 1.   57 Ibid., fr. 15.

shifted from philosophy to theology, which is no longer primarily a rational inquiry. What Plato metaphorically designated as number representing the idea has now become actual number, or more accurately, "numberness"; what he metaphorically provided with all the predicates of the personal has now truly become person.

Beside the paternal spirit, Xenocrates conceived a feminine godhead, the dyad, duality; it is the soul and mother of the cosmos. Plato's distinction of body and soul was thus given simple expression. But evil, the reality of which had first revealed itself to Plato, and which had compelled him to assume the existence of an evil world soul, now enters into the world soul as the "unlimited."[58] It is questionable whether Xenocrates was able to incorporate these basic ideas into a perfectly articulated system; most probably he was not, for he seems to have postulated three orders of gods, those of the fixed stars, those of the planets, and those of the elements.

This threefold division of the gods is almost congruent with the threefold structure of the cosmos:[59] the universe consists of the realm of the fixed stars, which is that of the spirit; the realm of the planets, which is that of the soul; the sublunar realm, which is that of man.[60] The region of the moon becomes here the true intermediary between heaven and earth, between the here and the beyond, between spirit and body.

In this way, Xenocrates arrived at a highly interesting structure of existence: although a certain element of the hypothetical is inevitable in view of our fragmentary knowledge of his work, let us attempt an elementary reconstruction of this system:

To the primal triad

world spirit	*world soul*	*cosmos*

corresponds the triad of physical theology

the gods of the fixed stars	*the gods of the planets*	*the gods of the elements.*

58 Ibid., pp. 66f.   59 Heinze, ibid., pp. 72f.
60 In part an old Academic idea, imputable perhaps to Eudoxus; Aristotle makes a similar distinction between the regions above and below the moon in *De caelo*, I, 3, 270, b5.

From this triad arises the archetypal cosmic triad

| *sun* | *moon* | *earth.* |

To this corresponds theologically and personally the triad

| *God the Father* | *God the Mother* | *God the Son.* |

To this corresponds in man the little triad

| *spirit* | *soul* | *body,* |

to which corresponds, on an epistemological plane,

| *thought* | *opinion* | *perception.* |

To this corresponds the triad of the fates:

| *Atropos* | *Lachesis* | *Clotho.* |

We need only call to mind the sun-metal gold and the moon-metal silver to realize that the emergence of alchemy was imminent.

In this astonishing system, the soul is the middle and intermediary between spirit and body, as is the moon between sun and earth.[61] As in all Greek systems of the spirit, a full correspondence is preserved between macrocosm and microcosm: just as the spirit enters into the soul, so does the world spirit enter the world soul. Here, in a unique way, these two Platonic motifs of the middle and of generation in beauty are applied to the spirit and its operation, and to the relation between spirit and soul. The fundamental problems of the pre-Platonic and Platonic quest of the spirit are retained and in a way solved in this compendium of "archetypal" associations: these are the question of the origin and nature of the cosmos and of man, the relation between man and the universe. At the same time, partly, it would seem, through the influence of Orphic conceptions, the spirit has become Zeus. Only one thing seems to be missing: the rhythmic dissolution of the All in the One, the exhaustion of the One in the All: that is to say, the cyclical waxing and waning of the cosmos.

These speculations of Xenocrates were to exert a decisive influence on all conceptions of the spirit from Posidonius to St. Augustine, but

---

61 This is stated by Plutarch in his dialogue "On the face of the moon," cited by Heinze, op. cit., pp. 125ff.

of equal importance was his peculiar endeavor to apprehend the eschatological life of the spirit as distinct from the soul. For this led him to demonology with all its far-reaching implications, and throughout the remainder of antiquity, spirits would be associated with the spirit! Fortunately Plutarch has preserved this doctrine of Xenocrates at the end of his dialogue "On the face of the moon." Here let us sketch it briefly: Man consists of spirit, soul, and body. The earth gave him his body, the moon his soul, the sun his spirit. When a man dies, that is his first death. This death separates soul and *nous* from the body. But soul and *nous* remain together. Every soul, after leaving the body, must wander about for a time between earth and moon and finally, after vicissitudes (depending on its spirit nature and its life on earth), reaches the moon. These souls sojourning on the moon are sharply divided according to good and evil: all together are demons. Yet their intervention in human affairs is generally favorable (in keeping with the preponderance of the good in the universe!). They sometimes descend to earth to administer oracles and to participate in mysteries (c 29).

Here on the moon the souls finally die their second death; the *nous,* yearning for the sun, separates from the soul; sovereign and free from all passion, it seeks the sun and unites with the primal spirit. The soul, parted from the spirit, remains on the moon and ultimately dissolves into the moon.

Scarcely any other text deals so thoroughly with the nature of the moon. It is an intermediary between sun and earth, exactly corresponding to the sun, which is intermediary between spirit and body.

This doctrine of Xenocrates is assuredly fantastic. Yet among the early Academics, the celebrated astronomer and physician Eudoxus, as well as Crantor, the commentator of the *Timaeus,* appear to have been close to it. Its influence was equaled only by the spirit doctrine of Aristotle, who today must be regarded merely as one among many Academics, and by no means the most original. For the demons, the good and bad spirits, have never died. More and more they would inhabit the space between God, the pure spirit, and man. But in still another respect Xenocrates represented a turning point in the history of the conception of the spirit; he was so certain of the spirit that to seek it and recognize it was for him less important than to consult it and make himself worthy of it. Plato's quest for the spirit became a basis for mystical life: the ordering of existence in the spirit and for the spirit. This is the meaning and aim of the spirit system of Xenocrates. The Gnostic summons to heed and obey the spirit-God begins exactly at this point.

6. The Stoa and the Logos Spermatikos

Possibly the quest of the spirit would have fallen into the hands of mere rational thinkers and their epigones, if it had not acquired a new force, outside the realm of thought. This force was not primarily Orphic as in many of the pre-Socratic philosophers and in Plato; it emanated from the religions of the East. It manifested itself among the Stoics, who now extended the Greek quest of the spirit over the whole Mediterranean and Near Eastern region, preparing the way for the Catholic doctrine of Rome and circumscribing it as though with a vast magic circle of space and time. The time: from the third century B.C. to the third century A.D.; and the space: the coasts of Asia Minor, Syria, Egypt, northern Africa, Spain, southern France, northern Italy, Greece, and Byzantium. The center of this circle would one day be Rome, not the Rome of Seneca, but of the Stoic and Apostle Paul. However, it is not of this that I wish to speak, but of the influence of Stoicism on the conceptions of the spirit, particularly in the period of its flowering, the second and first centuries B.C.

Alexander the Great had brought into the *oikoumene* a region which may be called the focus of these strivings for the spirit: the Cilician-Syrian coast. Here Stoicism became the dominant doctrine, this was its home. In this Stoicism, Persian and Babylonian conceptions were blended with Greek doctrines by thinkers of Semitic origin or Semitic imprint. Even Zeno, the founder, a native of Citium in Cyprus (he founded his school about 300 B.C. in Athens), appears to have been a Semite. Chrysippus, the third director of the school (about 220 B.C.), came from Tarsus in Cilicia, as did his successor, the younger Zeno. This was the same Tarsus where the Apostle Paul was born and raised. Between 140 and 60 B.C., the not far distant isle of Rhodes witnessed the teaching of two leaders of the middle Stoa, Panaetius, member of the philosophical group which had formed in Rome around

Scipio the younger, and Posidonius, whose lectures Cicero as a man of thirty attended in Rhodes, and who remained his friend and correspondent. From Tarsus came also Athenodorus, Stoic and director of the Pergamum library, who after 70 B.C. was tutor to Cato the Younger in Rome. From Cana near Tarsus came that other Athenodorus, teacher and adviser to Augustus. Finally, from the southeast corner of Cilicia came Sotion, well versed in the doctrine of Posidonius, who in his old age, from 18 to 20 A.D., instructed the philosopher Seneca. Rhodes was a Greco-Roman reservoir for diverse streams of Oriental thought, the region of Cilicia and Syria was an eastern and predominantly Semitic reservoir of Greek and Persian thought. And between the two, it must be added, ran many lines of intellectual communication.

It may be mentioned in passing that in the first century B.C. a strong Greek influence extended southward from Syria to Palestine.[62] This region became the principal home of the Neoplatonic doctrine of the spirit. Yet despite the influence of the Academy, the predominant word and concept was not the *nous,* but first the Heraclitean *logos* and later the *pneuma* of Anaximenes and the physicians.[63] But the words had ceased to be distinct in content; the *pneuma* connoted primarily the substance of the *logos.*

Zeno, founder of the Stoa, clearly followed the tradition of Heraclitus and Anaximenes; he never designated the godhead permeating the world as *pneuma,* but as πῦρ, "fire," and ἀήρ, "air."[64] It was Chrysippus who first called the substance of the godhead *pneuma,* breath and spirit, and from then on this term predominated among the Stoics. In both Zeno and Chrysippus, however, we find the most important peculiarity of the Syrian Stoa: despite strong Platonic influence, they both, by a return to Anaximenes and the physicians, conceived the *pneuma* corporeally.

Among the Stoics we encounter—and this we may call their first original trait—a new "materialization" of the spirit, of the world spirit as well as the human spirit, and this must be imputed to the

62 Eduard Wechssler, *Hellas im Evangelium* (Berlin, 1936), pp. 135ff.
63 Cf. the valuable philological investigations of Leisegang, in *Der Heilige Geist,* pp. 38ff.; and, on the word πνεῦμα, of Richard Reitzenstein, *Die hellenistischen Mysterienreligionen* (3rd edn., Leipzig, 1927), pp. 308ff.
64 Cf. Leisegang, op. cit., p. 50.

large part played by the Syrians in the school. Modern research[65] has repeatedly revealed that the Semites and Syrians could not conceive of a purely spiritual entity. The *pneuma,* which is spirit and world reason, is conceived as godhead, as a fiery, airy substance. This godhead—and this is a second peculiar trait—remains personified: Zeus. To him in his fiery, solar aspect Cleanthes, second director of the school, addressed his powerful Platonizing hymn. And a third characteristic of the Stoic doctrine of the *pneuma* is this: the act of generation, which in the lofty sublimation of Plato's *Symposium* is directed towards the archetype of the beautiful, is by the Stoics transferred to the cosmos. This experience, the archetypal experience of the mysteries, is deepened by the experience of the inner interrelation between macrocosm and microcosm, whereby the generation of man corresponds to a similar generation of the cosmos. Once arrived at this conception, the Stoics, even before Posidonius, gained the doctrine of the germinal spirit, the *logos spermatikos,* which under the impact of the twofold experience, of generation and of the parallelism between the universe and the self, became the core of their thinking, a conception of far-reaching consequence for all mystical and Christian thought. Simply and clearly, Diogenes Laertius, the Plutarch of ancient philosophical history, characterized the place of the *logos spermatikos* in Stoic thought:[66] "They also teach that God is unity, and that he is called Mind, and Fate, and Jupiter, and by many other names besides. And that, as he was in the beginning by himself, he turned into water the whole substance which pervaded the air; and as the seed is contained in the produce, so too, he being the seminal principle [*logos spermatikos*] of the world, remained behind in moisture, making matter fit to be employed by himself in the production of those things which were to come after. . . ."

The generative process of man and of the human spirit is one and the same. The sperm not only contains *logos,* but is substantially *pneuma,* spirit-breath.[67] Hence it is from the sperm that the *logos* develops in the child, and the *logos* begins to attain full growth when the child himself has acquired the power of generation. Then a human

65 I am referring to the work of Reitzenstein, Leisegang, and J. Heinemann on Gnosis, Philo, and Posidonius.
66 Diogenes Laertius, VII, 135ff. (tr. C. D. Yonge, London, 1853).
67 Chrysippus, in Diog. Laert., VII, 159.

period is at an end. We now understand the profound, truly Stoical word "generation." It is the generative cycle both in the corporeal and spiritual: the interval in which the seed from which the father had been engendered becomes seed again in the son,[68] the interval of thirty years. At death, the souls, with their generative power, return to the *logos spermatikos* of the universe. As in the universe the *logos* permeates all things, so in the sperm the *logos* permeates all men and is the foundation of the brotherhood of man.

Moreover: to the human cycle, in which the body grows from the seed, and seed grows from the new body, corresponds the cycle of the universe, from the complete dissolution of the cosmos in fire to the new ordering of the primal fire in a new cosmos and its new dissolution. Or, as Cleanthes put it:[69] "All nature must be transformed to fire, as to seed, and from it the cosmos must be restored as it was formerly." Thus the *logos spermatikos* is the one thing that remains eternally. And Cleanthes continues:[70] "Thus All grows out of the One and from All the One is again constituted."

In the doctrine of the *logos spermatikos,* the universe is seen not only in its rhythm but also in its cycle; to conform with nature the spirit of man must travel a similar cycle. Therefore the thinking of the spirit must be cyclical, annulling contradictions, thus differing from rational thought, which is rectilinear, which excludes contradiction, which progresses and is "progressive." Reason strives for "progress," the spirit despises it as a disease of childhood or at best looks upon it as a primitive period of growth.

Thus the *logos spermatikos* achieves its fulfillment rhythmically and in the cyclical movement of the universe. The Orphics and Heraclitus had conceived something very similar in the wandering of the souls from the One into individual lives, and back again from the individuals to the One; and likewise Plato had contemplated this migration of souls in its ultimate spiritual and metaphysical depth. In the doctrine of the generative spirit, the Stoics translate this Orphic-Platonic migration of souls into a material realm of the utmost subtlety; and this they do by a thoroughly syncretistic process. This

68 Heraclitus D 22 A 19; the true author is probably not Heraclitus but one of the Stoics.
69 Hans von Arnim, *Stoicorum Veterum Fragmenta,* Vol. I (Leipzig, 1905), fr. 107.
70 Ibid., fr. 497.

process occurred in Syria above all from the third to the first century
B.C. And the significance of the *logos spermatikos* in this process is
revealed by the central parable of the sower who went forth to sow,
in the New Testament, which has been shown to be a direct outgrowth
of the *logos spermatikos*.[71] And it should also be recalled that Seneca
has preserved this idea in several of his letters.[72]

*

In the cosmos as in man, according to Stoic doctrine, there are two
forms of spirit, "the spirit which fulfills the order of the universe"
(λόγος ἐνδιάθετος) and "the spirit which carries itself outward"
(λόγος προφορικός), which is as it were the product of the first.[73] In
this conception there remains an original Greek element; for just as in
early Greek thought thinking and the object of thinking coincide,
just as the Platonic idea becomes one with thinking about the idea,
similarly the word, the *logos prophorikos* (= *oratio*), is the principal
manifestation of the spirit. The word is not only a gift of the spirit,
it is the spirit itself bestowed upon us; it is the epiphany of the spirit,
it is revelation. This conviction accounts for the extraordinary love
of the Stoics for language and their passionate concern with it. It
accounts also for the special appeal of the Pentecost miracle to the
ancients and the ease with which the word was accepted as revelation.[74]

The significance of these two forms of the spirit for the ensuing
period may be seen in the fact that the Christians found God himself
in the *logos endiathetos*, the ordering spirit, and Christ, the son of
God, in the spirit turned outward. It was Plotinus, the great Neoplatonic mystic of the third century A.D., who, carrying Platonic
thought astonishingly close to Stoic conceptions, said:[75] "The first
beginning is *logos* and all things are *logos*. . . ." And close to this

---

71 Wechssler, op. cit., p. 283.   72 Seneca, *Epistles*, 38, 73, 81, 94.
73 Cf. PW (1927), XIII, 1057.
74 The Church Fathers were still animated by this attitude, which is excellently
characterized by Giuseppe Toffanin, *Geschichte des Humanismus* (Amsterdam,
1941; tr. from *Storia dell' umanesimo*, Naples, 1933), p. 85: "The entire patristic
literature assumes a hidden harmony between the truth which God entrusted
to the Bible and that which He entrusted to classical wisdom, between the sybils
and the prophets. For Dante the *Consolation of Philosophy* of Boethius set the
seal to the mission of the classical philosophers, and in the *Divine Comedy*, this
mission is proclaimed by Virgil."
75 Plotinus, *Enneads*, III, 2, 15, 118.

both in time and, despite distinctions, in meaning, is the first verse in the Gospel of St. John: "In the beginning was the Word [*logos*], and the Word was with God, and the Word was God."

Here it may reasonably be argued that the *logos* of Plotinus is truly immaterial and hence far removed from the *logos* of the Stoics. And indeed an explanation is needed. The Stoic doctrine of the spirit had been significantly purified and divested of materiality by Posidonius. Posidonius (135–51 B.C.) drew upon doctrines from the distant east, taking from the Chaldeans the light-ether which he assumed to be the dwelling place of a transcendent spirit-godhead. But at the same time, following Plato, he withdrew from the *pneuma* its subtly corporeal character and rediscovered it as pure spirit, opposed to substance in every possible way. And finally he ventured, again following Plato (*Timaeus* 90 a) and Xenocrates, to associate demonology with this dematerialized spirit. The new conception of the spirit finds its implicit formulation in its theory of sleep and dreams. In sleep the spirit does not rest, but lives its purest life separate from the senses, and is thus enabled in dreams to see the godhead and tell the future. How vastly this mysticism of Posidonius was to influence posterity is revealed by the dream oracle in Plutarch's little treatise *De genio Socratis*.

It is that mysticism of the spirit which was taken up and elaborated by Philo, who also transformed the demonology of Posidonius and Xenocrates into the first angelology. Posidonius' doctrine of dreams— in dreams the spirit is most immediately awake and becomes the "eye of the soul"[76]—won its first Roman adherent in none other than Cicero.[77] He was at the same time the most influential proponent of the Platonic and Posidonian doctrine of the spirit.

7. *Rudimenta Romana*

Cicero, whose philosophical knowledge and talent are so incomparably greater than his detractors of yesterday and today have wished to admit, and often than they themselves possess, was an adept of Posidonius, and, as we have said, his friend. We have Cicero to thank

---

76 Concerning this epithet and its elaboration by Philo, see Leisegang, *Der Heilige Geist*, pp. 216ff.
77 Cf. Wili in *Mensch und Gottheit in den Religionen* (Bern, 1942), p. 175.

that Platonism became the accepted doctrine of the highest Roman society, among men like Lucullus, M. Junius Brutus, Varro, and among many men of the next generation—Horace began as an Academic. This was the Platonism of the middle Academy, advocated by Cicero's teacher and friend Antiochus of Ascalon, who headed the school in Athens from approximately 88 to 68 B.C. He seems to have taught that not only in the ethical realm, but also in connection with the doctrine of the spirit, Plato and Aristotle would have found themselves in essential agreement with the Stoics. It is important to note that this Academic syncretism of Antiochus, in which Greek elements were mingled with Cilician-Syrian elements, influenced Cicero earlier than did Posidonius. Cicero did to be sure adopt the doctrine of Posidonius fully in his philosophico-religious writings, supported in this no doubt by the Stoic Diodotus of Sidon, who for many years served as his philosophical secretary. Diodotus came from Sidon in Syria, a place which Jesus later liked to visit.

We are now in a position to understand why in his work *On the Nature of the Gods,* the universe, in accordance with the doctrines both of the Academics and the Stoics, *"uno divino spiritu continetur."*[78] And moreover, that this *mens divina* is creative.[79] And finally, that the Posidonian world spirit, at the beginning of the great *Tusculan Disputations,* is one with the *mens divina* of the fifth book. Precisely these references show that the syncretism of Cicero works not only in the ethical but in the metaphysical sphere as well. And is it not Cicero who, with his certainty of the ordering world spirit, draws the political consequences of this belief in his *Laws,* and derives the hierarchy of governmental forms from the nature of the *mens divina* at work in the cosmos, as the highest law?

Later, Seneca was to adopt the most significant of Posidonius' ideas in his conception of the spirit. He was the first among the Roman Stoics who, unlike the older Stoics, stressed the opposition between spirit-God and matter; the first who, like Posidonius, juxtaposed passive matter to the creative spirit, to the spirit as artist and ruler. Despite all the rudimentary pantheism and monism in Seneca, this God-spirit, this *sacer spiritus creator,* is omnipotent and omniscient

78 Cicero, *De natura deorum,* II, 19, and III, 28.
79 Ibid., II, 136; for use of the word *mens,* I, 100, and II, 88; and *Timaeus,* 29.

and determines the future[80] by his providence. Aside from providence, justice and lovingkindness are characteristic of this personal God-spirit.[81] When Calvin, the commentator of Seneca, conceived his doctrine of predestination, the spirit-God of Posidonius and Seneca was again at work.

8. Humanistic Arabesques

The countless variations and forms of the *logos,* which are no mere logical exercises but partake of primal experience, the *pneuma* mysticism of Philo and the Gnostics, the *logos* doctrine of Clement of Alexandria, the discovery of the antispirit Satan, and the hierarchy of angels and devils—all these are matter for the historian of religion and for the theologian, and hence do not come within the scope of the present study.

But in conclusion let us at least broach the question of how the humanists received the forms of spirit found by the Greeks and Romans. First of all, it must be stated that long before the emergence of humanism, the most powerful interpretations of the spirit and of the antispirit Satan revealed themselves in the inexhaustible riches of the Latin hymn writers, in the ecclesiastical authors, in Augustine and Boethius, because they were nurtured from the deep springs of primal experience. In comparison to these, the humanistic interpretation seems trivial, above all it presupposes the spiritual experience already mentioned; it thus gains in breadth and diversity, but acquires no new depths. True, the humanist experienced the word as an epiphany of the spirit, the word of the poet as of the philosopher; true, as Sicco Polenton intimated in 1420, he looked on Latin literature as the layman's Bible, the record of a second, lesser divine revelation;[82] but in his *docta pietas,* he advanced only in times of crisis, as it were, from the arrangement of words to the structure of the original spirit. The first true humanists in the realm of the spirit were the Christian hymn writers; the creative humanists, in the realm of the spirit as in other realms, were Dante, Boccaccio, Petrarch, the discoverers of the *docta pietas;* Marsilio Ficino and Pico della Mirandola, who per-

---

80 Seneca, *Dialogues,* I, 5, 8.   81 Seneca, *Epistles,* 95.
82 Toffanin, op. cit., p. 457, note 67.

fected it; and as the last true humanists of the spirit we may regard those pneumatophoric natures, Leibniz and Newton.

All the rejoicing of the soul which has certainty of the spirit resounds in the Latin hymn. Because the word was here experienced by the singer as a pure epiphany of the spirit, it is truly great from Hilary of Poitiers, Ambrose, Prudentius, and Boethius, the heralds of the *spiritus creator,* up to St. Hildegarde of Bingen (1098–1179) who, filled with antiquity like Boethius, wrote one of the most amazing hymns of all time, which we shall quote. The creative spirit speaks:

> I am the supreme fiery force
> That kindles every spark of life;
> What I have breathed on will never die,
> I order the cycle of things in being:
> Hovering round it in sublime flight,
> Wisdom lends it rhythmic beauty.
>
> I am divine fiery life
> Blazing over the full-ripened grain;
> I gleam in the reflection of the waters,
> I burn in the sun and moon and stars,
> In the breeze I have secret life
> Animating all things and lending them cohesion.
>
> I am life in all its abundance,
> For I was not released from the rock of ages
> Nor did I bud from a branch
> Nor spring from man's begetting:
> In me is the root of life.
> Spirit is the root which buds in the word
> And God is rational spirit.[83]

We see how the great Heraclitean-Stoical heritage of thought concerning the spirit (at the end of the song we even encounter the *logos prophorikos*) entered into this nun, how in all the inspired simplicity of her Christian soul she made it her own and how she preserved it sacred.

Dante, in his *De monarchia,* glorified the same spirit. The order and gradation of the spirit in the universe demands a hierarchy of

83 [Rendered from a modern German tr. by Otto Karrer, *Schweizerische Rundschau* (1945), 147ff.—TRANS.]

104

men in the state:[84] this is the idea we have seen expressed in Cicero's *Laws*. Like Cicero, Dante grounds the monarchy in the spirit, and seems to draw on Cicero for his hierarchy of command and service. It is well to recall this at a time when the battle of spirit against anti-spirit has assumed such magnitude that it can end only in a peace and a state hierarchy built on the spirit, or in Satanic catastrophe.

There is a profound reason for the religious fervor with which the Italian humanists of the *quattrocento* received Cicero's divine rhetoric: the Latin language ennobled by rhetoric was the sole vehicle of the spirit and of wisdom, and Cicero was the greatest advocate of spiritual Rome.

Because language is spirit become word, these humanists were prepared to serve it and sacrifice to it after the manner of priests. Toffanin, one of the foremost students of Italian humanism, has formulated this as follows:[85] "And the great element of novelty is that though humanism retained the positively religious veneration of wisdom, which we find in innumerable passages in Dante, it reopened the battle between reason illumined by 'rhetoric,' the guardian of God's word, and pallid scientific reason, this battle which to St. Augustine had seemed the dominant motif of the centuries: '*magis ad poetas quam ad physicos fuisse populos inclinatos.*' "

Where *docta pietas* ceased to spring from the depths of the unconscious, man's word concerning the spirit was doomed to feebleness. The most learned humanist of all, Desiderius Erasmus, found little to say of it. This little we find in the *Enchiridion militis christiani*.[86] Following the Stoics and the Apostle Paul, he based his Christian ethic upon the Xenocratic-Stoic structure of man, whereby man consists of spirit, soul, and body, and the soul constitutes the middle and intermediary. But this truth, because it was apprehended only by the *ratio*, is a true platitude.

At this the Tuscans could only have been struck with horror. For in Tuscany, some decades previous, Marsilio Ficino, filled with the experience of Neoplatonic mysticism, had written a letter in his elegant Latin to Michele Mercati of San Miniato, in which he found these words for the relation of the spirit-God to the soul:

---

84 This is formulated with special incisiveness in *De monarchia*, III, 16.
85 Op. cit., p. 133.   86 B I, c 9f.

The spirit-God says of himself: "What things are good? Good is the sun of suns, the sunlight is good in the world today, good is the sunlight from the angelic intelligences. Such is my shadow, O soul, that it is the most beautiful of all corporeal things. . . ."

The soul replies: "Oh wonder exceeding wonder. What an exceeding fire devours me now. What a new sun, and whence does it shine upon me? What spirit, whence comes it so mightily and sweetly, and stings, bites, caresses, charms, and fills my marrow with joy? . . . The God of the universe has embraced me. The God of Gods flows into my marrow. God nourishes me entirely, and he who begot me creates me anew. He has begotten the soul, he elevates it to an angel, he transforms it into God."[87]

87 [Rendered from a German tr. by Marchese Karl von Montoriola, *Briefe des Mediceerkreises aus Ficinos Epistolarium* (Berlin, 1925), p. 100.—TRANS.]

Max Pulver

The Experience of the Pneuma in Philo

In commenting on Genesis 17:17, in his *On the change of names*,[1] Philo says of Abraham: "But to convict us, so often proud-necked at the smallest cause, he falls down and straightway laughs with the laughter of the soul [τὸν ψυχῆς γέλωτα], mournfulness in his face but smiles in his mind where joy vast and unalloyed has made its lodging. For the sage who receives an inheritance of good beyond his hope, these two things were simultaneous—to fall and to laugh. He falls as a pledge that the proved nothingness of mortality keeps him from vaunting; he laughs to show that the thought that God alone is the cause of good and gracious gifts makes strong his piety. Let created being fall with mourning in its face; it is only what nature demands, so feeble in footing is it, so sad of heart in itself. Then let it be raised up by God and laugh, for God alone is its support and its joy."

In §175 and §176 of the same work, Philo returns to the same thought: " 'And so Abraham fell and laughed.' He fell not from God, but from himself [. . . οὐκ ἀπὸ θεοῦ πεσών, ἀλλ' ἀφ' ἑαυτοῦ], for in clinging to the immovable Being he stood, but fell from his own conceit. And so when the Spirit which is wise in its own conceits had been thrown to the ground and the spirit of love to God raised up and firmly planted round Him who alone never bends, he laughed. . . ."[2]

And as he sets forth in §157, Isaac is his laughter.

There are few passages in Philo's compendious work that reveal his quality as distinctly as this interpretation of the passage in Genesis

1 *De mutatione nominum*, §§154–56, in *Philonis Alexandrini Opera qui supersunt*, ed. Paul Wendland, Leopold Cohn, and others (Berlin, 1896–1915, 6 vols.), Vol. III. Tr. F. H. Colson and G. H. Whitaker (Loeb Classical Library, London and New York, 1929– , 10 vols.), Vol. V, p. 221. [Hereafter these edns. are cited as WC and Loeb, respectively.—Ed.]

2 Loeb V, p. 233. I am indebted for much reference to Hans Leisegang's two works *Der Heilige Geist* (Leipzig, 1919) and *Pneuma Hagion* (Leipzig, 1922).

where God promises the hundred-year-old Abraham a son by Sarah, his ninety-year-old wife.

This style of exegesis, this symbolic interpretation of the Pentateuch, this *allegoresis,* was not invented by Philo; Aristobulus, of whose works only a few fragments have been preserved in the *Praeparatio evangelica* of Eusebius, and others used it before him. But peculiar to Philo is the pathos he brings to this method. What he understands under allegory is a symbolical vision[3]—ἐκ τῆς ἐν ἀλληγορίᾳ θεωρίας. And he describes its rules,[4] or canons. For Philo, Allegory, i.e., the art of expressing an idea in images, does not consist in an arbitrary manipulation of images; it is a regular method, governed by definite laws, for making intelligible that which is unintelligible in scripture; it rests on the immanent proportionality, the inner similarity (ὁμοιότροπον) between microcosm and macrocosm.

Allegory is based on an analogy between the microcosm of man and the macrocosm of the world; it rests on the assumption that "man is a little world and the world is a big man." This analogy presupposes an ontological (metaphysically real) correspondence; cosmos and man explain one another in accordance with the laws of symbolism.[5] "Everywhere, behind the historical allusions of the Pentateuch, one surmises a mysterious purpose; the symbols or actualizations of this purpose—the two are different in principle but are not kept apart—are the historical events."[6]

In this interpretation of *allegoresis* not only is the seemingly meaningless endowed with meaning, not only does a symbol become the expression of an essential truth, but through schooling in allegorical vision the philosopher, who for Philo is at the same time devotee and prophet, is also made aware of a spiritual world behind the world of historical fact.

If through this introductory example we have grasped the basic nature of Philo's piety; if we have understood his conception of allegory, we are in a position to understand what Philo means by the *pneuma.*

---

3 *De Josepho,* §28 (WC IV; Loeb VI, p. 155); *De specialibus legibus,* II §147 (WC V; Loeb VII, p. 397); *De posteritate Caini,* §7 (WC II; Loeb II, p. 331).

4 and 5 *De Abrahamo,* §131 (WC IV; Loeb VI, p. 69); *Quis rerum divinarum heres,* §70, §127 (WC III; Loeb IV, pp. 317, 347); *De spec. leg.,* I, §287 (WC V; Loeb VII, p. 267; *De somniis,* I, §102 (WC III; Loeb V, p. 351).

6 G. Kafka, *Der Ausklang der antiken Philosophie* (Munich, 1928), p. 172.

Philo was a Hellenistic Jew; in his conscious mind he was an apologist of the Mosaic religion, but in reality, though never quite clearly, he fused the monistic hylozoism of the Stoics with the ethical dualism of Plato; thus he became the forerunner of Gnosis, of Neoplatonism, and above all of the early Christian theology of the Church Fathers. "Jews and heathen have almost forgotten him, his memory lives almost entirely through the Christian church."[7]

Here I shall not have time to discuss his influence on Justin Martyr, on Clement of Alexandria, on Origen, Eusebius, Ambrose, St. John Damascene, Laurentius of Lydda, Basil the Great, St. Augustine, Sozomen, Anastasius of Sinai, and others; the Suidas said of him: "ἢ Πλάτων φιλονίζει, ἢ Φίλων πλατωνίζει—Either Plato philonizes or Philo platonizes—so similar is this man to Plato both in his thinking and in his expression."

One reason for his immense influence on the piety and dogma of nascent Christianity was his doctrine of the *pneuma*.

The term *pneuma* was in general use in the Hellenistic period. Even in the form of *hagion pneuma* (holy ghost), it occurs frequently in the literature of magic at the beginning of our era.[8]

The medical literature of the time also makes frequent use of the term, e.g., Chrysippus of Cnidus; in Erasistratos two *pneumas* make their appearance, the *pneuma* of life and the *pneuma* of the soul—πνεῦμα ζωτικόν and πνεῦμα ψυχικόν—whence there developed a pneumatological school of medicine which, with certain interruptions, has run through all medical history, even surviving Romanticism, as it would seem.

Similarly in the astrology of that period the *pneuma* of life played an important role. Here, as at first in Philo, the *pneuma* signifies the air as a sensory element, as *stoicheion* (which signifies both element and letter).

We have seen that according to the laws of allegory, every phenomenon is related to all other phenomena, the sensory is an indication of the spiritual. "Created things are brothers, since they all have one Father, the Maker of the universe."[9] And as there

7 Prolegomena of L. Cohn, WC I.
8 See Albrecht Dieterich, *Eine Mithrasliturgie* (Leipzig, 1903), and *Abraxas* (Leipzig, 1891), index.
9 *De decalogo*, §64 (WC IV; Loeb VII, p. 39).

are four elements in the universe, so also there are four elements in man.[10]

And conversely the human spirit is heaven on a small scale, it is the sun of the microcosm.[11] For Plato as for Philo, man is a celestial plant, a φυτὸν οὐράνιον.[12]

Thus it is Philo's first endeavor to remove the *pneuma*, this element of sensory air and breath, from the earthly sphere; for the human spirit is a fragment of the divine spirit.

Philo's *pneuma* is indeed air, but it also *means* something more, that is, a process at work in the spiritual world. "Now the name of the 'spirit of God' is used in one sense for the air which flows up from the land, the third element which rides upon the water, and thus we find in the Creation story: 'the Spirit of God was moving above the water' (Gen. 1:2), since the air through its lightness is lifted and rises upwards, having the water for its base. In another sense it is the pure knowledge—ἡ ἀκήρατος ἐπιστήμη—in which every wise man naturally shares."[13] Thus we have again two conceptions, the physical and the allegorical, the phenomenon and the higher truth to which it points. Philo, to be sure, does not separate the conceptions in this way, he sees them joined as though in a perspective, his philosophizing is only a *façon de parler,* he does not strive to impart insights but to describe what he has seen. But conglomerate and contradictory as his concepts may seem, they are susceptible to classification if we bear in mind the diverse levels of his thinking. Philo's vision cuts across all these strata, for it is always directed towards the quiddity of the divine spirit, towards the τὸ τί ἐστι πνεῦμα θεῖον. Even when he speaks of the *pneuma* of Moses that is transmitted to the seventy elders, this spirit that is upon him—τὸ ἐπ' αὐτῷ πνεῦμα—is "the wise, the divine, the excellent spirit, susceptible of neither severance nor division, diffused in its fullness everywhere and through all things, the spirit which helps, but suffers no hurt, which, though it be shared with others or added to others, suffers no diminution in understanding and knowledge and wisdom" (*De gigantibus,* §27). The primal being, the

10 *De opificio mundi,* §146 (WC I; Loeb I, p. 115).
11 *De somniis,* I, §77 (WC III; Loeb V, p. 337).
12 *Timaeus,* 90 A. Philo, *De plantatione,* §17 (WC II; Loeb III, p. 221).
13 Septuagint, Gen. 1:3. The entire passage in *De gigantibus,* §22 (WC II; Loeb II, p. 457).

godhead, is conceived in a Stoical, pantheistic sense; it is matter *and* spirit, a subtle, fiery *pneuma*.[14]

All the attributes thus far listed apply to this *pneuma*, though to God they cannot properly apply. Thus *pneuma* is both air, the third element, and pure (unmixed) knowledge. But this knowledge is not a philosophical concept; it is a divine force, which works in the cosmos as it works in man; it is a universal reason conceived as material fire, a distinct and self-contained breath, by which the cosmos is purified and held together in its order.

Philo introduces the *pneuma* as an incorporeal substance;[15] it is possible that he dimly anticipated the idea of a transcendental spirit. The beginning of the Creation was not the making of the earthly world, but of the κόσμος νοητός, the ideal world. This ideal world has seven parts; heaven, earth, air, empty space, water, air-*pneuma*, light.

For Philo this *pneuma* has life, while the air as such has not. Philo's conception of the *pneuma* is therefore not that of the Old Testament, in which the spirit of God is conceived as wind and storm, just as man's spirit is conceived as the breath from his lips. For Philo the *pneuma* is an incorporeal substance created by God, but not an attribute of God. But for him the air is also an incorporeal substance, and this is what makes his irrational conception possible; as the Creator, the *demiourgos* in Plato's *Timaeus,* creates the world soul, so Philo's God creates the *pneuma*. In Philo's conception this incorporeal substance, the air, is significant also because of its darkness; it is the black stratum surrounding the sublunar world. In it dwell the souls that hang between heaven and earth, every element—here Philo is in perfect accord with the alchemists—contains living creatures; and it is the darkness of the air that renders these creatures, the heroes, the demons, the souls of the dead, invisible. In the element of ether which lies above the air (and for Philo as for Zeno, the ether consists essentially of fire), in the fifth sphere, the πέμπτον κυκλοφορικὸν σῶμα,[16] in the quintessence, reside the heavenly bodies. The spirit can still be conceived only as bound to a body (perhaps this can be taken to

14 A. Schmekel, *Die Philosophie der mittleren Stoa* (Berlin, 1892), p. 239.
15 *De opif. mundi,* §29 (Loeb I, p. 23).
16 *De somniis,* I, §21 (WC III; Loeb V, p. 305).

mean that ideal essence has its material aspect), even though this body is represented as tenuous and unearthly. Light is seen as refined fire, the *pneuma* as refined air, the elements are divested of matter, the spirit is materialized, as occurs also in Posidonius. The *pneuma* becomes a fifth distinct substance, a πέμπτη τις οὐσία, but it remains an element. The cosmos is the first, man is the second. Here Philo's Platonic dualism, with its opposition of spiritual and material world, is hard pressed. Philo comments on the Bible, but in so doing he draws on the Hellenistic mysteries and on the conflicting philosophical schools. Thus the *pneuma* is not only an element, but also a cosmic principle. Intelligence, heaven, spirit converge. A strange agnosticism prevails. God is unknowable, the spirit is divine, the human spirit is also ἀπόσπασμα θεῖον—literally, a divine fragment. In the form of divine nutriment it descends from heaven into the human spirit, and must soar again heavenward. In a completely Stoic conception, the *pneuma* of the human soul is an emanation of the divine spirit that governs the cosmos.

At first, knowledge of the cosmos and of the stars seem to be prerequisite to knowledge of God and things divine. But then Philo perceives that this beginning offers no bridges. Intuitive vision, the power to see God, is not the product of such schooling, but of a fortunate natural disposition which God confers only on his elect.

Philo shows this by three figures, Abraham, the symbol of virtue acquired through instruction, Isaac, the symbol of innate virtue, and Jacob, the symbol of virtue acquired by practice; these three figures occur again and again in his writings.[17] There is Abraham, who starts from the astral lore of the Chaldeans and remains forever the Learner. Opposed to him stands Isaac, who is laughter (cf. Philo's commentary at the beginning of our article), who by natural, God-given predisposition attains to the vision of God at one bound, without the crutch of learning. He has the self-taught wisdom—αὐτομαθὴς σοφία—inculcated in his own heart. Learning for Philo serves a purpose only if it leads to an understanding of the creator, only if it gives rise to immersion in God.

It is not the physical eye that should be schooled but, to use a

17 E.g., *De Abrahamo*, §§50–55 (WC IV; Loeb VI, pp. 29ff.).

Platonic term, the eye of the soul—τὸ τῆς ψυχῆς ὄμμα.[18] Philo reconsiders and moves away from the Stoic, material *pneuma*. The *pneuma* ceases to be a refined substance and becomes the divine *logos* itself. *Pneuma, logos,* and *sophia* are now equated. There is in man a reflection of this trinity, a fragment, an *apospasma*—and it takes the form of a striving for wisdom and knowledge. Nevertheless, the *pneuma* retains its hylozoistic coloration. It is now a supernatural force that flows into the human spirit, rendering it susceptible to a kind of knowledge that has nothing in common with earthly knowledge. This knowledge is achieved through the eye of the soul; and what is seen is the increate world. This knowledge, this ἐπιστήμη, this science and lore, this understanding is *Gnosis;* Philo merely avoids the term. Philo's *sophia*—and analogously the *sapientia* of the Wisdom of Solomon written at approximately the same time—is and has a *pneuma*. This *pneuma* is still a "breath," descending from a supernatural being and entering into the human spirit. In this connection it is often called *aura,* αὔρα, "breath" or "breeze," derived from the verb ἄημι, "to blow or breathe." This *pneuma* quite literally inspires. It is a spiritual being, independent of God, and no mere hypostasis of an attribute of God. In Philo's psychology, this *pneuma* has two functions: (1) it is the spirit of God, the πνεῦμα θεοῦ, the vital force which God breathed into the first man and which is immanent in all men. And (2) it is a supernatural force in the nature of the Biblical Holy Spirit, flowing suddenly from God into the soul of man. But the significance of the *pneuma* in Philo's psychology can only be properly understood in the light of his cosmology and the doctrine of the *anthropos* which it implies.

For Philo all created things have their archetype and prototype, their ἀρχέτυπον παράδειγμα, in the world of ideas.[19] God begins his world-making (the Greeks had neither the concept of Creation nor any word for it), by constituting an ideal world, a κόσμος νοητός, containing all the prototypes; subsequently copies of these prototypes come into being on earth. This view is similar to the idea of the *I*

18 Plato, *Republic,* VII, 533.
19 *De spec. leg.,* I, §327 (WC V; Loeb VII, p. 291). *De opif. mundi,* §130 (WC I; Loeb I, p. 103).

Ching. It is the relation between prototype, παράδειγμα, and copy, μίμημα, created by the *Demiourgos.*[20]

"He wrought its archetypal seal and he also stamped with this an impression which was its close counterpart." Plato was still uncertain as to whether the *kosmos noetos* included an idea of the soul; Philo, however, postulates an idea of the human spirit, of the *nous,* through the divine *logos,* which he later equates with the *pneuma.* He also postulates an idea of sensibility, of *aisthesis.* For him this idea of the human spirit is identical with the ideal man. The ideal man is pure spirit, hence not identical with the γήινος νοῦς, the earthly *nous* which is bound up with the human body. This ideal man, this *anthropos-nous* is made in the image of God. Man's likeness to God does not extend to his body.[21]

The spirit of each individual man was copied from this prototypic spirit, the unique spirit governing the universe. The individual man "partakes"—μετέχειν—of this ideal man. The nature of the partaking is left undefined, as also in Plato, but through it the *anthropos* is somehow drawn down to earth, and in some measure resides in each individual man. This real man is the man created according to the idea, hence it is not the physical man who is created in God's image.[22] The ideal *anthropos* is the truly perfect man in body and soul, like Adam; he is the type of higher man in general, the ideal of the philosopher, in Stoic terms the philosopher and king, in Biblical terms the upright man. Furthermore, the ideal man is Enoch,[23] ancestor of the pure, the purified race, truly endowed with reason; and he is Moses, the man of God. The ideal man symbolizes the divine *nous* and is the conscience of man, and this conscience is both witness and accuser.[24]

". . . the true man, the Monitor of the soul, who, seeing its perplexity, its inquiring, its searching, is afraid lest it go astray and miss the right word." The spirit of God lives in each individual man as his conscience; the *logos* becomes the *logos elengchos,* the *logos* of ethical

20 *De ebrietate,* §133 (WC II; Loeb III, p. 389).
21 *De opif. mundi,* §69 (WC I; Loeb I, p. 55).
22 Ibid., §§72ff. (Loeb I, pp. 57f.).
23 *De Abr.,* §47 (WC IV; Loeb VI, p. 27).
24 *De fuga et inventione,* §131 (WC III; Loeb V, p. 81): ὁ ἀληθινὸς ἄνθρωπος, ὁ ἐπὶ ψυχῆς ἔλεγχος ("the true man, the Monitor, set over the soul").

testing, our conscience and hence the intermediary between man and God. Philo's divine *nous,* as the conscience in man, suggests the doctrine of the holy ghost.

Where then does Philo situate the *pneuma* in the structure of man? Starting from below, Philo follows the Stoics in distinguishing the ἕξις, the inanimate nature, the *physis,* the animate nature, the *psyche* or *anima vitalis,* whose substance is the blood, τὸ αἷμα, and finally the *nous* or *anima rationalis,* the rational soul—whose substance is the *pneuma.* Thus he arrives at the strange equation: *nous = pneuma = logos.*

The *nous* (and in view of the equation, the *pneuma* as well) is the divine in man and is, as in Aristotle, ϑύραϑεν—it enters into man from outside. But in the Bible the godhead does not, as Philo would have it, breathe pure spirit into man; it inspires life and soul in general in the form of the *pneuma.* In the Bible the *pneuma* is the life and soul of the body. But Philo discerns in the *soma,* the body, three vital forces: *psyche, nous,* and *pneuma.* The *nous* is the ruler of the soul and can therefore be called soul, just as the pupil might be spoken of as the eye. The *nous* is the man in man.[25] The substance of the lower vital forces resides in the blood. Each man is beast and man, blood and soul, αἷμα καὶ πνεῦμα. By man, Philo does not mean the hybrid (the psychic man of the Gnostics), but the likeness of God through which we think, the pneumatic man, whose roots extend to the outermost sphere of the "fixed stars," i.e., to the most perfect sphere that consists of quintessence. He distinguishes between vital force and spiritual force. How far we have travelled from Aristotle, for whom "the soul is the form of a physical body endowed with life."[26] But despite his tendency towards spiritualization, Philo cannot free himself from Stoic materialism, for which the spirit remains a refined substance, a πνεῦμα διάπυρον, a fiery breath. Philo is full of contradictions, and perhaps it is these very contradictions that have kept his work so very much alive; he assumes, for example, that the *pneuma* is indissoluble from the blood, but at the same time he says that the *pneuma* in present man is only a pale remnant of the divine spirit that was conferred on man

25 *De agricultura,* §9 (WC II; Loeb III, p. 113): ἄνθρωπος δὲ ὁ ἐν ἑκάστῳ ἡμῶν τίς ἂν εἴη πλὴν ὁ νοῦς.
26 *De anima,* B I 412 a 19: εἶδος σώματος φυσικοῦ δυνάμει ζωὴν ἔχοντος.

in the act of creation, and never since then. But he also believes that God continues to bestow the *pneuma* on certain of the elect, while in other men it continuously dwindles and pales. Philo's *pneuma* is not that of the Old Testament, but more in the nature of the Platonic and Aristotelian *nous*. It constitutes the basis of his anthropology. Despite all his assurances to the contrary, the godhead is equated with the human spirit.[27] Seneca gave this idea its classical expression:[28] *"Quem in hoc mundo locum deus obtinet, hunc in homine animus"*: "The place which God occupies in this world is filled by the spirit in man." In our opinion, Philo derived this conception of the *anthropos* from Stoic pantheism. But the idea of the god in man was already present in Plato, e.g., *Phaedo*,[29] *Timaeus*,[30] in which man is called a divine plant—φυτὸν οὐράνιον—and other passages. Man's God-given reason is conceived as a *daimon* that fate has allotted to man. In Philo, the demon and the demons are replaced by the angels. The conscience in man, the λόγος ἔλεγχος, is as we have seen, the man in man, but it is also the angel. The angels are also conceived as consisting, like everything spiritual, of a refined substance, they are called ἀσώματοι, disembodied souls, yet they are also described as airy, ethereal beings.[31] ". . . they are very much like the ideas of men"; the substances or essences of the angels are pneumatic and breathlike.

And yet the spiritual, the spirit, the human spirit, is supposed to exist as an independent personality, residing in the corporeal man.

Plutarch reveals a very similar conception when he tells us that the *daimon* of Socrates is the spirit, or *nous*, of Socrates, but is at the same time an independent spiritual entity, that is, a demon in the sense of popular belief. Philo foreshadows the Gnostic triad of human essences: the pneumatic, the psychic, and the hylic or sarkical.

The human soul is of the same nature as the heavenly bodies. The stars are gods, and human souls are likewise gods; after his separation from the flesh man becomes a star, an astral deity. The doctrine of the independent existence of the spiritual man goes far back, it is an Orphic conception. For the demonic nature of the soul is an old and recurrent experience, and under its impact man comes to look upon the soul as his double. We have seen that the *pneuma* was breathed

27 *De opif. mundi*, §69. 28 *Epistolae*, 65, 24.
29 107 D.   30 90 A.   31 *De Abr.*, §113 (WC IV; Loeb VI, p. 59).

into man only once, when the world was made and man created. But we have also seen that the *pneuma* is a supernatural, God-given force that can suddenly invade the elect. On the whole, the generations of man inherit and partake of the *pneuma* of Adam, but by an exception to His rule God keeps a special *pneuma* in readiness for His elect, and this *pneuma*, bestowed from time to time, is the food of the soul. Here Philo's *pneuma* becomes identical with knowledge, and with *sophia*. This knowledge is universal reason, the divine *logos*. From this all-pervading *logos* God takes some part, "as one takes light from a flame," and deposits it in certain chosen men. But this gift of God, this *pneuma-logos* (unlike the hereditary *pneuma*) remains in the human soul only for a limited time.[32] The reason for this is to be sought in man's participation in the flesh, his dual nature.[33] The two conceptions of the *pneuma* are mutually contradictory, for the *pneuma* that is vital force, or food for the soul, is seen as *hexis*, a principle of cohesion permanently holding together all things, including the inorganic, while the *pneuma* that God bestows on the elect is expressly defined as dwelling only temporarily in the human soul. The conception of the *pneuma* as vital force and universal cohesion does not have its source in the Old Testament, but in Posidonius, whose ideas haunt all the philosophical thinking of the first century B.C. Philo's equating of the *logos* with the *pneuma*, to which he ascribes such a diversity of meanings, presents definite advantages for the furtherance of his design. It enables him to establish an alchemistic and cabalistic connection between the *pneuma* and certain phenomena close to his own experience, such as ecstasy, revelation, prophecy, divination by dreams; and it permits him to associate the *pneuma* with the demons of the air, as they were popularly called, or the angels as Philo himself called them. In this way he became the precursor of the Christian angelology. It was he who first defined the nature and essence of the angels as pneumatic.[34]

For him they have pneumatic substance. Philo conceives the angels, like the ideas of the original creation, like all the divine forces, among which the angels are numbered, as united in a single fundamental

32 *De gigant.*, §§47 and 53 (WC II; Loeb II, pp. 469f.). *Quod Deus sit immutabilis*, §2 (WC II; Loeb III, p. 11).
33 *Quis rerum divinarum heres*, §57 (WC III; Loeb IV, pp. 311ff.).
34 *Fragments of Philo Judaeus*, ed. J. R. Harris (Cambridge, 1886), fr. 8, 18.

force, the *logos*. This *logos*, which for him is identical with the *pneuma*, becomes a fluid that governs the universe, and when the human spirit is detached from the body it mingles with this fluid, which is the material vehicle, the refined substance in which the mystical forms of knowledge are grounded. Philo constantly slips into material terminology even when speaking of the spiritual; he has, it is true, suggested[35] the idea of an immaterial but substantial structure of the spiritual, as for example when he reveals an intuition of its pure existence, free from any sensual quality—τὸ ψιλὴν ἄνευ χαρακτῆρος τὴν ὕπαρξινκαταλαμβάνεσθαι—but he could not give this idea an adequate formulation. Nevertheless, as E. von Hartmann noted, his thinking represents a step forward in the history of metaphysical thought.

In concluding our study of Philo's *pneuma*, let us briefly examine his theory of ecstasy. The *pneuma* is the vehicle both of the spiritual and ethical forces and of the forces of physiological cohesion, it is the pneumatic tension, the πνευματικὸς τόνος, the symphony, the bond and harmony between the separate entities. It is this circumstance that forms the basis of the relation between *pneuma*, divine madness (μανία: frenzy and possession), and ecstasy (rapture).

Philo distinguishes four types of ecstasy (or "standing out"):[36]

(1) "Ecstasy is a mad fury producing mental delusion, owing to old age or melancholy or other similar cause."—ἔκστασις ἡ μέν ἐστι λύττα μανιώδης παράνοιαν ἐμποιοῦσα κατὰ γῆρας ἢ μελαγχολίαν ἤ τινα ὁμοιότρον ἄλλην αἰτίαν.

(2) "Extreme amazement at the events which so often happen suddenly or unexpectedly."—ἡ δὲ σφοδρὰ κατάπληξις ἐπὶ τοῖς ἐξαπιναίως καὶ ἀπροσδοκήτως συμβαίνειν εἰωθόσιν.

(3) "A passivity of mind if indeed the mind can ever be at rest."—ἡ δὲ ἠρεμία διανοίας, εἰδὴ πέφυκέ ποτε ἡσυχάζειν.

(4) "And the best form of all is the divine possession and frenzy, to which the prophets as a class are subject."—ἡ δὲ πασῶν ἀρίστη ἔνθεος κατακωχή τε καὶ μανία, ᾗ τὸ προφητικὸν γένος χρῆται.

Philo gives examples for the ecstasy of the first kind, the ecstasy of rage, from Deuteronomy. His examples of the ecstasy of the second

35 *Quod Deus sit immut.*, §55 (Loeb III, p. 38).
36 *Quis rerum div. heres*, §249. Cf. the following. (Loeb IV, p. 409.)

kind, that of amazement, are drawn from Genesis 27:33 and 45:26, Exodus 19:18, and Leviticus 9:24.

Here again he bases his comments on the Septuagint; the original Hebrew would not always have allowed of his interpretation. One of his examples for the third kind of ecstasy, the passivity of the mind, is Genesis 2:21,[37] which reads, according to the Septuagint: "And the Lord God caused a deep sleep [*ekstasis*] to fall upon Adam, and he slept." And Philo writes: ". . . the sleep of the spirit is the waking of the senses, and the waking of the spirit is the disuse of the senses."— ὕπνος γὰρ νοῦ ἐγρήγορσίς ἐστιν αἰσθήσεως, καὶ γὰρ ἐγρήγορσις διανοίας αἰσθήσεως ἀπραξία.

Philo's definition of ecstasy as a passivity and repose of the mind has given rise to many erroneous interpretations. Philo does not mean sleep, but τροπή, a turning away of the mind from sensuality, a μετανάστασις (departure), whether in waking or in sleeping.

Thus the third kind of *ekstasis* is really an aspect of the fourth kind, the prophetic. This is the soul state of him who is inspired and borne aloft by God—ἐνθουσιῶντος καὶ θεοφορήτου τὸ πάθος.

An evil man cannot be God's interpreter,[38] the unethical man cannot receive God's inspiration; it comes only to the wise man, who alone is a resonant instrument of God, which He invisibly plucks and strikes. ἐπεὶ καὶ μόνος ὄργανον θεοῦ ἐστιν ἠχεῖον, κρουόμενον καὶ πληττόμενον ἀοράτως ὑπ' αὐτοῦ.

"But to the wise man the Holy Scripture manifests prophetic power." When a prophet speaks, it is not from within, he states a message that comes from outside him. For Philo prophet, wise man, and philosopher are synonymous, all are gifted with the ecstasy of the fourth kind; Moses for him is the archetype of the prophet. But the prophet does not merely prophesy, his function lies also in ἑρμηνεία, the interpretation of the divine. He can see and tell the future, because he has the eternal before his eyes. Philo's four kinds of ecstasy correspond exactly to the four kinds of *mania*, i.e., of divine frenzy, in Plato.[39]

Plato in this connection avoids the term *pneuma;* but it is trans-

---

37 Cf. *Legum allegoria*, II, §§25–30 (WC I; Loeb I, pp. 243ff.).
38 *Quis rerum div. heres*, §259 (Loeb IV, p. 417).
39 Philo, *Quis rerum div. heres*, §264. Plato, *Phaedrus*, 240 A– 250 C, summed up in 265 B ff.

mitted to Philo both by the Egyptian writers on magic and by the Stoics. Nevertheless, Plato's conception of the divine frenzy, the θεία μανία, enters into Philo's conception of ecstasy. The soul detaches itself from the body, the godhead penetrates man. But here too an essential difference between Philo and Plato is manifested. For Philo the pathological ecstasy plays a much larger role than in Plato. Philo imputes the states usually classified as ecstasy: the Bacchanalian frenzy and the intoxication of genius, to madness. For him the only authentic ecstasy is the ascent of the soul to God.

It is a "sober drunkenness," a μέθη νηφαλία,[40] and this term, which he often repeats, was a source of inspiration to all Eastern mysticism. In his treatment of ecstasy, Philo considers the whole history of man's conception of it. He begins with the primitive peoples, for whom the god or demon enters into man and for a time expels the human soul; and comes finally to Plato's notion[41] of the soul's separation from the body for the attainment of higher knowledge. Philo also considers ecstasy as the road to knowledge. It develops by the following stages: (1) renunciation of concern with the natural sciences; (2) self-knowledge, characterized by abandonment of the sense of self; (3) merging of the soul with the divine *logos*. The *pneuma* encounters the soul. God himself withdraws and thus enables the souls, *logoi*, angels and demons dwelling in the region of the air, to act upon the human soul. The intellectual and sensory faculties by which the soul otherwise obtains knowledge are temporarily excluded. As preparation for the advent of ecstasy, the novice must lead an ascetic life; only then, only if he observes the rules of asceticism, does the transformation occur through the divine breath (divine *pneuma*) of the *logos-pneuma;* man's ears becomes eyes, i.e., intuitive knowledge is born.

According to the ancient conception, sight penetrates more deeply into the essence of things than hearing, though today perhaps we should judge differently. Philo for example rejects the supposition that the spiritual is an audible voice.[42]

Hearing (the hearing of God) is vision. The spirit is the eye of the

40 E.g., *De vita Mosis,* I, §187 (WC IV; Loeb VI, p. 373); *De opif. mundi,* §71 (WC I; Loeb I, p. 57); *De vita contemplativa,* §85 (WC VI; Loeb IX, p. 165); and elsewhere. 41 *Phaedo,* 79 C and D.
42 *De migratione Abrahami,* §47 (WC II; Loeb IV, p. 159).

soul.[43] For Philo as for Aristotle, light is a pneumatic substance that serves as intermediary between the eye and the object to be perceived. In his conception the mystical sense requires a similar substance, the "eye of the soul" requires these (invisible) rays of light, whose source is God himself, it needs the divine *pneuma*. Here Plutarch is in agreement with Philo.[44] Presumably Posidonius was the preceptor of them both. Those gifted with sight are those endowed with the *pneuma*. The human soul can rise up to heaven (οὐρανοβατεῖν), while the body remains behind on earth.

Let us conclude as we have begun with a statement from Philo himself:[45]

> For the offspring of the soul's own travail are for the most part poor abortions, things untimely born; but those which God waters with the snows of heaven come to birth perfect, complete and peerless.
>
> I feel no shame in recording my own experience, a thing I know from its having happened to me a thousand times. On some occasions, after making up my mind to follow the usual course of writing on philosophical tenets, and knowing definitely the substance of what I was to set down, I have found my understanding incapable of giving birth to a single idea, and have given it up without accomplishing anything, reviling my understanding for its self-conceit, and filled with amazement at the might of Him that IS to Whom is due the opening and closing of the soul-wombs. On the other occasions, I have approached my work empty and suddenly become full, the ideas falling in a shower from above and being sown invisibly, so that under the influence of the Divine possession I have been filled with corybantic frenzy and been unconscious of anything, place, persons present, myself, words spoken, lines written. For I obtained language, ideas, an enjoyment of light, keenest vision, pellucid distinctness of objects, such as might be received through the eyes as the result of clearest showing.

43 *De spec. leg.*, III, §194 (WC III; Loeb VII, p. 597).
44 *De defectu oraculorum*, 433 D.
45 *De migr. Abr.*, §§33, 34, 35 (Loeb IV, pp. 151f.).

Hugo Rahner

Earth Spirit and Divine Spirit in Patristic Theology[1]

"Now we have received, not the spirit of the world, but the Spirit that is of God" (I Cor. 2:12).

These words of St. Paul open, as though with a resounding thunder clap, the drama of the spirit which is central to Christian life. We cannot do full justice to the New Testament doctrine of the revelation of the Holy Spirit, as person and as gift, unless we give some attention to the equally Christian doctrine of the unholy spirit, the "spirit of the earth," of the "prince of this world," which is driven out by the Holy Ghost. It is this counterpoint that makes drama of dogma; divine spirit and earth spirit fighting to the death. It is a veritable Divina Commedia: *mors et vita duello conflixere mirando:* "death and life were locked in marvelous battle." The spirit-giving victory which Christ won on the cross must continue in the souls of men. "For this purpose the Son of God appeared, that he might destroy the works of the devil" (I John 3:8). It is a war that shakes the whole cosmos, and it is waged in the innermost soul of man; here in the most secret and primordial depths of the psyche, the spirits are in direct contact with one another like two naked wrestlers; it is here that the prince of this world is cast out, and on the outcome of the battle depends the ultimate fate of the entire cosmos. *Pneuma* and *daimon* are bound up with one another, like light and darkness, like freedom and servitude. And we cannot understand the joyous message of deliverance, the final victory of the good, as long as we know (or

[1] The present article is an extract from the material presented at the Eranos meeting. Owing to external circumstances, particularly the want of a library, even this extract was reconstructed from notes and recollections. [Biblical citations are from the Douay Version.—TRANS.]

wish to know) nothing of the slavery of the demonic and of the struggle that the Church carries on in the name of Christ, when in the mystery of baptism, she says: "Get thee hence, accursed Devil, and make way for the Holy Ghost!" Dante was aware of this when (in the magnificent scene at the end of the *Inferno*) climbing on a ladder made of "the hair of the wicked Worm that pierces the world," he rose up to the light, to the mountain of *Purgatorio,* which corresponds exactly to the terrible cavern hollowed out by the falling earth spirit. Out of the abysmal depths of Satan, he rose up through a narrow cleft to the stars:

> . . . we mounted up, he first and I second, so far that through a round opening I saw some of the beautiful things which Heaven bears, and thence we issued forth again to see the Stars.[2]

And from here the ascent continues to the Heights of the Holy Ghost at the end of the *Paradiso,* to that divine love "which moves the sun and the stars." That is the Divine Comedy of the Christian. The theology of the early Church Fathers conceived of this drama both in Biblical and Greek terms: its vision of the universe comprises the depths of the earth spirit and the heights of the Holy Ghost; and in that vision the innermost soul of man is the area in which the issue is decided.

And so, if we wish to gain even a fleeting insight into the doctrine of the Holy Ghost, as it appears in the works of the ancient classical theologians, we must first speak of the counterpart of the Pneuma Hagion, of the "spirit of the world." Only then will it become clear to us why the spirit of God, which Christ bestowed upon us as a gift, is a "spirit of heaven."

1. The Earth Spirit

The patristic dogma of Satan and his evil spirits is based primarily on the teachings of the New Testament. According to the Fathers, devils and demons are real spiritual beings, whose existence and workings are known to us through the revelation of Jesus Christ, which in turn was prepared by the revelation of the Old Testament. The

2 Tr. Charles Eliot Norton (Boston, 1940).

"devil and his angels" (Matt. 25:41) are the adversaries of Christ's work of redemption; the battle which the victorious Christ wages against them throughout the course of church history ends with the fall of Satan "like lightning" (Luke 10:18); those who had once been sublime spirits of heaven fell to earth and became demons, and such they will remain: "And that great dragon was cast out, that old serpent, who is called the devil and Satan, who seduceth the whole world. And he was cast unto the earth: and his angels were thrown down with him" (Apoc. 12:9). Earth and world become here the embodiment and symbol of the moral remoteness from God to which the evil spirits descended from "heaven," through willful aversion from God. Satan is "prince of this world" (John 12:31; 14:30; 16:11), and once in sublime exaggeration St. Paul even calls him "god of this world" (II Cor. 4:4). The darkness, inertia, and heaviness that we call earth and matter become the tangible image of this otherwise so unfathomable tragedy that has been enacted in the realm of spirits. The attributes which the New Testament attaches to the "angels" sent forth by Satan come very close to a description of the demonic force that has taken possession of men on earth: they are unclean (Mark 3:30; Acts 5:16), they make blind and dumb (Matt. 12:22; Luke 11:14), they induce sickness and dropsy, they enter into swine and rage in the depths of the sea (Matt. 8:31, etc.); in a word, they are "evil spirits." All these varied images mean but one thing, that Satan and his demons are spirits of the "depths," that their drive is downward, that they are fallen creatures, whose only desire is to draw men with them in their descent from heaven. The New Testament demonology never takes on the aspect of a cosmic myth, it is always and exclusively an attempt to represent in images the ethical drama of the fall from God of spirits that had been created good: but no imagery could have been more apposite, more fundamentally human, than the imagery of the "fall" to the depths of this dark earth. It was in this sense that Paul, stating the ethical through a cosmic image, could write: You ". . . were dead in your offences and sins, wherein in time past you walked according to the course of this world, according to the prince of the power of this air, of the spirit that now worketh on the children of unbelief" (Eph. 2:1–2). And it was in the same sense that he could summon the Christians to battle against this earth spirit who governs the "darkness of this world": "For our wrestling is not against flesh and blood: but against principalities and powers, against the rulers of the world of this darkness, against the spirits of wickedness in the high places" (Eph. 6:12).

But though the New Testament is permeated with this belief in the terribly real existence of evil spirits, it is also full of the triumphant and joyful knowledge that this dark realm of the earth spirit can be conquered in Christ: and thus the earliest Christianity had already found the balance and mean between the rationalism of the Sadducees, for example, who "say that there is . . . neither angel, nor spirit" (Acts 23:8) and the helplessness of Hellenistic superstition, lost in a cosmos populated by omnipotent demons. In the Christian view, the evil spirits of the earth are real, we encounter them every day; but they are powerless, they can be conquered, indeed they have already been conquered in the depths by him who on the cross cast out the prince of this world, who, "despoiling the principalities and powers, . . . hath exposed them confidently in open show, triumphing over them in himself" (Col. 2:15). ". . . the devils also are subject to us in thy name," said the disciples (Luke 10:17). Satan cannot outwit the Christians, for his devices are known to them (II Cor. 2:11) and "the God of peace [shall] crush Satan under your feet speedily" (Rom. 16:20); the Devil may be a "roaring lion," but the Christian can "resist [him] strong in faith" (I Peter 5:9). Thus the early church recognized and translated into abundant life two truths which we today, in the midst of the demonisms of our times, recognize anew, almost envious of the soul-saving power and psychological greatness of the apostles: it recognized that demons exist and that demons can be conquered.

St. Paul's "prince of the power of the air" raises questions of religious history, and of these too we must speak if we wish to understand the sublime doctrine of the Church Fathers concerning the demonic earth spirit. For do we not hear a familiar note? Is the conception of the demon as a ruler of the dark realm of the air not a clear echo of the doctrines of Plato, Xenocrates, Plutarch, and Posidonius? The similarity is conspicuous, and the studies dealing with the question are innumerable. Nevertheless it seems far more likely that St. Paul built his conception on late Jewish demonology. Among the

Jews the belief was current that the evil spirits fell only as far as the air surrounding the earth, and that from this vantage point they exerted their evil dominion over the earth. In St. Paul this conception comes to symbolize a conflict that is no longer cosmic but purely ethical. The "world" is for him fundamentally man, earthly, earth-bound, sinful, immersed in darkness—this man is subject to the influence of evil spirits, but he can also raise himself "from darkness to light and from the power of Satan to God" (Acts 26:18). It is the Christian's act of faith that decides the battle between earth spirit and divine spirit, and the "power of the air" is only a reflection of what takes place in man's innermost ethical soul. The concept of "world" in St. John should be taken in the same sense: the prince of this world is "a murderer from the beginning" (John 8:44), and "the whole world is seated in wickedness" (I John 5:19), but only because those men who are not "born of God" still sin. Only in this light does it become intelligible and bearable for a Christian to speak of a demonization of the "world": for the same "world" that is in the power of the evil one "was made by Him." The destiny of the cosmos is decided in man: in the sin of the first man, in the redemption of the God-man, and in the faith of the Christian. Through the sinful, unethical act of the first man, the "world," the realm of the air, the corporeal, the abysses of the soul have indeed succumbed to the power of the evil spirit—and ever since then any worldly bliss, any full affirmation of the earthly and corporeal and human would be a demonic error. But the redemption on the Cross began to rid the world of Satan, to "cast out" the worldly spirit, and this process is continued in the ethical discernment of spirits which is the ferment of Christianity. Hence St. Paul can say that the "spirits of this air" still rule: the demons are still with us, the "mystery of iniquity [still] worketh" (II Thess. 2:7). Since man is still demonic, so is the world. And St. Paul's image of the spirits who rule the air reveals the extraordinary depth to which the ethical state of the world, which reacts upon its cosmic state, has fallen. When the liberation of man's soul is fulfilled at the end of time, the cosmos will also be saved from the rule of the earth spirit: it will enter "into the liberty of the glory of the children of God. For we know that every creature groaneth and travaileth in pain, even till now" (Rom. 8:21–22).

After this brief sketch of the New Testament theology of the "spirit of the earth," we shall perhaps be in a position to understand the approach of the Church Fathers to the subject. And it will also help us to distinguish the dogmatic core of their teachings from the cloak of Greek imagery which, as born Greeks, they cast around their Biblical faith. For there is no doubt that a great deal of Hellenistic lore has crept into the demonology of the Fathers. Without changing the Christian substance, without succumbing to a purely cosmic conception of the fall of the evil angels, they nevertheless speak of the demons who rule over the earth in a manner distinctly reminiscent of Plutarch or Posidonius. Here it will not be possible to give a complete picture of the patristic demonology, even in its essentials. Instead, we shall select one aspect of it that strikes us as particularly instructive: the doctrine of the demons as "earth spirits." We shall attempt to describe the nature and the activities of these "angels of the devil," who have gained power over the earth.

I

The patristic doctrine of the demons as the "spirits of the world" is intelligible only if we have some understanding of the cosmology of the ancients. The universe is formed of a series of realms, each consisting of an element. The heaviest, dullest element is earth, which lies bottommost; above it lies the element of the air, which likewise participates in the darkness of the earthly, though it also partakes to some extent of the spiritualization of the sphere of fire which lies over it. The air is the mediating element, corresponding to the region of the moon, which lies above it; the region of the air is still "under the moon," hence subjected to dull chance, the blind, inert, crassly tangible unspirituality of the material. Hence the sphere of the air is a proper dwelling for beings who, though spiritual, somehow partake of the terrestrial realm: the demons. "All the air is full of spirits which we call demons or heroes," runs a saying of Pythagoras, quoted by Diogenes Laertius.

The Church Fathers drew their demons from an entirely different cultural source: from Biblical revelation, in which the fall of spirits who had been created good constituted an ethical fall from grace;

thus objectively the patristic theology has nothing to do with the strange speculations of the late Greeks, who conceived the demons as cosmic intermediaries between God and men; it has nothing to do with the passage from Plato's *Symposium:* "Every demon is an intermediary between God and mortal man."[2a] But when the Fathers have to speak of the nature of these fallen spirits, the imagery and language of their Greek heritage come to mind, and the most tangible and plastic expression of the ethical fall from grace of the demons, of its diabolical influence on the earthly sphere, is the image of the evil spirits who have fallen into the dark realm of the air. Thus the cosmology of the Church Fathers is filled with demons. These angels of Satan dwell in the dark air, under the moon; they permeate everything that is earthly: the demon is an earth spirit, he has—for the present, despite the victory of Christ on the Cross—dominion over the earthly in man and around him. "Everything, yea the whole world is full of Satan and his angels, the streets and the marketplace and the baths and the stables,"[3] says Tertullian; moreover, "no man is without his demon."[4]

As we have seen, the dwelling place which accords with his nature and symbolically expresses it is the realm of the air. St. Augustine is drawing on a fully classical conception when he expressly contrasts this sphere of the dark air with "heaven," the realm of the radiant ethereal stars: the demons dwell "here below, where the dark clouds gather and the birds flit about."[5] In the introductory epistle to his famous *Historia Lausiaca,* Palladius draws a similar picture: "The demons fell from heaven and must now fly through the realm of the air as devils, because in times gone by they turned their backs upon their teachers in heaven."

"Satan fell from heaven like a flash of fire," say the *Acta Archelai,* "and crashed to earth. Yea, into the earthly he fell, and never more will he be admitted into the regions of heaven: and that is why he now creeps about in the hearts of men."[6] All this is eminently true of Satan himself, the chief of the demons. Why, Basilius once asked himself, is he called in the Scriptures "Prince of this world"? And the

---

2a *Symposium,* 202 E.   3 *De spectaculis,* ch. 8.   4 *De anima,* ch. 57, 4.
5 *De natura boni contra Manichaeos,* ch. 33.   6 Ch. 36.

answer runs: "Because his dominion extends over all the earth."[7] The cosmos is as though covered and wrapped in an atmosphere of diabolical air. "In this dark realm that is so close to us," says St. Augustine,[8] "lives the evil one, as though locked in a prison of air." And perhaps the most magnificent symbolic vision of the spirit realm ever written by the Fathers is to be found in the *City of God,* where St. Augustine, after rejecting all the Neoplatonic theories of demons, represents the Christian, ethical conception of the fall of the angels in the image of the demons who hang head downward in the realm of the air, and thus remain until the final sentence is passed upon them.[9] The demon rules the earth under a false banner; he is the father of lies, of perversity, of renegation. We have seen how this Augustinian conception assumes poetic form in Dante's *Divine Comedy:* Satan is the Antispirit, cast headlong into the earthly element. This conception is at once classical and patristic. *"Diabolus totus terra haeret,"* St. Jerome once said in a sermon. "The devil is wholly attached to the earth."[10] But to this earth (and this must be borne in mind if we are to understand the classical cosmology of the Church Fathers) belongs the sphere of the air, and to it likewise belongs the innermost heart of earthly man. The realm of the air and the realm of the heart are one and the same "earth": as for the "world" in the ascetic sense, the world that must be renounced, that must be rid of devils—it is the scene of the struggle between earth spirit and divine spirit—we shall have more to say of it later. Here we shall speak only of a doctrine that is highly characteristic of early Christian demonology and can only be understood if we keep well in mind the material that has been discussed up to now. The demons who in their capacity as earth spirits have cast their spell over everything that is earthly, who rule the region of the air surrounding the earth, have only a single desire: to draw man, who is striving for redemption, down with them in their headlong fall. Redeemed man strives upward towards the translucent realm of the divine ether, towards heaven. But the demons who rule the earth oppose his ascetic (and after his death his real) ascent. They are (to use an image frequent in the writings of the

---

7 J. P. Migne, *Patrologiae cursus completus,* Greek Series, Vol. XXXI, 352 A.
8 *Epistula* 102, qu. 3, 20.—*Enchiridion,* 9, 28.
9 *De civitate Dei,* IX, 9.   10 *Anecdota Maredsolana,* III, 2 (1897), p. 24.

ancient ascetics) the "customs guards"[11] who sit at the diverse stations of the celestial journey and examine the souls striving so eagerly upward, to see whether anything earthly (hence demonic) still clings to them. Only those who are free of all remnants of the earth, only those who rid themselves entirely of the demonic, can safely pass these diabolical customs stations. The power to free himself from all taint of the earthly, to pass in unharmed bliss through the demonic barrier, comes to the redeemed Christian through the spirit-giving crucifixion of Jesus. Therefore, says Athanasius, in a wonderful chapter of his book on the incarnation, the Cross of the Lord towered high into the air, in order to cleanse this region of demons and clear the way upward for us.[12] And Melania, the Roman patrician, prays on her deathbed in the cloister of the poor in Bethlehem:

"Purify thy maid, that my soul, free from every bond, may rise towards thee, that the evil spirits of this airy realm may not hold me back, but that I may be guided immaculate by thy holy angels to thee in thy heavenly abode."[13]

II

The nature of this demonic earth spirit becomes clearer to us when we investigate its workings. A study of the patristic teachings concerning the influence of the demons on the soul of man would lead us into a rich complexity of problems. To what degree, for example, do these spirits of the earth affect the relations between body and soul; how do they make themselves felt in matters of religion and sex —indeed in every conceivable aspect of man's inscrutable psychosomatic existence? The Church Fathers and early monks in their asceticism saw very clearly in these matters and knew far more of the "world" and its demonisms than we do with all our supposed psychological knowledge. But here we must deny ourselves this journey.

Much more might be said of what the ancient Church Fathers taught and knew concerning the influence of the demons of the air on the physical processes of the earth in which we men of nerves and blood live. They firmly believed that storm and hail, disease and war could

11 Cf. Origen, *Commentary on St. Luke,* 23; Athanasius, *Vita Antonii,* ch. 65 and 66; Pseudo-Macarius, *Pneumatic homilies,* 16, 3; 23, 9.
12 *De incarnatione verbi,* ch. 25.   13 *Vita Melaniae,* ch. 64.

come from demons. Demons were at work in the most ordinary and most extraordinary happenings. Or one might speak at length of the patristic doctrine of the part played by the earth spirits in necromancy, fortune-telling, and other ancient superstitions.

All this would lead us too far; instead let us select a very limited aspect: the influence of demons on the dream life of the human psyche. In dreams man is, we might say, at his "most earthly"; he is entirely immersed in his dark blood, he sinks back into the deepest region of his being, and lives intensively in a "world" which he excludes or refuses to recognize in his waking state, particularly if he is a Christian. Thus dream life, according to the Fathers, is the most frequent point of contact between soul and demon. Here we have a vast abundance of source material to draw on, for the Christian thinkers of the patristic age strove unremittingly to bring some measure of theological light into these mysteries. It was in dreams, they believed, that the demons of the air found their principal scene of action.

The Fathers first of all accepted a natural interpretation of dreams; they generally adhered to the very material view developed by the late Stoics and gracefully stated in the well-known verse of Petronius: "It is not the shrines of the gods, nor the powers of the air, that send the dreams which mock the mind with flitting shadows; each man makes dreams for himself. For the mind . . . pursues in the darkness whatever was its task by daylight."[14]

Tertullian expresses the same opinion in the highly informative chapter on dreams in his book *On the Soul*.[15] And Gregory of Nyssa says that for the most part dreams are nothing other than an "echo" of the impressions of the day: "We are of the opinion that the fantastic illusions of dreams are figures created by the sublogical power of the soul according to man's actual experiences."[16] But that is not all. The Fathers leave open the possibility that a divine spirit or an earth spirit, a God or a demon, may take possession of the soul

14 Poems, no. 31 (tr. Michael Heseltine, Loeb Classical Library, London and New York, 1925, p. 361):
Somnia quae mentes ludunt volitantibus umbris,
non delubra deum nec ab aethere numina mittunt,
sed sibi quisque facit . . .
quidquid luce fuit, tenebris agit.
15 *De anima*, ch. 47.   16 *De hominis opificio*, ch. 13.

in dreams. Lactantius, in arguing for these possibilities, goes so far as to cite the Homeric parable (repeated by Virgil in the sixth book of the *Aeneid*) to the effect that dreams enter the soul by two doors.[17] In rhythmic prose, Ephraim the Syrian gives a detailed account of the ways in which demons work through dreams. And though the Armenian Eznig of Kolb confutes the Manichaean belief in divination by dreams, as a Christian he considers it possible that the demons—as well as the Holy Ghost—may play upon the soul through nocturnal images:

> Dreams too have different causes. It may be something that a man has said during the day, and that the spirit, when the body is resting, takes up again. But sometimes a thing that has not been present in the thoughts at all, nevertheless appears in dreams—and for this there are two causes. Either it is a vision of some definite thing in visible form, induced by the efficacy of the grace of God, in order to spur man to virtue. Or it comes from the adversary: for he is incorporeal, as man's soul is also incorporeal. He creates various delusions, sometimes of women, sometimes of wild beasts and reptiles, in order to arouse fear or desire.[18]

For a full understanding of this demonic earth spirit which communicates with the soul in dreams of so strangely earthly a nature, we should need a complete survey of the enormous bulk of material relating to dreams in the patristic literature. So far this overwhelming task has not been undertaken. What a wealth of insight it would give us! Above all, the monks in the desert, with their almost uncanny power of psychological analysis, dealt constantly with these questions and recorded their dreams for the moral and ascetic lessons they embodied. If the demon cannot approach a Christian in his waking state, he torments and troubles him in his dreams: for the "sublogical power" of the soul (as Gregory of Nyssa called it) is especially vulnerable to such attacks; and for the desert Fathers it was a fixed principle that a vice could not be looked upon as eradicated if it was still loved or committed in dreams. Prudentius described these demonic attacks in the dream world in his fine hymn to sleep. In words which almost recall the passage we have cited from Petronius, he tells us that dreams arise first and foremost from the conscious life

17 *De opificio Dei*, 18, 8–9.   18 *Against the sects*, II, 20.

of the day, for even when the body is asleep, the soul retains a "very tenuous life."[19]

Which is to say: "In imitation of itself, the soul devises multiform images; swiftly running through them, it enjoys a tenuous life." This is still good Stoic doctrine. But there are also demonic dreams and against these the Christian has only a single weapon: he must ban them with the sign of the Cross. And the poet prays: "Begone, begone, ye magical and delusive dream fantasies! Begone O tortuous serpent that with a thousand windings and deceptions troublest the sleeping heart."[19a]

The same thought is to be found in the Ambrosian hymn which is still repeated each night in the liturgical prayer: "May dreams and the phantasms of night recede. Subdue (O God) our enemy, that our bodies be not polluted."[20] This is a reference to the earthly aspect of the dreams inspired by the evil spirit, whose immersion in darkness and elemental baseness is revealed above all in sexual lures. But the evil earth spirit can also confront the soul in terrifying dreams with all the other obstacles that draw the upward striving soul down into the sensual, that destroy it with care or sickness. Here the thinking of the Church Fathers admirably combines personal experience with Christian knowledge of hereditary sin and with Platonic longing for the realm of the pure and tranquil spirit. The same demons who lie in wait for the soul as it leaves the body, and obstruct its final ascent to the heavenly ether, strive here below to block the path of inner resurrection with temptations and lascivious dreams. Only the other spirit, the celestial *pneuma*, which the Christian possesses by virtue of Christ's demon-conquering death on the Cross, can overcome the weight that draws the soul downward. And that is why the prayer of man assailed by the earth passes from exorcism of demons into a hymn to the heavenly spirit, into a plea for the free, winged, chaste

19 *Cathemerinon VI*, "Hymnus ante somnum":
Imitata multiformes
facies sibi ipsa fingit,
per quas repente currens
tenui fruatur actu.

19a O tortuose serpens   20 Procul recedant somnia
qui mille per meandros   Et noctium phantasmata;
fraudesque flexuosas   Hostemque nostrum comprime
agitas quieta corda!   Ne polluantur corpora.

grace of the divine *pneuma*. It is in the innermost soul of man that the decisive and saving encounter between earth spirit and divine spirit occurs: the soul that has freed itself from the "demon of the earth" has become a ruler of the cosmos; even now, but how much more so after death, it has power over all the earth. I know of no text in all the abundant writings of the Church Fathers that has expressed this more profoundly than the hymn of Synesius of Cyrene. With this hymn we shall conclude our remarks on the earth spirit and introduce those on the divine spirit. It is a wonderful prayer to God for liberation from the earth spirit and for the gift of the divine spirit, an outcry of the Christian and Greek soul from the depths of the cosmos to the heights of the pure spirit. Therefore it will serve also to introduce our discussion of the divine, the heavenly spirit:

> Have pity, O Lord
> on an imploring soul:
> Dispel the sickness
> and the care
> That devour the soul.
> Cast out the monster,
> the earthly dog,
> the demon of earth
> from my soul,
> from my prayer,
> from my life,
> from my works!
> May the demon remain
> outside of my body,
> outside of my spirit,
> outside of everything
> that I have and am.
> May the demon of matter,
> the source of all torments,
> who stands athwart
> the ascending path,
> who kills the questing
> aspiration to God,
> may he flee and be gone!

And now, as in a sublime counterpoint, the prayer turns towards the divine spirit and implores God for this most precious of all gifts:

But send me, O Lord,
the companion,
the sacred messenger
of holy power,
the messenger of divine,
inspired prayer,
the friendly giver,
keeper of the soul,
keeper of life,
guardian of prayers,
guardian of works.
May he preserve my body
free from sickness,
and preserve my spirit
free from shame.
May he grant my soul
forgetfulness of sorrow:
That the wings of the spirit
by hymns to thee
may surpass this earth-bound life,
that shorn of destiny
free from burdensome fetters,
unweighted by matter,
I may fulfill my journey
to thy tent and to thy breast
whence the soul's fountain
welled in the beginning.
Give me thy hand
and lead my imploring soul
away from matter![20a]

2. *The Divine Spirit*

This hymn of Synesius reveals with the utmost clarity the human and Christian dilemma: man is thrust down between the demonic earth spirit and the heavenly spirit, his soul is the battlefield of the powers of light and darkness. One might be inclined to criticize this poem for an exaggerated Platonism, almost drowning out the Christian note. But fundamentally the prayer is entirely Christian, for it shows a knowledge of the demonism of the material, such as the Neoplatonists

20a Hymn IV, 240ff. [Rendered from a German tr. by F. Wolters, *Lobgesänge und Hymnen* (Berlin, 1923), pp. 96f.—TRANS.]

never revealed, and its supplication for redemption through the Holy
Ghost is not the plea for disembodiment of one who despises the flesh,
but rather the entreaty of St. Paul: Who will redeem me from the
body of this death? It is a Christian insight that the dominion of the
evil earth spirit embraces primarily the material, the carnal, in short,
everything "which stands athwart the ascending path, which kills
the questing aspiration to God." Yet this never implies a demonization of the wondrous cosmos, but merely that the demon still exerts a
partial power over the earthly, in order to draw down to himself the
soul that still dwells in the flesh. And conversely, the sacred spirit
of heaven fills the universe, it is the *pneuma* that blows through the
whole world and the cosmos, also in order to draw man's soul to
itself, to lure it, to inspire it, to carry it upward into the light of its
love. Here again, the cosmic battle between the two spirits becomes a
copy of the drama enacted in man's soul. And it is in the innermost
heart of man that *pneuma* and *daimon* meet for the *duellum
mirandum,* which will decide the fate of the cosmos. This idea was
dear to all the Church Fathers, it may even be said to lie at the very
center of their asceticism and their eschatology. Gregory the Great
once asked: "What is the meaning of the Lord's words 'the prince
of this world will be driven out of the cavern of our heart'?" "It
means," he replied, "that Satan is driven like a serpent from the cavern
of our heart."[21] The human heart is the scene of the cosmic decision
between Christ and Belial, between light and darkness. "When it is
written," says Macarius in his *Pneumatic Homilies,* "that Satan dwells
in the world, it means that he dwells in the abyss of the heart."[22]
Beyond any doubt these Fathers knew more than we do of the depths
of the human soul; they had not yet forgotten that in the lowest
"abyss" of this inferno, there dwells a *daimon* fallen headlong from
heaven, and they also knew that down in these ultimate depths, the
conversion and the triumph begins, because there is another spirit,
the divine spirit, that penetrates even deeper into the caverns of the
soul. "The devil is expelled from the hearts of those who have faith,"
says Victorinus of Pettau, the early Christian interpreter of the
Apocalypse; "consequently he takes possession of the godless, in whose

21 *Moralia in Job,* XVII, 32. Cf. also St. Augustine, *Tractatus in Joannem,* 79, 2.
22 Homily 23.

136

blinded hearts he burrows day after day as in a profound abyss."[23] But in the mystery of faith and baptism, he is driven out of this abyss, and then begins the slow but ultimately triumphant process of the soul's exorcism, that ascetic and mystical struggle which Cyril of Jerusalem proclaimed to his candidates for baptism: "As long as man is in his body, he must struggle with many wild demons. But God has given us an ally and defender, the Holy Ghost, and he is greater than the devil and subdues him!"[24] The church still prays and thinks thus in its mysteries. For each and every man it says in the ceremony of baptism: "Recognize then, accursed devil, thy sentence, and do honor to the Holy Ghost! I exorcise thee, unclean spirit; depart from this image of God, that it may become the temple of the living God and that the Holy Ghost may dwell therein." And when Mother Church, in her ineffable knowledge of the demonism of the earthly, bends over the salt and the water and the oil of the earth and by her prayers casts the demon out of them, once again the fundamental implication is that the decision in the struggle is arrived at solely in the human heart, where the whole cosmos comes together as in a focal point.

In speaking of this divine spirit in patristic terms, we may therefore draw a close parallel with the doctrine of the earth spirit that we have just set forth. We shall first speak of the essence of the divine spirit as the counterpart to the "prince of this world"; then when we proceed to its function, we shall again select a special aspect which forms a kind of counterpoint with the demonic doctrine of dreams.

I

The essence of the divine spirit is indescribable, for its nature is to "breatheth where he will" (John 3:8). The divine *pneuma* is the intimate, unfathomable element in the godhead, and that is why the Church Fathers like to call it the fragrance and rejoicing of God. We have, to be sure, the clear and sober though sacred utterances of New Testament revelation concerning the Holy Ghost as person and as Messianic gift; but here too it is implicit that even as Christians we cannot comprehend its all-embracing, all-permeating essence; and the patristic theology always preserved the diffidence which Cyril of Jerusa-

23 Migne, op. cit., Latin Series, V, 341.   24 *Catechesis*, XVI, 19.

lem expressed when he said: "Thou shalt not, in thy curiosity, strive to penetrate the nature and essence of the spirit. Concerning what is not written, we shall not venture to speak."[25] And so, for our part, we shall attempt only to catch a fleeting breath of this fragrance, speaking of the Holy Ghost only in its function of "heavenly spirit" which fills the whole cosmos because it dwells in the bottommost depths of the human heart.

There are three principal Bible passages underlying this patristic theology of the *pneuma* that fills the universe. The first is Genesis 1:2: "And the spirit of God moved over the waters." The other two, from the Book of Wisdom, were all-important for the early Christian doctrine of the spirit and were dear to the ancient liturgy, recurring again and again in the hymns to the *Creator spiritus*. The first of them (Wis. 1:7) runs: "For the spirit of the Lord hath filled the whole world: and that which containeth all things hath knowledge of the voice." The second (Wis. 7:22–23) is a true hymn of praise, in the Greek manner, to the *pneuma*. There is in God a spirit that is "holy, one, manifold, subtile, eloquent, active, undefiled, sure, sweet, loving that which is good, quick, which nothing hindereth, beneficent, gentle, kind, steadfast, assured, secure, having all power, overseeing all things, and containing all spirits, intelligible, pure, subtile." Precisely because of the inescapable parallel between these words and the Greek Stoic doctrine of the *pneuma*, they have become the best argument against the pantheistic immanence of the universal spirit. It was through them that the Church Fathers arrived at the powerful Christian conception of the Holy Ghost as a divine person, infinitely separate from any created world, and yet infinitely *"intimus,"* filling the world, guiding it, and in it carrying on the divine drama of its inspirations. It would be a most interesting study in classical Christian philosophy to show the process by which the Fathers found the delicate middle point between immanence and transcendence, between the otherworldly celestial spirit and the creative spirit that is immanent in the world; to show how they never sacrificed the sharply delineated personal character of the *pneuma* and how this Christian certainty enabled them to praise the same *pneuma* as the essential force that rules in the heart of all creation, in the innermost core of the great

25 *Cat.*, XVI, 24.

and beautiful things of the cosmos. But here we shall be able to deal only with certain partial aspects of the patristic concept of the spirit.

The heavenly spirit is the divine artist, who is at work throughout the created world. In their interpretations of the creation in Genesis, the Fathers proclaimed this again and again in hymnlike language: this is the root of their almost modern love of nature's beauties, of the lyrical freedom with which they write of flower and star, sea and man. "It had been ordained that the pole of heaven should be adorned, that the earth should put forth shoots, and therefore the spirit of God hovered over them. For through it the seeds of the newly formed creatures have their germinating force, as the prophet says: Send forth thy spirit, and they shall be created; and thou shalt renew the face of the earth. Indeed, according to the Syriac text, the spirit of God *brooded* over the waters. This means that God animated the earth, in order that it might begin a new creation and in order that the spirit might brood over things and awaken the breath of life in them." Thus preached Ambrose.[26] In the famous chapter in his *Confessions* in which St. Augustine speaks of love as the fundamental force of all creation (the last verses of Dante's *Paradiso* must be understood in this light), the innermost essence of man, his own power of love, is also included in the dynamic of the *pneuma:* the stone falls downward, fire flares upward, and thus it is with the spirit, it is weight and it is flame, it moved over the waters at the beginning of time, it draws everything to itself; and so it is with the spirit-filled man. *Pondus meum amor meus.*[27] Even more beautiful is St. Augustine's comparison between the heavenly spirit and the creative artist: "As the creative will of a sculptor hovers over a piece of wood, or as the spiritual soul spreads through all the limbs of the body; thus it is with the Holy Ghost; it hovers over all things with a creative and formative power [*vi quadam effectoria et fabricatoria*]."[28] It is "the ordering power" in all things present.[29] It moves all things and yet is itself eternally at rest. It is the measure which establishes order and at the same time the measureless inspiration that bursts order asunder; it is both falling stone and leaping flame (and only in these antitheses can the Fathers speak of the Holy Ghost). A hundred years before

26 *Hexameron,* I, 8, 29.
27 *Confessiones,* XIII, 9.
28 *De genesi ad litteram,* IV, 16.
29 *De diversis quaestionibus,* II, 5.

Dante, Adam of St. Victor still praised the spirit in Augustinian style
as the love "which moves the sun and the other stars":

> Love of Father, Son, together,
> Equal of them both, with either
> One, the same in every part!
> All Thou fillest, all Thou lovest,
> Stars Thou rulest, heaven Thou movest,
> Though immovable Thou art.[30]

But—and with this we have taken a step further in the knowledge
of this celestial spirit—at the innermost center of the cosmos stands
man, and in the innermost center of man stands his spiritual love:
and consequently the Holy Ghost dwells and acts in man's soul in an
entirely new and special way, first revealed to us by the message of the
spirit-giving Messiah; and it was for the sake of this efficacy in the
soul of man that the spirit filled the inanimate cosmos.

The Church Fathers could best conceive of the permeation of the
cosmos by the celestial spirit (and in this they are entirely in the
Greek tradition) as a parallel to the permeation of man's body by his
soul. It is highly instructive to note the tone in which St. Jerome,
otherwise so sober a theologian, speaks of this *pneuma* of the world
and the human soul. He interprets the passage in the prophet
Habacuc (2:19-20) in which it is said of the wooden idol: "Behold,
it is laid over with gold and silver and there is no spirit in the bowels
thereof. But the Lord is in his holy temple." This temple, Jerome
interprets, is the whole universe, the Holy Ghost inhabits heaven and
earth, the oceans, and the whole cosmos. And here, characteristic of
the classical thinking of these ancient Christian theologians, there
comes to his mind a verse of Virgil, which to be sure refers to the
human soul (entirely in the Stoic sense) but is here boldly related to
the divine *pneuma*:

30 Pentecostal sequence, "Qui procedis ab utroque," 2, 7-12, tr. D. S. Wrangham,
The Liturgical Poetry of Adam of St Victor (London, 1881), Vol. I, p. 100, from:
> Amor patris filiique,
> par amborum et utrique
>   compar et consimilis.
> Cuncta reples, cuncta foves,
> astra regis, caelum moves,
> permanens immobilis.

a spirit within sustains, and mind, pervading its members,
sways the whole mass and mingles with its mighty frame.[31]

And we can say conversely: the creative spirit acts in the soul as in
the whole cosmos, the heart of man is the epitome and abstract of the
universe, it is, one might say, the chaos, over which the fertilizing
pneuma hovers and broods. "The pneuma, since it holds all things
together, has knowledge of every voice": this means, in the patristic
theology of the spirit, that the effective force of the "world Spirit"
(here used in the divine sense of the spirit that fills the world) culminates in the knowledge of the voice, which comes to the man gifted
with the spirit, in the word, in the imparted truth, in the vision of
God. It was entirely in the spirit of this theology, which sees the
visible cosmos as a reflection of the drama of the soul, that Notker
Balbulus, the monk of St. Gall, wrote these verses of his profound
Pentecost sequence:

> When by the power of his word
> God created
> heaven, earth, and ocean,
> thy breath,
> O sublime Holy Ghost,
> hovered over the wide waters,
> fructifying them.
> For thy breath awakeneth life,
> it fructifieth the waters
> and awakeneth
> the spiritual forces of man.[31a]

The waters fructified by the spirit are conceived as a visible sign,
as a symbol of the supernaturally awakened spiritual forces of man:
this universal conception, with its cosmic and psychic harmony, is the
most precious heritage of the old theology, for which no gulf existed
between world and soul, the outward and the inward. In perhaps the
finest passage of his work *On the Holy Ghost*, the Greek Basilius illus-

---

31 Tr. H. R. Fairclough (Loeb Classical Library, Cambridge, Mass., rev. edn., 1935),
of *Aeneid*, VI, 726f.:
> spiritus intus alit: totamque infusa per artus
> mens agitat molem et magno se corpore miscet.

It is cited in Jerome, *Commentarium in Habacuc*, 1, 2.

31a [Rendered from a German tr. by Wolters, *Hymnen und Sequenzen* (Berlin,
1914), p. 96.—TRANS.]

trated the creative essence of the Holy Ghost, at work both in the immense universe and in the depths of the human heart, by another cosmic image, that of the sun: "The holy *pneuma* is undivided and whole in every individual, and it is everywhere undivided." Just as the sunbeam is entirely present for every single individual, and yet floods the whole earth and the waves of the sea, thus it is also with the gracious indwelling of the Holy Ghost in the heart of man: in each man it is at work according to his power of apprehension, and yet it unites all. Here the usually dry style of Basilius takes wing and becomes a stormy hymn to the spirit:

> For him who has once triumphed in the Spirit over all earthly passions and thus returned to primal beauty, for him the Holy Ghost becomes a sun. His spirit becomes like the clear, glittering eye of Helios, disclosing the image of the invisible. And blissfully gazing at this image, thou wilt see the ineffable beauty of the archetype [τὸ ἄρρητον τοῦ ἀρχετύπου κάλλος]. Through this *pneuma* we become spiritual, men illumined and illuminating, knowers of the mysteries, who will some day experience infinite bliss dancing with the angels, nay, who will enjoy the highest of all things desirable [τὸ ἀκρότατον τῶν ὀρεκτῶν], to become like God [θεὸν γενέσθαι].

II

Thus by an almost antithetical truth, the heavenly spirit becomes the "earth spirit," because it fills and creatively transforms the whole world and the heart of man. The evil spirit is only the pretended "earth spirit," its counterpart, its ape, which has taken possession of the world and thence of the heart of man. In the depths of the heart the battle between the two spirits is enacted: and by the contrasting effects of these spirits, man learns "to distinguish the spirits"—that sublime psychological art of which the ancient Church Fathers had so profound a knowledge. The ultimate states induced by these two spirit forces that meet in the human heart are the diabolical blindness of the earth spirit who has fallen to the center of the earth, and the celestial vision of God's radiant essence through the illumination of the divine spirit. The decision is renewed again and again in the course of man's term on earth, between heaven and hell, surrounded by the messengers of the good and of the evil spirit, the angels and the demons. The divine spirit purifies, the earth spirit darkens. Or, as Notker sang, entirely in the spirit of the Augustinian theology, in the Pentecost sequence just cited:

> O thou great purifier
> of all the shameful things
> that dwell in the spirit:
> cleanse soon the clouded eye
> of our inner man,
> that we may be worthy
> to behold
> the glory of the Creator.

We cannot fully describe the function of the divine spirit without going at length into the patristic doctrine of the "discernment of spirits," this dogmatically sound yet subtly observant psychotherapy. This would lead us too far astray, into a field that has as yet been little explored. By such a study we might learn (and what a gain that would be for our present-day therapy) that one can speak only stammeringly and imperfectly of the psyche and its mysterious forces, if one has forgotten about heaven and the demon, about the vision of God to which the divine spirit empowers us, and the blindness of Satan into which we can fall. "For it is clear," Origen wrote, "that the soul of man, so long as it dwells in this body, is exposed to two forces at work within it: the good and the evil spirit."[32] The same was known to that simple Christian of the early period, the author of the *Shepherd of Hermas*, when he wrote: "Through sin the Holy Ghost that dwells within thee is darkened by another spirit, an evil spirit. There is then no room within thee for the tender spirit, for the evil spirit seeks to stifle it. And when both spirits dwell together in a man, it is injurious to him in whom they dwell."[33] What psychological profundity in these childlike words! Since then this "discernment of spirits" has had a glorious history, through the inspired insights of the desert monks, up to the terse but psychologically so profound rules laid down in the *Spiritual Exercises* of Ignatius Loyola.

We now come to a second effect of the divine spirit, parallel to the influence of the earth spirit that winds its way into the human soul in dreams. The Holy Ghost can also enter into the soul that has

32 *De principiis*, III, 3, 4.   33 Mandate V, 1.

"parted" from the flesh in sleep. Here again an exhaustive study of the abundant patristic dream literature would be exceedingly worth while. Tertullian had already developed the profoundly Christian insight that dream images must be sifted on awaking and precisely with that "spiritual discretion" of which we have been speaking. "For confidence in dream images," he says with Latin succinctness, "rests not on the visions themselves but on their effects [*fides somniorum de effectu non de conspectu renuntiatur*]: for it is not because they are seen that they are true, but because they are fulfilled."[34] I do not know what a modern psychologist would say of the heavenly dream that is reported in a fourth-century martyrology: after dreaming the story of his own martyrdom, the martyr enters into a vision of God; he is overcome by a feeling of miraculous lightness, and his earthly body becomes translucent as glass, so that men may look into the middle of his heart: *"perlucida fuit caro nostra ut oculorum visum ad intima cordis admitteret."*[35] At all events, the Christians of antiquity were convinced that the divine spirit could beneficently impart itself in dreams to the man who was the object of grace, and Prudentius, in his *Hymn to Sleep,* speaks of the "radiant clear secrets that must be cloaked in pious silence" that are imparted in a dream of grace.[36] The martyrology of James and Marianus (to cite one rather unfamiliar example) tells how the martyr, prior to his martyrdom, anticipates in a dream the cooling libation from the heavenly springs, and the writer cries out: "O dreamer's sleep, more powerful than any waking! O peace, in which sleeps blissfully he who is awake in the faith! Sleep, thou capturest only the earthly members: but the spirit alone can see God."[37]

Here we can only suggest the infinite riches of this field, and again we shall single out one aspect of the patristic doctrine of the heavenly spirit which forms a kind of counterpoint to the earth spirit's seizure of the soul that descends to the depths. I am speaking of that other

34 *De anima,* ch. 57, 10.
35 Thierry Ruinart, *Acta primorum martyrum* (2nd edn., Amsterdam, 1713), p. 233: on the martyrdom of Sts. Montanus, Lucius, and others.
36 O quam profunda justis
   arcana per soporem
   aperit tuenda Christus,
   quam clara, quam tacenda!
37 Ruinart, p. 226.

"seizure" which can come upon the soul, that inspiration by the Holy Ghost which the classical theologians called "sober drunkenness." The Greeks revealed a foreknowledge of this state when they conceived the epiphany of Apollo in its indissoluble duality: as intoxication and as inspiration to clear beauty. In the rare moments when the divine spirit imparts itself to earthly man, the ultimate state of beatific vision is anticipated. That is what Plotinus meant in calling this mystical event a "drunkenness of the spirit,"[38] and no other image is possible. When the spirit seizes hold of the prophet, he becomes drunk and exalted, but it is a restrained, sober, and miraculously lucid drunkenness; this gift of the spirit is water and fire at once, the potion from the cup of the *pneuma* brings intoxication and sobriety at once. "Open thy mouth and drink," says the voice to the prophet in IV Esdras. "Then I opened my mouth, and lo! there was reached unto me a full cup, which was full as it were with water, but the color of it was like fire. And I took it and drank; and when I had drunk, my heart poured forth understanding, wisdom grew in my breast. . . ."[39] Philo expressed this spiritual experience in the oxymoron of "sober drunkenness," and the Alexandrian Fathers particularly Origen, took it over from him and filled it with Christian meaning and the experience of the Holy Ghost. Gregory of Nyssa and Ambrose, those best of Origen's pupils, heard it from him, and through St. Augustine it was preserved forever for Western mysticism. This is the very same realm of the spirit in which the hymn of Synesius was born: the soul, yearning to rise out of the dark depths of the earth spirit to the realm of the heavenly spirit, is seized by the *pneuma* and carried upward to the heights of ecstasy. In order to partake of such grace, the soul must drink from the cup of wisdom: "It must be filled with that good and sober drunkenness," says Gregory of Nyssa, "through which it is given to man to ascend from the material to the divine."[40]

"To be rapt away from matter"—that is the longing of the Christian Greek. His source of strength is the divine *pneuma,* not the impotent independent striving of the Gnostic, but the humble, forever sober

38 *Ennead* VI, 7, 35.
39 IV Esdras 14:38–40 (tr. G. H. Box in R. H. Charles, *The Apocrypha and Pseudepigrapha of the Old Testament,* Oxford, 1913, Vol. II, p. 623).
40 Homily 5, on the Canticle of Canticles.

strength that is given to us from above, through Christ the man and through the spirit which he poured out for us in his humble death on the Cross. That is what Ambrose meant when he spoke of the cup of the spirit "which from heaven is held out to the earth," full of the wine "that was pressed from the grape that as flesh was nailed to the Cross. From this grape comes the wine that gladdens the heart of man, that makes it drunk with sobriety, with the ecstasy and fragrance of faith, of the true godliness, the intoxication of purity."[41] Here lies the true Christian adaptation of the Greek heritage. The Latin Church never forgot the verse composed by Ambrose in his soberly Roman, clearcut prosody: "Joyfully let us drink the sober intoxication of the spirit."[42] This ecstasy that raises the soul from the earthly is, however, merely a momentary, fleeting anticipation of the blissful lot that will fall to man when, purified, he enters the realm of the heavenly spirit. The spirit-inspired Christian experiences this event in the radiant darkness of faith, in the drunkenness of a love that remains always simple. St. Augustine admonishes those whom he has newly baptized: "The Holy Ghost is now beginning to dwell within you. Exclude him not from your hearts. He is a good guest: he will make you drunk. He delights in the Lord and rejoicing sings the praises of the Lord. Is he not like unto a drunken man? This drunkenness I praise: for with thee, O Lord, is the fountain of life, and thou shalt make them drink of the torrent of thy pleasure!"[43] Here we have a true ecstasy, even here below, a departure from all normal, philistine, purely human thinking, a "losing of the reason," as Augustine (in a style reminiscent of Plotinus) says: "The Holy Ghost sought for words in which to utter his thoughts with regard to things human; and since when men are drunk they lose their reason, he too found, as it were, in drunkenness what he wished to say: for when one receives that ineffable joy, the human reason somehow vanishes [*perit quodammodo mens*], becomes divine, and grows intoxicated by virtue of the superabundant riches in the house of the Lord."[44] And so this earthly sober drunkenness becomes the beginning and the pivot of the divine intoxication in which men grown eternal can dwell forever without peril; it becomes the "longing for the fountain of life. . . . Such a drunkenness

41 *De fide ad Gratianum,* I, 135f.
42 Laeti bibamus sobriam ebrietatem Spiritus.
43 *Sermo ad Catechumenos,* 225, 4.
44 *Enarrationes in Psalmos,* 35.

does not cast the spirit down, but bears it aloft and brings forgetfulness of all earthly things."[45]

We have come to the end of the soul's journey from the depths of the earth spirit that dwells in the middle of the earth, to the heights of the heavenly spirit that carries it upward beyond all things earthly. The Divine Comedy of man, the divine battle of the spirits, is at an end. "To the high fantasy here power failed." With these words Dante introduces, at the end of the *Paradiso,* the lofty vision which permitted him a moment's glance, ending in dazed darkness, into the exalted sphere of the triune godhead. In that flash he beheld the goal of all human souls: the eternal love that in God is spirit, and that moves the sun and the stars. The earth spirit that for a time was permitted to hold the beautiful cosmos in its power is now infinitely remote; it has fallen headlong into the earthly chasm of its own alienation from God. But man, and with him the newly consecrated cosmos, has been borne aloft in the spirit; he returns home to the love that was his starting point: "to thy tent and to thy breast, whence the soul's fountain welled," as Synesius prayed. Stars and stones, sun and soul, will all be embraced in the holy spirit and blessed. Once again, and now forever, the preserving power of the spirit that moved on the face of the waters—God's love—will rule over creation.

The Fathers of the early Church were of the wise and humble opinion that the mystery of the heavenly spirit can be comprehended only by those men who have been previously seized by this same Holy Ghost. For only the spirit that comprehends and embraces all things has the "knowledge of the voice": *scientiam habet vocis.* The spirit hears only what he himself "ineffably speaks" within us, says St. Paul. And when this grace is bestowed upon a man, it transforms him into a spiritual man. The spiritual transformation can be described only in the antitheses of the patristic theology: the spiritual man in the Christian sense is a man of fire, but of wisdom; of drunkenness, but of sobriety; of world renunciation, because he is borne aloft by the heavenly spirit, but of world love, because he finds in the cosmos the world-filling spirit; the spiritual man knows of demons, but he can conquer them; he knows the soul, because he knows God. For him

45 *De agone christiano,* I, 9, 10.

the formlessness of the merely visible suddenly begins to sparkle like a crystal: for the more he frees himself from the dark, earthly, and shapeless demon, the more sharply he discerns the formative power of the heavenly spirit (*vis fabricatoria Spiritus Sancti,* as St. Augustine called it) which governs and underlies all created things.

It seems fitting to conclude this brief extract from the spirit theology of the ancient Church Fathers with some verses by an unknown poet (presumably a contemporary of the great Dante), who was impelled by an old tradition, but also by his own poetic intuition, to speak in those ineffable antitheses through which alone we can utter the truth of the Holy Ghost:

> He who knows knows thee his feast,
> Whom thou graspest wisdom grasps,
> Happy he who thee receives.
> Sweet thou to uncorrupted palate,
> Once thou art received, once tasted,
> All that is fleshly loses savor.[46]

46 Tr. from:

> Sapienti vere sapis,
> iste capit, quem tu capis,
> felix, qui te recipit.
> Sano dulcis es palato,
> te recepto, te gustato,
> omnis caro desipit.

—Anonymous sequence, "Aquilone pulso," Lower Rhine, 12th–13th cent., from *Analecta hymnica medii aevi,* ed. Clemens Blume and G. M. Dreves (Liturgische Prosen des Mittelalters, 4th series), Vol. XXXIV (Leipzig, 1900), p. 42, no. 42.

Fritz Meier

The Problem of Nature in the Esoteric
Monism of Islam[1]

See ye yon hanging moon?—
But half it can be seen,
  Yet 'tis round and beautiful!
Thus many things there be
That we mock complacently,
  For our eyes behold them not at all.
—MATTHIAS CLAUDIUS (1740–1815)

1. The Esoteric Attitude towards Theology

One of the most interesting figures in the history of the Islamic mind
is 'Azīz ibn-Muḥammad-i Nasafī, a Persian mystic of the seventh
century A.H., or the thirteenth century A.D. Although our information
concerning him is sparse and in part unreliable, his writings give a
good idea of his position within the general picture of Islamic mysticism. He was born in Turkestan, at the remote northeastern edge of
Islamic territory, and in his thinking he was also at the very edge of
Islam. Often mystics can be associated with one of the great theological
doctrines of Islam: Sunna, Shiah, etc., and where they are not amenable
to such classification, it is because the substance of their lives was so
far removed from these questions that they had nothing whatsoever
to say about them. As for Nasafī, he was wholly immersed in these
matters, and nevertheless he stood outside the parties.

---

1 [In translating Persian material into German, Professor Meier used Latin for
quotations in Arabic (i.e., the "classical" language), and this convention has
been followed in the English translation. The abbreviation A.H. follows a date
in the Mohammedan calendar, which reckons from the year of the hegira,
A.D. 622. The passages from the Koran are in the J. M. Rodwell tr. (Everyman's
Library; New York and London, 1907), modified where necessary to accord
with Professor Meier's reading.—ED.]

149

This was possible because his approach to truth was more realistic than that of other mystics. For him the truth did not lie within any of the numerous dogmatic sects of Islam, each of which laid claim to election and exclusive legitimacy. For Nasafī it lay between or above the different sects, to which it was related as a theme is to its variations; or rather, the truth was the unseen goal towards which all the particularized creeds aspired, and from which all remained equally removed.

We might therefore be tempted to regard Nasafī as a forerunner of modern comparative religion, or at least of the philosophy of religion, which is also expected to be, in a sense, above the parties. But an important distinction must be made. According to Rudolf Otto, one thing is deplorably lacking in the modern philosophy of religion: certainty concerning the true religion in relation to which the innumerable variations, sects, and denominations might be appraised and classified. "For," says Rudolf Otto, "the objects to be classified are not for the most part related as the various species within a genus, they are not parts of an *analytical* unity, but forces comprising a synthetic unity. It is as though we discerned parts of a big fish over the surface of the water, and tried to classify the back, the tip of the tail, the head, according to species and genus, failing to realize that these aspects must be seen in their proper place and context, as parts of a whole, which must be understood before the parts can be understood."[2]

Nasafī believed that he had found this whole, in the shape of a religion based on personal experience and transcending theology. This religion, it is true, bore the unquestionable stamp of Islam, as is to be expected in a thinker of Nasafī's time and origins. But it would be a mistake to regard his ideas as a weapon against non-Islamic religions. Nasafī did not set out to propagate Islam; he wished to show his fellow men that the true Islam was to be found, not in the systems of theology, but in the receptive heart of the religious individual. True religion and true Islam were one for him, but both lay outside of authoritarian faith.

> O dervish [he wrote], Learn that of three roads you must take one. If you have talent and strength to become a wise man,

2 *Das Heilige* (Munich, 1932), p. 172.

a knower of the truth, and to ascertain by logic and intellectual endeavor which of the various forms of faith is the
true faith, apply yourself to the task, and act; for dogmatic
faith [*taqlīd*] leads to nothing, and there is no purpose in
reciting Sura 43:23: "We found our fathers with a religion,
and in their tracks we tread." But if you have not the talent
and the strength, then seek at least a wise man, a knower
of the truth, a man of God, seek him in earnest, and do not
come forth with the excuse that you have found none; for he
who seeks will find. And do not claim by way of dispensation
that there are no men of God nowadays; for the world is never
without them. But once you have found one, hold him fast,
take pleasure in serving him, consider it the summit of happiness to be with him, devote yourself to him, cast out your
self and your own opinion, fill your innermost being with him,
his will and your love of him! If he drives you away and forbids you his house—for they cannot live and suffer personal
contact with all kinds of people—linger at his door, and strive
to become so that he cannot do otherwise than accept you. If
then he does accept you, you have found the right way and
may be counted among the saved. O dervish, by men of knowledge and truth, we do not mean those inactive theologians
and impious sheikhs who glory in their roles as theologians
and sheikhs; for they are a thousand times more doctrinaire,
more in error and more removed from God than yourself, and
far as they are from God, they think they are close to Him; in
sheer folly and darkness they look upon themselves as knowing and illumined, and when they recite Sura 24:40: "Or like
the darkness on the deep sea, when covered by billows riding
upon billows, above which are clouds: darkness upon darkness," they apply these words to China or India, but do not
think of themselves. . . . O dervish, you will not find this
wise man, this knower of truth in the mosques, preaching
from the pulpit, among the hypocritical and the worldly,
you will not find him in the religious academies, among the
bookish and idolatrous professors who sit on their carpets in
pomp and dignity, nor in the Sufi convents among the vision-
aries and egotists. In rare instances one among a thousand may
have attained to truth in these places, knowing God and acting
for His sake. O dervish, the wise men and knowers of truth,
the men of God, are hidden, and this hiddenness[3] is their
sentinel and their lance, their castle and their weapon, pre-

---

3 Literally, "hidden" = "under the cupolas"; "hiddenness" = "these cupolas."

serving them unsullied and clean. . . . O dervish, their outward appearance is that of the common people, but inwardly they are elect. They give no leader or chief access to themselves, but they also assert no claim to be leaders or chiefs. Each one is busy with someone and something, according to his need, and they earn their living through the labor of their hands. They shun the money of princes and oppressors and do not speculate for gain. If without effort and exertion they obtain more than they need, they give it away and do not set it aside. They do not invoke old age and family as a pretext [for getting more]. They are busy themselves with thought and with remembrance of God, pass most of their time in retirement and solitude; they do not favor intercourse with the worldly, they detest association with men of rank and dignity, but live when possible with the elect ['azīzān] and with dervishes; then, by perceiving and preserving each other's words and moods, they make day into night and night into day. And so they wait for death to come and free them from this tumultuous city, this stormy sea, this world of events, this so-called human body.[4]

Thus true religion is not achieved by mere membership in any denomination, but by an inner accomplishment that leads from appearance to being and from belief to knowledge, that is, by a road leading inward. Nasafī designates those possessed of the true religion as men of God, men who know God, wise men, and men who have attained to the truth, and later, as people of spiritual reality (ahl-i ḥaqīqat). By this term he means pious men who no longer base their religion, as he says, on authority but on personal experience and verification. We might call this mysticism, except that Nasafī sometimes reveals a distaste for the term. To his mind mysticism, Sufism—and the exact historical source of this view can be indicated—is only the way in which higher knowledge is acquired, not the knowledge itself, which might better be designated as esoteric insight. But in the following we shall not hold strictly to this distinction.

In the passage quoted above, Nasafī finds fault with Sufism, which he considers in very much the same light as theology. But he speaks very differently of Sufism in discussing the esoteric path. Sufism then becomes the beginning of esoteric knowledge, while theology is its anti-

4 'Azīz-i Nasafī, "Kashf ul-ḥaqā'iq," MS. Nuru Osmaniye (Istanbul) 4899, 23b penult. – 232b 17.

thesis. Whereas the theologian, "he who travels the path of religious dogma," learns each day something he did not know before, the mystic, he who "travels the path of the initiate," forgets each day something that he knew. Whereas the business of the theologian is each day to make white paper black, the concern of the mystic is each day to make some part of his black heart white.[5] Yet both strive after knowledge, for, as he indicates by calling the esoteric seer a wise man, ignorance plays no part in this plan of forgetfulness. "Some travelers of the path [the theologians]," he says, "spoke: Let us learn the craft of the scribe and inscribe all existing things on our hearts with the ink of study and the reed of repetition in order that a copy of everything sensory and supersensory that exists in the world may be written in our hearts. Whatever is inscribed and recorded[6] in our hearts is well preserved. Thus our heart will become the Well-preserved Tablet. But other travelers of the path [the mystics] spoke: Let us learn the polisher's trade and make the mirror of our heart clean and shining with the stone of spiritual struggle and the oil of contemplation of God, in order that our hearts may become transparent mirrors, reflecting everything sensory and supersensory that exists in the world. A reflection in the mirror is more accurate and free from doubt than writing, for in writing errors and fallacies are possible, while in the reflection they do not occur. Moreover, there are many branches of science, and even many categories of science, and life is short. Hence life is not long enough to make the heart the Well-preserved Tablet by means of study and repetition. But by means of spiritual struggle and contemplation of God, life can make the heart a mirror, disclosing the whole world."[7] And so some of them made "the eyes of the heart sharp-sighted and far-sighted, in order to read the unwritten book, while others made the ears of their heart keen and alert, in order to hear the unwritten word."[8]

5 'Azīz-i Nasafī, "Tanzīl ul-arwāḥ," MS. Shehit Ali Pasha (Istanbul) 1363, 142b 1–7. "Kashf ul-ḥaqā'iq," 269b 19–ult.

6 *Naqsh, munaqqash*, etc., in such cases, often means "inscribe, write down," and not "paint." Perhaps under the influence of Pers. *nigāshtan*. Examples can be found in other writers, e.g., Ghazzālī, *Naṣīhat ul-mulūk* (Teheran, 1317 A.H./1899 A.D.), 128, 4; Khwājjūy-i Kirmānī in Sa'id-i Nafīsī, *Ahwāl u muntakhab-i ash'ari-i Khwajjūy-i Kirmāni* (Teheran, 1307 A.H./1889 A.D.), 75 penult. But even in the Arabic the root means "engrave" or "inscribe," esp. of coins.

7 Tanzīl, 142b 7 – 143a 6.   8 Kashf, 270a 4–5.

This sharply defines the antithesis between mysticism and theology. It is not because he has read too little that the theologian's foundation is narrow. No, even if he read many times more, his foundation would not be broad enough to make possible those insights to which the esoteric seer can aspire. Only an exercise of the heart, only moral labor and spiritual struggle, in short, a *vita purgativa,* can give this broadening. In the passage where Nasafī likens the mystics to polishers cleansing the mirrors of the hearts, he calls the theologians eye doctors who (instead of cultivating their hearts) merely endeavor to make their outward eye sound and sharp-sighted.[9] He calls the casting off of reprehensible traits of character in the *vita purgativa* "inner death," as contrasted to "inner life," which is the acquisition of praiseworthy traits of character. The former are partitions separating man from higher knowledge and being.[10]

The aim towards which the mystic strives is circumscribed by the concepts "completeness," "full-grown-ness," and "freedom," the last two of course in a figurative sense:

> When the fruit on the tree is full-grown it is said to be ripe [grown-up: *bāligh*], and when it is taken from the tree, it is said to be free [*ḥurr*].[11] That is, as long as the fruit is advancing towards its goal, it is not yet ripe, and as long as it is bound to the tree, it is not free; for a thing that is bound is not free. The exercises and spiritual struggles of the travelers of the path serve to bring them to their goal [*nihāyat*]. And

9 Kashf, 269b ult. 270 a 4.
10 Tanzīl, 129a 1–8: "Life is of two kinds, the one is the outward, the other is the inner life [*ma'nawī*]. And death is also of two kinds, one is the outward, the other the inner death. . . . It is inner life when a man becomes alive through praiseworthy traits of character, when he acquires praiseworthy qualities. . . . And it is inner death when a man dies to his reprehensible traits of character before dying his outward death. *Morimini priusquam morimini!"* Ibid., 145a 7–penult.: "O dear friend, the true [mystical] way consists of two steps. The first consists in escaping from the partitions [veils] and the second in attaining to the moral stages. Whatever a man must create out of himself is a moral stage. Thus every man who has fully equipped himself with praiseworthy characteristics has attained to all the moral stages. He who has escaped from the partitions and he who has attained to all the moral stages has accomplished prayer; for the essence of purification is separation [*faṣl*] and the essence of prayer is connection [*waṣl*]."
11 Not in the current usage but as construed by Nasifī. — *Hurriya* occurs in 'Ammār al-Bidlīsī (12th cent. A.D.), "Bahjat at-tā'ifa," MS. Berlin 2842, and in Ibn 'Abbād ar-Rundī (d. 1390 A.D.)—see M. Asín Palacios, *Al-Andalus,* XI (1946), p. 10 —but also in the ancient mystics of Iraq. The moral implication of "free" in poetry was developed especially by Bustī.

their goal is maturity. The exercises and spiritual struggles of the mature, in turn, serve to bring them to their end [*ghāyat*]. And this end is freedom. Between the mature man and the free man there is no difference except that the latter has loosed his bond. He who is bound is a slave. Thus one man lies in the bonds of prophecy and desires to become a prophet, a second lies in the bonds of saintliness and desires to become a saint, a third in the bonds of wisdom and desires to become a wise man, a fourth in the bonds of rank and desires to become a sheikh, a fifth lies in the bonds of money, a sixth in the bonds of women, a seventh in the bonds of good food, an eighth in the bonds of fine clothes, etc. Each man who is in fetters, whether fetters of gold or brass, is fettered, and he who is fettered is a slave.[12]

The highest degree of freedom is the freedom of the saint, which requires that man die not only to honor, to possessions, to pleasure, to knowledge, to piety, to obedience, to the respect of his fellow men, to presumption, but that he "also die to himself, that he forget himself and become free of the fetters of his self."[13] For if the path of theologians is study and of the ascetics *(ahl-i ṭarīqat)* is exercise, that of the men of spiritual reality *(ahl-i ḥaqīqat)* is the negation of their own existence.[14] By this Nasafī means to say that the Islamic profession of faith, "There is no God but God," is fulfilled only by man transcending his own selfhood, which constitutes a God beside God.

Once this is done, Nasafī enters upon the highest stage, contentment *(riḍā)*, which he equates with freedom: ". . . for he who is content is free and in paradise" and "He who is in fetters is a slave and in hell." Therefore that man is content who dies to everything that is and to everyone who is, and who also dies to himself and becomes free of himself.[15]

Nasafī frequently states that intellectual insight is not adequate to such acts of self-sacrifice. He insists that love must aid the faculties of the intellect; indeed, he demands that the intellect be transcended through love. "Although the light of the intellect is sharp-sighted and far-sighted," he says, "the fire of love is even more sharp-sighted and

12 Tanzīl, 151a 2 – 151b 7 (abridged).   13 Kashf, 265a 2–3.   14 269b 12–13.
15 265a 6–9. Concerning contentment, see also 249b 1 – 250b 18 (end of the first risāla), 260a 10 – 265b (in the second risāla), 280a 5 – 281a 10 (end of the third risāla).

far-sighted. Sometimes the light of the intellect becomes overwhelming, as though it might illumine the whole house and make everything within the house visible to each man in his place, even though the fire of love has not yet combined with it: 'Whose oil would well nigh shine out, even though fire touched it not' (Sura 24:35). But without the fire of love, the light of the intellect cannot illumine the whole house. Not until the fire of love combines with the light of the intellect and becomes 'light upon light' [the same passage in the Koran] will the whole house be illumined."[16] For Nasafī the fire of love is the force with which the mystic strives to extinguish and can extinguish his selfhood, or mystically speaking, his existence:

> O dervish, it is the fire of love that takes the traveler of the path from the distraction of [spiritual] variability[17] and leads him to the collectedness of [inner] constancy,[18] that liberates him from multiplicity and polytheism, gives him monotheism and unity. For light gives being and fire consumes being. As long as your own being endures, there will be two beings: your being and that of God. But God's being suffers no rivalry and no rival. If thus through the fire of love your being is consumed and entirely destroyed, there remains but one being, the being of God.[19]

> By love [Nasafī continues, in order to make it clear that he is speaking not of a natural impulse but of the sacred force that distinguishes the man who has grown out of himself, the true "man"] we mean not what people bound to sensory form and conceptions so designate, not what is called temptation. For if such temptations arise in a traveler of the path, they succumb to his intellect and can never combine with it. By our love is meant the love that can only be kindled in the oil of the intellect. Once it enters the intellect of a traveler of the path, it burns all directions and colors in him and makes the traveler of the path one-colored[20] and of one direction.

16 Kashf, 278a 3 from bottom to 278b 4.
17 In which a man is now subjected to depression, now to gaiety, now to speech and now to silence, now to association with his fellow men and now to solitude, now to the wrath of God and now to mercy, unable to develop a will of his own (278a 10–12), in which he is a prisoner of desire and anger and a plaything of his qualities (278a 17–18).
18 In which man holds in his own hands and guides by his own will everything towards which in a state of variability he is helpless (278a 13ff).
19 Kashf, 278b 9–13.
20 The word that ordinarily means "honest, forthright" presumably means here something akin to "single-minded."

Thereafter it makes him without color and without direction, for once it fully consumes the being of the traveler of the path, all colors and directions cease. Here lies the border of the realm of unity. O dervish, then is the time of laboring and exertion [kōshish] past and the time of being drawn onward and giving [kashish] is at hand. Exercise and spiritual struggle have ceased, the day of contemplation and vision has dawned. The search for God is ended, God himself is revealed. The time in which the intellect wandered is passed, the time of the revelation of love is at hand. This is the place of which Gabriel said: "If I should come closer by one finger's breadth,[21] I should be burned." Gabriel was logical thought. But once the beauty of the beloved has been revealed and the veil has been lifted, what further need is there of logical proof?[22]

Often Nasafī, after an abstract explanation of some point, addresses himself to the reader and says, "I know you have not yet fully understood this; I shall therefore explain it more clearly." Then he goes over the whole problem in hand, considering it from a new aspect or adducing a concrete example. Nevertheless, he is convinced that his words can be truly understood only through inner experience.

It is useless to speak about the final state of the traveler of the path to one who is still in the straits of natural existence

21 *Anmalatan* instead of the usual *shibran* for "one span."
22 Kashf, 278b 13–ult. I have elsewhere pointed out that despite apparent arguments to the contrary, the disappearance of individual existence is never taken to mean the cessation of individual consciousness. Those who without going more deeply into the subject have stressed expressions such as "extinguishing of self," etc., have created a one-sided view. Actually Nasafī finds the highest value in man: "O dear friend, here and hereafter are so much prized among men only because they do not know their own worth. Once a man has recognized his own worth, here and hereafter and everything in them are worthless." (Tanzīl, 151b ult. – 152a 2.) The striving of the mystic to become God can therefore be interpreted as a strengthening of man. The continuous conquest of self which Nasafī demands aims at a diminution only of the false, not of the true self: "O dervish, assuredly the traveler of the path must first be in the multiplicity [of appearances] and can only afterwards attain to unity. For if he is not first in multiplicity, he cannot 'travel,' and anyone who, without having traveled, issues from multiplicity and believes himself to be at the stage of unity, remains forever immature, only deluding himself that he is mature; remains forever imperfect, only deluding himself that he is perfect. Such a man never obtains from himself what he seeks, nor do others obtain anything from him, for a transformed character and a cleansed faith, a pure bosom and a radiant heart can never come into being without exercises and spiritual struggles." (Ibid., 122b 4–10.) Here the attainment of the goal is made expressly dependent on a moral effort, hence on the improvement of man's nature.

[tabī'at], as useless as trying to explain to a child that is still in its mother's womb, nourished on blood, that outside of its dark, narrow world there is another world which is broad and bright, and flowing with milk that is an exceedingly tender and wholesome food. And this is true until the child has left that first vital element [maqām], until it has entered into the new vital element and sees the streams of milk with its own eyes. And then, however much one tells the suckling babe of a still wider world, in which there exist the most varied foods and dishes, it will avail nothing until, grown mature and independent, he finds this world for himself. No one, through the vital element in which he finds himself, can understand the next higher one, and since he does not understand it, his attitude towards it is one of rejection, he persecutes those who are based upon it and accuses them of disbelief and heresy.[23]

The worldly call those who live with a view to the hereafter mad, these call those who have penetrated to the spiritual world [ahl-i malakūt] mad, and these regard those who have pressed forward to the essential core [ahl-i jabarūt] as mad. But these last forgive all the others and consider each individual to be good in his place.[24]

"Hearing is not knowing and knowing is not living [maqām[25]]," he says.

From hearing to knowing is a long way, and from knowing to living, there are again innumerable difficulties to be overcome. Therefore, he who has read or heard the theses here set down by the author should not suppose that he has everywhere understood what the author meant, and he who has understood what the author meant should not suppose that it has already become the foundation of his life [maqām]. For he who has heard that there is something in the world called sugar cane is not nearly so far advanced as he who knows that there is a plant called sugar cane that is very sweet, that is cut and crushed at a certain time,[26] and the juice of which is thickened to make sugar and candy. He in turn[27] is never so far advanced as the man who sees how sugar is obtained and himself has sugar in his mouth.[28] In regard to the knowledge of sugar, the first is at the stage of hearing, the second at the stage of knowing, and the third at the stage of experi-

23 Kashf, 303a ult. – 303b 10.
25 Add. dīgar, hence maqām dīgar.
27 Lacuna in text.

24 254b 7–9.
26 Corr. burrand instead of burdand.
28 Text corrupt.

ence [*dhawq*]. Only in the last stage is the knowledge complete. The first has general knowledge of sugar, the second specific knowledge, while the third has the knowledge of experience. The first has heard of sugar, the second knows of sugar, the third has seen it and tasted it. Know that it is thus with all things.[29]

He who knows a thing as it really is, knows it. But he who does not know it in this way does not know it. The mark of the man who knows a thing as it really is, is that his knowledge of the thing cannot possibly deviate from what really is, it cannot be changed. The knowledge, for example, of the man who has seen and tasted sugar, and knows that it is sweet, cannot be turned aside from this fact and changed, even if the whole world should maintain that sugar were bitter. The knowledge of the man who knows that two times two is four will not be turned aside or changed, even if the whole world were of another opinion. O dear friend, by this I mean to say that in regard to knowledge most men are at the stage of opinion [*martaba-i pindār*], whereas they think they are at the stage of knowledge, or indeed that they have passed this stage and have reached the stage of experience. But the mark of the man who has attained to the stage of true knowledge is[30] that the more his knowledge increases, the more indulgent and modest, the humbler and more devoted he becomes, whereas the mark of a man who is at the stage of opinion is that the stronger his opinion becomes, the more of his indulgence, modesty, humility, and devotion he loses. O dear friend, real knowledge is one thing, and inauthentic knowledge is another. Real knowledge is not changed by the changing of times and religions, but inauthentic knowledge is changed by the changing of times and religions. Any knowledge that is changed by the changing of times and religions is not knowledge at all, but is called so only in a figurative sense. It is a popular term or the fiction of a wise man, who, for reasons of expediency, has so ordered it for the people. Inauthentic knowledge should therefore be acquired only according to the measure of necessity; for as such it is not a goal, and everything that is as such not a goal, becomes at the moment when it surpasses the necessary measure, a deterrent from the goal.[31]

29 Tanzīl, 140a 11 – 140b ult.   30 Text somewhat corrupt.
31 Tanzīl, 141a 1 – 141b 9.

Here Nasafī attacks exoteric thinking at its most vulnerable point. This lack of individual experience, of "verification," is just what the esoteric seer condemns in the theologian. For even the words of the holy tradition, which the theologians are forever invoking, are to Nasafī's mind merely helpful indications, appealing, like the words of profane communications, to previous knowledge. Anyone desiring real religious knowledge must acquire original experience of the matters with which religion is concerned; for this it is necessary that each man for himself become an esoteric seer and go through that process of inner clarification, after which, in Nasafī's opinion, the true picture of things is revealed to a man, and is mirrored in him. Then he discovers that all the innumerable contradictions over which exoteric thinkers rack their brains originate in verbal distinctions and have no basis in the matter itself. Nasafī shows this by citing the seemingly so contradictory traditions regarding the first thing created by God. There is, says Nasafī, the tradition that God first created reason. But there is another tradition according to which He first created Mohammed's light, or his spirit. Still another tradition declared that the (divine) reed pen was God's first creation, and so on. But by all these things only a single substance was meant. And by contemplating this one substance from a hundred points of view, one might give it a hundred names and still it would not disintegrate into a multiplicity. This original substance might be called reason, because it intrinsically knows and causes to know; for reason is at once *apprehensor (mudrik)* and *donator apprehensionis (mudarrik)*.[32] It is light because it both appears and causes to appear; for light is *apparens (zāhir)* and *aperiens (muzhir)*. Spirit because it lives and causes to live; for spirit is *vivens (ḥayy)* and *vivificator (muḥyī)*. Pen because it notes the objects of knowledge; for the pen is the *scriptor* of things. But in so far as the first substance is an intermediary or a mediator, one might call it angel or Gabriel.[33] And Nasafī continues:

32 Hardly *mudrak*, "*apprehensum*." Cf. Tanzīl, 109b 5–12, where the senses are described as merely perceiving, but the intellect-reason as perceiving and causing to perceive (*mdrk dar nafs-i khwad u mdrk mar ghayr-i khwadrā*). Both, senses and reason, are light, for light both appears and causes to appear, appearing in itself and causing other things to appear (*zāhir dar nafs-i kwad u muzhir mar ghayr-i khwad [rā]*). Tanzīl, 98a ult. actually uses "knowing" (*dānā*) for perceiving, and "causing to know" (*dānākunanda*) for causing to perceive.—Only the form *mudarrik* creates difficulties.

33 Kashf, 241b 1–13.

Know that over these various utterances of Mohammed, many men have fallen into confusion and are still falling into confusion. The whole disparity of religious currents that we now have originates in such outward words in the sayings of Mohammed and in the Koran. And the source of this confusion is that men wish to reach meaning through the outward word. But he who wishes to reach meaning through the outward word and who, starting with outward words, wishes to grasp the essence of things, never arrives at the meaning and will never find the essence of anything; for there are many different languages and modes of expression in the world. Each group in turn has its own special language and mode of expression, especially the prophets, whose task it is to admonish and threaten the people, in order that they may abjure their evil ways. But as long as they cast no evil before the people, little is accomplished by their admonitions and threats, and the people do not abjure their evil ways. It is possible to admonish and threaten only by casting a veil over certain things.[34] To him, therefore, who wishes to reach meaning through the outward word, the word will always be a source of error, leading him farther and farther astray, while conversely, to everyone who goes from the meaning to the word, the word will become a source of guidance, taking him closer and closer to his goal. That is, to him who by exercises and spiritual struggles, in association with wise men and by way of supersensory perception, perceives the meanings and essences of things, words in all their diverse usage will not be a cloak but, on the contrary, a source of greater knowledge. But he who goes from word to meaning, will perhaps take a single reality for ten things, he will splinter into multiplicity and fall into confusion; for a single reality he reads ten or more different names and then, because of the ten names, he erroneously construes them as ten different things. It goes without saying that such a man will never penetrate to the essence of any matter.[35]

Thus true religious knowledge is represented as requiring an identification of the human spirit with objective reality *(ḥaqīqat)*, and the psychic curriculum by which the mystic is distinguished from the ordinary believer becomes a sort of dam which, by preventing the psychic forces from flowing prematurely into the natural thought of

34 An example: Tanzīl, 120a 2 — 121b 2.
35 Kashf, 241b 13 — 242a 6. A similar passage in Tanzīl, 98a 6 — 98b 9 (second aṣl).

the theologians, makes possible an ascent to direct spiritual apperception.

This dam is an important element in Nasafī's thinking. Perhaps
we can arrive at a better understanding of it and thus of the relation
between esoteric and exoteric, by examining a parallel in the field of
zoology. Here the damming up refers to the metaphysical process
which, according to some zoologists, made possible the progression of
the animal species and particularly the leap from beast to man. The
various zoological classes are so specialized in their forms that a
development of the higher, i.e., more universal, forms from the lower
forms is, they say, inconceivable. The breakdown into individual
types must therefore have occurred "in the soul of nature," before the
types were physically manifested. Similarly, according to Nasafī,
esoteric knowledge did not arise through mere intensification and
extension of theological knowledge, but through a withdrawal of
forces and a rebirth out of the soul. But we must go still further.
According to the zoological theory we have described, man held himself in abeyance while the animals were advancing towards specializa-
tion and thus he accumulated a greater store of faculties. Similarly,
according to Nasafī, the esoteric seer held himself back, in order to
achieve a higher, more comprehensive knowledge, measured by which
the theologies are premature concretions, blind alleys, one-sided forms
of truth. Esoteric wisdom for Nasafī is the universal type of religion,
while the theologies are its variations.

Now we understand why Nasafī could not be content with any of
the various religious currents of Islam: Let that man confine himself
to a sectarian cult who cannot raise himself up to the higher unity in
which all such currents are reconciled! Viewed in the light of objective
truth, which esoteric wisdom aspires to represent, the conflict of
opinions must be considered a fight over nothing.

> The number of the different sects[36] [says Nasafī] is known to
> no one. And therefore, the origins of the sects are also un-
> known. But this much is certain: The source of their disparity
> is this: after men had heard through the prophets of a Lord
> over the things of existence, each man formed ideas concern-
> ing the essence and attributes of this Lord. When they ex-

36 Corr. *madhābib* and *rā* after *kasē*.

changed their ideas, each had a different conception. Each one found fault with the next, and began to advance proofs in support of his own view and in confutation of the opposing conception. In so doing, they all believed their proofs to be accurate and sound. But this very belief was a fallacy; for all men believe that *via rationis una* [i.e., that the truth is one]. How then, if the *via rationis* cannot be two, can seventy-three [the traditional number of Moslem sects] or even more beliefs all be sound?[37]

Thus, according to Nasafī, theologians (and exoteric thinkers in general) are men who have grasped only a part of the object of their study, and, not content with partial knowledge, have gone on to represent this part as the whole. Since the whole consists of different parts, the result is bound to be false and one-sided; and moreover, each result, according to the part on which it was based, is different and each contradicts the others. The battle of theological opinions can therefore be arbitrated only by one who knows the relation between the parts, and that is the esoteric seer who, by following the method indicated by Nasafī, has preserved or acquired an ability to see the whole. To elucidate this, Nasafī tells the familiar legend (of Buddhist origin) about the blind men and the elephant. The blind men, as might be expected, symbolize the theologians and exoteric thinkers, while the elephant represents God or the truth:

> Once there was a city, the inhabitants of which were all blind. They had heard of elephants and were curious to see [sic] one face to face. They were still full of this desire when one day a caravan arrived and camped outside the city. There was an elephant in the caravan. When the inhabitants of the city heard there was an elephant in the caravan, the wisest and most intelligent men of the city decided to go out and see the elephant. A number of them left the city and went to the place where the elephant was. One stretched out his hands, grasped the elephant's ear, and perceived something resembling a shield. This man decided that the elephant looked like a shield. Another stretched out his hands, grasped the elephant's trunk, and perceived something resembling a club [*'amūd*[38]]. This man decided that the elephant looked like a club. A third stretched out his hands, grasped the elephant's

37 Kashf, 230a 5 from below – 230b 4.
38 Fritz Wolff, *Glossar zu Firdosis Schahname* (Berlin, 1935), 596a.

leg, and perceived something like a pillar [*'imād*]. He decided
that the elephant looked like a pillar. A fourth stretched out
his hands, grasped the elephant's back, and perceived something like a seat [*takht*]. He decided that the elephant looked
like a seat. Delighted, they all returned to the city. After each
one had gone back to his quarter, the people asked: "Did you
see the elephant?" Each one answered yes. They asked: "What
does he look like? What kind of shape has he?" Then one man
in his quarter replied: "The elephant looks like a shield."
And the second man in the second quarter: "The elephant
looks like a club." The third man in the third quarter: "The
elephant looks like a pillar." And the fourth man in the
fourth quarter: "The elephant looks like a seat." And the
inhabitants of each quarter formed their opinion in accordance
with what they had heard.

Now when[39] the different conceptions came into contact
with one another, it became evident that they were contradictory. Each blind man found fault with the next, and began
to advance proofs in support of his own view and in confutation of the views of the others. They called these proofs
rational and scriptural proofs. One said: "It is written that
in war the elephant is sent out ahead of the army. Consequently the elephant must be a kind of shield." The second
said: "It is written that in war the elephant hurls himself at
the hostile army and that the hostile army is thereby shattered.
Consequently the elephant must be a kind of club." The third
said: "It is written that the elephant carries a weight of a
thousand men and more without effort. Consequently the elephant must be a kind of pillar." The fourth said: "It is
written that so and so many people can sit in comfort on an
elephant. Consequently the elephant must be a kind of seat."

Now you yourself consider [Nasafī continues] whether with
such proofs they can ever penetrate to the object of their
demonstrations, the elephant, and whether with such premises
they can ever arrive at the correct conclusion. Every rational
man knows that the more proofs of this sort they advance,
the farther they will be from knowledge of the elephant, that
they can never arrive at the object of their demonstrations,
the elephant, and consequently that the conflict in their
opinions will never be relieved, but will become more and
more pronounced.

But know this: Suppose by the grace of God one of them is

39 Add. *chūn*, after Tanzīl, 95b 6.

made seeing so that he perceives and knows the elephant as it really is, and says to them: "In what you have said of the elephant, you have indeed grasped some aspect of the elephant, but you do not know the rest. God has given me sight, I have seen and come to know the elephant as it really is." They will not even believe the seeing man, but will say: "You claim that God has given you sight, but that is only your imagination. Your brain is defective, and madness assails you. It is we who are the seeing." Only some few accept the word of the seer, for it is written in the Koran: "But few of my servants are the thankful" [Sura 34:13]. The others persist in their stupidity coupled with arrogance, refuse to be instructed, and call those among them who hear and accept the word of the seer, and who agree with the seer, unbelievers and heretics. But this only shows that "to hear about a thing is not the same as to see it for yourself."[40]

40 Kashf, 230b 6 – 231a 17. — The legend is related in almost literally the same version in Tanzīl, 95a 2 – 96b 7 (first aṣl), but with the difference that here the appearance of the seer is part of the legend and is narrated in the past: "But when by the grace of God, one among them had been made seeing, etc." The address to the reader interpolated before this passage is also present. But it should be remarked that in Tanzīl the legend is differently interpreted than in Kashf. In this version, surprisingly, blindness is related also to the esoteric: for just as the knowledge of the exoteric thinker can aways be extended by new insights, the knowledge of the esoteric seer can always be surpassed by higher knowledge. This interpretation is quite in keeping with the context in which the legend here appears, but conflicts with the intrinsic content of the legend. Nasafī's words are as follows: "This story refers to those men who, in dealing with the intelligible world, proceed by rational thought and demonstrations; for reason has different stages, and the wisdom that lies in things is infinite and unfathomable. But it applies also to those of supersensory perception and sight, in their dealing with the object of supersensory perception [makshūfāt]; for supersensory perception also has stages, and God's self-revelation in things is infinite and unfathomable. Of a hundred thousand who enter upon this path, one attains to the goal and experiences grace. All others remain at the way stations and take the way station for the goal." (Tanzīl, 96b 7–12.)

On the relation between Sufism and theology, I have noted also the following sentences [paraphrased—Ed.] from the "Fakhr us-sādāt" of Ḥusayn-i Ḥusaynī (d. 1318 A.D.), MS. Aya Sofya (Istanbul) 4133, 16b–17b: Originally, Sufi masters and theologians are one, but by the fact that the former purify their character and cleanse their innermost soul, they have a small headstart. The Sufi masters stand, in a manner of speaking, on the shoulders of the theologians. They have something to give the elite and not, like the theologians, merely something to give the crowd. In the gaining of "the knowledge that can be acquired" (ʿilm-i kasbī), Sufi and theologian stand at the same level, but through real emulation, through their vita purgativa, the Sufis distinguish themselves from the others (although among themselves they vary in progress) and attain to the "knowledge that is given" (ʿilm-i ʿātāʾi). They do not persevere in conflict over dogmatic questions and half truths; the overwhelming force of a raptus illorum raptuum Dei, qui

2. *Excursus: History of the Legend of the Blind Men and the Elephant*

According to T. W. Rhys Davids,[41] the legend of the Blind Men and the Elephant originated in the Pali "Udâna," a collection of Buddhist legends, constituting a part of the "Tripitaka" and apparently compiled in the second century B.C. This source has long been known to the Western world, particularly the Anglo-Saxon countries.[42]

In the cultural sphere of Islam, the legend appears to have been first taken up by Muḥammad al-Ghazzālī (d. 505 A.H./1111 A.D.) in his *Theology Revived*.[43] Ghazzālī cites the tale in a digression on the problem of human action, a problem in which the inadequacy of natural reason becomes most evident. He starts out by saying that the commission of an act through man requires certain conditions, the order of which was laid down by God. For example: a decision of the human will must always be preceded by a knowledge; the knowledge must be preceded by a being alive; and the being alive must be preceded by possession of a body *(qaḍā')*. And in each special case God predetermines whether (assuming all the requirements to be fulfilled) a projected action will or will not really be performed *(qadar)*. When a man does a thing, those who have only this world in mind would, it is true, say that he does it, but in the Koran it is written (and this is the truth) that God is the doer, and this causes great perplexity among those who sit in the midst of the world of concrete objects. There are some who postulate absolute compulsion *(jabr)*, others who

---

opus hominum et geniorum aequant, fires their endeavor to such a degree that they can never again return from the depth of the spirit ocean to the shore of appearances. A descent from the zenith of Being-with-God and of collectedness to the nadir of distraction and Separation-from-God must indeed be a mortal sin.

41 "Does Al Ghazzali Use an Indian Metaphor?," *Journal of the Royal Asiatic Society* (London), 1911, pp. 200–201.

42 A translation of the original text is to be found in Eugene W. Burlingame, *Buddhist Parables* (New Haven, 1922), pp. 75–77. (A free version in Swami Yatiswarananda, "Flüchtiger Blick auf religiöse Hindu-Symbolik in ihrer Beziehung zu geistigen Übungen und zur Höherentwicklung," *Eranos-Jahrbuch 1934,* pp. 492ff.) Helmuth von Glasenapp informs me that Zieseniss has written a monograph on the legend [subsequently published as "Zwei indische Lehrerzählungen in Islam," *Zeitschrift der deutschen morgenländischen Gesellschaft,* IC (1945–46), 267–73.—F. M.].

43 *Ihyā' 'ulūm ad-dīn* (Cairo, 1933), Vol. IV, p. 6, at the end of the section "Bayān wujūb at-tawba."

cling to the free autonomy of man *(ikhtirā')*, and a third group who take a middle position and say that the deed is "done" by God but "acquired" *(kasb)* by man. Ghazzālī now continues: "If the gates of heaven were opened to them and they could look into the supersensory world and the world of essence,[44] it would become evident to them that each of the theories is right in a certain sense, but all are inadequate. It would become clear that none of them had penetrated to the core of the matter and knew it fully, that the full truth can be known only if light streams in through a window opening out on the supersensory world."[45] Now, Ghazzālī goes on, it may be considered contradictory and unintelligible to say that all three assertions are right and yet wrong, but the truth of the matter may be shown by the story of the blind men and the elephant. By this story, he then sets out to show that a man may possess certain sound knowledge, and yet fall into error by representing the one part or aspect of a matter known to him as the whole and the exclusive truth. This is his version of the legend:

> A community of blind men once heard that an extraordinary beast called an elephant had been brought into the country. Since they did not know what it looked like and had never heard its name, they resolved to obtain a picture, and the knowledge they desired, by feeling the beast—the only possibility that was open to them! They went in search of the elephant, and when they had found it, they felt its body. One touched its leg, the other a tusk, the third an ear, and in the belief that they now knew the elephant, they returned home. But when they were questioned by the other blind men, their answers differed. The one who had felt the leg maintained that the elephant was nothing other than a pillar, extremely rough to the touch, and yet strangely soft. The one who had caught hold of the tusk denied this and described the elephant as hard and smooth, with nothing soft or rough about it, moreover the beast was by no means as stout as a pillar, but rather had the shape of a post ['amūd]. The third, who had held the ear in his hands, spoke: "By my faith, it is both soft and rough." Thus he agreed with one of the others, but went on to say: "Nevertheless, it is neither like a post nor a pillar, but

44 " 'Alam al-malakūt." With regard to its position in Ghazzālī, see A. J. Wensinck, *La Pensée de Ghazzali* (Paris, 1940), Ch. 3.
45 Iḥya', 4, 6, 18–20.

167

like a broad, thick piece of leather." Each was right in a certain sense, since each of them communicated that part of the elephant he had comprehended, but none was able to describe the elephant as it really was; for all three of them were unable to comprehend the entire form of the elephant.

The legend was also used by the Persian poet Sanā'i (died probably 545 A.H./1150 A.D.), also by way of illustrating the inadequacy of reason. But this time the truth to be revealed to the intellect is not a special but an absolute truth: God himself. If in the Koran and the sayings of Mohammed God is said to have hands and feet, if it is said that He descended, that He sits on a throne, that He has a face, etc., we should not let such expressions lead us to anthropomorphic conceptions, but must accept them as something alien to the reason, by faith. Discussions on the subject had always brought men into the situation of those blind men who could only comprehend a single part of the elephant, yet believed that they could determine the whole from that one part.[46]

> Men know not the Divine essence; into this subject the philosophers may not enter. . . .[47]
> Exalted be the name of Him who is exempt from "what" and "how"! The livers of the prophets have become blood! Reason is hamstrung by this saying; the sciences of the learned are folded up. All have come to acknowledge their weakness; woe to him who persists in his folly![48]

Mawlānā Jalāl ud-dīn-i Rūmī (d. 672 A.H./1273 A.D.) tells the story in his *Mathnawī*, but here the characters are no longer blind men. He likens those who cannot agree about the eternally immutable God, those in whom the spiritual eye has not yet awakened, to a group of people who seek out an elephant in a dark room and try to determine its appearance by feeling its body. As in Nasafī and the older authors, each one comes to a different conclusion, and again the difference in

46 John Stephenson, *The First Book of the Hadiqatu'l-Hiqīqat or The Enclosed Garden of the Truth of the Hakim Abu'l-Majd Majdud Sana'i of Ghazna* (Bibliotheca Indica, New Series No. 1272; Calcutta, 1911): Persian text, 8, 10 – 9, 22; translation, pp. 13–15.
47 Text 9, 10.
48 Text 9, 18–20. A metrical translation of Sanā'i's verses is to be found in Edward G. Browne, *A Literary History of Persia*, Vol. II (London, 1906), pp. 319f.

their statements is explained by the difference in the parts they touch, while the possibility of such error is ascribed to the absence of light.

> The elephant was in a dark house; some Hindus had brought it for exhibition.
> In order to see it, many people were going, every one, into that darkness.
> As seeing it with the eye was impossible, [each one] was feeling it in the dark with the palm of his hand.
> The hand of one fell on its trunk; he said: "This creature is like a water-pipe."
> The hand of another touched its ear: to him it appeared to be like a fan.
> Since another handled its leg, he said: "I found the elephant's shape to be like a pillar."
> Another laid his hand on its back: he said, "Truly, this elephant was like a throne."
> Similarly, whenever anyone heard [a description of the elephant], he understood [it only in respect of] the part that he had touched.
> On account of the [diverse] place [object] of view, their statements differed: one man titled it "dal," another "alif."[49]
> If there had been a candle in each one's hand, the difference would have gone out of their words.[50]

Confronted with the form of the elephant, the hand is groping and inadequate; equally imperfect is the sensory eye in the contemplation of God.

> O thou who hast gone to sleep in the body's boat, thou hast seen the water, [but] look on the Water of the water.
> The water hath a Water that is driving it; the Spirit hath a Spirit that is calling it.[51]

But since the words by which he, Mawlānā, strives to make this clear are inadequate, and the adequate word exists only in the transcendental world, it is difficult to communicate with men.

49 *Dal,* a crooked letter in the Arabic alphabet, and *alif,* a long, straight letter. The same contrast also in Asadi, *Garshāspnāma* (Teheran, 1317 A.H./1899 A.D.), §3, v. 16; Sultan Walad, *Waladnāma* (Teheran, 1315 A.H./1897 A.D.), 162, 13.
50 *The Mathnawi of Jalalu' ddin Rumi,* edited with critical notes, translation, and commentary by Reynold A. Nicholson, Vol. IV (Gibb Memorial New Series IV, London, 1930), Book 3, vv. 1259–68.
51 Ibid., vv. 1273–74.

This [manner of] speech, too, is imperfect and maimed; the
speech that is not imperfect is Yonder.

If he [the saint] speak from that [source], thy foot will stumble;
and if he speak naught of that, oh, alas for thee!

And if he speak in the likeness of a [material] form, thou wilt
stick to that form, O youth.

Thou art foot-bound on the earth, like grass: thou noddest thy
head at a [breath of] wind, [though thou art] without
certainty,

But thou hast no [spiritual] foot that thou shouldst make a
departure or perchance drag thy foot out of this mud.

How shouldst thou drag thy foot away? Thy life is from this
mud: 'tis mighty hard for this life of thine to go [on the Way
to God].

[But] when thou receivest life from God, O dependent one,[52]
then thou wilt become independent of the mud and wilt go
[aloft].

When the sucking [babe] is separated from its nurse, it becomes an eater of morsels and abandons her.

Thou, like seeds, art in bondage to the milk of earth: seek to
wean thyself by [partaking of] the spiritual food.

Drink the word of Wisdom, for it hath become a hidden
[veiled] light, O thou who art unable to receive the unveiled
Light,

To the end that thou mayst become able, O Soul, to receive
the Light, and that thou mayst behold without veils that
which [now] is hidden.

And traverse the sky like a star; nay, [that thou mayst] journey
unconditioned, without [any] sky.

['Twas] thus thou camest into being from non-existence. Say
now, how didst thou come? Thou camest drunken [uncon-
scious].

The ways of thy coming are not remembered by thee, but we
will recite to thee a hint [thereof].

Let thy mind go, and then be mindful! Close thine ear, and
then listen!

Nay, I will not tell [it], because thou still art unripe: thou
art in [thy] springtime, thou hast not seen [the month of]
Tamuz.[53]

52 Literally "rhyme letter" (rawī).
53 Mathnawi, tr. Nicholson, vv. 1277-92.

3. Nasafī's Monism

Concerning his own higher knowledge, Nasafī seems to cloak himself in silence. In the introduction to his encyclopedic work "Kashf ul-ḥaqā'iq" (The Unveiling of Realities), he writes:

> I have, as the dervishes desired, stated in each dissertation [of this work] first the view of the theologians, then of the philosophers, and finally of the monists. But in this book I have not set down my own opinion and my own point of view. And this because a man does not know everything; because it is not fitting for him to say everything he knows; and because it is not fitting for him to write everything he says. Of a hundred thousand men, there may be one who knows; of a hundred thousand things this man knows, there may be one that he should utter, and of a hundred thousand things he utters, there may be one that he should write. For what is written falls into the hands of the wrong as well as the right people, and may be read by the incompetent as well as the competent.[54]
>
> If my own opinion had been set down in this book, both friend and enemy might learn of it, both the competent and incompetent might read it. But the incompetent are forbidden to see the thoughts of the initiate ['azīzān], since the harm would be greater than the benefit, indeed there would only be harm. In olden days the initiate confided their secrets only to those among their associates whom they considered competent to receive them, and made them swear to disclose nothing, to keep the secrets hidden from the incompetent and unfit, and reveal them only to the competent and fit. And thus, since Mohammed, or indeed since Adam, everyone who has had knowledge of the essence of things obtained it through personal association with one who knew. Therefore he who seeks the mysteries and realities must make himself into a "man of personal association" [az ahl-i ṣuḥbat], and seek whatever he seeks in personal association; for from the book nothing emerges.[55]

By "mysteries" and "realities" Nasafī means not only the experience of evidence, but actual secret knowledge. This can be seen from certain hints which disclose a glimmer of this knowledge. In an earlier work, but also in the "Kashf," he reveals a strange theosophical

54 Kashf, 222b 15–22. 55 223b 5 from below – 224a 6.

conception, according to which the world passes through large and small cycles; each cycle culminates in a natural catastrophe followed by profound changes. The small cycles are of 1,000 to 7,000 years, while the large cycles number 49,000 (7 × 7,000) years. The 7,000-year cycle may be influenced by Saturn, by Jupiter, or most especially by the moon. Nasafī regarded his own period, the seventh century A.H. (thirteenth century A.D.), as a moon cycle, apparently constituting the last seventh of a large cycle. A moon cycle seems to be followed by a Saturn cycle. But Nasafī does not give a complete account.[56]

Perhaps the "Kashf ul-ḥaqāʿiq" will tell us something about the more philosophical aspect of his thinking. Is it not conceivable, is it not even probable, that Nasafī belonged to one of the four groups whose opinions he discusses—theologians, philosophers, believers in the transmigration of the soul (for these are also discussed), and monists—but that for the reason just given he does not identify his position? We cannot fail to notice the sympathy and emphasis with which he states the view of the monists. Not only does he take them up last, as though in conclusion, but in speaking of them he often introduces his remarks with the invocation "O dervish," thus entering into closer contact with the reader. Moreover, the sections on the monists are full of poetical quotations, apparently intended to spiritualize and transfigure the ideas here developed.[57] In this section he sometimes speaks of himself in illustrating an idea of the monists, and uses his first name: ʿAzīz.[58] Furthermore, he clearly reveals the limitations of theology and nonmonist mysticism;[59] he expressly rejects the theologians' view of heresy[60] and other conceptions of the theologians, philosophers, and grammarians,[61] but approves and recommends the attitude of the monists.[62] Once, at the end of a series of monist interpretations, he goes so far as to exclaim: "O dervish, the words that are said here are not all addressed to you. But soon men will come who will pay with their lives for every letter of this book."[63] All this would indicate that Nasafī secretly identified himself with monism.

---

56 Tanzīl, 136a. Kashf, 262a 18–19.
57 Particularly apt examples are the third risāla and 282a.
58 Kashf, 267a penult.; 285b 6ff.; 301a 3 from below ff.
59 253b 3–7.   60 226b 17–19.
61 237b 4–5. Another instance: 306b 5 from below ff.
62 280a 5ff., 288b 14ff.   63 249a 12–13.

And there is another reason for this assumption. In the introduction to the "Kashf" (in which he dissociates himself from the doctrines described in the book), Nasafī refers readers eager to know what the writer himself believes, to his earlier work: "Maqṣad-i aqṣā" (The Ultimate Goal). But if we consult the "Maqṣad," we find that there too—at least in the English paraphrase that is accessible to us[64]—he sets down the teachings of the Sufis and monists (ahl-i waḥdat), and does not speak in his own name. Although the accounts of monism in the two books are not in complete agreement, his reference to the "Maqṣad" does indirectly confirm his support of the monist trend and indicates that the monism in the "Kashf" is to be taken more or less as his own point of view.

But there are still other works at our disposal, above all, the "Tanzīl ul-arwāḥ" (Spirits Brought Down). Nowhere does Nasafī state that this work does not represent his opinion. And here again, though in a different way, he intimates that he himself is a monist. He even remarks that if, as in the "Tanzīl," he considers the problems of metaphysics from six different points of view, this does not imply that anyone should accept all six, or even that he should progress from the first to the sixth. The esoteric seer must, rather, espouse only one, but he must know the others, that is, he must have familiarized himself with their logic and arguments.[65] Applied to the "Kashf," which, despite the difference in its subject matter, follows the same method of examining each theme from different points of view, this principle would tend to support, if not actually prove, the hypothesis that one of the points of view described in the "Kashf" is that of Nasafī himself.

It should not be supposed, however, that a complete picture of Nasafī can be given by an account of his monism. What strikes me as perhaps even more characteristic of his thinking is that even where he is obviously not stating his own opinion, he tries to find some element of truth, some relation to the truth, and this endeavor is apparent in his treatment of each doctrine. In the "Kashf," for example, he does not attack theology, but compares it with other systems in such a way as to make the reader understand that it has its

64 E. H. Palmer, *Oriental Mysticism: A Treatise on the Sufistic and Unitarian Theosophy of the Persians* (2nd ed., London, 1938).
65 Tanzīl, 94b 5 – 95a 1.

justification but is too naïve for any radical inquiry and therefore obsolete. Similarly, the contradictions in the monist view which he leaves unresolved point to the existence of a still higher, third principle in which these contradictions are reconciled, and in which the deviations of the three other systems from monism as well as the inadequacies of monism itself are corrected. For a full understanding of Nasafī, we should have to examine his utterances from the vantage point of this third principle.

The supreme maxim of the monists as Nasafī sketches them is: there is but one being, and this being is identical with God. Their argument is as follows:

> If beside God's being there were something else, then God, with regard to being, would have His peers and a rival. He would have an opposite and an associate; but all thinkers and scholars are agreed that this is not the case. *Non habet oppositum nec simile neque aequale nec socium.* Moreover the two beings that would then exist would either have to be connected or separate. But as all thinkers and scholars agree,[66] God is connected with nothing and separate from nothing. The pluralists claim that the source of connection is substance and that God has no substance, so that, even if there is another being, this does not imply that God is connected with anything or separated from anything. In answer to this, it may be said that if substance were really the source of connection and separation, accident could be neither connected nor separate. If the source of connection and separation were accident, then substance could be neither connected nor separate. But in both there is connection and separation. Consequently there must be something that substance and accident have in common, and that is being.[67]
>
> If it is now clear that being is only one and cannot be two, it logically follows that being has no beginning and no end; for if it had, there would be two beings. Moreover, it must follow from this that what is can never not be and what is not can never be; otherwise we should again have two beings (to wit: the later and the earlier). Consequently, everything that is has always been, and everything that is not has never been and never will be.[68]

66 Text corrupt.
67 Kashf, 229b 4 from below – 230a 9; 282b 5 from below – 283a 9.
68 230 a 12–18.

Nasafī finds this view already expressed in the Islamic profession of faith:

> O dervish, if up to now you have not recognized the meaning of the profession of faith, if you have lived in folly, false conceptions, polytheism, and pluralism, believing that you had essence of your own, attributes, being and life of your own, and if despite your polytheism you thought yourself a believer in unity, it is now time that you rid yourself of false conceptions and of folly, that you free yourself of polytheism and pluralism, and correctly interpret the profession of faith. "There is no God but God" means "There is no being outside of God."[69]

This transformation of Islamic monotheism into philosophical monism immediately raises certain questions chiefly concerning the relation of being to the world of phenomena. Nasafī describes the various views of the monists (ahl-i waḥdat) side by side, with no expression of partisanship. He divides them (in accordance with his metaphor by which fire consumes being, while light bestows being) into two groups which he calls fire monists (aṣḥab-i nar) and light monists (aṣḥab-i nur). The fire monists are so called "because in each man who has arrived at this stage, folly and error [naṣb] are negated, and he himself is negated. For fire first consumes the thing in question and then consumes itself."[70] The light monists are so-called because "each man who has arrived at this stage knows that he will live forever. For light bestows being, while fire consumes being."[71] Or, to put it more clearly:

With regard to the relation between God's unique being and the world, the fire monists believe that the world, and they themselves, are nothing but idea (khayal) and appearance (numayish) with no more claim to reality than dream images or reflections in water or in a mirror, which have only an imaginary, figurative, shadowy existence. "True being, God's being," says Nasafī, "is a being that appears as nonbeing [nēst-numāy], but imaginary being, the being of the world, is a nonbeing that appears as being [hastnumāy]. The world is through God, God appears through the world. God is the reality of the world, the world is the form of God. There is not an atom in the world in which God is not present, for there cannot be idea without reality,

69 283a 12–16.   70 283a penult. – 283b 1.   71 285a 4–5.

or shadow without substance."[72] To make this clear, Nasafī likens God to the air, which according to natural scientists is also a being that appears as nonbeing, and the world to the reflection in the air, the mirage, which is a nonbeing that appears as being. "The mirage *is* through the air, and the air *appears* through the mirage. Air is the reality of the mirage and the mirage is the form of the air (the form in which the air becomes visible). God's being in the world [*ma'iyyat*] must be conceived as the presence of the air in the mirage."[73]

Another question concerns the concrete extent of the Maya which constitutes the world: where does true being begin? Here Nasafī distinguishes two subdivisions among the fire monists. For the first, necessary, unique being begins with the spirit world and God is merely the inner, spiritual core of the world; this group applies the metaphor of air and mirage to the duality of the spirit world and the corporeal world; the corporeal world is mere appearance while the spirit world is being.[74] But according to the second subdivision of the fire monists, neither the outer nor the inner world is God; for these two are opposed to one another, while God tolerates no opposition, and has no form. Consequently God is exalted above the spirit world as above the corporeal world, and since God alone is real, both corporeal world and spirit world are mere idea and appearance.[75]

From the fire monists with their doctrine of Maya, Nasafī distinguishes the light monists, whom we should call pantheists. They say:

> "Everything taken together is God's being; for there is only one being as such, since within being neither a duality nor a multiplicity with regard to being is possible. Since God alone and nothing else has being, everything that is, must necessarily be God. He is the first, He is the last, He is the outer and also the inner, He is the knowing and likewise He is the known."[76]

Therefore, this one being [says Nasafī] can, if you will, be

72 Tanzīl, 75a 4–10.
73 75a penult. – 75b 1. The names "fire monists" and "light monists" occur only in the "Kashf."
74 Kashf, 283b 1 – 284a 11. 'Abdullāh-i Anṣārī (d. 481 A.H./1088 A.D.) and Abu Ḥafṣ as-Suhrawardī (d. 632 A.H./1234 A.D.) are mentioned as adherents of this view. Nasafī claims to have encountered many supporters of this belief.
75 Kashf, 284a 11 – 284b 12. The "Sheikh of Sheikhs" (Ibn 'Arabī?) and the "Sheikhs of the West" are mentioned as adherents of this view. Nasafī also speaks of having met many of its supporters.
76 Kashf, 285a 9–13.

designated as world or as God, or it can be left undesignated, for it needs no name.[77]
Only forms and attributes of this being need names.[78]
If you shape a hundred things out of wax, with these hundred forms a hundred names will necessarily emerge, and for every name so and so many additional names. But the man of understanding knows that there is nothing but wax and that all these names refer to one and the same wax, which has taken different names from diverse aspects and points of view.[79]

Nasafī also divides the light monists into two subdivisions. It becomes evident that what he had in mind was not so much an historical inventory as a systematic picture of monistic thinking and its consequences. One of these subdivisions, like the first group of the fire monists, distinguishes two aspects of the world, an outer and an inner, but ascribes real being to both of them. The outward aspect, the corporeal world, is a world in itself, which in order to be, does not need the spirit world any more than the spirit world needs the corporeal world. But through the connection between the two—Nasafī emphasizes that it is no nominalist (ja'lī) connection but a bond of love (ittiṣāl-i 'ishqī)—children are born. These living creatures, if we understand correctly, are animated substance; and after the dissolution of the bond, i.e., at the death of each living creature, the spirit returns to the spirit world and the body to the corporeal world. But in this process only the bodies undergo change. The spirit world is a single spirit, which stands like a light behind the corporeal world and shines through each individual that is born as through a window. According to the nature and size of the window, more or less light shines into the world, but the light itself remains unchanged.[80]

From this group, which reminds us somewhat of Gustav Theodor Fechner, is distinguished a second subdivision of light monists, according to whom there is development in the spirit world as well as the corporeal world. Every existing thing, even the mineral, is endowed with spirit, and like corporeal substance this spirit develops through the stages of nature, plant, animal, man, to perfection, and then re-

77 Tanzīl, 77a ult. – 77b 2.   78 77b 5.
79 Kashf, 286a 14–17. The opposing views of the fire monists and the light monists are outlined briefly and in similar terms in an earlier passage, 262b 3 from bottom – 263a.
80 266b 11 – 267b 2.

turns from the summit in man to the mineral; this occurs once, twice, three times, and forever.[81] This seems, for Nasafī, to have been the outstanding form of monism, and it is to this form that he apparently gave the greatest measure of agreement and personal collaboration. In the following, we shall therefore concentrate on this second subdivision of the light monists.

For them, the world is God and its special name signifies only that it is also the form in which God is manifested. From this it follows, first, that the world cannot have come into being either by a sudden act of creation or by a slow development. For, according to Nasafī— and on this point all monists seem to agree[82]—if this were not so, God would at one time have been imperfect, achieving perfection only at a later date, and this is incompatible with the concept of God. Consequently, the hierarchy of the world structure, the scale of higher and lower forms of life, etc., cannot have been built up in a temporal sequence from above or below, but must always have existed, and merely represents the order in which absolute being appears to the senses. Being as a whole was never in a state of development, but only each "particular thing,"[83] each "part,"[84] each "substance,"[85] developed. Only the components of this being, not the being itself, migrate from mineral to man, etc.

> This being [says Nasafī] has two aspects, one from the standpoint of the parts, the other from the standpoint of the whole. If we contemplate the parts, we find multiplicity and imperfection inherent in them. Thus each separate part of this being is at its particular stage in a journey which continues forever. But if we contemplate the whole, unity and perfection are inherent in it. Thus everything that is (i.e., the sum of all things) has always been and will always be at the same stage as now, and it will always be in the same condition; for a whole is not otherwise conceivable, and perfection is not otherwise possible.[86] [This he illustrates by the following metaphor:]
> Consider a stream flowing in a circle; at various points in its circuit there are four pools [ḥawḍ] (to wit, the four realms of nature: mineral, plant, animal, man); each one of the four

81 Kashf, 267b 2–11.　　82 243a 4, from bottom – 243b from bottom.
83 244a 10ff (fard).　　84 244b 3ff (juzw).
85 Tanzīl, 99b 3 from bottom ff (jawhar).　　86 Kashf, 244b 2–7.

178

pools has in it a fixed quantity of water. . . . The quantity of water in each pool must always have existed and must continue forever to exist, although the parts of the water flow continuously from one to another; for while from one side the particular pool is emptied, from another it fills up again. Although constantly in flux, touching one pool after another and with each pool taking on a different form and name, the sum of the water in the four pools has always been and will always be.[87]

The number of individual things is, as this metaphor shows, immutable, and Nasafī knows exactly how many individuals occur at each stage of existence, that is, in each realm of nature. In view of the oriental tendency to exaggerate, his figures are astonishingly small. It therefore seems likely that they conceal mysteries which can be penetrated only through closer knowledge of the occult tradition of which Nasafī partook. Nasafī sets the number of mineral parts at 12,000, the number of plants at 8,000, of animals at 6,000, and of men at only 6,000. Altogether there are 30,000 parts distributed among the four realms of nature, or resting places. The caravan is continuously on the move from the resting place of the minerals to that of the plants, from the resting place of the plants to that of the animals, and further to the resting place of men, from which they turn back again to the resting place of the minerals, whence they repeat the journey, and so on to infinity.[88]

So far the cosmology of Nasafī, or of the monists, is relatively clear and simple. It becomes more complicated when the astronomical world is drawn into the picture. How is the world of the spheres connected with the circuit of the realms of nature and the hierarchy of appearances?

In Nasafī there is an intermingling of the most diverse views. Even if the addition of the spheres merely extends the circle in which, according to Nasafī, all earthly things move, the question of the starting point of this development is still unresolved, since a circle has no beginning. We may feel sure that this question was answered in many different ways. But another version placed the world of spheres outside of the earthly circuit (mineral, plant, animal, man), thus

87 244b 8–15.   88 245a 3–8.

creating two parallel realms. In this case the question arises: what is the connection between the two worlds?

a

Nasafī considers as typically monist the conception whereby the spheres constitute a parallel to the earthly realms of nature.[89] In this view, the nucleus and beginning of the world, including the spheres, is the earth substance (mineral), with which, by a kind of creationism which is not further explained, a "humor" *(ṭabīʿat)*, presumably dryness, is associated.[90] From this duality originate both the realms of nature and the spheres. In this connection Nasafī also refers to the earth substance as Eve and the "humor" as Adam, expressly stating that in this case Eve precedes Adam. A variant, in which spheres and realms of nature are likewise developed from a common fundament, has it that the first thing "to pass from the sea of potentiality to the mainland of actuality" is an original substance (which is not further defined); from this original substance emanate two seedlings, body and spirit. This of course is to be taken not in a temporal but in an ordinal sense.[91] It is this conception (since Nasafī particularly stresses[92] its universal validity) that, for simplicity's sake, we shall now develop.

According to this view, spirit and corporeity are both born of the original substance; in their primitive stage they are both, by a profound mystery, signed with the original words "water" *(m")* and "mother" *('mm)*.[93] These are the fundamental components of the world, from which not only the earthly realms of nature but the celestial spheres are composed. Each of them, however, breaks down into four parts—body into the four elements: fire, air, water, and earth; spirit into the four "humors": heat, cold, wetness, dryness. But, according to Nasafī, these never occur separately, i.e., heat never occurs without an admixture of cold, wetness, and dryness, fire never without

89 Kashf, 245b 1–19. 90 Ibid. 91 Tanzīl, 98b 9 – 101b 3.
92 105b 9–11. "All travelers of the path agree that concerning the existence of the world, its beginning and its end, it is as the second traveler of the path has said." The second traveler of the path has just developed this view.
93 99a 7–9: "The origin of the world of spirits was called water, in accordance with Sura 21:30: 'By means of water we give life to everything. Will they not then believe?' And the origin of the world of bodies was called mother, in accordance with Sura 13:39: 'What He pleaseth will God abrogate or confirm, for with Him is the mother of the book.'"

admixture of air, water, and earth, while spirit and body always cling together and hence even in the mineral a spirit belongs to a body, wetness to water, etc. Therefore, for simplicity's sake, he speaks mostly of the duality of spirit and body.[94] On the other hand, the manner in which the elements and humors are mixed is highly important for the classification of combinations. The more balanced the mixture, the higher stands the thing in question in the hierarchy. Nasafī now distinguishes combinations of body and spirit in which the mixtures of the elements and qualities are fully balanced and combinations in which only a certain degree of balance has been achieved. He finds complete balance in the spirit and body of the spheres. The balance of spirit and body in the minerals is at the opposite pole, that of the plants is halfway, and that of the animals, among which in this connection he counts men, approaches perfect balance. Since he regards the fully balanced mixtures as a special group, he arrives at two series: a perfectly balanced celestial series embracing the spheres of the moon, of Mercury, of Venus, of the sun, of Mars, of Jupiter, of Saturn, of the fixed stars, and of the sphere of spheres; and the earthly series of mineral, plant, man, in which the balance of mixtures is imperfect.[95]

In this conception, the most primitive phenomenon in the universe is the earth substance; the highest being on earth is man; and the pinnacle of the cosmos is the uppermost sphere. Nasafī brought the two series together in the earth substance, which he considered to be the original fundament [*Urgrund*] of both. Thus we have two divergent series emanating from the earth substance: the cosmic series consisting of earth, water, air, fire, the moon, Mercury, Venus, the sun, Mars, Jupiter, Saturn, the sphere of fixed stars, and the sphere of spheres; and the tellurian series consisting of mineral, plant, animal (including man).[96] Nasafī does not explicitly consider earth, water, air, and fire as a unit in the cosmic series, i.e., as the sphere of the earth, or as a sublunar world[97] (guided by the *intellectus agens);* but there is perhaps a suggestion of this arrangement in another passage when

94 Very unclearly stated in Tanzīl, 101b ult. – 102a 4. More clearly, Kashf, 267b 2 – 269a 4.
95 Tanzīl, 102a 8 – 103a 4; Kashf, 268a 2–14.
96 Kashf, 245b 5 from below – 246b 1.
97 A. M. Goichon, *La Philosophie d'Avicenne* (Paris, 1944), pp. 32, 41, 44ff.

he calls the uppermost sphere the tenth sphere,[98] for the number of ten can be arrived at only by reducing the four spheres of earth, water, air, and fire to a single, sublunar sphere, since we already have nine others: those of the moon, Mercury, Venus, the sun, Mars, Jupiter, Saturn, the fixed stars, and finally the sphere of spheres.

The conception of two divergent series originating in the earth substance is so strong in Nasafī that he does not hesitate to claim two different paths of perfection for spirit and body. One way leads them through the spheres, the other through the realms of nature. There are two poles of perfection: the spirit and body of the uppermost sphere; the intellect and body of man.

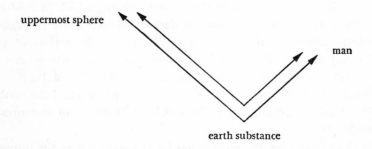

Nasafī tells us nothing more of the differentiation (*badal*,[99] *tabdīl*[100]) of the parts, that is, of the development of spirit and body through the spheres, but merely states that this development exerts an important nutritive force on the generation and progress of earthly forms, particularly of minerals. But he treats in detail the ascent of spirit and body through the realms of nature, giving particular emphasis to the transitions from one realm to another. The lowest plant form in the ascent of spirit and body is the water moss (*ṭiḥlib*),[101] the highest plant forms are the date palm, the mandrake,[102] and the legendary *waqwaq* tree, which, just as the mandrake has a man-shaped

98 Tanzīl, 128a 7 – 128b ult.   99 Kashf, 244a 3 from below.   100 245a 2.
101 "A green grass that grows in the water and, as all opinions agree, has no seed. In Transoxania it is called *chafn-rāwa* [not vocalized], in Fars it is called 'brooklet green' [*sabza-i jōy*]" (Kashf, 261a 17–19; Tanzīl, 133b 6). On this plant, see *Codex Vindobonensis sive . . . Muwaffak Heratensis Liber Fundamentorum Pharmacologiae*, ed. F. R. Seligmann (Vienna, 1859), s.v. *ṭuḥlub*.
102 Tanzīl, 133b 8. Corr. *luffah* instead of *tuffah*, "apple tree."

root, has fruits of human form.[103] The lowest animal is the long, thin red worm *(khirrāṭīn)* that is found in clay and in damp earth, then come gnats and flies, and so on up to the highest representatives of the animal kingdom, which are the elephant, the ape, and the legendary *nasnās,* which looks like a naked man, but has no intellective soul and hence does not speak. The lowest human type is the Negro, the highest the philosopher, the saint, and the prophet.[104]

The spirit that is never separate from body achieves greater differentiation with every realm of nature in which it is embodied. According to Nasafī's monists there are only three realms of nature: mineral, plant, and animal (including man); in the mineral stage, spirit is called natural property *(tabī'at)* (mythologically expressed as the four "angels of earth," the "angels of air, water, earth, and fire,"[105] a conception related to the Paracelsan elemental spirits); at the plant stage, it is called spirit, and at the animal stage reason.[106] The philosophers and believers in metempsychosis, Nasafī tells us, divide nature into four realms; but then spirit, or soul, begins only with plants and not with the minerals. In the plant the philosophers call it natural spirit, in the animal animal spirit, and in man soul spirit. The believers in metempsychosis speak of soul rather than spirit, and designate the three stages as natural soul, animal soul, and human soul. Man embodies all three varieties of spirit or soul,[107] natural spirit in his liver, i.e., on the right side, animal spirit in his heart, i.e., on the left side, and soul spirit in his brain.[108]

---

103 Kashf, 261a 3 from below. Cf. 261b 12ff.
104 Kashf, 261a 3 from below – 261b 8. Tanzīl, 133b 9 – 134a 6.
105 Kashf, 242b 4–5; 247b 2–5.   106 246a 12 – 246b 5.   107 257b 7 – 261b 12.
108 252a 12–14. Cf. 258a penult. – 258b 19 (paraphrased): Know that God has created four angels in the stomach: the attractive, the retentive, the digestive, and the repellent force. The philosophers call them forces, but the theologians call them angels. The stomach performs its functions with the help of these four angels. But these angels are also present and active in the liver, in the heart, in the brain and in all other organs. Not for a moment do they cease in their activity, and never are they weary or surfeited, not even in the future. When nutriment enters the stomach, where it is digested and distilled and turned to chyle, the liver absorbs the essence and extract of this nutriment through the mesentery. When it has then been digested and distilled a second time, and turned to chyle in the liver, the essence and extract becomes natural spirit and the residue becomes mucus, blood, yellow bile, and black bile. The natural spirit conveys these to their proper places. It is the distributor of nutriment in the body. From the liver, blood vessels lead to all the organs; they function as passages for nutriment and are called veins. But the heart attracts the essence

As the philosophers say, the soul spirit of man is capable of mirroring the souls of the spheres, and this defines man's position in the universe. We have heard that the body of the spheres differs fundamentally from that of the earthly realms by virtue of the balance in which its elements are mixed. But now we find that a closer bond and harmony with the spheres can be realized in the soul spirit. If by exercises and spiritual struggle man achieves the balance peculiar to the (corporeal) substantiality of the spheres, his soul spirit becomes receptive to the reflection of the souls of the spheres. And as the soul spirit achieves greater balance, becomes more transparent and mirrorlike, it reflects an ever higher sphere. The reflection of the souls of the spheres in man's soul spirit is called the human soul,[109] or the human spirit.[110]

This reflection is still perceived only by the so-called "common sense" that dwells in the soul spirit and also receives sensations from

and extract of the natural spirit. Here it is digested and distilled for a third time, and the essence and extract becomes animal spirit, which distributes the residue to the various organs. The animal spirit is the distributor of life in the body. From the heart, too, numerous blood vessels lead to all the organs. They serve as passages for life, and they are called arteries. But the essence and extract of the animal spirit is attracted by the brain, which digests and distills it a fourth time. The essence and extract of this process becomes soul spirit, which distributes the residue among the different organs. The soul spirit is the distributor of feeling and movement in the body. From the brain, nerves lead to all the organs, and these serve as passages for feeling and movement. (End of paraphrase.) Similarly Tanzīl, 112b ult. – 113b 2; here the natural spirit is called vegetative spirit.

109 Kashf, 257b 8–19: "Man has natural spirit, animal spirit and soul spirit. Thus far he resembles all animals. But he also has a human soul [nafs-i insānī]. This is the reflection [ʿaks] of the soul of the spheres, i.e., when the soul spirit that dwells in the brain of man comes to resemble [nazdīk shawad] the substantiality [jawhar] of the sphere, it reflects the soul of the sphere. . . . The corporeity of the spheres is neither hot nor cold, neither moist nor dry, neither heavy nor light. This is the meaning of balance [iʿtidāl] and uniformity [taswiya]. The more perfect uniformity the soul spirit attains through exercises and spiritual struggles, the more transparent and mirrorlike it becomes, the higher the sphere whose soul it is able to reflect. There can even be men whose soul spirit approaches the substantiality of the sphere of spheres and thus becomes receptive to the reflection of the sphere of spheres. The soul of the sphere of spheres, that is the all-soul, then becomes the soul of the man in question. . . . This human soul, that we have designated as the reflection of the soul of the sphere, is called also the emanation of the soul of the sphere. The believers in metempsychosis consider it only as emanation [fayḍ], not as reflection."
110 Tanzīl, 123b 8.

184

outside,[111] but man is now able to know more than the outward senses convey to him. For although the knowledge of the souls or spirits of the spheres is also not reality, according to Nasafī, but only a mirrored reality, it nevertheless is many times superior to the knowledge of the natural man, bound as it is to space and time.

> Everything that is present in the world of existent things [says Nasafī] is known by the spirits of the spheres, and the spirits of the spheres have knowledge of all existent things, indeed the spirits of the spheres have knowledge even of everything that is nonexistent or not yet present; for everything that will exist . . . as well as the supersensory is known to them. If a clean mirror is placed opposite them, everything that is in them is recreated in the mirror. This is what happens in the case of inspiration [ilhām].[112]
>
> Man has the power of raising himself to such a state that supersensory and sensory world become one for him, i.e., if by exercises and spiritual struggle a man makes his spirit so bright and radiant that it becomes a transparent mirror every image that is present in the spirits of the spheres is also present in his spirit, just as, when two clear mirrors are held facing one another, every image that appears in one also appears in the other and conversely.[113]

Here again, it goes without saying, speculative thinkers devised systems according to which man, with the knowledge of each new sphere that is mirrored in him, achieves a higher stage of inner development. We cannot treat this in detail, particularly as there is considerable inconsistency in Nasafī's classifications.[114] It may suffice

---

111 The soul spirit is the vehicle of feeling and movement, and as such is ascribed also to the animal.

112 Tanzīl, 126b 6 – ult. See my *Vom Wesen der islamischen Mystik* (Basel, 1943), pp. 31f., note 20.

113 Tanzīl, 126a ult. – 126b 6.

114 See, for example, in Kashf, 260a 3ff., a conception attributed to the philosophers, built on the concept of emanation rather than reflection: "The soul spirit that is in the brain becomes the lamp glass of the emanation of the soul of the moon sphere. The emanation [light in this instance] of the soul of the moon sphere becomes the lamp glass of the soul of the sphere of Mercury, etc." So that at each higher sphere the light of an earlier stage becomes a transparency, giving passage to a new light. But Nasafī's conception (in many respects unclear to me) that the soul spirit reflects the souls of the spheres is sometimes replaced or modified by other conceptions, as in Kashf, 260b 8–17: "He who by exercises and spiritual struggles frees and purifies himself of outer and inner bonds, re-

to note that when the spirit of the highest sphere is reflected in man, man's ascending development and with it the perfection of the tellurian series is concluded. God knows himself in the reflection of the spirit of the uppermost sphere and in the reflection of "man the perfecter" *(insān-i mukammil)*[115] and thus fulfills the purpose of creation—if it is permissible to use this term in connection with monism. Nasafī characterizes the mystical identity of the two summits of God's manifestation through a reference to the Koran, that is enchanting in its simplicity and profound as well: "Know that one name for the spirit of the uppermost sphere is The Compassionate (Raḥmān), and the corporeity of the uppermost sphere is the 'throne.' Upon it sits The Compassionate: 'The Compassionate sitteth on his throne' [Sura 20:5]. And a name of the spirit of man the perfecter

nounces and rids himself of [worldly] ties and obstacles, gains knowledge of everything that is to happen in the world before it happens. By exercises and spiritual struggles, the soul spirit achieves the balance that is peculiar to the corporeity [*jawhar*] of the sphere, and the intellective soul [*nafs-i nāṭiqa*] achieves the self-abnegation [*tajarrud*] and world renunciation [*inqiṭāʿ*] that is proper to the sphere of spheres. Through the correspondence that then arises between the intellective soul and the soul of the spheres, things pertaining to the soul of the sphere arise in the intellective soul, as though two polished mirrors were placed facing one another. What thus appears in the intellective soul is universal [*kullī*]. But though it appears *universaliter* in the intellective soul, the intellective soul conveys it *particulariter* [*ba-ṭarīq-i juzwī*] to the imagination [*mutakhayyila*]. From the imagination it then descends to the common sense, where it takes the form of a sensory perception. It makes no difference whether a thing enters into the common sense from outside or inside. Some have indeed called it common sense precisely because it perceives from two sides." Here the soul of the sphere is reflected not in the soul spirit but in the intellective soul of man. The former corresponds to the corporeity of the sphere.

115 Tanzīl, 123b 4ff. — The reading of *mkml* presents a certain difficulty. ʿAli Ḥusayn-i Kāshifī—*Rashaḥāt ʿayn il-ḥayāt* (lith.; Lucknow, 1905), 9, 4th line from bottom ff.—speaks of a man who, after achieving the stage of *kamāl u ikmāl*, began to educate the imperfect. Here we should have to read *mukmil*, and ibid. 12:9 we should similarly have to vocalize: *murshidī kāmil u mukmil*. On the other hand, in Shabistarī's "Gulshan i-raz," 169b 5 (MS. M III 45, Basel University Library), *sālik-i mukammal* rhymes with *awwal*, and this might appear to justify us in reading the passive form *mukammal*, "perfected," in Nasafī. In both Kashf, 254a 15 and the "Kitab Insān il-kāmil" (MS. Vienna No. 1952, Flugel's Catalog, 3, 431, note 1, line 7), Nasafī has the word pointed with double *m*, which makes the reading *mukmil* impossible or at least unlikely. But a passage in ʿAlāʾ ad-dawla as-Simnānī's "Safwat al-urwa" (MS. Laleli, Istanbul, 1432, 9a penult.), in which *al ʿārif al-mukammil* is expressly pointed with double *m*, taken in combination with the sense in which Nasafī used the word, makes it certain that *makammal* is also wrong and that the reading should actually be *mukammil*. Accordingly, E. H. Palmer in *Oriental Mysticism* (London, 1938), 11 ult., translates by "Perfecter."

is the Merciful (Raḥīm): 'Towards the faithful, compassionate, merciful' [Sura 9:129]. The body of man the perfecter is (likewise) the throne. On it sits the Merciful."[116]

Thus Nasafī makes the two names of God in the formula "In the name of God, the Compassionate, the Merciful" that precedes every Sura of the Koran, designations for two different persons, and detaches them from God. The result is something in the nature of a trinitarian creed, in which God, contrary to all conventional Islamic belief, becomes the "third of three," that is: absolute being. Raḥīm, the Merciful, essence and extract of the Little Man, might then be considered as the Son; Raḥmān, The Compassionate, the spirit of the sphere of spheres (essence and extract of the Big Man), might be likened to the Holy Ghost; and Allah, who, according to Nasafī, sits upon the two others, the ultimate stages of existence, which are his throne,[117] would be the Father.

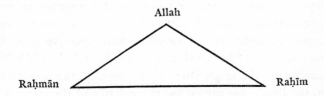

Nasafī of course does not employ this Christian formulation and does not clearly state the identity of the three persons. This is all the more understandable in that as a monist he attaches particular importance to differentiating the forms of being. But Nasafī's conception is nevertheless that man, by mystical growth into the knowledge of the All, ultimately arrives at a kind of coincidence with the All, and with God. All and Man the Perfecter are two all-embracing loci: the All in that it is nature, man in that he reflects this nature. And God is exalted above these two only to the extent that he is symbol and concept of their unity, wherein all antagonisms are resolved.

116 Tanzīl, 128b 4–8.
117 Tanzīl, 128b 8–10: "Raḥmān and Raḥīm which are the essence and extract of the Big Man and the Little Man, that are the ultimate things of existence and the end of all stages, are the throne of God, and upon this throne sits God."

b

This conception of God makes it understandable that Nasafī should also allow a different view of man's relation to the universe. Here man is not the terminal point of a parallel to the cosmos, but a kind of repetition on a small scale, a summary or copy of the cosmos; or conversely, the cosmos is an enlarged version of man. In this connection Nasafī calls the cosmos the Big Man and man himself the Little Man. Here we have no need to explain in what ways this conception contradicts, and in what ways it miraculously harmonizes with the other. It may suffice to state that Nasafī, with man as his point of departure, finds the following correspondences: The uppermost sphere, the sphere of spheres, which embraces all other spheres and thus the whole universe, is the skin of the Big Man. Nasafī likens the sphere below it, the sphere of the fixed stars, to head and feet; in the twelve signs of the zodiac he sees the twelve animal forces *(quwāy-i ḥayawānī)*: ten perceptive senses, that is, five inner and five outer senses (common sense, imagination, power of abstraction, memory, gift of combination[118]), and two motive senses (causative and executive force[119]). The other stars represent the vegetative forces *(quwāy-i nabātī)*.[120] The seven heavens are the seven viscera (the stomach, the duodenum, the jejunum, the ileum, the appendix, the colon, and the rectum),[121] the seven planets are the seven organs (brain, lungs, heart, liver, kidneys, bladder, and spleen), and the four elements are the four humors, etc.[122]

Man is a microcosm, a summary of the universe. Nasafī says:

> Being is formed [*muṣawwar*] and endowed with every form and quality that can exist, and in addition, with a form in which all forms and qualities are contained: man . . .
>
> O copy of the book of God that thou art,
> O mirror of royal beauty that thou art,

---

118 *Ḥiss-i mushtarak* (sensus communis), *khayāl* (virtus imaginativa), *wahm* (aestimativa), *ḥāfiza* (vis memorialis), *mutaṣarrifa* (the freely disposing = *mutafakkira* or *mutakhayyila*). Kashf, 258b ult. – 259a 11.

119 *Bāʿitha, Faʿila*—Kashf, 259a 6th from bottom.

120 *Cazwini's Kosmographie*, ed. Ferd. Wüstenfeld (Göttingen, 1849), Vol. I, pp. 245 and 356ff., lists the following vegetative forces: the attractive, retentive, digestive, repellent, and nutritive forces, and the forces of growth, reproduction, and form.

121 Ibid., p. 351.   122 Kashf, 248b 5 from bottom – 249a 4.

Whatever things there may be in the world, there is nothing
other than thou.
Whatever thou willst, demand it of thyself; for thou thyself
art that thing!

That is to say that although each of the various kinds of
existent things is a mirror, man is a mirror revealing the whole
universe; although each individual being in the existent world
is a goblet, the knowing man is the goblet that reveals the
whole cosmos.[123] Thus the knowing man is the union of all
stages (of being), the "great electuary" [ma'jūn-i akbar], the
goblet that reveals the world . . .

In quest of the goblet of Djam, I journeyed through the world.
Not one day did I sit down, and not one night did I give
myself to slumber,
When from the master I heard a description of the goblet of
Djam,
I knew that I myself was that goblet of Djam, revealing the
universe.[124]

Thus the whole universe is contained in the spirit of man, man
himself is a form of being, which in a small space corporeally and
spiritually resumes everything that the macrocosm displays in its vast
magnitudes, and also what it conceals. He is indeed the only form in
which Being, that is, God, has known and can know itself. "He who
says that the knowing man does not know God as He is, says that God
does not know Himself as He is."[125] Yet, Nasafī still considers it necessary to point out that all this does not imply an identity between
God and man.

O dervish, the house of God, Jerusalem, the Well-Appointed
House [in heaven], the Lotus Tree of the End, the Well-
preserved Tablet, the Great Throne, the Sublime Summit, are
all qualities and stages of man. Knowledge, Indifference,
Here, Hereafter, Paradise, Prophecy, Saintliness, are all qualities and stages of man. And the opposite: Ignorance, Satan,
Hell, the Lowest Depth, are all qualities and stages of man. It
is man who bears all these names. But, O Dervish, lest you
think falsely and fall from the zenith of faith in the one God
to the nadir of polytheism, and fall from the supreme summit

---

123 The Goblet of Djam: see my "Der Geistmensch bei dem persischen Dichter
'Aṭṭār," *Eranos-Jahrbuch 1945*, p. 300.
124 Kashf, 263b 6–15.   125 279b 18–20.

of unity to the lowest depth of multiplicity,—do not believe that the one being of which we have spoken is the being of man and that beside man there is nothing, for that would signify denial of God.[126]

But do not believe that God and man are both real; that would be to recognize two beings. O dervish, how often has it been said that there is only one being, God's being, and that everything else has no being! Thus man is only a form of this being. But this being has known itself in no other form, for knowledge has its seat in the heart, and the heart of Being is the knowing man, and in no mirror has it perfectly beheld itself except in this one; for man is a mirror that reveals the whole world.[127]

But this also eliminates the uppermost sphere as man's rival, and man alone becomes the quintessence and summit of creation. Here Nasafī calls him the "heart of existence" or the "fruit on the tree of existent things."[128] In this scheme, the uppermost sphere might be likened to the root of the tree; for now even the intelligences and souls (ʿuqūl, nufūs), the spheres and the stars (aflāk, anjum) seek their perfection in man.[129] "The aim of all things," says Nasafī, "is to attain to man. Once they have attained to man, the ascent [miʿrāj] of all things in the existent world is completed."[130] Here we no longer have two streams leading from earth substance to man and to the uppermost sphere, but only a single stream, which starts from the uppermost sphere, the original reason, descends to the earth by way of the spheres, and thence rises again to man, as the philosophers had already stated. "And so it is clear," says Nasafī, "that the ascent is in this world [īn ṭaraf]."[131]

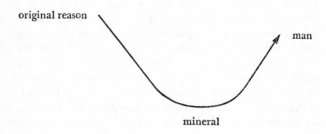

original reason

man

mineral

126 Kashf, 263b 15 – 264a 1.   127 264a 1–6.
128 248b 15–17.   129 279a ult.   130 279b 4–5.
131 279b 5. Nasafī also expresses this view in the "Maqṣad-i aqṣā."

c

How easy it is to pass from the first to the second conception becomes evident only when we have discovered their common fundament, which Nasafī does not disclose. But now, to find our way to a third conception which Nasafī also puts forward and which is no less different from the other two than the second is from the first, we must bear in mind a sense or feeling that seems to be inherent in the esoteric thinker. It is the sense of the middle, of centeredness. Through the revelations that come to him from his own inwardness, the esoteric seer regards himself, in a very different way from the exoteric thinker, as the objective center of the universe; and he can express this feeling in very diverse ways. He can do so through the conception by which man is the unique summit of the world of appearances; and it would not even be difficult to establish a connection between this sense of self and that other conception according to which there are two summits, man and the uppermost sphere; for in this conception not the sphere but man is the intruder, who sets himself beside the sphere. This fundamental esoteric mood becomes clearest however in the third conception of the monists, which like the others originated in exoteric thinking, but in this connection takes on an esoteric stamp. After listing the seven stages of spiritual and corporeal development from the element (mineral) through plant, animal, man, sphere of the planets, sphere of the fixed stars, to the sphere of spheres (here we have seven stages instead of the usual ten), Nasafī states that man occupies the fourth stage, which places him in the middle of the series. Developing this idea in meditations that are not fully intelligible from the context, he goes on to place man in the middle between reason and nature, light and darkness. Here the supralunar world is paradise, the sublunar world is hell; and man, who is composed of reason and nature, light and darkness, attains to bliss if he frees himself from nature and darkness and makes himself entirely into light; he succumbs to misery if he loses reason and light, and becomes all darkness. "Man has been called the 'heart of the world,' " says Nasafī, "because the heart is in the middle and has knowledge of all the parts, while the parts know nothing about the state of the heart."[132]

132 Kashf, 310b penult. – 311a 10.

And he continues:

> Now that you know that man is the fourth climate, know
> further that on the one side of man lie the climates of the
> angels, intelligences, and spirits, and on the other the climates
> of the devils, lusts, and humors. Thus it comes about that all
> are combined in man. That is to say, all the essences of these
> seven climates are combined in the fourth climate, man. For
> this reason there are three kinds of man. One kind inclines
> to the climates of the Devils, Lusts, and Humors. These are
> the "people of the left" and the dwellers in hell. Others incline
> towards the climates of the angels, intelligences, and spirits.
> These are the "people of the right" and the dwellers in para-
> dise. The third have progressed beyond the seven climates and
> attained to God. These are the "forerunners" and people of
> God. There are only these three kinds of men.[133]

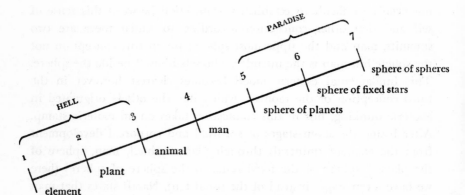

In this view, man is the middle rung of a ladder leading from
mineral through seven stages to the all-embracing sphere. Instead of
two divergents, earth-man and earth-cosmos, or an arc leading from
the uppermost sphere through the earth to man, we have here a
straight line, divided in two parts, with the realms of nature on the
left, the spheres on the right, and man at the center. Thus man is
placed at the middle point between two worlds, both of which stand
open to him. Perfection is sought in the upward (right) direction and
it is a regression for man to take the opposite direction, towards the
mineral. The lowest stage of the spirit, the humor or nature *(ṭabī'at)*

133 Kashf, 311a 10–18.

residing in the mineral, is then a diabolical form, contrasted with the human form, which is reason.

> Know, O dervish, [says Nasafī] that reason is in truth Gabriel [the divine intermediary of knowledge]; for through reason you possess knowledge. But reason is also Michael [the distributor of sustenance]; for through reason you obtain your sustenance. Reason is also Isrāfīl [who blows the trumpet at the Last Judgment]; for with one blast of the trumpet it causes you to die away from false conceptions and folly, and with another it makes you alive again by causing you to grasp the truth of things. And reason is Azrael [the Angel of Death]; for reason is a *Correptor spirituum* [*qābiḍ-i arwāḥ*]; whenever you know something as it really is, then you have grasped its spirit [or soul, *jān*]. — Know that reason is Adam, for it knows the names of things. . . . And nature [*ṭabi'at*] is the devil. For before the emergence of reason, nature is the chief of the angels, and all the angels stand under its command. But with the emergence of reason, nature is deposed from its command,[134] and all the angels fall down before Adam and obey reason, except for nature, which never submits to reason and never obeys reason. . . . Only the nature of some few submits to reason and obeys it, in accordance with the saying: "My Satan has become a Moslem through me." But, O dervish, between here, the aim and purpose which the prophets pursued, and there, the false conceptions and folly of men, ah, what endless darkness, what rolling, watery wastes, how many walls![135]
>
> O dervish, in the spiritual world as in the corporeal world, the angel is reason, and Satan is nature. When reason and nature were formed, the shape of Adam arose from them in the corporeal world. Thus Adam is composed of angel and Satan, i.e., of reason and nature. Consequently, each man in whom reason has the upper hand is an angel or even better than an angel, although he has human form, and each man in whom nature has the upper hand, is a Satan or a beast or even worse than the beasts.[136]

Thus the decision rests with man as to whether after death his soul will enter upon an ascending or descending transmigration; and according to Nasafī, the philosophers hint at this when they identify reason with Ṭūbā the Tree of Paradise and nature with Zaqqūm the

134 Corr. *sarwarī*.   135 Kashf, 247b ult. – 248a 14.   136 248b 1–6.

Tree of Hell. "The cultivation, indeed the setting and raising of this tree, lies entirely in your hand, for with every deed that goes out from you and that is done in reflection and rational thought, with every deed in which the lusting of the soul is repressed, you graft a branch to this Ṭūbā tree, or even plant a new tree of its kind."[137] Thus the ascending development of the forms of being, once they have reached man, are entrusted to his conscious guidance, and here Nasafī explains:

> Ascending transmigration [naskh] signifies that a thing casts off a form and assumes a new, higher form, as the part-soul first has the form of the elements, but casts it off and assumes the soul of the plant, then casts off the plant form and assumes the animal form, then casts this off and assumes the human form, and then casts off this form too, and assumes that of the angels. Descending transmigration [maskh] signifies that a thing casts off a form and assumes a new, lower[138] form, i.e., when the part-soul does not achieve its perfection at the human stage, it returns, after its separation from the human body, to the stage of the unreasoning beast,[139] reappearing [hashr] in the form of that animal whose character [ṣifat] predominated in it at the time of its separation. If thus, for example, the character of the ant or the mouse predominated, the soul reappears in the form of an ant or a mouse. But if the character of the dog or cat predominated, the soul reappears in the form of a dog or cat. If the character of the snake or scorpion predominated, the soul reappears in the form of a snake or scorpion. If the character of the cow or donkey predominated, the soul reappears in the form of a cow or donkey [etc.]. . . . From the animal stage it then goes back to the plant stage and from the plant stage to the mineral stage.[140] . . . Then it rises again by stages to the human stage. If again it fails to achieve its perfection . . . after its separation from the body it returns once again to the animal stage and by way of the plant stage to the mineral stage. Thus it goes up and down again until it achieves its perfection. But if it achieves its perfection, it is redeemed from this world of Becoming and Passing, from the world of natural properties and lusts, and attains to the world of permanence and steadfastness, the world of the intelligences and souls. Now if a man is knowing and righteous, he can attain to the stage of the

137 Kashf, 294b 16–19.   138 Read firōd.   139 Read ḥayawān.
140 Nasafī also says that the soul can migrate from a higher to a lower man, from a higher to a lower animal. Text corrupt.

All-soul and the All-reason, which are at the highest stage and constitute the highest summit, and thereby he can carry upwards with him all those who have adhered to him. But when a man is unknowing and unrighteous in the extreme, he can attain to the lowest level and the lowest depth, and he carries down with him all those who have adhered to him. This is the meaning of the words of the Koran: "One day we will gather the God-fearing before The Compassionate [*Rahmān*] . . . but the sinners we will drive unto Hell" [Sura 19:88–89].[141]

According to this version, the adversary of man is the natural property and thus a spirit in a primitive stage, and man's struggle takes place on the plane of the spirit, i.e., between spirit and spirit. Yet the other adversary, or the other aspect of the adversary, should not be forgotten. For to the extent that man's effort to overcome his "natural properties" can only be understood as an attempt to raise himself above the physical data, the old antagonism between spirit and body reappears. Instead of the "natural property," the body appears now as the darkness which must be overcome.

141 Tanzīl, 137b 1 – 138b 5. Text in many places corrupt. Tanzīl, 158a 9 – penult.: "Man is the producer of his own deeds, he is free [*mukhtār*] in bringing forth his deeds. He can bring forth good or evil according to his decision. If this were not so, the doer of good would not deserve reward and praise, and the doer of evil would not deserve punishment and blame, not now or ever." Later Nasafī states that not only the quality and possibilities, but also the functions of everything in the world are determined, but that man stands above this determination. Tanzīl, 159a 3 – 159b 10: "Earth cannot fulfill the function of water, nor water the function of earth. The almond tree cannot fulfill the function of the vine, nor the vine the function of the almond tree. The ass cannot fulfill the function of the horse, nor the horse the function of the ass. The eye cannot fulfill the function of the ear, nor the ear the function of the eye. The earth cannot fulfill the function of heaven, nor heaven the function of the earth. . . . Have you not recognized that each thing fulfills its fixed function, but that man can necessarily fulfill the function of all? Thus it comes about that although man is in outward form a man, in moral-spiritual structure [*ba-ma'nā*] he is sometimes an ant or a mouse, sometimes a wolf or a panther, or a demon and a Satan and other things as well. But he can also, outwardly as well as inwardly, be a man. Man in this sense is he whom all the things I have listed obey and follow, to whom they are all subject and submissive, before whom they all lie in the dust. He stands at the king stage and all other things are his subjects. . . . Only he who stands at this stage is really a man. He who does not attain to this stage is no man at all, but belongs rather among the brutes. . . . Thus man is defined in the sense that he can assume the qualities of every other creature and fulfill the functions of every other creature. According to whether he assumes the qualities of this or that creature, it is this or that creature that he becomes, even though outwardly he may have the form of a man."

Although man's body is [as] a substance without spirit and man's spirit is [as] a substance without body, the body is nevertheless *with* [*bā* = Arab. *ma'a*] the spirit and the spirit with the body, and although both spirit and body develop upwards by stages, and gradually attain to perfection, at the beginning the qualities and acts of the body have the upper hand, and the qualities and acts of the spirit are dominated, while at the end the qualities and acts of the spirit gain the upper hand and the qualities and acts of the body are dominated. To employ a metaphor, spirit and body are in the beginning as butter in milk and at the end as rider and mount. That is to say, in the beginning they are in one another, at the end they are with one another, in the beginning there is mixture, at the end contiguity. If butter is not separated from milk the spoiling of the milk results in the spoiling of the butter. . . . Thus all the exercises and spiritual struggles of the travelers of the path serve no other purpose than to separate the parts of light from the parts of darkness, in order that the light may become independent and solely dominant,[142] and that darkness may become the instrument of perfection and the implement[143] of its radiance; for darkness unifies light and is the reservoir of lights. O dear friend, men are differentiated in the beginning and also later, but the difference arises at first without conscious will and personal effort, but later by conscious will and effort. For that wherein men are differentiated in the beginning, is given them through inborn faculty, which is not subject to the free will; but later the difference is a result of their personal exertion and endeavor, both of which lie within the scope of man's free will. There are two kinds of faculty: the one is given to man at the very beginning, without conscious will and effort on the part of the child; this faculty is determined by time and place [of birth]; the other, later faculty, is acquired by conscious will and personal adaptation, it is a fruit of man's own exertion and endeavor.[144]

Thus if up to a certain degree man gives himself the impetus and direction towards perfection, this is understandable in the light of his nature as a self-conscious, rational being, who can choose one of two roads. But here we might ask: What of the mineral, plant and animal, who have no possibility of free decision, but apparently are subject

142 Corr. *mustabidd* for *mustabīd*.   143 Read *dast-afrāz*.
144 Tanzīl, 115b 1 – 116a 9. Text partly corrupt.

to compulsion? What manner of force is it that on the one hand enables man to ascend consciously, and on the other hand compels unfree nature to develop its aptitudes and to move always from the lower to the next higher form of existence, that transforms the lower plant into the higher, the higher plant into the animal, etc.? Nasafī designates this force reigning throughout nature as love. With Nasafī love is a broader concept than usual, more than a typically human striving, a quality of the whole cosmos by which each creature is oriented towards a goal and set in motion towards the achievement of this goal, not a cosmogonic eros to be sure, but a kind of libido, ὁρμή, a force of growth, which seizes upon each species or individual and guides its intrinsic predisposition to perfection, a dynamic entelechy. "O dear friend!" cries Nasafī—

> To travel the path is not an exclusively human thing. All the species of the existent world are journeying, to reach their goal and end. And the aim [nihāyat] of each thing is perfection, and the end [ghāyat] of all things is the human species, which is the perfection of the whole.[145] To their goal they journey in obedience and natural [ṭabī'ī] movement . . . but to their end they can also go against their will, in violent [qasrī] movement.[146] All things in the world of existence are on a journey to attain to their goal, and man too is on a journey. But the goal of man is maturity, his end freedom. The motive for the traveling of all these things is love ['ishq]. O dear friend, the seed of all plants and the sperm of all animals is filled with love, indeed all the parts of the world of existence are drunk with love; for if there were no love, the sphere would not turn, the plants would not grow, the animals would not be born. All are full of love for themselves, strive to behold themselves, desire to see themselves as they really are, and to disclose the beloved to the eyes of the lover.[147]

In man this striving toward perfection, toward his self, when it is a conscious discipline of moral self-perfection, is at the same time a striving toward God; and indeed this is quite consonant with monism,

---

145 Correction.

146 Cf. Kashf, 279b 8–10: "All things in the world of existence are commanded to ascend. . . . To their goal they go gladly and in natural motion, but to their end [ghāyat] they can go also against their will and in violent movement." This text makes it easy to correct the corrupt text in the Tanzīl passage.

147 Tanzīl, 143a 6 – 143b 5.

where man can become Raḥīm or with his perfect knowledge can be likened to the world-containing goblet of Djam. Only man, as Nasafī stresses, is capable of this striving: "Know that the striving for God is to be found in none of the species of the world of existence, excepting man; for only man is at the outset unrighteous and unknowing, and the striving for God is present only in a creature that is unrighteous and unknowing. Likewise, the knowledge of God is to be found in no species in the world of existence other than man; for when man attains to perfection, he becomes righteous and knowing, and the knowledge of God is possible only in one who is righteous and knowing."[148]

The question now arises: what is Nasafī's relation to nature worship? If, as the light monists maintain, the whole world is God, why should the worship of particular things be so contrary to reason?

Nasafī does not argue that man is then also God and therefore has no reason to worship any being that would be merely his equal. Instead, he elucidates the whole matter through the legend of the blind men. In the story, each blind man holds a part of the elephant in his hands but does not see the whole. Thus the veneration of things of the world is up to a certain point justified, but in so far as the part is represented as the whole, it is an error. Nasafī distinguishes three aspects of God: essence, countenance (or mode), and soul. The essence is the pure idea of God, the countenance is the form in which the idea is manifested, and the soul is both of these together. The point is elucidated by the example of water: the essence of water is for Nasafī water as such, the countenance or mode *(wajh)* of water is the common occurrence *('umūm)* of water in all plants, hence the presence of water in this or that form, and the soul *(nafs)* is the totality *(majmū')* of all water.

> With every plant one contemplates, one turns to the countenance [mode] of water. Know that it is likewise with the light of God; for God is the true light and there is no form in the world in[149] which the light of God is not present. But to see the being [*hastī*] of God's light is one thing, and to see the share in it [*'umūm*] that all things have in common is another, while to see the totality[150] of God's light is still another. God's

148 Kashf, 279b 14–18; Tanzīl, 144a 5–9.   149 Corr. *bā-ān* for *ba-ān*.
150 Corr. *majmū'* for *'umūm*.

being is tantamount to God's essence [*dhāt*], which has no need [*ghani*] of the world: "Verily God is rich enough to dispense with all creatures" [Sura 29:6]. The common presence of light in all things and the presence [*ma'iyyat*] of light in every particular form in the world is tantamount to the countenance (or mode) of God. And the totality is tantamount to God's soul. Whatever the form towards which man turns in the world, he has turned towards the countenance of God: "Whichever way ye turn, there is the countenance of God" [Sura 2:109]. . . . Thus each man who[151] has attained only to God's countenance and not to his essence is a polytheist, and each man who beyond His countenance (or mode) has attained to the essence, is a believer in one God. Thus he who worships everything worships, to be sure, nothing other than God, and he who turns towards everything turns only towards God. . . . But although all polytheists turned towards God's countenance and worshipped God,[152] they remained always fastened to a single countenance of God and turned their backs to the other countenances. But the recognition of particular countenances and the rejection of others was not pleasing to God. Therefore they were called away by the prophets from the circumscribed God [*ilāh-i maqayyad*] to the uncircumscribed God [*ilāh-i muṭlaq*], and instructed as follows: God is but one, and in all the things to which you have turned, you worship only the one God: "Maketh he the gods to be but one god? A strange thing forsooth is this!" [Sura 38:4]. It is a single light that has disclosed itself in the form of worshipped and worshipper, that has revealed itself in the form of believer and rejecter, of belief and unbelief, of the prophet and the congregation, of reward and punishment, of here and hereafter. It is impossible that a revelation of Him should not take some form. If He reveals himself in the form towards which a man has striven, that is the highest favor He can confer upon a man, as He did for example with Moses, and when He reveals himself to a man and discloses himself in this revelation, that is the highest grace He can show a man, as when, for example, He showed himself to Moses [?]. But there is no one at all to whom He has not disclosed himself, indeed all men are this disclosure, but to some He has made himself manifest, for others He has remained hidden. The miraculous part of all this is that when He manifests himself it is before himself, and when He hides himself it is from

---

151 Read *har ki* instead of *har yakē*.   152 Corr. *parastīdand* for *parastand*.

himself, and when He confers grace it is towards himself, and when He shows anger it is also towards himself, and when He sends an emissary He himself comes and stands before himself, and when He confers His faith He confers it[153] upon himself.[154]

Yet even if all the modes are taken together, the sum will not yet yield the being that Nasafī can worship as the Lord and the true object of worship.

Everything that is present in the world has three stages and two forms. The stages: essence [dhat], mode [wajh], soul [nafs] and the two forms: germ form[155] [jāmiʿa] and developed form [mutafarriqa]. For each thing must either have to develop all its inherencies in the future, so that they are present only potentially, as in the case of the egg, the sperm, the seed grain. This is the stage of so-called essence, its form is the so-called germ form. Or the thing has already exhausted the possibilities of its development, so that in it all is actually present, as in the case of the perfect man, the perfect tree.[156] This is the stage of the so-called mode, and its form is the so-called developed form. The unfolding [inbisāṭ] and extension [imtidād] of being beyond these stages is called the stage of the soul. By extension is meant the growth, the movement of the body; by unfolding is meant the diffusion of being, that is called soul. . . . The theologian calls this soul Lord [rabb], for the two words mean the same thing. That is the meaning of the saying: "He who knows himself (his soul) has known his Lord; he who knows the soul, has known the Lord." The stage of the soul that the theologian calls the Lord, stands above all stages, it is exalted above antagonisms and confrontations and free from figures and forms. Therefore men who are still bound to their senses and ideas have no access to this stage.[157]

But neither is the pure essence of God, here represented as the germ form, the true God. For to venerate an undeveloped form of

153 Read ba-khwad for waba-khwad. Perhaps more corrupt.
154 Tanzīl, 85b penult. – 87a 8. Text in many places corrupt. Compare also Sultan Walad (d. 712 A.H./1312 A.D.), "Rabābnāma," in A. Atesch and A. Tarzi, Farsca Grameri (Istanbul, 1942), Vol. I, p. 191.
155 Properly unifying form.   156 Might also be translated as "perfect plant."
157 Kashf, 237a 7 – 237b 3.

being as God would be to charge God with a former imperfection, and this, as we have seen, is unacceptable to Nasafī.

The monists never call God essence [*dhāt*], but only countenance < and > soul. For if they called Him essence, they would be saying that He had once been imperfect. But God has always been perfect and will always be perfect. Neither in the Koran nor in the sayings of Mohammed does the word essence [of God] occur. Each particle of this being rises out of the earth [*khāk*], attains to perfection[158] through the various stages, and then returns to the earth. Thus all these stages can be present in the particles. But the totality of this being, which with regard to being is a unique being and always at the stage of countenance, is without essence, because this being has always been thus and will always be thus, because it is, and never has been or will be a hair's breadth smaller or larger.[159]

No road leads from the particular things of existence to this being [Nasafī states emphatically], because the particular things of existence are themselves this being. If you do not understand this, know then that the relation of the particular things of existence to this being is a relation of breadth, not of length, i.e., the particular things of existence are to this being as the written letters are to the ink,[160] with the difference that the ink always exists before the particular letters that are written, while this being does not exist before the particular things of existence, for this being was never imperfect, but was perfect throughout its whole existence, and as long as it exists, it will remain perfect. Therefore it has been said: God has countenance and soul, but no essence. And that is why in the Koran as well as the sayings of Mohammed, the word essence [of God] nowhere occurs. Now since the ink existed before the written letters, the ink has the germ form and the written letters have the developed form; for ink is at the stage of essence and the written letters are at the stage of countenance. But the extension and development of the ink in these written letters represents the stage of the soul, and the theologian calls this soul Lord [*rabb*]; that is the meaning of the saying: "He who knows himself (his soul) has known his Lord." The lord of the microcosm is thus in one aspect sovereign [*rabb*], in another aspect subject [*marbūb*], in one

158 Corr. *wa ba-marātib ba-kamāl* for *ba-marātib wa ba-kamāl*.
159 Kashf, 238a 8–18.   160 Cf. Tanzīl, 106b–108b 6.

aspect Lord, in another aspect servant, in one aspect possessor, in another aspect possession. But the Lord of the macrocosm is in every aspect sovereign, lord, and possessor.[161]

Here Nasafī suggests that the right way to regard nature and universe is, not as an object of worship, but as a book of God. Nasafī compares the corporeal world with a Koran in which each genus is a Sura, each species a verse, and each individual thing a letter. The alternation of days and nights, the changes and variations "in horizons and souls," that is, in environment and feelings, are the inflective suffixes (*i'rāb*) of this book. Then he continues:

Each day destiny and the passage of time set this book before you, sura for sura, verse for verse, letter for letter, and read it to you . . . like one who sets a real book before you and reads it to you line for line, letter for letter, that you may learn the content of these lines and letters. This is the meaning of the words: "We will show them our signs in different countries and among themselves until it become plain to them that it is the truth" [Sura 41:53]. But what does it avail if you have no seeing eye and no hearing ear, i.e., no eye that sees things as they are, and no ear that hears things as they are? This is the meaning of the words: "They are like the brutes: yea, they go more astray: these are the heedless" [Sura 7:178]. O dervish, you must read this book. You do not read it because you have no eye for it. "It is not that . . . their eyes are blind, but the hearts in their breasts are blind" [Sura 22:45]. But if you yourself cannot read, then you must at least listen when someone reads to you, and accept what he reads. But you do not accept it because you have not the ear for it. "Who heareth the signs of God recited to him, and then, as though he heard them not, persisteth in proud disdain" [Sura 45:7], "as though his ears were heavy with deafness; announce to him therefore tidings of an afflictive punishment" [Sura 31:6]. . . . But he who finds for himself the eye of the eye and the ear of the ear, who transcends the world of creatures and attains to the world of the commandment [= the spiritual world], he obtains knowledge of the whole book in one moment, and he who has complete knowledge of the whole book, who frees his heart from this book, closes the book and sets it aside, he is like one who receives a book and reads it over and over until he fully knows its content;[162] such a man will close the book and set

161 Kashf, 286b 10 – 287a 2.   162 Text probably defective.

it aside. This is the sense of the words of the Koran: "On that day we will roll up the heaven as one rolleth up written scrolls" [Sura 21:104], and of that other passage: "And in his right hand shall the heavens be folded together" [Sura 39:67] whence it can be seen[163] that the "people of the left"[164] have no share in the folding together of the heavens.[165]

163 Text corrupt.   164 In this connection cf. p. 192.
165 Kashf, 309b penult.

Paul Masson-Oursel

1. The Indian Conception of Psychology

It is a common mistake to see our fellow men in our own image. There is no ground whatever for supposing that all mankind conceives the life of the mind in the same way as the European, and this has been particularly true since the sixteenth century, when we assumed the attitude which led us to construct the edifice of the "sciences."

The essence of this attitude is to recognize only "given" facts or phenomena, in the intention of determining their underlying laws. Since mathematics is the most satisfying of all the sciences, we have proceeded to formulate the concept of a mathematical physics as an objective study of nature. And parallel to this nature, we like to think of a kind of mental "nature," the knowledge of which would be the function of the psychologist.

The Orient, and most particularly India, has never known this curiosity about the "given," not to speak of our superstitious reverence for facts. The Indians have made no attempt to build up a natural science and have revealed even less interest in "psychology." But we shall here undertake to show that India has developed the most diverse attitudes towards the mind, and that such attitudes constitute psychologies.

Poetry, *kāvya*, and the other arts give a first example of psychology. The artist has experiences, less as a man than as an artist; he endeavors to communicate them through his talent. These experiences resemble love, terror, etc., but they transcend the love and terror of the common man; in so far as they belong to the realm of art, they exist outside of "nature." We are reminded of Diderot's saying that an actor should not entirely live his role, but play it, if he wishes to remain an actor. A poet, a musician, an architect, a sculptor, a painter, create works such as nature can never produce.

And there are other psychologies: Just as men can learn trades, they can be led into certain psychic channels by an apprenticeship, which the oriental serves with the gurus, pandits, yogis, etc. The Brahman religion, the teaching of which is a monopoly with the Brahmans, is a ritual technique. The revelation of the Upanishads postulates a gnosis, *jñāna,* in which the consciousness aspires to fuse with being itself and thus achieve perfect knowledge. This metaphysic has nothing in common with the artifices of the priest. The believer who in passive repose partakes *(bhakti)* of the anthropomorphic absolute confronts a different experience. And the ascetic in search of redemption enters upon yet another path. He begins by annulling that which is. How can he mold himself to Yoga since he is a living creature, impelled to the enjoyment of life? He must empty his thinking of its normal content. He may decide for the discipline of the Jaina or of the Buddhist. It may be his ambition to withdraw from the common conditions of human life, i.e., to renounce the action *(karman)* which chains him to the eternal servitude of transmigration. The Buddhist teaches that if a man extinguishes his accumulated acts and is careful to perform no new ones, he can evade spontaneous "nature"; but he must have understood that this nature itself was "a first habit," i.e., an attitude of servitude to enjoyment. Moreover, nature itself then appears as the outcome of a special, unconscious technique: the technique of egoistical desire, which engenders error.

Thus there are as many techniques as roads, while, on the other hand, there is no natural form of thinking that can be regarded as "necessary." Every man is free to choose among diverse psychologies, but one of them he is bound to accept, even if he lets himself be driven by life effortlessly and uncritically, for then, without knowing it, he follows the insidious and artificial—though spontaneous— technique of unconsidered enjoyment. But in so far as he is human, every man is highly pliable; by knowledge, tireless practice, and heroic self-mastery, he can cast off what he is by birth and become another.

If space permitted, a study of the psychological vocabulary of India might well indicate the heterogeneity of the various paths. From one philosophical system to another, from one religion to another, from one technical trade to another, the words for the essential psychological activities change. As we might expect, diverse roles are, for example, imputed to perception and memory. Yet it is noteworthy that the specialized technique of all the branches is designated by the same word: *pramāṇas,* sacrosanct rules, traditional with the group which practices them. The *pramāṇas* vary according to the aim which the group sets itself, but they are always *pramāṇas.* These canons are beyond a doubt the result of long gropings in the earliest times, but once established they prescribe a form for later experience. They are not conceived as valid a priori, like Kant's categories, but once accepted they govern with relative cogency.

I should like to venture the following comparison: With the same deck of cards we can play different games, each according to its established conventions. Each of these games has existed since the moment when its conditions and rules were established. These assure the player a certain emotional prospect—satisfaction or disappointment— and a certain psychological interest as well. There are as many types of experience as there are psychologies. The Indians play with the stakes of thought—and sometimes the game is tantamount to the loftiest speculations. They have the same approach to such adventures of the mind as to a handicraft; every discipline is similarly fixed by rules. The Indians are scholastics. Their technique of thought always retains something of the artisan's technique.

In India there is no such thing as what we call pure thought. In its stead we find the empty thought, the nonbeing of thought, towards which Yoga strives. What place would there be for a pure logic? Instead, there are relative and diverse logics, built upon *pramāṇas,* which in turn have reference to diverse theories of knowledge *(padārtha)* and other methods of discussion *(tarka).* There are several types of orthodox logic and many more heterodox types. Even within Buddhism we might find many. In short, there is no Indian thinking without rules which define its operations in advance—whether these operations are modest and simple, accessible to the most ignorant, or whether they are reserved for the metaphysical virtuosity of a Bodhisattva.

*

A study of the Chinese world would yield very similar findings. And an inquiry into the mentality of primitive peoples leads to the same inferences. What does this teach us? Have the orientals stopped half-way between the lower civilizations and positive thought? Do we think differently from them and should we consider ourselves fortunate in having assumed, in the structure of our scientific thought, an attitude different from theirs?

The Occident has a different conception of psychological phenomena. But why? Is it because we look upon mind, like nature, as an object of natural science, as a spiritual nature? But might this not be an illusion, a prejudice? What encourages this supposition is that even today, despite all our edifice of science, our behavior is not far different from that of the rest of the world.

Science is by no means "natural" to us. How much caution and critical thought we require in order to define and observe "objectivity"! Who among us practices pure thought? Only technical thought has produced results. We learn mathematical thinking in our scientific schools, juridical thought in our law schools, biological thinking at the Institut Pasteur, historical thinking at the École des chartes. Those who take up the study of logic learn that Aristotelian logic is merely the canon of noncontradiction, while logistics teaches that there are several logics. As for art, it has developed in the West as well as the East under the pressure first of a religious then of an aesthetic canon, and the old canons vanish only to make place for new ones which display their tyranny even before they have assumed fixed forms.

We like to believe in the existence of a reason which may pass for pure thought. But such a reason is more an ideal than a reality, and consubstantial with our "nature"; or else it gradually becomes a methodology underlying our diverse techniques: i.e., it is itself a technique. Those who fashion it in themselves by experience and reflection possess it, and nowhere does it exist in perfect form, as the ultimate formula for the intelligible.

In this respect occidental man remains comparable to the oriental. But in constructing the concept of psychological nature which is merely a copy of the physicomathematical nature, an abstraction of scientific thought, he appears to be the victim of an illusion which the thinkers of Asia have avoided. In any event, comparative psychology implies a critical approach to the concept of spirit.

2. Indian Techniques of Salvation

In our previous discussion we mentioned, among the many techniques of human thinking in general and Indian thinking in particular, the technique of salvation. This we shall now attempt to characterize.

The Indians have generally distinguished four modes of active behavior: *bhoga, artha, dharma, mokṣa.* The first of these words means the pursuit of pleasure; the second, the quest after gain; the third, a striving for harmony with the law, which embraces virtue, or moral worth, and the observance of religious ordinances. The last applies to redemption, i.e., more precisely, the technique of salvation. In our last year's lecture we pointed out that the millennium preceding the Christian era everywhere witnessed the emergence of doctrines which no longer, like the traditional ritual religions, aimed at acquiring the goods of this world through ritual actions, but at distilling and cultivating a spiritual principle capable of unfolding in another life. The mysteries of Egypt, Phrygia, Syria, and Greece; the reforms of Zoroaster, Jainism, and Buddhism, the revelations of the Upanishads, the religions of Jesus and of Mani: these are the most important among the techniques of salvation. Today we shall concern ourselves only with the Indian conceptions, particularly that of Mahayana Buddhism, and here too we shall limit ourselves to the bare essentials.

Enjoyment, gain, harmony with the religious laws—the Brahman law, for example—engender and store up *karma.* When a man has been sensual or egotistical, he burdens himself with sensuality or egotism. He becomes less worthy. When he has fulfilled the rites of orthodoxy, he burdens himself with merit: he becomes more worthy. In the latter case as in the former, he becomes ensnared in the eternal transmigration of the soul, for both moral and physical necessity requires that the worthy be rewarded and the guilty punished. Requital, good or bad, is always a bond, for it exacts an endless sequence of lives.

It was reserved for Buddhist insight to discern the servitude in good as in evil: to find egotism in traditional religion, in enjoyment and in gain. After it had recognized that a surrender to misery is inherent in each of these modes of conduct, it put forward the postulate that there must be a mode of conduct which is not subject to this oppressive fatality, for if this were not so, there would be no possibility of redemption.

To renounce all action: that was the solution found by the oldest Buddhism, that of the Lesser Vehicle. And indeed, if a man proceeds with the utmost circumspection—with clear insight and perfect self-mastery—he can expect his accumulated *karman* to exhaust itself, but he must take care that the store is not renewed by a continuance of self-seeking action. However, the steps by which this store is diminished require much time, numerous lives; asceticism to be sure accelerates the "ripening" of the seeds that sustain life, but not beyond a certain limit. Liberation by a gradual exclusion of the residue that oppresses us—and this is the only liberation implied in the *nirvāṇa* of earliest times—gives moreover a purely negative solution. This solution shuns any positive statement concerning the essence—if it is one—that is thus liberated. Might it not be, as the term "emptiness" would seem to indicate, a pure nothingness?

The liberation of a pure nothingness is no less absurd than its enslavement. The theoreticians of the Greater Vehicle knew that according to the teachings of the Brahman orthodoxy the object of liberation was a spiritual principle. The *ātman* of the Vedas, a slave where knowledge is relative, becomes free through perfect knowledge. Most of the *darśanas* assume, implicitly at least, the existence of a *vīrya;* of an essential efficacy, an οἰκεῖον ἔργον as it were, of this *puruṣa* which the Romans called *vir:* the act itself, the pure act of the spirit, which is very different from the activity in which it misunderstands itself and betrays its own essence; and this essential efficacy is never a source of misery. From all these considerations, the Buddhism of the Greater Vehicle draws its profit. Fundamentally, Buddhism excludes the substantiality of the spirit, not the spirit itself. It definitely does not negate life and its relativity; nor does it forbid the endeavor to work out a spiritual principle with the instruments provided by life—a principle that is spiritual because it is knowing and wise, but is nevertheless relative. The realization *(sādhanā)* of this principle is the goal of the magnificent ventures undertaken by the *yogācāras,* whose building of psychological worlds by the magic of thought approaches a systematic effort to create spirit.

The bold, ingenious, heroic initiations to which we refer begin only after the *nirvāṇa* of the narrow way has been attained; they are provisional and inadequate because they are negative. Since they begin only after the entire store of *karman* is exhausted, since they originate in an activity free from egotism, and beyond good and evil, they do not give rise to any new, enslaving *karman*. And yet they are activities in the truest sense of the word: activities devoid of all passion because they are free from all bonds. Moreover, they may be said to be actions which engender and create freedom. We no longer have to do with liberation, but with a fecund autonomy.

*

We shall better understand this pure act or spiritual freedom if, like the Indians, we envisage it through parallels with the highest creations of art.

The ancient languages of Asia have no word corresponding to our "art." Handicraft, from the humblest routine to the masterpiece, is a means of livelihood. The great artist may despise money, favor, fame; nevertheless he seeks to experience and to give pleasure. Whether poet, painter, or sculptor, he is, like the artisan, only a *śilpin,* who must work in accordance with the sacred norms. He would seem not to know the disinterestedness, the creation, to which the very great saints attain.

We find the pinnacles of what we call art in the religious life. In India and China, the most perfect works of painting and sculpture are monuments to Buddhist faith. Only under the impulsion of the highest spiritual vocation, and then only very exceptionally, has plastic creation freed itself from the schematism of the craft. But the highest religious creations, because they generate worlds in which the dialectic of concepts is complemented by sensory hallucinations in which sight, smell, hearing, and the tactile sense enjoy free play, can be likened to a complete art such as Richard Wagner saw in opera.

And it should not be argued that art aspires to please, whereas sanctity lies outside the realm of satisfaction. Although it is only the ignorant who confuse *nirvāṇa* with the prospect of a paradise, there is no doubt that it is conceived as inducing a beatitude, a state of contentment in which the spiritual principle flowers, and which in sculpture and painting is expressed by the ineffable smile of the Buddhas. Did not even orthodox Buddhism teach that the Living Redeemed One *(jīvanmukta)* attests his liberation by the radiations of euphoria: by *ānanda,* this ultimate grace of attained perfection? A thousand miles removed from sensual pleasure and self-seeking interest, which have been excluded or transcended, there still remains a *feeling,* sublime and transposed by perfect wisdom.

Thus that art which is most worthy of the name—an art such as that whose theory the German Romantics formulated—can help us to apprehend the meaning of religious ventures. The psychoanalytical conception of the nature of the artist confirms and clarifies this affinity. The projection of the work frees the mind for a time from the complexes which assailed it. Michelangelo analyzed himself in carrying out his commission in the Sistine Chapel. It is wrong to suppose that the value of art lies entirely in the work; even in the case of the eminent masterpiece, the art lies more in the mood than in the work. The true masterpiece is then the author. He is justified by the work. And that is what brings the titans of art so close to the Bodhisattvas.

*

By diverse ways we have arrived at this essential realization: beyond redemption, salvation embraces freedom. This excludes ontological realism. For if the function of the mind were merely to register a pre-existing objective reality, it would be condemned to an attitude of passivity. The mind would then have merely to know, but to do nothing. And if it is itself "essence," it need only know itself, and do nothing. For this reason the *sādhanās* were undertaken, not in Brahman realism, which believes in being and in the *ātman,* but in Buddhism, which rejects both. Even we Europeans—if as Christians we believe in the existence of a spiritual soul—are deterred by this belief from any strenuous effort to translate our spirituality into action. The Mahayanists and certain Tantrists endeavored, on the other hand, to carry out, with the sole instrumentality of a living body (which, to be sure, declines to "let itself live" and gives itself to an *"anti vita"),* vast programs of asceticism by which to create the spirit.

In reality there are two types of object or aim *(artha):* those which

211

are supposedly present or given, and those which exist only if we create them. The believer seeks his God and sometimes finds him—if this God exists. But the spiritual hero creates his God, who did not exist, and from himself he makes spirit, though he is nothing but life.

But let us not be dismayed; for even outside the sphere of sanctity there are men who do not await their destiny, but create it.

Ernesto Buonaiuti

Ecclesia Spiritualis

1. The Iranian, Greek, and Biblical Precursors of the Spiritual Church

As you know, I come from a country that is deeply enmeshed in traditions and memories; there is perhaps no other country on earth where traditions are preserved with such anxious solicitude. When I saunter out through the old Via di Porto, in Rome, past the ruins of Caesar's gardens, or when, not far from the Piazza Vittorio Emmanuele, I approach the ancient site of the gardens of Maecenas, I can sometimes almost see the poet Horace, making his way to the house of a friend or patron, or seeking to evade some unwelcome encounter. And when, as I look out into the plain beneath the present Villa Celimontana, the old Porta Capena arises in my mind's eye, and I seem to hear the voice of Juvenal, weaving his impressions of the turmoil of this poor quarter of the city into a satire. And again, as I descend the Colle Oppio and climb the Colle Celio, the present names of various streets bring me the echo of the old African quarter, which extended from the banks of the Tiber up to these hills. Whenever I walk through the Forum, I cannot help thinking that this ground which we tread today still conceals the old mortuaries, where the two great funeral rites of the aboriginal Italic peoples met, even before the first rectangular streets of Rome were laid on the Palatine: the rite of cremation and the rite of interment. When from the city as it stands today I travel northward, towards the old Etruscan centers, the entire region speaks to me of the ancient Central Italian culture that preceded the earliest history of Rome. And finally, when I turn southward, towards the foothills of the Apennines, to take part in the religious festivals of the modern descendants of the Hernicians,

Volscians, Sabines, and Pelignians, even today, at the very gates of Rome, I can observe, in religious rites and sacral usages, elements that carry me back thousands of years. Each year, on the day set aside by the Catholic Church for the festival of the Holy Trinity which, fluctuating with Easter, usually falls in the days between spring and summer, thousands of pilgrims from all the tributary valleys of the Simbrivio climb to the chapel situated in the mountain cleft known as the Tagliata del Monte Autore. Within this Christian chapel lies the ancient sanctuary which the earliest inhabitants dedicated to the numen of the distressed (Nume Indigete), which dwelt in the River Simbrivio. The votive offerings found near this holy site make it clear that a heathen cult was once practiced in this spot where the roads from the two slopes of the Apennines meet. And indeed, elements of the pre-Christian liturgy have survived in the ritual of the long and arduous pilgrimage to this shrine.

The pilgrims, arriving at the edge of the hallowed ground, must cross the Simbrivio at the point where it flows into the Aniene. Here they kneel down and cross the bridge backwards on their knees; in devout awe they throw stones to left and right over the parapet, raising their hands in so doing as if to exorcise the evil spirits which might be lurking in ambush at the entrance to this zone sacred to the deity. It may be presumed that these exact same motions were performed thousands of years ago by the old Italic tribes, summoned each year to the mountain heights to honor the tutelary deity who sent down the waters of the river to prosper the fields.

Human religiosity is nothing other than the performance of a number of "transitional rites" which serve to carry man unharmed through the most difficult and critical periods of transition. Primitive mankind was made up of wandering pilgrims, searching constantly for the safest and most fruitful stopping places. These pilgrims felt the need to take some measure against the obstacles that beset them in their slow progress, to seek some effective means of securing the benevolence of the forces dominant in nature. They followed the river valleys, sensing the risk involved in any deviation from their course, and thus they sought to avoid obstacles which it would have been hard to overcome. But as man very gradually passed from nomadic life to a settled existence and from the uncertainty of hunting and fishing to the most primitive forms of a sedentary agricultural life, the transitional rites ceased to consist in the magical exorcism of evil forces hidden in the earth and the mountains, and became symbolic actions connoting the admission of an individual into an alien clan, or his acceptance as a full member of his own clan.

A classical example of this second and higher stage of the transitional rites is circumcision. Thus the Yahwist writes, in the fourth chapter of Exodus (24–26 [A.V.[1]]): "And it came to pass by the way in the inn, that the Lord met him, and sought to kill him. Then Zipporah took a sharp stone, and cut off the foreskin of her son, and cast it at his feet, and said, Surely a bloody husband art thou to me. So he let him go: then she said, A bloody husband thou art, because of the circumcision." In its present form this story has of course been edited and reinterpreted, but it is not difficult to guess its original content and meaning.

The very fact that Zipporah used a stone to perform the bloody ritual act proves this to be an ancient rite, that originated in an age when the use of metal was still unknown. But the nature of the rite itself has undergone changes whose significance and purpose may be readily understood. It is quite evident that the myth was conceived by way of symbolizing the first meeting of Moses, who is assumed to be uncircumcised, with the God Yahweh. Yahweh is angry with Moses because Moses, though uncircumcised, is on the point of consummating his union with a Midianite woman, belonging to a clan which scrupulously observed the custom of circumcision. The woman intuitively realizes what must be done to conciliate Yahweh; with almost magical quickness she intervenes and circumcises her husband to save him from God's wrath. The final words of the story—"She said, A bloody husband thou art, because of the circumcision"—point clearly to the custom of circumcision as commonly administered to youths entering upon the age of puberty. It is Moses himself who is circumcised by his wife, and the version according to which the son of Moses is circumcised by his mother results evidently from a late interpretation. Actually Zipporah, by fastening her husband's bleed-

---

1 [Professor Buonaiuti was accustomed to making his own translations of Bible passages. For this volume, his scriptural quotations are given according to the Authorized Version, with occasional slight modifications to accord with his readings.—ED.]

ing foreskin to the image of Yahweh, succeeds in conciliating God and saving her husband from His anger, because by this barbaric, primitive procedure she has made Yahweh into her husband of the first night. And because by her magic act Zipporah had created this bond, Yahweh later reveals himself to Moses in the burning bush. This incident in the book of Exodus is our oldest record of the original character of the rite of circumcision, as the rite by which the youth on attaining puberty is admitted into the full life of his clan. This rite was indispensable for the admission of a foreigner into the clan; without it, his union with his young bride would offend God, who saw himself as linked by an exclusive and fearfully guarded bond with the clan that stood under His care and protection. Such is the original nature of circumcision. It is nothing other than an expression of the religious aspect of the collective consciousness of the clan, which feels the need of God's protection in the solemn, dramatic hour when its members progress from one physical stage of life to another. Up to this point the circumcision rite is of a primitive physiological-ethnical nature. During the wanderings of Israel, and up to the conquest of Canaan, warlike, aggressive implications seem inherent in the rite. In its period of victorious expansion, under the vigilant protection of Yahweh, the people of Israel had to husband its strength and required a rigid orthodoxy in order to keep its forces intact. But once it had settled in the land of Canaan, once it had achieved domination over the Canaanite tribes and established a unified kingdom, the people of Israel had no need to see anything more in circumcision than an official religious confirmation of its privileged position. Later, in the Greek cities, basic civic rights were conferred by official ceremony on those appointed to attend the public assemblies—and these assemblies always had a certain religious character.

When the people of Israel became accustomed to a sedentary life in the land of Canaan and began to incur that spiritual impoverishment which is a natural by-product of every politico-religious tradition, the stern, incisive voice of the prophets arose, striving to awaken the people from their state of spiritual torpor and indifference.

In the kingdoms of Judah and Israel there was an official school of prophecy, subservient to the wishes of the authorities. True prophecy however arose on the day when, under the pressure of the great empires in the northeast and southeast, the people of Israel came to recognize in its innermost consciousness the possibility of pursuing human ideals quite apart from any realistic political aims. The attitude of the prophets is altogether original in that it embraces both the spiritual and the moral quality of the Hebrew God and religion. And in this attitude there was something fundamental, destined to leave an eternal and ineradicable mark upon the whole religious development of the Mediterranean region. It is strange to note how the true prophetic message refers again and again to the experience of Israel as a nomadic people, when on its journey through the desert it was guided by the pillar of fire and by the living flame of its faith and hope in its God.

In invoking the rights of a tradition which they unconsciously idealized, the prophets called to life a spiritual religion in which inhered a presentiment of a better mankind and the awareness of a transcendent force that contributed to molding and realizing this better mankind on earth. The prophets were no philosophers. They were no thinkers. They were no socialist-tinged popular leaders. They were purely and exclusively idealists, stronger than all the contradictions of reality. Their calling was based upon an immoderately pessimistic conception of the world about them. This was first proclaimed by Amos, a shepherd of Tekoa, accustomed to the seasonal wanderings of the flocks between the Palestinian plateau and the banks of the Jordan. Before him, the "day of Yahweh" had been known as the day of His glorious apparition; it was the day on which God, with His whole people, triumphed over the enemies of Israel which were also His enemies. The evidence indicates that the usage did not have the universal significance ascribed to it by official exegesis up to the present time. It would seem rather that the formula originated in the liturgy of the great holy places where—no differently than in the temples of the Babylonians—the festival of the new year was celebrated with the enthronement of the god, a rite which was looked upon as the renewed consecration of his realm, both in nature and within the group of his devotees. Jerusalem had a festival of this sort. And Bethel is believed to have observed one of its own in honor of Yahweh the bull-god. Both festivals occurred in the autumn. It seems certain that, to the religious fervor of the faithful, the annual celebration of the return of Yahweh into his temple was a symbolic representation of the future triumph through which Yahweh would confer victory and prosperity on his people for all time. Thus it was a day of rejoicing, symbol and foretaste of an endless joy to come. It was on the very day of this annual festival that Amos came down from his plateau in the region of Jerusalem, appeared before the temple of Bethel, and uttered his words of menace and vengeance. For Amos the day of Yahweh was not a day of rejoicing and triumph, but a day of bitter punishment and devastation, because what Yahweh desired of his people was not ritual acts or outward obedience, but justice, peace, humanity, and brotherhood. The prophet was convinced that because Israel had favored outward piety over the repentance of the heart, a mightier people would come (here Amos is referring to the Assyrians) and banish the people of Israel from their land. According to Amos, Yahweh desired no other cult than social justice and simplicity of manners. Yahweh, the prophet proclaims, is weary of the elaborate feast days celebrated in his name, while the poor are oppressed and injustice prevails. Thus for him the practice of religion and the participation in the world of absolute values stood outside the customary sphere of cult observances. Foreshadowed is the conception, later clearly expressed in Jeremiah, that the original circumcision by which the sons of God are singled out and hallowed is not a circumcision of the flesh, but of the spirit. Thus, to be born in God constitutes an inner conversion. And this concept of a spiritual church runs through all the prophetic eloquence of Israel. In describing the trials reserved for Israel because of its recalcitrance against the true will of the Lord of Hosts, the prophets speak again and again of the "remnant," whose mission it will be to overcome these terrible trials by the true virtue that arises from the piety that is pleasing to God. This remnant is the spiritual church. And it is precisely through this remnant that Yahweh will restore the glory of Jacob and rebuild the tabernacle of David. This remnant, this spiritual church, will represent a bond between the original Israel, guided by Yahweh in the desert, and the new Israel which will have issued from the terrible trials of the day of justice and judgment.

Are ye not as children of the Ethiopians unto me, O children of Israel? saith the Lord. Have not I brought up Israel out of the land of Egypt? and the Philistines from Caphtor, and the Syrians from Kir? Behold, the eyes of the Lord God are upon the sinful kingdom, and I will destroy it from off the face of the earth; saving that I will not utterly destroy the house of Jacob, saith the Lord. For lo, I will command, and I will sift the house of Israel among all nations, like as corn is sifted in a sieve, yet shall not the least grain fall upon the earth. All the sinners of my people shall die by the sword, which say, The evil shall not overtake nor prevent us. In that day will I raise up the tabernacle of David that is fallen, and close up the breaches thereof; and I will raise up his ruins, and I will build it as in the days of old. [Amos 9:7–11.]

This conception of a last trial which awaits Israel in the development of its political destinies, but which at the same time will open up the way to a vast restoration of justice and peace, and extend to the hearts of the people of Israel the circumcision which they bear in their flesh, is increasingly stressed in the teachings of the prophets, so that at length it becomes not only the cornerstone of Judaistic eschatology, but the characteristic driving force of Christian eschatology as well. Jeremiah cries out (4:4): "Circumcise yourselves to the Lord, and take away the foreskins of your heart, ye men of Judah and inhabitants of Jerusalem: lest my fury come forth like fire, and burn that none can quench it, because of the evil of your doings." In the highest prophetic wisdom, as in Greek tragedy, the culminating motif is the idea that religious piety does not consist in obedience to outward laws, but in man's striving, through the alertness of his conscience, to live in accordance with the unwritten laws of revelation, which demand compassion towards his brothers and zeal in the search for the supreme divine values. Just as Heraclitus calls every man a barbarian who heeds only the testimony of his senses, to the exclusion of the divine harmonies which remain inaccessible to the corporeal ear, so Jeremiah makes his God utter an unmistakable threat against all those who are "circumcised and uncircumcised." And in this great category of the "circumcised and uncircumcised," the prophet includes without distinction "Egypt, and Judah, and Edom, and the children of Ammon, and Moab, and all that are in the utmost corners, that dwell in the wilderness: [and he adds:] For all these nations are uncircumcised, and all the house of Israel are uncircumcised in the heart" (9:26). And

219

in another passage: "To whom shall I speak, and give warning, that
they may hear? behold, their ear is uncircumcised, and they cannot
hearken; behold, the word of the Lord is unto them a reproach . . ."
(6:10).

To this people of the "circumcised and uncircumcised," Yahweh
proclaims through the mouth of the prophets, as later through the
mouth of Jesus, that salvation cannot be attained through outward
worship, that salvation is granted only to those who circumcise from
their hearts the foreskin of self-seeking, cruelty, and hatred. He who
in his innermost consciousness practices this higher form of circumcision, will enter into that remnant, that spiritual church, which is the
implement of God, with which He orders his household and carries
out his decisions with regard to the destiny of man.

None of the prophets sang the glory of this remnant more elo-
quently than Isaiah:

> And it shall come to pass, that he that is left in Zion, and he
> that remaineth in Jerusalem, shall be called holy, even every
> one that is written among the living in Jerusalem: When the
> Lord shall have washed away the filth of the daughters of
> Zion, and shall have purged the blood of Jerusalem from the
> midst thereof by the spirit of judgment, and by the spirit of
> burning [4:3-4].
> And it shall come to pass in that day, that the remnant of
> Israel, and such as are escaped of the house of Jacob, shall no
> more again stay upon him that smote them; but shall stay
> upon the Lord, the Holy One of Israel, in truth. The rem-
> nant shall return, even the remnant of Jacob, unto the mighty
> God. For though thy people Israel be as the sand of the
> sea, yet a remnant of them shall return. . . . [10:20-22.]

If there is any logical and intelligible reason for the inclusion in
the canonical book of Isaiah of that section which today we call
Deutero-Isaiah and ascribe to that great unknown who was the
prophet of exile, it consists in the extreme emphasis laid in Deutero-
Isaiah upon this supreme community of Yahweh, embracing all those
who are pure and upright on earth. "Hearken unto me, O house of
Jacob, and all the remnant of the house of Israel, which are borne by
me from the belly, which are carried from the womb: And even to
your old age I am he; and even to hoar hairs will I carry you; I have

made, and I will bear; even I will carry, and will deliver you" (46:3, 4). But the prophet who proclaimed these words of deliverance, who predicted this happy end for the remnant of Israel, had already conceived a universal vision of God's chosen people and the circumcision in the spirit. At this early date we perceive the conflict which for centuries would rend the very core of the Christian community, the conflict between a certainty that the circumcision of the spirit can only be the heritage of the few ("the salt of the earth") and an ardent desire to extend God's message of peace and salvation to all mankind. "Listen, O isles, unto me; and hearken, ye people, from far . . ." (49:1).

That the great poet who prophesied Israel's liberation from evil through the intervention of Cyrus, the Lord's anointed, foresaw the advent of a spiritual community which would mold its people in justice, in the circumcision of the spirit, and in universality, signifies that a strong revolutionary force had entered into the consciousness of Israel: this was the spirit of the teachings of Zoroaster.

Today no one can deny the influence of the Iranian cult of Zoroaster upon the postexilic Hebrew religion, and, more generally speaking, upon the whole development of spiritual life in the Mediterranean basin, from the end of the sixth century on. The Zoroastrian teachings would seem to have issued from an overwhelming need to discover sacred, eternal values amid the manifestations of empirical, worldly life. Embodying this need to distinguish the empirical from the superempirical, the profane from the sacred, the transient from the eternal, the relative from the absolute, the Zoroastrian religion, with its classical dualism, proved eminently suited to provide a theoretical justification for the earliest intimations of an *ecclesia spiritualis*. If the spiritual church represents a union of those who feel themselves bound together, not in the outward profession of a dogma and not in the practice of a physical rite, but in their awareness of a supramundane community of militants, into which one is received by virtue of a transcendent justice which surpasses all earthly frontiers, this vision must inevitably exact a dualistic view of the world.

Darkness veils the person of Zoroaster: the period he lived in, the circumstances of his life, the country of his origin, the region where he preached. And even the exact content of his message must be pieced together from records, which themselves represent the painstaking reconstruction of an old legend.

But if anything follows from all our protracted research into the later texts of the Avesta, it is the realization that Zoroaster transferred the center of religion to a realm distinct from any mythology or metaphysics: his religion is based upon the concept of being.

The religion of Zoroaster was the first among all the great reformed creeds to declare that the religious sentiment of the believer arises not from a theoretical contemplation of the primal sources of the world, but from a judgment concerning the ethical meaning of all that exists. The universe, or macrocosm, and the human heart, or microcosm, are, according to the Zoroastrian dualism, the arena of an open struggle between two transcendent realities. Ahura Mazda and Angra Mainyu are the two warring principles, and in their struggle is grounded the drama of cosmic life and human history. The one is the principle of light, truth, justice, and the good. The other is the principle of darkness, the lie, injustice, and evil. The battle between these two principles is finally decided through the victory of the good. But before the triumph of light over darkness is complete, the universe and mankind must pass through endless cycles of exhausting torment and untiring strife. Man in the world is confronted by the choice between these two principles; hence his life is the hard life of a warrior who must choose his banner. And since the conflict between the two principles is universal as to space and time, the choice which man must make is not differentiated and delimited by empirical boundary stones, but is a choice whose dividing lines lie in a supersensory sphere. Quite as a matter of course, those who are called to be followers of Ahura Mazda form among themselves bonds of spiritual solidarity having nothing to do with the empirical relations between them, with relations deriving from considerations of race, political allegiance, and social group.

In one of the main sections of the Avesta, we read: "The souls of the faithful of both sexes in the Aryan countries, the Turanian countries, the Sarmatian countries, the Synian countries, the Dacian countries, in all countries—all these do we venerate" (Yasht 13:143, 144).

One can conceive of no more explicit and succinct definition of a universal, religious community. All distinctions of race, caste, nationality, are done away with. A believer, wheresoever he be found, is an object of veneration, to be approached with a sense of deference which becomes second nature for all the community of faith and brotherhood in the grace of God. A "believer" in the Zoroastrian sense is one who, regardless of his political allegiance and earthly origin, has undertaken to be a warrior in the host of Ahura Mazda, in the pursuit of justice and peace. St. Paul goes no further in his Epistle to the Galatians when he proclaims (3:28) that in rebirth through the faith "there is neither Jew nor Greek . . . neither bond nor free . . . neither male nor female."

We have no knowledge of the channels by which the Zoroastrian teachings slowly descended to the shores of the Mediterranean where the ancient Greek colonists had established themselves. But unexpected developments may be assumed to have occurred in those profound strata of the collective unconscious where all significant spiritual fecundation takes place. The Ionian civilization and state of mind must have felt the fateful impact of the Iranian culture, when the empire of the Achaemenides established its great lines of communication between distant Susa and the Anatolian coast. Just as Iranian conceptions exerted a powerful influence on the postexilic Hebrew prophets, they may be presumed to have left an incalculable mark upon the Hellenic world. Just as Greece at a later day would subjugate her proud Roman conqueror, so Persia, though defeated at Marathon and Salamis, must have left a perceptible trace on the Hellenic world of the spirit.

And it is indeed true that immediately after the two great Athenian victories over the army and navy of the Persians, a vast transformation becomes apparent in Hellenic religious life. This was the great era of tragedy, so closely bound up with the Dionysian cult. And Dionysus, who plays a relatively minor role in the epics of Homer, now appears among the Olympian gods on the friezes of the Parthenon. Between these two dates the incursion of the Dionysian mysteries and the transformation of Greek religious life must be placed.

This transformation consists entirely in a sublimation and refinement of religious feeling transcending its old ethnicopolitical character.

The Dionysian cult, wherever it may have originated, represents the headlong incursion of a new mystical element into the traditional religion of the Hellenic world. The old gods of Olympus represented the epitome of material strength and warlike power. The Homeric mythology was nothing more than an anthropomorphism carried to its utmost possibilities. The Olympian gods are human beings, whose divinity is manifested in their power. The Dionysian religion is the religion of dreams and drunkenness, hence in a sense of physical weakness, corresponding to a predominance of the soul and the imagination. The religion of Dionysus developed with the spread of viticulture and is the religion of drunken unconsciousness. This loss of consciousness inevitably invites catastrophe. In the frenzy of her initiation, Agave does not realize that the trophy of victory she carries is the bleeding head of her son.

And yet, at a time in the spiritual development of the Mediterranean countries which cannot be determined but which was crucial none the less, this mad, licentious religion of intoxication—which, under the influence of Orpheus (a semimythical figure whom we cannot disengage from the shadow of his great legend), Euripides so masterfully represented in his spiritual testament the *Bacchae*—developed into a religion of sober drunkenness. It became a community of the intoxicated in the purest and most spiritual sense that can be ascribed to this word. The drunken adepts of Orphism resemble the Pythagoreans, intoxicated with music and contemplation. And the dualism of the Zoroastrian philosophy underlies the Orphic attitude. The empirical world is wretched, confused, tormented—it is what the Orphics and Pythagoreans called the "sphere of sensory existence." But through music, contemplation, love, man is given the possibility of liberating himself from the sphere of sensory experience and, thanks to his membership in the thiasos, of earning spiritual immortality even now. Thus the religious world of the Greeks became familiar with the concept of the spiritual community *(ecclesia spiritualis)*. The Orphics did not call the secret gatherings of their initiates *ecclesiai;* they preferred to use circumlocutions. We cannot determine exactly why, but such caution in the use of this word would seem to have a certain spiritual significance. In the everyday civic life of the Greeks, the word *"ecclesia"* was a technical term with a clear and simple meaning. The *ecclesia* was the assembly of the free citizens of a *polis,* summoned together by a herald to deal with affairs related to civic life. This word could not have been used for the members of a community of the elect without danger of grave misunderstandings. Moreover, the use of such a word would have suggested a certain parallelism between the civic *ecclesia* and the universalistic community of the elect, thus automatically bringing with it the danger of a relapse into the realm of the empirical and material, in which every political organism must operate. But once the *polis* had lost its position as a universal political organization to the Roman *oikoumene,* then the word *ecclesia* became suitable as a designation for the universal brotherhood of the reborn and renewed. It then became possible for St. Paul to call the thiasos of the believers in Christ an *ecclesia.*

But regardless of these distinctions in nomenclature, we can, without the least violence to the historical facts, recognize many forms of *ecclesia spiritualis* not only in the Orphic-Pythagorean communities but also in all other communities built on mystical religions. They all reveal the characteristic traits of that *ecclesia spiritualis* which has been the great historical reality throughout the centuries.

These are the communities and conclaves of men who recognize a solidarity unrelated to race, to nation, land, blood, politics, class, or caste; who, on the contrary, find the basis of their solidarity in a common belief in transcendental values and in their participation in divine grace. This enables them, even here on earth, to live the immortal life which constitutes the future triumph of beatitude and peace for the individual or the community. Thus in the course of the ascending development which marks the spiritual history of the Mediterranean world through the centuries, we have progressed from the transitional rite, which consecrated the dramatic moments in the primitive wanderings of the tribes and consecrated the admission of the individual into the full life of the clan, to the spiritual transitional rite, which consecrates a suprapolitical union, and makes the elect into instruments for the elevation of the civic community, to which from an empirical standpoint they belong, to a realm transcending political life.

Nowhere in history has this sublimation of transitional rites occurred without conflicts and upheavals.

There is an ancient Greek myth which gives magnificent expression to this gradual change in the forms of human society. It is the myth of Orestes. Orestes kills his mother in order to avenge his father. Clytemnestra, at the instigation of her lover, Aegisthus, has stabbed Agamemnon on his victorious return from Troy. Orestes is impelled to wreak vengeance. But precisely because he is the unconscious instrument of a nemesis that represents the ascent to higher forms of justice, the Areopagus acquits him. And in the temple, on the sacred hill of Athene, the Erinyes are transformed into Eumenides.

And in all history progress is signalized by matricide committed to avenge the murder of a father. Plato's predicament is that of Orestes. He kills his mother to avenge his father. His father is Socrates, his mother is Athens. Athens has killed Socrates. The universalistic and Orphic conception embodied in the Platonic Republic is the assassination of the Greek *polis*. Man arrives at the universal only through sacrifice of the particular. In Shakespeare's *Hamlet* a sublime and terrible matricide furthers the ends of justice.

But the myth of Orestes became a dramatic and terrible reality upon the day when a Hebrew of the Dispersion, Paul, killed the synagogue in order to avenge the death of his father, Christ, and in so doing, created the great, definitive *ecclesia spiritualis*.

2. The 'Ecclesia Spiritualis' through the Centuries

Even if the historian who deals with this second theme, "the destinies of the *ecclesia spiritualis* down through the ages," does no more than fulfill his proper function, the unearthing of data and facts, he must needs become a dramatist. For in the twenty centuries of Christian tradition, the history of the *ecclesia spiritualis* has been a continuous drama, both impassioned and sublime. It is the drama of the conflict in time between the irrepressible, forever-reborn striving towards spirituality, and the hard, unbending law of social life which imperiously calls forth dogmas, hierarchical doctrines, and juridical norms consonant with empirical and material phenomena.

It is possible that Jesus never uttered the Hebrew word *qahal* and the corresponding Aramaic term—words which the Greek translators commonly rendered by *ecclesia* and *synagoge*. Christ looked on his handful of disciples, not as an organized body, but as the little flock, the salt of the earth and the leaven of the world, elected to enter the future kingdom as a favored advance guard, which had been considered worthy of renunciation, suffering, and hope. In our canonical gospels the word *ecclesia* occurs only twice, in Matthew 16:18 and 18:17. And in these two passages it is not used in the same sense. The first, fundamental for the entire development of Christianity, is the well-known passage in which Christ appoints Peter to the leadership of the Church: "Thou art Peter, and upon this rock I will build my church." These words stand in strange contrast to the usual tenor of Christ's preachings in which he proclaims the approaching day of the Lord and sounds the call to repentance, i.e., a reversal of values, in order that man may be received into the kingdom. The idea that a long interval must precede the coming of the kingdom, and that this interval requires the foundation of a visible, hierarchically ordered church, is utterly alien to Christ's central thought. It is hard to say in what period and under the pressure of what circumstances a passage such as Matthew 16:18 can have found its way into the gospel text. There is good reason to think of it as a late interpolation. It may well be regarded, for example, as the expression of a reaction against the Marcionite spiritualism that throve at the end of the second century; and since this reaction appears to have been led by Hegesippus, who was active in Rome at the time of Bishop Eleutherius, it is not inconceivable that this passage, representing so unique a justification for the centralization of church power in Rome, actually was devised by Hegesippus. Eusebius tells us that he was highly proficient in Aramaic and made use of this knowledge to support the idea of an independent apostolic church. From the sources of Papias, it was well known that Matthew had originally written his gospel in Aramaic. Eusebius further tells us that Hegesippus had "borrowed various things from the Aramaic language." We may well be tempted to regard these vaguely mentioned "various things" as a reference to the pun on *Kephas,* Peter's Aramaic name, which the present version of the Gospel of Matthew places in the mouth of Jesus. The implication is that Hegesippus embellished the dialogue between Jesus and his disciples in Caesarea; that he put into the mouth of Jesus—and herein lies the special subtlety—a speech which in style deviated only imperceptibly from his authentic utterances, and which, at the end of the second century, could serve the Roman Church as authority for the position of pre-eminence it was even then beginning to assume over East and West alike. At an exceedingly critical moment in the development of church discipline, when the Marcionites were gaining in influence and the first indications of the Montanist crisis were already apparent, it must indeed have been taken as a stroke of rare good fortune that the learned pun of an Aramaist should provide a juridical basis for the power of Peter and his successors. The African members of the Roman congregation must have been amazed at such philological subtlety. And thus—perhaps—the words which one day were to appear in giant letters upon the majestic dome of St. Peter's originated in the learned gloss of a converted Hebrew, determined to introduce hierarchical and pontifical forms into the organism of the Christian church, in opposition to the spiritual anarchism of the Marcionites. How vastly these words were destined to prosper! So utterly devoid of logic, so infinitely romantic are the origins and pathways of human institutions in this world.

The other passage in which the word *ecclesia* appears, Matthew 18:17, would also seem to be apocryphal. In the preceding verses, Jesus declares: ". . . if thy brother shall trespass against thee, go and tell him his fault between thee and him alone: if he shall hear thee, thou hast gained thy brother. But if he will not hear thee, then take with thee one or two more, that in the mouth of two or three witnesses every word may be established." And if this too fail, Jesus concludes, "tell it unto the church [*ecclesia*]." This passage bears a clearly rabbinical character, in contrast to the directness and simplicity which distinguish the master's authentic utterances. Jesus opposes any recourse to the law courts. With gentle irony, he proposes that in case two brothers have quarreled and have set out to seek judgment from the court, they should stop along the way and try to come to terms, before incurring legal expenses that will be the ruin of them both. This passage in Matthew reflects a legalistic tendency, much purified and ennobled to be sure, which a copyist wishes to incorporate into the fervent Messianic message which is the true content of the gospel.

If the critical research of the last two centuries into those New Testament texts in which the earliest Christian teachings are set forth, has revealed anything at all, it is the strictly eschatological character of Jesus' message. This message is epitomized in these few words from the first chapter of Mark: "The time is fulfilled, and the kingdom of God is at hand: repent ye." And it may be a source of discomfiture to anxious, pusillanimous souls that this promise of a kingdom of God on earth, accompanied by a moral revolution, has been belied by time, that now, two thousand years later, the kingdom of God is still no more than a dream and a hope. Or, to put it more plainly, it may be a source of vexation to pseudoreligious souls, who presume that our frail and uncertain criteria of space and time can in any way bind or determine the judgment, the values, the promises of God. Miserable creatures that we are, forced by the ephemeral events of our lives into a schema of space and time, we are forever tempted to regard a promise which has not been confirmed by temporal events as an illusion if not a deception. God's guardianship and God's kingdom are close to us in so far as we yearn for them and dream of them. Oh if only our hearts' experience of the transcendent realities and absolute values, offered so abundantly in the revelation of the kingdom of God, might be strong enough to convince us that the kingdom of God stands at the portals of our corporeal and ethical life! The power of religious experience, one might paradoxically state, stands in direct proportion to the amount of illusion inherent in it. Any attempt to reduce the fervent yearning of religious enthusiasm to the level of everyday, empirical judgment is a reprehensible endeavor to force the divine into the narrow limits of a transient human perspective. And that is why a great religious thinker once said that Christianity has been fully lived only by Christ and the small group of his immediate successors, who went down from Galilee to Jerusalem in the certainty that God would soon establish his kingdom there.

It is true that this little band embodied the highest *ecclesia spiritualis* in history. Jesus was fully aware of this. When the Pharisees questioned him concerning the signs that would accompany the appearance of the kingdom of God on earth, he replied with a saying that might seem fearfully presumptuous had it not been uttered by Him: "The kingdom of God is in your midst." These famous words are ordinarily rendered as: "The kingdom of God is within you," but this version cannot possibly be accepted for the simple reason that Jesus is speaking to the Pharisees whom he consistently attacks for their falsity and hypocrisy and he is hardly likely to find the kingdom of God in souls sullied and benighted by the pretense of righteousness. Here Jesus means only to say that the kingdom of God is already present in the world of the Pharisees' false piety, because He has appeared who is to establish it, and who, with the small band of his faithful followers, is zealously preparing its coming.

But from this moment on, the *ecclesia spiritualis* bore within it the split which has made its historical development one continuous drama. For the *ecclesia spiritualis* is a spiritual community only in so far as it believes that everything unspiritual on earth is moving towards its decline and end. And accordingly, every delay and every obstacle standing in the way of the dissolution of the empirical world and the sudden manifestation of the beatific kingdom of God is at the same time an obstacle in the path of the inviolate and immaculate spiritual church itself.

Christ never spoke of a church. St. Paul, who made of Christ the innermost driving force of his experience and his teachings, was the founder of Christian ecclesiology. The congregations he established were churches. He looked upon himself as a messenger whose mission it was to summon together those whom God had elected to be free citizens in the new spiritual *polis,* those elected to deal in the great mysteries of revelation, grace, and salvation. And he saw all the congregations which he founded in the course of his untiring apostolic service as united and welded together in a single spiritual church, destined to spread over the whole known world. This organic conception of the community of the faithful is mystical through and through. The church praised by St. Paul is really an *ecclesia spiritualis,* because in its totality it represents nothing other than the mystical body of Christ, arduously built up everywhere by the successive generations of the baptized. Therefore St. Paul's vast historical vision of a spiritual organization to be founded anew each day, thanks to the union of its converts into a single body, which is at once visible and invisible. With these two adjectives we have indicated the coefficient which makes the uninterrupted development of the *ecclesia* an everlasting drama.

As a gospel of inner redemption and of union in a mystical body symbolizing the community of the kingdom of God on earth, Christianity in its earthly course is at the same time a summons to an aristocratic form of higher spiritual life and a message of universal salvation. Jesus desired his disciples to be the salt of the earth, the leaven of the world, the light in the darkness. A very pessimistic attitude towards life underlies these various comparisons: human life is a richly laid table upon which the salt is lacking, it is a vast field of darkness needful of a ray of light, it is a formless mass of dough requiring leaven. Light, leaven, salt—all symbolize a small group of men, whose mission it is to lend savor to a food that would otherwise be insipid, to carry light into a realm of darkness, to raise up a mess of dough which would otherwise rot and decompose. But side by side with this pessimism, Christianity envisages unlimited fields of conquest; for if the Christians had expected to remain an isolated minority, they would not have been Christians, since the sentiment of universal brotherhood is implicit in Christianity. Here we have the insoluble paradox which lies at the very root of the dialectic of Christian history, a paradox which can be resolved only through the divine gift which the religious soul calls grace. And in order to grasp the full import of this Christian paradox, one must bear in mind that an *ecclesia spiritualis*—a spiritual community—gains in spirituality only in so far as it presses towards a universality of the spirit, towards an all-embracing brotherhood.

It was from this need of universality that Christian propaganda embarked on its journey into the world. Not to have done so would have meant disloyalty to its mission. Once Christianity had begun its march of world conquest, it had to build up an organized apparatus, for while it is possible for small groups of enthusiasts and mystics to live in the dreamland of a universal metamorphosis which they look upon as accomplished, while they may dwell in an other-worldly kingdom of God, it is technically impossible to establish and maintain a large and far-flung body of believers without drawing upon confessional and disciplinary forms which, because of their self-imposed conceptual limitations, represent a weakening of spirituality.

As soon as we leave the world of the New Testament, we find human speculation and hierarchic forms laying hands on the Christian message. Even St. Paul, despite the burning zeal with which he believed in the imminent kingdom of God and the inviolability of the mystical body of Christ as it is constituted in history, was on several occasions

231

driven to theological speculations which are not without an admixture of rabbinicism, and to disciplinary measures which might well have found support among the authorities of the Sanhedrin. The post-apostolic congregations entered resolutely upon the path which had been imposed on St. Paul by the requirements of a large-scale propaganda.

The documents of what we call post-apostolic literature, which form a unified corpus even though we cannot fit them into any clearcut scheme on the basis of their dates and local origins, show us the Christian mind, at the close of the first and the beginning of the second century, endeavoring to translate the Christian message into generally intelligible terms, often with the help of intensive exegetic elaboration. Once it enters upon its career of outward growth and expansion, the *ecclesia spiritualis* of Jesus and St. Paul becomes inwardly deformed and impoverished.

The decline is so rapid and so profound, that as early as the second century we find innumerable groups making desperate efforts to preserve the *ecclesia spiritualis* as the higher aristocratic repository of the Christian message. Orthodox Christians called these men heretics.

Gnosticism, Marcionism, Montanism—the three great "heretical" movements of the second century—are all attempts to defend the *ecclesia spiritualis* against the forces of profanation which menaced its innermost being.

For the Gnostics the church was a "pleromatic" edifice which had existed before its appearance on earth in the unknowable eternity of God the Father. The *syzygiai* into which the Gnostics, by a progressive process of division, break down the pleromatic world, include "church and man," pointing, it would seem, to the eternal, primeval mystery of the union between man and the church. The church is regarded as the synthesis and symbol and fulfillment of everything that is most spiritual and most rare in the essence of a creation endowed with reason.

Marcion wished to cut every possible bond between the Old Testament regime—of violence, legalistic justice, canonical doctrine, hierarchical forms—and the New Testament world of the good God, who administers no punishments, imposes no laws, recognizes no hierarchy, whose only laws are grace, renunciation, forgiveness, and love. Montanism, which originated in distant Phrygia, proclaimed throughout Christendom, then rapidly spreading out along the Mediterranean coasts, the coming of the Paraclete who to the early Christian mind was the herald of the coming kingdom of God.

Amid these heretical currents, the *ecclesia spiritualis*, the church willed of Christ, defended itself against the snares and pitfalls of a nascent secularization. But—and is this not a play within the play?—these same heretical movements, which aimed more or less consciously at the defense of the spirituality of the mystical body of Christ, were compelled by their own propagandistic activity to take up the very weapons employed by the empirical, material, hierarchical church in its struggle against the spiritual church.

In order to prove that the spiritual church had existed even before the beginning of time, the Gnostics had recourse to speculations concerning the origin of the world, which made up the principal part of their higher religious gnosis. At the same time, in order to envelop their believers in a cloud of transcendent mysteries, they created the doctrine of the sacraments, intended to set their seal of consecration upon every significant act and every important step in life.

In order to oppose everything in the Christian teachings of their time that struck him as a Judaistic survival, Marcion undertook a massive revision of the gospels and the writings of the apostles.

In order to support the infallibility of prophetic inspiration and the sure coming of the Messiah, Montanus and his supporters were forced to engage in philosophical and juridical inquiries into the nature of God and of God's conduct of history.

In this way the so-called heretics provided the orthodox church with excellent weapons and lent *de facto* support to its religious speculations and hierarchical doctrines.

The orthodox doctrines of the creation took the wind out of the sails of the Gnostic speculations. The church doctrine of the sacraments is merely an emended version of the Gnostic liturgy. The organization of the Christian Church proceeded under the pressure and goad of Marcionist institutions, and it was the Montanist writer Tertullian who later cried out, forlornly, that he recognized only an *"ecclesia spiritus"* and not an *"ecclesia numerus episcoporum"*—that is to say, he acknowledged a community of the spirit, but not a community which was merely a band of bishops who had formulated the trinitarian doctrine and christology of the orthodox church, and which accordingly might better be designated as *"sub-spiritualis."*

Thus from the second century on we see in all its naked reality the struggle between the *"ecclesia spiritualis"* and the *"ecclesia carnalis"* —the congregation of the flesh—which has run through the whole subsequent history of Christianity.

There can be no doubt that Catholic orthodoxy was fully active at the end of the second century. But since that same time, the spiritual forces have been making a dramatic resistance, attempting to break out of the forms prescribed by the orthodox hierarchy, to live within the spiritual community of the believers in Christ, and to exert a continuous influence on the Church in the name of the spirit.

It goes without saying that this struggle has not always been carried on with the same violence or in the same tragic form. It becomes more violent when the aberrations of the *"ecclesia carnalis"* become most offensive, when it seeks to stifle and emasculate the resistance of the spiritual trends. Particularly in its relation to the political community, the carnal church shows itself inclined to compromises and concessions, which have repeatedly called forth strictures and countermoves on the part of the *ecclesia spiritualis*. This persistent duel reaches one of its climaxes in the fourth century, at the time of the so-called conversion of Constantine.

From the standpoint of secular society, an immediate and striking consequence of the growth of the Christian community was the clear-cut differentiation of religious and political values. In the social sphere, Christianity resulted in the establishment of a strictly spiritual community, which influenced the world by negating and transcending it. Thus it is fully understandable that the incorporation of political forms into the Christian message was bound to produce important repercussions upon the aims and functions of the spiritual church, and this has been true down to our own day.

The Christian conscience was for the first time faced by this problem in all its gravity on the day when, after three centuries of stubborn and violent hostility to Christianity, the Roman Empire sought to make it the state religion. In his *Apologetics,* Tertullian wisely declared: The rulers of Rome can introduce Christianity only if one of two things happens: if the world proves capable of dispensing with rulers, or if a Christian mounts the throne of the Caesars. When Constantine publicly embraced Christianity on the eve of the battle of the Saxa Rubra, and when he subsequently developed his vast pro-Christian policies, which of Tertullian's alternatives had been fulfilled? Was the century mature enough to dispense with Caesars, or had the Christians found a means of bringing their old religious vocation into harmony with the duties which political domination imposes? In reality, the so-called conversion of Constantine was not the conversion of a pagan to the Gospel, but rather a pagan's attempt to capture and subjugate Christianity by stealth. His attempt was not without its success, but the *ecclesia spiritualis* was vigilant and swift to counterattack.

Three separate crises now manifested themselves within the religious community which the crafty, farsighted emperor had invited to collaborate in his own political program: a philosophico-theological crisis, an organizational crisis, and a moral crisis. These crises constituted the history of the fourth Christian century and left discernible traces in the whole subsequent development of Catholic Christianity.

The philosophico-theological crisis owes its name to the Alexandrian priest Arius. The Arian system divests the Christian theodicy and soteriology of all mystical content and reduces them to the level of an ordinary rationalistic philosophy, on a par with all the various schools of metaphysical speculation, which in the eyes of the Roman state were perfectly harmless. No self-governing religious society, whose independence might be regarded as a threat to the state, had ever grown up on the basis of such metaphysical systems. Arianism was a resolute attempt to reduce Christian theology to rational proportions, to turn Christian thought into a purely human dialectic, from which the empire might freely borrow various philosophical ideas, for is not philosophy a useful instrument of government? God was removed to a position of unattainable aloofness, from which he emerges only in the moment set aside for creation. God as the Father is subjected to limitation in time. The Word becomes the beginning and prototype of all created things. The mysteries of Christ and the Trinity are suppressed, and all suprarational elements are eliminated from Christian dogma. Arius so mercilessly secularizes Christian doctrine that it becomes inadequate as a theoretical justification for a religious community miraculously called by God to create and maintain, between heaven and earth, spiritual relations secure against earthly infringements. Thus Arius suppressed the church in its original fragile essence. By silencing the mystery, he suppressed the autonomy of the community which administered it, and dealt a heavy blow to Christian sovereignty. His success would have meant the death of the *ecclesia spiritualis.*

The theological crisis which broke over the Christianity of the East immediately after its incorporation in the empire and the intervention of Constantine in the internal affairs of the church revolved around a purely political difficulty. Should the religion which had now been honored by official recognition preserve the same outward relations and the same position of inner independence towards the new political power as it had upheld in its dealings with the pagan state? It was very fortunate for the church of Rome that Constantine moved the capital of his empire to Byzantium. For, consequently, it was Constantinople and not Rome that was consumed by the poison of caesaropapism, while Rome, to a certain degree, might champion the *ecclesia spiritualis* up to the day when it too should be infected with political ambitions.

Official recognition of the legality of the Christian community, the rise of many Christians to high imperial office, the altered attitude of the rulers, conferred worldly wealth on a community that had been grounded in the expectation of the kingdom of God and in the practice of renunciation. This circumstance inevitably called forth a moral crisis which of all the crises provoked by the conversion of Constantine was, beyond question, the most shrewdly planned and startling.

The New Testament is not a collection of laws for an ascetic mode of life in the original, etymological sense of the word, that is to say, it does not inculcate a rule whereby the carnal man is repressed and an athlete of the spiritual arena emerges. There was, on the contrary, a wide gulf between New Testament Christianity and the asceticism preached by the Greek schools of philosophy. Christianity, as a strictly religious movement, expected to achieve the ideal of perfection through its ardent, enthusiastic, divine hope in a complete reversal of values, and it is this hope which the inner rebirth, the *metanoia* of the New Testament, seeks to kindle in the spirit of its converts. The asceticism of the Stoics, the Neopythagoreans, and the Neoplatonists taught, on the contrary, that perfection could be achieved through a gradual, personal process of purification, seen as a kind of daily gymnastic exercise. But as the enthusiasm that had driven the earliest Christian generations to total renunciation of the world began to dwindle, it became necessary to formulate the ascetic ideal, previously upheld by the great Messianic dream, in rules suited to the daily lives of the faithful, who had indeed increased in numbers but not in ardor and purity.

The first manifestations of a regulated asceticism at the beginning of the fourth century are anchoritism, as described in Athanasius' life of St. Anthony, and the Pachomian movement that succeeded the great wars of Constantine's time. Both of these movements reveal living memories of early Christian enthusiasm. But from the ethical standpoint, the regularly observed asceticism of the Christian church did not differ essentially from the asceticism practiced by the Neopythagoreans and the Therapeutics. A strong indication of this is that when Eusebius, in reading Philo's work on the contemplative life, came to the rites and usages of Egyptian contemplation, he was dumbfounded and could find no other way out of his perplexity than to relate these descriptions to Christian contemplation. The monastic orders of the fourth century made it possible for the Christian community to lead their Christian life amid the new political and social conditions created by the Constantinian revolution, without entirely surrendering the nature of their old autonomous administration; the orders now constituted an *ecclesia spiritualis,* and their founding served as a spur and goad to the secularized Church of Rome, which was striving to reconcile this age and the next within the bosom of its world-embracing administration.

Monasticism was the *ecclesia spiritualis* of the Middle Ages. Despite all the turmoil created by the various Reform movements and the rationalism of the Illuminati, the heart and essence of this era was a revival of the Orphic and Pythagorean thiasos of pre-Christian days. This we can establish irrefutably by the study not only of its organization but also, and to an even greater degree, of its artistic, liturgical, and cultural achievements. Monastic art is the great art of the Middle Ages. The monastic liturgy is a revival of the old Orphic-Dionysian liturgies. The Gregorian chant most probably finds its remote origin in the musical technique of Pythagoras and Orpheus. And still, in this world of monastic experience and culture, we find renewed the same drama of conflicts and contradictions that we have already witnessed in the spiritual movements of the second century. We find a renewal of Gnosticism and Marcionism.

Just as the Marcionism and Gnosticism of the second century strove to defend Christian spirituality against the forces of decay inherent in Christian proselytism and conquest, the great monastic orders were now impelled by a natural urge to combat the process of secularization that had seized upon the triumphant church. These monastic orders, which in a manner of speaking had grown up on the periphery of the official ecclesiastical community, now became its leaven and its salt. To the purely juridical disciplines of the visible church they opposed the mystical doctrine of grace that arose from an inward call to religious fulfillment. To the hierarchical forms of episcopal organization and the whole network of diplomatic relations with political, secular authorities, they juxtaposed the seclusion of the cloister and the atmosphere of the *opus Dei,* the work of God, which consisted only in song and contemplation. The monks were in reality the representatives and faithful adherents of a higher gnosis, conceived as complement and counterpart of the lower dialectical sciences which are needed to impose order and restraint upon social organisms. At a certain point, however, the same thing happened to monasticism as to the church in the days of its earliest outward successes. It was seduced into an attempt to dominate the visible church and at the same time tempted to remold its gnosis into systematic science and rational speculation. Monasticism now renounced its office as an *ecclesia spiritualis,* and undeterred by any salutary fear of contamination, engaged in the empirical, worldly, political life of the official church.

There is a certain savor of irony in the fact that the first medieval copies of the Aristotelian texts were undertaken in the mysterious darkness of the cloisters, under the protection of independent monasticism. But in later years, when, in accordance with the infallible law of historical repetition and prophetic revival, monasticism began to degenerate and seemed to be losing the essence of its special Christian mission, a new prophetic voice burst from the innermost depth of monastic spirituality with the call for a new *ecclesia spiritualis.* Where silence had reigned for hundreds of years, a monk now arose, who— like the Montanists of the second century—proclaimed the advent of the Paraclete and the end of the time of symbols. A Cistercian monk, Joachim of Floris, proclaimed loudly and persistently that the eras of the Father and the Son must now be followed by the era of the Holy Ghost, which would signify full revelation and the establishment of eternal peace among men. Joachim's message was to give the Franciscan movements its characteristic stamp and carry a new rhythm into the whole spiritual life of Europe. Joachim of Floris was fully aware of the revolutionary import of his teachings; he waited anxiously to see what reception the Church of Rome, the church of St. Peter, would accord the new spiritual church of St. John. But he indignantly rejected the very thought that the church of Rome might not accept the great new communication of the spirit. He preferred to imagine that the Roman Church, like the aged Simeon in the temple, would take the child begotten of the spirit in its arms, and would say, with humble devotion: "My mission is ended; the era of sacraments and symbols is ended, let it be followed by the era of reality and grace."

Joachim of Floris was a great optimist. The church of St. Peter scorned and condemned the new visitation of the spirit, proclaimed by the Calabrian seer. The *ecclesia spiritualis* was mercilessly driven from the enclosure of the visible church, and we may well say that from then on, from the beginning of the thirteenth century, the Christian message ceased to be an effective instrument of universal salvation in Europe. From this moment on, the whole religious history of Europe has been marked by this rejection of the spirit. The various reform movements were its inevitable, ruinous consequence. The Roman Church on the other hand has become more and more congealed in its Aristotelian speculations and Papal ordinances. And since that time, the *ecclesia spiritualis* has been dispersed, moving over secret esoteric paths, and yearning for the day when the evident and inevitable collapse of Christian values would open the eyes of men and lead them to recognize that all communal life is doomed unless it bears within it the inspiring dream of peace and truth in spirit.

3. Christian Mysticism as 'Ecclesia Spiritualis'

Mrs. Froebe has expressed the wish that this third part of my lecture should serve in a sense as a conclusion to this year's session.[2] This does not mean, of course, that my words are to be taken as a summation of all the excellent talks we have heard in the last few days. Yet it would be impossible for me not to stress the profound impression made upon me by the communication of such varied religious experience by so outstanding a group of scholars. And what the speakers have said affects me all the more strongly in that it seems to confirm me in my own inner conviction that the Christian message represents a synthesis of the religious development of the whole Mediterranean world, and that in Christianity all fundamental components of the civilization whose source and focus is the region of the Mediterranean find a meeting place.

At the opening of this year's session, Mrs. Froebe stated very aptly that we are not here to resuscitate dead and forgotten voices from the shades of the past, but rather to repair and replenish, in a religious spirit, a spiritual chain that has not been destroyed by time. We are here to receive the tradition of a life that is not extinct. We are here to carry on a tradition which, even though it does embrace the distant past, also looks towards the future with confidence and eager expectation. These gatherings in Ascona take their spirit from the great symbol contained in the Panathenaean games, where the weary runners handed the blazing torch of life to the fresher, swifter runners who relieved them: *"Quasi cusores vitai lampada tradunt. . . ."*

For the last four or five years the Eranos meetings have been devoted to the problem of salvation in the various religions. The problem itself presupposes an implicit conviction that man's physical life cannot be regarded as a perfect realization. Life is not a simple biological process and the problem of life is not a problem of the mechanical distribution of the means of satisfying our elementary physical needs. Life is the realization of a program of salvation or redemption. From whom and from what must we redeem ourselves? From what situation of inferiority and servitude must we be saved?

2 [The subject of the 1937 meeting was "The Formation of the Idea of Redemption in East and West."—Ed.]

From what dangers must we shield ourselves and against what snares must we secure ourselves? Is this redemption, this aim of our worldly existence, a physical or a moral redemption?

The answers vary, but always they point to the development of the human spirit, which from its fleeting appearances in prehistoric times ascends by an arduous path to the higher forms of mysticism.

The first intimations of human religiosity are the pure, simple expression of man's natural need to safeguard himself against the evil and treacherous forces that abound in nature, to parry them, as it were, in advance. Primitive man seeks redemption from the thousand dangers that menace him and strives to bring about circumstances favorable to the satisfaction of his physical needs. Magic is the earliest religious technique. It embraces the sum of all the means of preserving the individual and the community. Man's ignorance of the laws governing natural phenomena, his confused interpretations of nature's most striking manifestations, make this original, simple religiosity a seemingly infallible means of safeguarding himself against the calamities of material existence. Primitive religion is an endeavor to propitiate the forces that govern the universe, and by this means man sought to facilitate his physical life.

But man became increasingly familiar with the regularity and inevitability of natural processes, and availed himself more and more of this knowledge. His intelligence grew, he began to understand the conditions under which matter could be subjugated and turned to his use. And thus his belief in magical forces gave way to higher forms of striving for religious salvation. By this I do not mean to deny that man's attitude towards nature has preserved a certain element of primal magic. One might, for example, ask whether the scientist who believes he possesses infallible means of utilizing natural phenomena has not within him something of the primitive magician who was convinced that by a magical formula he could bend the imponderable, intangible natural forces around him to his will. In any event it is certain that the progress of human religiosity rests entirely on a transference of the mystical sense from the field of natural processes to the ethical sphere. Religion never ceases to be what it was in its origins and what is defined by the very concept of religion: an endeavor

241

to further and control the normal course of social life by transcendent doctrine and grace. The great religious reforms have never aimed at liberation from animism and magic, they have never sought to give the individual a sense of liberation from the superstition of the taboo. Rather they have been bold attempts to make man conscious that the great mystery surrounding his life resides first and foremost in his relation to his fellow men. The ascending stages of religious life are characterized by an increasing conviction that to win the favor of the numen, under whose imperious rule our existence moves, magical rites do not suffice. That is to say, it is not necessary to perform magical rites in order to evoke a natural phenomenon indispensable for our primary needs. What is necessary is that we subordinate our social life to another sphere—that of mutual service and universal love—which rests upon the conviction that there is a redemption capable of raising us from the sensory world into a transcendent world of the spirit.

Consequently, those higher religions which take their names from a reformer and may accordingly be called messianic, are those which have freed the magical forces of the human spirit from the lower natural sphere, and directed their spiritual force to its own proper sphere of activity, the mutual relations between men as social beings. These are the religions which have taught man to submit his life to guidance by the mysterious magic of the good, which have offered him the doctrine of salvation, of perfect redemption, which have taught him to attune his social morality to unwritten laws and higher ideals, and which have led him to the deep mystery in which the origins of men's spiritual relations are grounded. Prometheus declares, in the tragedy of Aeschylus: "I have planted blind hope in the hearts of men." To which the leader of the chorus replies: "On that day you made them a rare gift." Blind hope, the highest gift of immortals to mortals—the hope that has nourished all forms of religious experience—is the hope for liberation from sin, from death, from the cycle of the successive generations, and from the empirical world.

Hope presupposes a pessimistic view of life. The need for redemption implies the presence of conditions and circumstances from which man must seek escape, liberation. But where do these painful circumstances originate? The myth of original sin occurs in numerous versions. Here we have no need to seek its psychological basis. It is as old as the oldest human civilization. The Yahwist of Genesis makes Yahweh ask the fratricide Cain: "Where is Abel thy brother?" Cain, tortured by his conscience, replies defiantly: "I know not. Am I my brother's keeper?" And Yahweh answers with a terrible judgment: "The voice of thy brother's blood crieth unto me from the ground." And the earth shall therefore find no peace until the brother's blood with which Cain has sullied it is avenged. The earth has been tainted by the first fratricide, and the earth re-echoes the remorse which torments and pursues him. According to the legend of Genesis, Cain, in order to set a stone wall between himself and the inexorable voice of his conscience, builds the first city. In this moving and subtle Biblical myth, the civilization of the empirical world grew out of the fratricide's desperate effort to erect a dike of ostentation and spurious grandeur between himself and his guilt.

This is not the liberation of which the religious soul dreams. Religion points out other roads to liberation and redemption. All these roads converge and lead to the conquest of higher values. When man receives and partakes of these values, he is enabled to escape from the blind servitude of sensory experience and to achieve the absolute freedom that lies in the inner, intuitive vision of God. The fundament and touchstone of the spiritual church is a "gnosis," a subtle interwovenness with the realities of the spiritual world.

In the spiritual sense gnosis is something far different from what we ordinarily mean by knowledge. According to the gnosiology which, beginning with Aristotle we might say, gained universal currency in the culture of the Mediterranean countries, knowledge is the recognition and assimilation of universal ideas through a dialectical process. This process begins with empirical data; by elaborating them on the basis of metaphysical categories which are a part of man's intellectual structure, it attains to the innermost and most universal essence of things. From the religious standpoint gnosis is something entirely different. In the language of Plato, and to a far greater degree in that of Neoplatonic and Christian mysticism, gnosis is a voluntary but irresistible harmony with the deepest reality of the world around us and with the values that rise above it, inspired and sustained by the ethical force within us. In its essence, gnosis is not merely a higher intellectual virtue than the common, hackneyed, domesticated method

243

that characterizes our empirical, gnosiological development. It is its exact antithesis. For knowledge, in the current sense of the term, is a conceptual elaboration of the matter which reaches us through sensory experience; while gnosis is the power to recognize absolute values through inspiration, through a spiritual grasp, a psychic sensibility, without the intermediary of sense perception—which indeed it utterly rejects. From this standpoint gnosis and mysticism are fully synonymous and equivalent. Mysticism reveals its meaning in its etymology. Mysticism, derived from the Greek verb μύω ("I close"), implies the shutting of the eyes, ears, and lips, and this shutting is a prerequisite, an essential component of the concept. And if all forms of religious mysticism, whether of the East or West, have anything in common, it is the conception that in order to see in the world of supersensory reality, we must close our eyes to all sense perceptions. In order to hear the voices and melodies of the supernatural world, we must close our ears once and for all to the idle hubbub and noise of this world. In order to sing the one hymn of praise that is worthy of God, we must seal our lips in the presence of sacred things. A mystic therefore is one who wraps his life in the mantle of seclusion and closes off these avenues of communication with the outside world that have been well worn by experience, not in order to renounce his faculties of sight, hearing, and speech but, quite the contrary, in order to open the inner eye to supersensory visions, in order to capture the sounds that come to him from the world that stands above experience, and in order to sing in silence the ineffable hymn of praise to the supreme being.

The great religious upheavals, the innermost conversions, have always been marked by a sudden transition from indulgence of the vain life of the senses to a quest for the gifts of the supersensory life.

Today it is more urgent than ever that we regain our awareness of the profound gulf lying between conscious acceptance of the data of experience, between the dialectical process, scientific knowledge, and metaphysical ideology on the one hand, and the concrete possession of active and tangible reality on the other. Such concrete possession of reality emanates solely from our unquestioning reliance on the spiritual light of truth and goodness in the world. This is a light which cannot be seen with the eyes of the flesh. It is diffused when we vibrate in silence with the harmonious chords of the universe. It gushes forth from the silent hymn of recognition and praise which all creatures sing unceasingly in honor of their Father in heaven.

Today the *ecclesia spiritualis* needs for its foundation no geographically limited units, no official groups organized in accordance with ecclesiastical articles and rules. The *ecclesia spiritualis* comes into being when here and there, of their own free will but no less firmly and effectively, all those band together who have become aware that future salvation does not depend on the mechanical development of our industry and technology, or on any fixed regulation of our economic and social life, but solely on the revival of a world of mysterious values, which evade all empirical judgment, and reveal themselves only to faith and hope.

Of course mysticism is manifested in many forms. And anyone familiar with the history of philosophy and the higher religions knows that the various forms of mystical life can be classified according to a hierarchical scale. There would seem to be two sharply delineated forms of mysticism. The one is strictly solitary, the other strictly communal. In which of the two, it might be asked, can the human spirit best accomplish its "purification" from the confused realm of sensory perception and the consciousness of sin? The classical form of Neoplatonic mysticism seeks to liberate man's consciousness from the whole burden of materiality, to lead it, through zealous purification and inner elevation, to beatific reunion with the One and Eternal. Porphyry, in his account of the life of Plotinus, considers it highly important to describe the attitude of this sensitive, receptive spirit, who felt shame at being clad in a body. Here apparently we have to do with a personal form of mysticism, based on the belief that far-reaching purification can be achieved by a purely personal effort, and might be achieved even if the living reality of the outside world did not exist. It is possible to regard this as mysticism in its perfect form. Since mysticism rejects and suppresses the possibilities of communication with the outside world, the more fully it strives to destroy the very substance of our empirical experience the more mystical it becomes.

But there is another form of mystical experience. This form looks on the natural, outward world and the world of relations between us and other living creatures, not as two mutually repellent worlds which cannot be brought into harmony with one another, and which can undergo spiritual transformation only through ideal repression. This is the form of mystical experience that finds its highest expression in the experience and teaching of Christianity. This form of mysticism looks upon the reality of the outward world and the daily evidence of the bonds between men as the raw material for the highest spiritual transfiguration.

Here in truth we have the most subtle way of negating what is base and worthless in the sensory world, not by disregarding it but by overcoming it, not by absorbing it through empirical experience but by exercising our faculty for reading in symbols and seeing in the invisible. The teacher of this mysticism was St. Paul. In the most moving terms he spoke of the gulf between the flesh and the spirit, the knowledge of which had so shaken Plotinus. From man's feeling for the flesh, for the body, for material substance, St. Paul made an instrument and an aid for the reception of that body, that flesh, that higher substance, which constitutes the supersensory Christ, and which takes form with the progressive growth of God's kingdom in the world. The great Christian mystics have walked in the footsteps of St. Paul. The second great Christian teacher of mysticism, St. Augustine, also refers frequently to the doctrines of the Neoplatonists.

And indeed, as the *Confessions* make clear, the day on which the young teacher of rhetoric in Milan received a copy of the Latin translation of the *Enneads* from a friend was a great day in his spiritual life—and consequently in the history of the Christian mysticism of the West. However, it must not be forgotten that two conflicting forms of mysticism met and mingled in the soul of St. Augustine: the monistic mysticism of Plotinus and the dualistic mysticism of the Manichaeans. He himself admits that though he had found much in Plotinus, there were many other things he had not found. In the *Confessions* he does not fully state where he found these things that he did not find in Plotinus. For in the course of time his own opposition to Manichaeism, as evinced in his polemics, was bound to distort his memory of his own spiritual growth. But all recent inquiries into Augustine's life and work make it clear that much of the young Manichaean clings to the soteriology and ecclesiology of the great

African theologian. Essentially, dualistic mysticism consists in a sense of participation in a continuous drama, which is enacted outside the sensory world, in a spiritual realm embracing the beginnings of existence and the whole of life. In this transcendent realm God's light suffers and struggles for its survival in a battle to the death against the false light in which Satan's darkness cloaks itself. We may say that while philosophy is fundamentally monistic, religion, where it is manifested in its pure state, free from speculative admixture, is fundamentally dualistic. A more or less latent tendency to believe in an unremitting dualistic drama at the core of life and universal morality can be said to underlie all constituted religious forms. The more directly and immediately a religion partakes of its original idea, the more religious it can be said to be; and always this original religious idea bears the imprint of the suffering that assails life and the good in the world and of the fervent belief that this life and death struggle in the world is moving towards a restoration of perfect justice. The original spirit of philosophy, on the other hand, has been revealed by one of our greatest modern philosophers—Benedetto Croce. In discussing certain neodualistic trends in Italian culture, he tells us that if he were a dualist, he would be ashamed to admit it—as though there were not many things in human nature which, if we were to be perfectly honest, we would have to be ashamed of. But never should we be ashamed to confess the truth, whatever it may be, even though it may wound and shame our pride and presumption. There is but one thing to be ashamed of, and that is unwillingness to recognize the truth: the lie. It is not for nothing that in the religion of Zoroaster the lie is designated as the source of evil. And if our present culture is ashamed to recognize that the dualistic drama of the world is reality, it is most probably because, in the words of the New Testament, it is steeped in the evil which is the lie.

It is imperative that we understand how deeply ingrained is the eternal struggle between good and evil in the world.

Religiosity consists not in explaining the origin of the world, but in an endeavor, grounded in gnosis, to distill from the universe in which we live its ethical meaning and eschatological goal. For philosophy, which strives to go back to the world's first causes, the static fulcrum of existence may well be designated as "God," or as

Aristotle put it, "the idea of the idea." For the religion that is directed towards perceiving and proclaiming the enduring presence in the world of a watchful and benevolent being who calls upon comrades and children to help realize the good, there is no other word so expressive of the sentiments of veneration and affection as that of Father. It is not the existence of God that concerns the religious soul. It is rather God's presence in every manifestation of life, in every impulse implanted by grace in the depth of our hearts.

If God is what the philosophers make him, we may say (the idea may be bold but it is not arbitrary) that religion in general, and Christianity in particular, is godless, because piety never arises from recognition of the theoretical existence of a driving force that was originally at rest, but solely from a sense of love and trepidation, from a sense of kinship with the Father, without whose succor the whole world must instantly crumble into nothingness.

There are strange and mysterious realities. But the sound religious attitude towards them is to be sought not in the presumption that seeks to account for them and prove their existence but in the humility which, peering upward from the very dust, recognizes a sublime being to worship and serve.

Out of the countenance of our brother, God's divine radiance shines upon us. ("Hast thou seen thy brother?—Then thou hast seen God!" This was the motto of the early Christians, as reported by Clement of Alexandria and Tertullian.) Shall we then seek to prove the existence of our brother? And to seek proof of God's existence would seem to be a very refined means of evading the commandment to behave "respectfully" in His presence. Only a philosophy puffed up with pride presumes to prove the existence of God. The great religions have never presumed to do this. They have postulated a God, given by spiritual gnosis, and have sought to apprehend this already acquired possession in forms of worship, of veneration, and of obedience to all the living creation through which God works, suffers, and hopes. The great religions of history have never started from the idea that one must go far to seek God, that one must struggle through tedious inquiries into things of secondary importance which can always be traced back to one primal cause, beyond which no one has ever advanced. Any attempt to prove the existence of God is tantamount to the supposition that He might desire to capture by stealth man's halt and feeble powers of apprehension. Spiritual gnosis, the gnosis which germinates in the *ecclesia spiritus*—the community of the spirit—knows that there is a God and inquires only into his ways, his manifestation, his acts in the great drama of the world, which moves through pain and death towards the ultimate kingdom of truth and love.

Pascal, who had examined all the best traditions of Christian experience, correctly summed up the essence of Christian teaching in the term *"ecclesia spiritualis."* Jesus struggles with death until the end of the world. In this boundless Gethsemane, which is the life of the universe, Christ struggling with death is the sublime and living personification of all suffering and sorrow. Christ is sorrowful unto death —wherever a tear falls, wherever a heart is seized with despair, wherever an injustice or an act of violence is committed. To partake with Christ in the sufferings of the world is to be true to the teaching of his gospel, is to live within the *ecclesia spiritualis.*

All this is far removed from the views and usages of the official church, whose mission today, strange and monstrous as it may seem to say so, is none other than to suppress and stifle every breath of the spiritual church beneath a pall of theological circumlocutions and papal ordinances. Wherever in the world there are souls who feel the oppressive weight of religious dogmas and who, despite all obstacles, sense the urgency of a planned and widespread movement for religious revival in faith and divine grace—there the first rays of an *ecclesia spiritualis* are dawning. Today we are like wanderers and pilgrims in the world. In an age long past, the gift of mutual hospitality was ours, but since then we have defaced the signs we exchanged at our last parting, by which to recognize one another at the stopping places of our journey through life. These signs have become tarnished and unrecognizable, overlaid with alien matter. They communicate nothing, one sign does not speak to another.

These were the signs by which we should have known one another as brothers with a common aim in life, the ascent to the good, the aim and the work of the Father, who guides us on our way. We have surrounded our souls with a shell: our national pride, our racial isolation, our frozen articles of faith, the empty presumption of our castes and classes. And if along our path we meet a brother, we are like the wild beasts of the desert: we sense an enemy. The spiritual church will never be present reality, will never strike harbor in the stormy sea of modern history, until the day when there are many who, in meeting a fellow man along their road, greet him with an intelligible sign, the symbol of a common hope, of a single-minded striving to bring about the good, the truth, and peace in common cause with God.

Werner Kaegi

The Transformation of the Spirit in the Renaissance

I

In considering the topic that has been suggested to me—"The Transformation of the Spirit in the Renaissance"—I find myself obliged to cast a look around me at the landscape of concepts and ideas into which it leads us, before we can hold converse within the separate houses which these concepts designate.

Anyone who hears this title without having followed the preceding lectures of our cycle will be sure to associate the spirit that is transformed in the Renaissance with an entirely different idea than that which the initiates of the Eranos circle will form. Not only the layman, but even the historian who has not made a special study of the Renaissance, associates a very definite picture with the "transformation of the spirit in the Renaissance," even if he knows that all the formulas of Michelet and Burckhardt can no longer be taken for gospel. For, in any event, what is transformed in the Renaissance is "the spirit." Now then, what is "the spirit" in this case? Don't you know? Why, the general spirit of the age, of course, the spirit of the epoch. If I now have the courage to press my question, and to admit that I do not know exactly what the spirit of an age, or epoch, is, I run the risk of having some schoolmaster tap me on the shoulder and say pityingly, "You have studied the Renaissance too much, my good man, you no longer see the forest for the trees; the spirit of the Renaissance: why, it's obvious; everybody knows what that is; and from you of all people we might have expected something better than helpless questions."

Now for how long, actually, has everyone known what the spirit of the Renaissance is? Almost exactly one hundred years. Before 1830–40, it was customary in France, where the concept (as the word indicates) originated, to add what one meant: *La renaissance des lettres, la renaissance des arts.* Only since Jules Michelet and Jacob Burckhardt has one spoken more generally of the Renaissance pure and simple, of the age of the Renaissance. This means that a term relating specifically to the history of art or the history of literature was at that time extended into a general cultural and historical concept, and that this concept, whatever may be said of its content, achieved such universal currency that for ever since it has cost an effort to recollect how the idea was first meant. This extension of a specialized art-historical and literary concept into the general concept of an epoch could be effected so easily because the basic mold of thought, into which what had previously been a specific content was poured, already existed: the concept of a historical epoch as a spiritual entity, as a unit.

The historical epoch as a form of the revelation of the spirit might be a highly significant topic of research. We should have to pursue it from the speculations of late antiquity on the history of philosophy, through the medieval historians' doctrines concerning the ages of the world, to the strange ideas of the humanists and mystics of the fifteenth and sixteenth centuries, with their shifting, varied, astrological, spiritualistic, and historiographic emphasis, and finally to Giambattista Vico. But only after Hamann and Herder in Germany began to construe history as a self-revelation of God, after—in France —Edgar Quinet, the friend of Michelet, translated Herder, and Michelet immersed himself for years in Vico's *"scienza nuova,"* did scholars in northern Europe become generally interested in deciphering the individual words of this revelation, i.e., in discerning definite meanings in the different ages of history, in understanding them as spiritual entities, as epochs. If history was the self-revelation of God, then the individual peoples or epochs must be the words, or sentences, of this self-revelation. And these words or sentences must have a meaning that can be deciphered. And in every single case, this meaning implied a certain degree of unity.

Historiography had become a kind of secularized theology. Here too a rationalization of revelation had set in. Men like Ranke and Burckhardt, to be sure, were sometimes horrified at the monstrosities to which Schelling and Hegel gave birth in their philosophies of history. At Schelling's lectures, Burckhardt felt as though "some monstrous Asiatic god must come waddling along on twelve legs and remove six hats from six heads with twelve arms."[1] Nevertheless Burckhardt's thinking was quite permeated with Herder's ideas, and he too believed that he heard, distinctly in his youth, more faintly in his old age, the self-revelation of the spirit in history. "Self-revelation of God," Herder and Hamann had said.

> Dost thou not speak to the soul in the song of nature?
> Dost thou not speak to me in the mouth of history?
> Does not my own being
> Persistently call out thy name to me?

This was young Burckhardt's invocation to "providence."[2] After that the historiography of the nineteenth century proceeded to forget the whole theological and mystical background of its concept of epochs and found everything self-evident, for αὐτὸς ἔφα: Ranke had spoken, Burckhardt had spoken, and today every schoolmaster knows what the spirit of an epoch, the spirit of the Renaissance is, though indeed he prefers to keep the world spirit at a safe distance.

The second half of the strophe cited casts light on the destiny of Michelet:

> Does not my own being
> Persistently call out thy name to me?

The special form of modern thought that seeks a self-revelation of God in history implies the possibility that the age-old striving of all pious men for a reunion of their own soul with God has reappeared in the interpretation of history. Throughout Burckhardt's work on the Renaissance echoes of his personal conflict with the traditional religion of Basel at the time of his theological studies are still discernible; and Michelet, in his somewhat earlier writings on the Renaissance, delivered a *confession de foi* which everywhere recalls his break with the romantic Catholicism of his early period and his fight against the Jesuits in the days of Louis Philippe. His account of the Renaissance is not merely history, but also a more or less autobiographical demonstration that the world spirit itself, as it reveals itself in history, had as early as the sixteenth century made the break

1 Letter, June 13, 1842, to Gottfried Kinkel.
2 *Gedichte,* ed. K. E. Hoffmann (Basel, 1926), p. 7.

which Michelet himself, because of the deplorable delays which are inevitable in the course of history, had been compelled to repeat under such unpleasant circumstances. In any event, the decision of the world spirit in the sixteenth century had been no different from the position taken by Michelet in his difficult struggles of the 1840's: that was his opinion.

We recall these circumstances not for the sake of historical Pyrrhonism, but in order to indicate two things: first, that the spiritual unity of a historical epoch is a postulate that is certainly not the product of our specialized historical discipline, but existed before it; and secondly, that the spiritual content which the concept of the Renaissance acquired when it was first formulated a hundred years ago embraced considerable elements of a subjectivity that did not belong to the epoch represented but to the nineteenth century itself. More recent research has endeavored to re-examine and correct that first conception from very different points of view, to wipe out values that were historically false, and to stress the original coloration of the epoch itself. I think that we must first look into the results of this critical work. Then, in the second part of this lecture, we shall come back to certain vantage points, from which we may examine our topic afresh.

If one wishes to know how the concept of the Renaissance was originally intended, it is advisable to read not Burckhardt's masterwork, with its fine shadings, but the flaming manifesto of about one hundred pages, five years earlier in date, which Michelet wrote as the introduction to the seventh volume of his *Histoire de France,* published in 1855. Here Michelet takes as a starting point the traditional conception of the Renaissance as a revival of classical studies and Roman law and a renewal of the arts, and then fulminates against this view:

> These all too narrow minds have forgotten only two things, two little things to be sure, but two things which belonged to this epoch more than to any preceding it: the discovery of the world, the discovery of man.—The sixteenth century extends in its great and true breadth from Columbus to Copernicus, from Copernicus to Galileo, from the discovery of the earth to that of the heavens.—It was then that man rediscovered himself. While Vesalius and Servetus revealed life to him, he pene-

trated the secrets of his spiritual life through Luther and
Calvin, through Dumoulin and Cujas, through Rabelais,
Montaigne, Shakespeare, Cervantes. He perceived the profound foundations of his nature. He began to take his place
on the chairs of justice and reason [one can hear the fanfares
of the French Revolution], the doubters helped faith back on
its feet, and the boldest of all [Michelet has Rabelais in mind]
could write on the gateway of his temple of the will: *"Entrez
qu'on fonde ici la foi profonde."*[3]

Thus what Michelet regarded as the distinguishing feature of the
new epoch was nothing less than the founding of a new faith. And he
makes certain statements with regard to this new faith: revived
antiquity proved in its heart identical with the new era; the Orient,
understood at last, held out its hand to the Occident, and in space as
well as in time there began "a joyous reconciliation between the
members of the human family."[4]

This was written a few months before the outbreak of the Crimean
War, on the eve of the establishment by violence of the German
Empire, at the beginnings of an age which today all textbooks
designate as that of imperialism and in which the seeds for the world
wars of our own century were germinating.

But perhaps in January, 1855, Michelet was still entitled to regard
the modern era as a period of uninterrupted progress and to praise
the epoch of the Renaissance as the hour of its birth. His conception
of this epoch and its spirit can be seen from what he says about the
end of the Middle Ages: "How often they ended! They ended at the
end of the twelfth century when secular poetry opposed several dozen
epics to the Holy Legend, when Abelard opened the schools of Paris
and ventured the first attempt at critique and common sense.—They
ended in the thirteenth century when a bold mysticism went beyond
critique, when the historical gospel was replaced by the *evangelium
aeternum* and Jesus by the Holy Ghost.—They ended in the fourteenth
century when a layman"—Michelet is referring to Dante—"took possession of the three world spheres, embraced them in his *comédie
humaine* and thus remolded and delimited the realm of the vision.—
And finally they ended in the fifteenth and sixteenth centuries when
the printing press, the ancient world, America, the Orient, and the

3 Ed. Marpon and Flammarion, Vol. IX (1879), p. 8.   4 Ibid.

true system of the world: when all these flaming lights sent down their combined rays on that age."[5]

Now—at last!—these Middle Ages were ended for good, and what Michelet understood not as a transformation but as a rebirth, had taken place: the modern era had been born. One senses that Michelet speaks here not as a historian but as the bearer of a message of salvation; his words carry the accents of the prophet, the tone of a new gospel. And why? Because Michelet was not merely writing a given chapter of the *Histoire de France,* and was not merely introducing a random era in the history of mankind—no, he was proclaiming the new order, the new golden age, whose precursor had been the Renaissance and whose fulfillment had been the spirit of the Parisian people in the French Revolution. No doubt this is one of the main reasons why for many generations the concept of the Renaissance has been burdened with too much meaning and too many big words: the modern subjectivity had too much at stake in it. Here, in a sense, was the family tree of the modern spirit. It is customary to weave a legend around the ancestor, and family trees are represented rather differently from the trees in the textbooks of botany.

Without an avid hunger for self-glorification, it seems hardly likely that a brilliant but hastily conceived sketch from a history of France and Burckhardt's somewhat later, masterly picture of an Italian cultural epoch would have been forcibly amalgamated, and that these two, at best a chapter of French history and a chapter of Italian history, should have been proclaimed as the principal content of a universal epoch of the European spirit. Sixteenth-century Germany by no means fits into this picture, and if one wished to include Spain, one would either have to caricature it as a black gargoyle somewhere in the background, or else pick a few suitable motifs from the Spanish scene and discard the rest.

Rather than give a bibliographical summary of Renaissance studies in the ninety years that have passed since Michelet's *Introduction,* I shall attempt to give a brief survey of Michelet's sketch of 1855 from the vantage point of 1946, showing the scientific fate of each of his speculative figures, and to determine the present position of Michelet's

5 Ibid., pp. 10ff.

256

queens, bishops, castles, and pawns on the chessboard of scientific research.

Let us begin with his remarks about the end of the Middle Ages. "They ended in the twelfth century when secular poetry opposed several dozen epics to the Holy Legend, when Abelard opened the schools of Paris." No one today will claim that secular poetry as such was specifically modern, let alone typical of the Renaissance. In the *chansons de gestes* and the German chivalric and folk epics, classical influences and prototypes can occasionally be discovered, but today no one would think of characterizing them as contrary to the spirit of the Middle Ages, since we now know how much of medieval art rested, literally or figuratively, on ancient foundations. As for the Breton legends, chivalric poetry in general, and German folk epics of the type of the Nibelungenlied, studies in literary history have, quite aside from the classical-Byzantine traditions, disclosed or at least shown the probable existence of so rich a world of Celtic and Germanic poetry as the background of those epics of the High Middle Ages, that today the epic of the twelfth and thirteenth centuries is no longer regarded as a beginning of secular poetry, but as the late—and often the only surviving—expression of a rich poetic tradition which from the very beginning was carried on by laymen and beyond a doubt belongs to the very epitome of medieval poetry. No serious scholar will ascribe the demonic rebirth of Nordic heroism that we have experienced since the days of Michelet to the spirit embodied in the Renaissance. Especially when we consider the Renaissance treatment of the material of the medieval epic, in Pulci, Boiardo, and Ariosto, it becomes on the one hand self-evident (one might even go so far as to call it a commonplace) that these works were written by laymen, while on the other hand it is characteristic of these works that in them the old heroic content of the epic has faded and given way to a new content of a comical, courtly-convivial, or erotic character. Not the Renaissance is to be blamed for the modern *Kraftmensch,* but at most the questionable body of history and belles-lettres that has grown up around the Renaissance. The true Renaissance quality of Ariosto lies neither in the heroic nor the erotic, indeed not in any content, but in his narrative style, in that type of harmony and beauty which was basically alien to the epic genre.

257

And yet here a misgiving arises. We have passed from the secular element to the heroic. It was not Michelet, but Jacob Burckhardt, in the first section of "The State as a Work of Art,"[5a] who portrayed a human type which he unquestionably regarded as one of the embodiments of Renaissance culture; this was the ruler over a small despotic state, the *condottiere,* the man "thrown entirely on his own resources," who no longer ruled his state and performed his political functions as God's emissary, invoking the eternal laws of justice and peace, but who, depending only on himself, in the turmoil of a world grown lawless, fought for his possessions and his personal glory, or at best for the interests of his house. Here we shall not look into the literary origin of the type that Burckhardt has drawn in this first chapter. It might be found in Stendhal, but the German writers, Schiller, Heinse and Klinger, Platen and Tieck, are a more likely source. The question as to whether Burckhardt's first chapter is anything more than a captivating introduction and embodies any specific quality of the Renaissance turns today on another question: How shall we differentiate between nature and spirit in this field of political Renaissance history? Even Burckhardt suspected that there was no lack of unrestrained immoralists in the High Middle Ages, and the more we study the growth of the medieval states, with their dynasties, vicissitudes, and designs, the more numerous these figures become. In the decades around 1900, poets had no difficulty in finding prototypes for their dramatic immoralists in every epoch and country of European history, when they wished, for a change, to forego the Renaissance costume. Such types are found throughout history. It is entirely different with the spiritual aspect of the phenomenon: the consciousness of political action, its historical representation and possible justification. Only on the last point did the Renaissance contribute something new: the concept of *raison d'état.* In Machiavelli, however, this still remained more or less the knowledge of a disquieting natural phenomenon, a questionable, suspect, barely intimated occult doctrine. It can scarcely be maintained that Machiavelli's ideas exerted an essential influence on the crucial political events in Europe in the first half of his century. The great game between Francis I and Charles V was not played according to the instructions laid down in *The*

5a [Part I of *The Civilization of the Renaissance.*—Ed.]

Prince, but rather in accordance with the rules of family tradition, Imperial policy, and a long, living experience that needed no textbook. A man like Gattinara, in his boldest piece of diplomacy, his polemic against the Papal Curia that provoked the sack of Rome, seems far more likely to have drawn inspiration from the very medieval Dante than from Machiavelli.[6] The romantic Renaissance tyrant has become a dubious stock character not only in the dramas of our literati but also in the repertory of historical concepts.

"The Middle Ages ended when . . . Abelard opened the schools of Paris and ventured the first attempt at critique and common sense. . . ." This must have occurred at about 1110, when Abelard returned to Paris from his home in southern France and opened his school on Mont Sainte-Geneviève. It is well known, however, that Abelard did not stand at the end but at the beginning of scholasticism—that his use of critique and common sense did, to be sure, cause a crisis in early scholastic realism, but through this very crisis led to the development of the principal systems of high scholasticism. Critique and common sense, as they were understood at that time, were so fundamental a part of the Paris school debates, in which scholasticism lived and throve, that one must either claim the whole of scholasticism for the Renaissance, or omit critique and common sense from the factors constituting the Renaissance. Critique and common sense are not the heritage of any one epoch, and surely not a monopoly of the modern age.

"The Middle Ages ended in the thirteenth century when a bold mysticism went beyond critique, when the historical gospel was replaced by the *evangelium aeternum* and Jesus by the Holy Ghost." Here one is amazed at the assurance with which Michelet was able to formulate and toss out ideas which he had not thought through but scarcely surmised, and which were to occupy generations of scholars after him. Assuredly the spiritualistic tradition, which, rising from late classical sources, fructified and troubled Western thought long before the thirteenth century, cannot be claimed for the Renaissance alone. Surely nothing is more alien to the traditional central ideas of the Renaissance—ancient prototypes, classical form—than the idea of

6 Concerning the use of *De monarchia* in Imperial polemics, see Karl Brandi, *Kaiser Karl V* (Quellen und Erörterungen, Vol. II; Munich, 1941), p. 105.

Christian spiritualism. But today there is no doubt that with the *evangelium aeternum* of Joachim of Floris an astonishing new chord was struck, which was re-echoed by Franciscans, Waldensians, and Hussites, and then in the sixteenth century grew to such magnitude in the movements of the northern European Baptists and the Spanish-Italian anti-Trinitarians that this particular century cannot be understood at all without the influence of the spiritualist idea in its highly diversified forms. In the latter part of this lecture we shall pursue this very idea. But—granted that the interconnections in this field are even today more surmised than explored—we may, to be sure, associate the main accents of the Renaissance—classical form, the new simplicity in religion, literature, architecture, script, and fashions—with spiritualism, but we shall not derive them from spiritualism. Nevertheless: on this point in particular, we are glad to bow before the clairvoyance of Michelet, who saw and expressed in plain words spiritual connections in the presence of which many specialized scholars after him could only stammer helplessly.

"The Middle Ages ended in the fourteenth century when a layman" —Dante—"took possession of the three world spheres, embraced them in his *comédie humaine,* and thus remolded and delimited the realm of the vision." What these words actually imply is that Dante's Christian conception of the Beyond was a pure product of *clerical* imagination, which with Dante luckily fell for the first time into lay hands, and in him was transformed into psychology and poetry. But Michelet was already in a position to know how much the basic structure of Dante's *Inferno,* in particular, owed to Homeric and Virgilian traditions, that is, it goes without saying, to ancient secular sources. Subsequent research has shown, more and more convincingly, that these classical foundations in Dante are not attributable to the Renaissance but to a widely ramified body of classical tradition, which was taken for granted throughout the Middle Ages and even enriched by Celtic and Islamic conceptions. Like the poets of the northern European folk epic, Dante has today come to be regarded less as an initiator and founder than as a late perfecting genius. Even if he cannot entirely be separated from the ensuing Renaissance, it is certain that the great main accents of his thought and imagination are genuinely medieval. Attempts to divest his *Commedia* of its theological and metaphysical

260

content and to interpret it as a purely aesthetic work of art, or as a psychological human comedy à la Balzac, may from time to time be tolerated in newspaper articles, but surely do not befit the historian.

"And finally they ended in the fifteenth and sixteenth centuries when the printing press, the ancient world, America, the Orient, and the true system of the world: when all these flaming lights sent down their combined rays on that age." The Middle Ages did not finally end even in the sixteenth century. Thomism, the core of medieval theology, withstood the crisis of the Reformation and experienced a renewal in Spain and France, which only ill faith can efface from the picture of the ensuing epoch. But not only the ecclesiastical life but also the artistic life of the seventeenth century, its architecture as well as its painting and sculpture, is inconceivable without the new impulses of the Catholic reform. The idea that "baroque is the art of the Counter Reformation" has been one of the most fruitful for the interpretation of this style. The Counter Reformation, however, would be unthinkable without the survival of powerful medieval elements. Benedetto Croce has flung his aesthetic anathema ex cathedra at the stylistic principle of baroque, but the historian cannot close his eyes to this important phenomenon, and before he may venture to judge it he must understand it as the expression of a great positive will. Michelet saw the surviving influence of the Middle Ages as a dead mass and suffered the consequence: he could represent the French culture of the seventeenth and eighteenth centuries as nothing more than a caricature. This is what makes his later volumes, written in exile with inadequate resources, such painful reading. Since then, however, not only have serious scholars been unable to ignore the Catholic forces of the baroque period and their close ties with medieval traditions—Jacob Burckhardt himself traveled this road as an old man—but even out and out Protestants have noted that the era of confessionalism reveals medieval forms of organization and thought in many basic traits. Ernst Troeltsch and Max Weber have pointed out that the great caesura in the history of the modern world occurred not at the time of Luther but in the period around 1700. In any event, a final disappearance of the Middle Ages in 1500 is out of the question.

"The printing press, the ancient world, America, the Orient, and the true system of the world"! The new understanding of the ancient world will always be counted among the crowning glories of the Renaissance. What is meant for the development of form, both in the fine arts and in literature, has been shown in memorable aesthetic analyses respectively by Heinrich Wölfflin and Johan Huizinga. Here remains the kernel of that complex of ideas that will always be called Renaissance. The printing press—no spiritual content but a mere technical vehicle—also brought about so profound a change in the forms of intellectual communication, and is chronologically so well established, that it too will always be counted among the principal features of the Renaissance. But America, the Orient, the true system of the world! To be sure, the new discoveries beyond the sea and the new computations of the orbits of the planets fall into this period, and assuredly people were taking an increasing interest in the Islamic Orient in this period of the founding of the Turkish Empire, but by and large these factors did not bring about a transformation in European thought in the sixteenth century. They are to be counted among the great agencies that caused, between 1680 and 1710, that *crise de la conscience européenne* that has been described by Paul Hazard. He revealed in a masterly way the true beginnings of the modern consciousness in the dawning interest in the comparative study of civilizations, in the closer spiritual contact between Orient and Occident, America and Europe, and in the rich literature of travel accounts and letters that flourished about 1700.

And yet it is no accident that the discovery of America occurred shortly before 1500 and not in 1700, that Copernicus at the beginning of the sixteenth century inaugurated those calculations that were raised to the level of evidence by Galileo and Newton, that the circle of the Florentine Platonists and Guillaume Postel initiated discussions on the Orient which later bore fruit. An enormous thirst for reality, a quest for new fields of exploration, a frenzied preoccupation with the possibility of tangible new knowledge, animated leading spirits in the most divergent spheres. Among them were Columbus and Copernicus, but also Leonardo and Rabelais, Vesalius and Servetus. But let us consider a little more closely what this thirst for experience and reality meant, to Vesalius for example. The *De humani corporis fabrica* of 1543 was not the first textbook of anatomy, but one among the many that had been written since Galen. Nor was Vesalius the first man since late antiquity to make use of cadavers for anatomical studies. Animal cadavers had been dissected in Salerno throughout the Middle Ages, and human bodies had frequently been dismembered since the fourteenth century. What characterizes Vesalius is not only an increased intensity in the pursuit of an already existing line of investigation, which impelled him to descend from the lecturer's platform, take the knife from the surgeon's hand, and himself demonstrate on the cadaver; it was above all his passion for disclosing the errors of Galen, the master of the ancient anatomists. The entire effort of Vesalius was patently directed against the canonical acceptance of a classical authority. It was, in a certain sense, antihumanistic. But in this endeavor, Vesalius was in full agreement with his great precursor Leonardo and his significant successor Servetus. For these men the ancient authorities were dethroned. What captivated them was the nature of things themselves. Concerning the religious convictions of Vesalius, we know little beyond conjecture. But we know a great deal about those of that other physician, whom Michelet mentions in the same breath with Vesalius, and who, because of his discovery of the lesser circulatory system, will always stand close to Vesalius in the history of medicine: Miguel de Servedo. The special doctrine of the Holy Ghost which Servetus supported, and for which he was burned at the stake in Geneva, is of extreme interest because of its relation to the intuition of nature. This finally leads us to the actual core of our lectures: here, in the anatomists of the sixteenth century, the theme of nature and spirit assumes its true urgency. *"Et verbum caro factum est."* What rich new meaning this ancient phrase acquired in the mind of a physician like Servetus the Spaniard, who became the head of the Italian spiritualists and Baptists. *Caro factum est:* flesh of the human body, that the anatomist could dissect.

But in turning to this theme, we shall do well to remember that we are now entering the wings of the Renaissance stage. And the actors in the play, for which the historian, despite all his reservations towards a hypertrophied concept, must retain the term Renaissance, are not natural scientists or spiritualists. It is the drama of classical form and ancient inspiration. Architects, sculptors, and painters take part in it, humanists above all, i.e., philologists in Ciceronian Latin, historians in the style of Livy, poets writing Petrarchan sonnets, finally such clever women as the memorable Marguerite of Navarre, who made music and told stories animated by a mixture of realistic inspiration and classical form.

If we wish to define this drama of the Renaissance in concepts and if we search for categories with a broader validity than those formulated for the fine arts by Heinrich Wölfflin, we shall no longer seize upon Burckhardt's catchword about the awakening of the individual. This concept has become too ambiguous and formless. It is the very formlessness of modern individualism that has made it impossible to employ this term without certain reservations, if we wish to do justice to the extreme importance of form in the spiritual manifestations of the Renaissance. It is known that, as an old man, Burckhardt changed his own mind on this point. "Oh, individualism," he said, in his homely Swiss dialect, "I don't entirely believe in it any more, but I don't say so; it gives them so much pleasure."[7] Those who took such immoderate pleasure in it were the political radicals all over Europe, who, in their anticlerical exuberance, believed that the Renaissance had happily done away with the religious substratum of life and given full license to the arbitrary acts of the individual. People were still reading Burckhardt with the ideas of Michelet in their hearts—the anticlerical Italians, for example, as their editions of Burckhardt's work show—long after Burckhardt himself had inwardly abandoned those ideas. He now said of the Middle Ages: "That which is vital to us is rooted there," and without the slightest paternal piety exposed his work of 1860 to falsification and extension.[8] He had other things to think about.

---

7 *"Ach wisse Si, mit dem Individualismus, i glaub ganz nimmi dra, aber i sag nit; si han gar a Fraid."* I first published this remark, told to me by one of those present, in my introduction to Ernst Walser's *Gesammelte Studien zur Geistesgeschichte der Renaissance* (Basel, 1932), p. xxxvii. There can be little doubt as to its authenticity, although Burckhardt seems, as was his custom, to be forsaking one of his brain children a little too easily. A characteristic shift in his ideas on the individual can be noted in his lecture on the "Cultural History of the Middle Ages." Speaking of the cult of martyrs and relics, he says: "Buddhism venerates only relics of Buddha himself and has no special memory of its individual disseminators, because it regarded everything individual as unworthy of it. Christianity, on the other hand, since it takes the salvation of the individual seriously, attaches the highest glory to its individual heralds and actually transfers to their relics and tombs a large part of its cult and its idea of God." *Gesamtausgabe,* Vol. VII (Stuttgart, 1929), p. 257.

8 Ibid., p. 254.

And yet an important insight resided in Burckhardt's catchword. In opposition to Burckhardt's thesis Huizinga once argued that wherever the scant sources allow us to fathom the origin of medieval works of the spirit, individualities emerge with strong personal thoughts and intentions. "How was it possible to claim individualism for the Renaissance, when beyond the dividing line stood figures like Abelard, Guibert de Nogent, John of Salisbury, Bertrand de Born, Chrétien de Troyes, Wolfram von Eschenbach, Villard de Honnecourt, and a hundred others?"[9] Assuredly the folk spirit alone accomplished nothing significant in the Middle Ages. Without the work of the significant individual, and there already were significant individuals, that culture is inconceivable. Yet is it an accident, resulting only from the scantiness of our sources, that we possess no portrait, either in painting or sculpture, of any of the men Huizinga names?—While on this side of the dividing line, we have innumerable biographies and portraits. In the Middle Ages only rulers and saints were thus glorified. While in the Renaissance a bookseller like Vespasiano da Bisticci painted portraits of all his best customers, one after another; and not only notorious braggarts like Benvenuto Cellini, but even more modest men like Thomas Platter, the son of a Swiss peasant, have left detailed autobiographies.

Nevertheless, we cannot claim this trait for the Renaissance alone, we cannot characterize the Renaissance by the portrait. The great intimate self-portrait, based on intensive self-examination, flowered in the age of Rousseau's *Confessions* and lasted on through the nineteenth century. Perhaps this trait was a part of that more general hunger, which we have discussed, for the realities of existence, for knowledge of the individual and specific, and that does not typify the Renaissance alone but the entire modern epoch. It is to a certain extent the natural aspect of this spirit. And one of its great forms of expression is the natural sciences. Moreover one can, without robbing the Middle Ages, maintain that the so-called realism of late Gothic art contains an announcement of this spirit, expressed in Gothic forms, but emanating from the same bourgeois milieu later cultivated by the Renaissance.

9 "Das Problem der Renaissance," in *Wege der Kulturgeschichte,* tr. into German by W. Kaegi (Munich, 1930), p. 130.

The true spiritual element that characterizes the Renaissance and only the Renaissance is, it seems to me, to be sought far more in that tendency which art historians found long ago in their special field: in a new simplicity. The simple, sweeping forms of the High Renaissance, which Wölfflin has disengaged so convincingly from the more animated and broken forms of the *quattrocento,* are not limited to the arts. Without reference to Wölfflin, Lucien Febvre had a good deal to say of this quality in his recent book on Marguerite of Navarre. Apropos of the conversations of Marguerite of Navarre with Briçonnet, her priestly adviser, he raised the question:

> What indeed was the strongest constant for the people of this epoch? Impatience, horror, hatred of complications, flourishes and formalism. A need for purity and simplicity in every field. Nothing is more understandable—as a reaction. It is true of architecture: the fifteenth century had seen the excesses of the flamboyant style, it had seen the pure forms of the thirteenth century, the robust and solidly bourgeois forms of the fourteenth century masked and disguised under a plethora of ornaments, furbelows and interlacings, which sometimes resulted in a positive decorative jumble.—It is true of fashions, whether we turn our attention to the feet or the head: the fifteenth century had seen the complicated headdress, the horned bonnets of the women, the tall caps of the men, the beaked shoes, the shirred cuffs, the slashed costumes with contrasting colors.—It is true of literature: the fifteenth century had seen the mastersingers with their rhyming games, their sterile rivalries in word acrobatics, the childish foolery of their rhymes, ambiguous and otherwise.—It is true of philosophy: the fifteenth century had seen the logical excesses of the terminalists, the chimerical excursions to the heaven of second intentions, the contests of the apprentice logicians, who sat like young cocks on their ergos and fought till their spittle ran out, amid the envious admiration of rival connoisseurs.— Finally, it is true of religion: the fifteenth century had seen the sacred texts masked, denatured and stifled by the pullulation of commentators on commentaries, by the abuse of glosses superimposed on glosses. And the mechanical analysis of texts, the substitution of reflections on texts for texts, the divisions and complications of texts, kept dozens of quarrelsome interpreters so busy that they forgot the texts themselves.—All this disgusted the men of 1520. Architecture moved towards

simpler, fuller lines, fashion towards natural, sober forms. Literature towards health, philosophy towards simplicity. And religion finally towards a return to the texts.[10]

Huizinga himself arrived at similar ideas when describing the advent of the new forms and analyzing the impulses of the Erasmian spirit in his *Waning of the Middle Ages*.[10a] These are modest categories, but they delimit what we know as the High Renaissance, both from the preceding epoch of the *quattrocento* and the ensuing Baroque age. In a certain sense they apply even to the reformers, particularly as distinguished from the Protestant clergy that grew out of their spirit.

Moreover, it will be well to bear in mind that a historical epoch need not necessarily represent a unit, but that historical science should primarily examine each separate life form and field of endeavor, each theme in its special variations.

II

In turning from the broader sphere of general history to the more restricted sphere of the history of ideas, I should like to suggest that we question certain contemporaries concerning their opinions and experience in regard to this theme. Their answers will provide a certain spectrum of the possibilities of experience and perhaps at the same time a chronological sequence of forms that we shall be able to construe as a transformation.

Most of all, I should like to knock on the door of a man who in a sense lives close to the gate of our own age; I am thinking of Dante. But anyone who speaks to the *alto poeta* is certain to receive so rich an answer that for the rest of the day he will have no leisure for other things. Spirit and nature in Dante would be a theme imposing the loftiest demands, and a theme the study of which would throw light on some of the most difficult and most beautiful questions not only regarding the *Commedia,* but regarding the whole *Geistesgeschichte* of the Middle Ages. We must pass this door by, and if we have hesitated for a moment it is because the very least that we owe him is a silent reverence.

10 Lucien Febvre, *Autour de l'Heptaméron, Amour sacré, amour profane* (Paris, 1944), pp. 99f.
10a Tr. F. Hopman (London, 1937) from *Der Herbst des Mittelalters.*

Anyone who desires to know how, as early as the first years of the *quattrocento,* the voice of the spirit could be heard and its manifestation seen in pristine purity, will find answers in the simplest, and, it seems to me, the strongest personality of those decades: Jeanne, *la pucelle.* The judges, who took seriously their task of determining the true nature of Jeanne's inspiration, have left us the records of their proceedings, including transcripts of testimony, which lose nothing by comparison with modern psychiatric case histories and have the advantage of giving not only interpretations and inferences that are subject to doubt, but many genuine documents, the most beautiful of all being the statements of Jeanne herself. These judges, who for political reasons had to arrive at a conviction, attempted with much caution and guile to force upon Jeanne two interpretations of her voices, one emphasizing the sexual motive and the other stressing pagan prototypes. The firmness and humor with which Jeanne answered such questions are as inspiring as the simplicity with which she describes the origin and nature of her voices. After a period of hesitation and reticence, she decided, on February 22, 1431, at the sixth session, to make a complete statement, in which she declared that ever since the age of fourteen she had heard a voice from God which had helped her in matters relating to her conduct.[11] Thus her vision seems originally to have been a phenomenon comparable and perhaps related to the Socratic *daemonion.* Characteristic is the fear that came over her when she heard the voice for the first time, and perhaps also the high noon hour of this first summer visitation: it occurred in her father's garden, not far from the church. And from the very beginning the voice seems to have been accompanied by the vision: *"et raro eam (vocem) audit sine claritate."*[12] This apparition of light always came from the same direction as the voice. She related that she had heard the voice in her father's garden, then in the woods as well, and after this had happened three times, she knew that it was the voice of an angel. Apparently this voice ordered her at a very early date, not only to conduct herself well and go to church, but also to run away to France. It was St. Michael who appeared to her,

11 Pierre Champion, *Procès de condamnation de Jeanne d'Arc* (Paris, 1920), Vol. I, p. 38.
12 Ibid. ("She seldom heard it [the voice] without the vision.")

and here we are reminded that in more than one function St. Michael was in a sense the Christian successor of Hermes, the ancient *psychopompos* and messenger of the gods. In the case of Jeanne d'Arc, he presumably signifies above all the archangel who enjoyed the most popular cult in her native region and who was also the patron saint of France and the royal armies.

Jeanne's subsequent testimony adds a few more touches to our knowledge of her apparitions; they predict the future: Orléans would be recaptured; they make her clairvoyant: she recognizes Robert de Baudricourt and later the Dauphin, although she had never seen them before. But the essential point is still that the voices come *ex parte Dei* and exact obedience. Her future personal salvation and her present inner assurance are bound up with this obedience. She is convinced that her downfall, especially her failure before Paris, stems from her disobedience to the voices. Now, in the prison at Rouen, the voices after a long interruption are again heard frequently. *"Ego audivi heri et hodie,"* she says in answer to the judges' questions.[13] Sometimes she wakes in the morning to the sound of her voices, sometimes she hears them three times in a day: in the morning, at the hour of vespers, and in the evening when the Ave Maria is rung. When asked whether she had thanked the voice and knelt, she replied: yes, she had thanked it, "sitting in her bed with folded hands."[14] Also significant perhaps is her statement that one day on waking she heard the voice, but only indistinctly, and that not until she was fully awake could she understand the words. The relation of obedience is seen most clearly in her admission that she was far more afraid to displease her voices by her statement in court "than I am afraid to answer you."[15]

When we hear these manifestations of a truly medieval visionary piety, we are amazed that anyone should have seriously attempted to separate Jeanne from the Middle Ages. Jeanne's life was really nothing else than an act of obedience towards a voice that came to her *ex parte Dei*. Fortunately, there is no need here to argue further with those who claim Jeanne d'Arc for the Renaissance on the strength of her "personality," her character, and her temperament.[16] One point,

13 Ibid., p. 45. ("I heard them yesterday and today.")
14 Ibid.   15 Ibid., pp. 46f.
16 Cf. Huizinga, "Bernard Shaws Heilige," in *Wege der Kulturgeschichte*, pp. 171–207.

however, in the argument of Bernard Shaw, who claimed Jeanne for Protestantism, remains worthy of note: the assertion that Jeanne held obedience to her personal revelations above obedience to the visible church. Luckily for the Church, the trial in Rouen was conducted by a politically prejudiced court of questionable competence, so that this problem in any true sense did not arise. Yet the historian cannot entirely ignore the question of how things would have gone if the Archbishop of Reims had done his duty and taken over the trial or at least protested it, or if Rome itself, as it was then, had had to decide in the matter. Gerson's treatise *De distinctione verarum visionum a falsis* operates with categories not far different from those employed by the judges at Rouen. In the event of a trial at Rome, would English influence with the Curia have been stronger than French influence? How would the picture of Jeanne d'Arc have come down in history if in the face of an unfavorably disposed Roman court she had preserved the courage she displayed at Rouen? Luckily, the historian has no need to answer these questions, but even if we must make a certain concession to Bernard Shaw, a Jeanne d'Arc burned in Rome rather than at Rouen would still not be a Renaissance figure, but a figure more in line with the true medieval heretics.

For Jeanne d'Arc the spirit that spoke to her was still something coming entirely from outside: an objective, perceptible phenomenon of sound and light. And the strange part of it is that, applied either by her friends or enemies, the naïve theological criteria for distinguishing between spirits are of no avail with her. A true divine inspiration, it was said, could not make a demand that ran counter to God's commandments, i.e., counter to a daughter's duty to obey her parents, and to womanly modesty. This was the opinion of the judges at Rouen and indeed of Gerson as well. But it is these very commandments of God, which are at the same time ordinances of nature—obedience to parents and womanly modesty—against which Jeanne offends: she runs away from home without permission and wears men's clothes. So violent is the compulsion to obey the commandment of her voices. And this very compulsiveness of obedience is the medieval, the ascetic quality in her.

Entirely different seems the relation in those spirits who, although they still possess the entire heritage of the Middle Ages, nevertheless embody the fully developed Renaissance: in the Platonists of Florence. During the very same decade in which Jeanne was burned in Rouen, the first idea of an academy originated in the mind of Cosimo de' Medici. "Anyone who understands the correct relation of natural things to divine things will find that, just as nature leads to God, the Aristotelian doctrine represents the road to the wisdom of Plato," says Marsilio Ficino himself in one of his letters.[17] Not only Aristotle and Plato, but nature and spirit, are now seen in a relation of harmony rich in correspondences, as two aspects of the same being. The mind of the Renaissance now carries this polarization further; either on the road of the natural philosophers and natural scientists, for whom the spirit remains only a function of nature, or, traveling the other road, the road of spiritualism, it extends the opinion of the Florentine Platonists that nature is to be understood only as a reflection and objectivization of the spirit.

The scales of nature and spirit had for long years been evenly balanced in the human consciousness: now for a time that of nature seemed to weigh more heavily, even in the minds of such men as Erasmus and More, who were somewhat more removed from Italy with its hunger for reality. Concerning Erasmus we know—and Huizinga has reminded us in his memorial lecture at Basel—that he wrote his *Praise of Folly* only as part of a triptych, the other two parts of which were intended to be a praise of nature and a praise of grace. No one can say in any detail what this praise of nature, conceived as an antithesis to a praise of grace, would have been.[18] Yet surely it would not have been as irreverent as certain admirers of the Renaissance suppose; more probably it would have been consonant with, for example, that maxim on the relation between soul and body that we find in the *Convivium religiosum*. There, in the course of edifying reflections, one of the banqueters suddenly cries out: "But while we are treating our souls so sumptuously, let us not neglect our colleagues." "What do you mean by colleagues?" another asks. "I mean our bodies; are they not the colleagues of our souls? I would rather call them thus than implements or houses or tombs." In this sentence lies the whole Erasmus. He came of a spiritual environment

17 Cf. Giuseppe Toffanin, *Storia dell' umanesimo* (Naples, 1933), p. 211.
18 J. Huizinga, *Parerga* (Zurich, 1945), pp. 63ff., esp. pp. 75ff.

in which the medieval, ascetic contempt for nature was all the more universal, in that it was not so much scholastic as mystical and provincial in character. In this milieu bodies were regarded as the tombs, at best the houses or implements of the soul. Now Erasmus, who from long experience with the infirmities of his *corpusculum* knew how autonomously the body could behave, addressed them politely as colleagues.[19] Erasmus, it is true, had no share in the endeavors of contemporary natural scientists, seafarers, and discoverers. These matters did not touch him deeply. But human nature itself played a very significant role in his thinking. In some passages of *The Praise of Folly*, it is almost identical with the merry Stultitia. Read for example her narrative of her birth:

> I was not brought forth in floating Delos, or on the foaming sea, or "in hollow caverns," but right in the Fortunate Isles, where all things grow "without ploughing or planting." In those islands is no drudgery or old age, nor is there any sickness. In the fields one never sees a daffodil, mallow, leek, bean, or any of such kind of trash; but one's eyes and nose are enchanted at the same time by moly, panacea, nepenthes, sweet marjoram, ambrosia, lotus, rose, violet, hyacinth, and the gardens of Adonis. And being born among these delights, I did not enter upon life with weeping, but right off I laughed sweetly at my mother. Nor indeed do I envy great Jupiter his nurse, the she-goat, since two charming nymphs nourished me at their breasts—Drunkenness, offspring of Bacchus, and Ignorance, Pan's daughter.[20]

The Praise of Folly seems to contain many intimations of the unwritten "Praise of Nature." Folly is life impulse and courage to live; "Folly is spontaneous energy that no one can do without."[21] Throughout the world, folly and nature stand in contrast with the *sophia* of the philosophers. But even where Erasmus speaks seriously, one is frequently made aware of the importance he attached to a healthy nature: in his concern with the proper feeding of suckling babes, with the clothing of children, with protecting young girls from marriage against

19 Note the difference in accent between the *corpusculum* of Erasmus and the σωμάτιον of Epictetus.
20 Erasmus, *The Praise of Folly*, tr. H. H. Hudson (Princeton, 1941), pp. 12–13.
21 J. Huizinga, *Erasmus of Rotterdam*, tr. F. Hopman (London, 1952), p. 71.

their will. In his testament he stipulated that half his fortune be spent on scholarships for poor students and the other half on trousseaus for poor girls.[22]

What constitutes the Renaissance quality in Erasmus is precisely this love for the simple, natural things in life and the way in which he combines them with the spiritual and theological aspects of his activity. This same connection characterizes the man to whom *The Praise of Folly* is dedicated: Thomas More. Only in the last decades has the non-English world recalled what More meant to the church and the freedom of the spirit. For the last century, More had almost become the patron saint of socialism, at all events he was primarily the author of *Utopia,* and in Utopia, as everyone knows, Christianity was not yet preached. *"Virtutem definiunt secundum naturam vivere."* They define virtue as living according to nature. We know how this principle applied to the whole life of the Utopians: to their clothing, their games, their country life, their contempt of money, their education of children. In all this, the modern reader must be constantly reminded that Thomas More may very well have felt that his ideals could be realized in a well-conducted monastery, for the natural color of the clothes may mean Franciscan garb, contempt of money may mean apostolic poverty, and the country life may mean Benedictinism. Rabelais' Abbey of Thélème is not very far removed from Utopia. In the decade after *Utopia* was written, the young Rabelais found, to be sure, that the Franciscan cloister in which he lived was no longer the right place for him; he wished to leave. In order to come a little closer to his ideals, he doffed the Franciscan dress and became—a Benedictine.

If More's Utopian had been constrained to live amid the reality of the sixteenth century, we must always reckon with the possibility that he would have become a Benedictine or a Carthusian. It was from the Carthusian monastery in Basel that the humanism of Amerbach and Frobenius received its most vital inspiration. When Erasmus came to Basel, he undertook, with his editions of St. Jerome and St. Augustine, a half-completed work that had begun its spiritual growth

---

22 Cf. Carl Roth, "Das Legatum Erasmianum" in *Gedenkschrift zum 400. Todestag des Erasmus von Rotterdam* (published by the Historische und Antiquarische Gesellschaft zu Basel, 1936), pp. 282ff.

in this monastery.[23] Not far from Basel, where these works were printed under the auspices of humanism, stood the altar of Isenheim, on the outer doors of which are carved the church fathers of the Basel editions, St. Jerome and St. Augustine. In the interior of the altar, Grünewald himself had depicted the ideal of life which these fathers had proclaimed. In the one case this was the Imitation of Christ, in the other, the life of St. Anthony in the Thebaid. It should not be forgotten that old Amerbach named one of his sons after Bruno, the founder of the Carthusian order, another after Basil, the Greek church father, and only the third after Boniface, the Occidental wandering apostle. The picture of the early Christian pneumatologist still lived deep in the heart of this generation.

But it is time for us to cross the Alps and knock on Italian doors. The real, the true relation of the Renaissance to nature and spirit is best discerned in its artists. Here we encounter the relation between the Renaissance and realism. Half a century ago, a somewhat naïve conception saw Renaissance wherever it observed realism. This of course applied especially to the beloved *quattrocento*. In his polemic against these ideas, Heinrich Wölfflin formulated the main principles of his "classical art." But the idea was also transferred to the Dutch painting of the Brothers van Eyck, and there was talk of a "Renaissance septentrionale." This was the point of departure for Huizinga's *Waning of the Middle Ages,* in which he drew a parallel between the realism of the Dutch-Flemish painting and the general tendency of the late Middle Ages towards the materialization of spiritual and divine things, whether in poetry or in art. *The Waning of the Middle Ages* is a polemic against the idea of the "Renaissance septentrionale" and its equating of Renaissance and realism.[24] Significant in this connection are certain statements by Dürer which throw light on the relation between Renaissance and realism, as it was reflected in the spirit of those artists themselves. It is Melanchthon who tells us that towards the end of his life Dürer described his development as an artist as follows: In his youth he had liked to paint colorful pictures rich in forms, and to represent odd misshapen figures. Grown

23 Cf. in this connection *Die Amerbach-Korrespondenz,* ed. Alfred Hartmann (Basel, 1942/43), Vols. I and II.
24 On Renaissance and realism, cf. Huizinga, *Wege der Kulturgeschichte,* pp. 140ff.

more mature, he had begun, however, to observe nature and to imitate its *original face* as faithfully as possible, and he had learned that this simplicity was the highest ornament of art, but he had also learned how hard it was not to deviate from nature.[25] It is understandable that the nineteenth century should have taken such words as an avowal of its own naturalism. But in Dürer's notes, we find versions of the idea, which clearly express the spiritual part of the matter: "Life in nature reveals the truth of these things. Therefore observe it diligently, be guided by it, and depart not from nature in thy presumption that thou mayst find something better by thyself. For in that thou wouldst be led astray. For verily, art dwells in nature, that man who can wrest it out, he has it. . . . Therefore, never presume that thou canst or willst do something better than God has given His created nature the power to do. For thy strength is helpless against the creation of God."[26] In Dürer's magnificent German all this sounds simple-hearted and primitive. But we perceive that in reality an old Aristotelian tradition of medieval times stands behind these words, when we invoke a passage from Dante as a sort of commentary. The question in point is sins against nature, specifically the taking of interest and usury, and Virgil declares:

"Filosofia," mi disse, "a chi la 'ntende,
    nota non pure in una sola parte,
    come natura lo suo corso prende

dal divino intelletto e da sua arte;
    e se tu ben la tua Fisica note,
    tu troverai, non dopo molte carte,

che l'arte vostra quella, quanto puote,
    segue, come il maestro fa il discente;
    sì che vostr' arte a Dio quasi è nepote."[27]

25 J. Manlius, *Locorum communium collectanea . . . , tum ex lectionibus D. Philippi Melanchthonis tum ex aliorum doctissimorum virorum relationibus excerpta* (Basel, 1562), p. 212. Cf. Huizinga, op. cit., pp. 155ff.

26 E. Heidrich, *Dürer's schriftlicher Nachlass* (Berlin, 1910), pp. 277ff.

27 " 'Philosophy,' he said to me, 'points out to him who understands it, not only in one part alone, how Nature takes her course / from the Divine Intellect and from Its art. And if thou note thy Physics well thou wilt find, after not many pages, / that your art follows her so far as it can, as the disciple does the master, so that your art is as it were grandchild of God.' "—*Inferno*, XI, 97–105, tr. C. E. Norton (Boston, 1940).

Art then is a granddaughter of God through nature, her mother. The granddaughter, however, does not merely imitate, but acts creatively, like her mother, nature; and it is this that enables her, *God's* creature, to wrest out what is *in nature.*

It seems paradoxical that Dante, who stands far from the Renaissance, should, of all people, invoke his Aristotle like a humanist for an insight that Leonardo, the true master of the Renaissance, expresses precisely in attacking the humanism of the schools: "Even though I should not, like them, be able to adduce authors, a far greater and worthier thing to read is the invocation of experience, the master of their masters. Those people go about puffed up with pomp, clad and adorned not in their own but in other people's pains . . . and if they despise me, an inventor, how much more blameworthy are they, not inventors, but trumpeters and reciters of other people's works."[28] Here in Leonardo, to be sure, there speaks something more than the spirit of the Renaissance, and that is the spirit of natural science as opposed to the spirit of school humanism. This is exactly the attitude of Vesalius towards Galen. And it is strange that Leonardo, who embodies the Renaissance if anyone does, should herald the new principle of knowledge that points beyond the Renaissance: mathematics. "There is no certainty," he writes in his notes, "where one of the mathematical sciences cannot be applied, nor is there certainty in anything which cannot be connected with mathematics."[29] Combination of experience and calculation, of experiment and mathematics. Here, in the very heart of the Renaissance, lies the spirit of a hard future. But in Leonardo the awareness of nature's mysterious wealth in hidden spiritual possibilities is still perfectly intact. *"La natura è piena di infinite ragioni che non furono mai in esperienza."*[30]

It is evident that even where the classical sense of form has reached its high point, the culmination of its spiritual suggestion, the experience of nature achieves almost paramount power. And this is what connects Leonardo with that most unclassical spirit of his age, whose

28 *Leonardo da Vinci, der Denker, Forscher und Poet aus seinen veröffentlichen Handschriften,* ed. Marie Herzfeld (Jena, 1926), p. 11.

29 Ibid., p. 7, from *Les Manuscrits de Léonard de Vinci,* in phototype facsimile, edited by Charles Ravaisson-Mollien (Paris, 1881–91).

30 Ibid., p. 13, from MS. J, fol. 18 r, in Ravaisson-Mollien edn. ("Nature is full of infinite reasons that have never been found in experience.")

work had been a heroic hymn to nature: Rabelais. His hymn so intoxicated his contemporary, and even more so his modern readers, that the strangest misunderstandings have arisen. Abel Lefranc is an eminent student of Rabelais, deserving of the highest merit for his edition of Rabelais' works; he has frequently revealed a true insight into human nature. And yet, according to his interpretation, Maître Alcofribas, *abstracteur de quintessence,* is a declared enemy of Christianity and a militant atheist. Jean Platard's meticulous biographical research and critical studies of texts put this thesis in doubt; and Lucien Febvre's thorough investigation of the matter in his *Problème de l'incroyance au XVIme siècle*[31] confuted it completely. The statements of Rabelais' contemporaries who called him an atheist proved utterly worthless. Febvre was able to show that if this word were to be taken at its face value, we should also have to call Erasmus, even Luther and Calvin, atheists, for so said all their adversaries; on the other hand, the representatives of the Curia, even the popes themselves, were atheists, for so said the Protestants. The expression was an expletive of theological polemics, a vulgar insult, like the "Bolshevik" of our days. And incidentally: *Tout le monde est le nazi de quelqu'un.*

As to what Rabelais thought about matters spiritual and divine, the only fully valid testimony lies in his own writings. One of the most important is a letter, known as the "Lettre à Salignac," but proved to have been written to Erasmus.[32] Here Rabelais calls Erasmus "his father and mother at once," him from whose spirit he has nourished and shaped himself all his life: "such hast thou educated me, such hast thou nourished me on the chaste breasts of thy divine teachings, that, were I not to offer thee in thanks everything that I am and everything of which I am capable, I should be the most ungrateful of all men. And so I salute thee again and again, beloved father, ornament of the fatherland, pillar of the sciences, unexcelled champion of the truth." The letter was written in 1532. At that date, the Christian import of Erasmus' life work was no longer subject to doubt. It is hard to conceive of anyone supporting this work with greater enthusiasm than Rabelais. It has not been very difficult to recognize the central

31 Paris, 1942.
32 Rabelais, *Oeuvres complètes,* ed. Jacques Boulenger (Pléiade edn., Paris, 1934), pp. 978f.

ideas of Erasmus in Gargantua's well-known pedagogic letter to his son Pantagruel and even in the regulations of the Abbey of Thélème. Today the Erasmian attitude and piety of Rabelais are scarcely to be questioned.

The assertion that Rabelais did not believe in the immortality of the soul provoked a noteworthy piece of research. In the above-mentioned letter to his son, Gargantua counsels Pantagruel to take pains in forming his mind, partly in order that his father when facing death may be comforted by the thought that he will not entirely die, but will survive spiritually in his son: *"car, quand par le plaisir de luy, qui tout régist et modère, mon âme laissera ceste habitation humaine, je ne me réputeray totallement mourir, ains passer d'un lieu en aultre, attendu que en toy et par toy je demeure en mon image visible en ce monde, vivant, voyant et conversant."*[33] Abel Lefranc maintains that this is a profession of pure survival in the flesh of one's children, and that without this survival death would mean a total dying, that is, complete extinction, also of the soul. This interpretation might go hand in hand with Ronsard's ironical epitaph for Rabelais, in which he has a grapevine draw its nourishment from the rotting belly of the mighty eater and drinker that the legend makes of Rabelais, in order to show that *"d'un mort qui pourri repose, / Nature engendre quelque chose."*[34] This would be a survival entirely in keeping with the spirit of the medical admirers of Rabelais, who prior to 1940 offered potations to their great colleague in the taverns of France. It has not been very difficult to show that Rabelais' alleged denial of the immortality of the soul rests on a very artificial logic in the interpretation of texts, and that the *"totallement mourir"* of Gargantua's letter is contradicted by very positive statements of Rabelais with regard to eternal life. Gilson, the religious historian, has demonstrated Rabelais' thoroughly orthodox adherence to tradition in this point by comparison with the great theological texts of the Middle Ages, while Febvre, the philological historian, has explained Rabelais by Rabelais and shown that Maître Alcofribas represented a very conservative doc-

33 Ibid., p. 225.
34 "Epitaphe de François Rabelais" in Pierre de Ronsard, *Oeuvres complètes,* ed. Gustave Cohen (Pléiade edn., Paris, 1938), Vol. II, pp. 784f.

trine of the human soul: in Rabelais as in all his contemporaries, the natural spirits animate the separate parts of the body; their home is the liver and they travel through the veins; animated by the warmth of the heart, the vital spirits travel through the arteries, and the animal or life spirits, that are renewed in the brain, travel through the nerves.[35] To these three types of errant spirits in the body, all of which occur in Rabelais, correspond three different souls: a natural soul which sustains the vegetative life, a sensitive soul which sustains the animal life, and an intellective soul which sustains the actual spiritual life. As in creation, the vegetative soul is proper to plants, the sensitive soul to animals, and the intellective soul to man, thus in the individual man the three souls grow with his body. The foetus possesses the vegetative, the newborn babe also the sensitive, and the adult, in addition to the vegetative and the sensitive, possesses also the intellective soul. Through the possession of these three souls, man becomes capable of exercising all his functions, from the most primitive up to the highest, which is the contemplation of the Creator. When man dies, his vegetative soul dies in him as in plants, his sensitive soul also dies in him as in animals. These two souls are mortal, as plants and animals are mortal: this was the tradition, this was the belief of the sixteenth century, this was also the belief of Rabelais. The intellective soul, however, separates—as to how it does this let the theologians of the sixteenth century rack their brains—from the vegetative and sensitive soul; it also separates from the body and returns to its true home. Once when one of her waiting women lay dying, Marguerite de Navarre tried in vain to perceive physically the escape of the soul from her lips, or at least to hear a soft whistling sound. The spirit, the soul, and the animus: these were the three natures of the soul, and for Rabelais they were just as self-evident facts as for the physicians, poets, and theologians of his time. True, there were deviations in detail, variations in conception and terminology; but the underlying idea of a soul composed of several parts, of a mortal and immortal nature, remains. And Pantagruel in the *Quartlivre* expresses his fully conventional belief in immortality: *"Je croy— (dist Pantagruel) que toutes âmes intellectives sont exemptes des ciz-*

35 Cf. Febvre, *Le problème de l'incroyance au XVIme siècle*, pp. 183ff.

eaulx de Atropos; toutes sont immortelles: anges, daemons et humaines."[36] Here the human soul appears again in its intrinsic kinship with the immortal intellective souls of the angels and the demons.

Death, for the people of the sixteenth century as for those of the Middle Ages, is the dissolution of the complex union of the multiform material and spiritual forces that in their combination represent the living man. And this dissolution is complete, a *"totallement mourir,"* even if one of its parts, the intellective soul, survives. It is quite understandable that a giant like Gargantua, who in his lifetime took so much pleasure in the vegetative and sensitive functions of his existence, who was so mighty an eater and drinker, should be somewhat grieved at the thought of the complete dissolution of his earthly person. This does not necessarily make him a heathen, for even the good Christian looks on death as a punishment: the wages of sin. In this grief over the reality of his death, it gives Gargantua a certain comfort to think that not only his immortal soul, but also something of his earthly being, as it lived in the flesh, will endure in his son Pantagruel, if he becomes a true image of his father, not only in his physical but in his spiritual powers as well.

In the expectation of death, the people of the sixteenth century knew, in addition to the consolations of the church, another very specific comfort, highly typical of them and their age: music. Here again Michelet has given us a magnificent formulation: "A new mother of the human race had come into the world; the great enchantress and consoler, music had been born."[37] One of the daughters of Catherine de' Medici, when she felt the approach of death, sent for her musician: *"Julien, prenez votre violon et sonnez-moi toujours jusqu'à ce que vous me voyez morte."* The musician was ordered to play a song about the defeat of the Swiss at Marignano.[38] "And when you come to the place: *'tout est perdu,'* sonnez-le par quatre ou cinq fois le plus piteusement que vous pourrez." A humanist of the French circle, Etienne Dolet, who was later burned at the stake, tells us what music had meant for the advancement of his work: "To music I owe my life and the whole success of my literary labors. . . .

36 *Oeuvres complètes*, ed. Boulenger, p. 639.
37 *Histoire de France*, Vol. X, p. 88 ("La Reforme," Ch. V).
38 Cf. Febvre, op. cit., pp. 468ff.

I should never have been able to endure my gigantic, unremitting exertions, if music had not refreshed me." Here Etienne Dolet only repeats what Baldassare Castiglione, the great Italian master of all knowledge concerning education and the true intellectual life, had said of his *cortegiano:* "You must know that I am not content with the courtier unless he be also a musician and unless, besides understanding and being able to read notes, he can play upon divers instruments."[39] When one of the courtiers of Urbino, among whom the dialogue takes place, argues that music was "proper to women and perhaps to some that have the semblance of men, but not to those who really are men," Castiglione threatens: "Say not so, for I shall enter upon a vast sea in praise of music. And I shall call to mind how it was always celebrated and held sacred among the ancients, and how very sage philosophers were of opinion that the world is composed of music, that the heavens make harmony in their moving, and that the soul, being ordered in like fashion, awakes and as it were revives its powers through music."[40]

Nowhere, I believe, is the classical conception of the Renaissance concerning the relation of nature and spirit better expressed than in these words of Castiglione on music. In the practical life of those men, the law of harmony is sometimes harder to discover than in their theory. And yet, if we do not find it, the reality of the period is not so much to blame as our inadequate faculties of historical understanding. The cynical smile with which the modern observer views the harsh contrasts of that reality often attests nothing but our own ignorance. Recently Lucien Febvre attempted once more to solve, as far as possible, one of the most remarkable of those paradoxical contradictions. The paradox in this case is named Marguerite of Navarre.[41] In the history of the French Reformation she is known as the protectress of the young Calvin, as the woman who in her petty southern French kingdom granted a haven to many who were exiled for reasons of the spirit, whether humanists, Lutherans, or mystics. We know the religious writings of Marguerite herself, her pious correspondence with Briçonnet, the Bishop of Meaux. Her own attitude

39 *Il Cortegiano,* Lib. I, Cap. XLVII (*The Book of the Courtier,* tr. L. E. Opdycke, New York, 1903, p. 62).
40 Ibid. (Opdycke, p. 63).
41 *Autour de l'Heptaméron, Amour sacré, amour profane.*

has sometimes been described as humanistic-Neoplatonic, sometimes as Lutheran, sometimes as Calvinist. Yet we know that about 1500, even before the emergence of Luther, there was such a thing as Paulism: the Paulism of the Oxford Reformers and of Lefèvre d'Étaples. Among these Paulists must be numbered Briçonnet and Marguerite of Navarre. It is a pre-Lutheran Paulism, which, like that of More, remained a purely Catholic manifestation.

But side by side with the pious Marguerite of Navarre, who wrote the *Miroir de l'âme pécheresse* condemned by the Sorbonne, stands another Marguerite, author of the *Heptameron*, a collection of crude love stories in the manner of the *Decameron*, in which, for the attainment of the goal of love, every means, treachery, adultery, murder, is taken for granted without so much as a word wasted in justification. Concerning the relation between the actual conduct of those who wrote or listened to such stories and the spirit of the *Heptameron*, Burckhardt made a memorable remark. "Some readers will think," he said, "that a society capable of listening to such immoral tales was utterly worthless. It would be more correct to say: on what secure foundations must a society have rested, which despite such stories did not depart from external forms, did not get entirely out of hand."[42] For Marguerite of Navarre, author of the *Heptameron*, the corrected version of this observation is surely applicable. As to her listeners, it is true that they sometimes got out of hand, but this they could have done even without having read the *Heptameron*. The contrast remains loud and harsh, it lies in the reality of the spiritual life of that time. Marguerite encompassed its entire gamut of variations and possibilities. What form the dialogue between the different powers of the soul, the argument between spirit and nature, assumed in the individual, we scarcely know. We have, to be sure, a long series of splendid autobiographies, but they were all molded around an idea and stylized. The true *journal intime*, the confession, was not born until the eighteenth century. In the sixteenth, we sometimes have the impression that the individual forces of the soul still acted in full sovereignty, independently of one another, like the nobles under the monarchy, in harsh contradictions, but that the leap of consciousness from one sphere to another need not be regarded as hypocrisy or cynicism. To

42 *Gesamtausgabe,* Vol. V, p. 276.

us it seems almost a blasphemy that the whole company of the *Heptameron* and especially those who are to speak that day should have gone to mass every morning, and prayed the divine mercy to lend them the grace necessary for the telling of their spicy stories.

Glaring as the contrasts may seem to us, they were for the people of that epoch self-evident and natural. And they did not prevent those people from believing in a constantly renewed reconciliation with God. The Renaissance was far removed from drawing radical theological consequences from the contradiction between nature and grace, as the Reformers did. But the best of its representatives felt— like the Reformers—that to transcend that tension could not be the work of the human will, but must be a gift of heaven. *"La grazia non s'impara,"* says Castiglione.[43] Grace is not to be learned of schoolmasters. And yet, without this one gift of heaven—grace—the whole education of the courtier is imperfect. What Castiglione says about the origin of grace is highly remarkable. Sometimes it seems to him to lie in nature itself, for as one of the first prerequisites of the true courtier, he names the following: "endowed by nature not only with talent and beauty of person and feature, but with a certain grace and (as we say) air that shall make him at first sight pleasing and agreeable to all who see him."[44] And then, after listing all the abilities that the courtier must master: the handling of arms mounted and on foot, bull fighting, swimming, running, ball playing, good conversation, eloquence, knowledge of the poets both Latin and Greek—he must be able to write poetry, perform music, and at least know how to judge painting—after all this, Castiglione comes back to grace. For all these abilities are nothing without grace. But grace is *"don della natura e de' cieli."*[45] And "those men who are born so fortunate and so rich in this treasure as are some we see, seem to me in this to have little need of other master; because that benign favor of heaven almost in spite of themselves leads them higher than they will, and makes them not only pleasing but admirable to all the world. . . . But they who have received from nature only so much that they are capable of becoming graceful by pains . . ." are next to be discussed.[46] And Castiglione goes

43 *Il Cortegiano,* Lib. I, Cap. XXV (Opdycke, p. 34).
44 Ibid., Cap. XIV (p. 23).   45 Ibid., Cap. XXIV.
46 Ibid. (Opdycke, p. 33).

on to impart the nature of affectation and false grace, and to tell how these pitfalls of conduct can be avoided.

It seems to me that Castiglione did not realize how close he was here to a central problem of theology. When he wrote *Il Cortegiano*, the central problems with which Luther was concerned were not yet known in Italy. If I were now bidden to speak of "spirit and nature in the sixteenth century," the great question of the reflection of this theme in the spirit of the Reformers would force itself upon me. But here I shall limit myself to the Renaissance. Yet precisely this narrower topic demands a last word on that group of thinkers who, coming from the Renaissance, turn towards the Reformation: these are the Italian spiritualists and anti-Trinitarians, so-called, because they represent a special doctrine of the spirit and hence also of the Trinity. They include a number of significant figures: Ochino, the first vicar-general of the Capuchins, the two Sozzinis, the fathers of Socinianism, Gribaldi, Biandrata, and Curione, from whom Jacob Burckhardt was descended. All of them left Italy voluntarily or involuntarily. Locarno was the first haven of many who shared their destiny and their faith; most went on to Geneva, Zurich, Basel, some to Germany, Poland, or England. Significantly, they encountered on their wanderings northern spiritualism, whose destinies were molded by the Reformation. Personal friendships were formed, as between Curione and the Dutch Baptist David Joris in Basel, or between Ochino and the Silesian mystic Kaspar Schwenckfeld in Augsburg.[47] Today scholarship is concerned with this group mainly in connection with the history of the idea of tolerance.[48] In dealing with this problem, American scholars in particular have gone back to the men who, in 1554, after the burning of Servetus, issued the Basel protest against Calvin: *De haereticis an sint persequendi*. But to understand these men we need not call on the ideas of the Enlightenment; we may equally understand them as late Joachimites. They too lived in the expectation of a dawning new era, that of the Holy Ghost, and most of them expected the Last Judgment in their own lifetime. What

47 On this whole subject, cf. Delio Cantimori, *Eretici italiani del Cinquecento* (Florence, 1940).
48 Cf. Roland H. Bainton, *David Joris, Wiedertäufer und Kämpfer für Toleranz im 16. Jahrhundert* (Archiv für Reformationsgeschichte, Suppl. Vol. VI; Leipzig, 1937).

detains us here for a moment is their connection with the Renaissance. In their endeavor to sift the spiritual tradition of the late scholastic era, more than one of them proceeded from a philological point of departure: they are preoccupied with the exact meaning of words, especially in the text of the Bible. Lorenzo Valla is their first guide in the critical interpretation of the gospels. One of the main problems, which troubles them again and again, is the correct translation of the first sentence in the Gospel of St. John. Certain that the Greek λόγος is not simply the written Biblical word, the *verbum*, they search for new Latin versions that would render the wealth of meaning inherent in the concept. For the most part they preferred *sermo* instead of *verbum*, because it suggested continuous speech, the *eloquium Dei*. The Savoyard Castellio translates it in this way; and the Spaniard Servetus, who for a long time was the leader of the Italian spiritualists, opened the whole central dogmatic question that lay behind the problem of the word and of translation, and had already been discussed by Valla and Erasmus. It was the prophetic element in the concept of the *logos* that preoccupied these Italians: they construed St. John's *logos* as *oraculum, vox,* as *sermo* or *eloquium Dei*. In his *De Trinitatis erroribus* Servetus stresses that the Holy Ghost is a comprehensive and active principle with which inspired speech, preaching and prophecy, indeed every work of God, must be associated, *"quasi spiritus sanctus non rem aliquam separatam, sed Dei agitationem, energiam quandam seu inspirationem virtutis Dei designet."*[49] This doctrine, which was the source of the chasm separating the spiritualists from the Reformers who limited revelation to the word of the Holy Scriptures, and of the typically Baptist protest against the new paper Pope, made for a wealth of possibilities in the interpretation of the *logos*, leading to the most diverse tendencies of thought. In Camillo Renato, a leader of the Italian refugees living in concealment in Graubünden, the concept of spirit assumes a completely Platonizing coloration akin to the eros concept in Marsilio Ficino. It is a *vis Dei* that acts in the heart of Christians, making them capable of divine deeds, giving them the knowledge of truth and the

---

49 *De Trinitatis erroribus*, p. 28 v., according to Cantimori, op. cit., p. 39. (". . . just as the Holy Ghost does not designate any separate thing, but a movement of God, a certain energy or inspiration of the Divine spirit.")

intuition of God. In Curione, the Basel philologist, the *logos* becomes a principle animating the world, *"un certo animo o ver spirito eterno . . . il quale chiamiamo Iddio et quello doversi honorar et adorar da tutti gli uomini del mondo: la qual cosa ci è efficacemente dimostrata dalla quasi infinita bellezza di questo mondo et dall' ordine maraviglioso che vediamo nei celesti corpi et lumi."*[50] Here the emphasis is on the beauty of natural creation, on the hidden laws of nature and the heavenly bodies. The thinking of these men turns back into the main stream of Renaissance ideas: veneration of God in the beauty of His creations, in the mystery of nature, and also, as these spiritualists of the sixteenth century had already conceived, in the mysteries of history. Even then they sought a revelation of God not only in the spatial realm of nature, but in the temporal domain of historical events. Convinced that the end of history was approaching, that the Last Judgment was at hand, they looked back over the whole of human destiny. Many of them were inspired above all by a sense that all exalted human gifts would be lost in the ultimate confusion and exhaustion: and the historical road that had led to these sinful last days was for them an object of profound amazement. They not only believed that, like artists and natural scientists, they could recognize the workings of the divine spirit in the nature of tangible things, but also found its manifestation in the destinies of nations and great empires, even in the thought patterns of the different religions, dogmas, and heresies. The number of historians among the spiritualists is remarkable, and their thinking had a significant influence on the development of a philosophical historiography. Nowhere have these ideas been more fully expressed than in Sebastian Franck. With him we have returned close to the point from which we started today: to the idea of a self-revelation of God in the history of the human race. From Sebastian Franck's representation of history as a series of God's miraculous deeds, from his chronicle of heretics to Herder's philosophy of history, the road is not hard to find. Strange to say, a

---

[50] *Una familiare et paterna institutione della Christiana religione di M. Celio Secundo Curione, più copiosa et più chiara che la latina del medesimo. Con certe altre cose pie* (Basel, 1549), c. A[5] r. (". . . a certain eternal soul or rather spirit . . . whom we call God and who should be honored and worshiped by all men in the world: which thing is effectively demonstrated by the almost infinite beauty of this world and by the marvelous order that we see in the heavenly bodies and luminaries.")

related road leads directly to Michelet's concept of the Renaissance. This idea was nothing other than an attempt to reduce any given epoch of modern history to the simple formulation of a concept of providence. When, towards the end of his life, Michelet wished to set down the sum of his historical knowledge in a single book, he chose for this book the title *Bible de l'humanité* and began it with the words: *"L'humanité dépose incessamment son âme en une Bible commune. Chaque grand peuple y écrit son verset."* Michelet probably did not suspect that the title of his book of 1864 was an unconscious translation of another book title, which had reflected the sixteenth century spiritualist view of history. When, in 1531, Sebastian Franck, at the age of thirty-two, wished for the first time to express his idea of a revelation of God in the destinies of nations, he chose the title *Chronica, Zeitbuch, und Geschichtsbibel* (Chronicle, annals, and Bible of history). This universal history was to be a Bible, because it too was the expression of a word of God. "For there is scarcely a heathen, philosopher, or heretic who has not divined some good thing, which I do not for that reason reject, but worship as pure gold, and likewise in heathen and heretics I find some of my God, whom I love and honor. Just as He lets His sun shine on good and evil, He pours forth His loving-kindness on all the children of mankind."[51]

---

51 *Chronica, Zeitbuch, und Geschichtsbibel von Anbeginn bis in dies gegenwärtig 1531 Jahr* (Strassburg, 1531).

Friedrich Dessauer

Galileo and Newton: The Turning Point in Western Thought

1

"Spirit and nature" has been chosen as our central theme, and in her remarks at the opening of the meeting, Mrs. Froebe has made clear what this implies: by a responsible striving towards the truth, we must endeavor to bridge the distances which modern scientific methodology has created between the two great realms designated as sciences of the spirit [*Geisteswissenschaften*], or humanities on the one hand, and natural science and technology on the other. Is there an element common to them? Have they a common root? Is there any justification for setting a higher value on the humanities? It means to interpret the ambivalent terms "spirit" and "nature" in a very definite way; that is, from the standpoint of man's endeavor to achieve systematic knowledge. The question arises: what share has each of the two great spheres in determining the destiny of man and mankind? Where lie the decisions for the future of the human race?

Many who, without the slightest misgivings, used to let their basic attitude, their humanistic tradition, answer such questions for them, now show a certain hesitancy. For today the feeling has become widespread that some of the more recent scientific discoveries, such as that of atomic energy (though not that alone) make it necessary for man to pursue certain courses in order to avoid his own destruction; the statesmen of all countries are motivated by such a feeling. One cannot help wondering whether this has not been true for a long time— whether electrification, aviation, our increased knowledge of biology, and much earlier the printing press and many other discoveries and inventions, have not, for centuries, affected our lives more profoundly than anything else. Perhaps, after all, the great achievements of technology based on natural science have more than a merely pragmatic meaning.

Bearing in mind the dilemma of modern man, we wish to examine here the manner in which our present modes of thought and behavior were molded by a critical change that occurred three centuries ago. We shall find, perhaps to our surprise, that to a very great extent the present age, and particularly the way in which we react to our environment, was determined by the times of Galileo and Newton.

But before attempting to show this, I should like to make certain fundamental remarks:

Firstly: *Everything that the natural scientist discovers in his field is spiritual,* for it is rule, order, law. Chaos can be perceived by the mind but cannot be made an object of intellectual knowledge. Only order can be known. And a barely visible grain of dust bears within it more spirit than all man's wit has thus far been able to fathom. It consists of millions of molecules, which in turn consist of atoms, and we are just beginning to know something about the atom. The ancients knew that everything knowable in nature is spiritual. What in Plato appears independently as the idea and in Aristotle as μορφή, the form of a substantial, corporeal thing, and at the same time the fulfillment of a purpose, an entelechy, is the spiritual element of the object and combines being and intelligibility.

Secondly: In the history of civilization there have been epochs in which there was no schism in the quest for knowledge, when inquiring minds did not diverge but, looking through nature, man, and society, all turned in *one* direction, towards a universal first cause. It was only much later that in considering matter, nature, and the domain of the secular, rather than spirit, culture, and the divine, a changed attitude was felt to be necessary. This divergence and even opposition and conflict between the two positions is not necessarily inherent in the subject matter; does it not seem possible that it is grounded in human attitudes which are historically determined? We shall speak of two epochs in which the world was contemplated *uno aspectu.*

Finally: Let us explain simply what we mean when we speak of reality, or more specifically natural reality, in order not to be hampered by any difficulties that may arise out of a theory of knowledge. What reality does natural science aspire to know? "Real" in the naïve sense are this house, the beautiful lake outside the windows, the rocky mountains round us—things, in other words, bodies, substantial, material objects. But also the radiance of space, the light of the sun; the "object of the senses," so to speak, all lumped together. But light is an entirely different thing, it is not a body. In eight minutes' time, it passes through a space almost devoid of bodies from the sun to the earth, and we call it an energy. Certainly this is something real, for our whole life and being depend on the stream of energy emanating from the sun, it is the force underlying all our water power, all our machines. This hall in which we are gathered together is filled perhaps with innumerable electromagnetic waves, of which our senses tell us nothing. But we can establish their reality at once with the help of a radio receiving set. They belong indubitably to our natural reality, although none of our senses perceives them. By far the greater part of natural reality is hidden to our senses, which penetrate neither that which is too small nor that which is too large, which register only an infinitesimal segment of all the immense variety of waves, which are restricted to the narrow spatial and temporal limits of our most immediate human environment. The ancient philosophers thought that nothing of any importance in the cosmos could still be unknown to them, for otherwise there would be a special sensory organ for it. But natural science has shown that the sphere of reality is millions of times greater in breadth and depth than the unaided senses can tell us and than our forefathers believed. By far the most of it was unknown to the Greeks. When their historic hour struck in the pre-Socratic era, they opposed the cosmos to their own consciousness and construed the world "as an order" which also included man, an order that could be known, that the intellect could penetrate. Awakening from the animistic, Homeric world, in which every spring, every tree had its demigod, on whose will and grace the whole world process depended, the Greeks soared to amazing intellectual heights and attempted to explain the existence and nature of the world on the basis of ultimate principles. Since then, the object to be known has grown millions of times larger, new strata of being, new realities have been disclosed, and all of them must be included in the realm of natural reality.

For all these realities there is a criterion. Natural science is a realm of certainty. No one seriously doubts the reliability of a natural law that has once been established. Even those idealists whose theory of knowledge has led them to doubt the existence or the intelligibility of things transcending consciousness have, for practical purposes, fully relied on such things. We all feel perfectly certain that our electrical power plants, provided they are constructed in accordance with natural laws, will accomplish everything we have grown accustomed to expect from them; that the planets will move in their orbits; that drugs will soothe pain; that the airplane will rise off the ground; that radio waves will cross the sea; that our house will shelter us and our bridge support us. *Reality is recognized by its efficacy,* which is its criterion; *natural reality is reliable.*

If in the present discussion we concentrate on two names, Galileo and Newton, it is an unavoidable simplification, hence an inexactitude, for which I beg your indulgence. In addition to these two great men, many others, some of them very great scientists, helped to constitute the epoch on which I shall speak. It is perhaps impossible, for me I know it is impossible, to give a clear and penetrating picture of a great event in man's spiritual history without simplification, generalization and reduction to types. And moreover, in order to make the essentials intelligible, I shall have to leave far more unsaid than it will be possible for me to say (and this does not imply that what I omit is unimportant).

2

When Galileo, son of a cloth merchant of good family, was born in Pisa, in 1564, Michelangelo Buonarroti, the most representative figure of the Renaissance that was then drawing to a close, lay on his deathbed. Young Galileo Galilei's father, who was none too prosperous, desired his gifted son to study medicine, which he regarded as a lucrative profession. But Galileo's genius led him elsewhere. He was a zealous student of Aristotle, who then dominated all academic learning, and at an early age he turned his attention to the master's works on physics. Since Aristotle had, in a sense, explained all nature, the scientists of the time believed that all its important elements were known. Of all Aristotle's works that have come down to us, more than half are concerned with explaining the world on the basis of "last principles."

Only prejudice can deny that the conception of these "last principles" was a great intellectual accomplishment. As Aristotle himself tells us, he strove for a solution of the antinomy that is commonly designated by the names of Heraclitus and Parmenides. In Aristotle's view, Heraclitus saw the great, ultimate essence of all nature in change or, as it was then more frequently stated, in motion. For him, permanence is only slow change, and there is no static being. For this, the world of appearance offers innumerable arguments; as is even better known to us today than it was then. Parmenides on the other hand, the first true metaphysician and one of the greatest of all time, saw through motion and recognized that underlying it there must be a being without change and at rest. He divides the world into a real world of being and an illusory world, in which we are submerged, a kind of unreal being. At the gate between these two realms watches Dike, guardian of the law. It seems safe to assume that Parmenides' world of true being is a "nomic" world, a world of immutable laws, while the world of things with its constant change is actually a deceptive world of nonbeing.

Plato, Democritus, and Aristotle were faced with this dilemma: was change or permanent being the fundamental characteristic of the cosmos? Each solved the problem in his own way, and each solution, viewed with the eyes of the present, shows greatness, depth, and an element of truth. That of Aristotle became dominant two thousand years later, in the thirteenth century, when Albertus Magnus and Thomas Aquinas took over the Aristotelian philosophy, largely from Arabic sources, and used this grandiose system as a foundation for revelation that would be rational and philosophical, hence adequate to the human mind. St. Thomas was assuredly one of the ablest thinkers of all time; acutely differentiating, interpreting, clarifying, and ordering, he concerned himself with a wide range of problems. He took the heathen philosopher into his system in order to lead the intellective human spirit to God. After a period of tenacious resistance, his work conquered the schools of the Christian world. His integration of the metaphysical heritage into the sphere of theology was a masterful achievement, but the result of this ecclesiastical accept-ance of philosophical ideas was that an aura of the unassailable and sacrosanct fell upon the profane philosophy of Aristotle. Among the learned world it was well-nigh dogmatized, at all events it became dominant; in Galileo's day, it was the foundation even of most profane disciplines, of physics, astronomy, and, to a large extent, of medicine.

Aristotle arrived at the core of his doctrine by turning his atten-tion to the phenomenon of development. In order for a corporeal thing, a crystal, a plant, an animal, to develop, a readiness must be present, a "potentiality," which is seized upon by a formative prin-ciple, the "act." This is the first of his pairs of concepts. Potentiality and act are spiritual principles of being, constitutive for the objects of this world. "Matter" is what is ready. Readiness is its basic prin-ciple. "Form" takes hold of matter and molds it into a corporeal object, thus fulfilling its purpose and making it intelligible. The world as a whole consists essentially in the sum of all corporeal things, of the "substances," which are endowed with an independent existence and which carry within themselves the "accidental" qualities, the active and passive potentialities. Thus "matter" and "form," "substance" and "accident," constitute two further pairs of concepts, with the help of which Aristotle investigates the whole existing world.

It follows from this conception that the independent corporeal things, the substances, which in their totality constitute the world and which in their quantitative aspect, extension, constitute space, are at the same time the objects which reveal the world process to us. If one succeeds in knowing the essence of a corporeal substance, one knows how it will act, for the activity and passivity of substance result from its nature or essence, and thus the scientist's endeavors are di-rected towards corporeal things, that is, the substances.

The stone is heavy, the snowflake light, the action follows from the essence. The stone more than the snowflake strives downward, to the "natural place" of the heavy. The earth rests at the center, round it rotates the heavens of the fixed stars, composed of the fifth original element, ether, and not subject to change; it moves in the "most perfect" form of motion, the circular orbit. The planets have their own spheres, sublunar space is the region of mutability. From his last principles Aristotle, with remarkable zeal, explained absolutely all of the world as it was then known: from God to the saline content of the sea, from the stars to the origin of the lower forms of life, from the Nile floods to the grain of dust, he took everything into account. He possessed his time's knowledge of nature—an abundance of information, much of it inaccurate.

One more characteristic trait remains to be filled in: according to Aristotle, our senses give us an inward copy of the objects of the world. The *sensory qualities,* such as color and sound, are, for his school, not only categories of perceptions but *categories of being.* Thus an object is *really* red, if it gives us the sensory perception, the experience, of this color. Today we have absolute certainty that this is false. Colors, sounds, and many other qualities are part of our impression, they are immanent. Their external causes remain to be investigated, and that is a function of physics. There is no color and no sound in the transcendental object. The causes of our perceptions are of an entirely different nature: in the case of colors and sounds they are electromagnetic waves and sound waves.

Such was the fund of knowledge which young Galileo, like all other students of his time, zealously strove to master; throughout the European learned world it was regarded as complete and unassailable. Isolated disagreements had been expressed, to be sure, but the young medical student (although he read everything he could lay hands on) can scarcely have known of the Franciscan Roger Bacon, who had performed experiments three centuries earlier, had been suspected of magic, imprisoned, and freed only through the intercession of the pope. Independently Galileo had conceived the desire, so presumptuous for his time, to investigate and see for himself whether the natural laws of the great master Aristotle concurred with the actual phenomena. For us it is a matter of course that we must experiment, test, and verify, but in those days to doubt the doctrine of the schools, to doubt what Aristotle, St. Thomas and the commentators professed as a certainty, was inconceivably rash and presumptuous, particularly in one so young and immature. But the inner urge, the divine spark of genius, was strong in him. With the most primitive equipment he performed experiments, over and over again, and the more he experimented the greater grew his doubts. While teaching at

Padua, the university of the Venetian Republic, he read Copernicus and communicated with Kepler. On the basis of data brought to him from Holland by his students, he constructed a telescope and discovered the moons of Jupiter, which, in honor of the Florentine princes, he called the "Medicean stars." In the Milky Way he found an abundance of separate stars, thus confuting two theories: The conclusive catalog of approximately one thousand fixed stars was false, and the moons of Jupiter, according to his observations, moved in an orbit similar to that of the earth around the sun in the system of Copernicus. The discovery of a "nova," or new star, confuted the doctrine of the immutability of the ethereal zone. But more important than these astronomic discoveries, which brought him into the tragic conflict of his life, were Galileo's experiments with falling bodies.

It appears that he investigated falling bodies of every conceivable sort over a period of decades. To common sense it seems obvious that everything which is not supported must be driven downwards by its weight. But that is the crux of the matter: the obvious is that to which we have not yet given serious thought. The Aristotelian doctrine regarded falling as an expression of the essence of corporeal substances. It lay in their essence to strive downwards. Their action followed from their nature. Galileo dropped heavy and light objects from various heights, he tied weights together and dropped them, then he dropped them separately, and thus he established that the doctrine of the schools could not possibly be true. If Viviani is to be believed, he used the leaning tower of Pisa for some of his experiments.

Let us pursue this problem and see what he actually found out. He carried on a great many experiments and made many discoveries, but nowhere is his peculiar method of research, which has become our own, so clearly manifested. His new principle is, as we have said, experimentation, i.e., to question nature itself. But how is that to be done? *How can one force a clear, unequivocal answer from nature itself?* Clearly this is the decisive question. The manner of questioning nature and obtaining its answer is the greatest among all Galileo's discoveries, and the only one that we shall examine more closely today. It is known as the "inductive method." The term does not mean the same as "inductive syllogism," although to be sure the inductive method includes the inductive inference. Philosophers distinguished then, as now, between deductive and inductive syllogisms. From a fully certain major premise, we can deduce particulars with evident certainty. If all men are mortal and Titus is assuredly a man (the minor premise), then Titus is mortal. The ancients regarded a great number of major premises as entirely certain and held the deductive method in high esteem. For us moderns the question always arises: how do we arrive at the major premise?—and we frequently find such a premise to be less certain than we had supposed. Inductive reasoning, from the particular to the general, was not so highly valued, and, indeed, it is not logically cogent. Even the greatest accumulation of similar findings cannot in itself prove that all future cases will be the same. On the basis of all past experience, it is true, we fully expect the sun to rise tomorrow morning. To say that the sun will rise tomorrow at a certain time is an inductive inference. In times where there was no such certainty that the world operated according to laws, people were not so sure. Things might always turn out differently.

The inductive method, which Galileo mastered and adopted more and more clearly and completely in the course of his life, requires as its first step a hypothesis. For if one wishes to question nature, one must first form some idea of the object of the question. In our case, Galileo substituted a new idea for the Aristotelian principle that bodies fall faster or more slowly by virtue of their essence. From the proposition that bodies fall, he inferred that everywhere on the earth's surface a constantly operating principle was at work, a force everywhere the same, that acted upon bodies from outside and drew them towards the center of the earth; and this force governed the fall of any given object. He now set out to inquire of nature itself whether this was really true. Thus he had a hypothesis, a provisional assumption, such as every scientific experimenter sets up, because without one he cannot ask any question. He derives this provisional opinion from previous knowledge, from known factors presumed to be certain— but the decisive new element is that he does not take a dogmatic view of his assumption, he makes no claims for it, he does not herald it abroad, but keeps the question open and submits his opinion to the decision of nature itself, prepared to accept this decision without reserve. Thus the inductive method begins with the deductive establishment of a working hypothesis, a provisional opinion. The second step in the deductive method is analytical. How shall I question nature? All occurrences in nature are, in a manner of speaking, bundles of effects. Several effective causes nearly always participate in a single phenomenon. The falling body is affected not only by the outward force that we call gravitation, but also by the friction of the air or the inclined plane, by the wind, even, indeed, by the attractive forces of surrounding objects—of the moon, the sun, the stars—though of course only to an infinitesimal degree. If one wishes to obtain a clear answer from nature, one must question it in such a way that its answer clarifies one isolated chain of causality. One must avoid, or at least minimize, the influence of other natural forces, or when possible determine them separately. It is this *analytical and isolating process* within the inductive method that brings us to the actual experiment. Galileo performed experiments with falling bodies of all sorts: bodies falling freely through the air, serving as the weights of a pendulum, sliding down an inclined plane; he used bodies of every conceivable size, and minimized friction in every possible way. The heart of his experimentation, the precise formulation of his question was: How long will a falling body take to traverse a predetermined distance? He worked with many different distances, which we shall designate as d. This choice is open to the experimenter, and we call this factor the independent variable. Nature then answers with another magnitude, the time consumed by the falling of the body. This we designate as t. In modern terminology, this is the dependent variable. Each experiment now yields a pair of numbers: a value is assumed for d, let us say 30 metres, 50 metres, or any other, and by a delicate measuring device the time which the falling body takes to traverse this distance is determined.

Galileo made use of a highly ingenious contrivance for the measurement of time, without suspecting that Nicholas of Cusa had used it a hundred years before him. In those days there were no clocks in the present sense. He constructed a mechanism that would open a water faucet at the beginning of the fall and turn it off when the body reached the end of its trajectory. The weight of the accumulated water was the measure of the time elapsed.

Any experiment of this sort yields a pair of numbers. To any value for d, distance, nature answers with a numerical value for t, time, and at length we have a whole column of figures. Each pair embodies the result of an experiment. Now begins the synthetic step of coordinating and comparing these numbers which at first sight seem so haphazard, until we find a connection between them.

To the beginner in physics it is always a source of amazement to repeat Galileo's experiments, such as that of the inclined plane, to take down columns of figures which at first appear perfectly meaningless, and ultimately to find by comparing them that they are all bound together by a common "law." Galileo found that the distance traversed is proportionate to the square of the time: that is, for four times the distance, only double the time is required, for nine times the distance only triple the time, for sixteen times the distance only four times the time. Indeed, the synthesis results in Galileo's famous law of gravitation to the effect that when a body falls free and unobstructed, the distance is proportional to the square of the time. Thus Galileo established the relation between space and time when a constant force, such as he presupposed, acts upon a body. What follows is perhaps the strangest step of all: *the result obtained is postulated as universally valid.* Galileo must have performed thousands of experiments with falling bodies, and since then millions of experiments have been conducted, and they all result in the same law of gravitation or, to speak in more general terms, in the law of acceleration by a constant force, the great basic law of mechanics, which Newton later formulated as the second law of mechanics and applied to the orbits of the planets. But what justified Galileo, and what justifies modern scientists in maintaining that a natural law so obtained is universally valid and reliable? A strictly logical proof is not possible. Yet we can say that millions of experiments have yielded no exception. This has proved equally true of the other basic laws of mechanics and electrodynamics. The predictions based on these laws have been fulfilled. Laws arrived at through a relatively small number of carefully conducted experiments can confidently be used to calculate future or past occurrences. Predictions of eclipses of the planets, of their phases and paths, have been fulfilled even centuries later. This impressive accumulation of data provides in itself a certain assurance. But the second reason is much stronger. For a long time we have based our technology upon natural laws, that is to say, we have applied the natural laws arrived

at by scientists to the fashioning of implements and processes, telescopes, medicines, buildings, vehicles, the telegraph, the telephone,
lighting, heating, power plants, in short, millions of objects in time
and space, and we know that they can all be relied on to perform as
calculated, provided they have been purposively designed in accordance with natural laws. An incandescent lamp tells us in every second
of its burning that the natural laws on which it is based were correctly calculated and are always fulfilled, and each one of us is confident in the reliability of our transformers, generators, turbines,
automobiles, and locomotives, our buildings and bridges, cranes,
microscopes, and chemicals. In other words, we are fully convinced
of the validity of what has been revealed to us by the inductive method.
Furthermore, we can give a metaphysical reason for this validity, and
Newton formulated it in a fine phrase: "The Creator respects his
laws." If the world is a cosmos and not a chaos, if the inner skeleton
of its being is a νόμος, "law," and not arbitrary chance, if it constitutes
a unity of being and effect, it must be reliable.

Thus Galileo came to investigate the laws of nature and opened
a new world to man's vision. The world consists not only of bodies,
for behind the bodies, in a deeper layer of reality, there appear active
principles that reliably, calculably, and without exception determine
everything that happens. Indeed, in his great masterwork of 1638,
which through a stratagem he managed to have published in Holland
four years before his death (1642), when he was already blind, he
recognizes and discusses not only the action of external forces but also
the presence of forces within bodies. Bodies are really subject to
change, and corporeal entities are possible only because their material
ingredients are held together by inner forces in a very definite way.
Thus external and internal *forces* constitute corporeal being, corporeal
growth and decline. They are a new stratum of being, more profound
than bodies, new because they had never before been realized. Goethe
once said that Aristotle had the mind of a master builder. He meant
that Aristotle viewed the world with the understanding eye of an
architect, that by observing its structure he divined its meaning, its
spiritual content, and its beauty, as a connoisseur might contemplate
the façade of a cathedral. Now man's whole attitude changed. The
old passive acceptance of the cosmos, presenting itself to man in the

multiplicity of its corporeal substances, was replaced by a sense of cosmic dynamism, and it is this dynamism that now becomes the principal object of study. Invisible players called forces were playing a world game, and the visible, as St. Paul and St. Augustine had said, was merely an expression of the invisible. But man could actively question this invisible background, he could break through the silence of nature, he could compel nature to answer by observing the rules of the inductive method. Francis Bacon had said, *"Natura parendo vincitur."* Nature is conquered by obedience. Only by permitting ourselves to be instructed by the power of experiment, without obtruding the least prejudice, passion, *parti pris,* or desire, only *parendo,* do we learn the truth concerning this dynamic of being, and only then, only equipped with this knowledge, can we continue to build and change the world itself, adding to it such new things as drugs, telescopes, machines, buildings, chemicals.

Of all Galileo's achievements this was his greatest gift to posterity: the inductive method, the core of all exact science; extended in the years that followed, it proved to be the key to the mysteries of being, opening up ever new strata, ever new depths. And it is through the inductive method that our knowledge of the world has grown to be a million times greater than that of the ancients.

Galileo himself made many discoveries, and yet he remained all his life a restless, striving man, moved by an endless thirst for knowledge, and he remained a profoundly pious Christian. His support of the Copernican system, his whole new point of view, brought him into conflict with the learned world of his time. He was attacked not only by theologians, but even more sharply by profane scholars. In a sense, he had taken the ground from beneath their feet, for they owed their appointments, their reputations, their prestige to their knowledge of Aristotelian doctrine, which they confidently upheld. The idea that the earth, whose surface had been trodden by Christ, should be nothing but a tiny, second-rate planet, hurled through space and revolving around the sun—this shattering of the whole perfect structure of the cosmos, which for centuries had been taken for granted— involved a terrifying revolution, whose dangerous consequences for all human thought were even then surmised. We know Galileo's tragic fate. Except for his support of the Copernican theory, he made no outstanding contribution to astronomy; he did not follow the discoveries of Kepler. *But he did give us the inductive method, the fundamental method of the entire modern era, the source of all our knowledge of nature and power over nature.*

He did far more. He changed man himself. The man who knows what he can wrest from nature is not the same as the man who resigns himself to nature in passive contemplation. Once discovered, the dynamic of cosmic being awakened the dynamic of the human heart. The laws of nature, once known, are a portal through which inestimable power has come into the hands of man, up to the present day that finds us profoundly shaken by the discoveries in the field of atomic energy and the power they place at the disposal of humankind.

But we shall say no more of this until we have looked into Isaac Newton's equal enrichment of human knowledge.

3

It might be supposed that "the Muses are silent" in times of war and hardship. But history teaches us that this is not true. During the Thirty Years' War, which exterminated two thirds of the population of Germany, numerous discoveries were made. In these tormented, chaotic years Kepler lived and thought; Lord Napier and the Swiss Joost Bürgi invented logarithms; Galileo was at work; Grimaldi, the great Jesuit physicist and mathematician, was teaching in Bologna; Scheiner, the eminent astronomer, likewise a Jesuit, discovered the images on the retina; Mersenne carried out his pioneering investigations in acoustics. Descartes, in winter quarters at Neuburg on the Danube, created analytical geometry. Galileo's pupils Torricelli and Viviani, and Otto von Guericke, the gifted mayor of Magdeburg, investigated air pressure and the vacuum, and invented the barometer; von Guericke devised the first electrical machines; and Cavalieri, with his analysis of "indivisibles," prepared the way for Isaac Newton. This list might be expanded almost indefinitely. How was this possible? It might have been expected that the events of the day, the hardships of war, the bloodshed and misery would turn all human energies to the most primitive and urgent matters, the preservation of life, survival in the face of present danger. And for most men this is true. Yet, at the same time, suffering and upheaval work as a plow, breaking the hard, crusted earth of souls and spirits, so that it may receive new seed.

The World Wars of our own day have seen enormous progress in the natural sciences and technology. We shall realize this more fully when the advances, thus far kept secret, in the fields of synthetic fuels, aviation, radar, utilization of atomic energy, chemical therapy, bacteriology, and many others have been made public.

The lifetime of Isaac Newton was full of upheavals. Since the government of the violent Henry VIII, England had known no peace. The population was deeply split into hostile religious and social parties. Newton's youth coincided with Cromwell's military rule; during this time King Charles I was beheaded; the dictator's cavalry, the Ironsides, jangled through the countryside. Manners were uncouth. The famous colleges of Oxford and Cambridge lost much of their standing and wealth, discipline was relaxed, and the corporations of teachers and educators were weakened by political quarrels. Under Charles II, some semblance of order was restored; he founded the Royal Society; but the political atmosphere remained tense. After the death of Mazarin, Louis XIV took the political reins in his own hands, and from then on there was no peace. There came a long-drawn-out war with the Netherlands. An immense fire destroyed sixteen thousand houses in London. Twice the Black Plague ravaged the counties of England; the religious struggles continued: test acts, oath of supremacy, but also a great beam of light, the acts of habeas corpus. James II, Charles' unfortunate successor, attempted to restore absolutism. Revolution compelled him to take flight. The victorious insurgents called in William of Orange, who became William III and reigned jointly with Mary II, his queen. New struggles broke out with the Irish and the Scots, an attempt to restore the Stuarts to the throne failed. George I initiated the rule of the house of Hanover.

All this turbulence ran through the life of Isaac Newton, son of a small landowner, born in Woolsthorpe in January, 1643, shortly after the death of Galileo. He never saw his father, who died in the first year of his marriage, before his son was born. His mother was remarried to the pastor Barnabas Smith, but soon she was widowed a second time. A brother of Newton's excellent mother, the Reverend

William Ayscough, adopted the boy, who revealed amazing gifts in early childhood.

One episode may disclose his precocious genius. A great storm was raging through the countryside. The waves beat against the chalk cliffs, ships were torn from their anchors, and giant trees were uprooted. Cromwell lay dying at the time, and the population connected his death agony with the natural cataclysm: "God is summoning the hard man to judgment." People far and wide shut themselves up in their houses, but young Isaac did nothing of the sort. To everyone's amazement he remained outside, drawing lines with a stick and jumping from one to another with all his might. After a while, he went back into the house and began to reckon. Questioned about his strange behavior, he explained that he was trying to measure the force of the storm. In one direction, he explained, it supported the force of his leap. In the opposite direction, the forces combated one another, and he subtracted one from the other. Thus he measured the force of the storm compared to that of his own body, in order to calculate the pressure of the wind on the side of a ship, on a sail, on trees and houses. Since he was forever performing such experiments and studying everything he could about natural science and mathematics, it became clear that he was unsuited to become a farmer as had been intended; he distinguished himself in school, and it was decided to send him to Cambridge. There Isaac Barrow, his instructor in optics and mathematics, had much to do with determining his future career.

Until fame came to him at the age of fifty, Newton led the essentially lonely life that is so often the lot of great minds. The people around him were moved by entirely different interests, and after the early departure of his master Barrow, there was hardly anyone in Cambridge who understood the things that occupied him day and night. In his early youth, he formed the great conceptions that led to his discoveries. When, at the age of fifty, he was called to London and appointed master of the royal mint, he became a man of the world, highly esteemed and for the first time in his life quite comfortably off. He turned his attention to new tasks, of which we shall speak only briefly. He had conceived the basic outline of his greatest discoveries as a young man of twenty-three. The college had closed because of the plague, and Newton, returning home to live with his mother, had engaged in studies of his own.

His greatest achievements are his studies of light, his telescope, and analysis of the spectrum; the founding of classical mechanics in continuation of the work of Galileo and other precursors; the reduction of the planetary orbits to the laws of gravitation and the elaboration of an instrument which he needed for this purpose, the infinitesimal calculus. This is by no means all he accomplished. But even of his greatest works, we can only discuss one today, and we choose the third, the founding of mathematical analysis, of the differential and integral calculus, because in it we can best understand the intellectual transformation which, up to our own day, has determined the knowledge and activity of modern man. The problem of the infinitesimal—i.e., primarily, the problem of the infinitely diminishing and infinitely increasing, or as is often said, of the infinitely small and infinitely large—had become urgent. Many thinkers had given it their attention: Cavalieri, Mercator, Fermat, Descartes, Pascal, Wallis, Barrow, Kepler, to mention only a few names. But now further progress was impossible without its solution, and a solution offered incalculable possibilities for the future. The leading scientists of the time *sensed* this, and even in the ancient Greek mathematicians there are passages pointing to this question. Let us quell the *horror mathematicus* that frightens so many people away from such matters, and try to achieve a certain understanding of this universal problem and of the solution which changed the entire life of mankind, giving man new powers and an insight into new depths of being.

It will not, of course, be possible to explain the differential and integral calculus in this lecture, but perhaps we can throw some light on their subject matter. Essentially, geometry, arithmetic, and elementary algebra provide answers to so-called static problems, that is, they answer questions about relations that do not change: they tell us, for example, what qualities are proper to a triangle, a circle, an ellipse; what is the area of a room whose length, breadth, and height are given. But only a relatively limited number of the problems in nature are of this kind. By far the greater number arise through becoming, change, "motion." Suppose we simply ask: *what is a velocity?* The answer seems easy. The concept of velocity connects space and time; thus it signifies a distance traversed in a given time. We speak of a velocity of 60 m.p.h. for a railroad train or an automobile, of 300 m.p.h. for an airplane, or so and so many yards a second for a projectile. Let us again designate the distance as *s,* the time as *t,* and the velocity as *v;* the common relation will then be $v = s/t$; but obviously this is *only* true of constant velocities or for an *average* velocity. In reality a train or airplane, a projectile or a falling stone, is always changing its speed. Let us take a bullet: from muzzle to target, its velocity is reduced by air resistance; the important factor is the *velocity at the moment of impact, at the end of the trajectory.* But what is the meaning of velocity at the end of the trajectory? Or at any given point in the trajectory? *Can a moving body have a velocity at one point?* A point is ordinarily regarded as a something without extension, that is, a distance in which $s = 0$. In order to traverse a distance equal to zero, no time is required, therefore $t = 0$. Thus, for velocity at a given point, we arrive at the formula: $v = 0/0$. This, however, is contradictory to our thinking and strikes us as absurd; for nothing cannot be divided and something cannot be divided by zero. Our intuitive thought cannot follow, our conceptual thought is recalcitrant, and we thus conclude that at a point in its trajectory a body can have no velocity. But that, too, is impossible. Our logic tells us that if at any given point in its trajectory it had no velocity, it would stand still and not advance, and we must admit that our everyday thinking and the concepts arising from the customary and familiar, as well as dialectical and discursive thinking, *lead us to an antinomy* which we cannot resolve. But all natural science is filled with such problems and therefore dependent on their solution.

And now let us go back to the time of Euclid and other Greek mathematicians who were aware of these questions. Guided by our imagination, we might hear the following dialogue: Euclid speaks to one of his students: "Let us presuppose two lines, *a* and *b,* and co-ordinate them with two numbers, by saying that *a* is twice as long as *b;* that is $a = 2$ stadia, $b = 1$ stadion. We can also write $a = 2\,b$, or $a/b = 2$; or we can generalize and in place of 2 take any number indicating the ratio; for example, *a* may be 3, 7, or *n* times as large as *b*. Now divide *a* and *b* in equal parts, that is, cut them in half. In what relation does half of *a* stand to half of *b*?" The student answers: "This too seems an easy matter, master. If I cut both lines in half, the parts must stand to one another in the same ratio as before. The half of the first line = 1. Half of the second = ½, so that the ratio between the two remains 2:1." Euclid: "And if the ratio had been *n*:1 and you had divided both lines?" "Well, then the relation between the parts would also have remained *n*:1." Euclid: "Very well. Divide the halves again in half. In what ratio do the two parts now stand?" "In no other, master. The ratio remains 2:1 or *n*:1, as it was in the beginning." Euclid: "Now divide the two lines by a thousand, or by 100,000. Even though they may now be so small that you cannot see them, you can still do this in your mind. Now what is the relation between them?" "It can be no different, master. It must always remain 2:1, regardless how many times I divide them." "And is there any point, if you keep on dividing them, at which the ratio will be changed?" "No, there can be no such limit." "Now if you have divided *a* millions and millions of times and continue to divide, what have you then?" "I obtain less and less. The magnitude approaches zero. It vanishes, it becomes imperceptibly small, inconceivably small, so that I can no longer distinguish it from zero." "And that is true also of *b*?" "Of course. It also vanishes if it is divided into millions and millions of parts." Euclid: "Then we are guilty of no gross error if we designate both these vanishing quantities as 0, since they are now so infinitesimal that we can in no way distinguish between them. We therefore formulate it as 0/0, but this 0/0 has a very definite value, to wit, 2/1 or *n*/1. While the magnitudes themselves vanish into nothingness, the ratio between them remains 2:1 or *n*:1, or whatever the original ratio was. The term 0/0 thus has *a very definite and distinct value*, while the magnitudes whose ratio has this value themselves vanish."

Euclid continues his questioning. "How would it have been," he asks, "if I had instructed you not to divide *a* and *b*, but to double them, and then to double them again and again until they extended through the heavens as far as the stars? Would the ratio have been different?" The answer is: "No. Even when multiplied, the ratio remains the same, even if this equal multiplication should extend both magnitudes into the inconceivable, the unlimited, the infinite.

For the infinite we use the symbol ∞, that is the fraction $\frac{\infty}{\infty}$ would in our example have a clear value of 2 or n."

This is a simple case of proportionality. The two magnitudes remain proportional, that is, $a = nb;$ n is the coefficient. We have seen that in the process of infinitesimal reduction or infinite enlargement, the relation between the two is invariable; and thus for perfectly invisible quantities like the point in a trajectory or the time needed to traverse the point, we obtain clear relations on the basis of which we can calculate, while the quantities themselves have become quite unintelligible. We call the ratios between these tiny quantities differential quotients, the vanishing quantities themselves differentials. The example is very simple, and the problem is this: In natural phenomena variable quantities are bound to one another by some function, i.e., their relation to one another is determined by a law. In Galileo's law of gravitation, $s = t^2$. In other cases, the inductive method may find such a relation in a root, a cube, a logarithm, or some other function. What remains to be determined is the value of the ratio between dependent and independent variables, when the independent variable becomes infinitely small, that is, when it diminishes to a point. This is the core of the problem.

Kepler had found the orbits of the planets to be elliptical. Newton asked: Why is this so? What force acts upon the planet at each "point" in its orbit, in order to make it move in just this and no other way? Newton first studied the problem with the moon, because, while in Woolsthorpe during the Plague, he had conceived the inspired idea that the force governing the moon's orbit was nothing other than Galileo's gravitation. But in order to prove this, he needed a mathematical instrument that would enable him to derive from the equation of the ellipse the force of acceleration that would be exerted on the moon at every point in its orbit. It was for this purpose that he had to devise the new mathematics.

Newton was a stubborn, solitary thinker. He is said to have sat whole nights over his problems without so much as stirring. He was very lonely in these untrodden zones of knowledge, and because he was lonely, he did not believe that any other man then living could have entered the regions where his mind now dwelt. That is why it was later so inconceivable to him that Leibniz had independently discovered the new mathematics and had indeed penetrated it even more deeply than he. Newton could not bring himself to believe this and quite unjustly suspected Leibniz of stealing his ideas. This sense of having, by enormous exertions, penetrated realms of the spirit where no human thought had hitherto dwelt, this sense of being a pioneer, a misunderstood, distant wanderer, made Newton hostile and distrustful when he found that his equally inspired contemporary had arrived at the same results.

Although we cannot go much more deeply into the mathematics of it, we must add one more factor to complete the picture: The method of differentiation, that is, the establishment of the ratio between related vanishing quantities, is the *one* road of higher analysis. It leads from general laws, from descriptive, static laws like those governing the orbits of the planets, to specific laws; in the case of falling bodies, it leads from the general law: the distance is equal to the square of the time, to the concept of velocity at a given point; or with Newton from the planetary orbit to the force of gravitation which at every point in the orbit makes this orbit necessary. This operation is known as differentiation. But there are also cases when the inductive method yields the instantaneous laws, i.e., when the functions expressing an instantaneous effect are found experimentally. Then, by the reverse of the process, by integration, the general law can be found.

This was then the problem confronting Newton's age. Newton himself, like his time, had at first regarded geometry as the leading mathematical discipline, though even to geometry he had ascribed only a helping role, a subservient rank. He himself says this very plainly in the preface to his *Philosophiae naturalis principia mathematica.* "Geometry itself," he writes, "is based on mechanical practice and is indeed nothing other than that part of mechanics which exactly defines and explains the art of measurement."

The enormous importance of this achievement became clear only with time, but Newton's work gave an inkling of it. He observes that throughout the real world the finite is bound up with the infinite, just as it is in the examples we have cited in connection with distance, time, and velocity, and that the concept of the infinitesimal is essentially *dynamic.* In his *Geometry of the Indivisibles,* Cavalieri had conceived a curve as consisting of an infinite number of indivisible, infinitely small points. Fermat had corrected this view and shown that the elements of a geometrical line, even of a line in analytical geometry, must, however minute it may be, have finite extension. For Newton the curves and orbits of geometry, and especially of analytical geometry, are created *dynamically,* through motion, in much the same way as we, through motion—that is, spatial change in time, hence dynamically—make a line come into being on paper and study this coming into being. Thus Newton, in his approach to mathematics, turned his attention to change. He calls the quantities that change and are interconnected in their change, fluents; and the basic fluent, the type by which all other changing quantities can be measured, is time. Time is for him the prototype of the independent variable, and whatever grows or diminishes or changes in time, according to any law, is the other fluent. Change is functional interdependence. At every moment the value of the dependent fluents is determined by the value of the independent one—e.g., of time. He calls the relation between the two "fluxion," and this is what we designate by differential quotients. We can sum up by saying that the *invention of the differential and integral calculus* meant a dynamization of mathematics, a conquest of all the diverse and multiple change that occurs in growth and decline, in rising and falling, the intellectual conquest of the πάντα ῥεῖ of Heraclitus, through the knowledge that where intuitive, conceptual knowledge fails us, the fleeting reality can be reliably encompassed within the mesh of mathematical logic.

4

The inductive method and the conquest of the infinitesimal are the two channels through which a broad stream of scientific revelation has reached mankind ever since. In England the new method was slow to be accepted, except by a few advanced thinkers. Even in Newton's lifetime, it made discernible progress, but the hard struggle against the conservative tendency had not yet been won. While the new mathematics put forward by Leibniz and the Bernoullis was studied and applied throughout the continent, in England it remained for some time almost an occult science, while the new physics, stated in enduring form in Newton's most famous work, the *Principia mathematica,* scarcely penetrated English thinking. Even the English universities taught the peripatetic physics of Aristotle, or the newer physics of Descartes, which essentially was not much better. Descartes, whose influence was then at the zenith, was a great mathematician and an important philosopher. But in physics he cannot lay claim to equal rank. For he had made his own consciousness the foundation of objective knowledge (by his famous axiom *Cogito, ergo sum*), and in the light of this principle he undertook to mold all science according to the pattern of mathematics. This orientation leads inevitably to a criterion of certainty, similar to mathematical evidence. No rational being can reject the proof of a mathematical principle, such as the Pythagorean theorem. It is evident. And thus we come to the Cartesian view, which makes "intuition," or evident clarity, the criterion of truth. Descartes does not follow Galileo, but expresses the opinion that if inductive investigation were to give a result differing from evident intuition, he would trust reason and not experiment. Thus he *invented* a special physics of celestial movements (and other phenomena). Vortexes caused the planets to revolve and to rotate about the central stars. This appeared to him perfectly evident, and he regarded it as certain. Because of his authority, such philosophical opinions passed into textbooks of physics, and in England the Cartesian theories were gradually replacing the old scholastic physics. Not until the last years of Newton's life did one of his students, Samuel Clarke, manage, by a stratagem, to smuggle Newton's physics into the English schools. The usual textbook, written by Rohault on Cartesian principles, was out of print. Newton's disciple appended notes to the new edition, in which the Cartesian and Newtonian physics were juxtaposed. The comparison was so overpowering, the superior certainty of Newton's findings so obvious, that the reform of instruction in physics was launched (first in the Scottish universities of St. Andrews and Edinburgh).

Newton suffered greatly from the misunderstanding of his contemporaries, from the attacks which his work, like all pioneering efforts, was bound to call forth. When he broke down common light into the colors of the spectrum, his adversaries argued that this meant little, since he had discovered nothing concerning the *essence* of light. But this he had made no attempt to do. He had come to realize that the question of essence need not necessarily be stressed, that we can achieve much certainty concerning relations, structures, dependencies, causalities, and developments without coming any closer to the essence of things. He wished to set up no hypothesis about the nature of things themselves, and yet sometimes the controversy forced him to do so; concerning the nature of light rays, for example, he stated various views, finally saying that if compelled to do so, he would give preference to a corpuscular hypothesis. Yet, at the same time, he ascribed to his infinitesimal light corpuscles special properties not far removed from vibration, and in any event, he was far from committing himself. His students, however, were more dogmatic and thus obstructed the vibration theory of light for several decades. The loneliness that Newton felt round him, the general lack of understanding and hostility to his ideas, personal misfortunes such as the death of his mother, and protracted overexertion brought about the psychic collapse that for two years (1692–94) flung him into confusion and despair, making it impossible for him to work or sleep. This period of his stay in Cambridge remained for a long time unknown, and even today it is not fully understood. The turning point came in 1699, with his call to London. He had gained prosperity, social rank, world fame, he was received at court, but his great creative period in the realms of mathematics and physics was ended.[1]

What followed was often a source of profound concern to Newton. The discoveries of a genius are one thing, what the world makes of them is another. The scientist achieves knowledge, but knowledge is followed by disclosure, the publication of his discoveries to the world. He has carried on his inquiries with certain intentions in mind. His knowledge belongs to him as long as he is at work and as long as he keeps his insights to himself. But once he has published them, they are taken up by the current of time, by his contemporaries and by posterity. Here they work with a *force of their own* and are seen

---

1 A bibliography of works on Isaac Newton is found in my *Weltfahrt der Erkenntnis, Leben und Werk Isaac Newtons* (Zurich, 1945); a bibliography on Galileo in my *Der Fall Galilei und wir* (3rd edn., Frankfort, 1951).

through the intentions of others. Many a great man has been horrified at an independent force emanating from works which he has created and can no longer call back.

Newton was a profound believer. He often stressed that his discoveries proved the existence of God,[2] that Nature revealed Him. He compared the natural revelation that is given to the scientist with the revelation of the Gospels.[3] But to his consternation he saw that his contemporaries drew entirely different conclusions from his work. If the movements in the cosmos occur with mathematical certainty in accordance with ascertainable laws, if anonymous forces rule inexorably—where then, they asked, is there room for the rule of God, for the efficacy of prayer? Is there any point in praying for good weather at harvest time, when ironbound natural laws govern the sunshine and the rain? During the last years of Newton's life, scientific discoveries were made in abundance all over Europe with the new methods. The sphere of causality became larger and larger, while that of the religious was reduced to the vanishing point. Thomas Aquinas had presumed that angels governed the paths of the stars, and now there was no room for them. The discovery of a new stratum of being, that of effective forces, led, as such discoveries almost always do, to philosophical generalization, the overstressing of a principle. In this case the result was a system of dynamism that set out to explain the whole universe through mechanics. Newton had no such idea. In his view, the origin of the laws, the essence of things, such as light and gravitation—that was God's affair. The laws were reliable, for the Creator respects his own laws, as Newton himself said. For him, all his discoveries were one great proof of the existence of God, and he wrote of this at length in his letters to Pastor Bentley (I have quoted a number of important passages in my biography of Newton). But now the opposite of what he had intended occurred, and he could not help it. He would so gladly have given to the world not only his discoveries, but also a spiritual legacy, his opinion, intention, and vision. But in this he was not successful. Like so many great men, he was filled with horror to see what had become of his own work. And in

2 In the letter to Bentley of December 10, 1692, in the epilogue to his *Optics,* and in other works.

3 Most evident in the correspondence with Bentley. (See my *Leben und Werk Isaac Newtons,* p. 387.)

this case it was monstrous: a stream of discoveries and of inventions based on them poured into the life of man. Nature, once contemplatively accepted, was stormed with questions, to which she replied. The answers constituted a foundation on which stupendous things were built: telescopes that brought near the large and distant; microscopes that revealed the whole immense world of the minute; machines and devices without number, buildings, dams, floodgates, sewage systems, engines, pumping stations, cranes, steam engines, telegraph, new types of light! Suddenly creation was enriched by innumerable forms it had never before contained. And each one of these things had a power, each one influenced human existence, altered the course of everyday life, the relations between peoples, reduced the size of the earth, gave domination over nature, freed people from burdens, created prosperity, increased the efficacy and danger of weapons, altered the nature of armies and warfare, emancipated the lower classes, did away with guild restrictions, spread over the earth's surface, colonized strange peoples. The material world was found to be permeated by forces susceptible to mathematical formulation; this new knowledge made obscure, hidden things transparent to Reason, and man, becoming more and more powerful, boldly stretched forth his arms to more and more distant goals. *But man is only one.* Natural science and mathematics have led him from success to success, they have made him powerful and confident; he transfers his new-found method and his self-confidence to other fields. What he was able to do in the field of science and technology he now wishes to accomplish in the social sphere. He strives to solve all sorts of new problems *more physico et mathematico,* as best he can. It is hard for us to realize to what an extent our approach to problems was formed by this scientific frenzy. When, in the misery of his time, Francis of Assisi desired to help his fellow man, his "neighbor," according to the example of Christ, he did so through personal, human contact. In an act of love and sacrifice, he shared his scanty garment with the naked, his frugal fare with the hungry. He made his arduous pilgrimage from village to village, preaching and above all helping. He even went among the lepers who were shunned by all. By his example he exerted a compelling influence on his contemporaries. When we moderns wish to alleviate suffering, we use different and surely far more effective methods: objective research into the causes, statistics, computations, and on this basis, well-planned organization with a thousand technical devices, registration, card files—these are our methods, and those who administer such campaigns rarely have any human contact with the individual whom they want to help. There is a coldness in this activity organized according to the rational methods of empirical science and mathematical formulation. Science triumphant has been applied to almost every sphere of human life. Economic planning and management, factory organization, social projects, rational colonization, hygiene, even school organization, everything, everything has gained from this attitude. Surely a great gain, yet also a great loss. The *ratio* is the victor, and the *anima*, the sympathetic, partaking human soul, is relegated to the background.

It is inevitable that such activity should affect not only the outward shape of man's existence, but also his mode of life, his *habitus*. Man has become earthly, materialistic. Goethe expressed this truth in strong terms (*Faust*, Part II, Act 5):

> This earthly circle I know well enough.
> Towards the Beyond the view has been cut off;
> Fool—who directs that way his dazzled eye,
> Contrives himself a double in the sky!
> Let him look round him here, not stray beyond;
> To a sound man this world must needs respond.
> To roam into eternity is vain!
> What he perceives, he can attain.[4]

Goethe, as we know, was horrified at the transformation being wrought in the world around him by technical and scientific progress, though he knew it to be inevitable. And it is well to remember that the poet makes Faust, who utters these words, fail in his earthly undertakings. Everything that he has built with such bold defiance is swallowed up by the sea:

> In all respects you're lost and stranded,
> . . . .
> Annihilation is the law,[5]

says Mephisto, as he supervises the digging of Faust's grave.

4 Tr. Louis MacNeice (New York and London, 1952), p. 283.
5 Ibid., p. 286.

314

But inevitably too much success brings *hubris,* pride. Inexorably, accumulated triumphs bring narrowness and shortsightedness. If all this has gone so well, can we not expect *everything* to go equally well? And if force and matter govern with so much certainty, can we not assume that everything is force and matter? Power seduces. Unceasingly it whispers, "Use me!" Unceasingly it lures man to evade hard work, to acquire earthly goods and bask in pleasures, and in all this it offers its services. Thus it corrodes man's inner force; demoralizes his ethos, extinguishes his conscience, kills pity, and drives the possessor of power into the fatal abyss. Woe to the generation that has gained power and lost its sense of higher values. What untold horrors it must suffer. To this we can all of us bear witness.

The inductive method, as perfected over a period of centuries, is still the heart of all exact science. We too receive answers from nature when we question her correctly. To us, too, it reveals its secrets, and upon us, too, it bestows power. Since the days of Galileo new strata of being have opened up, and always the cosmos has been found to be far deeper and wider than any preceding generation ever imagined. For Copernicus, Kepler, Galileo, Newton, the universe consisted primarily of our solar system. But the galaxy to which we belong is a system of millions of suns. Newton's telescope, as perfected in recent times, goes beyond, and we know that there are millions of such astral systems as our galaxy. We, the inhabitants of *one* little planet, circling around *one* sun among millions in *one* system among millions, intellectually penetrate this system and the laws that govern it by means of the inductive method and the logical mesh of mathematics. And bodies are not, as they appear to us, the enduring, representative element in the world. They are only superficial, as it were. Underneath, there are stronger, more enduring elements, by which bodies are moved and transformed. Still deeper lie the levels that are now being revealed to us. The substances, the most trifling articles of everyday life, stones, wood, metal, clothing, and foodstuffs, all these familiar things contain within them the most gigantic stores of energy. A few grams of their substance, transformed into energy, can pulverize a big city in an instant. The bricks of the universe, protons, neutrons, electrons, are objects of an entirely unforeseen nature, comparable to nothing ever found in the world as previously known. As in the presence of the infinitesimal in the structure of the world, concept, language, logic, dialectic, are again at a loss. If we read the pre-Socratic philosophers, their manner of expressing themselves sometimes strikes us as strange, for they had no proper philosophical language. In order to describe their intuition of the world, they had to use images, words, analogies, symbols, from the world of the familiar. Only much later, with Plato and Aristotle, did a specialized philosophical language gradually develop. Again and again we have fallen into the same situation, and today this is again the case. When we want to describe atoms, we must use images that are not accurate, concepts that do not embrace everything they are intended to, words that do not express the objective reality. No other possibility is open to the human mind when it encounters new levels of being. For again and again we discover that in the depths everything is entirely different from what we had imagined.

Newton's era already heralded the cleavage that since then has threatened more and more to destroy the unity of the mind. The Greeks and to a very high degree the late scholastic philosophers strove to see through nature, cosmos, man, with *one* vision and in *one* direction, and to penetrate to the fundament. The age of Galileo believed in this unity of vision and struggled desperately to defend it. But then with each ensuing generation it seemed clearer that passing from the realm of the spirit to the realm of natural law and technology implied a change in the direction of man's thinking. It is forbidden to speak of God in considering technology—and in cultural matters it is not customary to speak of mechanics or chemistry. The spheres have grown apart and no longer understand one another. The great army of all those who work in the realm of natural science and technology have lost the cultural, traditional values which were assembled by our forefathers through long struggle and bitter experience. The representatives of tradition, the humanists, historians and all the rest, find science and technology difficult, dry, unintelligible, and essentially not worth the trouble. But more and more, the young people turn to the various branches of science and technology. A powerful social group has developed and in some countries has thrust aside the carriers of culture. This is in large part our own fault: we remained too much among ourselves, speaking and writing for each other. We did not concern ourselves with outsiders. We set no great store by them, but accepted their services and achievements without thanks. Who, for example, considers, when he picks up a book, a product of the printing technique, that it embodies human, *technological* endeavor based on natural science, that it embodies the studies, investigations, experience of thousands of unknown fellow men? Who among us gives thanks to the technicians and workers who built our railroads and highways, our ships and vehicles, our houses and meeting halls, who devised our medicines and all the other things that we use day after day, year after year? And yet all this was accomplished and given to us by the "Brothers Anonymous," who poured out their lives in their work. *Because we do not thank them and do not greet them in spirit, they do not turn to us.* One group among us is no longer in sight of the other, and that is one reason for the tragedy of our time.

The scientist and technologist dwell in a realm of certainty; they are certain of their success if only they persist in an attitude of loyal service. Natural science is the humblest science, for it brings results only if man masters every arbitrary desire, all wishful thinking, egotism, and weakness, only if he listens in silence to what nature discloses; and equally humble is the activity of the technician who cannot solve problems as he wishes, because over his drafting board, over his test equipment, Dike herself, the great goddess of nature, stands watch. Natural science and technology are an incentive, perhaps a primary incentive to discipline, one might even say asceticism.

If the scientist or technologist departs from this professional sphere, he easily becomes uncertain. The criteria of certainty which scientists found at home, i.e., in their own department, and which in principle negate struggle, are not present outside it. Every political party teaches struggle. The courts are filled with struggle over points of law. To every question of being and essence, the philosophers give a hundred different answers, and the sermons in the houses of worship do not agree. Thus the son of technology feels abandoned in the human world, which has become for him a place without certainty. Whether his machine will run, whether his airplane will rise into the air—this he can calculate, verify, ascertain. Here there is no room for doubt. But where in the social world will he find criteria which he feels

317

obligated to accept? If he does not find them and yet is faced with a decision (politically, for example, as in the German or the Russian Revolution), what is he to go by? By the most drastic, visible, brilliant symptoms of achievement. For lack of other criteria, he will be inclined to accept pomp and glitter, success and victory, as ersatz criteria. And thus we see the great host of technicians complaisantly bowing before the wielders of power, lending these men their impressive abilities throughout the world. For the technical and trade schools have no room for our cultural heritage, for tradition, and in them the name of God is not uttered. No one says what Newton never ceased to say, that decisions of the experiment are revelations of God's laws. No one says that God governs also in the workshop, in the factory; no one suggests that technical power implies responsibility; that it should not be used for destruction, for murder, for the inundation of cultivated soil. How to do it, that the schools have taught, but nothing has been said of the aims that our abilities serve, or should serve.

Is not this the source of much of our misfortune and anxiety? The abysmal truth is that tradition, reason, and order have been lost through technical progress. And the tragedy becomes even more profound when we consider that the rhythm of progress in science and in technology can be accelerated and is being accelerated. It is no exaggeration to say that what formerly would have taken two generations is now accomplished in a decade. Thus the situation in which we live is rapidly changed, the power at our disposal is increased at an inconceivable pace. But this is not true of the rhythm of human *behavior*. The way in which we classify things and invest them with meaning, the way in which we guide our lives—in other words our direction, our behavior in the face of rapidly changing possibilities, has lagged behind; it is bound up with biological seasons, with the succession of the generations. Thus we are tempted to slip away from tradition, which consequently no longer serves us, to let ourselves be carried away from it by the rushing stream of scientific and technical progress, which we are no longer able to dominate. Newton had a foreboding of this and never ceased to struggle for higher values, for the relation to God, until his death in the night of Sunday, March 19, 1727.

Is there no way out? Can we not regain the unity of the spirit, which once consisted in looking straight through the universe and mankind to the fundament? Is there no comprehensive pattern, no depth at which this cleavage will be resolved, since obviously everything that we know is spiritual? I believe that there is, and I shall attempt to indicate in a few words how, in my private opinion, all human endeavors in natural science, technology, culture, and history might be integrated, and under what sign a unity of vision might again be regained.

Any scientist or technologist who has had the good fortune to be present at the birth of a great discovery or invention will never forget this experience. Ordinarily such an hour is preceded by years of zealous searching and ardent endeavor, years of repeated disappointment, difficulties and more difficulties, until in a consecrated hour a veil falls, and the eye penetrates a new, never-trodden realm. Here it becomes perfectly plain that fulfillment can come to man only after he has heeded certain requirements. Yet in many cases, and this is one of the profoundest of human experiences, it is the idea that takes hold of the man rather than the other way around. Man is overpowered by a relation, an insight. This, in a word, is *revelation*. The scientist pursues a discovery, the technologist an invention. Sometimes, in either case, the search lasts for generations. Some do not live to see it, for the road passes through centuries, or millennia. But then it is *revealed*. In the days of Nicholas of Cusa many men were aware of this. The inspired German cardinal, who in a sense anticipated the Copernican system by a whole century, regarded the investigation of nature as a form of worship, a search for the revelation of the Creator and Lawgiver in His cosmos. He found eloquent words to describe this encounter with the creator in natural revelation. For him the study of nature was a way to God who was the fundament and goal of all things. This sentiment was almost lost when natural science departed from, or rather was thrust out of, the sphere of spiritual unity. But the insight is true: the study of nature is a journey towards the divine ideas of the Creator, a quest for natural revelation: a worship at a new altar, but dedicated to the same God.

But to travel this path to the ultimate fundament is long and arduous. It leads through centuries, and the term of human life is short. Such revelation is not enough. By its very nature, man's unity demands other, nearer sources, and they can be found. There is a second level that we may call historical revelation, in which we may find the fundament through the insights of the great intellects of all peoples and all eras. For the Christian, historical revelation culminates in the appearance of the Saviour, in his words and his example, and this revelation is humanly near, it has the full living warmth of an exemplary sacrifice. Here too God is revealed. But there is still a third level of revelation to which man strives. Man strives to come closer to the fundament than the long, though kingly road of the scientist can take him in a brief lifetime, closer than the exalted but remote example of the Saviour can lead him. He desires, he yearns, he strives for personal revelation, for a closeness of his own; he longs to hear the voice of God, and that is what Kant meant when, with a shudder of profound awe, he spoke of the voice of conscience. For him, who is disposed to search, there is revelation in dialogue with God, in prayer with Him, in struggle with Him.

Man is a creature who depends entirely upon revelation. In all his intellectual endeavor, he should always listen, always be intent to hear and see. He should not strive to superimpose the structures of his own mind, his systems of thought upon reality. That has been done again and again, and at a certain critical point it has always failed. The greatness of the human spirit does not consist in building out of itself; its true greatness is the suppleness with which it adapts itself to reality, wherever it is revealed. We all know that what to one generation was inconceivable and therefore impossible has often come to be taken for granted by a subsequent generation. This was the case with the infinitesimal in nature and mathematics; with the concepts of force and energy, with the system of the universe and in many, many other cases. The human mind is a master of adaptability, but for adaptation it requires biological time. Therefore it must listen in silence and not loudly proclaim itself. It must listen and give heed. At the beginning of all spiritual endeavor stands humility, and he who loses it can achieve no other heights than the heights of disillusionment. True, men stop and gape where a noise occurs, but the stars move silently along their course. *The truly great comes softly and what is loud is never great.*

For man is *in statu viatoris*, in the condition of the wanderer. This

metaphor seems to me to describe man's existence in the modern
world better than the condition of "being thrown into existence," of
hovering in fear and anxiety over the abyss of nothingness. Man is
a wanderer and he has a compass if he hearkens to revelation. He
senses the direction. But full arrival at the goal is denied to mortal
life. Man wanders; he comes asymptotically closer if he lets himself be
guided by revelation. Each one of us, and each one of mankind, is a
pilgrim to the absolute. And the absolute is not an earthly possession
but a mission. Man must not lose his orientation towards it; else he is
confounded and falls into the abyss.

We are witness to such loss of orientation and to the catastrophes
that have arisen from it. Let us, each one for himself, take care that
the catastrophe of cleavage, of lost unity, or revelation silenced, that
we have experienced in Europe, shall not occur within us!

Erwin Schrödinger

The Spirit of Science

1

The spirit is to an eminent degree subject and thus evades objective examination. It is the subject of cognition (Schopenhauer) and therefore strictly speaking can never be its object.

Permit me to read you a few passages from Shankara's famous commentary on the Vedanta-sutras; it treats of this matter far more clearly than many modern philosophers, not to mention scientists. The English version is by F. Max Müller.[1]

> As it is well known . . . that object and subject, which fall under the perception of *We* and *You* (or, as we should say, of the Ego and Non-Ego), are in their very essence opposed to each other like darkness and light, and that therefore one cannot take the place of the other, it follows all the more that their attributes also cannot be interchanged.

In his commentary of this passage, Max Müller writes: "Thus for example the Non-Ego can be seen, heard, felt, but the Ego can never be seen, heard, felt. Its nature is to know, not to be known."

Shankara continues:

> Therefore we may conclude that to transfer what is objective, that is what is perceived as *You,* the Non-Ego and its qualities, on what is subjective, that is what is perceived as *We,* the Ego, which consists of thought, or vice versa to transfer what is subjective on what is objective, must be altogether wrong.

In this sense all science is a doctrine of the objective, of the nonego. It has played such a subordinate part in Hindu thought that among thinkers who equal Plato, Spinoza, or Kant in depth and magnificence

1 *Three Lectures on the Vedanta Philosophy* (London, 1894), pp. 62ff.

of conception, we find utterly childlike and naïve views concerning the objective universe, although their people had dwelt in it for just as long, and they were in the same position for observing it as Western scientists. However, this should not surprise us. It was simply not their concern. The eminent goal of their contemplation was the "ego that consists of thought,"[2] the ego and its relation to the godhead.

Perhaps we may be permitted to designate this "ego that consists of thought" as "spirit," even if it involves us in a controversy with Vedanta scholars regarding "ego," "spirit," "soul," "reason," etc.

The German language—and only the German language—sets up an antithesis between the *natural* sciences and the *Geisteswissenschaften* (sciences of the spirit, or cultural sciences). This is not fully acceptable, any more than the usage of the Romance peoples and the English, who limit the old universal *scientia* to the natural sciences, and withhold it from philology, history, etc.—as though in these fields there were no *scire* at all.

The German usage is unacceptable, because it reverses the Vedantist's profound distinction between subject and object, between spirit and objective fact; because in both cases it cuts through living flesh at right angles to the organic dividing line.

The object that we can examine scientifically is in every case limited to the nonself, the object as Shankara calls it, the object κατ' ἐξοχήν. And the method of scientific inquiry is always that of natural science, adapted to the particular type of object. The philologist today sees language as a living organism, developing in a social and political environment. The methods of comparative philology are almost interchangeable with those of paleobiology. Not to mention those of the psychologist.

Thus the ego, the spirit, can never strictly speaking be the object of scientific inquiry, because objective knowledge of the spirit is a contradiction in terms. Yet, on the other hand, all knowledge relates to the spirit, or more properly, exists in it, and this is the sole reason for our interest in any field of knowledge whatsoever. The knowledge, or at least the intuition, of this circumstance is indeed as old as the

2 Compare to this the words of the Buddha: "All that we are is the result of what we have thought: It is founded on our thoughts, it is made up of our thoughts." F. Max Müller, *Introduction to the Science of Religion* (London, 1873), p. 24.

urge for knowledge itself. The naïve and the natural attitude is to conceive of everything in relation to ourselves, to our own Ego. But this naïve attitude was for a time submerged beneath our unfortunate scientific materialism. The sudden and spectacular progress of natural science deluded some of its most brilliant exponents into supposing that science was about to throw light on everything that was worth knowing, that outside of science nothing of the slightest interest would remain, and, above all, that science would soon solve the "problem of the spirit" with a fully objective picture of the thinking process. Perhaps the submersion of the naïve, natural, and philosophically sound relation of all knowledge to the universal human ego (which is the subject of all knowledge but is itself not susceptible to scientific inquiry) resulted in part from a process of inhibition. The intellectual relation of knowledge to the self was thrust aside by a physical relation. Through its technical by-products that often bordered on the miraculous, the knowledge of nature often proved serviceable to the physical Ego. Thus a material "Egoism" took the place of an ideal "Egoism," and perhaps helped many people to forget that the ideal Ego was being submerged.

The object of all science is nature in the broadest sense, i.e., our spatial and temporal environment in all its aspects. The subject of every science is always the spirit and—to vary a well-known saying of Kant—it contains only as much true science as it does spirit.

This insight is valuable in a twofold sense. First, we shall not, in concerning ourselves with the spirit, fall into the error of the Hindus and disregard the natural sciences as though they were utterly irrelevant. True, the spirit is not their object, but this does not mean that they are any less concerned with it than the *"Geisteswissenschaften."* For the spirit is never the object of science. But the sciences are a product of the spirit in which they are conducted.

On the other hand, we shall not expect the natural sciences to give us direct insight into the nature of the spirit; we shall not *hope* to penetrate it, however much we learn about the physics and chemistry of the bodily processes with which we find perception and thought objectively linked; and we shall not *fear* that even the most exact knowledge of the mechanism of these processes and the laws by which they operate—a knowledge the subject of which is and will always remain the spirit—can lay fetters upon the spirit itself, that is, can compel us to regard it as unfree, "mechanically determined," on the ground that it is linked with a physiological process that is mechanically determined and subject to laws of nature. Such an inference would be a παράβασις εἰς ἄλλο γένος, a transference of the qualities of the object to the subject, such as Shankara rightly stigmatizes as absolutely false.

2

After what I have said, it is evident that I shall not attempt to analyze objectively the "spirit of science." Instead, I shall try merely to put you as subjects in direct contact with those currents of thought which, it seems to me, have determined the development of the sciences in the last ninety or one hundred years. At first it may seem to you that I am merely picking out random examples; but I shall endeavor to show the common forces at work in remotely separate fields, and finally to compose the various trends of thought into a unified picture, a unified spiritual current. Perhaps I may be permitted to state at the outset that in this endeavor I myself—and this should scarcely seem surprising—shall be guided by this same basic force, this same basic trend, for it is nothing other than the increasing simplification and unification of our view of the physical universe. To make myself perfectly clear, I repeat that the endeavor to disclose a common, homogeneous basis in all the broad realms of scientific research is today particularly relevant, because this basic motif is itself simplification and unification.

To an observer outside the field of science, the contrary seems rather to be the case. Indeed it has become almost a commonplace to say that the more we learn and know, the richer but also the more complex the picture must become. Let us take physics, which would indeed have to constitute the basis for a real unification, for it forms, as it were, the alphabet at the base of all scientific discourse concerning the higher structures: the cosmos, the organism. What additions have been made to this alphabet in the last hundred years and at what a headlong pace! Magnetism, and with it the more exact knowledge

325

of electrical phenomena. The phenomena of refraction and inter-ference in light, so much more complex than Newton had imagined. Electromagnetic waves. Cathode rays. X-rays. Finally, radioactivity, so perplexing at first, with its three or four different types of rays that appeared to be of an entirely new kind, and the strange transforma-tions of one type of matter into another. Hardly had all these develop-ments been to some degree gathered into a system, hardly had scientists begun to hope that they might be able to manage with two types of fundamental particle, the light negative and heavy positive atom of electricity (electron and proton) and one type of waves, the electromagnetic, when first the quantum theory was "forced upon" us, with its odd conception that energy is transmitted discontinuously. Shortly thereafter we learned from Einstein that energy and matter were one and the same thing. Thus our old particles of matter were themselves quanta of energy, and the energy quanta in light waves had, in turn, to be regarded as a kind of particle. The subsequent develop-ment of the quantum theory into "wave mechanics" showed—and experiments made it increasingly certain—that there are not, as formerly supposed, two distinct types of radiation, one consisting of waves, the other of particles, but that every type of radiation must be regarded in some respects as a series of waves, in another as a stream of particles, difficult as it may be for our imagination to combine such contradictory characteristics.

So we had a third elementary particle, the atom of light, to which we gave the name of photon. It is only a slight exaggeration to say that from then on scarcely a year passed without the invention or dis-covery of some new kind of particle—or new kind of hybrid I should say, for each one, of course, was at the same time a variety of wave. Anderson photographed a particle which was unmistakably a light, positive particle, the exact counterpart of the electron. It is now known as positron. A negative heavy particle (as counterpart of the positive proton) is not known, but there is an uncharged heavy particle, the neutron. A light neutral particle has never been found, but was invented and called the neutrino. Then particles of medium mass came to light, positive, negative, and neutral, and these were collec-tively called mesons, while the uncharged ones are sometimes called neutrettos. Agreement has not yet been reached concerning the exact mass of these mesons; according to what I heard last month[3] in Cambridge, there may be a whole assortment of different masses.

I might continue at length about these developments, but I think I have said enough along these lines. Surely you realize that this brief, incomplete, and "spiritless" list is not intended to reveal the spirit of modern physics, but rather its seeming lack of spirit. Instead of physics, I might equally well have invoked the example of biology to show that natural science, left to itself, has a tendency to become more and more complicated and "spiritless." The number of species described has, I am told, reached the million mark, and grows each year by about twenty thousand. In the rapidly developing field of genetics and the related study of cytology, the originally so simple Mendelian laws have had to be considerably modified and complicated, from year to year new concepts arise, and the resultant terminology has left that of physics far behind both as to bulk and as to demands on Greek and Latin lexicography.

But enough of such examples. You need only open any work, any dissertation on a scientific subject, to convince yourselves how involved the discipline in question has become, and how unintelligible the technical terminology has grown to be for the layman. Let us now try to find the few broad lines along which the spirit is advancing towards simplification and unification of the general picture. Here the kinship of the motive and of the nature of the success that we encounter in widely remote ranges of research reveals to us that the spirit has indeed been active and productive in guiding scientific inquiry, that science has done more than list the answers to the questions asked of nature through experiments: that it has done more than piece together long, elaborate chains of electrons, protons, photons, neutrons, mesons, neutrettos, and neutrinos.

I shall give a brief outline of what I take to be the leading ideas of modern natural science.

In the nineteenth century:

1. Darwinism.
2. Statistical-mechanical theory of heat.

In the twentieth century:

3. Genetics.

3 [In July, 1946.—Ed.]

4. Quantum theory.
5. Theory of relativity.

From their intersection arise:

6. The problem of time (from 2, 5, and 4).
7. The cosmic problem of astronomy (from 5 and 4).
8. The physical substratum of life and thought (in which 1–4 meet with the chemistry of enzymes and viruses).

It goes without saying that I shall not "dispose of" this program today.

3

In the analysis of ideas, scientific ideas in any case, it is not always desirable to follow the order of their historical appearance. Often we enter the unknown edifice of a new scientific discipline through a lesser gate that leads us into a side passage; it may take us a long while to find our way to the main portal and view the whole structure in its proper perspective. But apart from this, even the briefest step by step account of the developments indicated in the above outline would in almost each case exceed the time allotted to my lecture. Moreover, this is not my appointed task; but rather, to indicate the basic, unifying ideas. Here I must ask your indulgence, for my undertaking is exceedingly difficult, and that for two entirely different reasons. The first is that in some of these matters I do not feel justified in assuming that the majority of my listeners possess even the most superficial knowledge of the facts and the ideas based on them. The second is that in hardly a single one of these disciplines is the development concluded. For the most part, beginning, say, with No. 3, we are still in the midst of developments. My work is therefore bound to be fragmentary, and I shall be quite glad if I succeed in giving you a clear idea of two or three of the fascinating leitmotivs.

Let us begin with the nineteenth century. If, scientifically speaking, I call it the century of Darwin and Boltzmann, I follow Ludwig Boltzmann himself, the actual founder of the statistical-mechanical theory (it is ordinarily called thermodynamics but it is far more). Boltzmann once (1886) declared very emphatically that his century would some day be designated not as the century of steam, electricity, the telegraph, the telephone, etc., but as the century of Darwin. He said Darwin. We can hardly expect him to have said Darwin and Boltzmann, but we may be permitted to wonder whether he surmised as much.

The boundless admiration of Boltzmann for Darwin's work points to a common trait in their thoughts and aims. What is that common trait?—In an article commemorating Boltzmann[4] I have pointed to the statistical law of averages as this common trait which constitutes the backbone, the vital nerve of both theories. In this, one might see merely a common instrument, akin to the hammer, which is used both by the shoemaker and the stone mason, though for entirely different purposes. But here the common trait is something far more profound. It is a spiritual trend, a trend towards rationality that emerges in the thinking of the century and finds in these two men its highest exponents, a trend that is today still fighting for complete acceptance, though already it has far more supporters than adversaries.

How shall I characterize this trend? Half a dozen phrases come to my lips, yet none of them fully comprehends the matter. Divesting nature of its mystery. Banishment of mysterious natural forces, not to mention teleological traits, from the picture of nature. Repudiation of illusory verbal explanations.—To state the matter more positively: it begins to appear that we are now able to give a common-sense explanation of certain universal and dominant traits of the natural process, where this seemed inherently impossible, where we seemed to have reached the limit of the explicable, where it appeared that we could no longer hope for anything more than a complete description of our findings: we find it to be so and so, but why it is so I cannot tell you; the question itself is perhaps without real meaning (!).

Here I cannot go into details. But you know that according to the Darwinian theory the species arise and are transformed *de facto* along lines of apparently teleological development; this Darwin reduces to mere calculable chance, to the fact that in the average, the slight, accidental, directionless variations (today we must say mutations) among the thousands of millions of individuals who are born and die are retained and passed on to the progeny if and only if they are of some

4 "The Statistical Law in Nature," *Nature* (London), CLIII (1944), 704.

slight advantage to the individual in its struggle for existence, while they are eliminated if they are disadvantageous. Thus teleological lines of development arise through calculable chance.

The mechanical theory of heat similarly bases the laws of physics and chemistry on calculable chance. Most of these laws are far sharper and more exact than the organic lines of development we have been discussing. But this again is no mystery. The greater the number of individual cases a statistic is based on, the clearer and the more reproducible its results will be. According to the mechanical theory of heat, almost every individual phenomenon we observe in nature is itself the result of the interplay of an enormous number of atoms and molecules and their collisions, etc. And the number of particular events that work together in the slightest phenomenon that we observe—that work together in accordance with pure calculable chance—is in general far higher than in the field of biology, running not into millions but into millions of billions of billions. This alone is the reason why, if we repeat the same observation under the same conditions, we again observe the same phenomenon, quantitatively unchanged. Today this is no longer a dubious hypothesis; we are dealing with facts that can be checked in all significant details, merely by setting up conditions in which the number of particular occurrences contributing to an observable phenomenon is not too enormous. The theory permits us to calculate in advance the exact degree of indeterminateness and irreproducibility in such a phenomenon, and this lack of precision finds exact quantitative confirmation in experiment.

Boltzmann's theory of natural law casts an interesting sidelight on the concept of time. I shall come back to this (see 6 below).

4

Let us now advance to the threshold of the twentieth century. It so happens that exactly in 1900 two completely new leitmotivs were sounded, which proved to be the two leading ideas of modern physics and biology respectively. In this year, Max Planck laid before the Prussian Academy his work on the theory of heat radiation, which subsequently led to the quantum theory. In the same year, the Mendelian laws of heredity were rediscovered and their far-reaching importance recognized, independently by Tschermak in Vienna, De Vries in Leyden, and Correns in Berlin. Soon thereafter, Mendel's ideas were extended in De Vries' theory of mutations. The history of the world-famous dissertation of the Augustinian abbot, which slumbered in the archives of the Scientific Society of Brünn from 1866 to 1900, is today generally known. An old friend of mine, a physicist, has given me a charming detail. Soon after the rediscovery, he took the volume in question from the library of his academy and found that the pages had not even been cut.

Now let us consider the reorientation in physics brought about by the work of Max Planck. This is one of the cases where, in pursuing the underlying idea, we shall do better not to follow the historical development exactly. Planck's discovery that energy was not transmitted between material systems in a steady, continuous stream, as had been believed, but apparently in definite amounts, or "quanta"—this discovery represented for the physicist an extraordinarily exciting and challenging paradox. Indeed, Planck himself was slow and reluctant to accept the revolutionary implications of his discovery, and kept searching for ways to avoid them. Yet this whole matter is so far removed from ordinary thinking that it is difficult to perceive its full profundity and import at first glance. But aside from the theory of radiation there is another approach to the new orientation in physics which brings it into a meaningful historical context that is hundreds, indeed thousands of years old. This approach is the discovery made by Einstein some years later that energy and mass are merely different aspects of the same thing, that they are indeed identical.

Energy is a dynamic concept—at first sight a very abstract one—to which we are led when we submit to mathematical analysis the interplay of forces by which different parts of matter affect each other's movements, as, for example, the sun and the planets and moons. To the mathematical physicist energy is primarily nothing more than an integration constant (a very important one, to be sure) in the equations of mechanical motion. Later heat was also found to be a "form of energy," since in actual physical motion the "constant" of energy is usually not constant but diminishes, while somewhere a certain quantity of heat is always produced. But according to the mechanical theory of heat, of which I have already spoken, heat is nothing more than the motion of the smallest particles of matter. The "inconstancy of the constant" is only apparent. A part of it slips into the hidden motion of the smallest particles. Up to a certain degree, the process can be reversed and the energy regained through certain contrivances such as heat-driven engines. Thus energy, though in a strictly mathematical sense not identical with motion, is, as a concept, equivalent to motion and to force generating motion.

Mass, on the other hand, is the essential characteristic of matter. Newton, by a naïve tautology, still defined mass as "*quantitas materiae.*" A better Latin word for it would be *moles.* For what we think of first in connection with mass is the inertia with which a body resists being set in motion by forces.

It was believed for a long time that to contrast energy and mass, or in older terms force and matter, was very fundamental. We remember Büchner's well-known work, which to be sure belongs to a rather dubious philosophical milieu. This belief did not always enjoy undivided support. At all times there have been some profound thinkers who were disturbed by the duality of force and matter, who sensed in the *vires* a mystery from which they tried to free themselves. I believe that even Democritus, with his theory of atoms, was obscurely aiming at the ideal of deriving a purely geometrical view of the whole natural process from the fixed size and shape of the atoms that collide and deflect each other in virtue of their mutual impenetrability. Certainly Descartes' views tended toward geometrization, which, by the way, was the forerunner of the modern theories of relativity. Perhaps I shall be able to devote a few more words to it later on.

But now to Einstein's discovery; his famous equation

$$E = M$$

(energy equals mass) has put an end once and for all to the duality of force and matter. In view of what I have said before about energy and mass, it appears paradoxical in the highest degree to equate them. But today this is no longer an hypothesis, it is unhappily for the world an indubitable fact. For the enormous energy produced by the atom bomb results from a relatively slight diminution in the mass of the substances involved; i.e., the substances resulting from the alchemistic reaction weigh slightly less than the original substances. I say alchemistic, because a transformation of elements actually takes place, and this transformation is accompanied by a loss of mass. The lost mass ultimately reappears as heat and produces the inconceivably high temperature.

Thus the fact is clear, though in this simple form it is of course purely programmatic. We must delve into its meaning, which implies an immense program. It will compel us to organize our view—our θεωρία—of nature in such a way as to obviate force as an explicit concept, retaining it merely as an auxiliary concept. Einstein in his *Meaning of Relativity* has already done this for the theory of gravitation; he has done it through geometrization, though in an entirely different way from what Democritus and Descartes may have conceived. But of this I hope I shall be able to say more later.

Now let us turn in another direction. After what has been said, it will not be hard for you to recognize the nature of Planck's famous quanta of energy. In view of Einstein's equation they turn out to be quanta of mass. The idea of the discontinuity of matter, the idea that it is not continuous but consists of discrete particles, has been familiar to us since Democritus. Since Democritus, the notion has never been entirely lost, although many thinkers were violently opposed to it up to the very end—that is, up to the time when incontrovertible experiments proved the soundness of the atomic theory.

Now we need simply transfer this discontinuity, this discreteness, from mass to energy: and there we have Planck's quantum theory. Of course it is not as simple as all that. This view of the physical world remains a revolution, and we are in the midst of it. How shall we conceive as discrete and discontinuous all the phenomena that have hitherto been regarded as the steady effect of a force that imparts, let us say, a gradually increasing velocity to a particle of mass? How shall we do so without sacrificing the clear, simple ideas that were contained in the older conception and which were very well adapted to explaining a large complex of facts that had been confirmed by experiment?—These ideas we must preserve unharmed. This is possible only if, on the basis of Einstein's equation, we also inversely transfer certain conceptions and working methods from the older theory of force to what used to be known as matter. An understanding of the wireless transmission, of light, even of the simplest electrical apparatus such

333

as the dynamo, the electric motor, the transformer, requires indispensably the conception of forces and waves continuously traversing space. But since on the other hand we must now adhere to the conception of energy exchanged in quanta, we arrive at a twofold nature of phenomena, which at first seems somewhat uncomfortable. Regardless how we ultimately reconcile ourselves to this twofold nature, we shall not obtain a general picture unless we ascribe such a twofold nature to particles of mass properly speaking, i.e., to those quanta of energy which we have always known as discontinuous and only as discontinuous. We must associate waves with particles of mass. But here I must warn against a common misunderstanding. Neither our imagination nor our linguistic usage is adequate to the comprehension and expression of so novel an idea. The meaning here is not that the particles of matter generate forces or waves, nor that they are surrounded by waves, but that they themselves can be regarded as waves, that they *are* waves.

But let us turn from these difficulties which, despite great partial successes, have not yet been solved and upon which I have scarcely time to touch, and turn back to our leitmotiv, the discontinuity or discreteness which, two thousand years after it was discovered or at least surmised for "matter," has been extended to force, so that in some way it will come to dominate our entire conception of nature.

Now what is so significant in this idea? Simply this, that discrete things can be counted; they can be counted with the help of the simplest, clearest mathematical equipment, of perhaps the one mathematical concept that is fully understood, the integer.[5] This allows us to hope for a real understanding, free from mystery, of many things that formerly we could only describe, or register as experienced. Boltzmann's theory of natural law, which I have characterized as one of the two great achievements of the nineteenth century, rests entirely on the method of counting discrete things, to wit, atoms, molecules, and their collisions. At first the method appeared rather accidental, a lucky chance. Cases were even found in which it was inapplicable, or applicable only with difficulty—with liquids, for example, because the molecules are so densely packed that it is impossible to speak of

5 Leopold Kronecker: "Integers were made by God, everything else is the work of man."

334

separate collisions, since every molecule is in constant interaction with dozens of neighbors.—But the universality of discreteness, as now recognized, appears to show that the method of enumeration, the method of the integer, is really the royal road, the only road by which we may hope to achieve real insight.

5

This view is confirmed when we realize that a truly astonishing inner kinship exists between the idea just stated and the second great scientific field that was opened to us in the fruitful year 1900: that of modern genetics.

Here, too, continuity has been replaced by discontinuity. The attention of biologists has shifted from the small, almost imperceptible variations of the phenotype, conceived by Darwin, to the mutations of the genotype, also small but discrete and therefore enumerable; the former, though they appear in the individual, are not transmissible, only the latter represent an hereditary change (precisely this consideration is expressed in the Greek technical terms). Thus the theory of mutations is an atomic theory of heredity. It is for the understanding of the origin of species what the quantum theory is for physics: the transformation does not take place evenly but in little jumps. That is so; it is a simple fact, not an idea. This fact enables us to count and thus for the first time to introduce an exact quantitative, mathematical method—indeed, the most exact of all—into the field of biology, so incomparably more complex than that of physics. Physics and chemistry on the one hand and biology on the other now approach one another to a degree and in a way which could never have been foreseen. Just as the physicochemist begins to realize that his "laws" are not really exact and inviolable, but follow merely from the law of averages; just as he is overcome by enthusiasm because he is enabled to corroborate his thesis and in cases where the numbers are not too large, really to observe the exceptions to his rigid "laws": at this very moment the biologist, the geneticist, is no less overjoyed to find that exact laws do exist in his field—even though, he says almost apologetically, they are "only" statistical laws, which become more and more exact as the number of subjects investigated increases.—Is there still any basic difference?—No.

I have explained elsewhere that this is no mere outward similarity between the sciences, no methodological analogy, but a direct, inner, essential connection in so far as the mutations are real, though sometimes exceedingly complex quantum transitions. A detailed discussion of this would lead us too far. But I should like to add one observation which seems to me of interest, though it quite possibly represents nothing more than an analogy.

In physics today we see relatively clearly that our conception of the atomism of matter and energy is somewhat too naïve, although we do not yet know how to improve on it. The particles are not separate entities of ascertainable individuality. Somehow the concept of the field enters into the picture, connecting the particles, interchanging their roles in a way that cannot be verified, and so on.—It is hard to express oneself clearly in the matter, because we do not yet understand it.

But it is highly interesting to note that recently a reaction has set in against the rigid atomism of heredity in the Mendel-Morgan theory. This reaction has given rise to the idea of "positional effect," according to which the genes are not strictly localized parts of the chromosome, with individuals responsible for this or that trait or mutation; the mutations are brought about by complex structural characteristics in the chromosome as a whole.

I know too little about this to say any more. It is possible that the common trait in the two developments can be reduced to the general rule that in every great discovery one tends to overshoot the mark and that, as in artillery fire, the next step is a process of range finding.

6

The time is growing short and I must abandon the greater part of the program we drew up at the start. Concerning the geometrization of force in the theories of relativity, I shall have some little to say a few days from now in Zurich.[6] The cosmic problem would in itself occupy at least a long lecture; concerning point 8, something is to be found in my little book *What Is Life?*:[7] much more than what I have written there I myself do not know.

6 Published in *Verhandlungen der Schweizer Naturforschenden Gesellschaft* (Zurich, 1946), 53–61.
7 New York and Cambridge, 1944.

And so I should like to ask your attention just a little while longer for a few sidelights that scientific thought has cast on the concept of time, because contemporary writers have seldom given this point (so important in the history of ideas) the attention it deserves.

The essential with regard to time is our knowledge of earlier and later. This seems to be a commonplace, almost a tautology. Therefore it will perhaps not be superfluous to point out the following: We are, it is true, accustomed to conceive of the subjective passage of time in the individual as a complete, indubitable, and well-ordered chain of experiences. But sometimes when we attach real importance to a decision regarding earlier or later, we find out that we cannot arrive at it intuitively, but must resort to rational inferences.

When was I given this paperweight that lies on my table? I recollect. I remember a remark that my friend X made about it the first time he saw it. But X hasn't been to see me in my own house since I lived in Zurich. The answer is therefore: in Zurich, or even earlier.—Each one of us is familiar with hundreds of instances of this kind of reasoning. Not to mention dreams, which *subjectively* are equivalent to the waking state. Here the time sequence is often completely confused, we speak with people who have long been dead. We worry about their future, and so on.

The widespread belief that the earlier and later of any two events is absolute and indubitable is therefore based not on immediate, subjective evidence, but on physics and chronology: on good watches, on a calendar approved by the state, and on the traces of individual and common experience that each day and each hour leaves in tens of thousands of newspapers, court records, official records, diaries, dated personal letters, etc. Thence we come to look upon the earlier-later relationship as an objective reality, independent of any records or other traces and inherent in the events themselves. Perhaps no trace can be found, but still one may exist. In the place and time in which a given event occurs, certain traces, repercussions, effects of some other event may already be present. And we feel certain that if this possibility exists, the opposite possibility is excluded. According to this rational criterion we then call the "other event" the earlier.

Here we see that the concept of time is closely bound up with the causal connection of the world: the earlier event can affect the later

337

event, not the other way round. When the special theory of relativity limited the sphere of causality very considerably by revealing that no physical cause could spread more rapidly than with the speed of light, our old, naïve concept of time had to be considerably revised. Consider two events, "simultaneous" in the naïve sense, taking place at A and B. A certain time must elapse before an effect from A can reach B.[8] Conversely, the event at B would have had to take place at an equal interval earlier, in order for an effect from B to have reached A. This double time interval at B embraces all the conceivable events at B which from the standpoint of the causal connection are neither earlier nor later than the event at A. But it further develops that the "simultaneous" event at B has no prerogative, no better right to be considered simultaneous with the event at A, than any other event occurring at B during the double time interval.

For places on the earth, this time interval is never greater than the fraction of a second. For cosmic distances the interval of simultaneity can amount to many years or even millennia.

From this conception, which is today uncontested, no very clear philosophical inference can be drawn. On the contrary, its significance lies perhaps in that it has blurred for the first time the supposed clarity of the space-time pattern by which man had always contemplated the universe, and shaken our faith in the monopoly of this pattern.

Suppose a friend of mine should board a space ship traveling at half the speed of light and reach the nearest fixed star in eight or ten years. Suppose he settled down there. At a certain moment I might wonder whether he were still alive, and I should have to realize that perhaps there is no objective answer to such a question. If he "has died," but only recently, so that a radio message carrying the news cannot yet have reached me, or if he is only "seriously ill" and "going to

8 The double-pointed arrows in the figure symbolize the two intervals of uncertainty.

die" before my next radiogram can reach him—in both cases, it is, from the standpoint of a physicist, a question of interpretation whether my friend is alive or not.

However, a far more incisive critique of the traditional concept of time comes to us from an entirely different source. But for a few exceptions, which really are exceptions, all events in nature are irreversible. A sequence of phenomena exactly opposite to that of real observation—as in a film run backwards—would almost always present a crass contradiction to natural laws. The most admired achievement of the mechanical theory was to make this specific direction of the world process really intelligible, intelligible without any *ad hoc* hypotheses embodied in the basic premises. According to Boltzmann, this direction is explained by the trivial circumstance that order "tends" to be transformed into disorder, but not the other way around. Conceive of a deck of cards in perfect order, 7, 8, 9, 10, jack, queen, king, ace, in all four suits. A violent shuffling motion would (probably) transform it from this condition into one of complete disorder. Now, mechanically speaking, the exact same motion might change it back again from disorder to order. But everyone would expect the former transformation and no one will expect the latter—for which one would wait in vain.

I must beg your pardon for the sketchy character of this explanation. In any event, the spontaneous transition from order to disorder is the quintessence of Boltzmann's theory of natural law and the temporal direction inherent in any natural law. This theory really grants an understanding and does not beg the question. For any attempt to reason away the observed dissymmetry of things by means of an a priori sense of direction or a line of direction of the time variables must be regarded as a begging of the question. No one who has once understood Boltzmann's theory will ever again have recourse to such expedients. It would be a scientific regression beside which a repudiation of Copernicus in favor of Ptolemy would seem trifling.

At first we may find it astonishing that nevertheless objections to the theory have been raised again and again in the course of the past decades, and not by fools but by fine thinkers. If we carefully consider these objections and eliminate the subtle misunderstandings and false inferences, we actually find remaining a small but exceedingly significant residue which we might express as follows:

First, my good friend, you state that the two directions of your time variables, from $-t$ to $+t$ and from $+t$ to $-t$, are a priori equivalent. Then by fine arguments appealing to common sense you show that disorder (or "entropy") must with overwhelming probability increase with time. Now, if you please, what do you mean by "with time"? Do you mean in the direction $-t$ to $+t$? But if your inferences are sound, they are equally valid for the direction $+t$ to $-t$. If these two directions are equivalent a priori, then they remain so a posteriori. The conclusions can never invalidate the premise. Then your inference is valid for both directions of time, and that is a contradiction.

Now it is not as bad as all that. But there is only one way out. It is not true that the inference must be valid for both directions of time, it must only be valid for either one of the two. For which one is irrelevant. It is irrelevant whether we begin with the plus or the minus sign. That it is the direction from past to future we must state by definition.

In a word, we must decide once and for all to determine the direction of time by means of Boltzmann's theory itself. The increasing disorder is itself the adequate measure of advancing time. Only as long as the statistical theory of heat itself is allowed to determine where the past lies and where the future, can it be maintained. It collapses as soon as there is any other independent criterion for the direction of time.

If we pursue these considerations, as Boltzmann himself did in full awareness of their implications, we may well be overcome by a slight dizziness—a dizziness in time, one might say. Boltzmann speaks seriously of the possibility that elsewhere in the universe time might run in the opposite direction, if the universe extended far enough in space and time.

This presumably it does not. It is not certain but fairly probable that straight lines run back into themselves after a distance of 10^{27} or at most 10^{30} centimeters and that the universe has not existed for more than 10^9 or 10^{10} years in a state bearing any resemblance to its present state. These dimensions are far too small to leave room for the extravagance of an occasional reversal of time.

340

Yet the fact remains that time no longer appears to us as a gigantic, world-dominating χρόνος, nor as a primitive entity, but as something derived from phenomena themselves. It is a figment of my thinking. That as such it might some day put an end to my thinking, as some believe, is beyond my comprehension. Even the old myth makes Kronos devour only his own children, not his begetter.

Adolf Portmann

Biology and the Phenomenon of the Spiritual

1

The conceptions of life and spirit have undergone such varied and complex changes in the course of historical development, that it might have been worth while to examine the attitude of biology to the phenomenon of the spiritual from this historical angle. If we do not dwell on the historical aspect of the matter, it is not because it is undeserving of our attention, but because another approach seems to me to be more important and more necessary on this occasion. What I should like to do is to give you an idea of those methods and findings of modern biological research which can throw light on the problems constituting the topic of our session.

"Spirit" is an archaic term, and when the biologist sets out to comment on the phenomena of the spirit, he must first of all state as exactly as possible which of the many things designated by this one word he is referring to. There are two groups of phenomena in which the biologist encounters the spiritual. First, there is that quality in man's works and in his mode of life that distinguishes him from even the highest of his animal relatives. This quality is said to be "spiritual," that is, determined by the spirit: it constitutes one of the aspects in which we encounter the spiritual.

But the dichotomy of "nature and spirit" points to still another meaning of this versatile word. This meaning refers to a realm above or beyond the things of nature, or in some mysterious way permeating the things of nature; it designates a transcendent order which philosophical theories of the world have related in the most different ways to the data of our sensory experience. This intangible realm is called the realm of the spirit. Now you will not expect the biologist to decide whether this refers to the same spirit which we have noted as the privilege of the human way of life. At the moment only one thing is important: we must keep in mind these two meanings of the word as we enter together upon the field of biology, and we shall attempt to exercise the greatest care in making it clear at every step which of the two meanings is intended, the more general one, or the one referring specifically to man.

The distinctions between nature and spirit: body and soul: body, soul, and spirit: reach far back into the past. But the foundations of biological research belong to the most recent period, the last centuries of human endeavor. The germ cell of a mammal was first seen in 1827 by Karl Ernst von Baer; the penetration of the sperm into the egg cell, or insemination, was first seen under the microscope between 1875 and 1877. Only since that time have we been able to speak with any certainty about the earliest stage of our own life and the beginning of individual development. I cannot overemphasize this contrast between the archaic origin of conceptual distinctions such as body and soul or nature and spirit, and the novelty of our knowledge regarding the first stages of the development to which we owe our existence. If you keep this contrast sharply in mind, if you let it permeate your thinking through and through, you will understand that the natural scientist cannot at first help distrusting such archaic separations into entities. Times which really believed that the lower animals were born out of muck and rot, which knew nothing of the spermatozoon or the human egg cell, were bound to have many conceptions at variance with our own.

Consequently, the biologist must for the time being disregard all these archaic distinctions. He must not allow himself to be guided by the a priori opinion that the spirit is something that enters earthly life from a foreign sphere, even though there may be theological or philosophical justification for such a view. But neither can he accept that other preconceived notion, according to which spirit is a product of material life, as a fruit is the product of a tree. The biologist cannot set to work with a preconceived conception of the spirit, either as an incursion from above or as an eruption from below.

What biology will have to say about the spiritual cannot be established in advance; we can only await the results. This would seem to be a very obvious truth—and yet it must be stated, for it is not hard to show that most biological works approach the phenomenon of the spirit from preconceived positions, resulting either from faith in certain religious ideas or from rejection of these same ideas. Both are a priori positions: one takes it for granted that the spiritual is beyond the scope of biological investigation, while the other includes it in the object of this investigation.

But on no account must biological method underestimate the phenomena comprised in the term spirit. This must be plainly stated. Shall it then be said that biology begins without premises? On the contrary: we shall attempt to elucidate the most general premises of modern biological research. Here I disregard such presuppositions as originate in the fact that the scientist is himself a living being. Their importance is never small, and they demand constant vigilance, since the object of our science is itself alive, and therefore leads us to so many essential problems of our human existence.

Our point of departure will be the present state of biological knowledge, the results of the work that has been done up to now. Modern biology considers the organism as a relatively closed or self-sufficient system. The self-sufficiency of the system is expressed in the continuity we can observe in the living organism from the germ cell to the death of the individual. This self-sufficiency is relative, however, since we know of emergences—for example, the abrupt origin of new systems and variations. We know of events which we call mutations and which are an important object of biological study.

The organisms also reveal the merely relative self-sufficiency of their systems in that they are always found in a relation to their environment as a whole, including all the realities that we cannot perceive directly with our senses and therefore seek to comprehend by indirect means. Bear in mind that for the biologist all the qualities of his object appears as qualities of an order, or system. And it is because we are dealing with a complex order that, as we have said, we do not permit our study of the organism to begin with archaic distinctions of body, soul, spirit. For such distinctions often give rise to pseudo problems by compelling us to set up hypotheses concerning the interaction of these supposedly separate entities. How do they act on one another and how are they connected?

I should like to convey some idea of the nature and consequences of

344

such pseudo problems by a glance at the cellular theory. Following the discoveries of the nucleus and of protoplasm, the belief was widely held that the cells were elementary organisms. It then became necessary to explain how these elementary organisms could order themselves into a higher structure, how they became specialized, what guided their division of labor. Up to the present day, the search after an intercellular force has been in vain—the more farsighted biologists realized long ago that such a force is already at work in the egg cell and that throughout the entire course of individual development it never ceases to exist. They realize that the plasmatic system, which was present from the very first, organizes itself—how it does so is a problem that leads us to the study of submicroscopic structures, a new field in which physicists, chemists, and biologists are all hard at work today. We must penetrate the structure of the plasma, not search for a secondary factor which orders the cells.

But we have set out to approach from the point of view of biology the phenomena in which the spiritual is manifested. To this end we shall choose one among the many branches of biological research. We shall leave aside many important fields of study; but I hope it will be clear to all of us that our choice is based solely on convenience and constitutes no value judgment, but only the direction of our present preoccupation. We shall omit from our survey fields of biological inquiry in which highly significant work is being done, yet as we follow the road that takes us to our specific problems, we shall do well to remember that these other fields exist.

First of all, biology leads us into the realm of the spiritual if only by its concern with the study of that special mode of existence which is best known to us from our own existence, and which the biologist designates by a word of his own, a scientific symbol, "inwardness," because the traditional terms seem to him too heavily loaded with extraneous meanings. What we call inwardness is the specific mode of existence of living beings. We know it best through our own experience, but find evidence of it in other organisms, though decreasingly as we move farther away from man.

Any study of inwardness must begin with that form of life whose interiority is best known to us: ourselves, the human species. Many biologists, fearing that this knowledge of our own rich interiority

345

might humanize and falsify our conceptions of other organisms, have avoided the whole sphere of inwardness. The results have sometimes been grotesque: mechanical description of animal behavior was regarded as the only valid biological method, much importance was attached to an "objective" nomenclature; it was considered better, for example, to say photoreceptor than eye. This school of biology denied any possibility of investigating the inwardness of animals and thought it best to disregard all signs of an experience in any way related to our own. For some time, however, scientists taking a more comprehensive and calmer view have begun slowly and cautiously to penetrate the inwardness of organisms, and this trend is becoming increasingly pronounced. These scholars know that on their road they will encounter the phenomena of the spiritual—they also know that the instrument of their own research is a part of this strange reality that is known as spiritual.

The first of the paths leading us into the realm of inwardness is the study of the motivation of animal drives, of those hidden systems that make the organism an active center and "express" inwardness. The relation of human motivation to these systems remains to be determined; the biologist who investigates these ordering systems is on the road to the manifestation of the spiritual in our directive mechanism. How much he will learn concerning this "spirit," no scientist can decide in advance. Thinking with regard to these different kinds of motivation was for a long time dominated by ideas of so-called instinctive behavior, based primarily on experiments with insects. Through the *Souvenirs entomologiques*,[1] the experiments of J. H. Fabre have entered into the literature and general knowledge of our time. The scientist whom Darwin called the incomparable observer, who so profoundly influenced Maeterlinck and Bergson, who was called the Homer, the Virgil of insect life—this J. H. Fabre drew so impressive a picture of the complexity of insect behavior, which he showed to be rigidly determined by inherited characteristics, that his examples have become genuine classics. Many of you no doubt remember, for example, his experiments with sand wasps and their care of their young, his observations of the scarabs, and so on.

The general impression that the rigid ways of insect life are hered-

1 Definitive edition in 10 vols., Paris, 1914–24.

itarily determined has led many biologists to conceive of instinctive kinds of motivation as behavior patterns typical for each species, almost without individual variation, stereotyped in all individuals, existing without any learning process, and preceding all experience. A picture thus emerged which offered a sharp contrast to our own mode of life, a picture markedly different from our hesitating, our groping and learning, from our possibility of change and individual contrasts. Small wonder that this one-sided conception of instinct was all too often regarded as the animal background against which our own freer behavior stands out as an exception.

Today we view instinctual behavior very differently. So differently, in fact, that we have come to regard the very word "instinct" with suspicion, as a term that has become devoid of meaning. As a result of painstaking research our old rigid conception of the instincts has become more supple: instances of flexibility within these hereditary systems have been demonstrated, instances where individuals of very different species can fulfill equivalent roles in the system and substitute for one another. Thus, for example, the place of the mother in the hereditary behavior pattern of the animal young can be filled by another creature, even by an automobile: the newborn gnu on the steppe runs after the motorcar whose owner has just shot its mother. The car moves, and that suffices to attach the child to it. Likewise a man or a hen can act as a mother to young geese, provided that this individual is the first that the goslings see as they break out of the egg. Lorenz designated this possibility of determining behavior as "imprinting"; numerous observations have shown it to be widespread.

Still another aspect of instinctive behavior has become highly questionable to us today: the release mechanism. Attention has been drawn to the peculiar character of the inner state preceding the setting in motion of the instinctive act: the restless searching for something, for a something which must exist in a structure within the animal but thus far is inaccessible to us, which corresponds to a structure in its environment. The observer is strongly impelled to believe in the existence of an image that releases expectancy, unrest, and a striving after the structure corresponding to the one that is already present. Whether we speak of "image" or "schema" is here irrelevant—in any case we have entered into the realm of inwardness and its mechanisms, and it

347

is understandable that in connection with discoveries in our own inwardness, some daring biologists have actually spoken of archetypes. Thus we are compelled to surmise the presence in the animal of stored-up potentialities closely akin to those which the student of man must assume as existing hidden within ourselves, if he is to understand certain mysterious encounters and correspondences. Let us at least observe that biologists today see the mystery of animal motivation in all its magnitude.

Since 1918, we have called the state of expectancy "appetence," to establish a connection with appetite and the appeasement of hunger. The underlying structure of appetence includes nervous elements as well as hormonal systems, and numerous internal and external organs as well. In this network we can at most localize certain regulatory nerve centers, and even this must be done with the greatest caution. On a summer day like this, the dovetail, a diurnal moth, is attracted to yellow or red blossoms, but when its eggs ripen a mood sets in, in which these colors cease to be attractive, and it will fly off in search of a certain green that occurs in the leaves of the bedstraw.

In extreme cases this searching may be directed toward extremely limited, specific schemata embodied in the mate, the offspring, or other members of the species. A particular marking of the head, or a color flash that appears in flight, then becomes as it were a symbol of the desired goal, a sort of flag or signal. We call such special characteristics "release signals" and at present they are the object of much industrious research. For a time such release signals were sought in all instinctive behavior, and the relation between release signal and inner schema was believed to be so close as to warrant the use of such terms as lock and key; each lock was held to have its own specific key. In the last five years, however, it has been recognized that such strict co-ordination of release signals and appetence occurs only in extreme cases, and that as a rule the appetence must seek its satisfaction in far more open situations through more complex behavior patterns.[2] A male robin redbreast *(Erithacus rubecula)* in the mating mood will drive any other male robin from his chosen territory. Sometimes he will be aroused to attack by a dummy made of red feathers but in

2 David Lack, "Some Aspects of Instinctive Behavior and Display in Birds," *The Ibis* (London), July, 1941.

no way resembling a bird. The same male may react to a birdlike shape of a different color. In a third experiment, the same individual fails to react to either of these dummies, and will only attack a real robin. This example should guard us from taking too schematic a view of the part played by release in instinctive behavior.

At still another point recent studies have invalidated the concept of rigid, hereditary behavior patterns. Careful observation of the higher animals reveals states in which action does not seem rigidly determined; we find types of behavior, free from appetite and susceptible to certain nuances. We hear birds singing a free, playful kind of song, we see them playfully chasing one another when, under optimal living conditions, they are free from the bonds of hunger and the sex urge. Bally has shown the significance of these phenomena and made it clear that play, free from appetite, occurs most frequently in the shelter of parental care. Free behavior seems to demand two conditions that are fulfilled among the higher animal groups: advanced development of the central nervous system and intensive, often protracted care of the young.

This free behavior, which may well be designated as playfulness, is characteristic of a complex system. It does not seem to originate at one point, that is, it does not seem to be a single new character, but rather a number of corresponding characters appearing at many points in the complex structure: characters of the nervous organization, or of the process of growth, and special characters of structure and behavior. In the following we shall augment this condensed statement by examining the richest of these systems, that of man. In any event, biological inquiry leads to the phenomena of freedom. And nothing could show more clearly how far our progress in the knowledge of animal behavior has led us from the rigid conceptions current at the turn of the century. In the play of the higher animals, we observe a peculiar variety of the inwardness that we count among the most important characteristics of our own species.[3]

Let us look back for a moment. On the road from external to internal characteristics, on the road of observation and biological experiment, we have penetrated to the dimension proper to living things, the dimension that we have called inwardness. The former dominant

3 Gustav Bally, *Vom Ursprung und von den Grenzen der Freiheit* (Basel, 1944).

picture of instinctive behavior as a ready-made, highly intricate lock
has, in the light of more intensive research, given way to a conception
that is not quite so clear and simple. We find to be sure a number
of built-in mechanisms, but we also find that new structures acquired
through experience can be mounted into these mechanisms and retained for the duration of the individual life span. The governing
directive systems, however, evade our understanding, because their
secret is the secret of protoplasm in general.

I shall now briefly touch on an experiment the results of which we
should never forget in our judgment of even the simplest animal
behavior. I cut the body of a worm in two parts, as you may often do
unintentionally in your garden. A regeneration occurs in which the
front part forms a new hind end, while the hind part forms a new
head, including a complete brain. Here we cannot follow this experiment in all its consequences; for the moment we wish to show only one
thing: that the system "worm" constructs its own brain; its nervous
center is only a link in a higher directive system, into the nature of
which the new submicroscopic investigation of protoplasm will perhaps
give us a deeper insight.

What the worm can do, man cannot! Part of the price we pay for
the complexity of our system is that it can only be constructed once.
But in the course of our embryonic development, our protoplasm
accomplishes the same thing. It also builds up its future directive
organ, its nervous system, thus clearly showing that the true sovereign
is the protoplasm, not its organs or their supreme hierarchic summit in
the mature organism. Here we can say no more concerning the nature
of this supreme direction. It is still hidden from us, yet since it resides
in the protoplasm it is open to further investigation. But even from
this summary account you will perhaps realize that it is not possible
to differentiate out of hand between the structure of this supreme
directive mechanism of animal life and that of man's highest systems
of motivation. Biological research admonishes us to restraint and to
the rare form of human asceticism known as patience.

Now let us turn to a different branch of biological research that
will also lead us to manifestations of the spiritual. I have in mind one
of the many aspects of the problem of outward form. Here again we

shall attempt to penetrate from the surface to the core in order to understand a small part of the great order of nature that we try to describe in our so-called "natural order of species."

Our present point of departure will be those phenomena that are summed up under the heading of "expression." In ourselves and in related organisms we observe many spontaneous external changes, disclosing momentary changes in internal being: bristling of hair and feathers, postures, sounds, even changes in color. We shall call them all "spontaneous expression" by way of emphasizing their momentary character. But you are all familiar with changes that are not momentary but continue for long periods of time, and which also are expressive of an inner change: for example, the ceremonial plumage which birds assume at mating times. Or consider the periodical shedding of the buck's antlers, which degrades him in his social group. Or the special dress of many young vertebrates, which not only informs us concerning the state of the animal, but communicates the same information to the animal group. For the present we shall call all these signs "temporary organs of expression."

But we further find that the whole outward appearance of the animal is in many ways related to its level of organization: certain formal elements, certain patterns, or seemingly ornamental forms, appear only beginning with certain degrees of brain development; they are characteristics of a given rank or stage of differentiation. An example: we classify the ruminants according to the degree of differentiation of their organism, particularly their brain; here we find a striking law: only in low forms do canine teeth serve as conspicuous sexual characteristics—these forms do not have antlers. Only high forms have complicated head ornaments, antlers or horns, and in them the canine teeth are reduced, as in the higher deer, the antelopes, and the bovines. We also know transitional forms with canine teeth and simple head ornaments in the male, as for example the muntjac deer.

The course of our description has led us into the midst of the rich and varied forms to be found in the garden of living creatures. Today, however, we must not travel too far along this path, but content ourselves with a glance. To sum up, we find the essential nature of animals expressed also in permanent outward characters.

This we might call "constant expression," but since the word "expression" is reserved for affective states, we shall do better to speak of the "representational value of forms."

A little-considered fact may serve to emphasize the expressive function of the animal exterior. If we compare the inner organs, such as liver, spleen, stomach, heart, it is very difficult to find in them any conspicuous traits characteristic of the species in question; their form is not very expressive. But if on the other hand we consider the coloration, head markings, and horn formation of a single group, such as the antelopes, what wealth of forms, what fertile invention, what striking originality, in contrast to the uniformity of the internal organs!

And now one more example which will perhaps lead us closer to an understanding of the hidden laws that govern animal forms. This example concerns the strange situation of the seminal glands in the higher mammals, including man. Innumerable facts justify us in regarding as "natural" the classification which places the great groups of vertebrates in a series ascending from the fishes via the amphibia and reptiles to the warm-blooded animals—in our present example, the mammals. "Natural" in this connection means that this series represents a segment of the process of development observed in nature, one of those morphological sequences which biologists are now endeavoring to explain through the study of mutations.

If in this natural sequence of animal types we study the situation of the seminal glands (for reasons of time we shall leave the comparable organs of the female out of account), we find that, in the ascending development from fish to mammal, the testicles move from the front or middle of the body towards the region of pelvis and groin and end up at the opposite, anal, pole in a sac outside of the abdominal cavity.

Scientists have made any number of attempts to account for this migration, which also occurs in our own prenatal development and which brings the procreative glands into so exposed a position. Here I cannot go into these "explanations." You may take my word for it (or see for yourself, by studying the technical literature) that there is no theory which accounts for this descent of the testicles. The phenomenon is of particular interest because it cannot possibly be explained by selection. The struggle for survival would hardly induce the testicles to emerge from the shelter of the abdominal cavity, and no theory of selection to date has been able to explain by what sexual selective processes the testicles could have been driven out in the first place.

I believe that this phenomenon can be understood only in the light of its representational value. As the brain develops, we find increasingly conspicuous head characters: in mammals, color pattern, manes, beards, horns, antlers, teeth, a trunk, etc. But parallel to this development of the frontal pole runs a development of the anal pole: ornamental configurations of the tail, varying hair lengths, conspicuous colorations in hoofed animals and apes, and strikingly symmetrical whorls of hair in dogs. The scrotum takes its place as one of the ornamental forms in the reproductive pole; it is indeed the supreme formal symbol of this pole. It is significant that those ruminants in which horns and color patterns attain their maximum development have a particularly large and protruding scrotum. With intuitive insight into their ornamental value, the heraldic representations of the ram include the testicles, while the pictures of the fifteenth century lansquenets and, in general, of the costumes of that period stress the codpiece.

By this illustration I have intended to show that as an animal rises in the hierarchy, it takes on certain formal characteristics which may serve elementary functions but which can be really understood only in the light of their representational function. The representational function of all the external organs of the higher animals is maximal, that of the internal organs slight. The visible—as well as the audible and olfactory—manifestation realizes in the higher species a maximum of individuality, specificity, and expressiveness of the special character of the plasmatic order. So far relatively little progress has been made in this field. We spend years in learning a human language—can it surprise us that we are very slow in penetrating the language of living forms?

I have given so much stress to the representational function, because it indicates the importance of externals, because it shows that the surface has far greater power of communication than the interior, which is devoted to more elementary functions. It is the surface organs of the animal that communicate inwardness, the peculiar essence behind the appearance.

353

This representational function extends far beyond the preservation of the species. To be sure, these superficial forms may be signals, release signals, for procreative functions, and thus play a role in societal relations, in enabling the members of the species, the sexes, to find one another—but this role might be fulfilled by any signal whatsoever. The specific nature of the individual form: the particular striping of the zebra, the particular curve of an antelope's horns, the particular shape of a wild goat's beard, the dewlap in a steer's neck, can never be explained solely with reference to their functional necessity. The representational value goes far beyond any possible utility of such a form for the organism. Yet this very fact indicates the limit of interpretation by biological method. For scientific explanation is possible only in a clearly defined system of relations: in our case we are ignorant of the frame of reference within which these forms might find an explanation.

By biological method I can determine the function of identification performed by a set of antlers or horns, a bird's plumage, a wedding dress. Here the frame of reference is the social life of the species, or more specifically the meeting of the sexes: at all events a perfectly intelligible reality. I can in general recognize the representational function, as such, of these same antlers or horns because the frame of reference, that is, the degree of differentiation of the species in question, is accessible to me through studies of the brain, the nervous system, and of behavior. But as a biologist I cannot explain the special character of these forms, I cannot tell why these horns, this mane, these head markings are exactly as they are. I cannot fit them into any frame of reference that is accessible to science. Here we encounter the limit of our knowledge. Yet even at this limit we find order, and this would suggest the existence of frames of reference that are at present beyond our reach.

Order at this limit—this brings us to realms with which the word "spirit," in one of its many meanings, is often associated. The biologist defines the borderline, but true to the nature of his discipline he does not pass beyond it. Nevertheless, he who has made his way to a borderline, who lives on this borderline, has in secret passed beyond it. And I hope that this excursion into the problem of external forms may also serve to indicate a point at which the realm of biological data touches upon the unknown. At the same time perhaps it has been made clear that biology, while investigating a relatively closed system, must itself remain an open system of analysis that allows for future additions and amplifications.

2

We now turn to our own, human form of life, which we shall examine with the methods of the biologist.

To the biologist, human life also appears primarily as a system: all observable peculiarities appear as links in a system that I shall now attempt to delimit. It embraces, of course, the single germ cell from the moment of its secretion in the mother's ovary, where so much is determined, through its subsequent fertilization, which brings narrower determination, to birth and the entire life of the individual up to death. We have little knowledge of some of the early phases, but we shall not for that reason underestimate their importance.

This individual is structurally correlated with a social organism, within which he lives in a sheltered state up to his fourteenth or sixteenth year, when he attains to maturity. This stage—though especially protracted in man—may readily be likened to the period of parental care, during which the higher animals often reveal a limited freedom. It is in this period that the whole social organism is assimilated. It is a time of gradual adaptation and growth into a social world that already exists. This social world is part and parcel of the individual; the individual is unthinkable without it.

The social quality of human life is primary and extends to its entire structure. This can be demonstrated with especial force for the early period after birth. Here we cannot go into detail, but it can be proved that human development in the womb is not prolonged proportionately to the complexity of our order, as is the case with the other higher mammals. It is approximately a year too short, if we take the mammals for our norm. The time needed for adaptation to the obligatory social world is thus prolonged not only through postponement of sexual maturity and late termination of growth, but also, most significantly, through our early birth.

Why is this so significant? Because this circumstance transfers a stage of development which in the higher mammals occurs in the womb, a constant environment poor in stimuli, to a shifting social world, rich in stimuli. It is precisely in this year that is snatched away from the uterine period that the faculties of standing, speaking, and thinking are developed—and in ways that can be shown to be peculiarly human: by a combination of maturation processes and socially conditioned learning processes which constitute an obligatory primary system no part of which can be changed without totally vitiating the subsequent development.

The development of the individual corresponds entirely to our peculiar form of existence, to its particular variety of social life ordered by tradition: form of existence and mode of development are fully correlated, they constitute the total system that is the object of biological investigation. The method by which this correlation is demonstrated withstood its test when a study of the different types of ontogeny in the higher vertebrates clearly showed the organic unity between mode of life and morphological development.[4]

Why do we stress this relative self-sufficiency of the system, this correlation between ontogeny and social life? Because of a theory of development which congealed into dogma at an early date and is still widely prevalent: the theory that the stages of our development repeat the stages of the history of the race. According to this view, the early phases of our development are merely a recapitulation—and this belief is so firmly entrenched that the period from birth to the second half of the first year has sometimes been called the chimpanzee age. This dogma is sharply contradicted by the fact that the ontogeny of all higher organisms is in its entire course correlated with the special character of the species, that in all stages it has an unmistakable special character belonging to this species.

If this theory were correct, the development of man would become human only in the last stage. But this is not the case, and it is easy to show that our uterine growth is early accelerated far beyond that of the other primates, and that this early acceleration of growth corresponds to the complexity of our central nervous system, that is realized only much later. It can be shown that in man the proportion of limbs

4 For further details, see my *Biologische Fragmente zu einer Lehre vom Menschen* (Basel, 1944).

to trunk deviates even in the womb from that found in apes, and that this early peculiarity is connected with our upright posture, acquired only much later. It might further be mentioned that the lumbar cleft in the spinal column typical of man is already present at the end of the second fetal month—and that this is the earliest distinguishing feature of the human spinal column, which acquires its characteristic form only after some years. There are many such signs of early ontogenic peculiarity.—The egg cell, in which up to the present time nothing particular has been found to distinguish it from the egg cell of other mammals, is nevertheless the germ of a man, extensively determined down to details of subsequent behavior and form. The study of identical twins gives us overwhelming proof of this determination.

What has this to do with the question of the spirit? It has very much to do with it, it seems to me. When we designate the human mode of existence as spiritual, we have in mind a certain special something which from the earliest historical times men have attempted to delimit as "spirit." In pursuing our biological tasks, we merely register the existence of this rich field of historical development; we do not enter upon it.

From the standpoint of the biologist, we must emphatically state that our whole system reveals this human uniqueness, and that neither the course of our development, nor the social world of mature man, contains any stage or fragment that does not clearly disclose this uniqueness. If I refrain from saying that our whole course of development is spiritual, it is because the biologist searches for the spirit and may therefore not employ the term in a priori definitions. Much less would I say with certain philosophers that the whole course of human development has been "spiritualized." The danger of a dualistic interpretation, that is, the tacit assumption of an outside principle working on the animal nature, would be too great. We must leave such words to other spheres of thought. But once again be it said that the special character of the human species is fully at work in every stage of its development, and that the spirit does not burst forth only at some late date—regardless of how late in life the individual may learn to express and give form to the "special something" that is at work from the very first.

By a single example I should like to throw further light on the

357

close relation between course of development and mature mode of life, to show how these two aspects of our organic system interpenetrate one another, and to clarify the complex unity of this system. Once again we choose the outward manifestations, the phenomena of expression, that show the biologist the way to the inner life.

If we survey the rich variety of human modes of expression, we shall find we have no difficulty in discerning the means of spontaneous expression we have discussed in connection with the animals. We too have hereditary responses to certain situations, corresponding to the roar of the lion, the wagging of the dog's tail, the arching of the cat's back. Screaming and stamping, the threatening gestures that enhance our stature, are of such an elementary nature. We may designate them as the one pole of our possibilities. It is interesting to note that at the higher levels of social life we strive to suppress all these modes of expression and to replace these embarrassing natural patterns by other patterns which we call civilized.

With this civilized sphere is associated our other mode of expression, which reaches its highest stage in speech: symbolic expression by means of words originating in history, established by convention, acquired by learning, perpetuated by tradition. We imply the relative freedom of this medium of expression, the possibility of deception, masked meaning, reserve, by calling it the mode of controlled expression. In this sense there is no animal language; we may evaluate this controlled expression as a distinctly human system of communication. Those who are especially addicted to abstract distinction may create such a cleavage between spontaneous and controlled expression. The biologist, however, in view of the inestimable richness of reality, maintains a high degree of reserve towards such distinctions. And indeed he immediately discovers a third, intermediary realm between the two extremes of expression, a twilight region, to which we shall now turn.

Consider, for example, laughing and crying, which are surely inseparable from human life, and yet cannot be defined either as controlled or as spontaneous expression. To the same intermediary realm belong blushing and blanching. They are indubitably connected with human experience, we might say with a sense of shame or consternation, yet they are far closer than laughing and crying to innate spontaneous responses. Our embarrassment in the face of these strange, ambivalent forms of expression is manifested in a conspicuous reluctance on the part of scientists to interpret them. For the present we shall restrict our attention to laughing and crying.

Immediately after birth, the number of new situations to which there is no response is exceedingly large, because the number of inherited responses is limited. The hereditary responses are localized in that region which, of all peripheral zones, is the most highly developed, the mouth muscles. Here, in the oral zone, a large number of nerve ends are developed at this early stage, and many types of motion are available. Perhaps I should add that the tactile function of the rest of the skin reaches this degree of development only in the ensuing months; the tactile corpuscles are fully formed only after the fifth month.

The first response after birth is wailing; smiling occurs only later, but as critical an observer as Stirnimann registered its presence in one case as early as the ninth day.[5] For a long time these are the infant's chief means of expression. They are two primary forms of response; crying from the very beginning is egotistical and unsocial, while smiling is more social, an expression of the need for company. When looked at, the newborn child can smile even in its sleep. The social bond in the infant is a certainty, and confutes all theories which try to interpret social life as a secondary, utilitarian development.

These two responses must serve the infant for all situations. How difficult the decision must be in some situations, when only such extreme opposites of expression are available. And it is a fact that up to the fourth month, the human voice often calls forth a smile, regardless whether it is menacing or friendly, severe or tender. Only after the seventh month is the smile distinctly limited to a friendly approach.

Before any speech, before standing or any development of technical faculties, these two earliest human modes of expression are, with increasing social experience, fixed and transformed into weeping—with tears observed from the third week on—and laughter, which appears in the seventh or eighth week. This development occurs in the same social medium as the first beginnings of speech. It is speech that brings the first possibility of a more varied response to different

5 Fritz Stirnimann, *Psychologie des neugeborenen Kindes* (Zurich, 1940).

situations; it is for us the most perfect form of response. Wailing and weeping, smiling and laughing, are the pre-speech modes of communication. With the development of speech arises the possibility of varied response in the social sphere. Or shall we say that language develops along with our understanding of situations? The two statements go hand in hand, and have reference to the same event.

But there still remain situations to which there is no adequate response, in which no available words help us, and the number of these situations is always large. It is for these occasions that the first developed, pre-speech modes of expression remain in function, and they remain allied to these situations for which there is no other response: weeping remains bound up with the sad situation, laughter with the cheerful one. This association endures throughout life. Wherever something unusual occurs to which we cannot respond in words or deeds, these two primary forms of expression remain in force: laughter in happy situations, tears in sad ones, such as the death of a loved one. But even late in life, these responses may be paradoxically reversed as in infancy; we may laugh in desperation and cry for joy.

Here I have no wish to study the complex relation between laughter and tears, but to indicate the continuous interaction between social life and the development of the individual. In each of us the development of civilized habits is concomitant with the development of controlled expression in dealing with situations. But the forms of expression anterior to the civilized sector persist for all situations that cannot be met by the acquired resources of controlled expression and intelligent action.

Thus far studies of tears do not tell us why we respond to these particular situations in such a strange way. At most, they show that these responses, if interpreted as a direct means of control, are futile, and that they take on meaning only in relation to social patterns.[6] But it seems to me that we can obtain a somewhat deeper insight into the matter by considering it in the light of general human ontogeny. The early concentration of all responses in the vital sucking zone of the mouth makes it understandable that the first primary social means of communication would be centered in this same region. In later life, moreover, these types of expression are still associated with situa-

6 Helmuth Plessner, *Lachen und Weinen* (Arnhem, 1941).

tions to which there is no adequate response, and such situations, as we have seen, are most predominant in infancy.

But we are interested not only in the understanding of these two modes of expression; through them, we wish to indicate the general specificity of human development and the biological approach to this specificity. Immediately after birth we find a creature, the product of prenatal development, which seeks contact in a human way: but its perceptions are not very precise, its understanding minimal, its responses limited to a relatively well developed apparatus localized in the oral zone. If such responses as laughing and crying persist throughout, it strongly indicates that man is specifically human from the very first. But in its early stages this human system may be likened to the rough sketch of a painting. The painting does not expand from a point through additions, it is present from the very first as a totality, but as a totality in process of transformation. Likewise the human system is present from the first in its full differentiation, sketched in all its parts, and developing its more definitive structures step by step. The sketch includes the primary social nature, equipped with rudimentary types of communication; these are extended in a changing social environment—not in the monotony of uterine existence.

I have been trying to show that the typical human qualities are clearly visible in all the stages of our growth, and that it is a mistake to speak of a development through various animal stages to the ape stage, which we transcend in the first year after birth. Such evolutionary characters take on paramount importance only if human specificity is argued away by abstraction—and for some decades this was the case. As late as the seventies of the last century, Wilhelm His the anatomist and Ludwig Rütimeyer the biologist tried in vain to counteract the extreme simplifications of Ernst Haeckel and obtain due consideration for the specific characters of the mammal groups. Their failure was in keeping with the times.

Human development reveals no stage at which a primate becomes a man. There is no indication that those characters we designate as "spiritual" appear only at a late stage. We must therefore reject all those theories which would make our specific nature a late product of human development. It is clear that our whole ontogeny is consistently directed towards the human form: the earliest stages reveal processes which are concluded only years later—beginning and end form a single unit.

We cannot—as has often been done—evaluate our human specificity as deficiency, or regression, or as a condition for which man has paid by the loss of all manner of faculties. Nor can the biologist support Scheler's view that the spirit is in itself impotent and derives its power from our animality.[7] I have no wish to vulgarize Scheler's idea; suffice it to say that the findings of biology cannot possibly be brought into harmony with such a restricted view of what is specifically human, the "spirit." Aside from his own bias, Scheler's attitudes were determined by the scientific opinions most current at his time and by a metaphysical preconception with regard to the spirit. Since then, things have occurred to bring about a change in biological approach. We also see the contradictions and disharmonies that Scheler saw, but we are not so ready as he to classify them as separate entities and place them in dramatic conflict with one another. Biological observation reveals human specificity not as deficient, but as directly productive and independent, on the basis of special characters which belong only to this biological system and are links in a relatively closed system.

Perhaps the biologist will be asked to define and disclose these links more clearly, since they are at work in the human plasma and, in our opinion, go back to the human specificity of the egg cell. For this egg cell is not the unicellular amoeba with which it is sometimes compared, but an extensively determined human germ. And I repeat that the full extent of this determination is revealed by the identical characters found in twins produced by the early division of a single germ. So far, to be sure, science tells us nothing about the specific structure of the human plasma, for the answer, in so far as any answer is possible, must be found in the realm of submicroscopic plasma research. Today physicists, biochemists, and geneticists are hard at work in this field and an increasing number of zoologists, botanists, and bacteriologists are turning to it. Nuclear studies, which provide so significant an understanding of certain phenomena of inheritance, throw no light on the central problem of plasmatic structure which is becoming one of the central problems of biology.

What then can we say of the structural basis of the human species?

7 Max Scheler, *Die Stellung des Menschen im Kosmos* (Darmstadt, 1930).

We do not yet know this structure: we are searching for it. But this negative answer has also its positive side, which you must bear in mind if you wish to understand the biologist's attitude towards the problem of man. In approximately three centuries of microscopic study, biologists have found again and again that the structures discovered had never been anticipated by theoretical methods, through rational deductions from known structures. Never did anyone foresee the specific form of a cell, a nucleus, or a chromosome, of a muscle fibril, a gland cell, a chloroplastid, or any of the innumerable other structures with which biological literature abounds. This circumstance has taught us great restraint in theorizing on invisible structures. Restraint does not mean abstention. But how rare are the lucky chances that bring us closer to structural reality. The biologist is confronted with far greater complexity than the chemist.

Consequently the biologist does not attempt to fill in the meaningless picture of the egg cell that we obtain from a microscopic section, with overhasty structural inventions. We must learn to endure this visual emptiness in the knowledge that it is not the full reality and in the expectation of further discoveries.

So far we have been speaking of human life in general. But human life occurs only in two polar differentiations: the male and female. With regard to this differentiation biology supplies an abundance of information which we may not pass by if we wish to obtain as faithful a picture of man, and also of his specific spiritual nature, as is possible today.

Their sexual differentiation is also a characteristic of the system as a whole: we know human beings only as male or female.

We have numerous indications to show that the fertilized human egg cell is bisexual. We also know certain decisive hereditary factors in the cellular nucleus, and know what material factors act on the bisexual egg cell to insure the normal unisexual structure of the individual. Today we also know the origin of forms which have the inherited characters of one sex, but to a varying degree realize the characters of the other sexual pole. These are never androgynous in the mythological sense: the human hermaphrodite is a fantasy, a reaction of the mind to the eternal division of the sexes: among the higher animals we find no hermaphrodites, but in the lower animal organisms they are frequent. It should be remembered, however, that biology has demonstrated full bisexual potentiality in the egg cell.

Here we must recall our metaphor of the sketch. We are not dealing with a sexless nucleus to which male or female attributes attach themselves, but with an unformed, ambivalent sketch of a system. Only in the execution does this sketch become a picture, and then in one of two possible forms. The structural bipotency remains a basic plasmatic fact throughout the life of the individual, and can be manifested in any number of ways.

But the little we know of the process by which this unfinished sketch assumes its definite forms leads to questions which no study of man can ignore. Observation reveals that the female retains a large number of characters proper to childhood before the tenth year, that in many respects she remains close to that type which in the male has been called pyknic (and this circumstance creates a number of difficulties for certain systems of typology). Such correspondences must be carefully considered in approaching the anthropological question: is it possible to conceive of a general human type, or prototype, which would be more than a forced abstraction? Here we shall render no judgments but limit ourselves to pointing out fields of research.

Having rejected the biological version of man as a deficient creature, we are compelled to give at least a passing glance to the theories, still much discussed by biologists, according to which the peculiar characters of man are regressive mutations resulting from self-domestication. Since the end of the eighteenth century, the idea has enjoyed some currency that man has arrived at his present state through becoming in a sense his own domestic animal. It is plain that the white variation of man would be particularly affected by such domestication.

Here we can only touch on this problem. Yet it should be mentioned that our brain is larger than that of the anthropoid apes, while in the domestication of mammals we find the opposite trend. Another supposed character of domestication is loss of hair, which an ancient tradition interprets as a sign of degeneration. But the biologist regards this hairlessness in quite a different light. We find striking distinctions between human loss of hair and the mutations of mammals in that direction, and moreover we observe a significant development of the human skin as a sensory organ. We find for example that the number of sensory nerves passing through the spinal cord is far greater in man than in other mammals. The importance of the skin in the development of the child, as an organ transmitting experience of his own body, the complex experience of having limbs and being able to use them, is inestimable. And these experiences form the basis of his first approach to the physical world and his social environment. The more closely we look into these relationships, the greater importance we shall ascribe to our periphery, to our naked body as a link in our specific spiritual system. The loss of hair takes on a positive aspect since it helps to create a new channel of experience. The road that might take us to the spiritual from this point is, however, almost untraveled: it must lead through a study of our prolonged child development.

Prolonged development! For a time these words stood at the center of biological discussions of man, after Louis Bolk had shown in a series of stimulating studies that the slowing down of animal development is a significant factor in producing a man. With this he associated a second fundamental idea, which became known as the hypothesis of fetalization. This hypothesis states that a maturation of the typically human form is induced in the fetal stage by altered hormonal influences. This is not the place to discuss these theories of human development. But I must stress Bolk's conception of retardation, because the attitude modern biologists have taken towards it is highly characteristic of the newer trends.

Until recently the dominant view among biologists was that human development represented a slowing down of the process of animal differentiation. And many writers have held that this slowing down implied degeneration. This idea, in combination with the older notion that the spirit is a disease that invades man, easily became a source of pessimism. I need not add that the dark character of our times provided a suitable background for such conceptions.

But anyone who approaches the events of our period of growth as links in the human system as a whole, soon arrives at a different sort of interpretation. He knows the immensity of the cultural heritage that is handed down by tradition. He knows also that the acquisition of this cultural heritage is for us a natural process. The acquisition

365

of speech, the molding of our specific instrument of communication, controlled expression, is a primary human development—and we must not underestimate the complexity of this development. Our area of objective behavior in the social sphere is the product of the long period preceding puberty. It is possible in the protection offered by the social group, and fully requires a period of this length.

In this primary human process, the slowness of development after birth is an important factor. And it is characteristic only of this stage of development. Observation of the prenatal period makes it clear that human growth in general is not retarded, for in this period, as we have seen in connection with brain development, we develop more rapidly than any related animals. This rapidity of early growth is correlated with the slowdown after birth. And this slackened pace, which has often been interpreted as a sign of degeneration, is an essential factor in the formation of our social world; it is an integral part of the system in which we find the characteristics known as spiritual. Every aspect of our development reveals from the very beginning a specificity closely related to the specificity of the mature man.

This phase of growth leads us to the problem of the diverse racial groups into which men are divided. The origin of these groups is unknown. We need only cite the opinion of two widely recognized authorities:[8] On the one hand, Eugen Fischer declares (1932): "The nature of the mutations needed to produce a man is an entirely open question." While, far removed from any such uncertainty, Egon von Eickstedt declares (1934): "The time is past when the origin and development of man were among the great mysteries of existence." The two years intervening between the publication of these two remarks do not account for the sharp difference of opinion, for they brought no decisive biological development. Serious research shows the question of origins to be still unsolved. And, moreover, it remains to be determined wherein the groups differ and wherein they resemble one another. We are far from a solution to these problems.

Racial features have been frequently described, and the usual emphasis is upon external differences. I shall therefore concentrate on certain common characters, which future anthropologists should bear in mind. Firstly, the newborn infant, of all races, regardless of adult

8 See my *Biologische Fragmente*.

366

stature, is relatively uniform in size. This can be understood only in relation to the approximate uniformity of brain size in all human types. Secondly, childhood growth is very similar in all races. Only with the phase of puberty do the characteristic racial differentiations in size appear. Thirdly, puberty occurs late in all human races, including the so-called primitive peoples. Recent studies among the natives of New Guinea, for example, show that puberty in the female does not occur until the fifteenth or sixteenth year. Early puberty, which, from the standpoint of Darwinism, we should expect to find in primitive races, is demonstrably the product of the highest civilization, occurring only in the big cities of the white race. Such observations should serve as a warning against precipitate conclusions.

Nor do I myself wish to base any bold theories upon these few facts; but they serve to remind us that all human groups are united by essential similarities which reside precisely in those ontogenic phenomena which we have found to be vital links in the over-all plan of our social development, hence of a primary human process. There would seem to be a common structural principle in all human development—and evidence of this is the ontogenetic similarity of human groups which differ greatly in their outward appearance. Such similarities, however, give no indication of the origin of the races: they might still be descended from a single group or from closely related groups. Or perhaps they are today in a state of balance which is the stabilized product of a very early mixture of types. What we know of mutations in animals and plants compels us to interpret such phenomena with the utmost reserve.

In the human species we encounter that special mode of behavior, experience, and method of coping with the tasks of life which since time immemorial has been called "spiritual." The biologist finds himself confronted by this traditional usage, but there is no need for him to tamper with it since everyone knows that the word cast off its original meaning years ago. Just as the word atom no longer designates the indivisible, and evolution has come to signify not the unfolding of a pre-existent multiplicity but rather a genuine development of new forms, so the word "spirit" in this context does not mean an immaterial something that permeates man and survives his body. "Spiritual" means here the special activity of man which creates the instrument of controlled expression, and which in languages and myth, in theory, art, and religion, builds up a system which helps him to master his peculiar existence.

Only amidst the wealth of these human instruments, in the isolations, transformations, and chains of influence created by the historical aspect of our social life, does that widespread contradiction arise that has been called the struggle between life and spirit. The significance and the tragic possibilities of this conflict are by no means diminished by this interpretation. To the biologist the struggle between these works of the spirit does not appear as a conflict between spirit and an isolated "life" or a soul: we see in these struggles and movements an inevitable clash between divergent means of mastering the environment. For the complexity of the world of controlled expression, which is subordinate to historical development but at the same time creates it, embraces both synergisms and antagonisms, while we must also reckon with limitations, with the inadequacy of our instruments of controlled expression, which cease to function at a certain point. The failure of these instruments calls forth all manner of attitudes, ranging from presumptuous illusion to despair, and involving a variety of social consequences.

The rich and varied forms of controlled expression are the highest creation of man. It constitutes at the same time the borderline at which special forces, alien to the animal world, appear, forces which psychology examines with its own techniques. The biologist sees this borderline. He will recognize that for the study of this special realm, which may be called the realm of the spirit, special instruments must be created by science, which is always basically *one*. But meanwhile he will conceive the world of controlled expression as a segment of the human system, and venture to study it with the methods proper to his discipline.

Up to now we have spoken only of the relatively closed system of the human species. It is time to recall that a relatively closed system must also be relatively open. And this would be the case with the rough sketch to which we have referred.

The study of external animal forms has shown us their role in communicating inwardness, and we are led to surmise further, hidden relationships. The same is true of the biological study of man. Our species is also embedded in broader contexts which are beyond the scope of biological research but whose existence must always be borne in mind. The knowledge that these broader contexts exist is one of the premises of biological study.

The biologist, to be sure, can only say of these contexts that they are pregnant with unknown things. Shall we interpret this fundamental mystery as the dark of night or as a supreme radiance? The language of symbols has for a long time taken both courses. Since the beginning of time, many of the best minds have searched for the hidden order that will make intelligible to us the forms and forces that govern this mysterious background.

Biology studies earthly forms. It contemplates the underlying order of the plant and animal world. And the more we learn of these worlds, the more immense become the possibilities of the underlying order. They are clearly revealed when we study the supraindividual complex of relations that unites natural forms, constructed to be perceived, with the structure of the perceiving organ—that, for instance, integrates into a higher unity the color of a flower, its shape, and the eye that perceives them. In ever increasing measure, the living forms of our earthly flora and fauna bear witness to the existence of mysterious laws, to forms not directly accessible to us, and to their modes of action.

Thus biology will approach with an open mind all disciplined methods which endeavor to explore the mysterious background. Biologists will in particular understand, and assist with all the means at their disposal, the intensive study of that field which is earthly and hence presumably within our scope but nevertheless represents the highest knowledge to which man can aspire: the study of the astonishing vital order that guides human existence: the human directive mechanism. Let us for the moment consider our brain as the most representative part of this directive mechanism: there is no objection to this, but we should not forget that we are forcibly tearing the brain out of the higher system to which it belongs. In order to define our position towards this most mysterious of all organs, I must invoke a metaphor:

Suppose we were to find on some virgin island a race of highly gifted people—such as those who may have lived on some of the Greek islands in ancient times with no knowledge of our recent centuries. And suppose we brought them a radio. They might be able to give the most detailed description of this mechanism, of its wires, coils, tubes, and switches—but even the fullest description would not tell them why voices and melodies issued from the radio. For though highly gifted, they would lack knowledge of the basic laws on which the construction of the radio is based. Their description could not possibly represent a meaningful context.

We are in the same position when it comes to our brain. We can carefully analyze it and describe various aspects of it—and this is done untiringly in countless laboratories. But the principle of its function is unknown to us: from our complicated picture of brain structures, we can derive no knowledge of its function, through which we live.

No biologist may close his eyes to this fact. And while he advances by his own means, he will understand that the work of our directive mechanism is being scientifically investigated from another angle, that attempts are being made to gain deeper knowledge of this central system of man from its acts. Thus when members of this circle attempt to investigate the infinite products of controlled expression, the myths and symbols of all times, the creatures of our unconscious dream life and other works of the symbolic world, and strive for insight into the structures of our directive mechanism, the biologist will find in this endeavor new roads to the old goals; he will remain as open to their possibilities as he should be towards new methods in his own field. For no one can define the limits of human investigation, not even of biology, when it seeks knowledge of the spiritual. But to realize and keep constantly in mind that there are limits, even when we cannot measure their proximity or remoteness, is one of the prerequisites of the scientific attitude.

370

C. G. Jung

The Spirit of Psychology

1. The Unconscious in Historical Perspective

More clearly, perhaps, than any other science psychology demonstrates the spiritual transition from the classical age to the modern. The history of psychology[1] up to the seventeenth century consists essentially in the enumeration of doctrines concerning the soul, without the soul's being able to get a word in edgeways as the object investigated. As the immediate datum of experience it seemed so completely known to every thinker that he was convinced there could be no need of any further, let alone objective, experience. This attitude is totally alien to the modern standpoint, for today we are of the opinion that, over and above all subjective certainty, objective experience is needed to establish an opinion that lays claim to be scientific. Notwithstanding this, however, it is still difficult, even today, to apply the purely empirical or phenomenological standpoint consistently in psychology, because the original naïve idea that the soul, being the immediate datum of experience, was the best known of all knowables is one of our most deeply rooted convictions. Not only does every layman presume to an opinion, but every psychologist too—and not merely with reference to the subject but, what is of greater consequence, with reference also to the object. He knows, or rather he thinks he knows, what is going on in another individual, and what is good for him. This is due less to a sovereign disregard of differences than to a tacit assumption that all individuals are the same. As a result, people incline unconsciously to a belief in the universal validity of subjective opinions. I mention this fact only to show that in spite of the growing empiricism of the last three hundred years the original attitude has by no means dis-

1 Hermann Siebeck, *Geschichte der Psychologie* (Gotha, 1880–84; 2 vols.).

appeared. Its continued existence only goes to prove how difficult is the transition from the old philosophical view to the modern empirical one.

Naturally it never occurred to the representatives of the old view that their doctrines were nothing but psychic phenomena, for it was naïvely assumed that with the help of intelligence or reason man could as it were climb out of his psychic condition and remove himself to one that was suprapsychic and rational. People had not yet begun to question whether the statements of the human spirit might not in the end be symptoms of certain psychic conditions.[2] This question would be entirely natural, but it has such far-reaching and revolutionary consequences that we can understand only too well why both past and present have done their best to ignore it. We are still very far today from Nietzsche's view of philosophy, and indeed of theology, as an *"ancilla psychologiae,"* for not even the psychologist is prepared to regard his statements outright as a subjectively conditioned confession. We can speak of a uniformity of individual subjects only in so far as they are in large measure unconscious—unconscious, that is, of their actual differences. The more unconscious a man is, the more he will conform to the general canon of psychic behavior. But the more conscious he becomes of his individuality, the more pronounced will be his difference from other subjects and the less he will come up to common expectations. Further, his reactions are much less predictable. This is due to the fact that an individual consciousness is always more highly differentiated and more extensive. But the more extensive it becomes the more differences it will perceive, and the more it will emancipate itself from the collective rules, for the empirical freedom of the will grows in proportion to the extension of consciousness.

As the individual differentiation of consciousness proceeds, so the objective validity of its views decreases and their subjectivity increases. It is no longer taken for granted that one's own preconceptions are applicable to others. This logical development had the consequence that in the seventeenth century—a century of great importance for the growth of science—psychology began to rise up by the side of philos-

---

2 Actually this is true only of the old psychology. In recent times there has been a considerable change of standpoint. Thus Wilhelm Dilthey says (*Gesammelte Schriften*, Leipzig, 1923, Vol. I, p. 406): "Any metaphysical system is representative only of the situation in which a soul has glimpsed the world riddle."

ophy, and it was Christian von Wolff (1679–1754) who was the first to speak of "empirical" or "experimental" psychology,[3] thus acknowledging the need to put psychology on a new footing. Psychology had to forgo the philosopher's rational definition of truth, because it gradually became clear that no philosophy had sufficient general validity to be uniformly fair to the diversity of individual subjects. And since on questions of principle, too, an indefinitely large number of different subjective statements was possible, whose validity in their turn could be maintained only subjectively, it naturally became necessary to abandon philosophical argument and to replace it by experience. Psychology thereupon turned into a natural science.

For the time being, however, philosophy retained its grip on the wide field of "rational" or "speculative" psychology, and only with the passage of the centuries could the latter gradually develop into a natural science. This process of change is not complete even today. Psychology, as a subject, still comes under the Philosophical Faculty in most universities, and "medical" psychology has to seek refuge with the Medical Faculty. So officially the situation is still largely medieval, since even the natural sciences are only admitted as "Phil. II," under the cloak of Natural Philosophy.[4] Although it has been obvious for at least two hundred years that philosophy above all is dependent on psychological premises, everything possible was done to obscure the autonomy of the empirical sciences when the discovery of the earth's rotation and the moons of Jupiter could no longer be suppressed. Of all the natural sciences, psychology has been the least able to win its independence.

This backwardness seems to me significant. The position of psychology is comparable with that of a psychic function which is inhibited by the conscious mind: only such components of it are admitted to exist as accord with the prevailing trend of consciousness. Whatever fails to accord is actually denied existence, in defiance of the fact that there are numerous phenomena or symptoms to prove the contrary. Anyone acquainted with these psychic processes knows with what subterfuges and self-deceiving maneuvers one sets about splitting off the inconvenience. It is precisely the same with empirical psy-

3 *Psychologia empirica* (1732).
4 In Anglo-Saxon countries there is the degree of "Doctor Scientiae."

373

chology: as the discipline subordinate to a general philosophical psychology, experimental psychology is admitted as a concession to the empiricism of natural science, but is cluttered up with technical philosophical terms. As for psychopathology, it stays put in the Medical Faculty as a curious appendix to psychiatry. "Medical" psychology, as might be expected, finds little or no recognition in the universities.

If I express myself somewhat drastically in this matter, it is with intent to throw into relief the position of psychology at the turn of the nineteenth and the beginning of the twentieth century. Wundt's standpoint is entirely representative of the situation as it then was—representative also because there emerged from his school a succession of notable psychologists who set the tone at the beginning of the twentieth century. In his *Outlines of Psychology*, Wundt says:

> Any psychical element that has disappeared from consciousness is to be called unconscious in the sense that we assume the possibility of its renewal, that is, its reappearance in the actual interconnection of psychical processes. Our knowledge of an element that has become unconscious does not extend beyond this possibility of its renewal. . . . Therefore it has no meaning except as a disposition for the rise of future components. . . . Assumptions as to the state of the "unconscious" or as to "unconscious processes" of any kind . . . are *entirely unproductive for psychology*. There are, of course, physical concomitants of the psychical dispositions mentioned, of which some can be directly demonstrated, some inferred from various experiences.[5]

A representative of the Wundt school opines that "a psychic state cannot be described as psychic unless it has reached at least the threshold of consciousness." This argument assumes, or rather asserts, that only the conscious is psychic and that therefore everything psychic is conscious. The author happens to say a "psychic" state: logically he should have said a "state," for whether such a state is psychic is precisely the point at issue. Another argument runs: the simplest psychic fact is sensation, since it cannot be analyzed into simpler facts. Consequently, that which precedes or underlies a sensation is never psychic, but only physiological. *Ergo*, there is no unconscious.

5 Tr. C. H. Judd (Leipzig, 1897), p. 208, from *Grundriss der Psychologie*. (My italics.)

J. F. Herbart once said: "When a representation [idea] falls below the threshold of consciousness it goes on living in a latent way, continually striving to recross the threshold and to displace the other representations." As it stands the proposition is undoubtedly incorrect, for unfortunately anything genuinely forgotten has no tendency to recross the threshold. Had Herbart said "complex" in the modern sense of the word instead of "representation," his proposition would have been absolutely right. We shall hardly be wrong in assuming that he really did mean something of the sort. In this connection a philosophical opponent of the unconscious makes the very illuminating remark: "Once this be admitted, one finds oneself at the mercy of all manner of hypotheses concerning this unconscious life, hypotheses which cannot be controlled by any observation."[6] It is evident that this thinker is not out to recognize facts, but that for him the fear of running into difficulties is decisive. And how does he know that these hypotheses cannot be controlled by observation? For him this is simply an a priori. But with Herbart's observation he does not deal at all.

I mention this incident not because of its positive significance but only because it is so thoroughly characteristic of the antiquated philosophical attitude towards empirical psychology. Wundt himself is of the opinion that as regards the "so-called unconscious processes it is not a question of unconscious psychic elements, but only of more dimly *conscious* ones," and that "for hypothetical unconscious processes we could substitute actually demonstrable or at any rate less hypothetical conscious processes."[7] This attitude implies a clear rejection of the unconscious as a psychological hypothesis. The cases of "double consciousness" he explains as "modifications of individual consciousness which very often occur continuously, in steady succession, and for which, by a violent misinterpretation of the facts, a plurality of individual consciousnesses is substituted." The latter, so Wundt argues, "would have to be simultaneously present in one and the same individual." This, he says, "is admittedly not the case." Doubtless it is hardly possible for two consciousnesses to express themselves simulta-

6 Guido Villa, *Einleitung in die Psychologie der Gegenwart* (Leipzig, 1902), p. 339.
7 Wilhelm Wundt, *Grundzüge der physiologischen Psychologie* (5th ed., Leipzig, 1903), Vol. III, p. 327.

neously in a single individual in a blatantly recognizable way. That is why these states usually alternate. Janet has shown that while the one consciousness controls the head, so to speak, the other simultaneously puts itself into communication with the observer by means of a code of expressive manual movements.[8] Double consciousness may therefore very well be simultaneous.

Wundt thinks that the idea of a double consciousness, and hence of a "superconsciousness" and "subconsciousness" in Fechner's sense,[9] is a "survival from the psychological mysticism" of the Schelling school. He obviously boggles at an unconscious representation being one which nobody "has."[10] In that case the word "representation" would naturally be obsolete too, since it suggests a subject to whom something is present or "presented." That is the basic reason for Wundt's rejection of the unconscious. But we can easily get round this difficulty by speaking, not of "representations" or "perceptions," but of *contents,* as I usually do. Here I must anticipate a point with which I shall be dealing at some length later on, namely the fact that something very like "representedness" or consciousness does attach to unconscious contents, so that the possibility of an unconscious subject becomes a serious question. Such a subject, however, is not identical with the ego. That it was principally the "representations" which were Wundt's bête noire is clear also from his emphatic rejection of "inborn ideas." How literally he takes this can be seen from the following: "If the newborn animal really had an idea beforehand of all the actions it purposes to do, what a wealth of anticipated life experiences would lie stored in the human and animal instincts, and how incomprehensible it would seem that not man alone, but animals too, acquire most things only through experience and practice!"[11] There is nevertheless an inborn "pattern of behavior" and just such a treasure house, not indeed of anticipated, but of accumulated, life experiences; only, it is not a question of "representations" but of sketches, plans, or images

8 Pierre Janet, *Automatisme psychologique* (Paris, 1913), pp. 243, 238ff.

9 Gustav Theodor Fechner, *Elemente der Psychophysik* (2nd ed., Leipzig, 1889), Vol. II, p. 438: ". . . the idea of a psychophysical threshold . . . gives a firm foundation to that of the unconscious generally. Psychology cannot abstract representations from unconscious perceptions, nor even from the effects of unconscious perceptions."

10 Ibid., p. 439.

11 *Grundzüge der physiologischen Psychologie,* p. 328.

which, though not actually "presented" to the ego, are yet just as real as Kant's hundred thalers, which had been sewn into the lining of a jacket and forgotten by the owner. Wundt might have remembered Christian von Wolff, whom he himself mentions, and his distinction with regard to "unconscious" states which "can be inferred only from what we find in our consciousness."[12]

To the category of "inborn ideas" also belong Adolf Bastian's "elementary ideas,"[13] by which we are to understand the fundamentally analogous forms of perception that are to be found everywhere, hence more or less what we know today as "archetypes." Wundt, of course, pooh-poohs this notion, still under the delusion that he is dealing here with "representations" and not with "dispositions." He says: "The origination of one and the same phenomenon in different places is not absolutely impossible, but, from the standpoint of empirical psychology, it is in the highest degree unlikely."[14] He denies a "common psychic heritage of humanity" in this sense and repudiates the very idea of an intelligible myth symbolism with the characteristic pronouncement that the supposition of a "system of ideas" hiding behind the myth is impossible.[15] The pedantic assumption that the unconscious is, of all things, a system of ideas would not hold water even in Wundt's day, let alone before or afterwards.

It would be incorrect to assume that the rejection of the idea of the unconscious in academic psychology at the turn of the century was anything like universal. That is by no means the case, for Fechner,[16] and after him Theodor Lipps, had given the unconscious a place of

---

12 Ibid., p. 326. Cited from Wolff's *Vernünftige Gedanken von Gott, der Welt, und der Seele des Menschen* (1719), §193.

13 *Ethnische Elementargedanken in der Lehre vom Menschen* (Berlin, 1895), and *Der Mensch in der Geschichte* (Leipzig, 1860), Vol. I, pp. 166ff., 213ff.; Vol. II, pp. 24ff.

14 *Völkerpsychologie* (2nd ed., Leipzig, 1911–20), Vol. V, Part II, p. 459.

15 Ibid., Vol. IV, Part I, p. 41.

16 Cf. Fechner's remark that "the idea of a psychophysical threshold is of the utmost importance because it gives a firm foundation to that of the unconscious generally." He goes on: "Perceptions and representations in the state of unconsciousness have, of course, ceased to exist as real ones . . . but something continues in us, psychophysical activity," etc. (op. cit., Vol. II, pp. 438f). This conclusion is a little incautious, because the psychic process remains more or less the same whether conscious or not. A "representation" exists not only through its "representedness," but—and this is the main point—it also exists in its own psychic right.

decisive importance.[17] Although for Lipps psychology is a "science of consciousness," he nevertheless speaks of "unconscious" perceptions and representations, which he regards as processes. "The nature or, more accurately, the idea of a 'psychic' process is not so much a conscious content or conscious experience as the psychic reality which must necessarily be thought to underlie the existence of such a process."[18] "Observation of conscious life persuades us that not only are unconscious perceptions and representations . . . at times to be found in us, but that psychic life *is therein principally enacted all the time, and only occasionally, at special points, does that which operates within us reveal its presence directly, in appropriate images.*"[19] "Thus psychic life always goes far beyond the bounds of what is or may be present in us in the form of conscious contents or images."

Theodor Lipps' remarks in no wise conflict with our modern views, on the contrary they form the theoretical basis for the psychology of the unconscious in general. Nevertheless resistance to the hypothesis of the unconscious persisted for a long time afterwards. For instance it is characteristic that Max Dessoir, in his history of modern German psychology,[20] does not even mention C. G. Carus and Eduard von Hartmann.

2. *The Significance of the Unconscious in Psychology*

The hypothesis of the unconscious puts a large question mark after the idea of the psyche. The soul, as hitherto postulated by the philosophical intellect and equipped with all the necessary faculties, threatened to emerge from its chrysalis as something with unexpected and uninvestigated properties. It no longer represented anything immediately known, about which nothing more remained to be discovered except a few more or less satisfying definitions. Rather it now appeared in strangely double guise, as both known and unknown. In consequence, the old psychology was thoroughly unseated and as

17 Cf. Lipps, *Der Begriff des Unbewussten in der Psychologie* (Third International Congress for Psychology, 1896), pp. 146ff.; and *Grundtatsachen des Seelenlebens* (Bonn, 1912), pp. 125ff.
18 *Leitfaden der Psychologie* (2nd ed., Leipzig, 1906), p. 64.
19 Ibid., pp. 65f. (My italics.)
20 *Geschichte der neuern deutschen Psychologie* (2nd edn., Berlin, 1902; 2 vols.).

much revolutionized[21] as classical physics had been by the discovery of radioactivity. These first experimental psychologists were in the same predicament as the mythical discoverer of the numerical sequence, who strung peas together in a row and simply went on adding another unit to those already present. When he contemplated the result, it looked as if there were nothing but a hundred identical units; but the numbers he had thought of only as names unexpectedly turned out to be peculiar entities with irreducible properties. For instance, there were even, uneven, and primary numbers; positive, negative, irrational, and imaginary numbers, etc.[22] So it is with psychology: if the soul is really only an idea, this idea has an alarming air of unpredictability about it—something with qualities no one would ever have imagined. One can go on asserting that the soul is consciousness and its contents, but that does not prevent, in fact it hastens, the discovery of a background not previously suspected, a true matrix of all conscious phenomena, a preconsciousness and a postconsciousness, a superconsciousness and a subconsciousness. The moment one forms an idea of a thing and successfully catches one of its aspects, one invariably succumbs to the illusion of having caught the whole. One never considers that a total apprehension is right out of the question. Not even an idea posited as total is total, for it is still an entity on its own with unpredictable qualities. This self-deception certainly promotes peace of mind: the unknown is named, the far has been brought near, so that one can lay one's finger on it. One has taken possession

21 I reproduce here what William James says about the importance of the discovery of the unconscious psyche (*Varieties of Religious Experience,* New York, 1902, p. 233): "I cannot but think that the most important step forward that has occurred in psychology since I have been a student of that science is the discovery, first made in 1886, that . . . there is not only the consciousness of the ordinary field, with its usual center and margin, but an addition thereto in the shape of a set of memories, thoughts, and feelings, which are extramarginal and outside of the primary consciousness altogether, but yet must be classed as conscious facts of some sort, able to reveal their presence by unmistakable signs. I call this the most important step forward because, unlike the other advances which psychology has made, this discovery has revealed to us an entirely unsuspected peculiarity in the constitution of human nature. No other step forward which psychology has made can proffer any such claim as this." The discovery of 1886 to which James refers is the positing of a "subliminal consciousness" by Frederic W. H. Myers. See note 44.

22 A mathematician once remarked that everything in science was man-made except numbers, which had been created by God himself.

of it, and it has become an inalienable piece of property, like a slain creature of the wild that can no longer run away. It is a magical procedure such as the primitive practices upon objects and the psychologist upon the soul. He is no longer at its mercy, but he never suspects that the very fact of grasping the object conceptually gives it a golden opportunity to display all those qualities which would never have made their appearance had it not been imprisoned in a concept (remember the numbers!).

The attempts that have been made, during the last three hundred years, to grasp the soul are all part and parcel of that tremendous expansion of knowledge which has brought the universe nearer to us in a way that staggers the imagination. The thousandfold magnifications made possible by the electron microscope vie with the five hundred million light-year distances which the telescope travels. Psychology is still a long way from a development similar to that which the other natural sciences have undergone; also, as we have seen, it has been much less able to shake off the trammels of philosophy. All the same, every science is a function of the soul and all knowledge is rooted in it. The psyche is the greatest of all cosmic wonders and the *sine qua non* of the world as an object. It is in the highest degree odd that Western man, with but very few—and ever fewer—exceptions, apparently pays so little regard to this fact. Swamped by the knowledge of external objects, the subject of all knowledge has been temporarily eclipsed to the point of seeming nonexistence.

The soul was a tacit assumption that seemed to know itself in every particular. With the discovery of a possible unconscious psychic realm, man had the opportunity to embark upon a great adventure of the spirit, and one might have expected that a passionate interest would be turned in this direction. Not only was this not the case at all, but there arose on all sides an outcry against such an hypothesis. Nobody drew the conclusion that if the subject of knowledge, the psyche, were in fact a veiled form of existence not immediately accessible to consciousness, then all our knowledge must be incomplete, and moreover to a degree that we cannot determine. The validity of conscious knowledge was questioned in an altogether different and more menacing way than it had ever been by the critical procedures of epistemology. The latter put certain bounds to human knowledge in general, from which post-Kantian German Idealism struggled to emancipate itself; but natural science and common sense accommodated themselves to it without much difficulty, if they condescended to notice it at all. Philosophy fought against it in the interests of an antiquated pretension of the human mind to be able to pull itself up by its own bootstrings and know things that were right outside the range of human understanding. The victory of Hegel over Kant dealt the gravest blow to reason and to the further spiritual development of the German and then of the European mind, all the more dangerous as Hegel was a psychologist in disguise who projected great truths out of the sphere of the subject into a cosmos he himself had created. We know how far Hegel's influence extends today. The forces compensating this calamitous development personified themselves partly in the later Schelling, partly in Schopenhauer and Carus, while on the other hand that unbridled "bacchantic God" whom Hegel had already scented in nature finally burst upon us in Nietzsche.

Carus' hypothesis of the unconscious was bound to hit the then prevailing trend of German philosophy all the harder, as the latter had apparently just got the better of Kantian criticism and had restored, or rather reinstated, the well-nigh godlike sovereignty of the human spirit—Spirit with a capital S. The spirit of medieval man was, in good and bad alike, still the spirit of the God whom he served. Epistemological criticism was on the one hand an expression of the modesty of medieval man, and on the other a renunciation of, or abdication from, the spirit of God, and consequently a modern extension and reinforcement of human consciousness within the limits of reason. Wherever the spirit of God is extruded from our human calculations, an unconscious substitute takes its place. In Schopenhauer we find the unconscious Will as the new definition of God, in Carus the unconscious, and in Hegel identification and inflation, the practical equation of philosophical reason with Spirit, thus making possible that intellectual juggling with the object which achieved such a horrid brilliance in his philosophy of the State. Hegel offered a solution of the problem raised by epistemological criticism in that he gave ideas a chance to prove their unknown power of autonomy. They induced that hybris of reason which led to Nietzsche's superman and hence to the catastrophe that bears the name of Germany. Not only artists, but philosophers too, are sometimes prophets.

I think it is obvious that all philosophical statements which transgress the bounds of reason are anthropomorphic and have no validity beyond that which falls to psychically conditioned statements. A philosophy like Hegel's is a self-revelation of the psychic background and, philosophically, a presumption. Psychologically, it amounts to an invasion by the unconscious. The peculiar high-flown language Hegel uses bears out this view: it is reminiscent of the megalomaniac language of schizophrenics, who use terrific spellbinding words to reduce the transcendent to subjective form, to give banalities the charm of novelty, or pass off commonplaces as searching wisdom. So bombastic a terminology is a symptom of weakness, ineptitude, and lack of substance. But that does not prevent the latest German philosophy from using the same crackpot power words and pretending that it is not unintentional psychology.

In face of this elemental inrush of the unconscious into the Western sphere of human reason, Schopenhauer and Carus had no solid ground under them from which to develop and apply their compensatory effect. Man's salutary submission to a benevolent Deity, and the *cordon sanitaire* between him and the demon of darkness—the great legacy of the past—remained unimpaired with Schopenhauer, at any rate in principle, while with Carus it was hardly touched at all, since he sought to tackle the problem at the root by leading it away from the overpresumptuous philosophical standpoint towards that of psychology. We have to close our eyes to his philosophical allure if we wish to give full weight to his essentially psychological hypothesis. He had at least come a step nearer to the conclusion we mentioned earlier, by trying to construct a world picture that included the dark part of the soul. This structure still lacked something whose unprecedented importance I would like to bring home to the reader.

For this purpose we must first make it quite clear to ourselves that all knowledge is the result of imposing some kind of order upon the reactions of the psychic system as they flow into our consciousness— an order which reflects the behavior of a *metapsychical* reality, of that which is in itself real. If, as certain modern points of view, too, would have it, the psychic system coincides and is identical with our conscious mind, then, in principle, we are in a position to know everything that can be known, i.e., everything that lies within the limits of the theory of knowledge. In that case there is no cause for disquiet, beyond that felt by anatomists and physiologists when contemplating the function of the eye or the organ of hearing. But should it turn out that the psyche does *not* coincide with consciousness, and, what is more, that it functions unconsciously in a way similar to, or *different* from, the conscious portion of it, then our disquiet must rise to the point of agitation. For it is then no longer a question of general epistemological limits, but of a flimsy threshold that separates us from the unconscious contents of the psyche. The hypothesis of the threshold and of the unconscious means that the indispensable raw material of all knowledge—namely psychic reactions—and perhaps even unconscious "thoughts" and "insights" lie close beside, above, or below consciousness, separated from us by the merest "threshold" and yet apparently unattainable. We have no knowledge of how this unconscious functions, but since it is conjectured to be a psychic system it may possibly have everything that consciousness has, including perception, apperception, memory, imagination, will, affectivity, feeling, reflection, judgment, etc., all in subliminal form.[23]

Here we are faced with Wundt's objection that one cannot possibly speak of unconscious "perceptions," "representations," "feelings," much less of "volitional actions," seeing that none of these phenomena can be represented without an experiencing subject. Moreover the idea of a threshold presupposes a mode of observation in terms of

---

23 G. H. Lewes (*The Physical Basis of Mind,* London, 1877) takes all this for granted. For instance, on p. 358, he says: "Science has various modes and degrees, such as Perception, Ideation, Emotion, Volition, which may be conscious, subconscious, or unconscious." On p. 363: "Consciousness and Unconsciousness are correlatives, both belonging to the sphere of Sentience. Every one of the unconscious processes is operant, changes the general state of the organism, and is capable of at once issuing in a discriminated sensation when the force which balances it is disturbed." On p. 367: "There are many involuntary actions of which we are distinctly conscious, and many voluntary actions of which we are at times subconscious and unconscious. . . . Just as the thought which at one moment passes unconsciously, at another consciously, is in itself the same thought . . . so the action which at one moment is voluntary, and at another involuntary, is itself the same action." Lewes certainly goes too far when he says (p. 373): "There is no real and essential distinction between voluntary and involuntary actions." Occasionally there is a world of difference.

energy, according to which consciousness of psychic contents is essentially dependent upon their intensity, that is, their energy. Just as only a stimulus of a certain intensity is powerful enough to cross the threshold, so it may with some justice be assumed that other psychic contents too must possess a higher energy potential if they are to get across. If they possess only a small amount of energy they remain subliminal, like the corresponding sense perceptions.

As Lipps has already pointed out, the first objection is nullified by the fact that the psychic process remains essentially the same whether it is "represented" or not. Anyone who takes the view that the phenomena of consciousness comprise the whole psyche must go a step further and say that "representations which we do not have"[24] can hardly be described as "representations." He must also deny any psychic quality to what is left over. For this rigorous point of view the psyche can only have the phantasmagoric existence that pertains to the ephemeral phenomena of consciousness. This view does not square with common experience, which speaks in favor of a possible psychic activity without consciousness. Lipps' idea of the existence of psychic processes *an sich* does more justice to the facts. I do not wish to waste time in proving this point, but will content myself with saying that never yet has any reasonable person doubted the existence of psychic processes in a dog, although no dog has, to our knowledge, ever expressed consciousness of its psychic contents.[25]

3. The Dissociability of the Psyche

There is no a priori reason for assuming that unconscious processes must inevitably have a subject, any more than there is for doubting the reality of psychic processes. Admittedly the problem becomes difficult when we suppose unconscious acts of the will. If this is not to be just a matter of "instincts" and "inclinations," but rather of considered "choice" and "decision" which are peculiar to the will, then one cannot very well get round the need for a controlling subject to whom something is "represented." But that, by definition, would

24 Fechner, op. cit., Vol. II, pp. 438f.
25 I am not counting "Clever Hans" and other "talking" animals. ["Clever Hans" was one of the famous trained horses of Elberfeld who tapped out answers to mathematical questions with his hoof.—TRANS.]

384

be to lodge a consciousness in the unconscious, though this is a conceptual operation which presents no great difficulties to the psychopathologist. He is familiar with a psychic phenomenon that seems to be quite unknown to "academic" psychology, namely the dissociation or dissociability of the psyche. This peculiarity arises from the fact that the connecting link between the psychic processes themselves is a very conditional one. Not only are unconscious processes sometimes strangely independent of the experiences of the conscious mind, but the conscious processes, too, show a distinct loosening or discreteness. We all know of the absurdities which are caused by complexes and are to be observed with the greatest accuracy in the association experiment. Just as the cases of double consciousness doubted by Wundt really do happen, so the cases where not the whole personality is split in half, but only smaller fragments are broken off, are much more probable and in fact more common. They constitute one of the age-old experiences of mankind which is reflected in the universal supposition of a plurality of souls in one and the same individual. As the plurality of psychic components felt at the primitive level shows, the original state is one where the psychic processes are very loosely knit and by no means form a self-contained unity. Moreover psychiatric experience indicates that it often takes only a little to shatter the unity of consciousness so laboriously built up in the course of development and to resolve it back into its original elements.

This dissociability also enables us to set aside the difficulties that flow from the logically necessary assumption of a threshold of consciousness. If it is correct to say that conscious contents become subliminal through loss of energy, and conversely that unconscious processes become conscious through accretion of energy, then, if unconscious acts of volition are to be possible, it follows that these must possess an energy which enables them to achieve consciousness, or at any rate to achieve a state of secondary consciousness which consists in the unconscious process being "represented" to a subliminal subject who chooses and decides. This process must necessarily possess the amount of energy required for it to achieve such a consciousness; in other words, it is bound eventually to reach its "bursting point."[26]

26 James, *Varieties of Religious Experience*, p. 232.

If that is so, the question arises as to why the unconscious process does not go right over the threshold and become perceptible to the ego? Since it obviously does not do this, but apparently remains suspended in the domain of a subliminal secondary subject, we must now explain why this subject, which is *ex hypothesi* charged with sufficient energy to become conscious, does not in its turn push over the threshold and articulate with the primary ego consciousness. Psychopathology has the material needed to answer this question. This secondary consciousness represents a personality component which has not been separated from ego consciousness by mere accident, but which owes its separation to definite causes. Such a dissociation has two distinct aspects: in the one case there is an originally conscious content that became subliminal because it was repressed on account of its incompatible nature; in the other case the secondary subject consists essentially in a process that never entered into consciousness at all because no possibilities exist there of apperceiving it. That is to say, ego consciousness cannot accept it for lack of understanding, and in consequence it remains for the most part subliminal, although, from the energy point of view, it is quite capable of becoming conscious. It owes its existence not to repression, but to subliminal processes that were never themselves conscious. Yet because there is in both cases sufficient energy to make it potentially conscious, the secondary subject does in fact have an effect upon ego consciousness—indirectly or, as we say, "symbolically," though the expression is not a particularly happy one. The point is that the contents that appear in consciousness are at first *symptomatic*. In so far as we know, or think we know, what they refer to or are based on, they are *semiotic*, even though Freudian literature constantly uses the term "symbolic," regardless of the fact that in reality symbols always express what we do *not* know. The symptomatic contents are in part truly symbolic, being the indirect representatives of unconscious states or processes whose nature can be only imperfectly inferred and realized from the contents that appear in consciousness. It is therefore possible that the unconscious harbors contents so powered with energy that under other conditions they would be bound to become perceptible to the ego. In the majority of cases they are not repressed contents, but simply contents that are not yet conscious and have not been subjectively realized, like the demons and gods of the primitives or the "isms" so fanatically believed in by modern man. This state is neither pathological nor in any way peculiar; it is on the contrary the original norm, whereas the psychic wholeness comprehended in the unity of consciousness is an ideal goal that has never yet been reached.

Not without justice we connect consciousness, by analogy, with the sense functions, from the physiology of which the whole idea of a "threshold" is derived. The sound frequencies perceptible to the human ear range from 20 to 20,000 vibrations per second; the wave lengths of light visible to the eye range from 7700 to 3900 angstrom units. This analogy makes it conceivable that there is a lower as well as an upper threshold for psychic events, and that consciousness, the perceptive system par excellence, may therefore be compared with the perceptible scale of sound or light, having like them a lower and upper limit. Maybe this comparison could be extended to the psyche in general, which would not be an impossibility if there were "psychoid" processes at both ends of the psychic scale. In accordance with the principle *"natura non facit saltus,"* such an hypothesis would not be altogether out of place.

In using the term "psychoid" I am aware that it comes into collision with the concept of the same name postulated by Driesch. By "the psychoid" he understands the directing principle, the "reaction determinant," the "prospective potency" of the germinal element. It is "the elemental agent discovered in action,"[27] the "entelechy of real acting."[28] As Eugen Bleuler has aptly pointed out, Driesch's concept is more philosophical than scientific. Bleuler, on the other hand, uses the expression *"die Psychoide"*[29] as a collective term chiefly for the subcortical processes, so far as they are concerned with biological "adaptive functions." Among these Bleuler lists "reflexes and the development of species." He defines it as follows: "The *Psychoide* is the sum of all the purposive, mnemonic, and life-preserving functions of

---

27 Hans A. E. Driesch, *The Science and Philosophy of the Organism* (London, 1908), Vol. II, p. 82.

28 Ibid., p. 231.

29 In *Die Psychoide als Prinzip der organischen Entwicklung* (Berlin, 1925), p. 11. A fem. sing. noun evidently constructed analogously to *Psyche* (ψυχοειδής = "soul-like").

the body and central nervous system, with the exception of those cortical functions which we have always been accustomed to regard as psychic."[30] Elsewhere he says: "The body-psyche of the individual and the phylopsyche together form a unity which, for the purposes of our present study, can most usefully be designated by the name 'Psychoide.' Common to both Psychoide and psyche are . . . conation and the utilization of previous experiences . . . in order to reach the goal. This would include memory (engraphy and ecphoria) and association, hence something analogous to thinking."[31] Although it is clear what is meant by the "Psychoide," in practice it often gets confused with "psyche," as the above passage shows. But it is not at all clear why the subcortical functions it is supposed to designate should then be described as "quasi-psychic." The confusion obviously springs from the organological standpoint, still observable in Bleuler, which operates with concepts like "cortical soul" and "medullary soul" and has a distinct tendency to derive the corresponding psychic functions from these parts of the brain, although it is always the function that creates its own organ, and maintains or modifies it. The organological standpoint has the disadvantage that all the purposeful activities inherent in living matter ultimately count as "psychic," with the result that "life" and "psyche" are equated, as in Bleuler's use of the words "phylopsyche" and "reflexes." It is extremely difficult, if not impossible, to think of a psychic function as independent of its organ, although in actual fact we experience the psychic process apart from its relation to the organic substrate. For the psychologist, however, it is the totality of these experiences that constitutes the object of investigation, and for this reason he must abjure a terminology borrowed from the anatomist. If I make use of the term "psychoid"[32] I do so with three reservations: firstly, I use it as an adjective, not as a noun; secondly, no psychic quality in the proper sense of the word is implied, but only a "quasi-psychic" one such as the reflex processes possess; and thirdly, it is meant to distinguish a category of events from

30 Ibid., p. 11.   31 Ibid., p. 33.
32 I can avail myself of the word "psychoid" all the more legitimately because, although my use of the term derives from a different field of perception, it nevertheless seeks to delineate roughly the same group of phenomena that Bleuler had in mind.

merely vitalist phenomena on the one hand and from specifically psychic processes on the other. The latter distinction also obliges us to define more closely the nature and extent of the psyche, and of the unconscious psyche in particular.

If the unconscious can contain everything that is known to be a function of consciousness, then we are faced with the possibility that it too, like consciousness, possesses a subject, a sort of ego. This conclusion finds expression in the common and ever-recurring use of the term "subconsciousness." The latter term is certainly open to misunderstanding, as either it means what is "below consciousness," or it postulates a "lower" and secondary consciousness. At the same time this hypothetical "subconsciousness," which is immediately associated with a "superconsciousness,"[33] brings out the real point of my argument: the fact, namely, that a second psychic system coexisting with consciousness—no matter what qualities we suspect it of possessing—is of absolutely revolutionary significance in that it could radically alter our view of the world. Even if no more than the perceptions taking place in such a second psychic system were carried over into ego consciousness, we should have the possibility of enormously extending the bounds of our mental horizon.

Once we give serious consideration to the hypothesis of the unconscious, it follows that our view of the world can be but a provisional one; for if we effect so radical an alteration in the subject of perception and cognition as this dual focus implies, the result must be a world view very different from any known before. This holds true only if the hypothesis of the unconscious holds true, which in turn can only be verified if unconscious contents can be changed into conscious ones—if, that is to say, the disturbances emanating from the unconscious, the effects of spontaneous manifestations, of dreams, fantasies, and complexes, can successfully be integrated into consciousness by the interpretative method.

33 Especial exception is taken to this "superconsciousness" by people who have come under the influence of Indian philosophy. They usually fail to appreciate that their objection only applies to the hypothesis of a "subconsciousness," which ambiguous term I avoid using. On the other hand my concept of the *unconscious* leaves the question of "above" or "below" completely open, as it embraces both aspects of the psyche.

4. Instinct and Will

Whereas, in the course of the nineteenth century, the main concern was to put the unconscious on a philosophical footing,[34] towards the end of the century various attempts were made in different parts of Europe, more or less simultaneously and independently of one another, to understand the unconscious experimentally or empirically. The pioneers in this field were Pierre Janet[35] in France and Sigmund Freud[36] in the old Austria. Janet made himself famous for his investigation of the formal aspect, Freud for his researches into the content of psychogenic symptoms.

I am not in a position here to describe in detail the transformation of unconscious contents into conscious ones, so must content myself with hints. In the first place the structure of psychogenic symptoms was successfully explained on the hypothesis of unconscious processes. Freud, starting from the symptomatology of the neuroses, made out a plausible case for dreams as the mediators of unconscious contents. What he elicited as contents of the unconscious seemed, on the face of it, to consist of elements of a personal nature that were quite capable of consciousness and had therefore been conscious under other conditions. It seemed to him that they had "got repressed" on account of their morally incompatible nature. Hence, like forgotten contents, they had once been conscious and had become subliminal, and more or less unrecoverable, owing to a countereffect exerted by the attitude of the conscious mind. By suitably concentrating the attention and letting oneself be guided by associations—that is, by the pointers still existing in consciousness—the associative recovery of lost contents went forward as in a mnemotechnical exercise. But whereas forgotten contents were unrecoverable because of their lowered threshold value,

---

34 Cf. in particular Eduard von Hartmann, *Philosophie des Unbewussten* (1869; tr., *Philosophy of the Unconscious*, London and New York, 1931).

35 An appreciation of his achievement is to be found in Jean Paulus, *Le Problème de l'hallucination et l'évolution de la psychologie d'Esquirol à Pierre Janet* (Paris, 1941).

36 In this connection we should also mention the important Swiss psychologist Théodore Flournoy and his chef d'oeuvre *Des Indes à la Planète Mars* (Paris and Geneva, 1900; tr., *From India to the Planet Mars*, New York, 1900). Other pioneers were W. B. Carpenter (*Principles of Mental Physiology*, London, 1874) and G. H. Lewes (*Problems of Life and Mind*, London, 1872–79). For Frederic W. H. Myers see note 44.

repressed contents owed their relative unrecoverability to a check exercised by the conscious mind.

This initial discovery logically led to the interpretation of the unconscious as a phenomenon of repression which could be understood in personalistic terms. Its contents were lost elements that had once been conscious. Freud later acknowledged the continued existence of archaic vestiges in the form of primitive modes of functioning, though even these were explained personalistically. On this view the unconscious psyche appears as a subliminal appendix to the conscious mind.

The contents that Freud raised to consciousness are those which are the most easily recoverable because they have the capacity to become conscious and were originally conscious. The only thing they prove with respect to the unconscious psyche is that there is a psychic limbo somewhere beyond consciousness. Forgotten contents which are still recoverable prove the same. This would tell us next to nothing about the nature of the unconscious psyche did there not exist an undoubted link between these contents and the instinctual sphere. We think of the latter as physiological, as in the main a function of the glands. The modern theory of internal secretions and hormones lends the strongest support to this view. But the theory of human instincts finds itself in a rather delicate situation, because it is uncommonly difficult not only to define the instincts conceptually, but even to establish their number and their limitations.[37] In this matter opinions diverge. All that can be ascertained with any certainty is that the instincts have a physiological and a psychological aspect.[38] Of great use for descriptive purposes is Pierre Janet's view of the *"partie supérieure et inférieure d'une fonction."*[39]

The fact that all the psychic processes accessible to our observation

37 This indistinctness and blurring of the instincts may, as E. N. Marais has shown in his experiments with apes (*The Soul of the White Ant,* London, 1937, p. 429 [tr. from Afrikaans]), have something to do with the superior learning capacity prevailing over the instincts, as is obviously the case with man too.

38 "The instincts are physiological and psychic dispositions which . . . cause the organism to move in a clearly defined direction" (W. Jerusalem, *Lehrbuch der Psychologie,* 3rd ed., Vienna and Leipzig, 1902, p. 188). From another point of view Oswald Külpe describes instinct as "a fusion of feelings and organic sensations" (*Grundriss der Psychologie,* Leipzig, 1895, p. 333).

39 *Les Névroses* (1909), pp. 384ff.

and experience are somehow bound to an organic substrate indicates that they are articulated with the life of the organism as a whole and therefore partake of its dynamism—in other words, they must have a share in its instincts or be in a certain sense the results of the action of those instincts. This is not to say that the psyche derives exclusively from the instinctual sphere and hence from its organic substrate. The psyche as such cannot be explained in terms of physiological chemistry, if only because, together with "life" itself, it is the only "natural factor" capable of converting statistical organizations which are subject to natural law into "higher" or "unnatural" states, in opposition to the rule of entropy that runs throughout the inorganic realm. How life produces complex organic systems from the inorganic we do not know, though we have direct experience of how the psyche does it. Life therefore has a specific law of its own which cannot be deduced from the known physical laws of nature. Even so the psyche is to some extent dependent upon processes in the organic substrate. At all events it is highly probable that this is so. The instinctual base governs the *partie inférieure* of the function, while the *partie supérieure* corresponds to its predominantly "psychic" component. The *partie inférieure* proves to be the relatively unalterable, automatic part of the function, and the *partie supérieure* the voluntary and alterable part.[40]

The question now arises: when are we entitled to speak of "psychic" and how in general do we define the "psychic" as distinct from the "physiological"? Both are life phenomena, but they differ in that the functional component characterized as the *partie inférieure* has an unmistakably physiological aspect. Its existence or nonexistence seems to be bound up with the hormones. Its functioning has a compulsive character: hence the designation "drive." Rivers asserts that the "all-

[40] Janet says (ibid., p. 384): "Il me semble nécessaire de distinguer dans toute fonction des parties inférieures et des parties supérieures. Quand une fonction s'exerce depuis longtemps elle contient des parties qui sont très anciennes, très faciles, et qui sont réprésentées par des organes très distincts et très spécialisés . . . ce sont là les parties inférieures de la fonction. Mais je crois qu'il y a aussi dans toute fonction des parties supérieures consistant dans l'adaptation de cette fonction à des circonstances plus récentes, beaucoup moins habituelles, qui sont réprésentées par des organes beaucoup moins différenciés." But the highest part of the function consists "dans son adaptation à la circonstance particulière qui existe au moment présent, au moment où nous devons l'employer."

or-none reaction"[41] is natural to it, i.e., the function acts altogether or not at all, which is specific of compulsion. On the other hand the *partie supérieure,* which is best described as psychic and is moreover sensed as such, has lost its compulsive character, can be subjected to the will[42] and even applied in a manner contrary to the original instinct.

From these reflections it appears that the psychic is an emancipation of function from its instinctual form and so from the compulsiveness which, as sole determinant of the function, causes it to harden into a mechanism. The psychic condition or quality begins where the function loses its outer and inner determinism and becomes capable of more extensive and freer application, that is, where it begins to show itself accessible to a will motivated from other sources. At the risk of anticipating my program, I cannot refrain from pointing out that if we delimit the psyche from the physiological sphere of instinct at the bottom, so to speak, a similar delimitation imposes itself at the top. For, with increasing freedom from sheer instinct the *partie supérieure* will ultimately reach a point at which the intrinsic energy of the function ceases altogether to be oriented by instinct in the original sense, and attains a so-called "spiritual" form. This does not imply a substantial alteration of the motive power of instinct, but merely a different mode of its application. The meaning or purpose of the instinct is not unambiguous, as the instinct may easily mask a sense of direction other than biological, which only becomes apparent in the course of development.

Within the psychic sphere the function can be deflected through the action of the will and modified in a great variety of ways. This is possible because the system of instincts is not truly harmonious in composition and is exposed to numerous internal collisions. One instinct disturbs and displaces the other, and although, taken as a whole, it is the instincts that make individual life possible, their blind compulsive character affords frequent occasion for mutual injury. Differentiation of function from compulsive instinctuality, and its voluntary application, are of paramount importance in the maintenance of life.

41 W. H. R. Rivers, "Instinct and the Unconscious," *British Journal of Psychology* (Cambridge), X (1919–20), 1–7.

42 This formulation is purely psychological and has nothing to do with the philosophical problem of indeterminism.

But this increases the possibility of collision and produces cleavages—the very dissociations which are forever putting the unity of consciousness in jeopardy.

In the psychic sphere, as we have seen, the will influences the function. It does this by virtue of the fact that it is itself a form of energy and has the power to overcome another form. In this sphere which I define as psychic the will is in the last resort motivated by instincts, not of course absolutely, otherwise it would not be a will, which by definition must have a certain freedom of choice. "Will" implies a certain amount of energy freely disposable by the psyche. There must be such amounts of disposable libido (or energy), or modifications of the functions would be impossible, since the latter would then be chained to the instincts—which are in themselves extremely conservative and correspondingly unalterable—so exclusively that no variations could take place, unless it were organic variations. As we have already said, the motivation of the will must in the first place be regarded as essentially biological. But at the (permitting such an expression) upper limit of the psyche where the function breaks free from its original goal, the instincts lose their influence as movers of the will. Through having its form altered the function is pressed into the service of other determinants or motivations which apparently have nothing further to do with the instincts. What I am trying to make clear is the remarkable fact that the will cannot transgress the bounds of the psychic sphere: it cannot coerce the instinct, nor has it power over the spirit, in so far as we understand by this something more than the intellect. Spirit and instinct are by nature autonomous and both limit in equal measure the applied field of the will. Later I shall show what constitutes the relation of spirit to instinct.

Just as, in its lower reaches, the psyche loses itself in the organic-material substrate, so in its upper reaches it resolves itself into a "spiritual" form about which we know as little as we do about the functional basis of instinct. What I would call the psyche proper extends to all functions which can be brought under the influence of a will. Pure instinctuality allows no consciousness to be conjectured and needs none. But because of its empirical freedom of choice the will needs a superordinate authority, something like a consciousness of itself, in order to modify the function. It must "know" of a goal different from the goal of the function. Otherwise it would coincide with the driving force of the function. Driesch rightly emphasizes: "There is no willing without knowing."[43] Volition presupposes a choosing subject who envisages different possibilities. Looked at from this angle, psyche is essentially conflict between blind instinct and will (freedom of choice). Where instinct predominates, *psychoid* processes set in which pertain to the sphere of the unconscious as elements incapable of consciousness. The psychoid process is not the unconscious as such, for this has a far greater extension. Apart from psychoid processes there are in the unconscious ideas and volitional acts, hence something akin to conscious processes; but in the instinctual sphere these phenomena retire so far into the background that the term "psychoid" is probably justified. If, however, we restrict the psyche to acts of the will, we arrive at the conclusion that psyche is more or less identical with consciousness, for we can hardly conceive of will and freedom of choice without consciousness. This apparently brings us back to where we always stood, to the axiom *psyche = consciousness*. What, then, has happened to the postulated psychic nature of the unconscious?

5. *Conscious and Unconscious*

This question, regarding the nature of the unconscious, brings with it the extraordinary intellectual difficulties with which the psychology of the unconscious confronts us. Such difficulties must inevitably arise whenever the mind launches forth boldly into the unknown and invisible. Our philosopher sets about it very cleverly, since, by his flat denial of the unconscious, he clears all complications out of his way at one sweep. A similar quandary faced the physicist of the old school, who believed exclusively in the wave theory of light and was then led to the discovery that there are phenomena which can only be explained by the corpuscular theory. Happily, physics has shown the psychologist that it too can cope with an apparent *contradictio in adiecto*. Encouraged by this example, the psychologist may be em-

43 *Die "Seele" als elementarer Naturfaktor* (Leipzig, 1903), p. 80. "Individualized stimuli inform . . . the 'primary knower' of the abnormal state, and now this 'knower' not only *wants* a remedy but *knows* what it is" (p. 82).

boldened to tackle this controversial problem without having the feeling that he has dropped out of the world of natural science altogether.

Before we scrutinize our dilemma more closely, I would like to clarify one aspect of the concept of the unconscious. The unconscious is not simply the unknown, it is rather the *unknown psychic;* and this we define on the one hand as all those things in us which, if they came to consciousness, would presumably differ in no respect from the known psychic contents, with the addition, on the other hand, of the psychoid system. So defined, the unconscious depicts an extremely fluid state of affairs: everything of which I know, but of which I am not at the moment thinking; everything of which I was once conscious but have now forgotten; everything perceived by my senses, but not noted by my conscious mind; everything which, involuntarily and without paying attention to it, I feel, think, remember, want, and do; all the future things that are taking shape in me and will sometime come to consciousness: all this is the content of the unconscious. These contents are all more or less capable, so to speak, of consciousness, or were once conscious and may become conscious again the next moment. Thus far the unconscious is "a fringe of consciousness," as William James puts it.[44] To this marginal phenomenon, which is born of alternating shades of light and darkness, there also belong the Freudian findings we have already noted.

We now come to the question: in what state do psychic contents find themselves when not related to the conscious ego? (This relation

---

44 James speaks also of a "transmarginal field" of consciousness and identifies it with the "subliminal consciousness" of F. W. H. Myers, one of the founders of the British Society for Psychical Research (cf. *Proceedings S.P.R.*, VII, 1891–92, 305, and William James, "Frederic Myers' Services to Psychology," *Proceedings S.P.R.*, XLII, May, 1901). Concerning the "field of consciousness" James says (*Varieties of Religious Experience*, p. 232): "The important fact which this 'field' formula commemorates is the indetermination of the margin. Inattentively realized as is the matter which the margin contains, it is nevertheless there, and helps both to guide our behavior and to determine the next movement of our attention. It lies around us like a 'magnetic field' inside of which our center of energy turns like a compass needle as the present phase of consciousness alters into its successor. Our whole past store of memories floats beyond this margin, ready at a touch to come in; and the entire mass of residual powers, impulses, and knowledges that constitute our empirical self stretches continuously beyond it. So vaguely drawn are the outlines between what is actual and what is only potential at any moment of our conscious life, that it is always hard to say of certain mental elements whether we are conscious of them or not."

constitutes all that can be called consciousness.) In accordance with "Occam's razor," *entia praeter necessitatem non sunt multiplicanda* ("principles are not to be multiplied beyond the necessary"), the most cautious conclusion would be that, except for the relation to the conscious ego, nothing is changed when a content becomes unconscious. For this reason I reject the view that momentarily unconscious contents are only physiological. The evidence is lacking, and apart from that the psychology of neurosis provides striking proofs to the contrary. One has only to think of the cases of double personality, *automatisme ambulatoire,* etc. Both Janet's and Freud's findings indicate that everything goes on functioning in the unconscious state just as though it were conscious. There is perception, thinking, feeling, volition, and intention, just as though a subject were present; indeed, there are not a few cases—e.g., the double personality above mentioned —where a second ego actually appears and vies with the first. Such findings seem to show that the unconscious is in fact a "subconscious." But from certain experiences—some of them known even to Freud— it is clear that the state of unconscious contents is not quite the same as the conscious state. For instance, feeling-toned complexes in the unconscious do not change in the same way that they do in consciousness. Although they may be enriched by associations, they are not corrected, but are conserved in their original form, as can easily be ascertained from the continuous and uniform effect they have upon the conscious mind. Similarly, they take on the uninfluenceable and compulsive character of an automatism, of which they can be divested only if they are made conscious. This latter procedure is rightly regarded as one of the most important therapeutic factors. In the end such complexes—presumably in proportion to their distance from consciousness—assume, by self-amplification, an archaic and mythological character and hence a certain numinosity, as is perfectly clear in schizophrenic dissociations. Numinosity, however, is wholly outside conscious volition, for it transports the subject into the state of rapture, which is a state of will-less surrender.

These peculiarities of the unconscious state contrast very strongly with the way complexes behave in the conscious mind. Here they can be corrected: they lose their automatic character and can be essentially transformed. They slough off their mythological envelope, and, by

397

entering into the adaptive process going forward in consciousness, they personalize and rationalize themselves to the point where a dialectical discussion becomes possible.[45] Evidently the unconscious state is different after all from the conscious. Although at first sight the process continues in the unconscious as though it were conscious, it seems, with increasing dissociation, to sink back to a more primitive (archaic-mythological) level, to approximate in character to the underlying instinctual pattern, and to assume the qualities which are the hallmarks of instinct: automatism, nonsusceptibility to influence, all-or-none reaction, and so forth. Using the analogy of the spectrum, we could compare the lowering of unconscious contents to a displacement towards the red end of the color band, a comparison which is especially edifying in that red, the blood color, has always signified emotion and instinct.[46]

The unconscious is accordingly a different medium from the conscious. In the near-conscious areas there is not much change, because here the alternation of light and shadow is too rapid. But it is just this no man's land which is of the greatest value in supplying the answer to the burning question of whether psyche = consciousness. It shows us how relative the unconscious state is, so relative, indeed, that one feels tempted to make use of a concept like "the subconscious" in order to define the darker part of the psyche. But consciousness is equally relative, for it embraces not only consciousness as such, but a whole scale of intensities of consciousness. Between "I do this" and "I am conscious of doing this" there is a world of difference, amounting sometimes to outright contradiction. Consequently there is a consciousness in which unconsciousness predominates, as well as a consciousness in which self-consciousness predominates. This paradox becomes immediately intelligible when we realize that there is no conscious content which can with absolute certainty be said to be totally conscious,[47]

---

45 In schizophrenic dissociation there is no such change in the conscious state, because the complexes are received not into a complete but into a fragmentary consciousness.

46 Red had a *spiritual* significance for Goethe, but that was in accord with his creed of feeling. Here we may conjecture the alchemical and Rosicrucian background, e.g., the red tincture and the carbuncle. Cf. *Psychology and Alchemy (Collected Works*, Vol. 12; New York and London, 1953), p. 449.

47 As already pointed out by E. Bleuler—*Naturgeschichte der Seele und ihres Bewusstwerdens* (Berlin, 1921), pp. 300f.

for that would necessitate an unimaginable totality of consciousness, and that in turn would presuppose an equally unimaginable wholeness and perfection in the human mind. So we come to the paradoxical conclusion that there is no conscious content which is not in some other respect unconscious. Maybe, too, there is no unconscious psychism which is not at the same time conscious.[48] The latter proposition is more difficult to prove than the first, because our ego, which alone could verify such an assertion, is the point of reference for all consciousness and has no such association with unconscious contents as would enable it to say anything about their nature. So far as the ego is concerned they are, for all practical purposes, unconscious, which is not to say that they are not conscious to it in another respect, for the ego may know these contents under one aspect, but not know them under another aspect, when they cause disturbances of consciousness. Besides, there are processes with regard to which no relation to the conscious ego can be demonstrated and which yet seem to be "represented" or "quasi-conscious." Finally, there are cases where an unconscious ego and hence a second consciousness are present, as we have already seen, though these are the exceptions.[49]

In the psychic sphere the compulsive pattern of behavior gives way to variations of behavior which are conditioned by experience and by volitional acts, that is, by conscious processes. With respect to the psychoid, reflective-instinctive state, therefore, the psyche implies a loosening of bonds and a steady recession of mechanical processes in favor of "selected" modifications. This selective activity takes place partly inside consciousness and partly outside it, i.e., without reference to the conscious ego, and hence unconsciously. In the latter case the process is "quasi-conscious," *as if* it were "represented" and conscious.

As there are no sufficient grounds for assuming that a second ego

48 With the explicit exception of the psychoid unconscious, as this includes things which are not capable of consciousness and are only "quasi-psychic."

49 In this connection I would mention that C. A. Meier associates observations of this kind with similar phenomena in physics. He says: "The relationship of complementarity between conscious and unconscious urges upon us yet another physical parallel, namely the need for a strict application of the 'principle of correspondence.' This might provide the key to the 'strict logic' of the unconscious (the logic of probability) which we so often experience in analytical psychology and which makes us think of an 'extended state of consciousness.' "—"Moderne Physik—Moderne Psychologie," in *Die kulturelle Bedeutung der komplexen Psychologie* (Berlin, 1935), p. 360.

exists in every individual or that everyone suffers from dissociation of personality, we have to discount the idea of a second ego consciousness as a source of voluntary decisions. But since the existence of highly complex, quasi-conscious processes in the unconscious has been shown, by the study of psychopathology and dream psychology, to be uncommonly probable, we are for better or worse driven to the conclusion that although the state of unconscious contents is not identical with that of conscious ones, it is somehow very "like" it. In these circumstances there is nothing for it but to suppose something midway between the conscious and unconscious state, namely an approximative consciousness. As we have immediate experience only of a reflected state, which is *ipso facto* conscious and known because it consists essentially in relating ideas or other contents to an ego complex that represents our empirical personality, it follows that any other kind of consciousness—either without an ego or without contents—is virtually unthinkable. But there is no need to frame the question so absolutely. On a somewhat more primitive human level ego consciousness loses much of its meaning, and consciousness is accordingly modified in a characteristic way. Above all it ceases to be reflected. And when we observe the psychic processes in the higher vertebrates and particularly in domestic animals, we find phenomena resembling consciousness which nevertheless do not allow us to conjecture the existence of an ego. As we know from direct experience, the light of consciousness has many degrees of brightness, and the ego complex many gradations of emphasis. On the animal and primitive level there is a mere "luminosity," differing hardly at all from the glancing fragments of a dissociated ego. Here, as on the infantile level, consciousness is not a unity, being as yet uncentered by a firmly-knit ego complex, and just flickering into life here and there wherever outer or inner events, instincts, and affects happen to call it awake. At this stage it is still like a chain of islands, or an archipelago. Nor is it a fully integrated whole even at the higher and highest stages; rather, it is capable of indefinite expansion. Gleaming islands, and indeed whole continents, can still add themselves to our modern consciousness—a phenomenon that has become the daily experience of the psychotherapist. Therefore we would do well to think of ego consciousness as being surrounded by a multitude of little luminosities.

6. *The Unconscious as a Multiple Consciousness*

The hypothesis of multiple luminosities rests partly, as we have seen, on the near-conscious state of unconscious contents, and partly on the incidence of certain images which must be regarded as symbolical. These are to be found in the dreams and visual fantasies of modern individuals, and can also be traced in historical records. As the reader may be aware, one of the most important sources for symbolical ideas in the past is alchemy. From this I take, first and foremost, the idea of the *scintillae*—sparks—which appear as visual illusions in the "arcane substance."[50] Thus the *Aurora Consurgens*, Part II, says: *"Scito quod terra foetida cito recipit scintillulas albas"* (Know that the foul earth quickly receives white sparks).[51] These sparks Khunrath explains as *"radii atque scintillae"* of the *"anima catholica,"* the world soul, which is identical with the spirit of God.[52] From this interpretation it is clear that certain of the alchemists had already divined the psychic nature of these luminosities. They were seeds of light broadcast in the chaos, which Khunrath calls *"mundi futuri seminarium"* (the seed plot of a world to come).[53] One such spark is the human mind.[54] The arcane substance—the watery earth or earthy water (*limus:* mud) of the World Essence—is "universally animated" by the "fiery spark of

50 *Psychology and Alchemy*, p. 126.
51 *Artis auriferae quam chemiam vocant* . . . (Basel, 1593), Vol. I, p. 208. Said to be a quotation from Morienus (cf. infra, p. 407), repeated by Johann Daniel Mylius, *Philosophia reformata* (Frankfort, 1622), p. 146. On p. 149 he adds *"scintillae aureas."*
52 ". . . *Variae eius radii atque Scintillae, per totius ingentem materiei primae massae molem hinc inde dispersae ac dissipatae: inque mundi partibus disiunctis etiam et loco et corporis mole, necnon circumscriptione, postea separatis . . . unius Animae universalis scintillae nunc etiam inhabitantes"* (. . . Its divers rays and sparks are dispersed and dissipated throughout the immense bulk of the whole mass of the *prima materia:* the sparks of the one universal soul now inhabiting those disunited parts of the world which were later separated from the place and mass of the body, and even from its circumference). Heinrich Conrad Khunrath, *Amphitheatrum sapientiae aeternae solius verae, Christiano-kabalisticum, divino-magicum* . . . *Tertriunum, Catholicon* (Hanau, 1604), pp. 195f., 198.
53 Ibid., p. 197. Cf. the Gnostic doctrine of the Seeds of Light harvested by the Virgin of Light, and the Manichaean doctrine of the light particles which have to be taken into one's body as ritual food, at a sort of Eucharist when melons were eaten. The earliest mention of this idea seems to be the καρπιστής (Irenaeus, *Contra haereses*, I, 2, 4).
54 *"Mens humani animi scintilla altior et lucidior"* (The mind of the human soul is a higher and more luminous spark). *Amphitheatrum*, p. 63.

the soul of the world," in accordance with the Wisdom of Solomon
1:7: "For the Spirit of the Lord filleth the world."[55] In the "Water
of the Art," in "our Water," which is also the chaos,[56] there are to
be found the "fiery sparks of the soul of the world as pure *Formae
Rerum essentiales.*"[57] These *formae*[58] correspond to the Platonic Ideas,
from which one could equate the *scintillae* with the archetypes on the
assumption that the Forms "stored up in some heavenly place" are a
philosophical version of the latter. One would have to conclude from
these alchemical visions that the archetypes have about them a certain
effulgence, and that numinosity entails luminosity. Paracelsus seems
to have had an inkling of this. The following is taken from his
Philosophia Sagax: "And as little as aught can exist in man without
the divine numen, so little can aught exist in man without the natural
lumen. A man is made perfect by numen and lumen and these two
alone. Everything springs from these two, and these two are in man,
but without them man is nothing, though they can be without man."[59]
In confirmation of this Khunrath writes: "There be . . . *Scintillae
Animae Mundi igneae, Luminis nimirum Naturae,* fiery sparks of the
world soul, i.e. of the light of nature . . . dispersed or sprinkled in
and throughout the structure of the great world into all fruits of the
elements everywhere."[60] The sparks come from the "Ruach Elohim,"
the Spirit of God.[61] From among the *scintillae* he distinguishes a
"scintilla perfecta Unici Potentis ac Fortis," which is the elixir and
hence the arcane substance itself.[62] If we may compare the sparks to
the archetypes, it is evident that Khunrath lays particular stress on

55 Khunrath, *Von hylealischen, das ist, pri-materialischen catholischen, oder alge-
meinen natürlichen Chaos* (Magdeburg, 1597), p. 63.
56 As synonyms Khunrath mentions *"forma aquina, pontica, limus terrae Adamae,
Azoth, Mercurius"* (a form watery and sea-like, the slime of the earth of Adama,
Azoth, Mercurius), etc. Ibid., p. 216. [*Adama* is Hebrew for "earth."—ED.]
57 Ibid., p. 216.
58 The *"formae scintillaeve Animae Mundi"* (forms or sparks of the world soul) are
also called by Khunrath (p. 189) *"rationes seminariae Naturae specificae"* (the
seed-ideas of Nature, the origin of species), thus reproducing an ancient idea.
In the same way he calls the *scintilla "Entelechia"* (p. 65).
59 *Paracelsus: Sämtliche Werke,* ed. Karl Sudhoff (Munich, Berlin, 1922–33), Vol.
XII, p. 231; . . . *Paracelsi . . . Philosophi und Medici Opera Bücher und
Schrifften,* ed. John Huser (Strasbourg, 1603, 1616–18), Vol. X, p. 206.
60 *Von hylealischen Chaos,* p. 94.   61 Ibid., p. 249.
62 Ibid., p. 54. In this he agrees with Paracelsus, who calls the *lumen naturae* the
Quintessence, extracted from the four elements by God himself.

THE SPIRIT OF PSYCHOLOGY

one of them. This One is also described as the Monad and the Sun, and they both indicate the Deity. A similar image is to be found in the letter of Ignatius of Antioch to the Ephesians, where he writes of the coming of Christ: "How, then, was he manifested to the ages? A star shone forth in heaven above all the other stars, the light of which was inexpressible, while its novelty struck men with astonishment. And all the rest of the stars, with the sun and moon, formed a chorus to this star. . . ."[63] Psychologically, the One Scintilla or Monad is to be regarded as a symbol of the self—an aspect I mention only in passing.

The sparks have a clear psychological meaning for Dorn. He says: "*Sic paulatim scintillas aliquot magis ac magis indies perlucere suis oculis mentalibus percipiet, ac in tantam excrescere lucem, ut successivo tempore quaevis innotescant, quae sibi necessaria fuerint.*"[64] This light is the *lumen naturae* which illuminates consciousness, and the *scintillae* are germinal luminosities shining forth from the darkness of the unconscious. Dorn, like Khunrath, owes much to Paracelsus, with whom he concurs when he supposes an "*invisibilem solem plurimis incognitum*" in man (an invisible sun unknown to many).[65] Of this natural light innate in man Dorn says: "*Lucet in nobis licet obscure vita lux hominum*[66] *tanquam in tenebris, quae non ex nobis quaerenda, tamen in et non a nobis, sed ab eo cuius est, qui etiam in nobis habitationem facere dignatur. . . . Hic eam lucem plantavit in nobis, ut in eius lumine qui lucem inaccessibilem inhabitat, videremus lucem; hoc ipso quoque caeteras eius praecelleremus creaturas; illi nimirum similes hac ratione facti, quod scintillam sui luminis dederit nobis. Est igitur veritas non in nobis quaerenda, sed in imagine Dei quae in nobis est.*"[67]

63 Ch. XIX, 1ff. (tr. in *The Writings of the Apostolic Fathers*, Ante-Nicene Christian Library, I; Edinburgh, 1883).
64 "Thus he will come to see with his spiritual eyes a number of sparks shining through day by day and more and more and growing into such a great light that thereafter all things needful to him will be made known." Gerhard Dorn, "De speculativa philosophia," in *Theatrum chemicum* (Ursel, 1602), Vol. I, p. 275.
65 "*Sol est invisibilis in hominibus, in terra vero visibilis, tamen ex uno et eodem sole sunt ambo*" (The sun is invisible in men, but visible in the world, yet both are of one and the same sun). Ibid., p. 308.
66 "*Et vita erat lux hominum. Et lux in tenebris lucet*" (And the life was the light of men. And the light shineth in the darkness). John 1:4, 5.
67 "For the life shineth in us, albeit dimly, as the light of men, and as though in darkness. It is not to be extracted from us, yet it is in us and not of us, but of

Thus the one archetype emphasized by Khunrath is known also to Dorn as the *sol invisibilis* or *imago Dei*. In Paracelsus the *lumen naturae* comes primarily from the *"astrum"* or *"sydus,"* the "star" in man.[68] The "firmament" (a synonym for the star) is the natural light.[69] Hence the "cornerstone" of all truth is "Astronomia," which is "a mother to all the other arts. . . . After her beginneth the divine wisdom, after her beginneth the light of nature,"[70] even the "most excellent Religiones" hang upon Astronomia.[71] For the star "desireth to drive man toward great wisdom . . . that he may appear wondrous in the light of nature, and the mysteria of God's wondrous work be discovered and revealed in their grandeur."[72] Indeed, man himself is an "Astrum": "not by himself alone, but for ever and ever with all apostles and saints; each and every one is an astrum, the heaven a star . . . therefore saith also the Scripture: ye are lights of the world."[73] "Now as in the star lieth the whole natural light, and from it man taketh the same like food from the earth into which he is born, so too must he be born into the star."[74] Also the animals have the natural light which is an "inborn spirit."[75] Man at his birth is "endowed with the perfect light of nature."[76] Paracelsus calls it *"primum ac optimum thesaurum, quem naturae Monarchia in se claudit"*[77] (the first and best treasure which the monarchy of nature hides within itself), in this concurring with the world-wide descriptions of the One as the pearl of

Him to Whom it belongs, and Who hath deigned to make us his dwelling place. . . . He has implanted that light in us that we may see in its light the light of Him Who dwells in the inaccessible light, and that we may excel His other creatures; in this wise we are made like unto Him, for He has given us a spark of His light. Thus the truth is to be sought not in ourselves, but in the image of God which is in us." "De philosophia meditativa," *Theatrum chemicum,* Vol. I, p. 460.
68 Ed. Sudhoff, Vol. XII, p. 23: "That which is in the light of nature, the same is the working of the star." (Ed. Huser, Vol. X, p. 19.)
69 *Philosophia sagax,* ed. Huser, Vol. X, p. 1 (ed. Sudhoff, Vol. XII, p. 3).
70 Ibid., ed. Huser, pp. 3f (ed. Sudhoff, pp. 5f.).
71 The apostles are *"Astrologi"*: ibid., p. 23 (p. 27). 72 Ibid., p. 54 (p. 62).
73 Ibid., p. 344 (p. 386). The last sentence refers to Matthew 5:14: *"Vos estis lux mundi."* 74 Ibid., p. 409 (pp. 456f.).
75 ". . . like the cocks which crow the coming weather and the peacocks the death of their master . . . all this is of the inborn spirit and is the light of nature." *Fragmenta medica,* cap. "De morbis somnii," ed. Huser, Vol. V, p. 130 (ed. Sudhoff, Vol. IX, p. 361).
76 *Liber de generatione hominis,* ed. Huser, Vol. VIII, p. 172 (ed. Sudhoff, Vol. I, p. 300).
77 *De vita longa,* ed. Adam von Bodenstein (Basel, 1562), Lib. V, c. ii.

great price, the hidden treasure, the "treasure hard to attain," etc. The light is given to the "inner man" or the inner body (*corpus subtile,* breath-body), as the following passage makes clear:

A man may come forth with sublimity and wisdom from his outer body, because the same wisdom and understanding which he needeth for this are coeval with this body and are the inner man;[78] thus he may live and not as an outer man. For such an inner man is eternally transfigured and true, and if in the mortal body he appeareth not perfect, yet he appeareth perfect after the separation of the same. That which we now tell of is called *lumen naturae* and is eternal. God hath given it to the inner body, that it may be ruled by the inner body and in accordance with reason . . . for the light of nature alone is reason and no other thing . . . the light is that which giveth faith . . . to each man God hath given sufficient predestined light that he not err. . . . But if we are to describe the origin of the inner man or body, mark that all inner bodies be but one body and one single thing in all men, albeit divided in accordance with the well-disposed numbers of the body, each one different. And should they all come together, it is but one light, and one reason.[79]

"Moreover the light of nature is a light that is lit from the Holy Ghost and goeth not out, for it is well lit . . . and the light is of a kind that desireth to burn,[80] and the longer [it burns] to shine the more, and the longer the greater . . . therefore in the light of nature is a fiery longing to enkindle."[81] It is an "invisible" light: "Now it follows that in the invisible alone hath man his wisdom, his art from the light of nature."[82] Man is "a prophet of the natural light."[83] He "learns" the *lumen naturae* through dreams,[84] among other things.

78 *Philosophia sagax,* ed. Huser, Vol. X, p. 341 (ed. Sudhoff, Vol. XII, p. 382): "Now it is clear that all the human wisdom of the earthly body lieth in the light of nature." It is "man's light of eternal wisdom": ibid., p. 395 (p. 441).
79 *Liber de generatione hominis,* ed. Huser, Vol. VIII, pp. 171f. (ed. Sudhoff, Vol. I, pp. 299f.).
80 "I am come to send fire on the earth; and what will I, if it be already kindled?" Luke (A. V.) 12:49.
81 *Fragmenta cum libro de fundamento sapientiae,* ed. Huser, Vol. IX, p. 448 (ed. Sudhoff, Vol. XIII, pp. 325f.).
82 *Philosophia sagax,* ed. Huser, Vol. X, p. 46 (ed. Sudhoff, Vol. XII, p. 53).
83 Ibid., p. 79 (p. 94).
84 *Practica in scientiam divinationis,* ed. Huser, Vol. X, p. 438 (ed. Sudhoff, Vol. XII, p. 488).

"As the light of nature cannot speak, it buildeth shapes in sleep from the power of the word" (of God).[85]

I have allowed myself to dwell at some length on Paracelsus and to cite a number of authentic texts, because I wanted to give the reader a rough idea of the way in which this author conceives the *lumen naturae*. It strikes me as significant, particularly in regard to our hypothesis of a multiple consciousness and its phenomena, that the characteristic alchemical vision of sparks scintillating in the blackness of the arcane substance should, for Paracelsus, change into the spectacle of the "interior firmament" and its stars. He beholds the darksome psyche as a star-strewn night sky, whose planets and fixed constellations represent the archetypes in all their luminosity and numinosity.[86] The starry vault of heaven is in truth the open book of cosmic projection, in which are reflected the mythologems, i.e., the archetypes. In this vision astrology and alchemy, the two classic functionaries of the psychology of the collective unconscious, join hands.

Paracelsus was directly influenced by Agrippa of Nettesheim,[87] who supposes a *"luminositas sensus naturae."* From this "gleams of prophecy came down to the four-footed beasts, the birds, and other living creatures," and enabled them to foretell future things.[88] He bases the *sensus naturae* on the authority of Gulielmus Parisiensis, who is none other than William of Auvergne (G. Alvernus; d. 1249), bishop of Paris from about 1228; author of many works, which influenced Albertus Magnus among others. Alvernus says that the *sensus naturae* is superior to the perceptive faculty in man, and he insists that animals also possess it.[89] The doctrine of the *sensus naturae* is developed from

85 *Liber de Caducis*, ed. Huser, Vol. IV, p. 274 (ed. Sudhoff, Vol. VIII, p. 298).
86 In the *Hieroglyphica* of Horapollo the starry sky signifies God as ultimate Fate, symbolized by a "5," presumably a quincunx. [Tr. George Boas (Bollingen Series XXIII; New York, 1950), p. 66.—ED.]
87 Cf. my *Paracelsica* (Zurich, 1942), pp. 47f.
88 Cornelius Heinrich Agrippa von Nettesheim, *De occulta philosophia* (Cologne, 1533), p. lxviii: *"Nam iuxta Platonicorum doctrinam, est rebus inferioribus vis quaedam insita, per quam magna ex parte cum superioribus conveniunt, unde etiam animalium taciti consensus cum divinis corporibus consentire videntur, atque his viribus eorum corpora et affectus affici."* (For according to the doctrine of the Platonists there is in the lower things a certain virtue through which they agree in large measure with the higher; whence it would seem that the tacit consent of animals is in agreement with divine bodies, and that their bodies and affections are touched by these virtues), etc.
89 Lynn Thorndike, *History of Magic and Experimental Science*, Vol. II (New York, 1929), pp. 348f.

406

the idea of the all-pervading world soul with which another Gulielmus Parisiensis was much concerned, a predecessor of Alvernus by name of Guillaume de Conches[90] (1080–1154), a Platonist scholastic who taught in Paris. He identified the *anima mundi,* this same *sensus naturae,* with the Holy Ghost, just as Abelard did. The world soul is a natural force which is responsible for all the phenomena of life and the psyche. As I have shown elsewhere, this view of the *anima mundi* ran through the whole tradition of alchemy in so far as Mercurius was interpreted now as *anima mundi* and now as the Holy Ghost.[91] In view of the importance of alchemical ideas for the psychology of the unconscious it may be worth our while to devote a little time to a very illuminating variant of this spark symbolism.

Even more common than the spark motif is that of the fish's eyes, which have the same significance. I said above that a Morienus passage is given by the authors as the source for the "doctrine" of the *scintillae.* This passage is indeed to be found in the treatise of Morienus Romanus. But it reads: ". . . *Purus laton tamdiu decoquitur, donec veluti oculi piscium elucescat . . .*"[92] Here too the saying seems to be a citation from a still earlier source. In later authors these fish's eyes are always cropping up. There is a variant in Sir George Ripley, stating that on the "desiccation of the sea" a substance is left behind which "glitters like a fish's eye"[93]—an obvious allusion to the gold and the sun (God's eye). Hence it is not to be wondered at if an alchemist[94] of the seventeenth century uses the words of Zacharias 4:10 as a motto for his edition of Nicholas Flamel: *"Et videbunt lapidem stanneum in manu Zorobabel. Septem isti oculi sunt Domini, qui discurrunt in universam terram"*[95] (And . . . they shall see the tin plummet in the hand of Zorobabel. These are the seven eyes of the Lord that run to and fro through the whole earth). These seven eyes are evidently the seven planets which, like the sun and moon,

90 François Picavet, *Essais sur l'histoire générale et comparée des Théologies et des Philosophies Médiévales* (Paris, 1913), p. 207.
91 Cf. *Psychology and Alchemy,* pp. 126, 178f., 405, and pp. 330f., 416f.
92 "Liber de compositione Alchemiae," in *Artis auriferae,* Vol. II, p. 32: "The pure lato is cooked until it has the lustre of fish's eyes." Thus, by the authors themselves, the *oculi piscium* are interpreted as *scintillae.*
93 *Opera omnia chemica* (Kassel, 1649), p. 159.
94 Eirenaeus Orandus, *Nicholas Flamel: His Exposition of the Hieroglyphicall Figures* etc. (London, 1624).
95 Zach. 3:9 is also relevant: ". . . upon one stone there are seven eyes." [Both Douay.]

are the eyes of God, never resting, ubiquitous and all-seeing. The same motif is probably at the bottom of the many-eyed giant Argus. He is nicknamed Πανόπτης, "the All-Seeing," and is supposed to symbolize the starry heavens. Sometimes he is one-eyed, sometimes four-eyed, sometimes hundred-eyed, and even myriad-eyed (μυριωπός). Besides which he never sleeps. Hera transferred the eyes of Argus Panoptes to the peacock's tail.⁹⁶ Like the guardian Argus, the constellation of the Dragon is also given an all-surveying position in the Aratus citations of Hippolytus. He is there described as the one "who from the height of the Pole looks down upon all things and sees all things, so that nothing that happens shall be hidden from him."⁹⁷ This dragon is sleepless, because the Pole "never sets." Often he appears to be confused with the sun's serpentine passage through the sky: *"C'est pour ce motif qu'on dispose parfois les signes du zodiaque entre les circonvolutions du reptile,"* says Cumont.⁹⁸ Sometimes the serpent bears the signs of the zodiac upon his back.⁹⁹ As Eisler has remarked, on account of the time symbolism the all-seeing quality of the dragon is transferred to Chronos, whom Sophocles names "ὁ πάντ' ὁρῶν Χρόνος," while in the memorial tablet for those who fell at Chaeronea he is called "πανεπίσκοπος δαίμων."¹⁰⁰ The Uroboros has the meaning of eternity (αἰών) and cosmos in Horapollo. The identification of the All-Seeing with Time probably explains the eyes on the wheels in Ezekiel's vision (A.V., 1:18: "As for their rings, they were so high that they were dreadful; and their rings were full of eyes round about them four"). We mention this identification because of its special importance: it indicates the relation between the *mundus archetypus* of the unconscious and the "phenomenon" of Time—in other words, it points to the *synchronicity* of archetypal events, of which I shall have more to say towards the end of this paper.

96 This mythologem is of importance in interpreting the *"cauda pavonis."*
97 "Τετάχθαι γὰρ νομίζουσι κατὰ τὸν ἀρκτικὸν πόλον τὸν Δράκοντα, τὸν ὄφιν, ἀπὸ τοῦ ὑψηλοτάτου πόλου πάντα ἐπιβλέποντα καὶ πάντα ἐφορῶντα, ἵνα μηδὲν τῶν πραττομένων αὐτὸν λάθῃ." *Elenchos*, IV, 47, 2, 3.
98 Franz Cumont, *Textes et monuments figurés relatifs aux mystères de Mithra*, Vol. I (Brussels, 1869), p. 80.
99 "Προσέταξε τὸν αὐτὸν δράκοντα βαστάζειν ἐξ ζῴδια ἐπὶ τοῦ νώτου αὐτοῦ." —Jean Baptiste Pitra, ed., *Analecta sacra* (Paris, 1876–91), Vol. V, 9, p. 300. Quoted in Robert Eisler, *Weltenmantel und Himmelszelt* (1910), Vol. II, p. 389, 5.
100 Eisler, op. cit., p. 388. "The All-seeing Chronos" and "the all-beholding daemon."

From Ignatius Loyola's autobiography, which he dictated to Loys Gonzales,[101] we learn that he used to see a bright light, and sometimes this apparition seemed to him to have the form of a serpent. It appeared to be full of shining eyes, which were yet no eyes. At first he was greatly comforted by the beauty of the vision, but later he recognized it to be an evil spirit.[102] This vision sums up all the aspects of our optic theme and presents a most impressive picture of the unconscious with its disseminated luminosities. One can easily imagine the perplexity which a medieval man would be bound to feel when confronted by such an eminently "psychological" intuition, especially as he had no dogmatic symbol and no adequate patristic allegory to come to his rescue. But, as a matter of fact, Ignatius was not so very wide of the mark, for multiple eyes are also a characteristic of Purusha, the Hindu Cosmic Man. The Rig-Veda (10. 90) says: "Thousand-headed is Purusha, thousand-eyed, thousand-footed. He encompasses the earth on every side and rules over the ten-finger space."[103] Monoïmos the Arabian, according to Hippolytus, taught that the First Man (Ἄνθρωπος) was a single Monad (μία μονάς), not composed (ἀσύνθετος), indivisible (ἀδιαίρετος), and at the same time composed (συνθετή) and divisible (διαιρετή). This Monad is the dot (μία κεραία), and this tiniest of units which corresponds to Khunrath's one *scintilla* has "many faces" (πολυπρόσωπος) and "many eyes" (πολυόμματος).[104] Monoïmos bases himself here mainly on the prologue to the Gospel of St. John! Like Purusha, his First Man is the universe (ἄνθρωπος εἶναι τὸ πᾶν).[105]

101 Ludovicus Consalvus, *Acta Antiquissima*, ii, 19 (tr. E. M. Rix, *The Testament of Ignatius Loyola*, London, 1900, p. 72).
102 Ignatius also had the vision of a *"res quaedam rotunda tanquam ex auro et magna"* that floated before his eyes: a thing round, as if made of gold, and great. He interpreted it as Christ appearing to him like a *sun*. Philipp Funk, *Ignatius von Loyola* (Berlin, 1913), pp. 57, 65, 74, 112.
103 [Tr. derived from various sources. As Ananda K. Coomaraswamy explains in the *Journal of the American Oriental Society*, LVI (1946), 145–61, "the ten-finger space" (lit. "the ten-fingered") refers "macrocosmically to the distance between sky and earth and microcosmically to the space between the top of the head and the chin" of a man. He continues: "I therefore consider it shown that what RV 10. 90. 1 . . . means is that Purusha, making the whole earth his footstool, fills the entire universe, and rules over it by means of the powers of vision, etc., that proceed from his face, and to which man's own powers of vision, etc., are analogous; this face, whether of God or man, being . . . itself an image of the whole threefold universe."—TRANS.]
104 *Elenchos,* VIII, 12, 5.   105 Ibid., VIII, 12, 2.

Such visions must be understood as introspective intuitions that somehow capture the state of the unconscious and, at the same time, as amalgams of the central Christian idea. Naturally enough, the motif has the same meaning in modern dreams and fantasies, where it appears as the star-strewn heavens, as stars reflected in dark water, as nuggets of gold or golden sand scattered in black earth,[106] as a regatta at night, with lanterns on the dark surface of the sea, as a solitary eye in the depths of the sea or earth, as a parapsychic vision of luminous globes, and so on. Since consciousness has always been described in terms derived from the behavior of light, it is in my view not too much to assume that these multiple luminosities correspond to tiny conscious phenomena. If the luminosity appears in monadic form as a single star, sun, or eye, it readily assumes the shape of a mandala and must then be interpreted as the self. It has nothing whatever to do with "double consciousness," because there is no indication of a dissociated personality. On the contrary, the symbols of the self have a "uniting" character.[107]

7. Patterns of Behavior and Archetypes

We have stated that the lower reaches of the psyche begin at the moment when the function emancipates itself from the compulsive force of instinct and becomes amenable to the will, and we have defined the will as disposable energy. But that, as said, presupposes a disposing subject, capable of judgment and endowed with consciousness. In this way we arrived at the position of proving, as it were, the very thing that we started by rejecting, namely the identification of psyche with consciousness. This dilemma resolves itself once we realize how very relative consciousness is, since its contents are conscious and unconscious at the same time, i.e., conscious under one aspect and unconscious under another. As is the way of paradoxes, this statement is not immediately comprehensible.[108] We must, however, accustom our-

106 Cf. the alchemical dictum: *"Seminate aurum in terram albam foliatam"* (Sow the gold in white foliated earth).

107 Cf. my remarks on the "uniting symbol" in *Psychological Types* (New York and London, 1923), def. 51; also Toni Wolff, "Einführung in die Grundlagen der komplexen Psychologie," in *Die kulturelle Bedeutung der komplexen Psychologie*, pp. 151ff., 161f.

108 Freud also arrived at similar paradoxical conclusions. Thus, in his article "The Unconscious" (*Collected Papers*, Vol. IV: "Papers on Metapsychology," Inter-

selves to the thought that conscious and unconscious have no clear demarcations, the one beginning where the other leaves off. It is rather the case that the psyche is a conscious-unconscious whole. As to the no man's land which I have called the "personal unconscious," it is fairly easy to prove that its contents correspond exactly to our definition of the psychic. But—as we define "psychic"—is there a psychic unconscious that is not a "fringe of consciousness" and not personal?

I have already mentioned that Freud established the existence of archaic vestiges and primitive modes of functioning in the unconscious. Subsequent investigations have confirmed this result and brought together a wealth of observational material. In view of the structure of the body it would be astonishing if the psyche were the only biological phenomenon not to show clear traces of its evolutionary history, and it is altogether probable that these marks are closely connected with the instinctual base. Instinct and the archaic mode meet in the biological conception of the "pattern of behavior." There are in fact no amorphous instincts, as every instinct bears in itself the pattern of its situation. Always it fulfills an image, and the image has fixed qualities. The instinct of the leaf-cutting ant fulfills the image of ant, tree, leaf, cutting, transport, and the little ant garden of fungi.[109] If any one of these conditions is lacking, the instinct does not function, because it cannot exist without its total pattern, without its image. Such an image is an a priori type. It is inborn in the ant prior to any activity, for there can be no activity at all unless an instinct of corresponding pattern initiates and makes it possible. This schema holds true of all instincts and is found in identical form in all individuals of the same species. The same is true also of man: he has in him these a priori instinct types which provide the occasion and the pattern for his activities, in so far as he functions instinctively. As a

---

national Psychoanalytical Library, No. 10, London, 1925, p. 109): he says: "An instinct can never be an object of consciousness—only the idea that represents the instinct. *Even in the unconscious, moreover, it can only be represented by the idea.*" (My italics.) As in my above account we were left asking, "Who is the subject of the unconscious will?" so we must ask here, "Exactly *who* has the idea of the instinct in the unconscious state?" For "unconscious" ideation is a *contradictio in adjecto.*

109 For details see C. Lloyd Morgan, *Habit and Instinct* (London and New York, 1896).

biological being he has no choice but to act in a specifically human way and fulfill his pattern of behavior. This sets narrow limits to his possible range of volition, the more narrow the more primitive he is, and the more his consciousness is dependent upon the instinctual sphere. Although from one point of view it is quite correct to speak of the pattern of behavior as a still existing archaic vestige, as Nietzsche did in respect of the function of dreams, such an attitude does scant justice to the biological and psychological meaning of these types. They are not just relics or residues of earlier functional modes; they are the ever-present and biologically necessary regulators of the instinctual sphere, whose range of action covers the whole realm of the psyche and only loses its absoluteness when limited by the relative freedom of the will. We may say that the image represents the *meaning* of the instinct.

Although the existence of an instinctual pattern in human biology is probable, it seems very difficult to prove the existence of distinct types empirically. For the organ with which we might apprehend them —consciousness—is not only itself a transformation of the original instinctual image, but also its transformer. It is therefore not surprising that the human mind finds it impossible to classify man into precise types similar to those we know in the animal kingdom. I must confess that I can see no direct way to solve this problem. And yet I have succeeded, or so I believe, in finding at least an indirect way of approach to the instinctual image.

In what follows I would like to give a brief description of how this discovery took place. I had often observed patients whose dreams pointed to a rich store of fantasy material. Equally, from the patients themselves, I got the impression that they were stuffed full of fantasies, without their being able to tell me just where the inner pressure lay. I therefore took up a dream image or an association of the patient's, and, with this as a point of departure, set him the task of elaborating or developing his theme by giving free rein to his fantasy. This, according to individual taste and talent, could be done in any number of ways, dramatic, dialectic, visual, acoustic, or in the form of dancing, painting, drawing, or modeling. The result of this technique was a vast number of complicated patterns whose diversity puzzled me for years, until I was able to recognize that in this method I was witnessing the spontaneous manifestation of an unconscious process which was merely assisted by the technical ability of the patient, and to which I later gave the name "individuation process." But long before this recognition dawned upon me I had made the discovery that this method often diminished, to a considerable degree, the frequency and intensity of the dreams, thus reducing the inexplicable pressure exerted by the unconscious. In many cases this brought a large measure of therapeutic success, which encouraged both myself and the patient to press forward despite the baffling nature of the results.[110] I felt bound to insist that they were baffling, if only to stop myself from framing, on the basis of certain theoretical assumptions, interpretations which I felt were not only inadequate but liable to prejudice the ingenuous patterns of the patient. The more I suspected these patterns of harboring a certain purposefulness, the less inclined I was to risk any theories about them. This reticence was not made easy for me, since in many cases I was dealing with patients who needed an intellectual *point d'appui* if they were not to get totally lost in the darkness. I had to try to give provisional interpretations at least, so far as I was able, interspersing them with innumerable "perhapses" and "ifs" and "buts" and never stepping beyond the bounds of the pattern lying before me. I always took good care to let the interpretation of each image tail off into a question whose answer was left to the free fantasy activity of the patient.

The chaotic assortment of images that at first confronted me reduced itself in the course of the work to certain well-defined themes and formal elements which repeated themselves in identical or analogous form with the most varied individuals. I mention, as the most salient characteristics, chaotic multiplicity and order, dualism, the opposition of light and dark, of upper and lower, right and left, the union of opposites in a third, the quaternity (square, cross), rotation (circle, sphere), and finally the centering process and a radial arrangement that usually followed some quaternary system. Triadic formations, apart from the *complexio oppositorum* in a third, were relatively rare and formed notable exceptions which could be explained by special con-

110 Cf. "Aims of Modern Psychotherapy" in *The Practice of Psychotherapy, Coll. Works*, Vol. 16, pars. 101ff.; and *Two Essays on Analytical Psychology, Coll. Works*, Vol. 7, pars. 343ff. (Both New York and London, resp. 1954 and 1953.)

ditions.[111] The centering process is, in my experience, the never-to-be-surpassed climax of the whole development,[112] and is characterized as such by the fact that it brings with it the greatest possible therapeutic effect. The distinctive features listed above go to the limits of abstraction, yet at the same time they are the simplest expressions of the formative principles here at work. In actual reality the patterns are infinitely more variegated and far more concrete. Their variety defies description. I can only say that there is probably no motif in any known mythology that does not at some time appear in these configurations. If there was any conscious knowledge of mythological motifs worth mentioning in my patients, it is left far behind by the ingenuities of creative fantasy.

These facts show in an unmistakable manner how fantasies guided by unconscious regulators coincide with the memorials of man's spiritual activity as known to us from tradition and ethnological research. All the abstract features I have mentioned are in a certain sense conscious: everyone can count up to four and knows what a circle is and a square, but, as formative principles, they are unconscious and by the same token their psychological meaning is not conscious either. My most fundamental views and ideas derive from these experiences. First I made the observations, and only then did I hammer out my views. And so it is with the hand that guides the crayon or brush, the foot that executes the dance step, with the eye and the ear, with the word and the thought: a dark impulse is the ultimate arbiter of the pattern, an unconscious a priori precipitates itself into plastic form, and one has no inkling that another person's consciousness is being steered by the same principles at the very point where one feels utterly exposed to the boundless subjective vagaries of chance. Over the whole procedure there seems to reign a dim fore-knowledge not only of the pattern, but of its meaning.[113] Image and meaning are identical; and as the first takes shape, so the latter becomes clear. Actually the pattern needs no interpretation: it portrays its own meaning. There are cases where I can let interpretation go as a therapeutic requirement. Scientific knowledge, of course, is

111 The same applies to the pentadic figures.
112 So far as the development can be ascertained from the objective material.
113 Cf. *Psychology and Alchemy*, pp. 211f.

another matter. Here we have to elicit from the sum total of our experience certain concepts of the greatest possible general validity, which are not given a priori. This particular work entails a translation of the timeless, ever-present operative archetype into the scientific language of the present.

These experiences and reflections lead me to believe that there are certain collective unconscious conditions which act as regulators and stimulators of creative fantasy activity and call forth corresponding formations by availing themselves of the existing conscious material. They behave exactly like the motive forces of dreams, for which reason active imagination, as I have called this method, to some extent takes the place of dreams. The existence of these unconscious regulators—I sometimes refer to them as "dominants"[114] because of their mode of functioning—seemed to me so important that I based upon it my hypothesis of an impersonal collective unconscious. The most remarkable thing about this method, I felt, was that it did not involve a *reductio in primam figuram,* but rather a synthesis—supported by an attitude voluntarily adopted, though for the rest wholly natural— of passive conscious material and unconscious influences, hence a kind of spontaneous amplification of the archetypes. The images are not to be thought of as a reduction of conscious contents to their simplest denominator, as this would be the direct road to the primordial images which I said previously was unimaginable; they only make their appearance in the course of amplification.

On this natural amplification process I also base my method of eliciting the meaning of dreams, for dreams behave in exactly the same way as active imagination, only the support of conscious contents is lacking. To the extent that the archetypes intervene in the shaping of conscious contents by regulating, modifying, and motivating them, they act like the instincts. It is therefore very natural to suppose that these factors are connected with the instincts and to inquire whether the typical situational patterns which these collective form-principles apparently represent are not in the end identical with the instinctual patterns, namely, with the patterns of behavior. I must admit that up to the present I have not got hold of any argument that would finally refute this possibility.

114 Cf. *Two Essays on Analytical Psychology,* par. 151.

Before I pursue my reflections further, I must stress one aspect of the archetypes which will be obvious to anybody who has practical experience of these matters. That is, the archetypes have, when they appear, a distinctly numinous character which can only be described as "spiritual," if "magical" is too strong a word. Consequently this phenomenon is of the utmost significance for the psychology of religion. In its effects it is anything but unambiguous. It can be healing or destructive, but never indifferent, provided of course that it has attained a certain degree of clarity.[115] This aspect deserves the epithet "spiritual" above all else. It not infrequently happens that the archetype appears in the form of a *spirit* in dreams or fantasy products, or even comports itself like a ghost. There is a mystical aura about its numinosity, and it has a corresponding effect upon the emotions. It mobilizes philosophical and religious convictions in the very people who deemed themselves miles above any such fits of weakness. Often it drives with unexampled passion and remorseless logic towards its goal and draws the subject under its spell, from which despite the most desperate resistance he is unable, and finally no longer even willing, to break free, because the experience brings with it a depth and fullness of meaning that was unthinkable before. I fully appreciate the resistance that all rooted convictions are bound to put up against psychological discoveries of this kind. With more foreboding than real knowledge most people feel afraid of the menacing power that lies fettered in each of us, only waiting for the magic word to release it from the spell. This magic word always rhymes with "ism" and works most successfully with those who have the least access to their interior selves and have strayed the furthest from their instinctual roots into the truly chaotic world of *collective consciousness*.

In spite or perhaps because of its affinity with instinct the archetype represents the authentic element of spirit, but a spirit which is not to

---

115 Occasionally it is associated with synchronistic or parapsychic effects. I mean by synchronicity, as I have explained elsewhere, the not uncommonly observed "coincidence" of subjective and objective happenings, which just cannot be explained causally, at least in the present state of our knowledge. On this premise astrology is based and the methods of the *I Ching*. These observations, like the astrological findings, are not generally accepted, though as we know this has never hurt the facts. I mention these special effects solely for the sake of completeness and solely for the benefit of those readers who have had occasion to convince themselves of the reality of parapsychic phenomena.

be identified with the human intellect, since it is the latter's *spiritus rector*. The essential content of all mythologies and all religions and all isms is archetypal. The archetype is spirit or pseudo spirit: what it ultimately proves to be depends on the attitude of the human mind. Archetype and instinct are the most polar opposites imaginable, as can easily be seen when one compares a man who is ruled by his instinctual drives with a man who is seized by the spirit. But, just as between all opposites there obtains so close a bond that no position can be established or even thought of without its corresponding negation, so in this case also *"les extrêmes se touchent."* They belong together as correspondences, which is not to say that the one is derivable from the other, but that they subsist side by side as reflections of the opposition that underlies all psychic energy. Man finds himself simultaneously driven to act and free to reflect. This contrariety in his nature has no moral significance, for instinct is not in itself bad any more than spirit is good. Both can be both. Negative electricity is as good as positive electricity: first and foremost it is electricity. The psychological opposites, too, must be regarded from a scientific standpoint. True opposites are never incommensurables; if they were they could never unite. All contrariety notwithstanding, they do show a constant propensity to union, and the Cusan defined God himself as a *complexio oppositorum*.

Opposites are extreme qualities in any state, by virtue of which that state is perceived to be real, for they form a potential. The psyche is made up of processes whose energy springs from the equilibration of all kinds of opposites. The spirit : instinct antithesis is only one of the commonest formulations, but it has the advantage of reducing the greatest number of the most important and most complex psychic processes to a common denominator. So regarded, psychic processes seem to be balances of energy flowing between spirit and instinct, though the question of whether a process is to be described as spiritual or as instinctual remains shrouded in darkness. Such evaluation or interpretation depends entirely upon the standpoint or state of the conscious mind. A poorly developed consciousness, for instance, which because of massed projections is inordinately impressed by concrete or apparently concrete things and states, will naturally see in the instinctual drives the source of all reality. It remains blissfully unaware of the spirituality of such a philosophical surmise, and is convinced that with this opinion it has established the essential instinctuality of all psychic processes. Conversely, a consciousness that finds itself in opposition to the instincts can, in consequence of the enormous influence then exerted by the archetypes, so subordinate instinct to spirit that the most grotesque "spiritual" complications may arise out of what are undoubtedly biological happenings. Here the instinctuality of the fanaticism needed for such an operation is ignored.

Psychic processes therefore behave like a scale along which consciousness "slides." At one moment it finds itself in the vicinity of instinct, and falls under its influence; at another, it slides along to the other end where spirit predominates and even assimilates the instinctual processes most opposed to it. These counterpositions, so fruitful of illusion, are by no means symptoms of the abnormal; on the contrary they form the twin poles of that psychic one-sidedness which is typical of the normal man of today. Naturally this does not manifest itself only in the sphere of the spirit : instinct antithesis; it assumes many other forms, as I have shown in my *Psychological Types*.

This "sliding" consciousness is thoroughly characteristic of modern man. But the one-sidedness it causes can be removed by what I have called the "realization of the shadow." A less "poetic" and more scientific-looking Greco-Latin neologism could easily have been coined for this operation. In psychology, however, one is to be dissuaded from ventures of this sort, at least when dealing with eminently practical problems. Among these is the "realization of the shadow," the growing awareness of the inferior part of the personality, which should not be twisted into an intellectual activity, for it has far more the meaning of a suffering and a passion that implicate the whole man. The essence of that which has to be realized and assimilated has been expressed so trenchantly and so plastically in poetic language by the word "shadow" that it would be almost presumptuous not to avail oneself of this linguistic heritage. Even the term "inferior part of the personality" is inadequate and misleading, whereas "shadow" presumes nothing that would rigidly fix its content. The "man without a shadow" is statistically the commonest human type, one who imagines he actually is only what he cares to know about himself. Unfortunately neither the so-called religious man nor the man of scientific pretensions forms any exception to this rule.[116]

Confrontation with an archetype or instinct is an *ethical* problem of the first magnitude, the urgency of which is felt only by people who find themselves faced with the need to assimilate the unconscious and integrate their personalities. This only falls to the lot of the man who realizes that he has a neurosis, or that all is not well with his psychic constitution. These are certainly not the majority. The "common man," who is preponderantly a mass man, acts on the principle of realizing nothing, nor does he need to, because for him the only thing that commits mistakes is that vast anonymity conventionally known as the "State" or "Society." But once a man knows that he is, or should be, responsible, he feels responsible also for his psychic constitution, the more so the more clearly he sees what he would have to be in order to become healthier, more stable, and more efficient. Once he is on the way to assimilating the unconscious he can be certain that he will escape no difficulty that is an integral part of his nature. The mass man, on the other hand, has the privilege of being at all times "not guilty" of his social and political catastrophes in which the whole world is engulfed. His final balance is thrown out accordingly; whereas the other at least has the possibility of finding a spiritual point of vantage, a kingdom that "is not of this world."

It would be an unpardonable sin of omission were one to overlook the *feeling value* of the archetype. This is extremely important both theoretically and therapeutically. As a numinous factor the archetype determines the manner of the structuring and the course it will follow, with seeming foreknowledge, or as though it were already in possession of the goal to be circumscribed by the centering process.[117] I would like to make the way in which the archetype functions clear from this simple example: While sojourning in equatorial east Africa, on the southern slopes of Mount Elgon, I found that the natives used to step

116 This was the truth upon which Philip Wylie based his vehement attack on modern civilization, here leveled exclusively at the United States (*Generation of Vipers*, New York, 1942). With few variations, however, it applies equally to Europeans. The development of consciousness in civilized man has its attendant and very serious dangers, which are still apparently not recognized for what they are, and are often misinterpreted in the most disastrous way.
117 Cf. *Psychology and Alchemy*, Part II, for evidence of this.

419

out of their huts at sunrise, hold their hands before their mouths, and spit or blow into them vigorously. Then they lifted their arms and held their hands with the palms toward the sun. I asked them the meaning of what they did, but nobody could give me an explanation. They had always done it like that, they said, and had learnt it from their parents. The medicine man, he would know what it meant. So I asked the medicine man. He knew as little as the others, but assured me that his grandfather had still known. It was just what people did at every sunrise, and at the first phase of the new moon. For these people, as I was able to show, the moment when the sun or the new moon appeared was *"mungu,"* which corresponds to the Melanesian words *"mana"* or *"mulungu"*[117a] and is translated by the missionaries as "God." Actually the word *"athista"* in Elgonyi means sun as well as God, although they deny that the sun is God. Only the moment when it rises is *mungu* or *athista*. Spittle and breath mean soul-substance. Hence they offer their soul to God, but do not know what they are doing and never have known. They do it, motivated by the same preconscious archetype which the ancient Egyptians, on their monuments, also ascribed to the sun-worshiping dog-headed baboon, albeit in full knowledge that this ritual gesture was in honor of God. The behavior of the Elgonyi certainly strikes us as exceedingly primitive, but we forget that the educated Westerner behaves no differently. What the meaning of the Christmas tree might be our forefathers knew even less than ourselves, and it is only quite recently that we have bothered to find out at all.

The archetype is pure, unvitiated nature,[118] and it is nature that causes man to utter words and perform actions whose meaning is unconscious to him, so unconscious that he no longer gives it a thought, even if he were capable of thinking, like the Westerner. A later, more conscious humanity, faced with such meaningful things whose meaning none could declare, hit upon the idea that these must be the last vestiges of a Golden Age, when there were men who knew all things and taught wisdom to the nations. In the degenerate days that followed, these teachings were forgotten and were now only repeated as mindless mechanical gestures. In view of the findings of

117a [*Mulungu* = "spirit, soul, daemonism, magic, prestige": *Two Essays,* par. 108.— ED.]

118 "Nature" here means simply that which is, and always was, given.

modern psychology it cannot be doubted that there are preconscious archetypes which were never conscious and can be established only indirectly through their effects upon the conscious contents. There is in my opinion no tenable argument against the hypothesis that all the psychic functions which today seem conscious to us were once unconscious and yet worked as if they *were* conscious. We could also say that all the psychic phenomena to be found in man were already present in the natural unconscious state. To this it might be objected that it would then be far from clear why there is such a thing as consciousness at all. I would however remind the reader that, as we have already seen, all unconscious functioning has the automatic character of an instinct, and that the instincts are always coming into collision or, because of their compulsiveness, pursuing their courses unaltered by any influence even under conditions that may positively endanger the life of the individual. As against this, consciousness enables him to adapt in an orderly way and to check the instincts, and consequently cannot be dispensed with. Man's capacity for consciousness alone makes him man.

The achievement of a synthesis of conscious and unconscious contents, and the conscious realization of the archetype's effects upon the conscious contents, represents the climax of a concentrated spiritual and psychic effort, in so far as this is undertaken consciously and of set purpose. That is to say, the synthesis can also be prepared in advance and brought to a certain point—James's "bursting point"— unconsciously, whereupon it irrupts into consciousness of its own volition and confronts the latter with the formidable task of assimilating the contents that have burst in upon it, yet without damaging the viability of the two systems, i.e., of ego consciousness on the one hand and the irrupted complex on the other. Classical examples of this process are Paul's conversion and the Trinity vision of Nicholas of Flüe.

By means of "active imagination" we are put in a position of advantage, for we can then make the discovery of the archetype without sinking back into the instinctual sphere, which would only lead to blank unconsciousness or, worse still, to some kind of intellectual substitute for instinct. This means—to employ once more the simile of the spectrum—that the instinctual image is to be located not at the red end but at the violet end of the color band. The dynamism of instinct is lodged as it were in the infrared part of the spectrum, whereas the instinctual image lies in the ultraviolet part. If we remember our color symbolism, then, as I have said, red is not such a bad match for instinct. But for spirit, as might be expected,[119] blue would be a better match than violet. Violet is the "mystic" color, and it certainly reflects the indubitably "mystic" or paradoxical quality of the archetype in a most satisfactory way. Violet is a compound of blue and red, although in the spectrum it is a color in its own right. Now, it is unfortunately rather more than just an edifying thought if we feel bound to emphasize that the archetype is more accurately characterized by violet, for, as well as being an image in its own right, it is at the same time a *dynamism* which makes itself felt in the numinosity and fascinating power of the archetypal image. The realization and assimilation of instinct never take place at the red end, i.e., by absorption into the instinctual sphere, but only through integration of the image which signifies and at the same time evokes the instinct, although in a form quite different from the one we meet on the biological level. When Faust remarks to Wagner: "You are conscious only of the single urge / O may you never learn to know the other!" this is a saying that could equally well be applied to instinct in general. It has two aspects: on the one hand it is experienced as physiological dynamism, while on the other hand its multitudinous forms enter into consciousness as images and groups of images, where they develop numinous effects which offer, or appear to offer, the strictest possible contrast to instinct physiologically regarded. For anyone acquainted with religious phenomenology it is an open secret that although physical and spiritual passion are deadly enemies, they are nevertheless brothers in arms, for which reason it often needs the merest touch to convert the one into the other. Both are real, and together they form a pair of opposites, which is one of the most fruitful sources of psychic energy. There is no point in deriving one from the other in order to give primacy to one of them. Even if we know only one at first, and do not notice the other until much later, that does not prove that the other was not there all the

---

119 This expectation is based on the experience that blue, the color of air and sky, is most readily used for depicting spiritual contents, whereas red, the "warm" color, is used for feelings and emotions.

time. Hot cannot be derived from cold, nor high from low. An opposition either exists in its binary form or it does not exist at all, and a being without opposites is completely unthinkable, as it would be impossible to establish its existence.

Absorption into the instinctual sphere, therefore, does not and cannot lead to conscious realization and assimilation of instinct, because consciousness struggles in a regular panic against being swallowed up in the primitivity and unconsciousness of sheer instinctuality. This fear is the eternal burden of the hero myth and the theme of countless taboos. The closer one comes to the instinct world, the more violent is the urge to shy away from it and to rescue the light of consciousness from the murks of the sultry abyss. Psychologically, however, the archetype as an image of instinct is a spiritual goal toward which the whole nature of man strives; it is the sea to which all rivers wend their way, the prize which the hero wrests from the fight with the dragon.

Because the archetype is a formative principle of instinctual power, its blue is contaminated with red: it appears to be violet, or again, we could interpret the simile as an apocatastasis of instinct raised to a higher frequency, just as we could easily derive instinct from a latent (i.e., transcendent) archetype that manifests itself on a longer wave length.[120] Although it can admittedly be no more than an analogy, I nevertheless feel tempted to recommend this violet image to my reader as an illustrative hint of the archetype's affinity with its own opposite. The creative fantasy of the alchemists sought to express this abstruse secret of nature by means of another, no less visual, symbol: the Uroboros, or tail-eating serpent.

I do not want to drive this simile to death, but, as the reader will understand, one is always delighted, when discussing difficult problems, to find support in a helpful analogy. In addition this simile helps to throw light on a question we have not yet asked ourselves, much less answered, the question regarding the *nature* of the archetype. The archetypal ideas mediated to us by the unconscious should not be confused with the archetype as such. They are very varied structures which all point back to one essentially nonvisual basic form. The

120 Sir James Jeans (*Physics and Philosophy*, Cambridge, 1942, pp. 282f.) points out that the shadows on the wall of Plato's cave are just as real as the invisible figures that throw them and whose presence can only be inferred mathematically.

latter is characterized by certain formal elements and by certain fundamental meanings, although these can be grasped only approximately. The archetype as such is a psychoid factor that belongs, as it were, to the invisible, ultraviolet end of the spectrum. It does not appear, in itself, to be capable of reaching consciousness. I venture this hypothesis because everything archetypal which is perceived by consciousness seems to represent a set of variations on a ground theme. One is most impressed by this fact when one studies the endless variations of the mandala motif. This is a relatively simple ground form whose meaning can be said to be "central." But although it looks like the structure of a center, it is still uncertain whether within that structure the center or the periphery, division or nondivision, is the more accentuated. Since other archetypes give rise to similar doubts, it seems to me probable that the real nature of the archetype is not capable of being made conscious, that it is transcendent, on which account I call it psychoid. Moreover every archetype, as a visual phenomenon, is already conscious and therefore differs to an indeterminable extent from the cause of the vision. As Theodore Lipps has stressed, the nature of the psychic is unconscious. Anything conscious is part of the phenomenal world which—so modern physics teaches— does not supply explanations of the kind that objective reality requires. Objective reality requires a mathematical model, and experience shows that this is built up of invisible and nonvisual—noumenal —factors. Psychology cannot evade the universal validity of this fact, the less so as the observing psyche is already included in any formulation of objective reality. Nor can psychological theory be formulated mathematically, because we have no measuring rod with which to measure psychic quantities. We have to rely solely upon qualities, that is, upon perceptible phenomena. Consequently psychology is incapacitated from making any valid statement about unconscious states, or to put it another way, there is no hope that the validity of any statement about unconscious states or processes will ever be verified scientifically. Whatever we say about the archetypes, they remain visualizations or concretizations which pertain to the field of consciousness. But—we cannot speak about archetypes in any other way. We must, however, constantly bear in mind that what we mean by "archetype" is intrinsically nonvisual and noumenal and has as much to do with the physical continuum as this has with it. Just as mathematical physics, in its psychological aspect, can do no more than establish the presence of an observer without being able to assert anything about the nature of that observer, so, thanks to the phenomenon of synchronicity, psychology can at least indicate a peculiar relation to the space-time continuum, though without being able to make out the least thing concerning its nature. For all we know, psychology might itself be the mathematically indeterminable, qualitative nature of that continuum. Certainly our present knowledge permits us no more than the comparison with two cones whose apices, meeting in an absolutely unextended point, a real zero point, touch and do not touch.

In my previous writings I have always treated archetypal phenomena as psychic, because the material to be expounded or investigated was concerned solely with ideas. The psychoid nature of the archetype, as put forward here, does not contradict these earlier formulations; it only means a further degree of conceptual differentiation, which became inevitable as soon as I saw myself obliged to undertake a more general analysis of the nature of the psyche and to clarify the empirical concepts concerning it, and their relation to one another.

Just as the "psychic infrared," the biological instinctual psyche, gradually passes over into the physiology of the organism and thus merges with its chemical and physical conditions, so the "psychic ultraviolet," the archetype, describes a field which exhibits none of the peculiarities of the physiological and yet, in the last analysis, can no longer be regarded as psychic, although it manifests itself psychically. But physiological processes behave in the same way, without on that account being declared psychic. Although there is no form of existence that is not mediated to us psychically and only psychically, it would hardly do to say that everything is merely psychic. We must apply this argument logically to the archetypes as well. Since their essential being is unconscious to us, and yet they are experienced as spontaneous agencies, there is probably no alternative at present but to describe their nature, in accordance with their chiefest effect, as "spirit," in the sense which I attempted to make plain in my paper "The Phenomenology of the Spirit in Fairy Tales."[121] If so, the position of the archetype would be located beyond the psychic sphere, analogous to the position of physiological instinct, which is immediately rooted in the stuff of the organism and, with its psychoid nature, forms the bridge to matter in general. In archetypal conceptions and instinctual perceptions, spirit and matter confront one another on the psychic plane. Matter as well as spirit appear in the psychic realm as distinctive qualities of conscious contents. The ultimate nature of both is transcendent, that is, noumenal, since the psyche and its contents are the only reality which is given to us *without a medium*.

8. General Considerations and Prospects

The problems of analytical psychology, as I have tried to outline them here, led to conclusions that astonished even me. I fancied I was working along the best scientific lines, establishing facts, observing, classifying, describing causal and functional relations, only to discover in the end that I had involved myself in a net of reflections which extend far beyond natural science and ramify into the fields of philosophy, theology, comparative religion, and the humane sciences in general. This transgression, as inevitable as it was suspect, has caused me no little worry. Quite apart from my personal incompetence in these fields, it seemed to me that my reflections were suspect also in principle, because I am profoundly convinced that the "personal equation" has a telling effect upon the results of psychological observation. The tragic thing is that psychology has no self-consistent mathematics at its disposal, but only a calculus of subjective prejudices. Also, it lacks the immense advantage of an Archimedean point such as physics enjoys. The latter observes the physical world from the psychic standpoint and can translate it into psychic terms. The psyche, on the other hand, observes itself and can only translate the psychic back into the psychic. Were physics in this position, it could do nothing except leave the physical process to its own devices, because in that way it would be most plainly itself. There is no medium for psychology to reflect itself in: it can only portray itself in itself, and describe

121 The first paper in this volume. [It had been given at the previous year's Eranos meeting.—Ed.]

itself. That, logically, is also the principle of my own method: it is, at bottom, a purely experiential process in which hit and miss, interpretation and error, theory and speculation, doctor and patient, form a *symptosis* (σύμπτωσις) or a *symptoma* (σύμπτωμα)—a coming together—and at the same time are symptoms of a certain process or run of events. What I am describing, therefore, is basically no more than an outline of psychic happenings which exhibit a certain statistical frequency. We have not, scientifically speaking, removed ourselves to a plane in any way "above" the psychic process, nor have we translated it into another medium. Physics, on the other hand, is in a position to detonate mathematical formulae—the product of pure psychic activity—and kill seventy-eight thousand persons at one blow.

This literally "devastating" argument is calculated to reduce psychology to silence. But we can, in all modesty, point out that mathematical thinking is also a psychic function, thanks to which matter can be organized in such a way as to burst asunder the mighty forces that bind the atoms together—which it would never occur to them to do in the natural course of things, at least not upon this earth. The psyche is a disturber of the natural laws of the cosmos, and should we ever succeed in doing something to Mars with the aid of atomic fission, this too will have been brought to pass by the psyche.

The psyche is the world's pivot: not only is it the one great condition for the existence of a world at all, it is also an intervention in the existing natural order, and no one can say with certainty where this intervention will finally end. It is hardly necessary to stress the dignity of the soul as an object of natural science. With all the more urgency, then, we must emphasize that the smallest alteration in the psychic factor, if it be an alteration of principle, is of the utmost significance as regards our knowledge of the world and the picture we make of it. The integration of unconscious contents into consciousness, which is the main endeavor of analytical psychology, is just such an alteration of principle, in that it does away with the sovereignty of the subjective ego and of collective consciousness and confronts the latter with collective unconscious contents. Accordingly the ego seems to be dependent on two factors: firstly, the conditions of collective, i.e., the social, consciousness, and secondly the collective unconscious dominants or archetypes. The latter fall phenomenologically into two categories:

instinctual and archetypal. The first includes the natural impulses, the second the dominants that emerge into consciousness as universal ideas. Between the contents of collective consciousness, which purport to be generally accepted truths, and those of the collective unconscious there is so pronounced a contrast that the latter are rejected as totally irrational, not to say meaningless, and are most unjustifiably excluded from the scientific purview as though they did not exist. However, psychic phenomena of this kind exist with a vengeance, and if they appear nonsensical to us, that only proves that we do not understand them. Once their existence is recognized they can no longer be banished from our world picture, especially as the prevailing conscious *Weltanschauung* proves to be incapable of grasping the phenomena in question. A conscientious study of these phenomena quickly reveals their uncommon significance, and we can hardly avoid the conclusion that between collective consciousness and the collective unconscious there is an almost unbridgeable gulf over which the subject finds himself suspended.

As a rule collective consciousness wins hands down with its "reasonable" generalities that cause the average intelligence no difficulty whatever. It still believes in the necessary connection of cause and effect and has scarcely taken note of the fact that causality has become relative. The shortest distance between two points is still, for it, a straight line, although physics has to reckon with innumerable shortest distances, which strikes the educated Philistine of today as exquisitely absurd. Nevertheless the impressive explosion at Hiroshima has induced an awestruck respect for even the most abstruse alembications of modern physics. The explosion which we recently had occasion to witness in Europe, though far more terrible in its repercussions, was recognized as an unmitigated psychic disaster only by the few. Rather than do this, people prefer the most preposterous political and economic theories, which are about as useful as explaining the Hiroshima explosion as the chance hit of a large meteorite.

If the subjective consciousness prefers the ideas and opinions of collective consciousness and identifies with them, then the contents of the collective unconscious are repressed. The repression has typical consequences: the energy charge of the repressed contents adds itself to that of the repressing factor, whose operational significance is

428

increased accordingly. The higher its charge mounts, the more the repressive attitude acquires a fanatical character and the nearer it comes to conversion into its opposite, i.e., an enantiodromia. And the more highly charged the collective consciousness, the more the ego forfeits its practical importance. It is as it were absorbed by the opinions and tendencies of collective consciousness, and the result of that is the mass man, the ever-ready victim of some wretched "ism." The ego keeps its integrity only if it does not identify with one of the opposites, and if it understands how to hold the balance between them. This is only possible if it remains conscious of both at once. However, the necessary insight is made exceedingly difficult not by one's social and political leaders alone, but also by one's religious mentors. They all want decision in favor of one thing, and therefore the utter identification of the individual with a necessarily one-sided "truth." Even if it were a question of some great truth, identification with it would still be a catastrophe, as it arrests all further spiritual development. Instead of knowledge one then has only belief, and sometimes that is more convenient and therefore more attractive.

If on the other hand the content of the collective unconscious is realized, if the existence and efficacy of archetypal ideas are made known, then a violent conflict usually breaks out between what Fechner has called the "daytime and the nighttime view." Medieval man (and modern man too in so far as he has kept the attitude of the past) lived fully conscious of the discord between worldliness, which was subject to the *princeps huius mundi* (St. John 12:31 and 16:11[122]), and the will of God. For centuries this contradiction was demonstrated before his very eyes by the struggle between imperial and papal power. On the moral plane the conflict swelled to the everlasting cosmic tug of war between good and evil in which man was implicated on account of original sin. This medieval man had not yet fallen such a helpless victim to worldliness as the contemporary mass man, for, to offset the notorious and so to speak tangible powers of this world, he still acknowledged the equally influential metaphysical potencies which de-

---

122 Although both passages hint that the devil was cast out during the lifetime of Jesus, in the Apocalypse the business of rendering him harmless is deferred until Doomsday (Rev. 20:2ff.).

manded to be taken into account. Although in one respect he was politically and socially unfree and without rights—e.g., as a serf—and also found himself in the extremely disagreeable situation of being tyrannized over by black superstition, he was at least biologically nearer to that unconscious wholeness which primitive man enjoys in even larger measure, and the wild animal possesses to perfection. Looked at from the standpoint of modern consciousness, the position of medieval man seems as deplorable as it is in need of improvement. But the much needed broadening of the mind by science has only replaced medieval one-sidedness—namely that age-old unconsciousness which once predominated and has gradually become defunctive—by a new one-sidedness, the overvaluation of "scientifically" attested views. These each and all relate to knowledge of the external object and in a chronically one-sided way, so that nowadays the backwardness of psychic development in general and of self-knowledge in particular has become one of the most pressing contemporary problems. As a result of the prevailing one-sidedness and in spite of the terrifying optical demonstration of an unconscious that has become alienated from the conscious, there are still vast numbers of people who are the blind and helpless victims of these conflicts, and who apply their scientific scrupulosity only to external objects, never to their own psychic condition. Yet the psychic facts are as much in need of objective scrutiny and acknowledgment. There are objective psychic factors which are every bit as important as radios and automobiles. Ultimately everything (particularly in the case of the atom bomb) depends on the uses to which these factors are put, and that is always conditioned by one's state of mind. The current "isms" are the most serious threat in this respect, because they are nothing but dangerous identifications of the subjective with the collective consciousness. Such an identity infallibly produces a mass psyche with its irresistible urge to catastrophe. Subjective consciousness must, in order to escape this doom, avoid identification with collective consciousness by recognizing its shadow as well as the existence and the importance of the archetypes. These latter are an effective defense against the brute force of collective consciousness and the mass psyche that goes with it. Talking of effectiveness, the religious outlook of medieval man corresponds roughly to the attitude induced in the ego by the integration of unconscious contents, with the difference that in the latter case suggestibility to environmental influences and unconsciousness are replaced by scientific objectivity and self-consciousness. But so far as religion, for the contemporary consciousness, still means, if anything, a creed, and hence a collectively accepted system of religious statements neatly codified as potted dogmatic precepts, it has more affinities with collective consciousness even though its symbols express the once operative archetypes. So long as the communal consciousness presided over by the Church is objectively present, the psyche, as said, continues to enjoy a certain equilibrium. At all events it constitutes a sufficiently effective defense against inflation of the ego. But once Mother Church and her motherly Eros fall into abeyance, the individual is at the mercy of any passing collectivism and the attendant mass psyche. He succumbs to social or national inflation, and the tragedy is that he does so with the same psychic attitude which had once bound him to a church.

But if he is independent enough to recognize the bigotedness of the social "ism," he may then be threatened with subjective inflation, for usually he is not capable of seeing that religious ideas do not, in psychological reality, rest solely upon tradition and faith, but originate with the archetypes, the "careful consideration" of which—*religere!*—constitutes the essence of religion. The archetypes are continuously present and active; as such they need no believing in, but only an intuition of their meaning and a certain sapient awe, a δεισιδαιμονία, which never loses sight of their import. A consciousness sharpened by experience knows the catastrophic consequences that disregard of this entails for the individual as well as for society. Just as the archetype is partly a spiritual factor, and partly like a hidden meaning immanent in the instincts, so the spirit, as I have shown in another Eranos lecture,[123] is two-faced and paradoxical: a great help and an equally great danger.[124] It seems as if man were destined to play a decisive role in solving this uncertainty, this doubt which arose eons before the birth of mankind, and to solve it moreover by virtue of his consciousness, which once started up like a light in the murk of the primeval world.

123 See supra, note 121.
124 Aptly put in the logion cited by Origen (*Homiliae in Jeremiam*, XX, 3): "He who is near unto me is near unto the fire. He who is far from me is far from the kingdom." This "unclaimed saying of the Master" refers to Isaiah 33:14.

Nowhere do we know for sure about these matters, but least of all where "isms" flourish, for they are only a sophisticated substitute for the lost link with psychic reality. The massing of the soul that infallibly results destroys the meaning of the individual and of culture generally.

From this it is clear that the psyche not only disturbs the natural order but, if it loses its balance, actually destroys its own creation. Therefore the careful consideration of psychic factors is of importance in restoring not merely the individual's balance, but society's as well, otherwise the destructive tendencies gain the upper hand. In the same way that the atom bomb is an unparalleled means of physical mass destruction, so the misguided development of the soul must lead to psychic mass destruction. The present situation is so sinister that one cannot suppress the suspicion that the Creator is planning another deluge that will finally exterminate the existing race of men. But if anyone imagines that a healthy belief in the existence of archetypes can be inculcated from outside, he is as simple as the people who want to outlaw war or the atom bomb. Such measures remind one of the bishop who excommunicated the cockchafers for their unseemly proliferation. Change of consciousness begins at home; it is a secular matter that depends entirely on how far the psyche's capacity for development extends. All we know at present is that there are single individuals who are capable of developing. How great their total number is we do not know, just as we do not know what the suggestive power of an extended consciousness may be, or what influence it may have upon the world at large. Effects of this kind never depend on the reasonableness of an idea, but far more on the question (which can only be answered *ex effectu*): is the time ripe for change, or not?

*

As I have said, the psychology of complex phenomena finds itself in an uncomfortable situation compared with the other natural sciences because it lacks a base outside its object. It can only translate itself back into its own language, or fashion itself in its own image. The more it extends its field of research and the more complicated its objects become, the more it feels the lack of a point which is distinct from those objects. And once the complexity has reached that of empirical man, his psychology inevitably merges with the psychic process itself. It can no longer be distinguished from the latter, and so turns into it. But the effect of this is that the process attains to consciousness. In this way psychology actualizes the unconscious urge to consciousness. It is in fact the coming to consciousness of the psychic process, but it is not, in the deeper sense, an explanation of this process, for no explanation of the psychic can be anything other than the living process of the psyche itself. Psychology is doomed to cancel itself out as a science and therein precisely it reaches its scientific goal. Every other science has so to speak an outside; not so psychology, whose object is the inside of all science.

Psychology therefore culminates of necessity in a developmental process which is peculiar to the psyche and consists in integrating the unconscious contents into consciousness. This means that the psychic human being becomes a whole, and becoming whole has remarkable effects on ego consciousness which are extremely difficult to describe. I doubt my ability to give a proper account of the change that comes over the subject under the influence of the individuation process; it is a relatively rare occurrence which is experienced only by those who have gone through the wearisome but, if the unconscious is to be integrated, indispensable business of coming to terms with the unconscious components of the personality. Once these unconscious components are made conscious, it results not only in their assimilation to the already existing ego personality, but in a transformation of the latter. The main difficulty is to describe the manner of this transformation. Generally speaking the ego is a hard-and-fast complex which, because tied to consciousness and its continuity, cannot easily be altered, and should not be altered unless one wants to bring on pathological disturbances. The closest analogies to an alteration of the ego are to be found in the field of psychopathology, where we meet not only with neurotic dissociations but also with the schizophrenic fragmentation, or even dissolution, of the ego. In this field, too, we can observe pathological attempts at integration—if such an expression be permitted. These consist in more or less violent irruptions of unconscious contents into consciousness, the ego proving itself incapable of assimilating the intruders. But if the structure of the ego complex is strong enough to withstand their assault without having its structure

433

fatally dislocated, then assimilation can take place. In that event there is an alteration of the ego as well as of the unconscious contents. Although it is able to preserve its structure, the ego is ousted from its central and dominating position and thus finds itself in the role of a passive observer who lacks the power to assert his will under all circumstances, not so much because it has been weakened in any way, as because certain considerations give it pause. That is, the ego cannot help discovering that the afflux of unconscious contents has vitalized the personality, enriched it and created a figure that somehow dwarfs the ego in scope and intensity. This experience paralyzes an over-egocentric will and convinces the ego that in spite of all difficulties it is better to be taken down a peg than to get involved in a hopeless struggle in which one is invariably handed the dirty end of the stick. In this way the will, as disposable energy, gradually subordinates itself to the stronger factor, namely to the new totality figure I call the *self*. Naturally in these circumstances there is the greatest temptation simply to follow the power instinct and to identify the ego with the self outright, in order to keep up the illusion of the ego's mastery. In other cases the ego proves too weak to offer the necessary resistance to the influx of unconscious contents and is thereupon assimilated by the unconscious, which produces a blurring or darkening of ego consciousness and its identification with a preconscious wholeness. Both these developments make the realization of the self on the one hand, and the existence of empirical ego consciousness on the other, impossible. They amount therefore to pathological effects. The psychic phenomena recently observable in Germany fall into this category. It is abundantly clear that such an *abaissement du niveau mental,* i.e., the overpowering of the ego by unconscious contents and the consequent identification with a preconscious wholeness, possesses a prodigious psychic virulence, or power of contagion, and is capable of the most disastrous effects. Developments of this kind should therefore be watched very carefully and require the closest control. I would recommend anyone who feels himself threatened by such tendencies to hang a picture of St. Christopher on the wall and to meditate upon it. For the self has a functional meaning only when it can act compensatorily to ego consciousness. If the ego is dissolved in identification with the self, it gives rise to a sort of nebulous superman with a puffed up ego and a deflated self. Such a personage, however saviorlike or baleful his demeanor, lacks the *scintilla,* the soul spark, the little wisp of divine light that never burns more brightly than when it has to struggle against the invading darkness. What would the rainbow be were it not limned against the lowering cloud?

This simile is intended to remind the reader that pathological analogies of the individuation process are not the only ones. There are spiritual monuments of quite another kind, and they are positive illustrations of our process. Above all I would mention the *koans* of Zen Buddhism, those sublime paradoxes that light up, as with a flash of lightning, the inscrutable interrelations between ego and self. In very different language St. John of the Cross has made the same problem more readily accessible to the Westerner in his account of the "dark night of the soul." That we find it needful to draw analogies from psychopathology and from Eastern and Western mysticism is only to be expected: the individuation process is, psychically, a borderline phenomenon which requires special conditions in order to become conscious. Perhaps it is the first step along a path of development to be trodden by the men of the future—a path which for the time being has taken a pathological turn and landed Europe in catastrophe.

To one familiar with our psychology, it may seem a waste of time to keep harping on the old established difference between becoming conscious and the coming-to-be of the self (individuation). But again and again I note that the individuation process is confused with becoming conscious of the ego and that the ego is in consequence identified with the self, which naturally produces a hopeless conceptual muddle. Individuation is then nothing but egocenteredness and autoeroticism. But the self comprises infinitely more than a mere ego, as the symbolism has shown from of old. It is as much one's self, and the other selves, as the ego. Individuation does not shut one out from the world, but gathers the world to oneself.

With this I would like to bring my exposition to an end. I have tried to sketch out the development and basic problems of a modern psychology and to communicate the quintessence, the very spirit, of this psychology. In view of the unusual difficulties of my theme the reader

435

may pardon the undue demands I have made upon his goodwill and attention. Fundamental discussions are among the things that mold a science into shape, but they are seldom entertaining.

Supplement

As the points of view that have to be considered in elucidating the unconscious are often misunderstood, I would like, in connection with the foregoing discussions of principle, to examine at least two of the main prejudices somewhat more closely.

What above all stultifies understanding is the arrant assumption that "archetype" means an inborn idea. No biologist would ever dream of assuming that each individual acquires his general mode of behavior afresh each time. It is much more probable that the young weaverbird builds his characteristic nest because he is a weaverbird and not a rabbit. Similarly, it is more probable that man is born with a specifically human mode of behavior and not with that of a hippopotamus or with none at all. Integral to his characteristic behavior is his psychic phenomenology, which differs from that of a bird or quadruped. Archetypes are typical forms of behavior which, once they become conscious, naturally present themselves as ideas and images, like everything else that becomes a content of consciousness. Because it is a question of characteristically human modes, it is hardly to be wondered at that we can find psychic forms in the individual which occur not only at the antipodes but also in other epochs with which archaeology provides the only link.

Now if we wish to prove that a certain psychic form is not a unique, but a typical occurrence, this can only be done if I myself testify that, having taken the necessary precautions, I have observed the same thing in different individuals. Then other observers, too, must confirm that they have made the same or similar observations. Finally we have to establish that the same or similar phenomena can be shown to occur in the folklore of other peoples and races and in the texts that have come down to us from earlier centuries and epochs. My method and whole outlook therefore begin with individual psychic facts which not I alone have established, but other observers as well. The material brought forward—folkloristic, mythological, or historical—serves in

436

the first place to demonstrate the uniformity of psychic events in time and space. But, since the meaning and substance of the typical individual forms are of the utmost importance in practice, and knowledge of them plays a considerable role in each individual case, it is inevitable that the mythologem and its content will also be drawn into the limelight. This is not to say that the purpose of the investigation is to interpret the mythologem. But precisely in this connection a widespread prejudice reigns that the psychology of unconscious processes is a sort of *philosophy* designed to explain mythologems. This unfortunately rather common prejudice assiduously overlooks the crucial point, namely, that our psychology starts with observable facts and not with philosophical speculations. If for instance we study the mandala structures that are always cropping up in dreams and fantasies, ill-considered criticism might raise, and indeed has raised, the objection that we are reading Indian or Chinese philosophy into the psyche. But in reality all we have done is to compare individual psychic occurrences with obviously related collective phenomena. The introspective trend of Eastern philosophy has brought to light material which all introspective attitudes bring to light all over the world, at all times and places. The great snag so far as the critic is concerned is that he has no personal experience of the facts in question, any more than he has of the state of mind of a lama engaged in "constructing" a mandala. These two prejudices render any access to modern psychology impossible for not a few heads with scientific pretensions. There are in addition many other stumbling blocks that cannot be overcome by reason. We shall therefore refrain from discussing them.

Inability to understand, or the ignorance of the public, cannot however prevent the scientist from employing certain calculations of probability, of whose treacherous nature he is sufficiently well informed. We are fully aware that we have no more knowledge of the various states and processes of the unconscious *an sich* than the physicist has of the process underlying physical phenomena. Of what lies beyond the phenomenal world we can have absolutely no idea, for there is no idea that could have any other source than the phenomenal world. If we are to engage in fundamental calculations about the nature of the psychic, we need an Archimedean point which alone

437

makes an opinion possible. This can only be the nonpsychic, for, as a living phenomenon, the psychic lies embedded in something that appears to be of a nonpsychic nature. Although we perceive the latter as a psychic datum only, there are sufficient reasons for believing in its objective reality. This reality, so far as it lies outside our body's limits, is mediated to us chiefly by particles of light impinging on the retina of the eye. The organization of these particles produces a picture of the phenomenal world which depends essentially upon the constitution of the apperceiving psyche on the one hand, and upon that of the light medium on the other. The apperceiving consciousness has proved capable of a high degree of development, and constructs instruments with the help of which our range of seeing and hearing has been extended by many octaves. Consequently the postulated reality of the phenomenal world as well as the subjective world of consciousness have undergone an unparalleled expansion. The existence of this remarkable correlation between consciousness and the phenomenal world, between subjective perception and objectively real processes, i.e., their energic effects, requires no further proof.

As the phenomenal world is an aggregate of processes of atomic magnitude, it is naturally of the greatest importance to find out whether, and if so how, the photons (shall we say) enable us to gain a definite knowledge of the reality underlying the mediative energy processes. Experience has shown that light and matter both behave like separate particles and also like waves. This paradoxical conclusion obliged us to abandon, on the plane of atomic magnitudes, a causal description of nature in the ordinary space-time system, and in its place to set up invisible fields of probability in multidimensional spaces, which do in fact represent the state of our knowledge at present. Basic to this abstract scheme of explanation is a conception of reality that takes account of the uncontrollable effects the observer has upon the system observed, the result being that reality forfeits something of its objective character and that a subjective element attaches to the physicist's picture of the world.[125]

The application of statistical laws to processes of atomic magnitude in physics has a noteworthy correspondence in psychology, so far as psychology investigates the bases of consciousness by pursuing the

125 I owe this formulation to the kind help of Professor W. Pauli.

conscious processes until they lose themselves in darkness and unintelligibility, and nothing more can be seen but effects which have an *organizing* influence on the contents of consciousness.[126] Investigation of these effects yields the singular fact that they proceed from an unconscious, i.e., objective, reality which behaves at the same time like a subjective one—in other words, like a consciousness. Hence the reality underlying the unconscious effects includes the observing subject and is therefore constituted in a way that we cannot conceive. It is, at one and the same time, absolute subjectivity and universal truth, for in principle it can be shown to be present everywhere, which certainly cannot be said of conscious contents of a personalistic nature. The elusiveness, capriciousness, haziness, and uniqueness that the lay mind always associates with the idea of the psyche applies only to consciousness, and not to the absolute unconscious. The qualitatively rather than quantitatively definable units with which the unconscious works, namely the archetypes, therefore have a nature that *cannot with certainty be designated as psychic.*

126 It may interest the reader to hear the opinion of a physicist on this point. Professor Pauli, who was good enough to glance through the MS. of this supplement, writes: "As a matter of fact the physicist would expect a psychological correspondence at this point, because the epistemological situation with regard to the concepts 'conscious' and 'unconscious' seems to offer a pretty close analogy to the undermentioned 'complementarity' situation in physics. On the one hand the unconscious can only be inferred indirectly from its (organizing) effects on conscious contents. On the other hand every 'observation of the unconscious,' i.e., every conscious realization of unconscious contents, has an uncontrollable reactive effect on these same contents (which as we know precludes in principle the possibility of 'exhausting' the unconscious by making it conscious). Thus the physicist will conclude *per analogiam* that this uncontrollable reactive effect of the observing subject on the unconscious limits the objective character of the latter's reality and lends it at the same time a certain subjectivity. Although the *position* of the 'cut' between conscious and unconscious is (at least up to a point) left to the free choice of the 'psychological experimenter,' the *existence* of this 'cut' remains an unavoidable necessity. Accordingly, from the standpoint of the psychologist, the 'observed system' would consist not of physical objects only, but would also include the unconscious, while consciousness would be assigned the role of 'observing medium.' It is undeniable that the development of 'microphysics' has brought the way in which nature is described in this science very much closer to that of the newer psychology: but whereas the former, on account of the basic 'complementarity' situation, is faced with the impossibility of eliminating the effects of the observer by determinable correctives, and has therefore to abandon in principle any objective understanding of physical phenomena, the latter can supplement the purely subjective psychology of consciousness by postulating the existence of an unconscious that possesses a large measure of objective reality."

Although I have been led by purely psychological considerations to doubt the exclusively psychic nature of the archetypes, psychology sees itself obliged to revise its "only psychic" assumptions in the light of the physical findings also. Physics has demonstrated, as plainly as could be wished, that in the realm of atomic magnitudes objective reality presupposes an observer, and that only on this condition is a satisfactory scheme of explanation possible. This means that a subjective element attaches to the physicist's world picture, and secondly that a connection necessarily exists between the psyche to be explained and the objective space-time continuum. Since the physical continuum is inconceivable it follows that we can form no picture of its psychic aspect, which also necessarily exists. Nevertheless, the relative or partial identity of psyche and physical continuum is of the greatest importance theoretically, because it brings with it a tremendous simplification by bridging over the seeming incommensurability between the physical world and the psychic, not of course in any concrete way, but from the physical side by means of mathematical equations, and from the psychological side by means of empirically derived postulates—archetypes—whose content, if any, cannot be represented to the mind. Archetypes, so far as we can observe and experience them at all, only manifest themselves through their ability to organize images and ideas, and this is always an unconscious process which cannot be detected until afterwards. By assimilating ideational material whose provenance in the phenomenal world is not to be contested, they become visible and *psychic*. Therefore they are recognized at first only as psychic quantities and are conceived as such, with the same right with which we base the physical phenomena of immediate perception on Euclidean space. Only when it comes to explaining psychic phenomena of a minimal degree of clarity are we driven to assume that archetypes must have a nonpsychic aspect. Grounds for such a conclusion are supplied by the phenomena of synchronicity,[127] which are

---

127 "Synchronicity," a term for which I am to blame, is an unsatisfactory expression in so far as it only takes account of time phenomena. The reason for this is that in practice the phenomena of psychic simultaneity are far more common than "spatial clairvoyance," as it is sometimes called. In my view the findings of the series of experiments conducted by Dr. J. B. Rhine (*New Frontiers of the Mind*, New York, 1937) rest more upon synchronicity than upon extrasensory perception in space. It is still an open question whether the predominance of the time factor is connected in any deeper way with the marked nonspatiality of the psyche.

associated with the activity of unconscious operators and have hitherto been regarded, or repudiated, as "telepathy," etc.[128] Skepticism should, however, be levelled only at incorrect theories and not at facts which exist in their own right. No unbiased observer can deny them. Resistance to the recognition of such facts rests principally on the repugnance people feel for an allegedly supernatural faculty tacked on to the psyche, like "clairvoyance." The very diverse and confusing aspects of these phenomena are, so far as I can see at present, completely explicable on the assumption of a psychically relative space-time continuum, or rather by postulating an observer in this continuum. As soon as a psychic content crosses the threshold of consciousness, the synchronistic marginal phenomena disappear,[129] time and space resume their accustomed sway, and consciousness is once more isolated in its subjectivity. We have here one of those instances which can best be understood in terms of the physicist's idea of "complementarity." When an unconscious content passes over into consciousness its synchronistic manifestation ceases; conversely, synchronistic phenomena can be evoked by putting the subject into an unconscious state (trance). The same relationship of complementarity can be observed just as easily in all those extremely common medical cases in which certain clinical symptoms disappear when the corresponding unconscious contents are made conscious. We also know that a number of psychosomatic phenomena which are otherwise outside the control of the will can be induced by hypnosis, that is, by this same restriction of consciousness. Professor Pauli formulates the physical side of the complementarity relationship here expressed, as follows: "It rests with the free choice of the experimenter (or observer) to decide . . . which insights he will gain and which he will lose; or, to put it in popular language, whether he will measure A and ruin B or ruin A and measure B. It does *not* rest with him, however, to gain only insights and not lose any."[130] This is particularly true of the relation between the physical standpoint and the psychological. Physics determines quantities and their relation to one another; psychology

---

128 The physicist Pascual Jordan ("Positivistische Bemerkungen über die parapsychischen Erscheinungen," *Zentralblatt für Psychotherapie* (Leipzig), IX (1936), 14ff.) has already used the idea of relative space to explain telepathic phenomena.

129 The extraordinary spatial orientation exhibited by certain birds and fishes corresponds to an essentially unconscious state.

130 Communicated by letter.

determines qualities without being able to measure quantities. Despite that, both sciences arrive at ideas which come tellingly close to one another. The parallelism of psychological and physical explanations has already been pointed out by C. A. Meier in his essay "Moderne Physik—Moderne Psychologie."[131] He says: "Both sciences have, in the course of many years of independent work, amassed observations and systems of thought to match them. Both sciences have come up against certain barriers which . . . display similar basic characteristics. The object to be investigated, and the human investigator with his organs of sense and knowledge and their extensions (measuring instruments and procedures), are indissolubly bound together. That is complementarity in physics as well as in psychology." Between physics and psychology there is in fact "a genuine and authentic relationship of complementarity."

Once we can rid ourselves of the highly unscientific pretense that it is merely a question of chance coincidence, we shall see that synchronistic phenomena are not unusual occurrences at all, but are relatively common, not to say banal. This fact is in entire agreement with Rhine's "probability-exceeding" results. The psyche is not a chaos made up of random whims and accidents, but is an objective reality to which the investigator can gain access by the methods of natural science. There are indications that psychic processes stand in some sort of energy relation to the physiological substrate. These processes, so far as they are objective events, can hardly be interpreted as anything but energy processes,[132] or to put it another way: in spite of the nonmeasurability of psychic processes, the perceptible changes effected by the psyche cannot possibly be understood except as a phenomenon of energy. This places the psychologist in a situation which is highly repugnant to the physicist: the psychologist also talks of energy although he has nothing measurable to manipulate, besides which the concept of energy is a strictly defined mathematical quantity which cannot be applied as such to anything psychic. The formula for kinetic energy, $E = \dfrac{mv^2}{2}$, contains the factors m (mass) and v

---

131 *Die kulturelle Bedeutung der komplexen Psychologie*, p. 362.

132 By this I only mean that psychic phenomena have a specific energy-aspect by virtue of which they can be described as "phenomena." I do not mean that the energy-aspect embraces or explains the whole of the psyche.

(velocity), and these would appear to be incommensurable with the nature of the empirical psyche. If psychology nevertheless insists on employing its own concept of energy for the purpose of expressing the activity (ἐνέργεια) of the psyche, it is not of course being used as a mathematical formula, but only as its analogy. But note: this analogy is itself an older intuitive idea from which the concept of physical energy originally developed. The latter rests on earlier applications of an ἐνέργεια not mathematically defined, which can be traced back to the primitive or archaic idea of the "extraordinarily potent." This mana concept is not confined to Melanesia, but can also be found in Indonesia and on the east coast of Africa;[133] and it still echoes in the Latin *numen* and, more faintly, in *genius* (e.g., *genius loci*). The use of the term *libido* in the newer medical psychology has surprising affinities with the primitive mana (one has only to think of Freud's "libido investment").[134] This archetypal idea is therefore far from being only primitive, but differs from the physicist's conception of energy by the fact that it is essentially qualitative and not quantitative. In psychology the exact measurement of quantities is replaced by an approximate determination of intensities, for which purpose, in strictest contrast to physics, we enlist the function of *feeling* (valuation). The latter takes the place, in psychology, of concrete measurement in physics (which is co-ordinated with sensation). The psychic intensities and their graduated differences point to quantitative processes which are inaccessible to direct observation and measurement. While psychological data are essentially qualitative, they also have a sort of latent physical energy, since psychic phenomena exhibit a certain quantitative aspect. Could these quantities be measured the psyche would be bound to appear as having motion in space, something to which the energy formula would be applicable. Therefore, since mass and energy are of the same nature, mass and velocity must be adequate concepts for characterizing the psyche so far as it has any detectable effects in space: in other words, it must have an aspect under which it would appear as mass in motion. If one is unwilling to postulate a prestabilized harmony of physical and

133 [Cf. the discussion of *mungu*, p. 420 supra.—ED.]
134 Cf. my "On Psychical Energy," *Contributions to Analytical Psychology* (New York and London), 1928.

443

psychic events, then they can only be in a state of interaction. But the latter hypothesis requires a psyche that touches matter at some point, and, conversely, a matter with a latent psyche, a postulate not so very far removed from certain formulations of modern physics (Eddington, Jeans, and others). In this connection I would remind the reader of the existence of parapsychic phenomena whose reality value can only be appreciated by those who have had occasion to satisfy themselves by personal observation.

If these reflections are justified, they must have weighty consequences with regard to the nature of the psyche, since as an objective fact it would then be intimately connected not only with physiological and biological phenomena but with physical events too—and, so it would appear, most intimately of all with those that pertain to the realm of atomic physics. As my remarks may have made clear, we are concerned first and foremost to establish certain analogies, and no more than that; the existence of such analogies does not entitle one to conclude that the connection is already proven. One must, in the present state of our physical and psychological knowledge, be content with the mere resemblance to one another of certain basic reflections. The existing analogies, however, are significant enough in themselves to warrant the prominence we have given them.

APPENDICES

Biographical Notes

ERNESTO BUONAIUTI, Ph.D., Theol.D. Born 1880, Rome; died 1946. Professor of the history of early Christianity at the University of Rome from 1915 to 1931, when his appointment ended owing to his refusal to take the Fascist oath of allegiance. After the second World War, in 1945, the Italian Government restored him to his chair, but he had not actually resumed teaching when he died in 1946. A friend of Buonaiuti's has written: "A leading spirit of the Modernist movement, Buonaiuti advocated a return to the primal social values of Christianity implied in the brotherhood of man, values which in his opinion had been obscured by the rigid doctrinalism of an age-old hierarchy. Despite repeated official condemnation of his views, he never in his heart departed from the Catholic Church." He was under the ban of excommunication during the last two decades of his life. Among nearly a hundred publications, the following are chosen for mention here: *Lo gnosticismo* (Rome, 1907); *Il cristianesimo medioevale* (Citta di Castello, 1914); *Le Modernisme catholique* (Paris, 1937); *Il cristianesimo nell' Africa romana* (Bari, 1928); *Storia del cristianesimo* (3 vols., Milan, 1942–43); *La fede dei nostri Padri* (Modena, 1944); *I maestri della tradizione mediterranea* (Rome, 1945); *Pellegrino di Roma* (autobiography; Rome, 1945); *Lutero e la Riforma in Germania* (2nd edn., Rome, 1945). Buonaiuti lectured at eight Eranos meetings, the last in 1940.

FRIEDRICH DESSAUER, Ph.D., M.D. (hon., Frankfort on the Main), D.D. (hon., Würzburg). Born 1881, Aschaffenburg. Since 1937, professor of experimental physics and director of the Institute of Physics, University of Fribourg (Switzerland). 1921–33, professor and director of the Institute of Biophysics, University of Frankfort. In 1924, he became a member of the Reichstag; he actively opposed the rise of National Socialism and was persecuted by the Hitler regime. 1934–37, professor of radiology and experimental physics at the University of Istanbul. Dr. Dessauer is a pioneer of deep x-ray therapy. Among some four hundred publications, the following are of special interest to the reader in philosophy and religion: *W. C. Röntgen* (Olten, 1945); *Weltfahrt der Erkenntnis* (biography of Newton; Zurich, 1945); *Der Fall*

Galilei und wir (Frankfort, 1943); *Religion im Lichte der Naturwissenschaft* (Frankfort, 3rd edn., 1952); *Am Rande der Dinge* (Frankfort, 2nd edn., 1952); *Die Teleologie in der Natur* (Basel, 1949); *Atomenergie und Atombombe* (Zurich, 1945); with X. von Hornstein, *Seele im Bannkreis der Technik* (Olten, 1945). Dr. Dessauer lectured at the Eranos meetings of 1946 and 1947.

C. G. JUNG, M.D., Litt.D. (hon., Clark), Sc.D. (hon., Harvard), Litt.D. (hon., Benares), Litt.D. (hon., Allahabad), Sc.D. (hon., Oxford), Sc.D. (hon., Calcutta). Born 1875, Kesswil, Canton Thurgau, Switzerland. 1905–1909, privatdocent, University of Zurich. 1907–13, associated with Bleuler and Freud in experimental research. 1933–42, taught at the Federal Polytechnic Institute, Zurich. He was called to the University of Basel in 1944 to occupy the chair of medical psychology, established for him, but was forced to resign owing to illness after only a year. His principal works, among more than 150 publications, include (in English translation): *Psychology of the Unconscious* (New York, 1916; now superseded by a revision, *Symbols of Transformation,* tr. in preparation); *Psychological Types* (London and New York, 1923); *Two Essays on Analytical Psychology* (London, 1928; published in the Collected Works, Vol. 7, New York and London, 1953); with Richard Wilhelm, *The Secret of the Golden Flower* (London and New York, 1931); *Psychology and Religion* (Terry Lectures, New Haven, 1938); *Psychology and Alchemy* (Collected Works, Vol. 12, New York and London, 1953). Jung has lectured at thirteen Eranos meetings, beginning with the first, in 1933.

WERNER KAEGI, Ph.D. Born 1901, Oetwil am See. Since 1936, professor of history, University of Basel. Corresponding member, Commission for a Scientific and Cultural History of Mankind, of the United Nations Educational, Scientific, and Cultural Organization. Principal works include *Michelet und Deutschland* (Basel, 1936); *Historische Meditationen* (Zurich, Vol. I, 1942; Vol. II, 1946); *Jacob Burckhardt* (Basel, 2 vols, 1947, 1950). He has translated several works of Johan Huizinga from Dutch into German.

C. KERÉNYI, Ph.D. Born 1897, Temesvár, (then) Hungary. Formerly professor of classical studies and the history of religion, Universities of Szeged and Pécs, Hungary. Resident of Switzerland since 1943. Lecturer, C. G. Jung Institute, Zurich. Founder and editor of the Albae Vigiliae series (Zurich) on mythology, art, and related subjects. Principal works: *Apollon* (2nd edn., Amsterdam, 1940); *Die antike Religion* (3rd edn., Düsseldorf, 1951); with C. G. Jung, *Essays on a Science of Mythology* (New York, 1949; London, 1950, as *Introduction to a Science, etc.*); *Niobe* (Zurich, 1949); *The Gods of the Greeks*

(New York and London, 1951). Dr. Kerényi has lectured frequently at Eranos meetings since 1941.

PAUL MASSON-OURSEL, Ph.D. Born 1882, Paris. Directeur d'études, École des Hautes-Études, Sorbonne. Special field, the comparative study of Western and Eastern philosophy. Principal publications: *Philosophie comparée* (Paris, 1923); *Esquisse d'une histoire de la philosophie indienne* (Paris, 1923); *L'Inde antique* (Paris, 1933); *La Philosophie en Orient* (Histoire de philosophie de Brehier, final vol.; Paris, 1937); *Le Fait metaphysique* (Paris, 1941); *La Pensée en Orient* (Paris, 1943). Dr. Masson-Oursel lectured at the Eranos meetings of 1936 and 1937.

FRITZ MEIER, Ph.D. Born 1912, Basel. Since 1949, professor of Oriental philology, University of Basel. Philological research in the mosque libraries of Istanbul (1936) and Iran (1937). 1946–48, maître de conférences, University of Farouk I, Alexandria. His special field is Islamic religion and mysticism. Principal publications: *Vom Wesen der islamischen Mystik* (Basel, 1943); *Die Vita des Scheich Abū Isḥāq al-Kāzarūnī* (Bibliotheca Islamica, vol. 14; Leipzig, 1948); *Die 'Fawā'iḥ al-ǧamāl wa fawātih al-ǧalāl' des Naǧm ad-dīn al-Kubrā* (A study of Islamic mysticism from 1200 A.D.; Basel, 1953). He has lectured at the Eranos meetings of 1944, 1945, and 1946.

ADOLF PORTMANN, Ph.D. Born 1897, Basel. Since 1931, professor of zoology, University of Basel. Early studies as a painter turned his interest to general questions of animal form and pattern and to the comparative morphology of vertebrates. He began his studies in marine biology at laboratories in France and Germany. Principal publications: *Biologische Fragmente zu einer Lehre vom Menschen* (Basel, 1944); *Einführung in die vergleichende Morphologie der Wirbeltiere* (Basel, 1948); *Animal Forms and Pattern* (London, 1952); and numerous popular works, among them *Vom Ursprung des Menschen* (Basel, 1944). He has spoken at several Eranos meetings since 1946.

MAX PULVER, Ph.D. Born 1889, Bern; died 1952. Writer and poet. In his later years, an internationally known graphologist, working in Zurich. He had a special interest in Gnosticism, and lectured on this and related subjects at several Eranos meetings. Principal works: *Symbolik der Handschrift* (Zurich, 1931); *Trieb und Verbrechen* (Zurich, 1934); *Person, Charakter, Schicksal* (Zurich, 1944); *Intelligenz im Schriftausdruck* (Zurich, 1949); and several volumes of belles-lettres, drama, and poetry.

449

HUGO RAHNER, S.J., Ph.D., Theol.D. Born 1900. Since 1937, professor of Church history, University of Innsbruck. His special field of historical research is that of early Christianity. Principal works: *Abendländische Kirchenfreiheit* (Einsiedeln, 1943); *Griechische Mythen in christlicher Deutung* (Zurich, 1945); *Der spielende Mensch* (Einsiedeln, 1952). He has lectured at a number of Eranos meetings since 1943.

ERWIN SCHRÖDINGER, Ph.D. Born 1887, Vienna. Since 1939, director of the Dublin Institute for Advanced Studies, which he founded. Taught previously at the universities of Zurich, Berlin, Oxford, Graz, and Ghent. He was awarded the Nobel Prize in 1933 for his work in wave mechanics, the branch of physics in which he is distinguished. He has received the Planck Medal and the Matteucci Medal and is a Foreign Member of the (London) Royal Society. His publications include, in English, a volume of collected papers (1928); *What Is Life?* (New York, 1945); and books on statistical thermodynamics, space-time structure, and the humanistic aspects of science.

WALTER WILI, Ph.D. Born 1900, Lucerne. Since 1932, professor of classical philology, University of Bern. Special fields of interest, Roman literature and culture and the Latin literature of the Middle Ages and the Renaissance. Principal publications: *Vergil* (Munich, 1930); *Europaisches Tagebuch* (Bern and Hamburg, 1939); *Tibulls 10. Elegie* (Basel, 1942); *Horaz und die august-eische Kultur* (Basel, 1948). He is president of Thesaurus Mundi, a scholarly society whose purpose is to publish critical editions of important medieval and Renaissance texts. Dr. Wili has lectured at the Eranos meetings of 1943, 1944, and 1945.

Contents of the *Eranos-Jahrbücher*

The contents of the *Eranos-Jahrbücher*, consisting up to the present time of twenty-two volumes, are here listed in translation as a reference aid and an indication of the scope of the Eranos meetings. The lectures were originally delivered in German, with a few exceptions in French, English, and Italian. In the first eight *Jahrbücher*, all of the papers were published in German; in the later volumes, the papers were published respectively in the language in which each lecture had been given.

In the following list, the places of residence of the lecturers at the time they spoke are noted the first time each name appears, and again if the place of residence changed. An index of names is on page 459.

I: 1933: Yoga and Meditation in the East and the West

HEINRICH ZIMMER (Heidelberg): On the Meaning of the Indian Tantric Yoga

Mrs. RHYS DAVIDS (London): Religious Exercises in India and the Religious Man

ERWIN ROUSSELLE (Frankfort on the Main): Spiritual Guidance in Living Taoism

C. G. JUNG (Zurich): A Study in the Process of Individuation

G. R. HEYER (Munich): The Meaning of Eastern Wisdom for Western Spiritual Guidance

FRIEDRICH HEILER (Marburg): Contemplation in Christian Mysticism

ERNESTO BUONAIUTI (Rome): Meditation and Contemplation in the Roman Catholic Church

II: 1934: Symbolism and Spiritual Guidance in the East and the West

ERWIN ROUSSELLE: Dragon and Mare, Figures of Primordial Chinese Mythology

J. W. HAUER (Tübingen): Symbols and Experience of the Self in Indo-Aryan Mysticism

HEINRICH ZIMMER: Indian Myths as Symbols

Mrs. RHYS DAVIDS: On the History of the Symbol of the Wheel

C. G. JUNG: The Archetypes of the Collective Unconscious

451

G. R. Heyer: The Symbolism of Dürer's Melancholia
Friedrich Heiler: The Madonna as a Religious Symbol
Ernesto Buonaiuti: Symbols and Rites in the Religious Life of Various Monastic Orders
Martin Buber (Heppenheim): Symbolic and Sacramental Existence in Judaism
Rudolf Bernoulli (Zurich): On the Symbolism of Geometrical Figures and of Numbers
Sigrid Strauss-Kloebe (Munich): On the Psychological Significance of the Astrological Symbol
C. M. von Cammerloher (Vienna): The Position of Art in the Psychology of Our Time.
Swami Yatiswarananda (Ramakrishna-Vivekenanda Mission): A Brief Survey of Hindu Religious Symbolism in Its Relation to Spiritual Exercises and Higher Development

III: 1935: Spiritual Guidance in the East and the West

C. G. Jung: Dream Symbols of the Individuation Process
G. R. Heyer: On Getting Along with Oneself
Erwin Rousselle: Lao-tse's Journey through Soul, History, and World
Mrs. Rhys Davids: Man, the Search, and Nirvana
Rudolf Bernoulli: Psychic Development in the Mirror of Alchemy and Related Disciplines
Ernesto Buonaiuti: I. Gnostic Initiation and Early Christianity. II. The Exercises of St. Ignatius Loyola
Robert Eisler (Unterach): The Riddle of the Gospel of St. John
J. B. Lang (Locarno): Pauline and Analytical Spiritual Guidance

IV: 1936: The Shaping of the Idea of Redemption in the East and the West

C. G. Jung: The Idea of Redemption in Alchemy
Paul Masson-Oursel (Paris): I. The Indian Theories of Redemption in the Framework of the Religions of Salvation. II. The Theory of Grace in the Religious Thinking of India
Mrs. Rhys Davids: Redemption in India's Past and in Our Present
Ernesto Buonaiuti: Redemption in the Orphic Mysteries
Henri-Charles Puech (Paris): The Concept of Redemption in Manichaeism
Boris Vysheslawzeff (Paris): Two Ways of Redemption: Redemption as a Solution of the Tragic Contradiction

V: 1937: The Shaping of the Idea of Redemption in the East and the West

C. G. Jung: Some Observations on the Visions of Zosimos
Louis Massignon (Paris): The Origins and Significance of Gnosticism in Islam

452

454

WERNER KAEGI (Basel): The Transformation of the Spirit in the Renaissance
FRIEDRICH DESSAUER (Fribourg): Galileo and Newton: The Turning Point in Western Thought
PAUL SCHMITT: Nature and Spirit in Goethe's Relation to the Natural Sciences
C. G. JUNG: The Spirit of Psychology
ERWIN SCHRÖDINGER (Dublin): The Spirit of Science
ADOLF PORTMANN (Basel): Biology and the Phenomenon of the Spiritual

XV: 1947: Man

ADOLF PORTMANN: The Problem of Origins
C. KERÉNYI: Primordial Man and Mystery
FRIEDRICH DESSAUER: Man and Cosmos
KARL LUDWIG SCHMIDT: Man as the Image of God in the Old and the New Testament
HUGO RAHNER: Origen's View of Man
GILLES QUISPEL (Leiden): The Conception of Man in Valentinian Gnosis
LOUIS MASSIGNON: The Perfect Man in Islam and Its Eschatological Originality
VICTOR WHITE (Oxford): Anthropologia rationalis: The Aristotelian-Thomist Conception of Man
LEO BAECK (London): Individuum ineffabile

XVI: 1948: Man

HUGO RAHNER: Man as Player
GILLES QUISPEL: Gnostic Man: The Doctrine of Basilides
GERARDUS VAN DER LEEUW (Groningen): Man and Civilization: The Implications of the Term "Evolution of Man"
C. KERÉNYI: Man and Mask
JOHN LAYARD: The Making of Man in Malekula
C. G. JUNG: On the Self
ERICH NEUMANN (Tel-Aviv): Mystical Man
HERMANN WEYL (Princeton): Science as Symbolic Construction of Man
MARKUS FIERZ (Basel): On Physical Knowledge
ADOLF PORTMANN: Man as Student of Nature

XVII: 1949: Man and the Mythical World

GERARDUS VAN DER LEEUW: World Beginning and End
C. KERÉNYI (Ponte Brolla): The Orphic Cosmogony and the Origin of Orphism
E. O. JAMES (London): Myth and Ritual
HENRY CORBIN (Teheran): The "Narrative of Initiation" and Hermeticism in Iran

456

457

GILLES QUISPEL (Utrecht): Time and History in Patristic Christianity
LOUIS MASSIGNON: Time in Islamic Thought
HENRY CORBIN: Cyclical Time in Mazdaism and Ismailism
MIRCEA ELIADE: Time and Eternity in Indian Thought
LANCELOT LAW WHYTE (London): Time and the Mind-Body Problem: A Changed Scientific Conception of Progress
C. G. JUNG: On Synchronicity
ERWIN R. GOODENOUGH (New Haven): The Evaluation of Symbols Recurrent in Time, as Illustrated in Judaism
HELLMUT WILHELM (Seattle): The Concept of Time in the Book of Changes
HELMUTH PLESSNER (Göttingen): On the Relation of Time to Death
MAX KNOLL (Princeton): The Transformations of Science in Our Time
ADOLF PORTMANN: Time in the Life of the Organism

XXI: 1952: Man and Energy

MIRCEA ELIADE: Power and Sacrality in the History of Religions
GERSHOM G. SCHOLEM: On the Development of the Cabalistic Conception of the Shekhinah
GILLES QUISPEL: Man and Energy in Patristic Christianity
ERICH NEUMANN: The Psyche and the Transformation of the Planes of Reality
KARL LÖWITH (Heidelberg): The Dynamics of History, and Historicism
HERBERT READ (London): The Dynamics of Art
MARTIN D'ARCY (London): The Power of Caritas and the Holy Spirit
ADOLF PORTMANN: The Significance of Images in the Living Transformation of Energy
MAX KNOLL: Quantum Conceptions of Energy in Physics and Psychology
LANCELOT LAW WHYTE: A Scientific View of the "Creative Energy" of Man

XXII: 1953: Man and Earth

ERICH NEUMANN: The Significance of the Earth Archetype for Modern Times
MIRCEA ELIADE: Terra Mater and Cosmic Hierogamies
GILLES QUISPEL: Gnosis and Earth
HENRY CORBIN: Celestial Earth and the Body of the Resurrection according to Various Iranian Traditions: I. Mazdean Imago Terrae. II. Hurqalya's Mystical Earth (Shaikhism)
GERSHOM G. SCHOLEM: The Conception of the Golem and Its Tellurian and Magical Contexts
GIUSEPPE TUCCI (Rome): Earth as Conceived of in Indian and Tibetan Religion, with Special Regard to the Tantras
DAISETZ SUZUKI (Enkakuji, Kamakura, Japan): The Role of Nature in Zen

Index of Lecturers

References are to volumes in the foregoing list.

459

INDEX

INDEX

A

Abel, 243
Abelard, Peter, 255, 257, 259, 265, 407
Abraham, 107, 108, 112
absolute, 321
abstraction, power of, 188
Academics, 77, 87, 91-96, 102
Academy, 91, 92&n, 97, 102
accident, concept of, 293
Achaemenides, 223
Achilles, 52, 59, 68
acoustics, 301
Acta Archelai, quoted, 128
action, 293; human, 166-67, 210, 370, 383n, 387; renunciation of, 209
Adam, 114, 117, 119, 171, 180, 193
Adam of St. Victor, quoted, 140&n
Adama, 402n
Admetus, 53
Aegisthus, 226
Aelian (Claudius Aelianus), 32n, 69n
Aeneid, see Virgil
Aeschylus, 65, 70, 73, 242; *The Eumenides,* 65-73; quoted, 66
Aëtius, 86n
Africa, 443
Agamemnon, 226
Agathyrsians, 56&n
Agave, 224
agnosticism, 112
Agrippa von Nettesheim, Cornelius Heinrich, 406; quoted, 406&n
Ahura Mazda, 222, 223
air, 80, 82, 83-85, 86, 87, 89, 97, 98, 109, 110, 111, 112, 127, 128, 129, 176, 180, 181, 182; God as, 83-84
air pressure, 301
aisthesis, 114

Albertus Magnus (Albert of Bollstädt), St., 292, 406
Alcaeus, 56
alchemists, 4, 11, 19, 29, 36&n, 45n, 111, 423
alchemy, 29, 30, 39, 44&n, 46, 94, 117, 398n, 401-410
Alcibiades, 74
Alcinous, 60
Alcmaeon, 78&n, 82, 83, 84, 86
Alexander III (the Great), of Macedonia, 96
Alexandria, 55
algebra, 304
Allah, 187
allegory, 108, 109
all-or-none reaction, 392-93, 398
All-soul, 187, 195
amazement, as ecstasy, 119
Ambrose, St., 104, 109, 133, 145; quoted, 139, 146&n
Amerbach, Hans, 273, 274
America, 255, 261, 262
Ammon, 219
amoeba, 362
Amos, 217, 218
Amphrysus (river), 53
anamnesis, purpose of, 14
ānanda, 211
Anastasius of Sinai, 109
anatomical studies, 262-63
Anaxagoras, 78, 83n, 87-89, 91
Anaximander, 79-80&n, 81n
Anaximenes of Miletus, 80&n, 81, 82, 83, 84, 88, 89, 97
anchoritism, 237
Anderson, Carl David, 326
angels, 34, 101, 103, 116, 117-18, 120,

463

gene, 336

generation, 90, 94, 98-99

genetics, 327, 335

Geneva, 284

genius, 443

genotype, 335

geometry, 304, 308-309; analytical, 301, 309

George I, king of England, 302

German language, 323

Germany, 255, 256, 257, 284, 301, 382, 434

germ cell, 343, 344, 355, 357, 362

Gerson, Jean de, 270

Gethsemane, 249

Ghazzālī, Abu-Hāmid Muḥammad al-, 153n, 166-68; quoted, 167-68

ghost, as spirit, 5, 6, 416

Gigon, O., 80n

Gilson, Étienne Henry, 278

glands, 363, 391

Glasenapp, Helmuth von, 166n

gnats, 183

gnomes, 19

gnosiology, 243-44, 247, 249

Gnosis, 98n, 109, 113

Gnostics, 87, 96, 103, 115, 116, 145, 232, 233, 238, 401n

God, 8, 13, 41n, 100&n, 101, 122, 125, 126, 128, 132, 133, 134, 135, 136, 215, 216, 243, 244, 258, 264n, 268, 270, 271, 283, 285, 292, 294, 303, 334n, 379n, 417, 429; air as, 83-84; and Arianism, 235-36; and art, 275-76; *vs.* Devil, 43, 124, 127; existence of, proof of, 248-49; and Gnostics, 232; of Hebrews, 217, 218, 219, 220, 221; history as self-revelation of, 252-53, 286-87; kingdom of, 229-30, 231, 233, 236, 246; and light, 402n, 405, 406&n; God's love, 147; in Mahayana Buddhism, 212; man image of, 114; in monism of Islam, 151-70 *passim*, 180n, 183n, 186-90, 192, 195, 197, 198-203; and nature, 286&n, 299, 312, 319; one being, 174-78; in Philo, 107-17 *passim*, 120; philosophy as, 247-48;

as prime mover, 88; and science, 316, 318, 319, 320; as spirit, 4, 7, 9, 78, 86, 90, 91, 92, 95, 96, 102-103, 104, 105, 106, 123, 137-48, 401, 402; as sun, 403, 404&n, 407-408, 409n, 420; triunity of, 39, 94; unconscious substitutes for, 381-82; is unity, 98; unknowability of, 112, 168; wise old man as, 21, 431; work of, 238; world as, 178, 198; in Zoroastrianism, 223

God-image, 41, 43

God-man, 37, 126

gods, 116, 387; Greek, 51-74 *passim*; secret names of, 62; theriomorphism of, 25; threefold division of, in Xenocrates, 93-94

Goethe, Johann Wolfgang von, 5, 19, 29, 85n, 299, 314, 398n; *Faust*, 29, quoted, 314, 422

Goetz, Bruno, 11n

Goichon, A. M., 181n

gold, 94, 407

Gonzales, Loys, 409

good, 89-90, 95, 222, 242, 248, 249, 250; and evil, 11, 12, 25, 30, 48, 195n, 247, 429; servitude in, 208-209

Gorgon, 67n

Gothic art, 265

grace, 127, 128, 132, 134, 144, 145, 147, 225, 230, 231, 232, 238, 242, 249, 271, 283-84

grammarians, 172

gravitation, 297, 312, 333; laws of, 298, 304, 307

Great Mother, 33

Greater Vehicle, 209

Greece, 208, 216, 223-26, 290

Greek thought, spirit in, 49-74, 77-78&n, 79-101, 102, 103, 113, 123, 127, 128, 145

Greene, Jane Bannard (tr.), 51n

Gregorian chant, 237-38

Gregory I (the Great), St., quoted, 136

Gregory of Nyssa, St., quoted, 131, 132, 145

Gribaldi, Matteo, 284

Grimaldi, Francesco Maria, 301
Grimm, Jacob and Wilhelm, 18n, 77n
Grünewald, Matthias, 274
Guericke, Otto von, 301
Guibert de Nogent, 265
Guigniot, J. D., 62n
Guillaume de Conches, 407
Guillaume de Paris (William of Auvergne), 406, 407
guilt, 12, 85, 88, 243
guru, 11&n, 205

H

habeas corpus, 302
Hades, 67
Haeckel, Ernst, 361
hair, loss of, 364-65
half-gods, 42, 45, 46
Halliday, W. R., 70n
hallucination, 10n
Hamann, Johann Georg, 252, 253
handicraft, 210
Hanover, house of, 302
harmony, 81, 82, 208, 243, 281
Harris, J. R., 117n
Harrison, J. E., 63n, 72n
Hartmann, Alfred, 274n
Hartmann, Eduard von, 118, 378, 390n
Hazard, Paul, 262
health, 85
hearing, 120, 158
heart, 83, 129, 136, 137, 141, 142, 153, 154, 183&n, 184n, 191, 222, 279
heat, 180, 331, 333; statistical-mechanical theory of, 327, 328, 330, 331-32, 339, 340
Heath, Thomas H., 86n
heaven, 61, 92, 93, 110, 111, 112, 121, 123, 124, 128, 129, 142, 143
heavens, seven, 188
Hector, 67
Heden, E., 55n
Hegel, Georg Wilhelm Friedrich, 5n, 76&n, 77, 78, 252, 381-82
Hegesippus, 227

Heidrich, E., 275n
Heinemann, J., 98n
Heinse, Wilhelm, 258
Heinze, R., 90n, 91n, 92n, 93n, 94n
Helbig, Wolfgang, 73n
Helios, 62&n, 73
hell, 142, 155, 189, 191, 192, 194
Hellas, 55
Henry VIII, king of England, 302
Hera, 70, 408
Heracleides Ponticus, 92n
Heraclitus, 80-82, 83, 84, 88, 89, 97, 99&n, 104, 219, 292, 309
Herakles, 36n, 67, 68
Herbart, Johann Friedrich, quoted, 375
Herder, Johann Gottfried von, 76&n, 77, 252, 253, 286
here, 50, 157n, 189
hereafter, 157n, 158, 189
heredity, 330-31, 335, 336, 346-47, 349, 358, 359, 362, 363
heresy, 158, 172, 232-33, 234, 270, 286
hermaphrodites, 363-64
Hermes, 22, 66, 74, 269; Homeric hymn to, 73-74
Hernicians, 213
hero, 24, 35-36, 40, 41, 42, 43, 111, 212, 257, 423
Herodotus, 58n, 67n, 79
Herrmann, Paul, 72n
Herzfeld, Marie, 276n
Heseltine, Michael (tr.), 131n
Hesiod, 74n, 80&n, 81n
Hesychius, 71n
hexis, 117
hieros gamos, 25
Hilary, St., of Poitiers, 104
Hildegarde, St., of Bingen, quoted, 104
Himerius, 56n
Hindu philosophy, *see* India
Hippocrates, 80, 82-83, 84-85&n, 89
Hippolytus, quoted, 408&n, 409
Hiroshima, 428
His, Wilhelm, 361
history, and spirit, 76; as self-revelation of God, 252-53, 286-87
Hölderlin, Friedrich, 76

475

M

O

W